Frommer's®

Caribbean Ports of Call

9th Edition

by Robin Andersen
with Christina Colón & Felisa Mahabal

WILEY

John Wiley & Sons, Inc.

Published by:

JOHN WILEY & SONS, INC.

111 River St.

Hoboken, NJ 07030-5774

ISBN 978-1-118-36906-7 (paper); ISBN 978-1-118-51806-9 (ebk); ISBN 978-1-118-51810-6 (ebk)

Editor: Christine Ryan
Production Editor: Heather Wilcox
Cartographer: Guy Ruggiero
Photo Editor: Richard Fox
Production by Wiley Indianapolis Composition Services

Front Cover Photo: Half Moon Cay, Bahamas ©Interface Images - Cruise Travel & Life / Alamy Images
Back Cover Photo: San Juan, Puerto Rico ©Katja Kreder / imagebroker / Alamy Images

For information on our other products and services or to obtain technical support, please contact our Customer Care Department within the U.S. at 877/762-2974, outside the U.S. at 317/572-3993 or fax 317/572-4002.

Wiley also publishes its books in a variety of electronic formats. Some content that appears in print may not be available in electronic formats.

Manufactured in the United States of America

5 4 3 2 1

CONTENTS

LIST OF MAPS

ABOUT THE AUTHORS

Robin Andersen is a professor of communications and media studies at Fordham University in the Bronx, and an award-winning author of non-fiction books on media analysis and criticism. After negotiating the virtual landscapes of media of all sorts, it has been a natural transition to negotiating the real, and incalculably more fun, landscapes of the Caribbean. Growing up in California and exploring beaches from the top to the bottom of the state before moving the New York, traveling to the Caribbean seemed like returning home. A sign discovered at one port said it best: Home Is Where the Beach Is.

Through travel writing, **Christina Paulette Colón** has merged her passion for research, education and ecotourism. With a Ph.D. in ecology and an M.A. in environmental conservation education her academic research has taken her to the jungles of Borneo, rainforests of Belize, and shores of Bora Bora. Her work as a travel writer began as a science consultant for other authors over ten years ago. Since then she has explored nearly every island and port in the Caribbean. When not abroad, she makes her home in New York, where she enjoys exploring the parks of Manhattan, woodlands of the Bronx and beaches of Brooklyn.

Felisa Mahabal has an uncanny knack for fact checking and updating guidebooks. In her spare time, of course, as if running a full time day care, managing a household and raising four children is not enough. Perhaps it is her love for reading guidebooks, planning trips, and exploring exotic destinations that accounts for this skill. Or it could be her passion for traveling to the Caribbean. With a father from Puerto Rico, a husband from Trinidad, and timeshares in The Bahamas and Florida, it is clear that the Caribbean is in her blood, close to her heart, and always on her mind.

ACKNOWLEDGEMENTS

With so many spectacular port destinations in the Caribbean, this volume wouldn't be possible without the generous support of so many. I'd like to thank my co-authors for their contributions, and also Angelo Berkowitz and writer Matt Hannafin. Our editor Christine Ryan was steadfast throughout the process. Bevan Springer keeps us up-to-date on people and places throughout the Caribbean. The weary travel writer cannot scout out destinations for cruise passengers without being guided and driven, lodged, and fed, scheduled and organized by the people who know what they are doing and love the places they live and work. In New Orleans, thanks to Christine DeCuir, Kelly Schulz, Lea Sinclair, and from another remarkable port of embarkation, Fort Lauderdale, thanks to Kaymi Malave, Jessica Taylor, and the wonderful people at Lago Mar, Debbie Banks and James Pancallo, and Michael Copper for his encyclopedic knowledge of eateries.

Cruzing Cozumel with Pablo Aguilar was fun and revealing, and dinner at Casa Mission with host Damian Miranda made it also a culinary delight. Without Emma Gomez I would never have caught the ferry to Playa del Carmen, and kudos to Paulina Feltrin for putting me up at the Fairmont Mayakoba. Cesar Lizarraga Gonzalez, a man of many talents, planed an extensive itinerary up and down the Yucatan Peninsula to wild places and amazing Mayan geographies. Special appreciation goes to Roberta Iniguea at Explorean, and to jungle expert Xavier, for allowing me to appreciate the sounds of night crickets. For their sense of humor and endless patience, my wonderful guides Harley Che and Denneric Polanco, made Chetulal my favorite capital city. I learned much from Raul Andrade while eating fresh fish along the Bahia. Ernesto Parra is an athlete as well as cultural historian; everyone should have him as a guide. The team from Ogilvy, Randee Ulsh, Marie Manning and Lauren Simpson, made travel in Puerto Rico a delight, and special thanks to Kathleen Krumhansl and Marta Albanese for their careful guidance. I am indebted to Judith Andujar and Efrain Rosa for extraordinary hospitality at the historic El Convento in Old San Juan, and the very same can be said for Lourdes Martinez and Stephanie Trabal at the Rincon Beach Resort.

The team from Cheryl Andrews Marketing Communications, especially Cheryl, is one of the best in the business, and many thanks to the charming Jennifer Johnson. Sue Cordray made traveling a breeze. We explored every inch of the tiny but fantastical island of Tobago guided by Jesille Peters with the help of Alex Nedd from Waterholics. My excellent eco-adventure in Trinidad with the folks at Paria Springs will remain an indelible memory, made more notable by Courtenay Rooks and Sheldon. No one appreciates a professional drive more than I do. They keep you safe and comfortable and offer an education, all at the same time. Thanks to Jose, Sugie, Victor Cruz, Tino Genchi and all those not named, past and future, who I will always value just as much.

—Robin Andersen

HOW TO CONTACT US

In researching this book, we discovered many wonderful places—hotels, restaurants, shops, and more. We're sure you'll find others. Please tell us about them, so we can share the information with your fellow travelers in upcoming editions. If you were disappointed with a recommendation, we'd love to know that, too. Please write to:

Frommer's Caribbean Ports of Call, 9th Edition
John Wiley & Sons, Inc. • 111 River St. • Hoboken, NJ 07030-5774
frommersfeedback@wiley.com

ADVISORY & DISCLAIMER

Travel information can change quickly and unexpectedly, and we strongly advise you to confirm important details locally before traveling, including information on visas, health and safety, traffic and transport, accommodation, shopping and eating out. We also encourage you to stay alert while traveling and to remain aware of your surroundings. Avoid civil disturbances, and keep a close eye on cameras, purses, wallets and other valuables.

While we have endeavored to ensure that the information contained within this guide is accurate and up-to-date at the time of publication, we make no representations or warranties with respect to the accuracy or completeness of the contents of this work and specifically disclaim all warranties, including without limitation warranties of fitness for a particular purpose. We accept no responsibility or liability for any inaccuracy or errors or omissions, or for any inconvenience, loss, damage, costs or expenses of any nature whatsoever incurred or suffered by anyone as a result of any advice or information contained in this guide.

The inclusion of a company, organization or Website in this guide as a service provider and/or potential source of further information does not mean that we endorse them or the information they provide. Be aware that information provided through some Websites may be unreliable and can change without notice. Neither the publisher or author shall be liable for any damages arising herefrom.

FROMMER'S STAR RATINGS, ICONS & ABBREVIATIONS

Every hotel, restaurant, and attraction listing in this guide has been ranked for quality, value, service, amenities, and special features using a **star-rating system.** In country, state, and regional guides, we also rate towns and regions to help you narrow down your choices and budget your time accordingly. Hotels and restaurants are rated on a scale of zero (recommended) to three stars (exceptional). Attractions, shopping, nightlife, towns, and regions are rated according to the following scale: zero stars (recommended), one star (highly recommended), two stars (very highly recommended), and three stars (must-see).

In addition to the star-rating system, we also use **seven feature icons** that point you to the great deals, in-the-know advice, and unique experiences that separate travelers from tourists. Throughout the book, look for:

special finds—those places only insiders know about

fun facts—details that make travelers more informed and their trips more fun

kids—best bets for kids and advice for the whole family

special moments—those experiences that memories are made of

overrated—places or experiences not worth your time or money

insider tips—great ways to save time and money

great values—where to get the best deals

The following abbreviations are used for credit cards:

AE American Express	DISC Discover	V Visa
DC Diners Club	MC MasterCard	

TRAVEL RESOURCES AT FROMMERS.COM

Frommer's travel resources don't end with this guide. Frommer's website, **www.frommers.com,** has travel information on more than 4,000 destinations. We update features regularly, giving you access to the most current trip-planning information and the best airfare, lodging, and car-rental bargains. You can also listen to podcasts, connect with other Frommers.com members through our active-reader forums, share your travel photos, read blogs from guide-book editors and fellow travelers, and much more.

INTRODUCTION: CRUISING TO THE PORTS OF CALL

The Caribbean cruise as we know it today is less than 50 years young, but the folks who boarded those first 700-passenger NCL and Carnival ships would be stunned at the 5,000-passenger behemoths that sail the region today. But despite all the technical innovations, some things about the experience never change.

Picture pulling up in your big white ship to a patch of sand-and-palm-tree paradise, a steel band playing as you stroll down the gangway in shorts and flip-flops. Throughout the Caribbean, you're guaranteed nearly constant sunshine, plenty of beaches, and relaxation, but you're also likely to find rich culture and (depending on the port) Mayan ruins, European colonial architecture, lush rainforests, winding mountain roads, beautiful tropical flowers and marine life, and opportunities to be as active or as laid-back as you want to be. And it's all so easy: Between the major Florida port cities (Miami, Fort Lauderdale, Cape Canaveral, and Tampa) and the other big regional home ports (New York, Charleston, Galveston, New Orleans, and others), most people in the northeastern and southeastern U.S. can easily drive to their ship, if they want to. Once there, it's all smooth sailing.

CHOOSING AN ITINERARY & THE BEST SHORE EXCURSIONS

If you count every rocky little outcropping and sandbar, there are hundreds of islands in the Caribbean, but of the 40 or 50 that make it onto the map, cruise ships regularly visit only about 25 of them. Most Caribbean cruises are 7 nights long and visit anywhere from three to six different ports, with the 2,000- to 4,000-passenger-plus megaships tending toward the lower number and spending the rest of their time on leisurely (and more profitable) days at sea. There are also 3- and 4-night cruises out of Florida visiting the Bahamas and/or ports along Mexico's Yucatán

ATLANTIC OCEAN

BAHAMAS

Freeport/
Lucaya

Nassau

Andros Is.

Turks & Caicos
Islands

Great
Inagua

VIRGIN ISLANDS

St. Martin/
Sint Maarten

San Juan

Barbuda

CUBA

Camagüey

DOMINICAN
REPUBLIC

Puerto
Rico

Antigua

St. Kitts
& Nevis

Montserrat

Guadeloupe

HAITI

Santo
Domingo

Dominica

IS.

Port-au-Prince

GREATER ANTILLES

Martinique

See "Eastern Caribbean" map
on following page

St. Lucia

Kingston

Barbados

JAMAICA

St. Vincent

Grenada

Caribbean Sea

Tobago

LESSER ANTILLES

Trinidad

Aruba

Curaçao

Bonaire

Caracas

Maracaibo

Barranquilla

Orinoco

Caroni

PANAMA

Colón

Panama
City

San Cristóbal

VENEZUELA

Apure

Gulf of
Panama

Cauca

Medellín

COLOMBIA

Magdalena

Bogotá

Meta

Uraricuera

BRAZIL

1 | DAYS AT sea VS. DAYS IN PORT

When evaluating an itinerary, take a look at its day-by-day schedule. A few ships will visit a different port every day, but it's much more typical for them to have at least 1 or 2 days at sea—either because they have to sail a long way between ports or because sea days are more profitable, with a captive audience of passengers hitting the bars, shops, and other extracost options. Many cruises these days—especially ones that sail from more northerly home ports to Caribbean destinations—spend up to 3 days at sea on 7-night itineraries, and 4 on 8-night itineraries. That's fine if your main vacation goal is to decompress, but if your goal is to see a lot of different ports, this is not an ideal situation. Ditto if you think you'll get "are we there yet?" antsy between ports.

Peninsula; 4- and 5-night cruises out of Tampa, Miami, New Orleans, and Galveston that follow western Caribbean itineraries; and 10- to 14-night Caribbean cruises that transit the Panama Canal, sailing either round-trip from Florida or one-way between Florida and Mexico's west coast, visiting three to seven ports.

Though pretty much all the Caribbean islands and ports are appealing in some way, they're not all created equal. Some are better for shopping, others for beaches or scenic drives. Some are quite built-up, whereas others are hardly developed at all. Some have piers that can accommodate several megaships at one time; others require that ships anchor as much as a mile offshore and shuttle passengers back and forth in small, motorized launches called "tenders." Big ships tend to visit the more commercialized, developed islands, while small ships are able to access the less-developed, off-the-beaten-path islands. Typically, cruise lines divide Caribbean itineraries into eastern, western, and southern routings, but as ships become faster and able to sail greater distances between ports, more and more of those distinctions are blurring.

Megaship Itineraries

EASTERN CARIBBEAN   Eastern Caribbean itineraries typically sail out of Florida or from one of the other home ports along the eastern seaboard, and may include visits to San Juan (Puerto Rico), the U.S. Virgin Islands (particularly St. Thomas), St. Martin, Grand Turk (in the Turks and Caicos Islands, east of the Bahamas), and Nassau or Freeport in the Bahamas—all very popular and busy ports of call, especially St. Thomas, Nassau, and San Juan.

WESTERN CARIBBEAN   Western Caribbean itineraries depart from Miami, Fort Lauderdale, Tampa, New Orleans, and Galveston, and usually visit Grand Cayman, Jamaica (Ocho Rios, Montego Bay, or the new port of Historic Falmouth), and Cozumel or one of the other ports on Mexico's Yucatán Peninsula. This is a popular itinerary for many lines, so you'll see throngs of other cruise passengers in each port—often three or four (or more) ships will be visiting at a time. Key West, Belize City, Grand Turk, and the Bay Islands of Honduras also pop up frequently on western Caribbean itineraries.

SOUTHERN CARIBBEAN   Southern itineraries typically sail round-trip out of San Juan or sometimes out of Aruba or Barbados. They often overlap with eastern Caribbean itineraries and may visit St. Thomas, St. Martin, St. Lucia, Martinique,

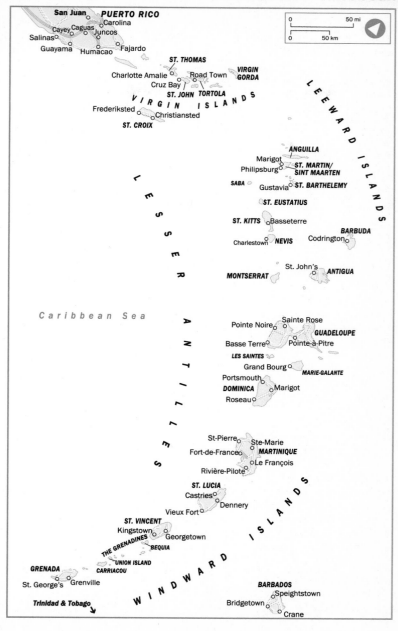

Antigua, and maybe Dominica, Guadeloupe, Aruba, and Grenada, or one of the other islands in the Grenadines.

Small-Ship Itineraries

Most small ships cruise in the eastern and southern Caribbean, where distances between islands are shorter. Instead of Florida, they may sail out of Barbados, Grenada, St. Kitts, or San Juan and visit more remote islands.

EASTERN CARIBBEAN   These itineraries may include visits to St. Barts, the British Virgin Islands, and the U.S. Virgin Islands (lush St. John as well as more touristy St. Thomas).

SOUTHERN CARIBBEAN   Southern Caribbean cruises may visit Guadeloupe, Dominica, Les Saintes, St. Kitts, Nevis, Martinique, St. Lucia, St. Vincent, Grenada, and Bequia, and maybe the truly unspoiled and remote Palm, Canouan, Mayreau, and Carriacou islands.

Shorter Itineraries

Short and affordable **2- and 3-night cruises** offer a more action-packed, nonstop party ambience than longer 7-night Caribbean itineraries. It's obvious why: These are weekend cruises, departing on Thursday or Friday afternoon, so people are ready to squeeze in as much fun, relaxation, drinking, gambling, dancing, and eating as possible before going back to work on Monday. Though you'll definitely find more 20- and 30-somethings on these shorties than on any other type of cruise, you'll still see a wide range of ages. Aside from the fun factor, short cruises are a great way for first-time cruisers to test the waters (so to speak) before committing to a full week—but keep in mind that the more party-oriented vibe of a short cruise is not an accurate representation of a longer 7-nights-plus itinerary. They're also a good idea if you're short on time or moola.

The ships that offer these minicruises tend to be the oldest in their fleets and are a bit beat up compared to the newest megaships. We've also noticed that service tends to not be as good on the short party cruises. Then again, most passengers don't notice the difference—they're too busy having fun.

Because they typically depart on Sunday or Monday afternoon and sail through the workweek, **4- and 5-night cruises** represent the opposite end of the liveliness spectrum, tending to attract an older and less party-oriented crowd.

Matching Your Habits to Your Itinerary

Some ports are better for certain things than others. Here's a short rundown; see p. 109 for a comparison chart that rates shore excursions, activities, beaches, shopping, and dining for all the Caribbean ports. The island reviews in chapter 5, "The Ports of Call," provide detailed information.

PORTS FOR SHOPPERS
Eastern Caribbean: Nassau, St. Martin, St. Thomas, San Juan. **Western Caribbean:** Cozumel, Grand Cayman, Historic Falmouth, Playa del Carmen. **Southern Caribbean:** Aruba, Barbados.

PORTS FOR BEACH LOVERS
Eastern Caribbean: Antigua, British Virgin Islands, St. Barts, St. John, St. Martin. **Western Caribbean:** Grand Cayman, Grand Turk, Jamaica. **Southern Caribbean:** Aruba, Barbados, Bequia, Grenada, Martinique, Nevis.

PORTS FOR SCUBA DIVERS & SNORKELERS

Eastern Caribbean: St. Croix, St. John, St. Thomas. **Western Caribbean:** Belize, Costa Maya, Cozumel, Grand Cayman, Grand Turk. **Southern Caribbean:** Bonaire, Curaçao, Dominica.

PORTS FOR HISTORY & ARCHAEOLOGY ENTHUSIASTS

Eastern Caribbean: San Juan. **Western Caribbean:** Cozumel and the other Yucatán ports. **Southern Caribbean:** Barbados, Curaçao.

PORTS FOR NATURE BUFFS

Eastern Caribbean: St. John, San Juan. **Western Caribbean:** Belize. **Southern Caribbean:** Aruba, Bonaire, Dominica, Grenada, St. Kitts, Trinidad.

PORTS FOR FRANCOPHILES

Eastern Caribbean: Guadeloupe, Les Saintes, Martinique, St. Barts, St. Martin.

Shore Excursions: The What, Why & How

Sometimes a port's real attractions may be miles (sometimes a lot of miles) from where your ship is docked. In such cases, touring on your own could be an inefficient use of your time, entailing lots of hassles and planning, and possibly costing more. In these places, the shore excursions offered by the cruise lines are a good way to go. Shore excursions run the gamut, from snoresville bus tours and booze cruises to more stimulating options such as snorkeling and jungle walks. For those who like a little sweat in their port visits, there are physically challenging options such as kayaking, horseback riding, mountain biking, and zip lining. Some things to keep in mind:

○ In almost every case, the cruise lines themselves do not operate the excursions; instead, they contract them out to operators in each individual port. That's why most lines seem to offer the same tours, though prices often vary slightly.

○ Excursion prices are often (but not always) lower for kids.

○ Excursions often fill up fast, especially on the megaships, so don't dawdle in signing up. If your cruise line offers the option to prebook online before your trip, do it. If not, sign up on the first day of your cruise.

In chapter 5, I discuss shore excursions in more depth, providing information on the best excursions and noting when you may want to skip the excursions entirely and set out on your own.

WHEN TO GO

The greatest number of ships sail the Caribbean from late November to mid-April, though many ships take advantage of the year-round good weather. The only trouble in paradise is **hurricane season,** which officially runs June 1 to November 30 but rarely causes cruisers any problems bigger than a few days of rain and a bit of rocking and rolling. I've taken many cruises in the Caribbean during this period and have only occasionally run into stormy weather; it's rare, but it's a risk you take. The chance of actually getting caught in the perfect storm is next to nil, as modern communications (and generally speedy vessels) allow captains to change course and pilot their ships out of danger as soon as they get word of a storm.

Defining seasons as "low" and "high" is hardly a science, but it's generally accepted that **high season** in the Caribbean is mid-December to mid-April. During this time, weather will most likely be perfect, the islands and ships will be packed, and the prices will be higher. The **holiday weeks** of Christmas, New Year's, Presidents' Day, and Easter are the absolute busiest and most expensive periods, especially on the family-oriented megaships—these are the few times in the year when the cruise lines usually don't offer deep discounts.

Despite falling within hurricane season, the **summer months** of June, July, and August are the next-busiest times; in fact, many lines consider these months high season, along with December through April, because families traditionally vacation during the summer and because many ships migrate to Alaska and Europe for the season, leaving fewer (and thus more in-demand) vessels in the Caribbean. Temperatures may be hotter in summer, but the islands' flowering trees are also at their most colorful and lush.

September, October, and early November are considered **low season** (aka "value season") and are the months when you'll encounter the fewest crowds onshore and on board, as well as some of the lowest rates. Sometimes there will be a lull during the first 2 weeks of January, just after the rush of the holidays, and sometimes in late April and May, so look for good prices then as well.

The **Panama Canal cruise season** generally parallels the Caribbean high season, with most cruises departing between November and April. Some ships offer only two Panama Canal cruises annually, when repositioning between their summer season in Alaska and their fall/winter season in the Caribbean. These days, many cruise lines include **partial canal crossings** as part of extended western Caribbean itineraries from Florida, sailing through the canal's locks westbound to Gatun Lake, docking for a day of excursions, and then sailing back out in the evening.

THE CRUISE LINES IN BRIEF

People feel very strongly about ships. For centuries, mariners have imbued their vessels with human attributes, and even though cruise passengers are typically aboard for only a week at a time, they really do bond with their vessels, and often find themselves buying T-shirts with the ship's name on the front, or getting into friendly but competitive "whose ship is best?" discussions with other cruisers they meet. We know people who have sailed the same ship a dozen times or more, and feel as warmly about it as though it were their own summer cottage.

Following is a quick primer on the cruise lines operating in the Caribbean. If you're an experienced cruiser, you may already have a favorite, but if not, this will give you a little background to help you make your choice. The important thing is to find a cruise line and a ship that says "you." To make your selection easier (and to make sure you're not comparing apples to oranges), I've divided the cruise lines into three distinct categories based on the type of experiences they offer: mainstream, ultraluxury, and small-ship/adventure cruises (which include both motorized and sailing vessels).

THE MAINSTREAM LINES

These are the cruise lines you know even if you've never set foot on one. They're the ones with the catchy TV spots, glossy magazine spreads, and omnipresent website banner ads that make cruises seem like sheer paradise—and for many people, they really are.

Today's mainstream ships are part theme park, part shopping mall, part gym, and part faux downtown entertainment and dining district, all packaged in a sleek hull with an oceanview resort perched on top. The biggest are *really* big: 14 stories tall, 1,000 feet long, with cabin space for between 2,000 and 5,000-plus passengers and a couple thousand crew. Most of the mainstream lines have spent the past decade pumping billions into ever-newer, bigger, and fancier ships, and the intense competition means they're constantly trying to outdo each other with entertainment and activities. The newer the ship, the more whoopee you can expect: open-air boardwalk districts, bowling alleys, water parks, ice-skating rinks, outdoor movie theaters, surfing simulators, zip lines, giant spas, rock-climbing walls, full-size basketball courts, and virtual reality golf, plus classics like hot tubs, theaters, water slides, and bars, bars, bars. The action is just outside your cabin door, though if you crave some downtime, there's always your private balcony or some quiet lounge that's deserted while everybody else is living it up.

The more elegant and refined of the mainstream lines are commonly referred to as premium, a notch up in the sophistication department from others that are described as mass-market. Quality-wise, they're all more similar than they are different, especially in regard to dining and entertainment. Ditto for lines such as Azamara and Oceania (and half the Holland America fleet), whose **midsize ships** are almost a throwback to the days before supersizing. Though these lines' vessels are tiny compared with the Royal Caribbeans, Carnivals, and Princesses of the world, I count them among the mainstream lines because they offer similar well-rounded cruises for a diverse mix of passengers, and because their prices (and amenities) aren't quite up there with the ultraluxury lines.

Azamara Club Cruises

1050 Caribbean Way, Miami, FL 33132. www.azamaraclubcruises.com. ✆ **877/999-9553** or 305/539-6000.

THE LINE IN A NUTSHELL   Launched in mid-2007, Azamara Club Cruises is a more high-end and adult-oriented sister brand to Celebrity and Royal Caribbean, offering more out-of-the-way itineraries, better service and cuisine, more enrichment opportunities, and lots of little extras that make the experience extraspecial. The line's two, near-identical ships, *Azamara Journey* and *Azamara Quest*, are midsize gems that were originally built for now-defunct Renaissance Cruises.

THE EXPERIENCE   The idea behind Azamara is pretty much the same idea that animates all the other former Renaissance vessels (some of which are also operated by Oceania and Princess): smaller, more intimate ships sailing longer itineraries, visiting out-of-the-ordinary ports, and offering a casual yet country-clubbish experience, with great service. That's not to call Azamara a copycat, though. Fact is, there are only so many different kinds of cruise experiences you can offer, and this is the kind that these ships were made for. In an age dominated by bigger and bigger megaships, it's nice to see that the midsize option is still alive and kicking.

Overall (and like Oceania), Azamara offers an experience that straddles the mainstream and luxury segments of the cruise biz—somewhere between Celebrity and Crystal or Regent, though luxury initiatives like complimentary house wines at lunch and dinner, free specialty coffees and bottled water, more overnights in port, and high-end excursions nudge the line awfully close to the high end. Ditto for other aspects of the experience. On the Pool Deck, for instance, there's a quiet jazz trio instead of the kind of loud pop/reggae band found on most mainstream ships, and in the cafe you'll often find a harpist plucking out traditional and classical tunes, spiced with pop standards. Service is exceptional, from the butlers who attend to all cabins to little touches such as the cold towels offered at the gangway after a hot day in port, and you don't have to worry about tips—gratuities are included in the fare. At dinner, things are entirely flexible—just show up when you like, at the main restaurant, at two reservations-only alternatives, or at a casual but still waiter-serviced option in the buffet restaurant. Onboard activities run from the usual (bingo, napkin folding, team trivia) to the unusual, including poetry reading/writing get-togethers and seminars on etiquette and art. At night you can take in a floor show at the theater, catch a performance by a guest magician or comedian, do the karaoke thing, watch a late-night movie, or take in music in several of the public rooms.

PASSENGER PROFILE The line draws from the typical cruise demographic, roughly ages 45 and up. The relatively long and unusual itineraries and the quiet onboard atmosphere appeal to a more cultured, accomplished crowd, while the higher-than-mass-market prices and the length of the itineraries favor retirees. The lack of children's programming limits the number of families with kids who book this line, while the stringent smoking regulations mean few smokers sail Azamara. (Smoking is prohibited everywhere on board except in the aft port-side section of the Looking Glass Lounge and in the forward starboard section of the Pool Deck.)

Carnival Cruise Lines

3655 NW 87th Ave., Miami, FL 33178-2428. www.carnival.com. ℂ **800/227-6482** or 305/599-2200. Fax 305/405-4855.

THE LINE IN A NUTSHELL The everyman cruise line, Carnival has the most recognized name in the biz and serves up a very casual, down-to-earth, all-American Caribbean vacation aboard colorful, jumbo-size resort ships. If you like the flash of Vegas mixed with a big dose of beach party, you'll love Carnival's brand of flamboyant fun.

THE EXPERIENCE Like the frat boy who graduated to a button-down shirt and an office job, Carnival has definitely moved up and on to some extent from its riotous, party-boat beginnings. But like that reformed frat boy who still meets his old pals for happy hour once a week, the line hasn't lost touch with its past. Sure, the ships' decor, like the clientele, has mellowed more and more in recent years (with 2012's *Carnival Breeze* being downright simple and elegant in places), but overall the 24-ship fleet is still dominated by a design vibe that borders on nutty, offering an eye-melting collage of textures, shapes, and images. Where else but on these floating play lands would you find a giant octopus-like chandelier with lights that change color, bar stools designed to look like baseball bats, or real oyster-shell wallpaper? The outrageousness is part of the fun. On many ships in the fleet, you'll also find sushi bars, supper clubs, wine bars, coffee bars, and great amenities for children. Food and service are also pretty decent, and Carnival gets points for upping the quality of its passenger experience over the years, and for trying new things. The "Fun Ship 2.0" initiative of 2012, for instance, is retooling Carnival's old "Fun Ship" brand for the times, introducing new dining choices, bars/lounges, and entertainment options based on partnerships with name entertainers like comedian George Lopez and star Food Network chef Guy Fieri.

PASSENGER PROFILE A Carnival cruise is a huge melting pot—couples, singles, and families; young, old, and lots in between. I've met doctors as well as truck drivers on Carnival cruises. And no matter what their profession, you'll see people wearing everything from Ralph Lauren shirts and Gucci glasses to Harley-Davidson T-shirts and tattoos. About one-third of passengers are under age 35, another third or so are between 35 and 55, and the other third is over 55. At least half of all passengers are first-time cruisers. Although it's one of the best lines to choose if you're single, families and couples are definitely in the majority. The line's 3-, 4-, and 5-night cruises tend to attract the most families with kids and the highest number of 20- and 30-something single friends traveling together in groups.

Regardless of their age, passengers tend to be young at heart, ready to party, and keyed up for nonstop fun and games. Many have visited the casinos of Las Vegas and Atlantic City, and the resorts of Cancún and Jamaica, and are no strangers to soaking in sardine-can hot tubs, sunbathing, hitting the piña coladas and beer before lunch, and dancing late into the night.

Celebrity Cruises

1050 Caribbean Way, Miami, FL 33132. www.celebrity.com. ℂ **800/437-3111** or 305/539-6000. Fax 800/722-5329.

THE LINE IN A NUTSHELL   Celebrity is the most stylish of the mainstream lines, operating big megaships spiced up with above-average service and a cutting-edge sense of design and style.

THE EXPERIENCE   Celebrity juices up the mainstream cruise experience with a big dose of refinement and class, all the while keeping things fun, active, and within the price range of Joe and Sally Cruiser. Each ship is glamorous, exciting, and comfortable, offering sleek modern styles accented with cutting-edge art collections. Its most recent ships, the five Solstice-class sisters, are, bar none, the most elegant megaships in the cruise world, and the line delivers the goods in a lot of subcategories too: Its spas are among the most attractive at sea, its decor the most original, its art collections the most compelling, and its restaurants among the most appealing (especially aboard the Solstice-class ships, but also the alternative restaurants on its Millennium class). An exceedingly polite and professional staff contributes greatly to the overall mood.

Like all the big-ship lines, Celebrity offers lots for its passengers to do, but its focus on mellower pursuits and innovative programming sets it apart. Such niceties as roving a cappella groups lend a warmly personal touch, and seminars on such topics as astronomy, scrapbooking, languages, and history offer a little more cerebral meat than the usual cruise line offerings.

PASSENGER PROFILE   Celebrity tries to focus on middle- to upper-middle-income cruisers, and even wealthy patrons who want the best megaship experience out there (while happily nestled in one of the line's amazing high-end suites). But because its rates are more or less comparable to those of Carnival and Royal Caribbean, you'll find a very wide range of folks aboard—those who appreciate the elegance of its ships as well as those who could care less.

Many passengers are couples in their 40s and 50s, though you'll see people of all ages, with a decent number of honeymooners, couples celebrating anniversaries, and older couples, plus families with children in summer and during the holidays.

Costa Cruises

200 S. Park Rd., Ste. 200, Hollywood, FL 33021-8541. www.costacruises.com. ℂ **800/462-6782** or 954/266-5600. Fax 954/266-2100.

THE LINE IN A NUTSHELL   Imagine a Carnival megaship hijacked by an Italian circus troupe: That's Costa. The words of the day are *fun, festive,* and *international,* with big, bright, new megaships providing the venue. Expect a really good time, but don't set your sights too high for cuisine (with the exception of the pizza and pasta).

Oh, and yes—this is the line whose giant *Costa Concordia* sank so disastrously off Giglio, Italy, in January 2012, taking the lives of more than 30 passengers and crew. It's going to take them a long time to live that one down.

THE EXPERIENCE   For years, Costa has played up its Italian heritage as the main factor that distinguishes it from Carnival, Royal Caribbean, and the rest—even though the line is part of the Carnival Corporation empire, and many members of the service staff are no more Italian than Chico Marx (though most officers and the "animation staff" really are). Still, there's an Italianate essence here, with more pasta dishes on the menu than on any other line; more classical Italian music among the entertainment offerings; Italian-flavored activities facilitated by the aforementioned animation staff (a young, energetic, and usually ridiculously attractive group); and a large number of Italian Americans among the passengers. The interiors of the line's huge new ships are by Carnival's former designer-in-chief Joe Farcus, who took inspiration from Italy's traditions of painting and architecture but filtered it all through his signature "more is more" style—think Venice à la Vegas.

PASSENGER PROFILE Costa attracts passengers of all ages who want lots of fun and action and who like the idea of a more European cruise flavor in the Caribbean. Italian Americans are heavily represented aboard the line's Caribbean cruises, and, in general, Costa passengers are big on participation—the goofier, the better: I've never seen as many guests crowding the dance floor, participating in contests, dressing up for costume galas, or having a go at mask painting or other crafts as I have aboard Costa's ships.

Typically, all but one of Costa's ships sail in Europe, as Costa focuses more on its Europe business, where the passengers are 80% to 85% Europeans. On that one Caribbean ship, though, about half the passengers are from North America, and the remaining half are mostly from Europe and South America. Costa's Caribbean cruises appeal to retirees and young couples alike, although there are more passengers over 50 than under. Typically, you won't see more than 40 or 50 kids on any one cruise except during holidays such as Christmas and spring break, when there may be as many as 500 children on board. Because of the international mix, public announcements, lifeboat drills, and some entertainment are given in both English and Italian. For Caribbean sailings, the cruise director is often American or British, but many of the activities staff members are multilingual Italians.

Cunard Line

24303 Town Center Dr., Ste. 200, Valencia, CA 91355-0908. www.cunard.com. *©* **800/728-6273** or 661/753-1000. Fax 661/284-4773.

THE LINE IN A NUTSHELL The most venerable line in the cruise industry, Cunard is a classic, offering a link to the golden age of passenger ships.

THE EXPERIENCE The Cunard of today is not the Cunard of yesterday, but then again, it is. Formed in 1840 by Sir Samuel Cunard, the line provided the first regular steamship service between Europe and North America. It was one of the dominant players during the great years of steamship travel, which lasted roughly from 1905 to the mid-1960s. From the early '70s on, it was the only line offering scheduled transatlantic crossings (aboard the legendary *QE2*), a tradition that continues today with *QE2*'s successor, the massive *Queen Mary 2*. *QM2* also sails the Caribbean every year, as occasionally do her smaller, newer fleet mates, the new *Queen Elizabeth* and the *Queen Victoria*. All three ships (though especially *QM2*) are modern reinterpretations of the golden-age luxury liner, offering oversize grandeur, old-world formality, new-world technology, and even a dose of blatant class structure: Some restaurants and outdoor decks are set aside specifically for suite guests only, if you please. For regular, nonsuite passengers, though, Cunard really doesn't offer an experience that's markedly different from the other mainstream cruise lines—it just does so with a heckuva lot more history backing it up.

PASSENGER PROFILE   In general, Cunard attracts a well-traveled crowd of passengers mostly in their 50s and up, many of them repeaters who appreciate the line's pedigree. It's more the 4 o'clock tea crowd than the hot tub–and–umbrella drink set. The nationality mix on board depends on where the ships depart from: Caribbean sailings that depart from U.S. ports will, of course, carry predominantly American passengers; those that depart from the U.K. will carry mostly Brits.

Disney Cruise Line

P.O. Box 10299, Lake Buena Vista, FL 32830. www.disneycruise.com. ℭ **800/951-3532** or 888/325-2500. Fax 407/566-3541.

THE LINE IN A NUTSHELL   Hands down, Disney is at the top of the heap when it comes to family fun, and its cruises overall are among the very best in the mainstream category in terms of entertainment and cabin amenities. Though Royal Caribbean, Carnival, Celebrity, NCL, and Princess all devote significant attention to kids, it took Disney to create vessels in which both kids and adults are really catered to equally, and with a nice mix of style and friendliness.

THE EXPERIENCE   Both classic and ultramodern, Disney's ships are like no others in the industry, designed to evoke the grand transatlantic liners of yesteryear but also boasting some truly innovative features, including extralarge cabins for families, several restaurants through which passengers rotate on every cruise, fantastic Disney-inspired entertainment, separate adult pools and lounges, and the biggest kids' facilities at sea. In many ways, the experience is more Disney than it is cruise (for instance, there's no casino), but, on the other hand, the ships are surprisingly elegant and well laid out, with the Disneyisms sprinkled around subtly amid the Art Deco and Art Nouveau design motifs. Head to toe, inside and out, they're a class act. More than a decade separates the line's older ships (Magic and Wonder) from its newer ships (Dream and Fantasy), but the older vessels have held up surprisingly well, and aren't too far behind their younger fleet mates in most regards. The exceptions are the dedicated children's facilities and dedicated adult entertainment areas, which are all larger and more compelling aboard the newer ships.

Disney is nothing if not organized, so its 3- and 4-night cruises out of Port Canaveral, Florida, are designed to be combined seamlessly with a Disney theme park and hotel package to create a weeklong land/sea vacation. You can also book these short cruises separately, or opt for a full weeklong Caribbean cruise.

PASSENGER PROFILE   Disney's ships attract a wide mix of passengers, from honeymooners to seniors, but naturally a huge percentage of guests are young families with children (most of them American). Because of this, the overall demographic tends to be younger than that aboard many of the other mainstream ships, with many passengers in their 30s and early to mid-40s.

Holland America Line

300 Elliott Ave. W., Seattle, WA 98119. www.hollandamerica.com. ℭ **877/724-5425** or 206/281-3535. Fax 800/628-4855.

THE LINE IN A NUTSHELL   Holland America, in business since 1873, has managed to hang on to more of its seafaring history and tradition than any line today except Cunard. It offers a moderately priced, classic, and casual yet refined cruise experience.

THE EXPERIENCE   Holland America is a classy operation, offering all-around appealing cruises with a touch of old-world elegance and cushy amenities such as plush bedding and flat-panel TVs with DVD players in all cabins. Though the line has been retooling itself to attract younger passengers and families, it still caters mostly to older folks and so generally offers a more sedate and stately experience than other mainstream lines (plus excellent service for the money). Its fleet is diverse, composed equally of midsize, classically styled ships and of larger, brighter, bolder megaships. New or old, the vessels are all well maintained and have excellent (and remarkably similar) layouts that ease passenger movement. In the ships' public areas, you'll see flowers that represent Holland's prominent place in the floral industry, Indonesian fabrics and woodcarvings that evoke the country's relationship with its former colony, and seafaring memorabilia that often hark back to Holland America's own history.

PASSENGER PROFILE   For years, HAL was known for catering to an almost exclusively older crowd, with most passengers in their 70s on up. Today, following intense efforts to attract younger passengers, about 40% of the line's guests are under 55, with a few young families peppering the mix, especially in summers and during holiday weeks. While the average age skews a bit lower on the newish Signature-class and Vista-class ships, HAL just isn't Carnival or Disney, and its older ships especially were designed with older folks in mind—a few even have fold-down seats in the elevators.

   Passengers tend to be amiable, low-key, and better educated than their equivalents aboard some of the other big mainstream lines, and much more amenable to dressing up—you'll spot lots of tuxedos and evening gowns on formal nights. Though you'll see some people walking laps on the Promenade Deck, others taking advantage of the ships' large gyms, and some taking athletic or semiadventurous shore excursions, these aren't terribly active cruises, and passengers overall tend to be sedentary. HAL has a very high repeat-passenger rate, so many of the people you'll see aboard will have sailed with the line before.

MSC Cruises

6750 N. Andrews Ave., Ste. 100, Fort Lauderdale, FL 33309. www.msccruises.com. ℂ **800/666-9333** or 954/772-6262.

THE LINE IN A NUTSHELL   MSC is "the other Italian cruise line" (after more established Costa) that would really, really like to join the front ranks of the cruise business. Toward that end, it's invested gazillions in a new megaship fleet that's the youngest in the cruise biz, offering a European-style cruise experience and good prices to boot. All it needs to do is polish up its delivery and it'll be good to go.

THE EXPERIENCE   An adjunct of Mediterranean Shipping Company (the world's second-largest container-shipping operation), MSC is all about "Italian style": Italian menus, lots of Italians (and other Europeans) on board, European-style entertainment, and a laid-back, nearly laissez-faire attitude. Its large, modern ships leaven their generally contemporary cruise experience with elements of what cruising was like in the distant and not-so-distant past, when it was more about interacting with other passengers than riding a surfing simulator or playing glorified video games. The activities it does program tend to be social and fun, while its entertainment includes unusual touches such as jugglers, magicians, classical pianists, and opera singers. Its Italian cuisine (especially its distinctive regional dishes) may be among the best Italian dishes at sea, and the evening pizza is superb. Ditto for the Italian wine list:

excellent and quite reasonable. The major downside to the experience is its service, which can often (though not always) seem surprisingly inattentive, provoking one guest I met aboard to comment: "You get the feeling that everyone has something more important to do than focus on you."

PASSENGER PROFILE   MSC has for years attempted a balancing act, trying to cater to a mostly European audience when it's in Europe (which is most of the time) and a mostly American audience on the one or two ships it dedicates to the North American market. It doesn't quite work, though, with the Italians on the staff often particularly gawky at trying to appeal to American sensibilities. Though the line doesn't carry as many kids in the Caribbean as it does in Europe, it should, considering its "kids travel free" policy, in which kids 11 and younger pay only port charges, and kids 12 to 17 pay a reduced rate. To accommodate the generally wide cultural mix on board, announcements in the Caribbean are made in English and Italian (in that order) and sometimes in Spanish, French, and German as well.

Norwegian Cruise Line

7665 Corporate Center Dr., Miami, FL 33126. www.ncl.com. ℂ **866/234-7350** or 305/436-4000. Fax 305/436-4126.

THE LINE IN A NUTSHELL   NCL may be the most mainstream of the main-stream lines these days—and we mean that in a good way. At a time when every cruise line seems to be pushing the "luxury" elements of their onboard programs, NCL hews to the upper center, with always-casual dining (and lots of it), cheerful and creative decor, and hip innovations like onboard bowling alleys, outdoor night-clubs, gourmet beer bars, and inside cabins with adjustable mood lighting. Nutshell? NCL's the kind of cruise line you want to sit down and have a beer with.

THE EXPERIENCE   Back in the '90s, NCL operated a mixed-bag fleet of older ships whose onboard vibe was only a couple steps above budget. What a difference a decade or two make. Today, NCL is one of the top players in the industry, offering a fun, pretension-free experience aboard ships that are designed like bright, interactive playrooms for adults. NCL was the first to dump the old system of formal/informal/casual nights, going totally casual in 2000 and starting a trend that totally changed the cruise experience. Today, its ships offer between 6 and 20 different places to grab a meal or a snack, and its entertainment is among the best at sea, consisting of both standard-issue (if higher quality) cruise fare like big stage shows and musical groups and also marquee entertainment like the Second City comedy troupe and the Blue Man Group, the latter of which does shows on every cruise aboard *Norwegian Epic*.

PASSENGER PROFILE   Passengers in general are younger, more price conscious, and more active than those aboard lines such as HAL, Celebrity, and Princess. Typical NCL passengers are couples between 25 and 60, including a fair number of honeymooners and families with kids during summers and holidays. The atmosphere aboard all NCL vessels is informal and well suited to casual types, party makers, and first-time cruisers.

Oceania Cruises

8300 NW 33rd St., Ste. 308, Miami, FL 33122. www.oceaniacruises.com. ℂ **800/531-5619** or 305/514-2300.

THE LINE IN A NUTSHELL   Oceania is the phoenix that rose from the ashes of Renaissance Cruises, which went belly up in September 2001. Founded by former

Renaissance and Crystal Cruises executives, the line began by operating three of Renaissance's ships, but has now blossomed into its own flower, launching two gorgeous midsize vessels that cement the line's rare position in the cruise industry, right in between the luxury and mainstream blocs. Oceania mimics some attributes of much pricier lines (including excellent service and cuisine and a quiet, refined onboard feel), but its rates are generally much more reasonable.

THE EXPERIENCE   Oceania is positioned as an "upper-premium" line intended to fill the gap between big-ship premium lines, such as Celebrity, and real luxe lines, such as Regent, in terms of both ship size and level of luxury. It's going for a kind of floating country-club feel, with a mellow ambience; few organized activities; low-key entertainment; a casual, sporty dress code; an emphasis on cabin comfort; and long itineraries that favor smaller, less visited ports such as St. Kitts and St. Barts. Prices are higher than those of premium competitors like Azamara, Celebrity, Holland America, and Princess, though they often include airfare to the port of embarkation.

Oceania's high points are its excellent cuisine (in both the main dining room and the specialty restaurants, of which the newer ships have a surprising number considering their smallish size); its exceptional, personal service; and its overall low-key onboard vibe.

PASSENGER PROFILE   Due partially to the length of these cruises (mostly 10, 12, and 14 days) and partially to the low-key onboard atmosphere, Oceania tends to attract older passengers who prefer to entertain themselves, reading in the library and enjoying the destination-heavy itineraries. Most are Americans, with many from the West Coast and many "returning," having sailed previously with Oceania. A sprinkling of younger couples usually find themselves on board as well, though children are rare enough to be surprising. Whatever their age, passengers tend to be drawn by the line's 100% casual dress code and ambience.

Princess Cruises

24305 Town Center Dr., Santa Clarita, CA 91355. www.princess.com. ℰ **800/774-6237** or 661/753-0000. Fax 661/259-3108.

THE LINE IN A NUTSHELL   With a fleet of mostly large and extralarge megaships, L.A.-based Princess offers a quality mainstream cruise experience with a nice balance of tradition and innovation, relaxation and excitement, casualness and glamour.

THE EXPERIENCE   If you were to put Royal Caribbean, Holland America, and Cunard in a blender and mix them together, then add a pinch of California style, you'd come up with something like Princess. Dining, entertainment, and activities are geared to a wide cross section of cruisers: The more tradition-minded can spend time in the library, join a bridge tournament, enjoy a meal in a grand dining room, and then take in a show. Those seeking something different can spin a pottery wheel, take a computer or scrapbooking class, grab a bite in an intimate Italian restaurant, or take in a jazz set. The line's largest vessels are some of the biggest at sea, yet they still manage to offer intimate spaces for quiet time, as well as lots to do.

PASSENGER PROFILE   The majority of Princess's passengers are in their 50s, 60s, and older, though you'll also find 30- and 40-somethings (and their families) sailing these days, particularly during summer school holidays. Overall, Princess passengers are less boisterous than those aboard Carnival and not quite as staid as those aboard Holland America. Its ships all have extensive kids' facilities and activities, making them suitable for families, while their balance of formal and informal makes them a good bet for a romantic vacation too, with opportunities for doing your own thing mixed in among more traditional cruise experiences. For serious Love Boat–style romance, Princess has things covered, offering secret proposal packages and onboard weddings in which the captain officiates.

Royal Caribbean International

1050 Caribbean Way, Miami, FL 33132. www.royalcaribbean.com. ℂ **800/327-6700** or 305/539-6000. Fax 800/722-5329.

THE LINE IN A NUTSHELL   Royal Caribbean has basically been *the* innovator in the mainstream sector of the cruise business over the past decade, transforming the architectural look and layout of big cruise ships and also rewriting the book on what's possible at sea: rock climbing, ice-skating, boxing, surfing on deck, zip lining . . . what's next? The line's fleet includes the 10 biggest cruise ships ever built, and although sheer size alone doesn't justify choosing these ships, the fact that Royal Caribbean puts the extra space to good use does. These big ships really do deliver the goods in terms of variety, comfort, design, and amenities.

THE EXPERIENCE   Royal Caribbean prides itself on being ultrainnovative and cutting edge, pushing the envelope with each new class of ship it builds. If there's something that's never been done at sea before, Royal Caribbean will figure out how to do it. The newest ships, sisters Oasis and Allure of the Seas, give new meaning to the phrase over the top, carrying a whopping 5,400 passengers apiece and designed with citylike neighborhoods and an incredible design that opens up the center of the ship to sunlight and fresh air. The supersize megacruisers were preceded by the three Freedom-class ships, which introduced a surfing simulator, full-size boxing ring, and "sprayground" kids' aqua park to the cruise world. These and the line's older ships all provide a fun, active, and glamorous experience for a wide range of people, whether your idea of a good time is riding a wave or relaxing in the Solarium pool. There are huge children's centers for the kids and elegant jazz clubs, kick-back sports bars, and flashy entertainment for adults. Decor-wise, these ships project fun without venturing into Carnival over-the-topitude.

PASSENGER PROFILE   You'll find all walks of life on a Royal Caribbean cruise: passengers in their 20s to 60s and older, mostly couples (including a good number of honeymooners), some singles traveling with friends, and also lots of families. The majority of passengers come from somewhere in North America, but the huge Oasis-, Freedom-, and Voyager-class ships, in particular, attract a lot of foreigners, including many Asians and Latin Americans. Overall, passengers are energetic, social, and looking for a good time, no matter what their age. And they want a less glitzy, theme-parkish, and party-on experience than they'll get with RCI's main competitor, Carnival. RCI's shorter 3- and 4-night cruises do tend to attract more of the partying crowd, however, as is the case with most short cruises.

THE ULTRALUXURY LINES

If you've got taste, tend to avoid the mass market, and have lots and lots of money, then these are the cruise lines for you. Most people attracted to these types of cruises are wealthy, sophisticated, and social. They're well-traveled if not necessarily adventurous, tend to stick to five-star experiences, and don't blink at paying top dollar to be pampered—which is exactly what they will be on these lines.

On these ships, elbowroom is abundant and service is very personal, with staff getting to know your likes and dislikes early on. The onboard atmosphere is much like a private club, with guests trading tales over drinks or over delicious French, Italian, Mediterranean, and Asian meals that often rival what's served in respected shoreside restaurants. It might not quite be up to the three-star Michelin level, but it's absolutely the best you'll find at sea, served in high style by gracious waiters who know their jobs. A full dinner can, of course, be served in your cabin, course by course if you like.

Entertainment and organized activities are both more dignified and more limited than on the mainstream ships. Guests tend to amuse themselves, enjoying cocktails and conversation in a piano bar, listening to singers or musicians, and attending lectures just for the fun of it. Itineraries tend to shun the big megaship ports in favor of yachting destinations like St. Barts, Bequia, and Jost Van Dyke.

All ships in the luxury market are considerably smaller than all but the smallest mainstream vessels, which lets them visit smaller ports and aids the staff in providing truly personalized service. The smallest vessels (the two SeaDream yachts, plus Seabourn's *Pride, Legend,* and *Spirit*) carry only about 100 to 200 passengers, while the largest would barely be midsize by mainstream standards, carrying only 700 to 1,100 passengers apiece.

While the high-end lines have not been immune to the economic marketplace and have adjusted their individual pricing policies and programs to meet the times, they'll still cost lots more than your typical mainstream cruise. Expect to pay at least $2,500 per person for a week in the Caribbean, and easily twice that or more if you opt for a large suite or if you cruise during the busiest times of the year. Balancing the high fares is the fact that all these luxury lines include a lot of extras in their rates, including gratuities; free unlimited wine, liquor, and other beverages; and niceties like high-end bath products from Bulgari, Molton Brown, Ferragamo, and so on. Regent goes a step further and includes most shore excursions in its rates, too.

These ships are not geared to children, although aboard Crystal, the kid-friendliest of the lot, you might see 100 or more during holidays or school vacation months. Babysitting can often be arranged privately with an off-duty crew member.

Crystal Cruises

2049 Century Park E., Ste. 1400, Los Angeles, CA 90067. www.crystalcruises.com. ℂ **888/799-4625** or 310/785-9300. Fax 310/785-0011.

THE LINE IN A NUTSHELL   Fine-tuned and fashionable, Crystal offers top-shelf service and cuisine on ships large enough to offer lots of outdoor deck space, generous fitness facilities, tons of activities, multiple restaurants, and more than half a dozen bars and entertainment venues.

THE EXPERIENCE   Crystal has the only truly upscale large-ish ships in the industry. Carrying 940 to 1,070 passengers, they aren't huge, but they're big enough to offer much more activities and entertainments than their high-end peers. You won't feel hemmed in, and you likely won't be twiddling your thumbs from lack of stimulation. Unlike Seabourn's smaller ships, which tend to be more calm and staid, Crystal's sociable California ethic and large passenger capacity tend to keep things mingley, chatty, and more active. If you want to learn something while you're on vacation, the line's enrichment program is one of the best at sea, and there are also dozens of themed sailings focused on food and wine, art, film, jazz, wellness, and other subjects.

Both service and dining are excellent, with passengers free to choose from several different types of restaurants: a formal dining room, three alternative restaurants (two with Asian cuisine by famed chef Nobu Matsuhisa), plus a poolside grill, an indoor cafe, and a casual restaurant that puts on great theme luncheon buffets. The ships' reservations-only Asian restaurants serve up utterly delicious, authentic Japanese food, including sushi. At least once per cruise, a themed buffet lunch features an awesome spread focused on Asian, Mediterranean, or some other scrumptious cuisine.

PASSENGER PROFILE   Like other high-end lines, Crystal draws a lot of repeat passengers. On many cruises, more than 50% hail from affluent regions of California, and most are on their second, third, or fourth Crystal cruise. There's commonly a small contingent of passengers (about 15% of the mix) from the United Kingdom, Australia, Japan, Hong Kong, Mexico, Europe, and South America. Most passengers are well-heeled couples over 55. A good number of passengers step up to Crystal from lines such as Princess and Holland America. Many enjoy dressing up for dinner.

Though not a kid-centric line compared to the mainstream options, Crystal is the most accommodating high-end choice for families with kids. Each ship has a dedicated playroom, and supervised activities for children 3 and up are offered when demand warrants it. During holidays and the summer vacation months of July and August, 100 or so kids on board is not that unusual.

Regent Seven Seas Cruises

8300 NW 33rd St., Ste. 100, Miami, FL 33122. www.rssc.com. © **877/505-5370.** Fax 402/501-5599.

THE LINE IN A NUTSHELL   Operating a fleet of stylish and extremely comfortable midsize vessels, Regent offers a casually elegant and understated luxury cruise experience. Its service is as good as it gets, and its cuisine is near the top. Having spent over $100 million on refurbishment in the past few years, the line has kept its three ships up-to-date and comparable with the younger ships in the luxury category.

THE EXPERIENCE   If you insist on luxury but like to keep it subtle, Regent might be your cruise line of choice. Its ships are spacious and understated, with a relaxed onboard vibe that tends to be less stuffy than Seabourn and Silversea. As is the case aboard all the luxury ships, entertainment and activities are relatively low-key, with passengers left to enjoy their vacations at their own pace. Dress tends toward casual, though tuxedos and gowns aren't uncommon on formal evenings. Service is friendly and absolutely spot on, and the cuisine is some of the best at sea, in both the formal dining rooms and the alternative restaurants. Even if what tickles your fancy isn't on the menu, the chef will prepare it for you.

PASSENGER PROFILE   This line appeals primarily to well-traveled and well-heeled passengers in their 50s and 60s, but younger passengers and honeymooners pepper the mix. Many clients are frequent cruisers who have also sailed on Silversea, Seabourn, and Crystal, or are taking a step up from Holland America, Celebrity, or one of the other mainstream lines. The passengers tend to be unpretentiously wealthy; though they have sophisticated tastes (and can do without inane activities such as napkin-folding classes), they also appreciate the line's less formal ambience. On my recent cruises, casual nights in the formal dining room saw some passengers dressed in polo shirts and jackets, and others in nice T-shirts with khakis and sneakers. You're also likely to find some women in full makeup, coifed hairdos, and coordinated jewelry, shoes, and handbags strolling the pool deck, and many men sporting gold Rolexes. A kids' program on summer sailings and some holiday sailings attracts some families, but the limited number of third berths in cabins tends to keep those numbers down.

Seabourn Cruise Line

300 Elliott Ave. W., Ste. 100, Seattle, WA 98119. www.seabourn.com. © **866/755-5619.**

THE LINE IN A NUTSHELL   Genteel and refined, these megayachts are intimate, quiet, and very comfortable, lavishing guests with plenty of personal attention and very fine cuisine.

THE EXPERIENCE   Strictly upper-crust Seabourn caters to guests who are well mannered and prefer their fellow vacationers to be the same. Generally, these folks aren't into pool games and deck parties, instead preferring a good book and cocktail chatter, or a taste of the line's special complimentary goodies, such as free minimassages on deck and soothing eucalyptus-oil baths drawn in suites upon request. Due to the ships' small size (with a capacity for just 208 passengers on its three older vessels and 450 on its three newest), everybody mingles easily and enjoys mellow pursuits such as trivia games and presentations by guest lecturers. With a higher staff-to-guest ratio than on almost any other line, service is very personal; staff members greet you by name from the moment you check in, and your wish is their command.

PASSENGER PROFILE   Seabourn's guests are mature adults mostly in their 50s, 60s, and 70s who are used to the five-star treatment. Many have net worths in the millions. You are likely to encounter former CEOs, lawyers, investment bankers, real estate tycoons, and entrepreneurs. The majority of passengers are couples, but there is always a handful of singles as well, usually widows or widowers. A few British, German, Swiss, and Australian guests might spice up the mix, but no matter what their nationality, these are experienced globe-trotting travelers. They also tend to be a bit on the (yawn) staid side. While you'll occasionally see families with children during the holidays and summers, it's the exception rather than the rule. These ships do not cater to kids at all, and passengers prefer it that way. These ships are like floating private clubs for the traveling elite.

SeaDream Yacht Club

601 Brickell Key Dr., Ste. 1050, Miami, FL 33131. www.seadream.com. © **800/707-4911** or 305/631-6100. Fax 305/631-6110.

THE LINE IN A NUTSHELL   Intimate cruise/yachting vessels, SeaDream's two 110-passenger ships deliver an upscale yet casual experience without the regimentation of traditional cruise itineraries and activities.

THE EXPERIENCE   SeaDream was created for independent-minded travelers craving high-end service and food sans formality and rigid schedules. Step aboard one of these yachts, and you're entering a floating club of mostly like-minded travelers who cringe at the thought of sailing en masse to the St. Thomases of the world. It's an intimate group that wants to feel like it's inhabiting an exclusive and remote seaside hamlet on some hard-to-reach, difficult-to-spell island, where the food is transcendent, the spa is ethereal, and the drinks are smooth and abundant. On these ships, you won't ever have to contend with art auctions, roving photographers, or "special" restaurants vying for your money. Instead, you'll get appealing Caribbean ports off the megaship drag, such as St. Barts, Bequia, Nevis, and Jost Van Dyke; cool adult toys such as WaveRunners; and pampering service that includes complimentary orders of shrimp cocktail served to you in the hot tub (or wherever) whenever you like.

PASSENGER PROFILE   Most passengers are in their 40s to 60s, 70% are American (with British, Canadians, and other Europeans making up most of the remainder), and many are not veteran cruisers. They're the kind who have refined tastes and want top-notch service and gourmet food, but are secure enough to dispense with a stuffy atmosphere. Many passengers have previously chartered their own small yachts or actually own one. On a recent sailing aboard the *SeaDream I,* the mix included a fun-loving middle-aged doctor and his wife from Texas, a 30-something couple-next-door from Pennsylvania who ran a successful baking business and liked to swig beer from the bottle, a retired travel executive who was clearly used to the good life, and a group of well-dressed, hard-drinking friends celebrating a 40th birthday. Passengers were friendly and mingled easily, and by day 3, alliances had been made and clusters of new friends enjoyed drinks by the pool and dined together in the open-seating restaurants.

Silversea Cruises

110 E. Broward Blvd., Fort Lauderdale, FL 33301. www.silversea.com. (C) **800/722-9955** or 954/522-4477. Fax 954/522-4499.

THE LINE IN A NUTSHELL   It doesn't get better than Silversea if you're looking for a total luxury experience at sea. From exquisite service and cuisine to such niceties as free-flowing Drappier champagne and Ferragamo and Bulgari bath products in the marble cabin bathrooms, the line's ships offer the best of everything.

THE EXPERIENCE   Fine-tuned and genteel, a Silversea cruise caters to guests who won't settle for anything but the best. The food and service are the finest at sea, and nothing seems to have been forgotten in the creation of the plush fleet, which features warm and inviting Italian-style decor and tables set with Christofle silver and Schott Zwiesel crystal. Each ship has two alternative venues for dinner, buffets are bountiful, and the room-service menu includes creative treats such as ceviche served in a martini glass. These are dignified vessels for a dignified crowd that likes to dress for dinner. If you want the VIP treatment 24/7, this is your cruise line.

PASSENGER PROFILE   Silversea's typical passenger mix is on the old side, but shorter cruises and Caribbean sailings often skew the mix a tad younger, adding at least a handful of 30- and 40-something couples to the pot. Typically, about 70% of passengers are Americans who are well traveled, well heeled, well dressed, and well accessorized. Most guests are couples, though singles and small groups of friends traveling together are usually part of the scene. Many have cruised with Silversea before, and they expect the best of everything.

SAILING SHIPS & COASTAL CRUISERS

Aside from the fact that they both sail in water, mainstream cruise ships and the ships in this section have hardly anything in common. Whereas big ships allow you to see a region while immersed in a resortlike onboard atmosphere, these vessels allow you to see it from down near the waterline, without much in the way of distractions or crowds. You're part of the destination from the minute you wake up until the minute you fall asleep, and for the most part, you're left alone to form your own opinions.

Like the traditional vessels of yore, the ships of Island Windjammers, Star Clippers, Sea Cloud, and Windstar are all, to a greater or lesser degree, powered by wind and sail (plus engines, which are essential to their being able to sail regular schedules). Sea Cloud, Star Clippers, and Windstar all offer a yachtlike vibe (way up toward the luxury end in the case of Sea Cloud, and fairly luxe for Windstar), while Island Windjammers is more like summer camp for adults.

The only nonsailing vessels in this section are operated by Blount Small Ship Adventures, which offers Belize/Guatemala sailings in winter aboard a 96-passenger motorized coastal cruiser that's able to nudge up right onto beaches when no port facilities are available.

Blount Small Ship Adventures

461 Water St., Warren, RI 02885. www.blountsmallshipadventures.com. ✆ **800/556-7450** or 401/247-0955. Fax 401/247-2350.

THE LINE IN A NUTSHELL   A family-owned New England line, Blount (formerly American Canadian Caribbean Line) operates tiny, no-frills ships that sail in offbeat places and attract a well-traveled, extremely casual, and down-to-earth older crowd.

THE EXPERIENCE   Blount began in 1966 when Rhode Island shipbuilder Luther Blount realized there was a demand for small-ship sailing on the rivers, canals, and coasts of New England and Canada. Over the years (and beyond Blount's own death; the line is now managed by his family), his vessels have gone well beyond their regional home and now offer cruises down the Intracoastal Waterway and into Central America, sailing among the islands and coastal areas of Belize and Guatemala. The line's extremely informal small ships won't win any awards for decor (they are, in fact, about the most bare-bones vessels you'll find in terms of amenities, service, and meals), but that's not what they're all about. Instead, this is a line that gets passengers close to the real life of the regions it visits, stopping at small islands and sometimes even debarking passengers right from the ship onto the beach, courtesy of the ships' shallow draft and long bow ramp.

PASSENGER PROFILE   This ultracasual line appeals to a sensible, early-to-bed crowd of mostly senior couples in their 60s to 80s, with the average age being around 72. While some are physically fit, there are usually a few walking with canes and using hearing aids. Besides senior couples, there may be a few mother-daughter teams. All are attracted by the line's casual atmosphere (windbreakers and wash-and-wear sportswear are about as fancy as these folks get on vacation) and want to visit some unusual, interesting ports while simultaneously avoiding overcrowded ones. Repeat passengers (who make up 65%–70% of the guests on an average cruise) appreciate the line's lack of glitz and gimmicks, as well as the "just us folks" features, such as a BYOB liquor policy, which can save travelers scads of cash. While trips are generally low impact, some adventurous options are available, including kayaking and snorkeling. A naturalist also sails on Central America cruises to provide perspective on what you're seeing.

Blount's ships won't appeal to the vast majority of young couples, singles, honeymooners, and families. Children 13 and under are prohibited, and the line offers no children's facilities or activities.

Island Windjammers

165 Shaw Dr., Acworth, GA 30102. www.islandwindjammers.com. ☎ **877/772-4549.** Fax 877/766-6502.

THE LINE IN A NUTSHELL Remember Windjammer Barefoot Cruises? A decade ago, they were the self-styled pirates of the cruise business, offering cruises on a fleet of old-fashioned, rum-soaked tall ships. It was terrific fun—until it finally fell off the ethical and financial tightrope it'd been walking, collapsing with a reverberating kaboom in 2007. Two years later, Island Windjammers was created by former Barefoot crew and passengers to fill the gap left behind, though this line is a bit more mature and less, shall we say, illegal.

THE EXPERIENCE Island Windjammers offers weekly 6-night cruises from Grenada aboard the 101-foot, 12-passenger brigantine schooner *Diamant,* sailing among the Grenadine Islands (an absolutely ideal locale for this type of ship), visiting Carriacou, Mayreau, Tobago Cays, Union Island, Palm Island, and Bequia. The vessel was built in 1978 and is more akin to the small windjammers that sail the Maine coast than to the bigger vessels that were operated by Windjammer Barefoot, or the even bigger ones operated today by Sea Cloud, Star Clippers, and Windstar. *Diamant* is tight and simple, with six air-conditioned cabins with portholes and private bathrooms, a combo lounge/dining room, an outdoor dining area, and lots of open deck space. Oh, and there's this: She's *gorgeous,* with a beautiful profile, lovely detailing, and shiny woodwork throughout.

   Though the line consciously tries to emulate the ultracasual Windjammer Barefoot vibe and does whip up the iconic rum swizzles in the evening, it shies away from the heavy drinking and risqué party atmosphere that sometimes sent Windjammer ships over the edge.

PASSENGER PROFILE Like Windjammer Barefoot Cruises before it, Island Windjammers' passengers run the gamut in age but are uniformly young at heart, enjoying a good time and not wanting to dress any fancier than shorts and T-shirts while having it.

Sea Cloud Cruises

282 Grand Ave., Ste. 3, Englewood, NJ 07631. www.seacloud.com. ☎ **888/SEA-CLOUD** (732-2568) or 201/227-9404. Fax 201/227-9424.

THE LINE IN A NUTSHELL Germany-based Sea Cloud Cruises caters to a well-traveled clientele looking for a deliciously exotic five-star sailing adventure. A trip aboard one of the line's sailing ships—the 2,532-ton, 64-passenger *Sea Cloud* or the 3,849-ton, 94-passenger replica *Sea Cloud II*—will spoil small-ship lovers forever.

THE EXPERIENCE It's all about history. In 1931, Wall Street tycoon E. F. Hutton commissioned construction of the four-masted sailing ship *Hussar* from the Krupp family shipyard in Kiel, Germany. Outfitting of her interior was left to Hutton's wife, heiress and businesswoman Marjorie Merriweather Post, who spent 2 years on the task, eventually drafting a full-scale diagram showing every detail of her design, down to the placement of antiques. After the couple's divorce, Post renamed the vessel *Sea Cloud* and sailed her to Leningrad, where second husband Joseph E. Davies was serving as U.S. ambassador. World War II saw the vessel commissioned to the U.S. Navy, which removed her masts and used her as a floating weather station. After the war, the vessel passed through numerous hands: first back to Post, then to Dominican dictator Rafael Leonidas Trujillo Montinas, then to a number of American owners before she was purchased by German economist and seaman Hartmut Paschberg. A lover of great ships, Paschberg and a group of Hamburg investors put up the money for an 8-month overhaul that restored *Sea Cloud*'s original grandeur, full of marble, gold, and mahogany detailing. Today, the line is owned by the Hansa Treuhand Group based in Hamburg, Germany. The ship has cabins for 64 passengers, the luckiest (and richest) of whom can stay in Post's own museum-like suite, with its Louis XIV–style bed and nightstands, marble fireplace and bathroom, chandeliers, and intricate moldings. The other original suites are similarly if less sumptuously furnished. Standard cabins are comfortable, but lack the suites' time-machine quality. Still, everyone aboard gets to enjoy a taste of the past in the main restaurant, with its dark-wood paneling, brass trimmings, and nautical paintings.

The larger, three-masted *Sea Cloud II* is a modern reinterpretation of the classics, built in 2001. Her elegant lounge has rich mahogany woodwork, ornate ceiling moldings, leather club couches, and overstuffed bucket chairs, and she has several opulent suites, one with burled wood paneling and a canopy bed. On both ships, standard cabins are very comfortable and designed with true yachting elegance. Those on *II* have small sitting areas, and all cabins have TV/VCRs, telephones, safes, hair dryers, bathrobes, and bathrooms with showers and marble sinks.

These being small sailing ships, organized activities are few; it's the ships themselves that entertain, and passengers can watch the crew work the riggings, plus count on visits to less touristed ports such as Les Saintes, Dominica, Bequia, Tobago, and St. Barts.

PASSENGER PROFILE Typical Caribbean cruises draw about 30% American passengers, 30% German, 20% British, and the rest from elsewhere in Europe. The international mix of adventurous, well-to-do, dress-up-for-dinner globe-trotters tend to shun the traditional cruise experience in favor of unique experiences that only outfits like Sea Cloud can offer.

Star Clippers

760 NW 107th Ave., Ste. 100, Miami, FL 33172. www.starclippers.com. © **800/442-0551** or 305/442-0550. Fax 305/442-1611.

THE LINE IN A NUTSHELL It's easy to fall in love with the Star Clippers experience—it's simply intoxicating. With the sails and rigging of a classic clipper ship and some of the cushy amenities of modern megaships, these beauties spell both adventure and comfort.

THE EXPERIENCE Star Clippers operates a small fleet of gorgeous sailing ships—the 170-passenger twins *Star Clipper* and *Star Flyer* and the larger, more elaborate, 227-passenger *Royal Clipper*—and the more I've sailed on other ships, the more Star Clippers' stock goes up. Few other lines offer the best of two worlds in such an appealing package. On the one hand, the ships feature comfortable, almost cushy public rooms and cabins. On the other, they espouse an unstructured, let-your-hair-down, hands-on ethic—you can climb the masts (with a harness), help raise the sails, crawl into the bow netting, or chat with the captain on the open-air bridge. Ducking under booms, stepping over coils of rope, leaning against railings just feet above the sea, and watching sailors work the winches are constant reminders that you're on a real working ship. Furthermore, as you listen to the captain's daily talk about the next port of call, the history of sailing, or some other nautical subject, you'll feel like you're exploring some of the Caribbean's more remote stretches in a ship that really belongs there—exotic ships for an exotic locale. In a sea of look-alike megaships, the *Royal Clipper, Star Clipper,* and *Star Flyer* stand out, recalling a romantic, intoxicating, swashbuckling era of ship travel.

PASSENGER PROFILE With so few passengers on board, each Star Clippers cruise seems like a triumph of individuality and intimacy. The line's unusual niche appeals to passengers who might recoil at the lethargy and/or sometimes forced enthusiasm of cruises aboard larger, more typical vessels.

Although you're likely to find a handful of late-20-something honeymoon-type couples and an extended-family group or two, the majority of passengers are well-traveled couples in their 40s to 60s, mostly active and intellectually curious professionals (such as executives, lawyers, and doctors) who appreciate a casual yet sophisticated ambience and enjoy mixing socially. During the day, polo shirts, shorts, and topsiders are standard issue; for dinner, many passengers simply change into cleaner and better-pressed versions of the same, with perhaps a switch from shorts to slacks for most men. Caribbean cruises typically carry a nearly even mix of North Americans and Europeans, most often from Germany, Austria, Switzerland, France, and the U.K. Announcements are made in English, German, and French.

Windstar Cruises

2101 Fourth Ave., Ste. 210, Seattle, WA 98121. www.windstarcruises.com. 📞 **800/258-7245** or 206/292-9606. Fax 206/340-0975.

THE LINE IN A NUTSHELL Windstar walks a tightrope between luxury line and sailing-ship line, with an always-casual onboard vibe, beyond-the-norm itineraries, and first-class service and cuisine. Its three ships—the 148-passenger twins *Wind Spirit* and *Wind Star* and the 312-passenger *Wind Surf*—combine 19th-century sailing-ship technology with modern engineering, with particularly gratifying, romantic results.

THE EXPERIENCE You say you want a cruise that visits interesting ports, boasts friendly yet efficient service, serves excellent cuisine, offers watersports from a retractable platform in the stern, has sails for a romantic vibe, and still doesn't cost an arm and a leg? You pretty much have only one option: Windstar.

This is no barefoot, rigging-pulling, paper-plates-in-lap, sleep-on-the-deck kind of cruise, but rather a refined yet down-to-earth, yachtlike experience for a sophisticated, well-traveled crowd who wouldn't be comfortable on a big ship with throngs of tourists, or on a more formal high-end ship. Days are loose and languid, with passengers exploring ashore (the itineraries visit a port almost every day) or kicking back and relaxing aboard ship with pretty much zero distraction. At dinner, few small ships can match Windstar for cuisine and ambience, with meals served in open-seating restaurants where guests can usually get a table for two. Service by mostly Indonesian and Filipino staff is extremely professional and friendly.

The ships themselves are lovely, with recently renovated interiors designed to resemble private yachts, with a palate that combines warm woods with sand and marine colors. Outside, the ships' huge white sails cut a traditional profile, but they're also state-of-the-art, controlled by a computer so that they can be furled or unfurled at the touch of a button. Despite the vessels' relatively large size (*Wind Surf* is one of the world's largest sailing ships, if not the largest), they're able to travel at upward of

12 knots under sail power alone, though usually the ships' sails are up only as a fuel-saving aid to the diesel engines.

PASSENGER PROFILE   These cruises are for those who are seeking a romantic escape, who like to visit islands and ports not often touched by regular cruise ships, and who can happily live without a large menu of onboard activities. Most passengers are couples in their late 30s to early 60s, with the average around 50. There are also usually a handful of honeymoon couples aboard any given sailing—a good choice on their part, as Windstar ranks high on my list of most romantic cruise lines. The line gets very few families with young kids—perhaps six or seven during school holiday periods, and they are usually in the 10-and-over age range.

Sailing Ships & Coastal Cruisers

THINGS TO KNOW BEFORE YOU GO

3

Although cruise ships are designed to cater to your every need, it's important to be familiar with the practical ins and outs of your line. Before you slip into relaxation mode, take a look at the general information included in this chapter—a little preparation will guarantee a stress-free cruise vacation.

PASSPORTS & VISAS

Got a passport? Virtually every air traveler entering the U.S. is required to show a passport. In addition, all persons, including U.S. citizens, traveling by air between the United States and Canada, Mexico, Central and South America, the Caribbean, and Bermuda are required to present a valid passport. *Note:* U.S. and Canadian citizens entering the U.S. at land and sea ports of entry from within the western hemisphere must now also present a passport or other documents compliant with the Western Hemisphere Travel Initiative (WHTI; see www.getyouhome.gov for details). Children 15 and under may continue entering with only a U.S. birth certificate, or other proof of U.S. citizenship.

Non-U.S./Canadian citizens departing from and/or returning to the U.S./Canada should check with their travel agent or cruise line to determine the required paperwork. Generally, you'll need a valid passport, alien-registration card as applicable, and occasionally a visa, as required by individual countries you're visiting.

If you need a passport, contact the issuing agency for your country:

- **Australia** Australian Passport Information Service (www.passports. gov.au; ✆ 131-232).
- **Canada** Passport Office, Department of Foreign Affairs and International Trade, Ottawa, ON K1A 0G3 (www.ppt.gc.ca; ✆ 800/567-6868 in Canada and U.S. or 819/997-8338).
- **Ireland** Passport Office, Frederick Buildings, Molesworth Street, Dublin 2 (www.foreignaffairs.gov.ie; ✆ 01/671-1633).
- **New Zealand** Passports Office, Department of Internal Affairs, Level 3, 109 Featherston St., Wellington, 6011 (www.passports.govt. nz; ✆ 0800/225-050 in New Zealand or 04/474-8100).
- **United Kingdom** Visit your nearest passport office, major post office, or travel agency, or contact the Identity and Passport Service

Travel to the Caribbean, Mexico, and Central America does not generally warrant inoculations against tropical diseases, though there have been recent cholera outbreaks in Haiti and the Dominican Republic. The Centers for Disease Control (CDC) sometimes recommends prescription antimalarial drugs if conditions in certain destinations warrant. CDC recommendations and warnings can be viewed at wwwnc.cdc.gov/travel/default.aspx.

(IPS), 89 Eccleston Sq., London, SW1V 1PN (www.ips.gov.uk; ✆ 0300/222-0000).

● **United States**   To find your regional passport office, check the U.S. State Department website (www.travel.state.gov/passport) or call the National Passport Information Center (✆ 877/487-2778) for automated information.

As you would before any trip abroad, make two photocopies of your documents and ID. Take one copy with you as a backup (keeping it in a different piece of luggage from the one holding your originals), and keep one copy at home.

After accepting your passport to board ship at the beginning of your cruise, the cruise line might hang onto it for the duration of your cruise, thus allowing the line to facilitate clearance procedures quickly at each port. Don't worry, this is normal. Your documents will be returned after the ship has departed its last foreign port of call, en route back to your home port.

CUSTOMS

All cruises to the Caribbean visit at least one foreign port on their itinerary, meaning you'll have to go through Customs and be subject to duty-free purchase allowances when you return. We've found clearing Customs at U.S. cruise ports usually painless and speedy, with officials rarely asking for anything more than your filled-out declaration form as they nod you through. Better safe than sorry, though: Keep receipts for all purchases you make abroad. And if you're carrying a particularly new-looking camera and expensive jewelry, you may want to consider carrying proof that you purchased them before your trip. Similarly, if you use any medication containing controlled substances or requiring injection, carry an original prescription or a note from your doctor.

In addition to items purchased, you will also want to consider those seemingly harmless souvenirs that you collected along the beach or along a trail, such as a beautiful conch shell, piece of coral, sand dollar, or interesting seed. A number of **plants and animals** are protected by law in a number of Caribbean nations and/or by international trade agreements such as CITES (Convention on International Trade in Endangered Species of Flora and Fauna). These agreements are in place to monitor and reduce international trade in species of plants and animals that are declining, are vulnerable to overharvesting, or are outright endangered. While in many cases it is perfectly legal to harvest or sell these species domestically, the regulations prevent illegal import or export of these species or parts thereof. Examples include black coral and conch shells. Another note of caution is for any **local remedies** you may have purchased or been given as a gift that are composed of fresh or dried seeds, fruit, leaves, or bark; these may be in violation of international plant conservation laws or USDA regulations to prevent accidental introduction of fungal pathogens or insect pests. In some cases, these items are allowable if "preserved" in "alcohol," which explains why some male—*ahem*—"vitality" tonics are sold in a bottle topped up with local rum or other spirits. While these are usually fine, be warned that any liquor above 80 proof may be too high a concentration of alcohol to be legally taken aboard your flight. Also be warned that because it is illegal to bring liquids in your carry-on, you will have to check it in your luggage, and that may be messy if the bottle breaks. You are better off with something from the duty-free shop in the airport, which is permissible in all cases.

Note that most meat or meat products, fruits, plants, vegetables, or plant-derived products will be seized by U.S. Customs agents unless they're accompanied by an import license from a U.S. government agency. The same import rules apply even if you are returning from Puerto Rico, Hawaii, or the U.S. Virgin Islands.

For more specifics, visit the **U.S. Customs & Border Protection** website at **www.cbp.gov** or call ✆ **877/CBP-5511** (227-5511). Canadian citizens should look at the **Canada Border Services Agency** site at www.cbsa.gc.ca, while citizens of the U.K. should visit the **U.K. Customs and Excise** site at www.hmce.gov.uk.

MONEY MATTERS

You know how they say cruises are all-inclusive vacations? They're lying. True, the bulk of your vacation expenses are covered in your fare, but there are plenty of extras. In this section, we'll examine the way monetary transactions are handled on board and in port.

Onboard Charge Cards

Cruise ships operate on a cashless basis. Basically, this means you have a running tab and simply sign for what you buy on board during your cruise—bar drinks, meals at specialty restaurants, spa treatments, shore excursions, gift-shop purchases, and so on—and then pay up at the end. Very convenient, yes—and also very, very easy to forget your limits and spend more than you intended.

Shortly before or after embarkation, a purser or check-in clerk will take an imprint of your credit card and issue you an **onboard charge card,** which, on most ships, also serves as your room key and as your cruise ID—you swipe it through a scanner every time you leave or return to the ship. Very few ships issue separate cards for these functions, or a card and an old-fashioned room key.

On the last night of your cruise, an **itemized account** of all you've charged will be slipped under your cabin door. If you agree with the charges, they'll automatically be billed to your credit card. If you'd rather pay in cash or if you dispute any charge, you'll need to stop by the office of the ship's cashier or purser. There may be a long line, so don't go if you don't have to.

Bringing Cash Ashore

The cashless system works just fine on board, but remember, you'll need cash in port. Many people get so used to not carrying their wallets aboard ship that they get off in port and find themselves without any money in their pockets—an annoyance if your ship is docked and it means trudging back aboard for cash, but a major, time-sucking hassle if your ship is anchored offshore and you have to spend an hour or more ferrying back and forth by tender.

Credit cards are accepted at most port shops, but we recommend having some real cash, ideally in small denominations, to cover the cost of taxi rides, tips to tour leaders, or purchases you make from crafts markets and street vendors. Information on local currency is included in the ports chapter of this book, but, for the most part, if you have U.S. dollars on hand you don't have to worry about exchanging money at all. In the Caribbean, the **U.S. dollar** is the legal currency of the U.S. Virgin Islands, Puerto Rico, and (oddly enough) the British Virgin Islands, but vendors on islands that have their own currency will also usually also accept dollars. Even on islands such as Guadeloupe and Les Saintes (both French possessions), where they may prefer euros, most vendors will accept dollars. Mexican and Central American ports are similarly dollar-friendly. Be warned that you will receive change in local currency, so factor that in when deciding what size bill to use when paying for purchases.

If you're running low on cash, **ATMs** are easy to find in nearly every cruise port covered in this guide, often right at the cruise terminal. Remember that you'll get local currency from machines where the dollar isn't the legal tender, so don't withdraw more than you need. Many megaships also have ATMs (surprise, surprise: usually near the casino), but you can expect to be charged a hefty fee for using them—up to $5 in addition to what your bank charges you.

Many lines will cash **traveler's checks** at the purser's desk, and sometimes **personal checks** of up to about $200 to $250 (but sometimes only when accompanied by an American Express card, for guarantee). You can also often get a **cash advance** through your Visa, MasterCard, or Discover card—but keep in mind that when you use your credit card to get cash, interest will start accruing right away.

Tipping the Crew

Most cruise lines pay their service staff low base wages with the understanding that the bulk of their income will come from tips. Each line has clear guidelines for gratuities, which are usually printed in its brochures and on its website, on your cruise documents, and in the daily schedule toward the end of your trip. The traditional way of tipping was to simply hand your waiter, assistant waiter, and cabin steward cash in a little envelope, but these days most lines add an **automatic gratuity** (sometimes called a "service charge") to passengers' onboard account—generally between $8.50 and $12 per person, per day total, with the amount adjustable up or down if you request it at the purser's desk before the end of the cruise. Many lines will allow you to opt out of the automatic payment if you prefer to give your servers cash directly. The ultraluxury lines (Crystal, Regent, Seabourn, SeaDream, and Silversea) include tips in their cruise rates.

Among lines that don't add an automatic charge, **suggested tipping amounts** vary slightly with the line and its degree of luxury, from about $8 to $14 total per passenger, per day, and half that for children in most cases As a rule of thumb, each passenger (not each couple) should expect to tip at least $4 per day for the cabin steward, $4 for the dining-room waiter, about $2.50 for the assistant waiter, and sometimes $1 for the headwaiter. Some lines suggest you tip the maitre d' about $5 per person for the week and slip another couple bucks to the chief housekeeper, but it's your choice. If you've never even met these people, don't bother. Guests staying in suites with butler service should also send $4 per day his or her way. A 15% gratuity is usually included on every **bar bill** to cover gratuities to bartenders and wine stewards. The captain and other professional officers definitely do not get tips—that would be like tipping your doctor.

On lines that follow traditional person-to-person gratuity policies, tip your waiter and assistant waiter during the cruise's final dinner, and leave your cabin steward his or her tip on the final night or morning, just before you debark. Tip **spa personnel** immediately after they work on you, but note that on some ships the spa will automatically add a tip to your account unless you indicate otherwise, so inquire before adding one yourself.

KEEPING IN TOUCH WHILE AT SEA

Some people take a cruise to get away from it all, but others are communication addicts. For them, today's mainstream and luxury vessels (and some small ships) offer a spectrum of ways to keep in touch.

Cellphones & Satellite Phones

All of the mainstream and most of the luxury lines in this book are wired with technology that enables cellphone users to make and receive calls aboard ship, even when far out at sea. With the exception of Windstar, the sailing ships and coastal cruisers listed in chapter 2 do not offer this service.

Cellphone service is enabled once a ship sails beyond the range of shoreside towers, typically at about 20km (12 miles). Calls are billed through your regular carrier according to its usual roaming rates, which can vary depending on the provider and sometimes on where in the world you're calling from. Rates typically range between $2.50 and $5 per minute. That's not cheap, but it's nowhere near the average $8 or $9 per minute (and sometimes up to $15 a min.) that cruise lines typically charge for **in-cabin satellite-phone service.** Text messages and e-mails sent from smartphones are more affordable, sometimes costing only a few cents, making them a great idea for couples and families trying to find each other aboard megaships.

In addition to cell service and in-cabin SAT phones, each ship has a **central phone number, fax number, and e-mail address,** which are sometimes in the cruise line's brochure and usually in the documents you'll get with your tickets. Distribute these to family members or friends, in case they have to contact you in an emergency. It's also a good idea to leave behind the numbers of the cruise line's headquarters and/or reservations department, both of which will be able to put people in touch with you.

Plugging In Your Gadgets

All ships reviewed in chapter 2 run on 110 AC current; many also run on 220. Outlets typically accept North American–style plugs (two flat, parallel prongs). Adaptors and converters are usually available for purchase on board if you need them and haven't brought them with you.

E-Mail & Internet Access at Sea

Aside from some of the sailing vessels and coastal cruisers, pretty much every cruise ship has computers from which passengers can send and receive e-mail and browse the Internet. In many cases, these computer centers are decked out with state-of-the-art flatscreen monitors, plush chairs, coffee bars, and webcams so users can send their vacation pictures to family and friends. They're often open around the clock, and many offer basic classes for computer novices. Most ships these days also offer **Wireless Internet (Wi-Fi),** allowing you to access the Internet either in designated Wi-Fi hotspots or, in some cases, from anywhere on the ship. To take advantage of this service, you must have a wireless card for your laptop, rent a card, or rent a laptop, then purchase minutes either on an as-used basis or in packages, just as you would if you were using the ship's Internet center. Per-minute rates tend to run between 50¢ and $1; packages vary by cruise length, but might run (for example) $50 for a 3- or 4-night cruise or $100 for a 7-night cruise.

Keeping on Top of the News

Most ships have news stations as part of their regular TV lineup. Some ships also maintain the old tradition of reprinting headline news stories pulled off the wire and slipping them under passengers' doors each morning.

WHAT TO PACK

Cruise lines don't place restrictions on the amount of luggage you can bring on board, but if you're flying to your ship's port, you might want to pack light to avoid airline fees. If you can't fit everything into a carry-on bag, at least be sure to pack a change of light clothes and a pair of flip-flops in your carry-on luggage, just in case your suitcase doesn't make it to the pier before your ship sets sail. Also, keep in mind that when you check your luggage as you're boarding the ship, you may not see it again for several hours, so be sure you carry whatever clothing and medications you need.

Shipboard Dress Codes (or Lack Thereof)

Ever since Norwegian Cruise Line started the casual trend back at the turn of the 20th century, cruise lines have been toning down or eliminating their dress codes. During the day, no matter what the itinerary, you'll find T-shirts, polo shirts, and shorts or khakis predominating, plus casual dresses for women, and sweatshirts or light sweaters to compensate for the air-conditioning. The vibe is about the same on the luxury lines, though those polos and khakis probably sport more expensive labels.

Evenings aboard ship used to be a lot more complicated, requiring passengers to pack for more situations than today's cruises demand. On most lines these days, **formal nights** have either melted away entirely or slid closer to what used to be considered semiformal. When Oceania Cruises started up in 2003, its dress code was set as "country-club casual" every single night, on every voyage. NCL has also pretty much ditched formal nights completely, though its "optional formal" captain's cocktail night accommodates those who choose to dress up. Disney Cruise Line has toned down formality to the point that a sport jacket is considered dressy enough. Most other mainstream lines still have 2 traditional formal nights during any 7-night itinerary—usually the second and second-to-last nights of the cruise, the former for the captain's cocktail party. For these, imagine what you'd wear to a nice wedding: Men are encouraged to don dark suits or tuxedos; women are attired in cocktail dresses, sequined jackets, gowns, or other fancy attire. For those who just hate dressing up, men can get away with a blue blazer and tie, while women can wear a blouse and skirt or pants—and, of course, jewelry, scarves, and other accessories can doll up an otherwise nondescript outfit. (Most cabins have personal safes where you can keep your good jewelry when you're not wearing it.) **Casual nights** (sometimes called "smart casual" or something similar) make up the rest of the week, though some lines still cling to an old distinction between full casual (decent pants and collared shirts for men, and maybe a sport jacket; dresses, skirts, or pantsuits for women) and informal or semiformal (suits or sport jackets; stylish dresses or pantsuits). Suggested dress for the evening is usually printed in the ship's daily schedule. Cruise lines also usually describe their dress codes in their brochures and on their websites.

Most of the **ultraluxury lines** maintain the same ratio of formal, semiformal, and casual nights, with passengers tending to dress on the high end of all those categories. Tuxedos are very common. That said, even the luxe lines are relaxing their dress standards. Seabourn doesn't even request ties for men anymore, except on formal nights, and SeaDream has a casual "no jackets required" policy every single day, though dinners usually see some men in sport jackets and women in nice dresses.

Aboard all the **sailing ship and small-ship lines,** it's very rare to see anything dressier than a sport jacket at any time, and those usually appear only for the captain's dinner. Most of these lines are 100% casual, 100% of the time, with passengers sometimes changing into clean shirts, trousers, or dresses at dinner.

Dressing for Your Destination

In the **Caribbean,** the temperature stays within a fairly narrow range year-round, averaging between 75°F and 85°F (24°C–29°C), though in summer the combination of sun and humidity can get very intense, especially in midafternoon. Trade winds help cool things off on many of the islands, as does rainfall, which differs from island to island—Aruba, for instance, is very dry, while it seems to rain briefly every other time I'm in Nassau. Winter is generally the driest season throughout the region, but even then it can be wet in mountainous areas, and afternoon showers often give the shores a good soaking—sometimes just for a few minutes, sometimes for hours. Temperatures on Mexico's **Yucatán Peninsula** and in **Central America** can feel much hotter, especially on shore excursions to the humid interior. Hurricane season lasts officially from June 1 to November 30, traditionally the low cruise season.

Casual daytime wear aboard ship means shorts, T-shirts or polos, sundresses, and bathing suits. The same dress code works in port, too, but in many places it's best to cover the skimpy bikini top if straying from the beach area. If you plan on hitting the gym, don't forget **sneakers** and **workout clothes.** Bring a good pair of **walking shoes** or **sandals** if you intend to do more than lie on the beach; **aqua-socks** might also be a good idea if you plan to snorkel, take inflatable launches to shore, or participate in watersports. They're also very good for shore excursions that traverse wet, rocky terrain, such as Jamaica's Dunn's River Falls trip, although take care to avoid using them to stand or walk on the delicate coral when out snorkeling. They're cheap to buy, but if you forget, some cruise lines rent them for excursions for about $5 a pair. A folding **umbrella** or lightweight **poncho** or raincoat is a good idea for destinations that experience regular tropical showers.

Lastly, remember to pack **sunglasses,** a **hat, light coverup,** and **high-SPF UVA/UVB sunscreen.** All are available aboard ship and in the ports, but sunscreen, in particular, will be a lot cheaper at your local market than in a gift shop. If you're flying to port, take care to pack all liquids and/or gels in your checked luggage, rather than your carry-on, unless it is in containers 100mL (3.4 oz.) or less and can all fit in a 1-quart Ziploc bag, in order to comply with most in-cabin safety regulations. If in doubt, contact your carrier before you fly. You might also consider bringing a **plastic water bottle** that you can refill aboard ship, rather than buying overpriced bottled water in port.

Sundries

Except on the small ships, most vessels have a **laundry service** on board and some dry cleaning, too, with generally about a 24-hour turnaround time; a price list will be in your cabin. Cleaning services tend not to be cheap—$1 or $1.50 per pair of socks, $2.50 to $3 for a T-shirt, and $10 to dry-clean a suit—so if you plan to pack light and wear the same outfit several times, consider the self-service laundry rooms that are available aboard many of the megaships and some luxury ships.

Like hotel rooms, most cabins (especially those aboard the newest and the most high-end ships) come with **toiletries** such as soap, shampoo, conditioner, and lotion, although you may still want to bring your own products—the ones provided often seem watered down (plus, many mainstream lines, including Royal Caribbean, do not offer conditioner or lotion in standard cabins). If you forget something, all but a few of the smallest ships in this book have at least one onboard shop selling razor blades, toothbrushes, sunscreen, film, and other sundries, usually at inflated prices.

Most cabins also have **hair dryers,** but they tend to be weak, so don't expect miracles—if you have a lot of hair, bring your own, or save yourself the trouble and bring clips to put your hair in an updo instead.

You don't need to pack a **beach towel,** as they're almost always supplied on board (again, except aboard some sailing- and small-ship lines). If you insist on big and fluffy, however, you might want to pack your own. Bird-watchers will want their **binoculars** and manuals, golfers their **golf clubs** (unless they intend to rent), and snorkelers their **snorkel gear** (which can also be rented, usually through the cruise lines).

Most ships of all sizes have libraries stocked with books and magazines. Some are more extensive than others. Most ships also stock paperback bestsellers in their shops.

THE PORTS OF EMBARKATION

This chapter describes the major ports of embarkation, tells you how to get to them, and suggests things to see and do there, including shopping and hitting the beach. You'll also find a sampling of restaurants and places to stay.

4

Hands down, the busiest of the ports of embarkation is **Miami,** followed by **Port Everglades** in Fort Lauderdale; **Port Canaveral** at Cape Canaveral, directly east of Orlando; **Tampa,** on Florida's west coast; and downtown **New Orleans,** which has made an impressive post-Katrina comeback as a port for ships sailing to Mexico and the western Caribbean. Fast on their heels are places such as **Charleston,** South Carolina; **Galveston,** Texas; and **New York City,** which each host a number of ships. I profile all of these ports in detail in this chapter. **San Juan,** Puerto Rico, is both a major port of embarkation in the eastern Caribbean and a major port of call, so you'll find its review in chapter 5.

These ports of embarkation are tourist destinations themselves, so most cruise lines now offer special deals that allow passengers to extend their vacations with a stay in the port of embarkation either before or after their cruise. These packages, for 2, 3, or 4 days, often offer hotel and car-rental discounts, as well as sightseeing savings. Have your travel agent or cruise specialist check for the best deals.

Note that the hotel prices listed here are winter rates for standard double rooms unless stated otherwise. Prices in the off season will be lower.

All the ports in this chapter can be reached by train as well as by air and car. **Amtrak** (www.amtrak.com; Ⓒ **800/872-7245**) has a New York–Miami route that stops in Miami, Fort Lauderdale, and Orlando (for Cape Canaveral); a New York–Tampa route that stops in Tampa; a Los Angeles–Orlando route that stops in Orlando, New Orleans, and Houston (for Galveston); and a route from Chicago to New Orleans.

For more information about each destination, check out *Frommer's Florida, Frommer's South Florida, Frommer's New Orleans, Frommer's Texas, Frommer's New York City, Frommer's The Carolinas & Georgia,* and *Frommer's Puerto Rico.*

MIAMI

The most Latin city in the U.S. offers a hot-hot-hot club scene, sparkling beaches, crystal-clear waters, and more palm fronds, glittering hotels, and red sports cars than you'd find just about anywhere else, save maybe Monte Carlo and Rio de Janeiro. On top of all that, Miami is the

ATTRACTIONS & SHOPPING ●

Art Deco District **10**
Bal Harbour Shops **3**
Bass Museum of Art **6**
Bayside Marketplace **12**
CocoWalk and the Streets
  of Mayfair **21**

Coral Gables Merrick House **15**
Crandon Beach Park **25**
Jungle Island **13**
Lincoln Road Shopping **10**
Miami Children's Museum **13**

Miami Science Museum **22**
Miami Seaquarium **24**
Monkey Jungle **27**
The Shops at Midtown **7**
Vizcaya Museum & Gardens **22**

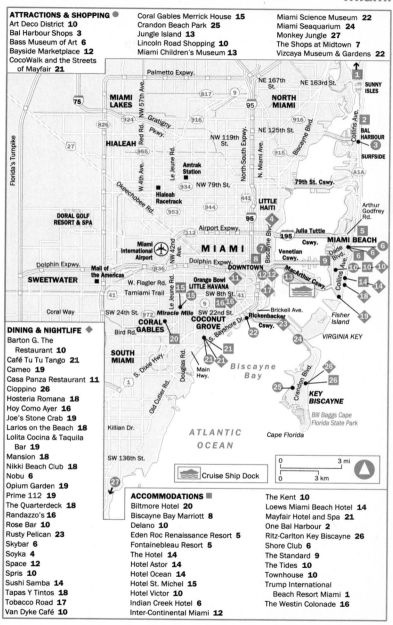

DINING & NIGHTLIFE ◆

Barton G. The
  Restaurant **10**
Café Tu Tu Tango **21**
Cameo **19**
Casa Panza Restaurant **11**
Cioppino **26**
Hosteria Romana **18**
Hoy Como Ayer **16**
Joe's Stone Crab **19**
Larios on the Beach **18**
Lolita Cocina & Taquila
  Bar **19**
Mansion **18**
Nikki Beach Club **18**
Nobu **6**
Opium Garden **19**
Prime 112 **19**
The Quarterdeck **18**
Randazzo's **16**
Rose Bar **10**
Rusty Pelican **23**
Skybar **6**
Soyka **4**
Space **12**
Spris **10**
Sushi Samba **14**
Tapas Y Tintos **18**
Tobacco Road **17**
Van Dyke Café **10**

ACCOMMODATIONS ■

Biltmore Hotel **20**
Biscayne Bay Marriott **8**
Delano **10**
Eden Roc Renaissance Resort **5**
Fontainebleau Resort **5**
The Hotel **14**
Hotel Astor **14**
Hotel Ocean **14**
Hotel St. Michel **15**
Hotel Victor **10**
Indian Creek Hotel **6**
Inter-Continental Miami **12**

The Kent **10**
Loews Miami Beach Hotel **14**
Mayfair Hotel and Spa **21**
One Bal Harbour **2**
Ritz-Carlton Key Biscayne **26**
Shore Club **6**
The Standard **9**
The Tides **10**
Townhouse **10**
Trump International
  Beach Resort Miami **1**
The Westin Colonade **16**

undisputed cruise capital of the world. More cruise ships, especially supersize ones, berth here than anywhere else on earth, and more than three million cruise passengers pass through yearly. Not surprisingly, the city's port facilities are extensive and state-of-the-art; and Miami International Airport is only 13km (8 miles) away from the port, about a 15-minute drive.

Industry giants **Carnival** and **Royal Caribbean** both have long-term agreements with the port, and to accommodate the influx of new ships over the past few years, Miami has spent $76 million on major improvements to terminals 3, 4, and 5, plus added a 750-space parking facility.

VISITOR INFORMATION Contact or visit the **Greater Miami Convention & Visitors Bureau,** 701 Brickell Ave., Ste. 2700, Miami, FL 33131 (www.miamiand beaches.com; ✆ **800/933-8448** for a free vacation planner and questions).

Getting to Miami & the Port

The **Port of Miami** is at 1015 N. America Way, in central Miami. It's on Dodge Island, accessible via a four-lane bridge from the downtown district. For information, call ✆ **305/371-7678.**

BY PLANE **Miami International Airport** is about 13km (8 miles) west of downtown Miami and the port. If you've arranged air transportation and/or transfers through the cruise line, a cruise line rep will meet you at the airport and direct you to shuttle buses to the port. Taxis are also available; the fare is a flat rate of $25. Some leading taxi companies include **Central Taxicab Service** (✆ **305/532-5555**), **Diamond Cab Company** (✆ 305/545-5555), **Yellow Cab Company** (✆ 305/444-4444), and **Metro Taxicab Company** (✆ **305/888-8888**).

SuperShuttle (www.supershuttle.com; ✆ **305/871-2000**) charges about $16 per person, with two pieces of luggage ($2 for each additional piece), for a ride within Dade County, which includes the Port of Miami. Its vans operate 24 hours a day. Call to make a reservation.

BY CAR The Florida Turnpike (a toll road) and I-95 are the main arteries for those arriving from the north. Continue south on I-95 to I-395, and head east on I-395, exiting at Biscayne Boulevard. Make a right and go south to Port Boulevard. Make a left and go over the Port Bridge. Coming in from the northwest, take I-75 to S.R. 826 (Palmetto Expwy.) S. to S.R. 836 E. Exit at Biscayne Boulevard. Make a right and go south to Port Boulevard. Make a left and go over the Port Bridge. Parking lots right at street level face the cruise terminals. Parking runs $20 per day. Porters can carry your luggage to the terminals.

GETTING AROUND See above for taxi contact information. The meter starts at $2.50 and ticks up another $2.40 for each mile and 40¢ for each additional minute, with standard flat-rate charges for frequently traveled routes. **Metromover** (✆ 305/770-3131), a free 6.5km (4-mile) elevated line, circles downtown, stopping near important attractions and the shopping and business districts. It runs daily from about 5am to 1:45am, offering a fun way to see the sights if you've got time to kill.

Exploring Miami

Miami's finest attraction is a part of the city itself. Located at the southern end of Miami Beach below 20th Street, **South Beach's Art Deco District** is filled with outrageous and fanciful 1920s and 1930s architecture that shouldn't be missed. This treasure-trove, called "the Beach" or "SoBe," features more than 900 pastel, Pez-colored buildings in the

4

Miami

THE PORTS OF EMBARKATION

Art Deco, Streamline Moderne, and Spanish Mediterranean Revival styles. The district stretches from 6th to 23rd streets, and from the Atlantic Ocean to Lennox Court. Ocean Drive boasts many of the premier Art Deco hotels.

Also in South Beach is the **Bass Museum of Art,** 2121 Park Ave. (www.bass museum.org; © 305/673-7530), which has a permanent collection of old masters, along with textiles, period furnishings, objets d'art, ecclesiastical artifacts, and sculpture. Rotating exhibits cover subjects such as pop art, fashion, and photography. The museum is open Wednesday through Sunday from noon to 5pm. Admission is $8 for adults, $6 for seniors and students, and free for children 5 and under.

On the causeway between the port and South Beach, the **Miami Children's Museum,** 980 MacArthur Causeway (www.miamichildrensmuseum.org; © 305/373-5437), gives kids of all ages an introduction to South Florida, with hands-on, playgroundlike exhibits that let little ones learn about the Everglades, the different neighborhoods of Miami, and the importing and exporting process at the Port of Miami. There's even a miniature version of a cruise ship for kids to explore in preparation for the journey ahead. The museum is open from 10am to 6pm daily. The cost is $15 for children and adults, $12 for Florida residents, and free for children under 12 months.

The adjoining **Coral Gables** and **Coconut Grove** neighborhoods are also fun to visit for their architecture and ambience. In Coral Gables, the Old World meets the New, with curving boulevards, sidewalks, plazas, fountains, and arched entrances evoking Seville. Today, the area is an epicurean's Eden, boasting some of Miami's most renowned eateries as well as the University of Miami and the nearly 1km-long (½-mile) Miracle Mile, a 5-block retail mecca (see "Shopping," below). You can even visit the boyhood home of George Merrick, the man who developed Coral Gables. The **Coral Gables Merrick House,** 907 Coral Way (www.coralgables.com; © 305/460-5361), has been restored to its 1920s look and is filled with Merrick memorabilia. Tours are on Wednesday and Sunday at 1, 2, and 3pm. Admission is $5 for adults, $3 for seniors and students, and $1 for children 6 to 12.

Coconut Grove, South Florida's oldest settlement, remains a village surrounded by the urban sprawl of Miami. It dates back to the early 1800s, when Bahamian seamen first came to salvage treasure from the wrecked vessels stranded along the Great Florida Reef. Mostly people come here to shop, drink, dine, or simply walk around and explore. Don't miss the **Vizcaya Museum & Gardens,** 3251 S. Miami Ave. (www.vizcayamuseum.org; © 305/250-9133), a spectacular 70-room Italian Renaissance–style villa. It's open every day except Christmas from 9:30am to 4:30pm. Admission, which includes a guided tour, is $15 for adults; $10 for seniors, students, and visitors in wheelchairs; and $6 for children 6 to 12.

The **Miami Science Museum,** 3280 S. Miami Ave. (www.miamisci.org; © 305/646-4200), is adjacent to the Vizcaya gardens, but it couldn't be more different. The museum has hosted a series of rolling exhibits describing everything from dinosaurs in China to a history of the Titanic; the permanent exhibitions of the museum include the planetarium and the wildlife center, filled with snakes, birds, and reptiles. The museum is open daily from 10am to 6pm. The cost is $15 for adults; $11 for students, seniors, and children 3 to 12; and free for children 2 and under. Admission prices include entrance to museum galleries, the planetarium, and the wildlife center.

Organized Tours

BY BOAT From September to May, **Miami Aqua Tours** (www.miamiaquatours. com; © 305/860-8854) offers daily 2-hour jaunts at 1:30, 3:30, 5:30, and 7:30pm aboard the 26m (85-ft.) schooner *Heritage of Miami II* or *El Loro Pirate Ship,* a replica of a Spanish galleon, departing from the Bayside Marketplace. Tickets cost $25 for adults and $15 for children 11 and under. On Friday, Saturday, and Sunday evenings, 1-hour tours at 9, 10, and 11pm show off the lights of the city ($15 adults, $10 children).

The city of Miami has a special relationship with the ocean—it's practically built on top of it—so it's no surprise that deep-sea fishing is a favorite hobby for locals and tourists alike. Bayside Marina and Haulover Marina are both full of fishing charters that'll take you out for 4-hour or 8-hour fishing excursions in search of whatever you want to catch: sailfish, tuna, dolphin (the local name for mahimahi), and even sharks. One of the best-known charters at Bayside is the **Thomas Flyer** (www.thomasflyer fishing.com; ℂ **305/374-4133**), where $800 gets you a half-day private charter. You can also contact **Capt. Joe Cotter** at **Finway Sportfishing** (www.fishfinway.com; ℂ **786/457-1930**), where a half-day private charter will run you $650.

ON FOOT An **Art Deco District Walking Tour,** sponsored by the Miami Design Preservation League (www.mdpl.org; ℂ **305/672-2014**), leaves every Thursday at 6:30pm and every Wednesday, Friday, Saturday, and Sunday at 10:30am from the Art Deco Welcome Center at 1001 Ocean Dr. The 90-minute tour costs $20, or $15 for students and seniors.

The Design District, Miami's not-quite-gentrified but up-and-coming neighborhood of boutiques and art galleries, sponsors **Art & Design Night** (www.artcircuits.com; ℂ **305/661-0511**) on the second Saturday of each month from 7 to 10pm. Galleries open their doors (and usually also their wine bottles) free to artsy types for browsing and mingling throughout the night. To participate, just head to Northeast 40th Street between North Miami Avenue and Northeast 2nd Avenue and follow the crowds.

Hitting the Beach

A 90m-wide (300-ft.) sand beach (that's really wide for a beach) runs for about 15km (9 miles) from the south of **Miami Beach** to **Haulover Beach Park** in the north. (For those of you who like to get an all-around tan, Haulover is a known nude beach.) Although most of this stretch is lined with a solid wall of hotels, beach access is plentiful, and you are free to frolic along the entire strip. A wooden boardwalk runs along the hotel side from 21st to 46th streets—about 2.5km (1½ miles).

You'll find lots of public beach areas along this stretch, wide and well maintained, with lifeguards, concession stands, metered parking (bring lots of quarters), and toilet facilities, including 21st Street, at the beginning of the boardwalk; 35th Street, popular with an older crowd; 46th Street, next to the Fontainebleau Hilton; 53rd Street, a narrower, more sedate beach; 64th Street, one of the quietest strips around; and 72nd Street, a local old-timers' spot. There are also public garages on 7th, 9th, 13th, and 16th streets; prices range from $15 to $35. At the southern tip of the beach is family-favorite **South Point Park,** where you can watch the cruise ships.

In Key Biscayne, **Crandon Park,** 4000 Crandon Blvd. (ℂ **305/361-5421**), is one of metropolitan Miami's finest white-sand beaches, stretching for nearly 6km (4 miles). It has lifeguards and rental cabanas with a shower and chairs ($38 per day). The beach can be extremely crowded on Saturday and Sunday. Parking nearby is $6 for cars and $15 for campers and buses.

Shopping

Most cruise ship passengers shop right near the Port of Miami at **Bayside Market-place,** 401 Biscayne Blvd. (www.baysidemarketplace.com; ℂ **305/577-3344**), a mall with 150 specialty shops, street performers, live music, and some 30 eateries, many of which have outdoor seating right along the bay for picturesque views of the yachts harbored there. Bayside Marketplace can be reached via regular shuttle service from the port or by walking over the Port Bridge.

For high-end shopping head to **Bal Harbour Shops,** 9700 Collins Ave. (www.balharbourshops.com; ℂ **305/866-0311**). This complex features big-name stores, from Chanel and Prada to Lacoste and Neiman Marcus (and Florida's largest Saks Fifth Avenue), and doubles as a celebrity-sighting hot spot (think Jennifer Lopez, Lindsay Lohan, Paris Hilton, and the like).

In South Beach, **Lincoln Road,** an 8-block pedestrian mall, runs between Washington Avenue and Alton Road, near the northern tier of the Art Deco District. It's filled with popular shops, such as Gap and Banana Republic, interior-design stores, art galleries, and even vintage-clothing outlets, as well as coffeehouses, restaurants, and cafes. Despite the recent influx of commercial anchor stores, Lincoln Road manages to maintain its funky, arty flair, attracting an eclectic, colorful crowd.

Coconut Grove, centered on Main Highway and Grand Avenue, is the heart of the city's boutique district and features two open-air shopping and entertainment complexes, **CocoWalk** and the **Streets of Mayfair.**

In Coral Gables, **Miracle Mile,** actually a nearly 1km (½-mile) stretch of Southwest 22nd Street between Douglas and Le Jeune roads (37th and 42nd aves.), features more than 150 shops.

For more local flavor, head north on North Miami Avenue to the **Design District.** You'll find plenty of art galleries, as well as furniture and home-goods stores with couches and shelves that look like art. Start exploring on Northeast 40th Street between North Miami Avenue and Northeast 2nd Avenue.

For a change from the fast-paced glitz of South Beach or the serene luxury of Coral Gables, head for **Little Havana,** where Cubans commingle with the young artists who have begun to set up performance spaces in the area. Little Havana is located just west of downtown Miami on Southwest 8th Street. In addition to authentic Cuban cuisine, you'll find a lively Cubano cafe culture.

Where to Stay

Thanks to its network of highways, you can stay virtually anywhere in greater Miami and still be within 10 to 20 minutes of your ship.

DOWNTOWN   Two hotels—the 34-story **InterContinental Miami,** 100 Chopin Plaza (www.intercontinental.com/miami; ℂ **800/327-3005** or 305/577-1000; rates: $399), and the **Biscayne Bay Marriott,** 1633 N. Bayshore Dr. (www.marriott.com; ℂ **800/228-9290** or 305/374-3900; rates: $219)—are right across the bay from the cruise ship piers, near Bayside Marketplace, a mecca of shops and restaurants.

SOUTH BEACH   The Art Deco, comfy-chic **Hotel Astor,** 956 Washington Ave. (www.hotelastor.com; ℂ **800/270-4981** or 305/531-8081), originally built in 1936, reopened in 1995 after a massive renovation. Rates: $219. The Astor is only 2 blocks from the beach, but if that's still too far for you, the upscale **Hotel Ocean,** 1230–38 Ocean Dr. (www.hotelocean.com; ℂ **800/783-1725** or 305/672-2579), may be the right choice. Rates: $229.

The **Delano,** 1685 Collins Ave. (www.delano-hotel.com; ℂ **800/555-5001** or 305/672-2000), is a sleek, postmodern, self-consciously hip celebrity hot spot; it's worth at least a peek. Rates: $475. **The Hotel,** 801 Collins Ave., at 8th Street (www.thehotelofsouthbeach.com; ℂ **305/531-5796**), formerly known as the Tiffany Hotel (until the folks behind the little blue box threatened to sue), is a Deco gem—and the most fashionable hotel on South Beach, thanks to the whimsical interior designed by Todd Oldham. Rates: $255.

Hotel Victor, 1144 Ocean Dr. (www.hotelvictorsouthbeach.com; ✆ 305/428-1234), is one of the most posh places to stay on Ocean Drive, with a high-fashion aesthetic that attracts plenty of pretty people to its rooms and restaurant. Rates: $650. Meanwhile, **The Tides,** 1220 Ocean Dr. (www.tidessouthbeach.com; ✆ 305/604-5070), has more of a nouveau-Renaissance feel, and doubles as the best place for people-watching on Ocean, thanks to its massive, elevated front steps outfitted with plush chairs and couches. Rates: $500. Both of those, unsurprisingly, are boutique hotels; the **Loews Miami Beach Hotel,** 1601 Collins Ave. (www.loewshotels. com; ✆ 305/804-1601), on the other hand, is a more traditional high-rise resort with its own shopping center attached, plus a location convenient to both Lincoln Road and the beach. Rates: $549.

The **Townhouse,** 150 20th St. (www.townhousehotel.com; ✆ 877/534-3800 or 305/534-3800), a funky newcomer with exercise bikes in the hallways and free Wi-Fi in all rooms, caters to young, trendy movers and shakers. Rates: $275. **The Kent,** 1131 Collins Ave. (www.thekenthotel.com; ✆ 866/826-5368 or 305/604-5068), attracts a less upwardly mobile yet no-less-chic crowd of young, hip travelers. Rates: $239. **The Standard,** 40 Island Ave. (www.standardhotels.com/miami; ✆ 305/673-1717), is a chic spa oasis that also attracts a younger crowd, though it's set a bit apart from the SoBe madness out on the Venetian Causeway. Hipsters tend to stop by the resort restaurant on weekends for bingo (played ironically, of course) and Guitar Hero tournaments. Rates: $369. Finally, the trendy **Shore Club,** 1901 Collins Ave. (www. shoreclub.com; ✆ 877/640-9500 or 305/695-3100), is where you'll find Miami's very first Nobu, a branch of the Japanese restaurant that took Manhattan by storm some years ago. Rates: $505.

MIAMI BEACH At the **Indian Creek Hotel,** 2727 Indian Creek Dr., at 28th Street (www.indiancreekhotel.com; ✆ 800/491-2772 or 305/531-2727), each room has hardwood floors and modern decor. Rates: $179.

The **Eden Roc Renaissance Resort and Spa,** 4525 Collins Ave. (www.edenroc miami.com; ✆ 800/319-5354 or 305/531-5000), has reopened with fully renovated rooms, spa, and public areas. Rates: $459. Next door, the **Fontainebleau Resort,** 4441 Collins Ave. (www.fontainebleauresorts.net; ✆ 800/548-8886 or 305/538-2000), is another popular, updated 1950s resort that evokes the bygone Rat Pack era, with health clubs, outdoor pools, and beach access. Rates: $599.

Bal Harbour is home to Miami Beach's newest resort, **One Bal Harbour Resort & Spa,** 10295 Collins Ave. (www.oneluxuryhotels.com; ✆ 305/455-5400), a luxury property on a 230m (750-ft.) stretch of shoreline. Rates: $525. Just up the road from Bal Harbour, the **Trump International Beach Resort Miami,** 18001 Collins Ave. (www.trumpmiami.com; ✆ 866/628-1197 or 305/692-5600), offers direct access to Sunny Isles Beach. Every room, from standard all the way up to two-bedroom suites, has a balcony. Rates: $479.

COCONUT GROVE The **Mayfair Hotel & Spa,** 3000 Florida Ave. (www.mayfair hotelandspa.com; ✆ 800/433-4555 or 305/441-0000), is a shopper's dream destination, located right across from the CocoWalk shops. Rates: $309. The **Ritz-Carlton Coconut Grove,** 3300 SW 27th Ave. (www.ritzcarlton.com; ✆ 800/241-3333 or 305/644-4680), the third and smallest of Miami's Ritz-Carlton hotels, is surrounded by nearly a hectare (2½ acres) of tropical gardens and overlooks Biscayne Bay and the Miami skyline. Decorated in an Italian Renaissance style, the hotel's understated luxury is a welcome addition to an area known for its gaudiness. Biscaya is the hotel's extremely elegant restaurant—we're talking footstools for women to put their purses on! Rates: $499.

CORAL GABLES   The famous **Biltmore Hotel,** 1200 Anastasia Ave. (www. biltmorehotel.com; © **305/445-1926**), exudes an old-world, stately glamour and is rumored to be haunted by ghosts of travel days past. Rates: $429. The **Hotel St. Michel,** 162 Alcazar Ave. (www.hotelstmichel.com; © **800/848-4683** or 305/444-1666), is a three-story establishment reminiscent of an inn in provincial France. Rates: $189. **The Westin Colonnade,** 180 Aragon Ave. (www.starwoodhotels.com; © **800/937-8461** or 305/441-2600), has a classy, European feel, and is popular with business travelers. Rates: $349.

KEY BISCAYNE   The **Ritz-Carlton, Key Biscayne,** 455 Grand Bay Dr. (www. ritzcarlton.com; © **800/241-3333** or 305/365-4500), offers a to-die-for spa, not to mention stunning ocean views. Rates: $519.

Where to Eat

DOWNTOWN   Up Biscayne Boulevard near the burgeoning Miami Design District is **Soyka,** 5556 NE Fourth Court (www.soykarestaurant.com; © **305/759-3117**), the hip downtown sibling of South Beach's Van Dyke cafe, serving American food. Dinner main courses: $15 to $32.

SOUTH BEACH   For a "burlesque-inspired" Mexican dining experience try **Lolita Cocina & Tequila Bar,** 100 Collins Ave. (© **305/532-4550**). Dinner main courses: $16 to $32. Take time to stroll down the pedestrian mall on Lincoln Road, which offers art galleries, specialty shops, and several excellent outdoor cafes such as **Spris,** a pizzeria at 731 Lincoln Rd. (www.spris.cc; © **305/673-2020**), and the **Van Dyke Cafe,** 846 Lincoln Rd. (www.thevandykecafe.com; © **305/534-3600**). Prices range from $5 to $16 at Spris, $10 to $24 at the Van Dyke.

Lincoln Road is home to haute eateries-cum-lounges imported from New York (or at least inspired by the city's hot spots). Selections include **Sushi Samba,** 600 Lincoln Rd. (www.sushisamba.com; © **305/673-5337;** dinner main courses: $21–$44), which features a delectable fusion of South American and Japanese cuisine; and **Nobu,** 1901 Collins Ave. (www.noburestaurants.com; © **305/695-3232;** dinner main courses: $21–$90), the revered name in nouvelle Japanese cuisine.

At the legendary **Joe's Stone Crab,** 11 Washington Ave., between South Point Drive and First Street (www.joesstonecrab.com; © **305/673-0365**), about a ton of stone-crab claws are served daily during stone-crab season from October to May (the joint is usually closed May 15–Oct 15), when people wait for up to 2 hours for a table. Crab prices vary depending on the market rate, but start around $35 per order. Even if Gloria Estefan weren't co-owner of **Larios on the Beach,** 820 Ocean Dr. (© **305/532-9577**), the crowds would flock to this bistro, which serves old-fashioned Cuban dishes such as *masitas de puerco* (fried pork chunks). Dinner main courses: $13 to $19.

About a block and a half south of Lincoln Road, **Espanola Way** is a charming, stucco-lined street with the feel of a rural Mediterranean village. It's blocked to traffic, so pedestrians can wander at whim, and it's also home to some great midpriced restaurants. **Tapas y Tintos,** 448 Espanola Way (www.tapasytintos.com; © **305/538-8272**), serves up authentic Spanish tapas with an emphasis on Galician dishes, as well as a wide variety of cocktails that include sangrias and mojitos. Tapas cost anywhere from $9 to $15 per dish. Across the way, **Hosteria Romana,** 429 Espanola Way (www.hosteriaromana.com; ℂ **305/532-4299**), offers a rowdy experience of old Italy with enormous pasta and pizza dishes, as well as boisterous waiters belting out Italian tunes and playing cymbals. Main courses: $15 to $40.

If you're in need of a casual place to catch the game—whatever game you're looking for—try **the Quarterdeck,** 1430 Alton Rd. (www.quarterdeckrestaurants.net; ℂ **305/531-2441**). It's one of South Beach's only sports bars, and its walls are filled with flatscreen TVs showing everything from college football to ice-skating. Main courses: $7 to $20.

The southern tip of South Beach—known as SoFi, or "South of Fifth"—is a less flashy, more serene side of the beach, and it's also home to some of its best dining. **Prime 112,** 112 Ocean Dr. (www.prime112.com; ℂ **305/532-8112**), is a traditional steakhouse with South Beach styling. Dinner main courses: $40 to $110.

COCONUT GROVE   If you want to people-watch while you eat, head for **Café Tu Tu Tango,** 3015 Grand Ave., Ste. 250 (www.cafetututango.com; ℂ **305/529-2222**), on the second floor of CocoWalk. Designed to look like a disheveled artist's loft, it has original paintings (some half-finished) on easels or hanging from the walls. The tapas courses range from $7 to $12.

CORAL GABLES   **Randazzo's,** 385 Miracle Mile (www.randazzoslittleitaly.com; ℂ **305/448-7002**), is a tiny little Italian restaurant with the biggest portions around. Owned by a former boxing champ, it can get a bit crowded, but it's worth it for the food (try the spicy calamari), the ambience (screens running *The Godfather* movies on a loop), and the witty menu ("Shut up and eat a cannoli. What are you, a supermodel?"). Main courses: $16 to $40.

KEY BISCAYNE   The surf and turf is routine at the **Rusty Pelican,** 3201 Rickenbacker Causeway (www.therustypelican.com; ℂ **305/361-3818**), but it's worth a visit for a drink and the spectacular sunset view. Dinner main courses: $17 to $68. **Cioppino,** at the Ritz-Carlton, 455 Grand Bay Dr. (ℂ **305/365-4286**), serves Tuscan fare. Dinner main courses: $34 to $50.

LITTLE HAVANA   Little Havana offers excellent Cuban and Spanish cuisine. **Casa Panza Restaurant,** 1620 SW Eighth St. (ℂ **305/644-3444**), a taste of Old Seville in Little Havana, is a feast for the senses with flamenco dancers, tempting tapas, and a lively atmosphere that reels in crowds nightly. At 11pm on Thursday, everyone, no matter what their religion, is given a candle to pray to La Virgen del Rocio, one of Seville's most revered saints—it's a party with piety! Dinner main courses: $15 to $35. Another place to check out is **Versailles,** 3555 SW Eighth St. (www.versaillescuban.com; ℂ **305/444-0240**), a palatial, late-night (Sun–Fri until 2am, Sat until 4am), mirrored diner serving all the Cuban mainstays in large and reasonably priced portions. Dinner main courses: $10 to $23.

Miami After Dark

Miami's nightlife is as varied as its population, and the sizzling scene is no stranger to A-list celebrities, from Leonardo DiCaprio and Gwyneth Paltrow to Al Pacino, Sylvester Stallone, and Madonna. Look for the klieg lights to direct you to the hot spots of South Beach. The blocks of Washington Avenue, Collins Avenue, and Ocean Drive are the main nightlife thoroughfares, but you're more likely to spot a celebrity in an off-the-beaten-path eatery like **Barton G. the Restaurant,** 1427 West Ave., Miami Beach (www.bartong.com; ✆ **305/672-8881**). Dinner main courses: $25 to $70.

Restaurants and bars are open late—usually until 5am. Hotel bars are very popular, particularly the **Rose Bar** at the Delano, 1685 Collins Ave. (www.delano-hotel.com; ✆ **305/672-2000**), and the Shore Club's hot, hauter-than-thou celeb magnet **Skybar,** 1901 Collins Ave. (www.shoreclub.com; ✆ **786/276-6772**). Command central for the chic elite at all hours of the night includes the restaurants-cum-lounges Sushi Samba and Nobu, listed in the "Where to Eat" section, above.

As trends come and go, so do clubs, so before you head out for a decadent night of dancing, make sure the place is still in business! At press time, some of the clubs at which to see, be seen, and, of course, dance, include **Cameo,** 1445 Washington Ave. (www.cameomiami.com; ✆ **786/235-5800**), formerly Crobar; **Mansion,** 1235 Washington Ave. (www.theopiumgroup.com; ✆ **305/531-5535**); and **Opium Garden,** 136 Collins Ave. (www.theopiumgroup.com; ✆ **305/531-5535**), an open-air nightclub that's a magnet for the trendoid brass (be sure to check out the hot new V-VIP lounge, called Privé). For a Playboy Mansion–type scene by day, check out the **Nikki Beach Club,** 1 Ocean Dr. (www.nikkibeach.com; ✆ **305/538-1111**), complete with Tiki huts and tepees on the beach.

But South Beach isn't the only place for nightlife in Miami. Not too far from the Miami River is the city's oldest bar, **Tobacco Road,** 626 S. Miami Ave. (www.tobacco-road.com; ✆ **305/374-1198**), a gritty place that still attracts some of the city's storied, pre–*Miami Vice* natives. Downtown Miami is also home to the city's biggest warehouse-size clubs. There's **Space,** 142 NE 11th St. (www.clubspace.com; ✆ **305/372-9378**), which occupies a very large warehouse in downtown Miami and is vaguely reminiscent of a funky, SoHo-style dance palace.

Down in Little Havana is **Hoy Como Ayer,** 2212 SW Eighth St. (✆ **305/541-2631**), where salsa is not a condiment, but a way of life.

Other nocturnal options abound in Coconut Grove and Coral Gables and, slowly but surely, the Design District. Check the *Miami Herald, Miami New Times,* and **www.miami.citysearch.com** for specific events.

FORT LAUDERDALE

Broward County's **Port Everglades** one of the busiest cruise ports in the world, with more home-ported cruise ships than any other cruise port. It draws more than three million cruise passengers a year and boasts the deepest harbor on the eastern seaboard south of Norfolk, 12 ultramodern cruise ship terminals, and an easy access route to the Fort Lauderdale–Hollywood International Airport, less than a 10-minute drive away. In addition, Port Everglades is embarking on a $54-million project to renovate four existing cruise terminals that will feature juried, Florida-themed artwork. Details on the renovations and the latest cruise offerings are available at www.port everglades.net.

The port itself is fairly free of congestion, offering covered loading zones, drop-off and pickup staging, and curbside baggage handlers. Terminals are comfortable and safe, with seating areas, snack bars, lots of taxis, and clean restrooms. Parking lots have recently been expanded to offer a total of 4,500 spaces.

VISITOR INFORMATION   The **Greater Fort Lauderdale Convention & Visitors Bureau,** 100 E. Broward Blvd., Fort Lauderdale, FL 33316 (www.sunny.org; ✆ **800/22-SUNNY** [227-8669] or 954/765-4466), is an excellent resource, distributing a comprehensive guide on accommodations, events, and sightseeing in Broward County.

Getting to Fort Lauderdale & the Port

Port Everglades is located about 37km (23 miles) north of Miami within the city boundaries of Fort Lauderdale, Hollywood, and Dania Beach. I-595 will take you right onto the grounds. For information, contact **Port Everglades** (www.broward. org/port; ☎ **954/523-3404**).

BY PLANE   Small and extremely user-friendly, the **Fort Lauderdale–Hollywood International Airport** (www.broward.org/airport; ☎ **866/435-9355**) is about 3km (2 miles) from Port Everglades (5 min. by bus or taxi), making this the easiest airport-to-cruise-port trip in Florida. (Port Canaveral, by contrast, is about a 45-min. drive from the Orlando airport.) If you've booked air or transfers through the cruise line, a representative will show you to your shuttle bus after you land at the airport. If not, taking a taxi to the port costs about $18.

BY CAR   The port has three passenger entrances: Spangler Boulevard, an extension of S.R. 84 E.; Eisenhower Boulevard, running south from the 17th Street Causeway/A1A; and Eller Drive, connecting directly with I-595. I-595 runs east-west, with connections to the Fort Lauderdale–Hollywood Airport, I-95, S.R. 7 (441), Florida's Turnpike, Sawgrass Expressway, and I-75. Parking is available at the port in two large garages. The 2,500-space Northport Parking Garage, next to the Greater Fort Lauderdale/Broward County Convention Center, serves terminals 1, 2, and 4. The 2,000-space Midport Parking Garage serves terminals 18, 19, 21, 22, 24, 25, and 26. Garages are well lit, security patrolled, and designed to accommodate RVs and buses. The 24-hour parking fee is $15 daily.

GETTING AROUND   For a taxi, call **Yellow Cab** (☎ **954/565-5400**). Rates start at $4.50 for the first mile and $2.40 for each additional mile. **Broward County Mass Transit** (www.broward.org/bct; ☎ **954/357-8400**) runs bus service throughout the county. One-day passes are $4. **Water Taxi** (www.watertaxi.com; ☎ **954/467-6677**) offers all-day passes for $20 for adults and $13 for seniors and kids.

Exploring Ft. Lauderdale

With its lovely and expansive beach promenade, its numerous inlets and waterways, its boating history, and the Florida art and culture found along the elegant Las Olas Boulevard, Fort Lauderdale is an excellent choice for a south Florida port. The beach at Fort Lauderdale was featured in the popular 1950s movie *Where the Boys Are* and became infamous as a chaotic spring-break playground in the 1980s. Since then the place has changed dramatically. The Beach Promenade underwent a $30-million renovation not long ago, and today it looks marvelous.

In addition to miles of beautiful wide beaches, Fort Lauderdale has more than 480km (300 miles) of navigable natural waterways as well as innumerable artificial canals that permit thousands of residents to anchor boats in their backyards (and that have led to the city's nickname: "Venice of the Americas"). You can easily get onto the water by renting a boat or hiring a private, moderately priced water taxi (see "Getting Around," above).

The **Museum of Discovery & Science,** 401 SW Second St. (www.mods.org; ☎ **954/467-6637**), is an excellent interactive science museum with an IMAX theater. Check out the 16m-tall (52-ft.) "Great Gravity Clock" in the museum's atrium.

Fort Lauderdale

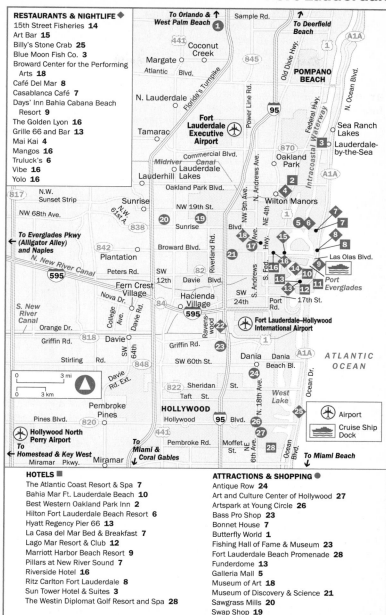

RESTAURANTS & NIGHTLIFE ◆
15th Street Fisheries **14**
Art Bar **15**
Billy's Stone Crab **25**
Blue Moon Fish Co. **3**
Broward Center for the Performing Arts **18**
Café Del Mar **8**
Casablanca Café **7**
Days' Inn Bahia Cabana Beach Resort **9**
The Golden Lyon **16**
Grille 66 and Bar **13**
Mai Kai **4**
Mangos **16**
Truluck's **6**
Vibe **16**
Yolo **16**

HOTELS ■
The Atlantic Coast Resort & Spa **7**
Bahia Mar Ft. Lauderdale Beach **10**
Best Western Oakland Park Inn **2**
Hilton Fort Lauderdale Beach Resort **6**
Hyatt Regency Pier 66 **13**
La Casa del Mar Bed & Breakfast **7**
Lago Mar Resort & Club **12**
Marriott Harbor Beach Resort **9**
Pillars at New River Sound **7**
Riverside Hotel **16**
Ritz Carlton Fort Lauderdale **8**
Sun Tower Hotel & Suites **3**
The Westin Diplomat Golf Resort and Spa **28**

ATTRACTIONS & SHOPPING ●
Antique Row **24**
Art and Culture Center of Hollywood **27**
Artspark at Young Circle **26**
Bass Pro Shop **23**
Bonnet House **7**
Butterfly World **1**
Fishing Hall of Fame & Museum **23**
Fort Lauderdale Beach Promenade **28**
Funderdome **13**
Galleria Mall **5**
Museum of Art **18**
Museum of Discovery & Science **21**
Sawgrass Mills **20**
Swap Shop **19**

THE PORTS OF EMBARKATION | Fort Lauderdale

4

47

Admission is $18 for adults, $14 for children 2 to 12, and $17 for seniors. It's open Monday through Saturday from 10am to 5pm, Sunday from noon to 6pm.

The **Museum of Art,** 1 E. Las Olas Blvd. (www.moaflnsu.org; ✆ **954/525-5500**), is a truly terrific small museum whose permanent collection of 20th-century European and American art includes works by Picasso, Calder, Warhol, Mapplethorpe, Dalí, Stella, and William Glackens. African, South Pacific, pre-Columbian, Native American, and Cuban art are also on display. Admission is $10 for adults, $7 for seniors and students, and free for kids 4 and under. The museum is open Tuesday through Saturday from 11am to 5pm, Sunday from noon to 5pm.

For an alternative to the beach or other (weather-dependent) outdoor activities, try the new 9,000-square-foot play center, **Funderdome,** 1455 Southeast 17th St. (www.funderdome.net; ✆ **954/525-1816**), near the port. In addition to a giant indoor playground, the facility is equipped with a climbing wall, a sky trail ropes challenge course, a ball blasting arena, a high-energy laser maze, and an interactive game floor. A separate section is available for toddlers, and parents can relax in the cafe, which offers free Wi-Fi. Open daily 9am; entrance fee $20.

Bonnet House, 900 N. Birch Rd. (www.bonnethouse.org; ✆ **954/563-5393**), a plantation-style home and 14-hectare (35-acre) estate, survives in the middle of an otherwise highly developed beachfront condominium area, offering a glimpse into the lives of Fort Lauderdale's pioneers. Guided tours are offered Tuesday through Saturday from 10am to 4pm, and the museum is closed during the month of September each year. Admission is $20 for adults, $18 for seniors, $16 for kids ages 6 to 12, and free for children 5 and under.

Butterfly World, Tradewinds Park South, 3600 W. Sample Rd., Coconut Creek, west of the Florida Turnpike (www.butterflyworld.com; ✆ **954/977-4400**), is home to more than 150 species. In the park's walk-through, screened-in aviary, visitors can watch newly hatched butterflies emerge from their cocoons and flutter around as they learn to fly. It's open Monday through Saturday from 9am to 5pm, Sunday from 11am to 5pm. Admission is $25 for adults and $20 for kids 3 to 11.

In South Florida, fishing isn't just a hobby—it's an obsession, and for many locals, a way of life. So it's no surprise that the International Game Fish Association chose Fort Lauderdale as the site for its **Fishing Hall of Fame & Museum,** 300 Gulf Stream Way (www.igfa.org; ✆ **954/922-4212**). In addition to historical information and facts about fish, the museum offers a simulated fishing experience, just in case you didn't have time for the real thing. It's open Monday to Saturday from 10am to 6pm and Sunday from noon to 6pm, closed only on Thanksgiving Day and Christmas Day. Admission is $8 for adults, and $6 for kids ages 3 to 16 and seniors 62 and over.

Where people-watching and casual dining are concerned, Downtown Hollywood, the stretch of Hollywood Boulevard between Dixie Highway and 17th Avenue, is a destination in itself. Here, the streets are lined with quaint cafes and laid-back restaurants, with a sprinkling of art galleries and one-of-a-kind boutiques. The area is often taken over by street festivals and antique shows; contact the **Hollywood Office of Tourism,** 101 N. Ocean Dr., Ste. 204 (www.visithollywoodfl.org; ✆ **877/672-2468**), to check for special events during your stay.

At the center of Downtown Hollywood is the **ArtsPark at Young Circle,** a 4-hectare (10-acre) park with walking promenades, a playground, and a Japanese-designed interactive fountain. In addition to being a rosy patch of grass for a picnic, **ArtsPark** also hosts fitness lessons such as yoga and circuit training. For a full schedule, visit www.hollywoodfl.org or call ✆ **954/921-3404.**

As the name of its park suggests, Downtown Hollywood is one artsy place. For modern art that can border on the wacky, visit the **Art and Culture Center of Hollywood,** 1650 Harrison St. (www.artandculturecenter.org; ✆ **954/921-3274**), which has been known to showcase pieces such as 3m-tall (10-ft.) puppets and an entire collection of artwork banned for using copyrighted images. The center also screens an eclectic selection of independent films. The gallery is open Monday through Saturday from 10am to 5pm, and on Sunday from noon to 4pm. Admission is $7 for adults; $4 for student, seniors, and kids age 4 to 13; and free for children 3 and under.

Organized Tours

The Mississippi-style riverboat *Jungle Queen,* Bahia Mar Yacht Center, Florida A1A (www.junglequeen.com; ✆ **954/462-5596**), is one of Fort Lauderdale's best-known attractions. Four-hour dinner cruises and 3-hour sightseeing tours take visitors up the New River past Millionaires' Row, Old Fort Lauderdale, the new downtown, and the Port Everglades cruise ship port. Call for prices and departure times.

Water Taxis of Fort Lauderdale, 651 Seabreeze Blvd. (www.watertaxi.com; ✆ **954/467-6677**), operates a fleet of old port boats that offer taxi service on demand around this city of canals, carrying up to 72 passengers each. You can be picked up at your hotel and shuttled to the dozens of restaurants and bars on the route for the rest of the night. The service operates daily from 10am to 11pm. The cost is $20 per person before 5pm, or $10 for a moonlight madness ticket after 5pm.

If you'd rather see the city by land, choose the **Fort Lauderdale Trolley Tour,** 419 S. Fort Lauderdale Beach Blvd. (www.southfloridatourismcouncil.com; ✆ **954/522-1770**), a 2-hour exhaustive narrated tour of the port, marina, Fort Lauderdale Beach, Riverwalk, Las Olas Boulevard, and other important and historic sites. The tour runs four times daily, leaving at 9:30am, 11:30am, 1:30pm, and 3:30pm. Admission is $25 for adults, $15 for children.

Hitting the Beach

The stunning 8km (5-mile) **Fort Lauderdale Beach** is located along A1A, also known as the Fort Lauderdale Beach Boulevard, between Southeast 17th Street and Sunrise Boulevard. The fabled strip from *Where the Boys Are* is **Ocean Boulevard,** between Las Olas and Sunrise boulevards. On weekends, parking at the oceanside meters is difficult to find, but there is a parking lot 1 block west of A1A that charges $10 for the day.

The beach is environmentally certified by Blue Water, as a clean beach. Lifeguards can be found all along the strip with posted information on water temperature, currents, and daily swimming conditions. You can also call the lifeguard service (✆ **954/828-4597**) for swimming conditions. Although the water along Florida's Atlantic coast is beautiful and mostly calm, it can also get a little choppy. The beach at the Howard Johnson is a perennial local favorite. A jetty bounds the beach on the south side, making it rather private. High-school and college students share this area with an older crowd. One of the main beach entrances is at 4660 N. Ocean Dr., in Lauderdale-by-the-Sea. Just south of Fort Lauderdale, Hollywood Beach boasts its own boardwalk, which is a favorite among local runners, bicyclists, and in-line skaters. The beach itself is a venue for volleyball games and yoga and tai chi classes; cultural events and musical performances take place periodically at the Beach Theater.

Shopping

Not counting the discount "fashion" stores on Hallandale Beach Boulevard, there are a few places visitors should know about, including **Antique Row,** a strip of U.S. 1 around North Dania Beach Boulevard (in Dania, about a mile south of Fort Lauderdale–Hollywood International Airport) that holds about 200 antiques shops. Most shops are closed on Sunday.

The **Swap Shop,** 3291 W. Sunrise Blvd. (www.floridaswapshop.com; ✆ 954/791-7927), is one of the world's largest flea markets. In addition to endless acres of vendors, there's a mini–amusement park and a 14-screen drive-in movie theater. It's open daily.

For mall-style shops, **Sawgrass Mills,** 12801 W. Sunrise Blvd. (✆ 954/846-2300), is the largest retail center in the area, with 350 stores and restaurants. The Colonnade Outlets offer discounts on luxury items, while the Wannado City indoor theme park keeps kids entertained by letting them try out such professions as doctor and firefighter. Sawgrass Mills is open Monday through Saturday from 10am to 9:30pm, and on Sundays from 11am to 8pm. **The Galleria Mall,** 2414 E. Sunrise Blvd. (✆ 954/564-1015; www.galleriamall-fl.com), in the center of Fort Lauderdale, is anchored by Neiman Marcus, Macy's, and Dillards. It's large and upscale, and with its attractive architecture and ambience, it's also a popular place for dining.

Far from your typical shopping experience, the 15,000-sq.-m (160,000-sq.-ft.) **Bass Pro Shops Outdoor World,** 200 Gulf Stream Way (www.basspro.com; ✆ 954/929-7710), is a showroom for fishing, boating, camping, and hunting gear, as well as a shooting range, an aquarium, and a restaurant. Plus, it's conveniently located next to the IGFA Hall of Fame (see above).

Where to Stay

Fort Lauderdale Beach has a hotel or motel on nearly every block, and the selection ranges from run-down to luxurious. Call the **Greater Fort Lauderdale Convention & Visitors Bureau** (www.sunny.org; ✆ 954/765-4466) for a copy of *Superior Small Lodgings,* a guide to small accommodations in the area. It also has a list of hotels that offer shuttle services to cruisers during your stay.

Located very close to the port, the **Hyatt Regency Pier 66,** 2301 Southeast 17th St. (www.pier66.hyatt.com; ✆ 800/233-1234 or 954/525-6666), is a circular landmark with larger rooms than those at some equivalently priced hotels in town. Its famous Piertop Lounge, a revolving bar on the roof, is often filled with cruise ship patrons. Rates: $175 to $385.

Located just south of Fort Lauderdale's strip, the **Marriott Harbor Beach Resort,** 3030 Holiday Dr. (www.marriottharborbeach.com; ✆ 800/222-6543 or 954/525-4000), is set on 6.5 hectares (16 acres) of beachfront property. Most rooms have private balconies overlooking either the ocean or the Intracoastal Waterway. Rates: $309 to $529.

Aimed at ultra-high-end travelers, **the Westin Diplomat Golf Resort & Spa,** 501 Diplomat Pkwy., Hallandale (www.diplomatresort.com; ✆ 954/602-6000), is a massive complex that attracts large conference groups as well as golfers, who flock to its 18-hole, par-72 golf course with a signature island hole. Rates: $339 to $735. The Diplomat's sister property, **the Atlantic Resort & Spa,** 601 N. Fort Lauderdale Beach Blvd. (www.atlantichotelfl.com; ✆ 954/567-8020), is more of a spa retreat, with its own European-style Spa Atlantic, as well as tasty Mediterranean cuisine at its Trina Restaurant. Rates: $559 to $1,345.

Another high-end hide-out, the **Ritz Carlton Fort Lauderdale,** 1 N. Fort Lauderdale Beach Blvd. (www.ritzcarlton.com; ✆ **954/465-2300**), looks out over the ocean at 24 stories, with a nostalgic design reminiscent of the 1940s. Rates: $529 to $1,500.

The family-owned **Lago Mar Resort & Club,** 1700 S. Ocean Lane (www.lago mar.com; ✆ **800/524-6627**), exudes old Florida charm; has big, well-furnished rooms; and sits on the largest private beach in Fort Lauderdale. It's family-friendly, with tow pools (one for adults only) as well as a full-service spa. Rates: $385 to $580.

The **Hilton Fort Lauderdale Beach Resort,** 505 N. Fort Lauderdale Beach Blvd. (www.hilton.com; ✆ **954/414-2222**), in addition to having luxury appeal, enjoys excellent placement between Sunrise and Las Olas boulevards, meaning that guests here have easy walking access to plenty of bars, restaurants, shops, and galleries. Rates: $309 to $1,399.

Bahia Mar Ft. Lauderdale Beach, 801 Seabreeze Blvd. (www.bahiamarhotel. com; ✆ **800/708-1590** or 954/764-2233), is scattered over 17 hectares (42 acres) of seacoast. The 4-story and 16-story rows of units are adjacent to Florida's largest marina. Rates: $149 to $499.

The **Riverside Hotel,** 620 E. Las Olas Blvd. (www.riversidehotel.com; ✆ **800/325-3280** or 954/467-0671), which opened in 1936, is a local favorite. Try for one of the ground-floor rooms, which have higher ceilings and more space. Rates: $219 to $289.

The Spanish Mediterranean–style **La Casa del Mar Bed & Breakfast,** 3003 Granada St. (www.lacasadelmar.com; ✆ **954/467-2037**), has 10 individually furnished rooms and is only a block away from Fort Lauderdale Beach. Rates: $149 to $242. **The Pillars at New River Sound,** 111 N. Birch Rd. (www.pillarshotel.com; ✆ **954/467-9639**), is a small 23-room hotel, the best of its size in the region. Rates: $259 to $525.

Also newly renovated, the boutique-style **Sun Tower Hotel & Suites,** 2030 N. Ocean Dr. (www.iwantbeach.com; ✆ **954/565-5700**), is located directly on Fort Lauderdale beach. All 23 oceanfront accommodations have private balconies or verandas. Rates: $99 to $259.

Several area properties associated with **Best Western** (www.bestwestern.com) are reasonably priced and located within 8km (5 miles) of the airport and port: **Best Western Airport/Cruise,** 1221 W. S.R. 84 (✆ **800/528-1234** or 954/462-7005; rates: $149–$199); **Best Western Oakland Park Inn,** 3001 N. Federal Hwy. (✆ **800/633-6279** or 954/565-4601; rates: $149–$209); and **Best Western Oceanside Inn,** 1180 Seabreeze Blvd. (✆ **800/367-1007** or 954/525-8115; rates: $188–$289).

Where to Eat

Garlic crabs are the specialty at the **Rustic Inn Crabhouse,** 4331 Anglers Ave. (www.rusticinn.com; ✆ **954/584-1637**), located west of the airport. This riverside dining choice has an open deck over the water. Dinner main courses: $16 to $42. **Grille 66 and Bar,** 2301 SE 17th St. (www.grille66andbar.com; ✆ **954/728-3500**), serves steak, seafood, and pasta dishes at affordable prices. Dinner main courses: $24 to $52.

The restaurant and patio bar at the **Day's Inn Bahia Cabana Beach Resort,** 3001 Harbor Dr. (www.bahiacabanaresort.com; ✆ **954/524-1555**), are charming and laid-back, serving inexpensive American-style dishes on a covered open-air deck overlooking Fort Lauderdale's largest marina. The Fort Lauderdale water taxi makes a stop here. Dinner main courses: $13 to $20.

Don't let its outward appearance fool you: Though **15th Street Fisheries,** 1900 SE 15th St. (www.15streetfisheries.com; ✆ **954/763-2777**), looks like just another seafood stop for boaters, its selection of fresh catches and stellar preparation make it one of the best seafood restaurants in the area. What's better, you can take a water taxi right to its dock for an authentic South Florida experience. Dinner main courses: $25 to $38.

Café Del Mar, 213 S. Fort Lauderdale Beach Blvd. (www.cafedelmarfl.com; ✆ **954/767-8223**), offers a Mediterranean take on seafood, plus a schedule of local and international musicians on its beachfront stage. Dinner main courses: $15 to $40. **Casablanca Café,** 3049 Alhambra St. (www.casablancacafeonline.com; ✆ **954/764-3500**), serves up a preview of the islands you'll be visiting on your cruise, with Caribbean-tinged seafood and steak options. Dinner main courses: $17 to $38.

For dockside dining, the **Blue Moon Fish Co.,** 4405 W. Tradewinds Ave. (www.bluemoonfishco.com; ✆ **954/267-9888**), is a local favorite with a wonderful Art Deco style mixed with an underwater theme done up in wood and glass. Main courses: $29 to $39. **Truluck's,** 2584A E. Sunrise Blvd. (www.trulucks.com; ✆ **954/396-5656**), is an award-winning seafood restaurant and steakhouse. Main courses: $22 to $36.

In Hollywood, you'll find the best crab at **Billy's Stone Crab,** 400 N. Ocean Dr. (www.crabs.com; ✆ **954/923-2300**). It serves only domestic fish and seafood, and nothing is farmed. Open seasonally; all you can eat crab $65.

Fort Lauderdale After Dark

Fort Lauderdale's Riverwalk promenade is primarily a venue for dining and strolling, but after dark, it also heats up with clubs and bars. **ArtBar,** 300 SW 1st Ave. (www.artbarftlauderdale.com; ✆ **954/525-0044**), is a top-40 dance club that doubles as a mecca for spring breakers. **The Golden Lyon** at the Riverside Hotel, 620 E. Las Olas Blvd. (www.riversidehotel.com; ✆ **954/467-0671**), is a cozier people-watching spot. **Mangos,** 904 E. Las Olas Blvd. (www.mangosonlasolas.com; ✆ **954/523-5001**), features some of the best live music in the area while serving up inspiring fresh fish and inventive cocktails.

If you are in the mood for a dressy, more urban, trendy attitude, try **Yolo,** 333 E. Las Olas Blvd. (www.yolorestaurant.com; ✆ **954/523-1000**), or the adjacent bar **Vibe,** 301 E. Las Olas Blvd. (www.vibelasolas.com; ✆ **954/713-7313**), both with an international jet-set feel.

Closer to the beach, at **Blue Jean Blues,** 3320 Northeast 33rd St., 2 blocks north of Oak Park Boulevard and A1A (www.bluejeanblues.net; ✆ **954/306-6330**), live jazz plays 7 nights a week. It's an inviting, atmospheric club with cozy seating and good service.

The **Mai-Kai Restaurant and Polynesian Show,** 3599 N. Federal Hwy. (www.maikai.com; ✆ **954/563-3272**), is fun, popular, and extravagant. The wood-covered walls and South Seas island decor (complete with masks, thatch, and coconuts), together with the extreme cocktails, are quite entertaining, and the show features talented dancers. The food is very good. Dinner main courses: $20 to $45.

The **Broward Center for the Performing Arts,** 201 Southwest Fifth Ave. (www.browardcenter.org; ✆ **954/462-0222**), hosts top opera, symphony, dance, and

Broadway productions. Check online for upcoming shows and events, or look for listings in the *Sun-Sentinel* or the *Miami Herald*.

CAPE CANAVERAL & COCOA BEACH

Known as the Space Coast because of nearby Kennedy Space Center, the Cape Canaveral/Cocoa Beach area boasts 116km (72 miles) of beaches, plus fishing, golfing, surfing, and proximity to Orlando's theme parks, which are only about an hour west—this is exactly why long-underutilized Port Canaveral is now busier than ever before, offering many 3- and 4-night cruise options (often sold as packages with pre- or postcruise visits to the Orlando resorts) as well as weeklong itineraries. Port Canaveral has even become a port of call, with NCL's *Norwegian Dawn* visiting on round-trip Florida/Caribbean itineraries from New York.

Outside the port area, Cape Canaveral is . . . well, it's no Miami. Highways, strip malls, chain stores, and tracts of suburban homes predominate from the port area south into Cocoa Beach, where most of the hotels, restaurants, and beaches discussed here are located. The central areas of Cocoa Beach are mildly more interesting, with some great '50s and '60s condo and hotel architecture—but stylish they're not.

Port Canaveral probably wouldn't be on the cruise industry's radar if it weren't so close to Orlando; most passengers shuttle directly from theme park to pier rather than spending any significant time here. Nevertheless, anyone interested in the space program and its history should plan to arrive a day early (or stay a day after) to check out Kennedy Space Center and the Astronaut Hall of Fame.

VISITOR INFORMATION   Contact the **Florida Space Coast Office of Tourism,** 2725 Judge Fran Jamieson Way, Vierra, FL 32940 (www.space-coast.com; ✆ **877/572-3224** or 321/433-4470; to request a vacation planner, call ✆ **800/936-2326**). Its office is open Monday through Friday from 8am to 5pm.

Getting to Cape Canaveral & the Port

Port Canaveral is located at the eastern end of the Bennett Causeway, just off S.R. 528 (the Beachline Expwy.), the direct route from Orlando. For information about the port, contact the **Canaveral Port Authority** (www.portcanaveral.org; ✆ **888/767-8226** or 321/783-7831).

BY PLANE   The nearest airport is **Orlando International Airport** (www.orlando airports.net; ✆ **407/825-2001**), a 72km (45-mile) drive from Port Canaveral via the S.R. 528/Beachline Expressway. Cruise line representatives will meet you at the airport, if you've booked air and/or transfers through the line. **Cocoa Beach Shuttle** (✆ **888/784-4144** or 321/631-4144) offers shuttle service between Orlando's airport and Port Canaveral; group rates start at $60 for two people each way.

BY CAR   Port Canaveral and Cocoa Beach are about 72km (45 miles) east of Orlando and 300km (185 miles) north of Miami. They're accessible from virtually every interstate highway along the East Coast. Most visitors arrive via Route 1, I-95, or S.R. 528. At the port, park in the North Lots for north terminals 5 and 10, or the South Lots for terminals 2, 3, and 4. Parking costs $20 a day for vehicles up to 6m (20 ft.), $35 a day for vehicles 6m (20 ft.) and over.

GETTING AROUND   For a cab, call **Yellow Top Taxi** (✆ **321/636-1234**).

The Orlando Theme Parks

All it took was a sprinkle of pixie dust in the 1970s to begin the almost-magical transformation of Orlando from a large swath of swampland into the most-visited tourist destination in the world. Today the city is home to three giants—**Walt Disney World, Universal Orlando,** and **SeaWorld**—and to seven of the eight most-popular theme parks in the United States.

Many cruises from Port Canaveral are sold as land/sea packages that include park stays; if you decide to visit Orlando before or after your cruise, it's essential to plan ahead. Otherwise, the number of attractions begging for your time and the hypercommercial atmosphere can put a serious dent in your psyche as well as your wallet and stamina. Even if you had 2 weeks, it wouldn't be long enough to hit everything, so don't even try. Stay selective, stay sane. That's our motto.

It would take a significant portion of this book to detail everything to do in Orlando, but you'll find some basic information on the major theme parks and other attractions below. For more information, pick up a copy of *Frommer's Walt Disney World & Orlando.*

WALT DISNEY WORLD

Walt Disney World is the umbrella covering four theme parks: the Magic Kingdom, Epcot, Hollywood Studios, and Animal Kingdom. Besides its theme parks, Disney has an assortment of other attractions, including three water parks, several entertainment venues, and a number of shopping spots.

VISITOR INFORMATION   Walt Disney World is located southwest of Orlando off I-4, west of the Florida Turnpike. For information, vacation brochures, and videos, call *✆* **407/934-7639;** for general information, visit www.disneyworld.com or call *✆* **407/824-2222.**

TICKET PRICES   At press time, **1-day/one-park tickets,** for admission to the Magic Kingdom, Epcot, Hollywood Studios, or Animal Kingdom, were $91 for adults, $85 for children 3 to 9, and free for children 2 and under. Discounted multiday, multipark passes are available, and many land/sea cruise packages include these passes.

OPERATING HOURS   Park hours vary and are influenced by special events and the economy, so call ahead or go to www.disneyworld.com to check. Generally, expect Animal Kingdom to be open daily from 9am to 5 or 6pm, Epcot to be open from 9am to 9pm, and Magic Kingdom and Hollywood Studios to be open from 9am to 8 or 9pm. All may open or close earlier or later.

The Parks

MAGIC KINGDOM   The most popular theme park on the planet offers some 40 attractions, plus restaurants and shops, in a 43-hectare (106-acre) package. Its symbol, Cinderella Castle, forms the hub of a wheel whose spokes reach to seven "lands" simulating everything from an Amazonian jungle to Colonial America. The classic **it's a small world** ride is still here, as well as the original 1970s **Pirates of the Caribbean** attraction, though it's undergone a recent upgrade to include the Captain Jack character of movie fame, along with his enemy Barbosa. New special effects—including animatronic technology to make the pirates look a bit more convincing—have turned the ride into a more modern version of the one you might remember from your childhood. The Magic Kingdom is also home base for some of Disney's most beloved characters: Mickey and Minnie, of course, as well as characters from *Aladdin,*

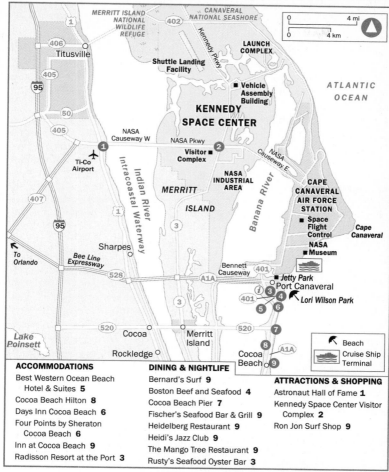

ACCOMMODATIONS

Best Western Ocean Beach
  Hotel & Suites **5**
Cocoa Beach Hilton **8**
Days Inn Cocoa Beach **6**
Four Points by Sheraton
  Cocoa Beach **6**
Inn at Cocoa Beach **9**
Radisson Resort at the Port **3**

DINING & NIGHTLIFE

Bernard's Surf **9**
Boston Beef and Seafood **4**
Cocoa Beach Pier **7**
Fischer's Seafood Bar & Grill **9**
Heidelberg Restaurant **9**
Heidi's Jazz Club **9**
The Mango Tree Restaurant **9**
Rusty's Seafood Oyster Bar **3**

ATTRACTIONS & SHOPPING

Astronaut Hall of Fame **1**
Kennedy Space Center Visitor
  Complex **2**
Ron Jon Surf Shop **9**

Cinderella, Pinocchio, and *Monsters, Inc.* If you're traveling with little kids, this is the place to go.

EPCOT   This 105-hectare (260-acre) park (the acronym stands for Experimental Prototype Community of Tomorrow) has two sections. **Future World** is centered on Epcot's icon, a giant geosphere that looks like a big golf ball. Major corporations sponsor the park's 10 themed areas, and the focus is on discovery, scientific achievements, and tomorrow's technologies in areas ranging from energy to undersea exploration. The **World Showcase** is a community of 11 miniaturized nations surrounding a 16-hectare (40-acre) lagoon. All of these "countries" have indigenous architecture, landscaping, restaurants, and shops; cultural facets are explored in art exhibits, dance or other live performances, and innovative films. EPCOT definitely appeals more to adults than children. It has few thrill rides, so if that's a requirement, go elsewhere. A few notable exceptions are **Soarin',** a hang gliding simulation that takes passengers on a thrill ride over the treetops of California's Yosemite and redwood forests; **Mission: SPACE,** which challenges teams of visitors to avoid meteors and navigate a spaceship through a simulated adventure in open space; and the **GM Test Track,** which lets you know what it's like to be a crash test dummy (minus the actual crash, of course), strapping in for tight turns, bumpy terrain, and changes in temperature. **Note:** Hiking through this park will often exhaust even the fittest person—some folks say *Epcot* really stands for "Every Person Comes Out Tired"—so I recommend splitting your visit over 2 days, if possible.

DISNEY'S HOLLYWOOD STUDIOS   You'll probably spy the Earful Tower—a water tower outfitted with gigantic mouse ears—before you enter this 45-hectare (111-acre) park, which Disney bills as "the Hollywood that never was and always will be." You'll find pulse-quickening rides such as the Aerosmith-themed **Rock 'n' Roller Coaster** and the **Twilight Zone Tower of Terror,** plus movie- and TV-themed shows such as Jim Henson's **Muppet*Vision 3D,** as well as some wonderful street performers. The newest attraction here is **Toy Story Mania,** a 3-D simulation that lets visitors compete in games hosted by Woody, Buzz, and the rest of the *Toy Story* gang. Adults and kids both love this park; best of all, it can be done comfortably in a day.

ANIMAL KINGDOM   This 200-hectare (500-acre) park opened in 1998, combining animals, elaborate landscapes, and a handful of rides. It's a conservation venue as much as an attraction, so it's easy for most of the animals to escape your eyes here (unlike at Tampa's Busch Gardens, the state's other major animal park). Though the thrill rides are better at Busch, Animal Kingdom's **Expedition Everest** roller coaster and **DINOSAUR** ride through primeval times both offer family-friendly, if slightly tamer, thrills. Animal Kingdom also has much better shows, such as *Finding Nemo—The Musical* and *Festival of the Lion King.* The park is good for both adults and children, and can be done in a single outing, but if you come on a hot summer day, get here early—or it's unlikely you'll see many of the primo animals, which are smart enough to seek shade.

WATER PARKS   If you're stopping by Disney World on a particularly hot day in the summer, chances are that you'll need a place to cool off and relax for an afternoon. Enter **Blizzard Beach** and **Typhoon Lagoon,** Disney's laid-back alternatives to braving the beating-down sun back on land.

For the truly overheated, Blizzard Beach holds the most appeal, designed to look like a snow-capped ski resort. Slides include individual "toboggan" racers, **Teamboat Springs,** a winding family raft ride, and the **Slush Gusher** speed slide. The **Cross Country Creek** lazy river and **Tike's Peak** kids' area offer more low-key ways to play.

Typhoon Lagoon, on the other hand, lets visitors slip and slide their way through a deserted Caribbean island. You can try your hand at surfing in one of the world's largest wave pools here, or climb in a raft and shoot down **Mayday Falls** or **Gang Plank Falls.** Still, the top thriller here is the opportunity to snorkel with sharks and other tropical sea life at the **Shark Reef.** Like Blizzard Beach, Typhoon Lagoon also has lazy river and kids' water facilities, so the whole family is covered.

UNIVERSAL ORLANDO

Universal Orlando is Disney World's number-one competitor in the ongoing Orlando-area "anything you can do we can do better" theme brawl. Although it's a distant

Cape Canaveral & Cocoa Beach

second in terms of attendance, it's unquestionably the champion at entertaining teenagers and the older members of the thrill-ride crowd, with two major parks—the original Universal Studios Florida and the newer Islands of Adventure—plus a water park, an entertainment district, and several resorts.

VISITOR INFORMATION The parks are located at Universal Boulevard, Orlando, off I-4. For information, go to www.universalorlando.com or call ✆ **800/837-2273** or 407/363-8000.

TICKET PRICES A **1-day/one-park** ticket costs $85 (plus 6.5% sales tax) for adults, $79 for children 3 to 9. A **Universal Orlando Park to Park Unlimited Admission Ticket** gets you admission at Universal Studios and Islands of Adventure, as well as the Universal CityWalk nightlife hub; a 2-day pass is $136 for adults and $126 for kids ages 3 to 9 (available online only).

OPERATING HOURS The parks are open 365 days a year, generally from 9am to 6pm, though often later, especially in summer and around holidays, when they're sometimes open until 9pm. Call before you go for exact hours on the days you're visiting.

The Parks

UNIVERSAL STUDIOS FLORIDA Even with fast-paced, grown-up rides such as **Back to the Future, Terminator,** and **Men in Black Alien Attack,** Universal Studios Florida is fun for kids. While the **E.T. Adventure** has been a staple at this park for years, newer rides such as **Shrek 4-D, Revenge of the Mummy,** and **Jimmy Neutron's Nicktoon Blast** keep the place up to speed with current pop culture, meaning that there are a handful of rides that appeal to every age group. Case in point: **The Simpsons,** Universal's newest ride, takes visitors on an adventure through a theme park within a theme park—this one set in Springfield, and hosted by Krusty the Clown.

Universal is also a working motion-picture and TV studio, so filming is often going on at Nickelodeon's sound stages or elsewhere in the park. Talented actors portraying a range of characters from Universal films usually roam the park. You can do the park in a day, although you'll be a bit breathless when you get to the finish line.

ISLANDS OF ADVENTURE This 45-hectare (111-acre) theme park opened in 1999 and is, bar none, *the* Orlando theme park for thrill-ride junkies. With areas inspired by Dr. Seuss, Jurassic Park, and Marvel comics, the park successfully combines nostalgia with state-of-the-art technology. The **Amazing Adventures of Spider-Man** is a 3-D track ride that is arguably the best all-around attraction in Orlando, and the **Jurassic Park River Adventure** has a 21m (69-ft.) drop that scared Steven Spielberg into jumping ship before going over. **Dueling Dragons,** a ride that draws more raves from coaster crazies than any other in Orlando, has been renamed **the Dragon Challenge** to fit into the brand-new **Wizarding World of Harry Potter.** Similarly, the Flying Unicorn will now be known as the **Flying Hippogriff.** The only new attraction, **Harry Potter and the Forbidden Journey,** is a high-tech simulator-style ride that is housed in a replica of Hogwarts castle. Unless it's the height of high season, the park can be done in a day. It is not, however, a place for families with young kids: 10 of the park's 15 major rides have height restrictions.

WET 'N WILD Universal's answer to Disney's water parks, Wet 'n Wild gives grown-ups a whole host of slides all their own, including **Disco H2O,** which is every bit as nostalgic as it sounds. Most slides here are multiperson-tube slides, which means that it's a great place for groups traveling together. But don't worry about the little ones—they'll be at the **Kids Park,** riding miniature versions of the "big kid" slides.

SEAWORLD

An 80-hectare (200-acre) marine-life park, SeaWorld explores the deep in a format that combines conservation awareness with entertainment—pretty much what Disney is attempting at Animal Kingdom, but SeaWorld got here first, and its message is subtler and a more integrated part of the experience. The park is fun for everyone from small children to adults (who doesn't like dolphins and whales?) and you can easily tour it in a single day. The pace is much more laid-back than Universal or Disney, so it makes for a nice break if you're in the area for several days. SeaWorld has a handful of high-tech water rides such as **Journey to Atlantis** and **Kraken,** but all in all, the park can't compete in this category with Disney and Universal. On the other hand, those parks don't let you discover the crushed-velvet texture of a stingray or the song of a sea lion, not to mention the killer whale **Shamu,** the park's star attraction, and the six other resident orcas. Such attractions as **Dolphin Cove,** the **Manatee Rescue,** and **Penguin Encounter** will put you closer to the critters than just about anyplace else in the area, which is a different kind of thrill altogether.

VISITOR INFORMATION   The park entrance is at the intersection of I-4 and S.R. 528 (the Beachline Expwy.), 10 minutes south of downtown Orlando and 15 minutes from Orlando International Airport. For information, go to www.seaworld.com or call ✆ **888/800-5447** or 407/351-3600.

TICKET PRICES   A **1-day ticket** costs $82 for ages 10 and over, $74 for children 3 to 9, plus 6% sales tax; kids 2 and under get in free.

OPERATING HOURS   The park is usually open daily from 9am to at least 6pm, and later during summer months and holidays, when there are additional shows at night.

Kennedy Space Center & the Astronaut Hall of Fame

Set amid 61,000 hectares (150,000 acres) of marshy wetlands favored by birds, reptiles, and amphibians, the **Kennedy Space Center** (www.kennedyspacecenter.com; ✆ **321/449-4444**) is where astronauts left for the moon in 1969, where the shuttles have lifted off since 1981, and where America's components of the International Space Station are sent into orbit. Even if you've never really considered yourself a science or space buff, you can't help but be impressed by the achievements this place represents.

Security restrictions mean that most of the center is off-limits, but the **Visitor Complex** is designed to offer a glimpse of the works, with real NASA spacecraft; exhibits; hands-on activities for kids; a daily question-and-answer session with a real astronaut; IMAX 3-D movies; a space-shuttle mock-up; a Launch Status Center where presentations are given on current shuttle missions; an outdoor rocket garden displaying now-obsolete *Redstone, Atlas, Saturn,* and *Titan* rockets; and more. There's also the obligatory gift shop and several ridiculously pricey stops where you can grab a bite (you're better off planning to eat before or after your visit).

Some people stick to the Visitor Complex, but for a more complete insight into the space age, take the **bus tour** of the larger complex. Buses depart at 15-minute intervals, but the wait to get aboard can easily take an hour or more, so figure this into your planning. Buses stop at three sites—Launch Complex 39, the International Space Station Center, and the *Apollo/Saturn V* Center—with visitors allowed to spend as much time at each as they like before catching the next bus. You can experience a narrated simulation of the *Apollo 8* launch while looking into an actual Mission Control room that was used for the mission. Following the show, you'll enter an enormous hall where an entire *Saturn V* rocket is on display, held up horizontally by huge metal supports. Numerous exhibits cover various aspects of the Apollo program, and a lunar module hangs from the ceiling above the snack bar.

The **Astronaut Hall of Fame,** located about 10km (6 miles) west of the Space Center Visitor Complex on S.R. 405, near the intersection with U.S. 1, focuses on the heroic human element of the space program and holds the world's largest collection of astronaut memorabilia. And the displays of NASA memorabilia are just plain awesome: actual Mission Control terminals at which you can sit to access interactive information; Jim Lovell's logbook from *Gemini VII;* and, most mind-blowing of all, the actual Apollo 14 command module *Kitty Hawk,* whose plaque bears the inscription "This spacecraft flew to the moon and back January 31–February 9, 1971." 'Nuff said.

But let's get down to brass tacks. The Astronaut Hall of Fame offers one main thing the rest of the KSC Visitors Complex doesn't: the chance to pretend you're an astronaut through various simulations. In the G-force simulator, two wannabe spacemen at a time are strapped tightly into pods at opposite ends of what looks like a giant barbell, which then whirls around on its axis so fast that your cheeks start to flap, just like in the movies. A film projected in the pod simulates a high-speed test flight. Just across the room, the 3-D 360 simulator takes a group of passengers on a simulated shuttle flight to the new International Space Station, pitching you backward, forward, sideways, and upside down along the way. At the Walk on the Moon simulator, visitors are strapped into a harness, which is then counterbalanced to their weight so that they can bounce around as if weightless, doing their "one small step for man" imitation. Now the warnings: Simulators are off-limits to folks under 1.2m (4 ft.). Also, if you tend to suffer from motion sickness, you'll probably want to avoid everything except the weightlessness simulation. Lastly, on the off chance you're there on a slow day, be sure to allow at least a few minutes between simulations, even if you've got a cast-iron constitution. Trust me on this one.

Kennedy Space Center is accessible via S.R. 405, just off U.S. 1. The Visitor Complex is open daily, except Christmas and certain launch days, from 9am to 6pm. The Astronaut Hall of Fame is open daily from 10am to 6pm. The last bus tour departs at 2:15pm from the Visitor Complex. Admission to the Visitor Complex is $43 for adults, $33 for children 3 to 11; admission to the Hall of Fame is $20 for adults, $16 for children. Parking at the Visitor Complex and Hall of Fame is free, but there is no shuttle between the two. Be sure to pick up maps as you enter each branch, and expect to spend most of the day here to get the full experience.

Hitting the Beach

Though the Cape Canaveral/Cocoa Beach area doesn't have the spectacular beach culture of Miami, it doesn't lack for pleasant coastline. The following beaches (or "parks," in the local lingo) are located within an easy drive of the port area.

Closest to the cruise ship port and actually part of the larger port complex, the clean, nicely landscaped **Jetty Park,** 400 E. Jetty Rd. (www.jettyparkbeachand campground.com; ☎ 321/783-7111), is the most elaborate and possibly the nicest of the local beaches, perched at a point from which the whole expanse of the Cape Canaveral/Cocoa Beach coastline stretches away to the south. It's some view. A massive stone jetty juts seaward as protection for the mouth of Port Canaveral, and alongside is an elevated platform from which fishermen dangle their lines right into the surf. A snack bar, bathrooms, picnic facilities, children's playground, and fishing are among the perks here. Parking costs $10 per car. Follow the signs after entering the port area, near where S.R. 528 and S.R. A1A intersect.

A series of beaches are accessible (and generally signposted) off the A1A heading south from the port. The **Cocoa Beach Pier** (www.cocoabeachpier.com) area, off the A1A at Meade Avenue, is a great surfing spot with volleyball, an open-air bar, and a party atmosphere. **Lori Wilson Park,** farther south at 1500 N. Atlantic Ave., is another nicely landscaped area on the order of Jetty Park, with bathrooms and showers; a rustic boardwalk with some shaded picnic areas and benches; a nature center; and the Hammock, a short boardwalk nature trail that winds through ferns, twisted trees, and other *Jurassic Park*–looking foliage, while butterflies flutter by and spiders eye them from their webs. Parking is free.

Shopping

Let's be unkind: You could shop here, but why bother? The offerings in Cape Canaveral and Cocoa Beach are mostly the kind of national mall chains that you've probably got at home, so save your energy and dollars for the Caribbean. An exception—as much for the experience as for the goods—is the **Ron Jon Surf Shop,** 4151 N. Atlantic Ave./S.R. A1A (www.ronjons.com; ✆ 321/799-8888). Inside the blue-and-yellow South Beach–looking Art Deco building is enough au courant beachwear to transform you and a good-size army into surfer dudes. The store also rents beach bikes, body boards, surfboards, kayaks, beach chairs, and other equipment by the hour, day, or week. It's open 24 hours a day, 365 days a year.

Where to Stay

Only a 5-minute drive from the port, **Radisson Resort at the Port,** 8701 Astronaut Blvd./S.R. A1A (www.radisson.com/capecanaveralfl; ✆ 800/333-3333 or 321/784-0000), offers comfortable standard rooms, but families will want to go for the two-room suites that feature a kitchenette with microwave and fridge, a living room with sofa bed and giant TV, and a bedroom with Jacuzzi and second giant TV. The jungle-motif front courtyard has a large amoeba-shaped pool, and a second courtyard has tennis courts. Cruise passengers who are arriving by car can leave their vehicles in the hotel's lot for free during their cruise and can take advantage of the complimentary Radisson shuttle to and from the port. Rates: $117 to $223.

At the other end of the spectrum, the **Inn at Cocoa Beach,** 4300 Ocean Beach Blvd., just off the A1A behind the Ron Jon Surf Shop (www.theinnatcocoabeach.com; ✆ 800/343-5307 or 321/799-3460), is almost entirely couples-oriented, presenting itself as more of a personalized inn than a traditional hotel. Almost all of its 50 comfortable rooms face the ocean and include rocking chairs on their balconies, king- or queen-size beds, TVs, and large bathrooms. A bar off the lobby operates on the honor system (just sign for what you take), and two lobby dogs and four tropical birds in cages around the property add to the homey, low-key atmosphere. Rates: $145 to $235.

Located near Lori Wilson Park on the A1A (and, for you '60s TV fans, near a street called I Dream of Jeannie Lane), the **Cocoa Beach Hilton,** 1550 N. Atlantic

Ave./S.R. A1A (www.cocoabeachhilton.com; ✆ **800/526-2609** or 321/799-0003), is the most upscale of the mainstream beachfront hotels, though it looks like a downtown business hotel that's been transplanted to the seashore. Rooms are spacious but have smallish picture windows only, and none offers a balcony. Rates: $109 to $219.

You'll also find plenty of budget accommodations surrounding the port. **Four Points by Sheraton Cocoa Beach,** 4001 N. Atlantic Ave. (www.starwoodhotels. com/fourpoints; ✆ **321/783-8717**), is a colorful, surfer-inspired property with a 21,000-liter shark tank at the ultracasual Shark Pit Bar & Grill. Rates: $160. The **Best Western Ocean Beach Hotel & Suites,** 5600 N. Atlantic Ave. (www.best westerncocoabeach.com; ✆ **800/962-0028** or 321/783-7621), puts its guests right on the beach. Rates: $129 to $179. Likewise, the **Days Inn Cocoa Beach,** 5500 N. Atlantic Ave. (www.daysinn.com; ✆ **321/784-2550**), sits a mere 90m (300 ft.) from the water's edge. Rates: $125.

Where to Eat

It seems that everywhere you turn down here, you're facing a crab shack or beat-up restaurant or bar. That, in a nutshell, is the dining scene in this area: very casual, very open air, and very, very fried. They all have plenty of character, but one of my favorites is **Boston Beef & Seafood,** 6910 N. Atlantic Ave. (✆ **321/784-4000**), which serves up seafood, New England style. (That means homemade chowder, Ipswich Belly Clams, and plenty of Red Sox pride on the side.)

If you are looking for a casual option, try **Rusty's Seafood & Oyster Bar,** on the south side of Port Canaveral Harbor at 628 Glen Cheek Dr. (www.rustysseafood.com; ✆ **321/783-2033**). On the menu: spicy seafood gumbo, raw or steamed oysters, burgers and sandwiches, pasta, and so on—accompanied by views of the fishing boats and cruise ships heading in and out of the port. Main courses: $15 to $25; sandwiches and salads: $7 to $13.

The Mango Tree Restaurant, 118 N. Atlantic Ave./S.R. A1A, between North First and North Second streets (www.mangotree-restaurant.com; ✆ **321/799-0513**), is the most beautiful and sophisticated restaurant in Cocoa Beach, featuring gourmet seafood, pasta, chicken, and Continental dishes in a plantation-home atmosphere. Dinner main courses: $16 to $39.

In downtown Cocoa Beach, the **Heidelberg Restaurant,** 7 N. Orlando Ave./S.R. A1A, at the Minuteman Causeway (http://heidelbergcocoabeach.com; ✆ **321/783-4559**), serves German and Continental cuisine such as beef stroganoff, goulash, roast duck, sauerbraten, and grilled loin pork chops, in a middling-elegant atmosphere. The adjoining Heidi's Jazz Club (see below) has music Tuesday through Sunday nights. Dinner main courses: $21 to $34.

Port Canaveral After Dark

The **Cocoa Beach Pier,** 401 Meade Ave., off the A1A, less than 1km (½ mile) north of S.R. 520 (www.cocoabeachpier.com; ✆ **321/783-7549**), juts out 150m (500 ft.) over the Atlantic, where it offers a casual beer-and-fruity-drinks atmosphere, an open-air bar with live music most nights, an ice-cream shop, sit-down seafood restaurants, and an arcade, plus beach-equipment rentals and volleyball right next door on the sand.

At the Heidelberg Restaurant (see above), **Heidi's Jazz Club,** 7 N. Orlando Ave./S.R. A1A, at the Minuteman Causeway (http://heidisjazzclub.com; ✆ **321/783-4559**), offers live jazz and blues Tuesday through Sunday, with featured performers

Cape Canaveral & Cocoa Beach

on selected Friday and Saturday evenings and an open jam session Sunday at 7pm. Check out the website for a schedule of performances. The cover is $5.

If you're willing to make the drive to Orlando for your after-dark entertainment, Universal Orlando is the place to be. The resort lives up to its reputation as "Disney for adults" by providing entertainment long after the sun sets and the rides close down. **CityWalk** is the resort's dining and nightlife district, stocked with restaurants, clubs, bars, and even a movie theater. Browsing the clubs here is similar to walking through Epcot Center's World Showcase, in terms of variety: There's a salsa club, an Irish pub, a jazz hangout, a reggae bar, and a South Beach–style ultralounge, all lining the same walkway. Cover charges vary from club to club, but a CityWalk Party Pass will get you in everywhere at no extra charge. A 1-night Party Pass costs $14, and they're often bundled with resort packages, so be sure to check before going out on the town.

TAMPA & ST. PETERSBURG

Tampa was a sleepy port until Cuban immigrants founded Ybor City's cigar industry in the 1880s. A few years later, Henry B. Plant built a railroad to carry tourists into town and constructed his garish Tampa Bay Hotel (now the Henry B. Plant Museum). During the Spanish-American War, Teddy Roosevelt trained his Rough Riders here and walked the Ybor City streets with Cuban revolutionary José Marti. A land boom in the 1920s gave the city its charming, Victorian-style Hyde Park suburb (now a gentrified area, just across the Hillsborough River from downtown), and the go-go 1980s and 1990s brought skyscrapers, a convention center, a performing-arts center, and lots of shopping and dining options to the downtown area.

On the western shore of Tampa Bay, St. Petersburg is the picturesque and pleasant contrast to busy, industrial, business-filled Tampa. Originally conceived and built primarily for tourists and wintering snowbirds, it has a nice downtown area, some quality museums, and a few good restaurants.

The Port of Tampa is set amid a complicated network of channels and harbors near historic Ybor City and its deepwater Ybor Channel. Ships sailing from here head primarily to the western Caribbean, the Yucatán, and Central America.

Tampa is best explored by car, as only the commercial district can be covered on foot. If you want to go to the beach, you'll have to head to neighboring St. Petersburg.

VISITOR INFORMATION Contact the **Tampa Bay Convention & Visitors Bureau,** 400 N. Tampa St., Ste. 2800, Tampa, FL 33602 (www.visittampabay.com; ✆ **800/448-2672** or 813/223-2752). You can also stop by the **Tampa Bay Visitor Information Center,** 3601 E. Busch Blvd. (✆ **813/985-3601**), north of downtown, in the Busch Gardens area.

Getting to Tampa & the Port

The **Tampa Port Authority** is located at 1101 Channelside Dr. (www.tampaport. com; ✆ **813/905-7678**). The Garrison Seaport Center's Cruise Terminal 2 is located at 651 Channelside Dr.; Terminal 3, 815 Channelside Dr.; Terminal 6, 1333 E. McKay St.; and Terminal 7, 2303 Guy N. Verger Blvd.

BY PLANE **Tampa International Airport** (www.tampaairport.com; ✆ **813/870-8700**) is 8km (5 miles) west of downtown Tampa, near the junction of Florida 60 and Memorial Highway. If you haven't arranged for transfers with the cruise line, the

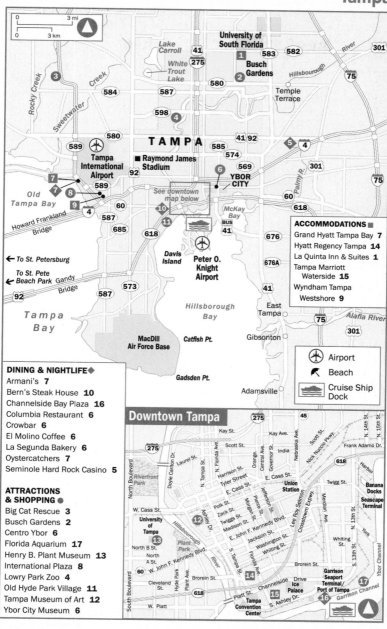

Tampa

University of
South Florida **1**
Busch Gardens **2**

Temple Terrace

T A M P A

Tampa International Airport

■ Raymond James Stadium

YBOR CITY **6**

Old Tampa Bay

See downtown map below

McKay Bay

BUS

Davis Island

Peter O. Knight Airport

Howard Frankland Bridge

← To St. Petersburg

To St. Pete
← Beach Park Gandy Bridge

Tampa Bay

Hillsborough Bay

East Tampa

MacDill Air Force Base

Catfish Pt.

Gibsonton

Gadsden Pt.

Adamsville

Alafia River

ACCOMMODATIONS ■
Grand Hyatt Tampa Bay **7**
Hyatt Regency Tampa **14**
La Quinta Inn & Suites **1**
Tampa Marriott
  Waterside **15**
Wyndham Tampa
  Westshore **9**

Airport
Beach
Cruise Ship Dock

DINING & NIGHTLIFE◆
Armani's **7**
Bern's Steak House **10**
Channelside Bay Plaza **16**
Columbia Restaurant **6**
Crowbar **6**
El Molino Coffee **6**
La Segunda Bakery **6**
Oystercatchers **7**
Seminole Hard Rock Casino **5**

ATTRACTIONS & SHOPPING ●
Big Cat Rescue **3**
Busch Gardens **2**
Centro Ybor **6**
Florida Aquarium **17**
Henry B. Plant Museum **13**
International Plaza **8**
Lowry Park Zoo **4**
Old Hyde Park Village **11**
Tampa Museum of Art **12**
Ybor City Museum **6**

Downtown Tampa

Riverfront Park

Union Station

Banana Docks

Seascape Terminal

University of Tampa **13**

Plant Park

Henry B. Plant Museum

Tampa Museum of Art **12**

Garrison Seaport Terminal/Port of Tampa

Ice Palace

Tampa Convention Center **15**

Garrison Channel

Ybor Channel

4

THE PORTS OF EMBARKATION | Tampa & St. Petersburg

63

port is an easy 30-minute taxi ride away; the fare is about $25 per person via **Yellow Cab** (© 813/253-0121) or **United Cab** (© 813/253-2424). You can also take the shared-ride **Bay Shuttle** (www.tampabayshuttle.com; © 813/259-9998) to the port for $25. **SuperShuttle** (www.supershuttle.com; © 800/282-6817 or 727/572-1111) will take you via town car for $57 or van share ride for $14.

BY CAR   Tampa lies 303km (188 miles) southwest of Jacksonville, 80km (50 miles) north of Sarasota, and 395km (245 miles) northwest of Miami. **From I-75 and I-4:** To terminals 2 and 6, take I-4 west to exit 1 (Ybor City), go south on 21st Street, then turn right on Adamo Drive (Hwy. 60) and then left on Channelside Drive; for Terminal 7, go south on 21st Street (21st St. merges with 22nd St. after crossing Adamo Dr.), turn right on Maritime Boulevard, and then go left on Guy N. Verger to Hooker's Point. **From Tampa International Airport:** To terminals 2 and 6, follow signs to I-275 north, go to I-4 east and then to exit 1 (Ybor City), go south on 21st Street, turn right on Adamo Drive (Hwy. 60), and then turn left on Channelside Drive; for Terminal 7, use directions from I-75 above. The port has ample parking (at $15 per day), with good security. Valet parking is also available.

GETTING AROUND   Taxis in Tampa do not normally cruise the streets for fares; instead, they line up at public loading places, such as the airport, the cruise terminal, and major hotels. **Yellowcab of Tampa** (© 813/872-8294) and **United Cab** (© 813/251-5555) charge about $2.25 per mile; the meter starts at $2.

The **Hillsborough Area Regional Transit/HARTline** (© 813/254-4278) provides regularly scheduled bus service between downtown Tampa and the suburbs. Fares are $1.75 for local service and $2.75 for express routes; exact change is required.

Exploring Tampa
BUSCH GARDENS
Yes, admission prices are high, but **Busch Gardens,** 3605 E. Bougainvillea Ave. (www.buschgardens.com; © 888/800-5447), remains Tampa Bay's most popular attraction. The 136-hectare (336-acre) family entertainment park features thrill rides, animal habitats, live entertainment, shops, restaurants, and games. The park's safari ranks among the best in the country, with nearly 3,400 animals.

Sesame Street Safari of Fun is a land filled with kid-size attractions, both wet and dry. Fly through the desert with Grover, climb in Elmo's Tree House, and splash in Bert and Ernie's Watering Hole. You can also dine with the characters, which, depending on your child, is either thrilling or terrifying. In my experience, it's the former (except for the toddler set), so bring your camera and get ready for some hugs.

Jungala is a 1.6-hectare (4-acre) imitation of a jungle nature preserve where visitors make their way through trees and waterfalls to discover such animals as tigers and orangutans in their faux-natural habitats. The Jungala area is also home to two new rides: Jungle Flyers, a zip-line adventure above the treetops, and the Wild Surge, which shoots passengers out of a crater in a mountain to a towering height above one of Jungala's waterfalls, affording one of the best views of the park.

The park's thrill ride **Sheikra** has gotten more exciting as well, with redesigned "floorless" cars, that give passengers a view from the tips of their toes all the way down to the ground 60m (200 ft.) below (as they're rushing toward it, of course).

Rhino Rally is another recent addition. It's an off-road adventure in 16-passenger "Ralliers," or Land Rovers, that travel a bumpy course with views of Asian elephants,

Tampa & St. Petersburg

THE PORTS OF EMBARKATION

buffalo, antelope, and more. Hang on to your hat when a flash flood whisks away the bridge—and your vehicle.

Montu, once the world's tallest and longest inverted roller coaster, is part of **Egypt,** one of the park's themed areas, which also includes a replica of King Tutankhamen's tomb and a sand-dig area for kids. **Timbuktu** is a replica of the ancient desert-trading center, complete with African craftspersons at work. It also features a sandstorm ride, a boat-swing ride, a roller coaster, and a video-game arcade. **Morocco,** a walled area with exotic architecture, has Moroccan crafts demonstrations and a sultan's tent with snake charmers. The **Congo** features white-water raft rides; **Kumba,** once the largest steel roller coaster in the southeastern United States; and **Claw Island,** a display of rare white Bengal tigers in a natural setting.

The **Serengeti Plain** is an open area with more than 500 African animals roaming in herds. This 32-hectare (79-acre) natural grassy veldt can be viewed from a tram, the **Trans-Veldt Railway,** or the **Skyride,** a sky tram. **Nairobi** is home to a natural habitat for various species of gorillas and chimpanzees, a baby-animal nursery, a petting zoo, reptile displays, and Curiosity Caverns, where visitors can observe animals active at night. **Bird Gardens,** the original core of Busch Gardens, offers rich foliage, lagoons, and a free-flight aviary holding hundreds of exotic birds, including golden and American bald eagles, hawks, owls, and falcons. This area also features **Land of the Dragons,** a children's land and water play area.

The **Crown Colony** area encompasses the **Crown Colony House Restaurant,** overlooking the Serengeti Plain; stables with a team of Clydesdale horses; and the Anheuser-Busch hospitality center. **Akbar's Adventure Tours,** which offers a flight simulator, is located here and offers behind-the-scenes tours.

To get here, take I-275 northeast of downtown to Busch Boulevard (exit 33) and go east 3km (2 miles) to the entrance on 40th Street (McKinley Ave.). Admission is $85 for adults and $77 for kids 3 to 9 (plus 7% tax)—if you book tickets online ahead of time you can get a discount off those prices. Parking is $12. Park hours are at least daily 10am to 6pm; hours are extended during summer. See the website for exact opening and closing times.

OTHER ATTRACTIONS

Only steps from the Garrison Seaport Center, the **Florida Aquarium** (www.flaquarium.org; © 813/273-4000) celebrates the role of water in the development and maintenance of Florida's topography and ecosystems, with more than 10,000 aquatic plants and animals. One exhibit follows a drop of water as it bubbles through Florida limestone and winds its way to the sea. Another popular attraction: the Penguin Promenade, a meet and greet with the aquarium's tiny, tuxedoed birds, held daily at 10am, 1:30pm, and 3pm. Admission is $22 for ages 12 and over, $19 for seniors, $17 for children 3 to 12, and free for children 2 and under. Open daily from 9:30am to 5pm.

Back on land, you'll find even more animals at the **Lowry Park Zoo,** 1101 W. Sligh Ave. (www.lowryparkzoo.com; © 813/935-8552). The facility is home to animals of all sorts, from white tiger cubs to African penguins to several species of birds of prey. Throughout the day, zookeepers put on shows, playing, feeding, and otherwise interacting with species of meerkat, primates, alligators, manatees, and more. A 1-day pass costs $24 for adults, $22 for seniors age 60 and up, $19 for children ages 3 to 11, and free for kids 2 and under. It's open daily 9:30am to 5pm and parking is always free.

You'll see even more creatures in the wild at the **Big Cat Rescue,** 12802 Easy St. (www.bigcatrescue.org; ✆ 813/920-4130), a sanctuary for tigers, lions, leopards, jaguars, and other big cats. Walking tours run Monday through Friday at 9am and 3pm, and Saturday at 9:30am, 11:30am, and 1:30pm. The cost is $29, and visitors must be age 10 or older. Special tours for kids 9 and under take place on Saturdays at 9am at a cost of $19 per child and $25 per adult.

Dinosaur World, 5145 Harvey Tew Rd. in Plant City, about a 20-minute drive from Tampa (www.dinoworld.net; ✆ 813/717-9865), may be one of the cheesier attractions the Tampa area has to offer—but if your young children are going through that "dinosaur" phase, they'll be talking about it for months. The park features more than 150 life-size replicas of dinosaurs standing amid the trees, as well as a museum offering more information on the enormous creatures, a bone yard/sandbox for digging up bones, and picnic areas. The park is open daily from 9am to 6pm; in December and January, the park is open 9am to 5pm. The cost is $15 for adults, $12 for children 3 to 12, and $13 for seniors 60 and over.

Distinctive Moorish architecture and 13 silver minarets make the stunning **Henry B. Plant Museum,** 401 W. Kennedy Blvd. (www.plantmuseum.com; ✆ 813/254-1891), the focal point of the Tampa skyline. This national historic landmark, built in 1891 as the Tampa Bay Hotel, is filled with European and Oriental furnishings and decorative arts from the original hotel collection. It's open Tuesday through Saturday from 10am to 5pm, Sunday from noon to 5pm. A donation of $10 for adults, $7 for seniors and students, and $5 for children 11 and under is suggested.

Ybor City is only about a mile or so from the cruise ship docks. It's Tampa's historic Latin enclave and one of only three national historic districts in Florida. Once known as the cigar capital of the world, Ybor offers a charming slice of the past with its Spanish architecture, antique street lamps, wrought-iron balconies, ornate grillwork, and renovated cigar factories. Stroll along Seventh Avenue, the main artery (closed to traffic at night), where you'll find cigar shops, boutiques, nightclubs, and the famous 100-year-old Columbia Restaurant (see "Where to Eat," below).

The **Ybor City Museum State Park,** 1818 Ninth Ave., between 18th and 19th streets (www.ybormuseum.org; ✆ 813/247-6323), relates the city's history, with special attention paid to the importance of the cigar to the area. You'll see a collection of cigar labels, cigar memorabilia, and works by local artisans. Admission is $4 per person, free for children 4 and under. The museum is open daily from 9am to 5pm.

At **Centro Ybor,** a shopping/entertainment complex between Seventh and Eighth avenues and 16th and 17th streets (www.centroybor.com; ✆ 813/242-4660), you'll find a multiscreen cinema, several restaurants, a comedy club, a large open-air bar, a bunch of typical mall-type stores, and GameWorks, a high-tech entertainment center designed by Steven Spielberg's Dreamworks and Universal Studios. The Ybor City Chamber of Commerce has its Cigar Museum & Visitor Center here (on Eighth Ave., next to Centro Español).

The permanent collection of the **Tampa Museum of Art,** 600 N. Ashley Dr. (www.tampamuseum.com; ✆ 813/274-8130), is especially strong in ancient Greek, Etruscan, and Roman artifacts, as well as 20th-century art. The museum grounds, fronting the Hillsborough River, contain a sculpture garden and a decorative fountain. It's open Tuesday, Wednesday, and Friday from 11am to 7pm; Thursday 11am to 9pm; and Saturday and Sunday 11am to 5pm. Admission is $10 for adults, $7.50 for seniors, $5 for students with ID cards and children, and free for kids 6 and under.

Tampa & St. Petersburg

THE PORTS OF EMBARKATION

About a half-hour drive from Tampa, the **Salvador Dalí Museum,** 1000 Third St. S., in St. Petersburg (www.thedali.org; ℭ **727/822-6270**), boasts the world's biggest collection of Dalí's trippy, lavish paintings, watercolors, drawings, photographs, and more. The museum is open Monday through Saturday from 10am to 5:30pm (Thurs until 8pm), and Sunday from noon to 5:30pm. The cost is $21 for adults; $19 for seniors 66 and over, military, and police; $15 for children 13 to 18 and students 18 and over with ID; $7 for children 6 to 12; and free for kids 5 and under. Visitors from 5 to 8pm on Thursdays pay $10.

Organized Tours

BY BUS   Swiss Chalet Tours, 3601 E. Busch Blvd. (ℭ **813/985-3601**), operates guided tours of Tampa, Ybor City, and the surrounding region, including beaches and museums. Four-hour (10am–2pm) tours run most every day; they cost $55 for adults and $45 for children 3 to 12. Seven-hour tours (10am–5pm), which also run virtually every day, visit Tampa, Clearwater, and St. Petersburg. Cost is $85 for adults and $75 for children. Your tour guide, a Tampa native, will pick you up at your hotel. Both tours include a restaurant stop, but you have to pay for your own lunch. Reservations for both tours must be made a day in advance.

ON FOOT   Ybor City walking tours are available through the Ybor City Museum (see "Other Attractions," above). Tours are $8 for ages 6 and over.

Hitting the Beach

Start at **St. Petersburg,** across the bay, for a north-to-south string of interconnected white sandy shores. Most beaches have restrooms, refreshment stands, and picnic areas. You can park either on the street at a meter (usually 25¢ for each half-hour) or at one of the four major parking lots located, from north to south, at Sand Key Park in Clearwater, beside Gulf Boulevard (also known as Rte. 699), just south of the Clearwater Pass Bridge; Redington Shores Beach Park, beside Gulf Boulevard at 182nd Street; Treasure Island Park, on Gulf Boulevard just north of 108th Avenue; and St. Pete Beach Park, beside Gulf Boulevard at 46th Street.

Shopping

On and around Seventh Avenue in **Ybor City,** you'll find a variety of interesting boutiques and shops, plus lots of cigar stores selling handmade stogies.

Some 60 upscale shops, plus restaurants and movie theaters, are located at **Old Hyde Park Village,** an outdoor European-style market at Swann and Dakota avenues near Bayshore Boulevard (www.oldhydeparkvillage.com; ℭ **813/251-3500**). **International Plaza,** 2223 N. West Shore Blvd. (www.shopinternationalplaza.com; ℭ **813/342-3790**), is more of a traditional indoor mall, set right next to the Renaissance Tampa Hotel. There's nothing particularly "Tampa" about either of these, but if you need a new Brooks Brothers suit or Ann Taylor dress for your cruise, you'll find them here.

Where to Stay

TAMPA   Tampa has two Hyatts. The **Grand Hyatt Tampa Bay,** 2900 Bayport Dr. (www.grandtampabay.hyatt.com; ℭ **800/233-1234** or 813/874-1234), sits in a 14-hectare (35-acre) wildlife preserve at the Tampa end of the long causeway traversing Tampa Bay, about 3km (2 miles) from the airport and 13km (8 miles) from downtown. Choose from regular rooms and suites in the main hotel building, or one of 45 Spanish-style villas set about a kilometer (½ mile) away. Rates: $250. The **Hyatt Regency Tampa,** 211 N. Tampa St. (www.tamparegency.hyatt.com; ✆ **800/233-1234** or 813/225-1234), sits in Tampa's commercial center and caters mostly to the corporate crowd. Rates: $250.

At the other big downtown hotel, the **Tampa Marriott Waterside,** 700 S. Florida Ave. (www.marriott.com; ✆ **800/228-9290** or 813/221-4900), about half of the rooms have balconies overlooking the bay or city (the best views are high up on the south side). Rates: $349.

La Quinta Inn & Suites, 3701 E. Fowler Ave. (www.lq.com; ✆ **800/687-6667** or 813/910-7500), is a motel with a pinch of upscale thrown in. Guest rooms come with coffeemakers and dataports, and it's only 2.5km (1½ miles) from Busch Gardens. Rates: $99.

Wyndham Tampa Westshore, 700 N. Westshore Blvd. (www.wyndhamhotel tampa.com; ✆ **813/289-8200**), offers a sleep-and-sail package which includes free transportation to the port. Its free business center makes it the perfect place for workaholics hoping to telecommute before the trip. Rates: $169.

ST. PETERSBURG   Overlooking Tampa Bay, the **Vinoy Renaissance St. Petersburg Resort & Golf Club,** 501 Fifth Ave. NE, at Beach Drive (www.renaissance hotels.com; ✆ **800/468-3571** or 727/894-1000), is the grande dame of the region's hotels. Built as the Vinoy Park in 1925, this elegant Spanish-style establishment reopened in 1992 after a meticulous $93-million restoration. Many of the guest rooms offer lovely views of the bay. Accommodations in the newer wing ("the Tower") are slightly larger than those in the hotel's original core. Rates: $329.

Another striking example of historical elegance is the **Don CeSar Beach Resort,** 3400 Gulf Blvd., on St. Pete Beach (www.doncesar.com; ✆ **866/728-2206**). Known affectionately as the Pink Palace, the original 1928 construction was once a hangout for the likes of F. Scott Fitzgerald, Lou Gehrig, and Al Capone. Today, guests stop by for killer spa treatments and fine dining, as well as the Art Deco atmosphere. Rates: $408.

Where to Eat

On the 14th floor of the Grand Hyatt Tampa, **Armani's,** 2900 Bayport Dr. (www. grandhyatttampabay.com; ✆ **813/207-6800**), is a stylish northern Italian restaurant with a panoramic view of the city skyline and the bay. Jackets are recommended, but not required. Dinner main courses: $28 to $39.

The best fish in Tampa is served at the Grand Hyatt's **Oystercatchers,** 2900 Bayport Dr. (www.oystercatchersrestaurant.com; ✆ **813/207-6815**). Pick your desired fish from a glass-fronted buffet, or enjoy mesquite-grilled steaks, chicken parmigiana, and shellfish. Dinner main courses: $24 to $38.

At **Bern's Steak House,** 1208 S. Howard Ave. (www.bernssteakhouse.com; ✆ **813/ 251-2421**), the steaks are close to perfect. You order according to thickness and weight. Dinner main courses: $31 to $72.

In Ybor City, the nearly 100-year-old **Columbia Restaurant,** 2117 Seventh Ave. E., between 21st and 22nd streets (www.columbiarestaurant.com; ✆ **813/248-4961**), occupies an attractive tile-sheathed building that fills an entire city block about a mile from the cruise docks. The aura is pre-Castro Cuba and the food is primarily Cuban. The simpler your dish is, the better it's likely to be. Filet mignon, roasted pork, black beans, yellow rice, and plantains are flavorful and well prepared.

Catch a flamenco show on the dance floor Monday through Saturday. Dinner main courses: $13 to $30.

La Segunda Bakery, 2512 N. 15th St. (www.lasegundabakery.com; © 813/248-1531) is one of the city's oldest bakeries; La Primera (the first) bakery opened in 1915, and when it burned in the 1950s, family members opened La Segunda (the second). The same family has been baking Cuban bread in Tampa for nearly a century now, and it shows. La Segunda churns out some 7,000 loaves daily. Lunch main courses: $6 to $9.

Another standout family business success story is **El Molino Coffee,** 2012 E. 7th Ave. (www.elmolinocoffee.com; © 800/531-9587). Four generations of coffee roasters have contributed to El Molino's reputation for an exceptional brew since the coffee shop opened in 1921. Stop by and enjoy a cup while watching the coffee being roasted. Coffee costs as little as $1.75 per cup.

It may be a bit out of the way, but **Lenny's Restaurant,** 21220 U.S. 19 N, Clearwater (© 727/799-0402), has been a local favorite here for nearly 3 decades. Breakfast is the restaurant's standout meal, with homemade hash browns, pastry baskets, and bacon cooked to diners' requests. Lunch main courses: $6 to $20.

Tampa After Dark

Nightfall transforms Ybor City, Tampa's century-old Latin Quarter, into an orgy of music, ethnic food, poetry readings, and after-midnight coffee and dessert. Seventh Avenue, one of Ybor City's main arteries, is closed to all but pedestrian traffic Wednesday through Saturday evenings. Many nightclubs pepper the streets here; one of your options is **Side Splitters Comedy Club,** 12938 N. Dale Mabry Hwy. (www.sidesplitterscomedy.com; © 813/960-1197), which features stand-up pros. The cover is $17 for general admission and $19 for preferred admission. **Crowbar,** 1812 17th St. (www.crowbarlive.com; © 813/241-8600), is the newest hot venue for live music, big on the punk and indie varieties.

In north Tampa, **Skipper's Smokehouse,** 910 Skipper Rd., at Nebraska Avenue (www.skipperssmokehouse.com; © 813/971-0666), is a favorite evening spot, with an all-purpose restaurant and bar where oysters and fresh shellfish are sold by the dozen and half dozen. You'll find live music back in the Skipper Dome, a sprawling deck sheltered by a canopy of oak trees. **Dallas Bull,** 3322 U.S. Hwy. 301 (www.dallasbull.com; © 813/987-2855), on the other hand, is a down-and-dirty honkytonk bar, complete with a mechanical bull and line dancing on Wednesday nights.

Northeast of town, at exit 6 off the I-4, the **Seminole Hard Rock Hotel & Casino,** 5223 N. Orient Rd., at Hillsborough Avenue (www.seminolehardrock.com; © 813/621-1302), is open 24 hours every day of the year, offering poker and slots. At **Floyd's,** the Hard Rock's restaurant-nightclub combo, guests can enjoy a late meal and then hit the dance floor all night long, to the sounds of local DJs or live bands. Meanwhile, the **Lobby Bar** pours over 30 kinds of tequila.

Channelside Bay Plaza, 615 Channelside Dr. (www.channelsidebayplaza.com; © 813/223-4250), is home to a mainstream lineup of piano bars, island-style Tiki spots, and laid-back country saloons. The following destinations are all located on 615 Channelside Dr., just east of the Harbor island bridge. **Stumps Supper Club** (www.stumpssupperclub.com; © 813/228-7300) is a classic barbeque joint with a rock-'n'-roll twist. **Howl at the Moon** (www.howlatthemoontampa.com; © 813/226-2261) is your typical piano bar, with a live musician taking requests and encouraging the occasional singalong. **Slingshots** (© 813/228-7300) bills itself as a "country pop saloon." You'll also find **Splitsville** (www.splitsvillelanes.com; ✆ 813/514-2695), an upscale bowling alley and bar, as well as **Channelside Cinema and IMAX Theater** (www.channelsideimax.com; ✆ 813/221-0006), showing the latest movie releases on the biggest of the big screens.

NEW ORLEANS

Exploring New Orleans, especially the French Quarter, is a culinary and musical extravaganza, all the more intense because there is so much to see in a compact space. European history (first French, then Spanish, then French again) mixes with Afro-Caribbean influences, creating the rhythms of a culture unique to this city. Walking through the streets of the French Quarter, or the Vieux Carre, as Tennessee Williams called it, you will see intricate ironwork and architectural gems, smell shrimp gumbos and crawfish jambalayas, and hear Cajun, Creole, rock, R & B, and zydeco music as it pours out of open club doors. And, of course, plenty of jazz, which was born here—a mix based on the drumming of African slaves and free people of color who danced in Congo square.

The devastation from Hurricane Katrina that flooded 80% of the city in 2005 can still be seen in places. But seven years later it has "come back strong," as your guide will tell you if take the 3-hour Katrina bus tour, on which you'll also learn more than you probably want to about how the levees hold the water back now.

Cruise ships depart from the **Erato Street Cruise Terminal** and the **Julia Street Wharf,** located adjacent to each other on the east bank of the Mississippi, south of the French Quarter. Both are operated by the **Port of New Orleans** (www.portno.com; ✆ **504/522-2551**). Parking is available at both terminals, at a cost of $16 per day.

The French Quarter is the most celebrated and oldest part of the city, but don't miss the Warehouse and Arts District, Faubourgs Marigny and Tremé, Lakeview, the Garden District with its impressive homes, and Magazine Street and St. Charles Avenue; all are fully restored. After Katrina, less wealthy districts such as Center City and the Lower Ninth Ward took longer to bounce back, but the eco-friendly, multi-colored designer homes built with the help of Brad Pitt in the Lower Ninth have former residents returning.

VISITOR INFORMATION Contact or visit the **New Orleans Convention & Visitors Bureau,** 2020 St. Charles Ave., New Orleans, LA 70130 (www.neworleanscvb.com; ✆ **800/672-6124** or 504/566-5011), for brochures, pamphlets, and information.

Getting to New Orleans & the Port

The **Julia Street Cruise Terminal Complex** sits at the foot of Julia Street on the Mississippi River, in the convention center district, a 10-minute walk or a short streetcar or taxi ride away from the edge of the French Quarter. For information, check out www.portno.com or call the **Port of New Orleans** at ✆ **504/522-2551.**

BY PLANE The **Louis Armstrong New Orleans International Airport** (www.flymsy.com; ✆ **504/464-0831**) is about 24km (15 miles) northwest of the port. Cruise line representatives meet all passengers who have booked transfers through the line. For those who haven't, a taxi to the port costs about $40 and takes about 45 minutes. **Airport Shuttle** (www.airportshuttleneworleans.com; ✆ **866/596-2699**)

Greater New Orleans

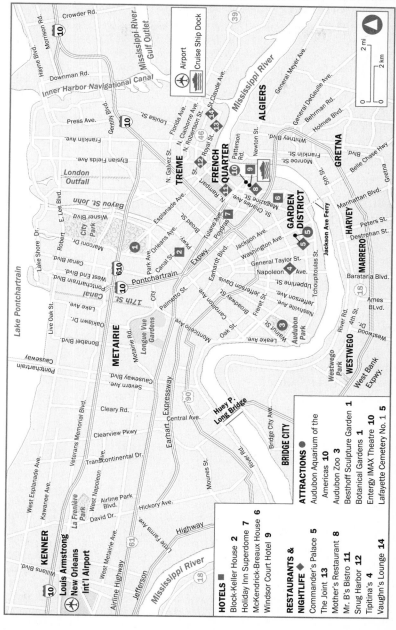

HOTELS ■
Block-Keller House **2**
Holiday Inn Superdome **7**
McKendrick-Breaux House **6**
Windsor Court Hotel **9**

**RESTAURANTS &
NIGHTLIFE** ◆
Commander's Palace **5**
The Joint **13**
Mother's Restaurant **8**
Mr. B's Bistro **11**
Snug Harbor **12**
Tipitina's **4**
Vaughn's Lounge **14**

ATTRACTIONS ●
Audubon Aquarium of the
  Americas **10**
Audubon Zoo **3**
Besthoff Sculpture Garden **1**
Botanical Gardens **1**
Entergy IMAX Theatre **10**
Lafayette Cemetery No. 1 **5**

runs vans at 30-minute intervals from outside the airport's baggage claim to the port and other points in town. It costs $20 per passenger each way, $38 round-trip, free for children 4 and under.

BY CAR   Take I-10 downtown. Then take the Tchoupitoulas/St. Peters Street exit, the last one before you cross the Mississippi. Stay to the right, and head toward the New Orleans Convention Center. Turn right onto Convention Center Boulevard, then left onto Henderson Street, which will take you to Port of New Orleans Place. Turn left and continue on to the cruise ship terminal. You can park your car in long-term parking at the port; inquire through your cruise line. You must present a boarding pass or ticket before parking.

GETTING AROUND   Taxis are plentiful. If you're not near a taxi stand, call **United Cabs** (✆ **504/522-9771**) and a car will come in 10 minutes. The meter begins at $3.50, plus $1 for each additional person, and goes to $2 per mile thereafter.

The city buses are a reliable and affordable means to get around, as are the adorable antique trolley cars that tool up and down Canal Street and other main thoroughfares, affording a good view of the local scenery. You can board the streetcar at the **French Market Riverfront** stop (where Esplanade Ave. meets the river, at the entrance of the French Market). The **Riverfront** line runs daily from 7am to 7pm. A **Canal Street** route also runs from the Esplanade to the historic former Krauss Building (near Basin St.). It operates daily from 6:30am to 10pm. Take it for a trip out to City Park, where the stately Live Oaks mingle with the Besthoff Sculpture Garden, and while you're there visit the Museum of Art and the Botanical Gardens all in one day. The cooling branches of oak trees also line the historic **St. Charles** route, which will take you through the Garden District to the Audubon Zoo. Contact the New Orleans Regional Transit Authority for current information (www.norta.com; ✆ **504/248-3900**). The fare is $1.25 for a single ride and $5 for an all-day pass.

From Jackson Square (at Decatur St.), you can take a 30-minute carriage ride through the French Quarter. **Royal Carriage Tour Co.** (www.neworleanscarriages. com; ✆ **504/943-8820**) offers private rides for up to four passengers in a Cinderella carriage for $75, or $15 per person if you are willing to travel with strangers, daily from 9am to midnight. The funny-looking horses with big ears are actually mules, which fare much better in the sweltering summer heat that would make your average horse weak in the knees.

Exploring New Orleans

The **Audubon Aquarium of the Americas,** 1 Canal St., at the Mississippi River (www.auduboninstitute.org; ✆ **800/774-7394** or 504/581-4629), is a great destination for young and old. Check out the frog exhibit on the second floor—it is full of exotic plants such as orchids that provide a backdrop for the amphibians, which come in almost as many colors and patterns as the flowers. From here, head over to the Caribbean Reef exhibit and walk through a 9m (30-ft.) aquatic tunnel, where you will be surrounded by dozens of marine creatures and see them from all angles. Adventure Island has lots of interactive exhibits, including a 9,800-liter pool full of cownose rays that you can reach out and touch, or even help feed. Admission is $21 for adults, $14 for children 2 to 12. The aquarium is open Tuesday to Sunday from 10am to 5pm.

After cleaning up from Hurricane Katrina, the **Audubon Zoo,** 6500 Magazine St. (www.auduboninstitute.org; ✆ **800/774-7394** or 504/581-4629), created a few new

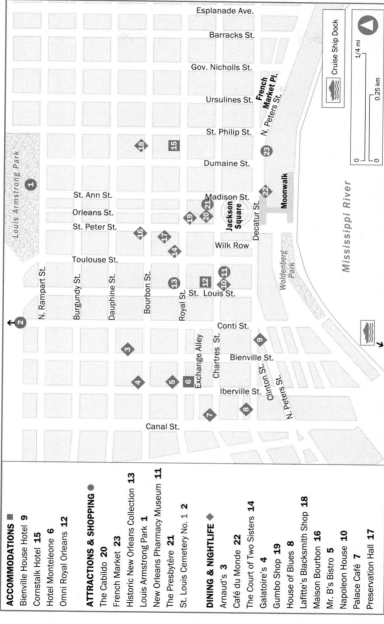

The French Quarter

Esplanade Ave.

Barracks St.

Gov. Nicholls St.

Ursulines St.

St. Philip St.

Dumaine St.

St. Ann St.

Orleans St.

St. Peter St.

Toulouse St.

St. Louis St.

Conti St.

Bienville St.

Iberville St.

Canal St.

Louis Armstrong Park

N. Rampart St.

Burgundy St.

Dauphine St.

Bourbon St.

Royal St.

Exchange Alley

Chartres St.

Clinton St.

N. Peters St.

Decatur St.

French Market Pl.

N. Peters St.

Madison St.

Wilk Row

Jackson Square

Moonwalk

Woldenberg Park

Mississippi River

Cruise Ship Dock

1/4 mi

0.25 km

THE PORTS OF EMBARKATION | New Orleans

4

ACCOMMODATIONS
Bienville House Hotel **9**
Cornstalk Hotel **15**
Hotel Monteleone **6**
Omni Royal Orleans **12**

ATTRACTIONS & SHOPPING
The Cabildo **20**
French Market **23**
Historic New Orleans Collection **13**
Louis Armstrong Park **1**
New Orleans Pharmacy Museum **11**
The Presbytère **21**
St. Louis Cemetery No. 1 **2**

DINING & NIGHTLIFE
Arnaud's **3**
Café du Monde **22**
The Court of Two Sisters **14**
Galatoire's **4**
Gumbo Shop **19**
House of Blues **8**
Lafitte's Blacksmith Shop **18**
Maison Bourbon **16**
Mr. B's Bistro **5**
Napoleon House **10**
Palace Café **7**
Preservation Hall **17**

attractions, including an endangered species carousel, a simulator ride, and a rock-climbing wall. The prices for these are separate from the admission fees and range from $3 to $6. The real attractions are the animals, including two "white" tigers, which are actually highly inbred Bengals missing the gene that would give them their orange fur. One not-to-be-missed attraction is the Louisiana Swamp, a re-created wetland that houses a myriad of local wildlife that would naturally be found down on the bayou, including alligators and black bears, amid a mock-up of a trapper's cottage, cypress trees, and Spanish moss. Hours of operation are Tuesday to Sunday from 10am to 5pm. Admission is $16 for adults and $11 for children ages 2 to 12.

The Entergy IMAX Theatre (www.auduboninstitute.org; ✆ **504/581-4629**) shows an ever-changing selection of spectacular high-definition IMAX movies that are projected onto a screen that is more than five stories tall. Perhaps the most astounding film you can see here is one that takes you into the backyards and local swamps of Louisiana. *Hurricane on the Bayou* tells the dramatic tale of the devastation and recovery from Hurricane Katrina and the vital role that wetlands play in mitigating the damage from hurricanes and storms. The IMAX lobby opens at 9:30am for ticket sales and to seat the 10am show. Shows run every hour throughout the day and the last movie at 5pm ends at 5:45pm. Admission is $11 for adults and $7.50 for children ages 2 to 12.

Audubon Insectarium (www.auduboninstitute.org; ✆ **504/581-4629**) encourages you to use all five senses as you explore North America's largest museum devoted to insects and their relatives. Thousands of live and preserved specimens plus hands-on interactive exhibits come together for a true tribute to insects. Hours are Tuesday through Sunday 10am to 5pm. Admission costs $16 for adults and $11 for children.

Because the aquarium, zoo, insectarium, and IMAX are all run by the **Audubon Nature Institute,** packages are available to visit any combination of the four attractions. The price for all four is $35 for adults and $20 for children ages 2 to 12. The Audubon Institute also runs **Audubon Park,** which is full of activities and is beautifully landscaped.

You can saddle up and ride at **Cascade Stables** (www.cascadestables.net; ✆ **504/891-2246**), which are open Tuesday to Sunday from 9am to 4pm, or play a round of golf at the par-62, 4,220-yard **Audubon Park Golf Course** (www.auduboninstitute. org/visit/golf; ✆ **504/212-5290**), which is the only municipal course to reopen since Hurricane Katrina, and remains one of the state's top public courses. The **Audubon Park Tennis Courts** (www.auduboninstitute.org/visit/parks/tennis; ✆ **504/895-1042**) are on Tchoupitoulas Street at the southeastern end of the park. An hour of court time runs $10, and lessons are also available.

Incorporating seven historic buildings connected by a brick courtyard, the **Historic New Orleans Collection,** 533 Royal St., between St. Louis and Toulouse streets (www.hnoc.org; ✆ **504/523-4662**), evokes the New Orleans of 200 years ago. The oldest building in the complex escaped the tragic fire of 1794. The others hold exhibitions on Louisiana's culture and history. All are open Tuesday through Saturday from 9:30am to 4:30pm. Admission is free.

Founded in 1950, the **New Orleans Pharmacy Museum,** 514 Chartres St., at St. Louis Street (www.pharmacymuseum.org; ✆ **504/565-8027**), is just what the name implies. In 1823, the first licensed pharmacist in the United States, Louis J. Dufilho, Jr., opened an apothecary shop here. Today, you'll find old apothecary bottles, voodoo potions, pill tiles, and suppository molds, as well as the old glass cosmetics counter and a jar of leeches, in case you feel the need to be bled. Hours of operation are Tuesday through Saturday 11am to 5pm; admission is $5 for adults, $4 for children and students, free for children 5 and under.

Constructed from 1795 to 1799 as the Spanish government seat in New Orleans, the **Cabildo,** 701 Chartres St., at Jackson Square (http://lsm.crt.state.la.us; ✆ **800/568-6968** or 504/568-6968), was the site of the signing of the Louisiana Purchase transfer. The building is now the center of the Louisiana State Museum's facilities in the French Quarter, with a multiroom exhibition that traces the history of Louisiana from exploration through Reconstruction, covering all aspects of life, including antebellum music, mourning and burial customs, immigrants, and the changing roles of women in the South. It's open Tuesday through Sunday from 10am to 4pm; admission is $6 for adults, $5 for students and seniors, and free for children 11 and under.

Also on Jackson Square is the **Presbytère,** 751 Chartres St. (http://lsm.crt.state.la.us; ✆ **800/568-6968** or 504/568-6968), planned as housing for clergy but now serving as a Mardi Gras museum that traces the history of the annual event, with everything from elaborate Mardi Gras Indian costumes to Rex Queen jewelry from the turn of the 20th century on display. The museum is open Tuesday through Sunday from 10am to 4pm; admission is $6 for adults, $5 for seniors and students, and free for children 11 and under.

The city's **cemeteries** are a bit peculiar: Because New Orleans has always been prone to flooding, bodies have been interred aboveground since the city's earliest days, in sometimes very elaborate tombs that are definitely worth a visit. **St. Louis Cemetery No. 1,** at Basin Street between Conti and St. Louis streets, at the top of the French Quarter, is the oldest extant cemetery (1789) in the area and the most iconic and famous. In the Garden District, **Lafayette Cemetery No. 1,** 1427 Sixth St., right across the street from the Commander's Palace restaurant, is another old cemetery that's been beautifully restored. Though both of these cemeteries are usually full of visitors during the day, you should exercise caution when touring, as they've seen some crime over the years.

Organized Tours

BY BUS   **Gray Line,** 1 Toulouse St. (www.graylineneworleans.com; ✆ **800/535-7786** or 504/587-0861), offers two different 2-hour bus tours: One is a general city overview, and the other is a Hurricane Katrina tour of the breached levies and harder-hit neighborhoods. The cost is $43 for adults and $15 for children 6 to 12; advance booking is required. To escape the city and travel back in time, book a tour of one of the few remaining plantation houses that provide a glimpse into life in the 1800s. The tour to **Oak Alley Plantation** (www.oakalleyplantation.com; ✆ **800/44-ALLEY** [442-5539] or 225/265-2151) will begin with a spectacular view of the plantation house through an allee (or tree-lined promenade) of sprawling oak trees, some over 250 years old. A tour of the grounds and interior, complete with mint juleps and guides in full hoop skirts, will leave you feeling as flush as Scarlett when she first laid eyes on that rascal Rhett. The cost of this 4½-hour tour is $54 for adults and $34 for children 6 to 12. The bus ride to and from the house is about an hour each way.

You can now tour the neighborhood called Tremé, also of the name of the HBO series about New Orleans after Katrina. Tremé gave rise to jazz and brass bands, incredible Creole architectural style, Mardi Gras Indians, and several pioneers of the civil rights movement, and is now home to such key cultural institutions as the New Orleans African American Museum, Backstreet Cultural Museum, St. Augustine Church, and Lois Armstrong Park (www.treme2012.com).

ON FOOT There are a lot of theatrical walking tours offered in New Orleans, many at night, but some are better than others. Many capitalize on sensational ghost stories and, while entertaining, offer little in the way of real information. If history and authenticity rather than legend are what you crave, **Historic Tours** (www. tourneworleans.com; © **504/947-2120**) is the one to select. The company offers tours of the French Quarter and the Garden District (including Lafayette Cemetery), plus a cemetery and voodoo tour. Prices are about $35 to $49 per person.

Seven museums in the French Quarter are operated by the Louisiana State Museum System, and you can easily walk between them. The **Cabildo** focuses on history, while the **Presbytere, Mardi Gras Museum,** and the **Arsenal** exhibit local artifacts. The **1850 House** attempts to recapture the look and feel of the 1800s, and **the Old Mint** has exhibits on Mardi Gras and jazz. The **"Madam John's Legacy,"** a French Colonial home, focuses on folk art. All proceeds from tours go to the preservation of these historic sites. For a tour of one or all of these national treasures, contact **the Friends of the Cabildo** (www.friendsofthecabildo.org), located in the historic Creole House at 619 St. Peter St. City-licensed guides conduct the tours, which start at the **1850 House Museum Store** (523 St. Ann St., on Jackson Sq.), and emphasize the history, architecture, and folklore of this fascinating city. Tours run Tuesday to Sunday at 10am and 1:30pm, except on state holidays. No reservations are needed, but please arrive 15 minutes before the start of the tour. Guided tours last 2 hours and are $15 for adults, $10 for students and seniors, and free for children 11 and under.

If you get tired, take a rest on the lush grass under a tree at **Louis Armstrong Park.** Walk out St. Ann Street from the French Quarter, cross Ramparts Street, and go under the big white arch. You will be greeted by a jazz band, one of the many sculptures on the grounds. Yes, there is one of Satchmo, and more, including Mahalia Jackson, and Big Chief Tootie Montana, a famous Mardi Gras Indian. The ample pond with its fountains and ducks is on the right; walk to your left to find Congo Square.

Shopping

Despite what you may think while making your first walk down **Bourbon Street,** there's more to New Orleans shopping than tourist traps selling cheap T-shirts, and even cheaper beads. The city's antiques stores are especially good, as are the art galleries.

On Decatur Street, across from Jackson Square, the **French Market** (www. frenchmarket.org; © **504/522-2621**) has shops selling candy, cookware, fashion, crafts, candles, toys, and New Orleans memorabilia. There's a lot of kitsch, but some good buys are mixed in, and it's always fun to stroll through and grab a few beignets at **Café du Monde** (see "Snacks & Sweets," below). The French Market is open daily from 9am to 6pm; Café du Monde is open 24 hours.

From Camp Street down to the river on Julia Street, you'll find many of the city's best contemporary **art galleries.** Of course, some of the works are a bit pricey, but there are good deals to be had if you're collecting, and fine art to be seen if you're not.

Magazine Street is the Garden District's premier shopping street, with countless antiques stores, art galleries, boutiques, and crafts shops among the 19th-century brick storefronts and cottages.

For those who want a glitzy indoor shopping experience with high-end stores such as Saks Fifth Avenue and Brooks Brothers, you should head over to **One Canal**

Place Shopping Mall, which is only partially filled with stores and has an eerily desolate feel to it.

Where to Stay

In the Garden District, the **McKendrick-Breaux House,** 1474 Magazine St. (www. mckendrick-breaux.com; ☎ **888/570-1700** or 504/586-1700), was built at the end of the Civil War by a wealthy plumber and Scottish immigrant. Today, it's one of the best guesthouses for value. It's been completely restored to its original charming state, and each room is furnished with antiques, family collectibles, and fresh flowers. Rates: $145 to $235.

Located in the French Quarter, **Bienville House Hotel,** 320 Decatur St., between Conti Street and Bienville (www.bienvillehouse.com; ☎ **800/535-9603** or **504/529-2345**), is part of the National Trust for Historic Preservation and is a member of Historic Hotels of America. This intimate property was once a rice mill and a syrup manufacturer. It is now a charming and romantic inn with classic wrought-iron balconies, a courtyard with tropical plants, and a serene pool. Some rooms have balconies or dark-wood four-poster beds, but all 83 units are appointed with coffeemaker, bathrobe, hair dryer, and complementary newspaper. Rates: $159 to $499.

Canal Street Inn, 3620 Canal St. (www.canalstreetinn.com; ☎ **504/483-3033**), was restored to its original Victorian splendor with stunning detail and excess true to the period. Despite the accuracy of the decor, the amenities are pure modern, with Jacuzzi tubs, plush carpeting, and all the rich appointments of a full hotel, especially in the larger upstairs rooms. Telephone, TV, and Wi-Fi will jolt you back into the 21st century. All guests are served a substantial continental-plus breakfast. The new owner is enthusiastic and accommodating. Rates: $130 to $170.

In the Central Business District, the **Windsor Court Hotel,** 300 Gravier St. (www.windsorcourthotel.com; ☎ **800/262-2662** or 504/523-6000), was named "Best Hotel in North America" by *Condé Nast Traveler,* so feel free to hold it to a high standard. Accommodations are exceptionally spacious and classy, with large bay windows or a private balcony overlooking the river or the city. Downstairs, two corridors display original 17th-, 18th-, and 19th-century art. A plush reading area with international newspapers is on the second floor. Rates: $260 to $595.

The Holiday Inn Superdome, 330 Loyola Ave. (☎ **800/315-2621**), is an exceptionally nice version of the brand, with good views and a restaurant featuring a replica of a streetcar. In addition to the huge clarinet mural that livens up the west bank area, its unique offering is "park and cruise"; if you book a room, you get free parking for up to 8 nights while you are on a cruise. Rates begin at $197.

About 7 blocks from the cruise ship terminal is the atmospheric **Hotel Monteleone,** 214 Royal St., between Iberville and Bienville streets (www.hotelmonteleone. com; ☎ **800/535-9595** or 504/523-3341). It's the oldest hotel in the city and also the largest one in the French Quarter (because of its size, you can almost always get a room here, even when other places are booked). Everyone who stays here loves it, probably because its staff is among the most helpful in town. Room decor and floor layouts differ slightly, so ask to see yours, if you care. If it feels like you're moving while having a drink in the Carousel Bar, it's because you are! The famous, newly renovated circular bar rotates. Rates: $289 to $779.

The Omni Royal Orleans, 621 St. Louis St., between Royal and Chartres streets (www.omnihotels.com; ☎ **800/843-6664** or 504/529-5333), is an elegant hotel located smack in the center of the French Quarter. The lobby is a small sea of marble, and the rooms are sizable and elegant, filled with muted tones, plush furniture, and windows that let you gaze out over the Quarter. Service varies, but can be exceptional. Rates: $197 to $279.

The **Cornstalk Hotel,** 915 Royal St. (www.cornstalkhotel.com; © **800/759-6112** or 504/523-1515), is a charming Victorian building with elegant French decor and 13 rooms. Sitting on the upstairs balcony, you may see a mule-drawn carriage stop and tell visitors about the hotel's ornate cast-iron fence depicting ripe ears of corn. It was commissioned by Dr. Secondo Biamanti in 1856 for his young wife, who missed the cornfields of Iowa. Louis, the manager, will tell you not to worry if you hear children running in the halls at night; they are only ghosts. Possibly more informative are the extensive lists of tours and local cafes he keeps in books for visitors. Breakfast is not included. Rates: $120 to $315.

Where to Eat

New Orleans is essentially one giant restaurant filled with famous chefs, and you could spend all your time here tasting what's being whipped up at 3 or 4 or 8 or 40 of the city's best. Most are in the French Quarter, but there are notable exceptions.

In business since 1918 and still mighty fine, the legendary **Arnaud's,** 813 Bienville St. (www.arnauds.com; © **504/523-2847**), is set in three interconnected, once-private houses from the 1700s. The restaurant's three Belle Epoque dining rooms are lush with Edwardian embellishments. Especially delicious menu items include snapper or trout topped with crabmeat, filet mignon, oysters stewed in cream, roasted duck in blueberry sauce, and a classic bananas Foster flamed at the table. Dinner main courses: $22 to $40.

Walk into **The Court of Two Sisters,** 613 Royal St. (www.courtoftwosisters.com; © **504/522-7261**), from either Bourbon Street or Royal Street, and enter an enchanted wisteria-covered courtyard that's consistently recognized as the best place for outdoor dining in New Orleans. It's been family-owned since it was opened by sisters Emma and Bertha, both born just before the Civil War. The place has oodles of atmosphere and a daily Jazz Brunch served from 9am to 3pm. More than 60 hot and cold dishes are on the buffet, with plenty of crawfish. The buffet costs $29, or $13 for children, and kids 3 and under eat free. Dinner main courses: $25 to $35.

Galatoire's, 209 Bourbon St., at Iberville Street (www.galatoires.com; © **504/525-2021**), feels like a bistro in turn-of-the-20th-century Paris. It's one of the city's most legendary places—and one of the spots that locals head to for a good meal. Menu items include trout (meunière or amandine), rémoulade of shrimp, oysters *en brochette,* and a savory Creole-style bouillabaisse. Dinner main courses: $19 to $40.

The **Gumbo Shop,** 630 St. Peter St., at Royal Street (www.gumboshop.com; © **504/525-1486**), is a cheap and convenient place to get solid, classic Creole food. The menu reads like a textbook list of traditional local food: red beans and rice, shrimp Creole, crawfish étouffée. The seafood gumbo with okra is a meal in itself, and do try the jambalaya. Dinner main courses: $9 to $25.

For the best BBQ anywhere, you will have to go to **The Joint,** 701 Mazant St., at Royal Street, in the Bywater (www.alwayssmokin.com; © **504/949-3232**). Though you order at a counter, don't be fooled; this is not a fast-food joint. A sign above the register warns not to rush them; they're moving at the speed of BBQ. Pork Ribs Lunch Plate: $12.

Café du Monde, 800 Decatur St. (www. cafedumonde.com; ✆ **504/525-4544**), right on the river, is basically a 24-hour coffee shop that specializes in beignets—square, really yummy French doughnut–type things, served hot and covered in powdered sugar. This is a great spot for people-watching, but if you don't want to wait for a table, you can always get a bag of beignets to go. Grab lots of napkins. Premoistened towelettes would be a good idea, too.

Not far outside the quarter, **Mother's Restaurant,** 401 Poydras St., at Tchoupitoulas Street (www.mothersrestaurant.net; ✆ **504/523-9656**), has long lines and zero atmosphere, but damn, those po' boys! Customers have been flocking here since 1938 for homemade biscuits and red-bean omelets at breakfast, po' boys at lunch, and soft-shell crabs and jambalaya at dinner. Everything's between $8 and $25.

Despite major damage from Katrina, the fully renovated **Mr. B's Bistro,** 201 Royal St. (www.mrbsbistro.com; ✆ **504/523-2078**), has the demure charm, look, and feel of a 19th-century French bistro. The menu adds a modern twist to classic French Creole. For dinner, start with the pan-seared jumbo sea scallops on a risotto cake with arugula pesto, or the fried oysters on the half shell topped with bacon and horseradish sauce. As a main course try the pecan-crusted redfish or the shrimp and grits, which is much more elegant than it sounds. The hot buttered pecan pie is not to be missed for dessert. Dinner main courses: $23 to $48.

Napoleon House, 500 Chartres St., at St. Louis Street (www.napoleonhouse. com; ✆ **504/524-9752**), would have been the home of the emperor himself if some locals' wild plan to bring him here to live out his exile had panned out. A landmark 1797 building with an incredible atmosphere, this place is a hangout for drinking and good times, but also serves food. The specialty is Italian muffuletta, with ham, Genoa salami, pastrami, Swiss cheese, and provolone. Po' boys start at $6.

Right on the border of the French Quarter, the open kitchen at **Palace Café,** 605 Canal St., between Royal and Chartres streets (www.palacecafe.com; ✆ **504/523-1661**), serves contemporary Creole food with a big emphasis on seafood: catfish pecan meunière, andouille-crusted fish of the day, and lots more. Don't miss the white-chocolate bread pudding. Walk up the curved iron staircase for a real treat; the second floor is ringed with murals depicting local jazz legends. Dinner main courses: $19 to $38.

Outside the quarter, at the corner of Washington Avenue and Coliseum Street in the Garden District, **Commander's Palace,** 1403 Washington Ave. (www. commanderspalace.com; ✆ **504/899-8221**), still reigns as one of the finest dining choices not only in New Orleans, but in the whole United States—the James Beard Foundation voted it the country's best restaurant in 1996. The cuisine is haute Creole. Try anything with shrimp or crawfish, or the Mississippi quail, or . . . oh, just try anything. Dinner main courses: $26 to $45.

New Orleans After Dark

Life in the Big Easy has always been conducive to all manner of nighttime entertainment—usually raucous—and that spirit is still very much alive. There's a reason jazz was born in this town.

Do what most people do: Start at one end of **Bourbon Street** (say, around Iberville St.) and walk down to the other end. Along the way, you'll hear R & B, blues, and jazz pouring out of dozens of bars; be beckoned by touts from the numerous strip clubs; and see one tiny little storefront stall after another sporting hand-lettered signs that say OUR BEER IS CHEAPER THAN NEXT DOOR. It's a scene. Bacchanalian? Yes. Will you spend time in purgatory for it? Maybe, but it's loads of fun.

Preservation Hall, 726 St. Peter St., just off Bourbon Street (www.preservation hall.com; © **504/522-2841** during the day, 504/523-8939 after 8pm), is usually open daily; check their website for the nightly schedule. This deliberately shabby little hall, with very few places to sit and no air-conditioning, will inevitably be packed with people there to see the house band, a bunch of mostly older musicians who have been at this for eons. Don't request "When the Saints Go Marching In" 'cause the band won't play it—even classics get to be old smelly hats when you've played them 45,000 times. Admission $15.

Close by, **Maison Bourbon,** 641 Bourbon St. (www.maisonbourbon.com; © **504/522-8818**), presents authentic and often fantastic Dixieland and traditional jazz. Stepping into the brick-walled room, or even just peering in from the street, takes you away from the mayhem outside. There's a one-drink minimum.

House of Blues, 225 Decatur St. (www.houseofblues.com; © **504/529-2583**), is one of the city's largest live-music venues. Patrons stand and move among the several bars that pepper the club. There's also a restaurant.

For a taste of history, make your way to the **Lafitte's Blacksmith Shop,** 941 Bourbon St. (www.lafittesblacksmithshop.com; © **504/593-9761**), which dates from the 1770s and is the oldest building in the French Quarter. It was allegedly owned by two notorious brothers who used it as a front to cover their trade in contraband. True or not, you will feel like you stepped back in time when you enter at night, as the entire place is lit by candles.

Just out of the quarter, in the Marigney, Frenchmen Street is the current epicenter of live music in New Orleans. On the 3 blocks between Washington Square and Royal Street, about a dozen clubs bill music almost every night with no cover charge, and most serve food. **Snug Harbor,** 626 Frenchman St. (www.snugjazz.com; © **504/949-0696**), one of the oldest on the street, is jazz in a cozy setting. There's a full dinner menu in the restaurant, but only appetizers are served in the club. Other favorites include Maison, The Spotted Cat, d.b.a., Café Negril, and The Three Muses, among others, but take a stroll, peruse the menus and performers prominently displayed outside each club, and decide for yourself.

Jazz, blues, and Dixieland pour out of the nostalgia-laden bar and concert hall **Tipitina's,** way uptown, at 501 Napoleon Ave. (www.tipitinas.com; © **504/891-8477**).

Legendary local trumpet player Kermit Ruffins, featured on HBO's *Treme,* with a style often described as Armstrong-esque, can still be heard live every Thursday night playing with his Barbecue Swingers at 8pm at **Vaughn's Lounge,** 800 Lesseps St. (© **504/947-5562**), in the Bywater.

GALVESTON

Some 80km (50 miles) south of Houston, Galveston, Texas, is located on a 43km-long (27-mile) barrier island that averages only 3km (2 miles) wide. Ships departing from here can reach the open sea in about 30 minutes, compared to several hours of lag time from the Port of Houston. The city's main attractions are the downtown historic

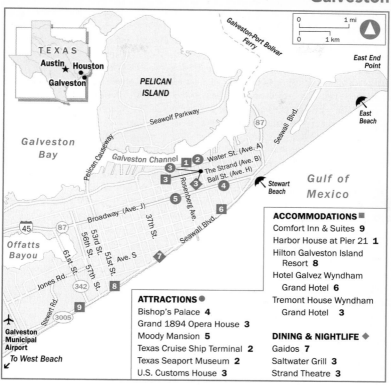

ACCOMMODATIONS ■
Comfort Inn & Suites **9**
Harbor House at Pier 21 **1**
Hilton Galveston Island
    Resort **8**
Hotel Galvez Wyndham
    Grand Hotel **6**
Tremont House Wyndham
    Grand Hotel **3**

DINING & NIGHTLIFE ◆
Gaidos **7**
Saltwater Grill **3**
Strand Theatre **3**

ATTRACTIONS ●
Bishop's Palace **4**
Grand 1894 Opera House **3**
Moody Mansion **5**
Texas Cruise Ship Terminal **2**
Texas Seaport Museum **2**
U.S. Customs House **3**

district; the Strand, with its Victorian commercial buildings and houses; and the beaches, which draw crowds of Houstonians and other Texans during the summer.

At the end of the 19th century, Galveston was the largest city in Texas and the third-busiest port in the country. But then, on September 8, 1900, a massive storm came ashore, carrying with it 225kmph (140-mph) winds and a 6m (20-ft.) surge that washed completely over the island. Houses were smashed into matchwood, and more than 6,000 islanders—a sixth of the island's population—drowned. Those who remained went to work to prevent a recurrence of the disaster, raising the city's ground level by up to 5m (16 ft.) and erecting a stout sea wall that now stretches along 15km (9 miles) of shoreline, with several jetties of large granite blocks projecting out into the water. Today, Galveston is a vibrant port city and a hub for cruises to the western Caribbean.

VISITOR INFORMATION   Contact **Galveston Island, Texas Tourism & Marketing** at ☎ **888/425-4753** or visit www.galveston.com for brochures, pamphlets, and information.

Getting to Galveston & the Port

The **Texas Cruise Ship Terminal** at the Port of Galveston (www.portofgalveston. com; ☎ **409/766-6113**) is at Harborside Drive and 25th Street, on Galveston

Island. It's reached via I-45 south from Houston. If you're flying in, you'll land at one of two Houston airports: **William P. Hobby Airport** (south of downtown Houston, about 50km/30 miles, or a 45-min. drive, from the terminal) or the larger **George Bush Intercontinental Airport** (just north of downtown Houston, and about 87km/54 miles, or an 80-min. drive, from the terminal). Information on both is available at **www.fly2houston.com**. Because it's a long way from both airports to the cruise ship terminal (and because taxi prices are correspondingly high), it's a good idea to arrange transfers through your cruise line. You can also call **Galveston Limousine Service** (www.galvestonlimosineservice.com; ✆ **800/640-4826** or 409/744-5466), which charges $45 per person for its shuttle from Hobby and $55 from Bush. **Taxis** cost about $75 from Hobby Airport and $125 from Bush.

If you're driving to the port, I-45 is the main artery for those arriving from the north. To get to the terminal, follow I-45 south to exit 1C (at Harborside Dr./Hwy. 275); it's the first exit after the causeway. Turn left (east) onto Harborside Drive and continue for about 8km (5 miles) to the cruise terminal. Long-term parking at the port is available. The lots are less than 1km (½ mile) from the cruise ship terminal; shuttle buses transport passengers between the lots and the terminal, where porters are available to carry luggage. Parking costs about $10 per day for an uncovered lot.

GETTING AROUND Within walking distance of the port's two terminals is the historic **Strand District,** Galveston's revitalized downtown, with shops, art galleries, museums, and eateries lining its quaint brick streets. Most of Galveston's hotels, motels, and restaurants are located along the sea wall from where Broadway meets the shore all the way west past 60th Street. If you're on the sea wall around 25th Street (near the visitor center), you can take the **Galveston Island Rail Trolley** (www.islandtransit.net; ✆ **409/797-3900**) to the Strand District for $1.50.

Exploring Galveston

If you have only a few hours before you have to board your cruise, focus on the Strand National Historic Landmark District, the heart of Galveston in the late 1800s and early 1900s, and the East End Historic District, both located north of Broadway.

The **Strand District** is the restored commercial district that runs from 19th to 25th streets between Church Street and the harbor piers. When cotton was king, the Strand was dubbed the "Wall Street of the Southwest." Today, its three- and four-story Victorian iron-fronts (so called because of their ironwork facades) are full of shopping and dining options. Near the cruise dock, at Pier 21, the **Texas Seaport Museum** (www.tsm-elissa.org; ✆ **409/763-1877**) is centered on the three-masted, iron-hulled sailing ship *Elissa,* built in 1877 in Aberdeen, Scotland, and still fully functional today. You can also browse a computer database listing the names of 133,000 immigrants who first entered the U.S. through Galveston in the 19th and early 20th centuries. Admission is $8.

The **East End Historic District** is the old-silk-stocking neighborhood that runs from 9th to 19th streets between Broadway and Church Street. It has many lovely houses that have been completely restored. The **Galveston Historical Foundation** (www.galvestonhistory.org) offers regular tours of several mansions-turned-museums including the ornate Victorian **Bishop's Palace,** 1402 Broadway (✆ **409/762-2475**), Galveston's grandest and best-known historic building, built between 1887 and 1893; and the **Moody Mansion,** 2618 Broadway (www.moodymansion.org; ✆ **409/762-7668**), whose ornately furnished rooms depict the home life of the wealthy Moody family, who built the house in 1895. Admission to each of the historic homes is $10 for adults, $7 for children 6 to 18, and free for children 5 and under.

Elsewhere in town, Postoffice Street is a restored historic district with more than 25 buildings, including the **Grand 1894 Opera House,** still in operation, and the **U.S. Customs House,** now home of the Galveston Historical Foundation.

Organized Tours

If you have a late-departing flight after your cruise, consider the 3½-hour **City Tour** bus tour. It passes through Galveston's scenic and historic Strand District, then travels to Houston, touring the downtown theater and museum districts; Hermann Park, home to the Houston Zoo; and River Oaks, Houston's most prestigious residential neighborhood, before ending at Bush airport. You can book it as a **shore excursion** on your cruise ship. The tour costs $60.

Hitting the Beach

The beaches are another of Galveston's most popular attractions, with light-tan sand and warm waters much of the year. **East Beach** and **Stewart Beach,** operated by the city, have pavilions with dressing rooms, showers, and restrooms, ideal for daytrippers. Stewart Beach is located at the end of Broadway, while East Beach is about a mile farther east. All of the beaches are free. Another activity popular with visitors and locals alike is walking, skating, or riding bikes atop the **sea wall,** which extends 15km (9 miles) along the shoreline.

Shopping

Galveston has more than 20 art galleries on the Strand, Pier 21, and in the Postoffice Street Entertainment District. The Strand is also known for its quaint antiques, art, and memorabilia shops.

Where to Stay

The **Wyndham Grand Tremont House Hotel,** 2300 Ship's Mechanic Row (www.galveston.com/thetremonthouse; © 877/999-3223 or 409/763-0300), is a 117-room gem located in the heart of the Strand neighborhood. A replica of the original 1839-built hotel, which stood nearby, this Tremont occupies the 1879-built Leon & H. Blum Building, and has been designed to re-create the atmosphere of its 19th-century namesake. Rates: from $179.

Harbor House at Pier 21, No. 28–Pier 21 (www.harborhousepier21.com; © 800/874-3721 or 409/763-3321), is a 42-unit hotel built on a pier and overlooking the harbor. It has very modern styling and is very close to the Strand District and many restaurants. Rates: from $99.

Hotel Galvez & Spa, A Wyndham Grand Hotel, 2024 Seawall Blvd. (www.wyndham.com; © 800/996-3426 or 409/765-7721), Galveston's historic grand hotel, is located on the shore facing the sea wall and one of the municipal beaches. It has 231 rooms and is on the trolley line leading to the Strand District. Rates: from $1,259.

Other properties on Seawall Boulevard include the 149-unit **Hilton Galveston Island Resort,** 5400 Seawall Blvd. (www.hilton.com; © 800/445-8667 or 409/744-5000; rates: from $189); and the 100-unit **Comfort Inn & Suites Stewart Beach,** 6302 Seawall Blvd. (www.comfortinn.com; © 800/221-2222; rates: from $89).

Restaurants & Nightlife

Seafood is the reason people come to Galveston, and there's quite a variety. **Gaidos,** 3800 Seawall Blvd. (www.gaidos.com; ✆ **409/762-9625**), is a Galveston favorite that's been owned and operated by the Gaido family for four generations, offering fresh seafood and attentive service. The soups and side dishes are mostly traditional Southern and Gulf Coast recipes that are comfort food for longtime customers. The stuffed snapper is the best I've had. Main courses: $16 to $35. **Saltwater Grill,** 2017 Postoffice St. (www.saltwatergrill.com; ✆ **409/762-3474**), located in an old building near the Strand, prints a daily menu that usually includes some inventive seafood pastas, a fish dish with an Asian bent, gumbo or bouillabaisse, and a few nonseafood options. Main courses: $16 to $30.

There are enough bars and restaurants along the sea wall and in the historic Strand and Postoffice Street districts to pleasantly while away an evening. For concerts, musicals, and plays, check out the 200-seat **ETC at the Strand Theatre,** 2317 Mechanic St. (www.islandetc.org; ✆ **888/762-3556**), in the heart of the historic district, or the elegant **Grand 1894 Opera House,** 2020 Postoffice St. (www.the grand.com; ✆ **800/821-1894**), for Broadway productions, orchestral performances, country music, and more.

BALTIMORE

Baltimore's Inner Harbor is one of the most popular areas of the city and has been one of America's major seaports since the 1700s. It became a cultural hub of Baltimore in the 1970s with the opening of **Harborplace,** the cornerstone of the Inner Harbor of Baltimore. Harborplace has transformed a once industrial area of Baltimore into a prime vacation destination. The shops, restaurants, entertainment, waterfront, and events that take place daily at Harborplace have made it the number-one attraction in Baltimore.

The Inner Harbor is also home to many of the city's most important attractions, including the Maryland Science Center, the National Aquarium, and Oriole Park at Camden Yards, home of Major League Baseball's Baltimore Orioles and among the most beautiful stadiums in all of baseball.

VISITOR INFORMATION Contact **Visit Baltimore** at ✆ **410/659-7300,** or visit www.baltimore.org for brochures, pamphlets, and information.

Getting to Baltimore & the Port

The **Baltimore Cruise Ship Terminal** (www.cruisemaryland.com; ✆ **410/962-8701**) is at 2001 E. McComas St., on Baltimore's Inner Harbor. It can be reached via I-95 from points both north and south. If you're flying in, you'll likely land at **Baltimore-Washington International Thurgood Marshall** (www.bwiairport.com/en), which is southwest of downtown Baltimore, about 18km (11 miles), or a 15-minute drive, from the terminal. BWI provides extensive taxi service from the airport to all Baltimore locations. A trip to the Inner Harbor will run you about $35.

If you're driving to the port, I-95 is the main artery for those arriving from both north and south. To get to the terminal:

From points north: Drive south on I-95 through the Fort McHenry Tunnel. Stay in the right lane when going through the tunnel. Take Exit 55, Key Highway. Turn left

Baltimore

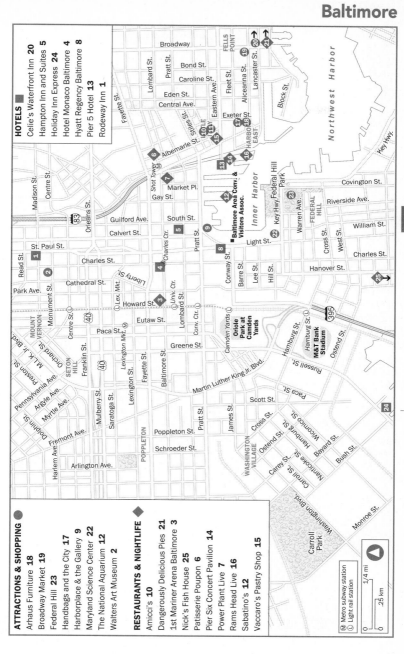

HOTELS ■
Celie's Waterfront Inn **20**
Hampton Inn and Suites **5**
Holiday Inn Express **24**
Hotel Monaco Baltimore **4**
Hyatt Regency Baltimore **8**
Pier 5 Hotel **13**
Rodeway Inn **1**

ATTRACTIONS & SHOPPING ●
Arhaus Furniture **18**
Broadway Market **19**
Federal Hill **23**
Handbags and the City **17**
Harborplace & the Gallery **9**
Maryland Science Center **22**
The National Aquarium **12**
Walters Art Museum **2**

RESTAURANTS & NIGHTLIFE ◆
Amicci's **10**
Dangerously Delicious Pies **21**
1st Mariner Arena Baltimore **3**
Nick's Fish House **25**
Patisserie Poupon **6**
Pier Six Concert Pavilion **14**
Power Plant Live **7**
Rams Head Live **16**
Sabatino's **12**
Vaccaro's Pastry Shop **15**

Ⓜ Metro subway station
Ⓛ Light rail station

at the traffic light onto East McComas Street. Follow the signs to the South Locust Point Cruise Terminal entrance on the right.

From points south: Drive north on I-95 to Exit 55, Key Highway. From the ramp stay straight on East McComas Street. The South Locust Point Cruise Terminal entrance is on the right.

GETTING AROUND   The port's cruise terminals are nestled in the city's historic **Inner Harbor,** Baltimore's revitalized downtown, beginning with the aforementioned Harborplace Mall (www.harborplace.com) with its shops, eateries, and entertainment venues. Most of the Inner Harbor's hotels, motels, and restaurants are all within walking distance of the Port of Baltimore.

Exploring Baltimore

If you have a limited amount of time before your cruise, the **Inner Harbor** provides more than enough entertainment. You can spend an entire day or more exploring its many attractions.

It all begins with **Harborplace & the Gallery,** a waterfront complex featuring more than 100 stores and dozens of eating establishments. This waterfront complex is connected by a public plaza that hosts street performers of all types and concerts on weekends.

Alongside Harborplace, **The National Aquarium** (www.aqua.org; ℭ **410/576-3800**) features a 225,000-gallon ring-shaped shark walk that lets you get up close and personal with various encircling species, an eerie jellyfish exhibit, and daily dolphin shows. Admission is $40 for adults, $30 for children.

On Harborplace's opposite flank is the **Maryland Science Center** (www.mdsci.org; ℭ **410/685-2370**); with its full-sized dinosaurs, IMAX theatre, and planetarium, the Science center has something for every species of science buff. Admission is $15 for adults, $12 for children (IMAX shows cost an extra $4 per ticket).

A prime destination by all accounts is the **Walters Art Museum** (www.thewalters.org; ℭ **410/547-9000**), at 600 N. Charles St. Begun with the 22,000-object collection of William and Henry Walters, this gem's ancient and medieval galleries practically sparkle. The Knight's Hall displays tapestries, furnishings, and armor from the Middle Ages. The Egyptian collection is one of the best in the U.S. The original Palazzo building features 1,500 works from the Renaissance and baroque periods. Hackerman House, open Saturday and Sunday, features Asian art. The Palace of Wonders is the gallery of a 17th-century Flemish nobleman, with art, collections from nature, and artifacts from around the world. Docents offer free tours Sunday at 2pm. The cafe serves light fare.

For a delightfully cost-free outdoor excursion to a scenic park with plenty of gardens and a great view of the city, head over to **Federal Hill** overlooking the Inner Harbor. Take the 100 steps on the Battery Avenue side, or enter from Warren Avenue, where you won't have any steps to contend with at all, except maybe a curbstone. The hill has been valued for its scenic views since the first Baltimoreans came here to watch construction around the harbor. A single cannon recalls the Civil War, when federal guns were trained on the city. There's even a fenced-in playground for the kids.

Shopping

You can find anything from onion rings to diamond rings at the 160 shops that make up **Harborplace Mall** (www.harborplace.com; ℭ **410/332-4191**), which is actually three separate venues: two stand-alone pavilions on Light and Pratt streets, and the Gallery, a vertical mall in the Renaissance Harborplace Hotel. The **Light Street Pavilion** has the most food stalls and restaurants, plus some souvenir shops. The **Pratt Street Pavilion** offers specialty stores, clothing and jewelry shops, and more restaurants. The **Gallery** has three floors of shops, plus a fourth-floor food court. Most of the stores are franchises of national chains (such as Banana Republic, Brooks Brothers, Ann Taylor, and Coach), and are open Monday through Saturday from 10am to 9pm and Sunday from noon to 6pm.

For something more quaint and local, you can wander over to **Broadway Market,** a 200-year-old market with two large covered buildings. This is the nation's oldest continually running market. It's staffed by local vendors selling produce and ethnic and raw-bar foods, and makes an ideal spot for a quick lunch.

Harbor East is a neighborhood that didn't even exist a few years ago, but is now thriving, and the shopping is *très* chic. Most shops are on **Exeter** or **Fleet Street.** Look for something hot to carry your stuff in at **Handbags and the City,** 612 S. Exeter St. (℅ **410/528-1443**), or something cool to sit on at **Arhaus Furniture,** 660 S. Exeter St. (www.arhaus.com; ℅ **410/244-6376**).

Where to Stay

Baltimore caters to business travelers, but loves families. With more than 9,000 rooms on offer, you're sure to find something that suits you.

The 488-unit **Hyatt Regency Baltimore,** 300 Light St. (www.baltimore.hyatt.com; ℅ **410/528-1234**), is located along the waterway on Baltimore's picturesque Inner Harbor. If you're planning a trip to Baltimore, the Hyatt's location and its spiffy new decor make it a must. The staff here, as well as the incomparable view and the Inner Harbor location, make this more than "just a Hyatt." Rates: from $199.

Built in 1906, the **Hotel Monaco Baltimore,** 2 N. Charles St. (www.monaco-baltimore.com; ℅ **888/752-2636** or 443/692-6170), on the Inner Harbor, features an elegant three-story lobby with its original marble floor and Tiffany stained-glass windows and 202 beautifully appointed guest rooms and suites. Rates: from $280.

Pier 5 Hotel, 711 Eastern Ave. (www.harbormagic.com; ℅ **410/539-2000**), is Baltimore's premier waterfront boutique hotel delivering harbor views, unrivaled dining options, and an exclusive guest experience directly adjacent to the National Aquarium. Rates: from $219.

Rodeway Inn, 723 St. Paul St. (www.rodewayinn.com; ℅ **410/244-6630**), in Maryland's historic Mount Vernon area, provides inviting accommodations in downtown Baltimore. The **Inner Harbor** port area is just minutes away. Rates: from $65.

Other properties on the Inner Harbor include the 116-unit **Hampton Inn and Suites,** 131 E. Redwood St. (www.hamptoninn.hilton.com; ℅ **410/539-7888;** rates: from $169); and the 123-unit **Holiday Inn Express,** 1701 Russel St. (www.hiexpress.com; ℅ **410/727-1818;** rates: from $119).

Celie's Waterfront Inn, 1714 Thames St. (www.celieswaterfront.com; ℅ **800/432-0184**), housed in an 18th-century townhouse, provides a quiet refuge in bustling Fell's Point. Two units have fireplaces, whirlpool tubs, and harbor views, while two others—with just as nice city views—have private balconies and whirlpools. Two interior rooms overlooking the flower-filled courtyard are particularly quiet. Two suites (with full kitchens) can accommodate four or six comfortably. Enjoy breakfast in your room, on the deck, or in the garden. Rates: from $159.

Restaurants & Nightlife

Baltimore is known for its seafood, but the city is also home to a variety of ethnic and regional cuisines. There are plenty of good restaurants in the main tourist areas, with excellent choices in **Little Italy, Fell's Point, Harbor East,** and **Mount Vernon.** In recent years, the **Inner Harbor** has become overrun with chain restaurants serving mediocre fare, but such places as the **Hard Rock Cafe** and **ESPN Zone** continue to draw crowds. **Power Plant Live,** with its mix of restaurants and clubs, is also packed for dinner. You'll find it a block north of **Pratt Street,** a short walk from the **Inner Harbor.**

No visit to Baltimore is complete without tasting the city's signature seafood favorite—crab cakes—but what makes a good crab cake is a topic of heated debate. You can expect jumbo lump mixed with a bit of mayo; fried or broiled is often the diner's choice. But each recipe is different. Is Old Bay seasoning required? How much filler is too much? Should you see a fleck of any plant material besides parsley? Keep in mind a few things: Crabs run from May to September (more or less), so you have a better chance of getting local crab then (as opposed to Louisiana or Asia imports). You don't have to go to a crab house for a decent crab cake. In fact, the number of crab houses has dwindled in recent years, but you can find good seafood at just about every restaurant around. Expect to pay $12 to $18 for a crab-cake sandwich (served on crackers or a bun). A crab-cake platter will be at least $25 and usually comes with fries, coleslaw, and sliced tomato.

South of the pier, on the waterfront, is **Nick's Fish House,** 2600 Insulator Dr., South Baltimore (www.nicksfishhouse.com; ✆ 410/347-4123). Maybe the old South Baltimore feel of this casual place swayed me, but this is a great traditional crab cake in a traditional (but new) crab house. Open every day for lunch and dinner.

You'll find all the pasta, cannoli, and chianti you could want in Baltimore's **Little Italy,** a few packed blocks conveniently located adjacent to the Inner Harbor. Make a reservation if you know where you want to eat beforehand. But if you prefer to wander, plan to eat early or late and choose a place as you stroll through the basil-scented streets. *Tip:* Parking is fairly easy. Choose the garage at Pratt and President streets, opt for the valet parking many restaurants offer, or look for a spot on the street.

For more than 50 years, **Sabatino's,** 901 Fawn St. (www.sabatinos.com; ✆ 410/727-9414) has been known for its exceptional cuisine. Everyone will tell you to get the house salad with the house dressing, which is thick and garlicky. Simple pasta dishes come in very large portions. The menu also has seafood and meat dishes, and their *brasciola* (a roll of beef, prosciutto, cheeses, and marinara) rivals my own Grandma Scalici's. Dining rooms fill three floors of this narrow building. It's worth the wait to be seated upstairs, where it's quieter. This is a good spot for late-night dining and people-watching after the bars have closed.

Perfect for families and easy on the wallet, you'll usually find casual **Amicci's,** 231 S. High St. (www.amiccis.com; ✆ 410/528-1096) crowded with local families and young couples who don't want to spend a lot on good Italian food. Don't be fooled by the small storefront—the restaurant is a maze of dining rooms. If you have to wait, it won't be too long. Start with Amicci's signature *pane rotundo* appetizer (a round loaf of bread topped with shrimp in a creamy, garlicky sauce). Seafood lovers will enjoy that or one of their seafood and pasta dishes, but the pasta should satisfy everyone, even vegetarians. A $5 children's menu is offered all day. Desserts here come from the famed **Vaccaro's Pastry Shop,** 222 Albermarle St. (www.vaccarospastry.com; **© 410/685-4905**).

Sometimes you just need a sweet—and there are a couple sweet spots around town that shouldn't be missed if you're in the neighborhood. The most famous baker in town, Food Network's *Ace of Cakes* chef, Duff Goldman, has his Charm City Cakes shop in Remington, but it isn't open to the public. **Dangerously Delicious Pies,** 2839 O'Donnell St. (www.dangerouspies.com; **© 410/522-7437**), serves up honest, homemade, fresh-out-of-the-oven pies. The rock-'n'-roll guys here make all kinds, including fruit, Key (Bridge) lime, derby, and a towering lemon meringue. Open Tuesday through Sunday from 7am to 6pm. **Patisserie Poupon,** 820 E. Baltimore St. (**© 410/332-0390**), is a delightful French pastry shop located in the shadow of the Shot Tower and near Port Discovery and Little Italy. (It's safer to drive here, due to traffic.) Stop for coffee and a croissant or a fabulously decorated pastry. Open Monday through Saturday from 7am to 6pm.

Baltimore is jumping when the sun sets: **The Inner Harbor, Federal Hill, Canton,** and **Mount Vernon** have all developed lives after dark. **Fell's Point** also has plenty of options for drinking and merriment.

Baltimore has a nice variety of small live-performance venues. Major national acts come to the **1st Mariner Arena Baltimore** near the Inner Harbor, 201 W. Baltimore St. (www.baltimorearena.com; **© 410/347-2020**); **Pier Six Concert Pavilion** at the Inner Harbor, 731 Eastern Ave. (www.piersixpavilion.com; **© 410/783-4189**); and **Rams Head Live** at Power Plant Live, 20 Market Place (www.ramsheadlive.com; **© 410/244-1131**). Get tickets at **www.ticketmaster.com** for 1st Mariner Arena and at Rams Head Live for Pier Six and Rams Head.

Power Plant Live, a mix of restaurants and bars, is a short walk from the Inner Harbor, at Water Street and Market Place. It packs in young singles, especially on weekend nights, who come for the gigantic **Lucky's Tavern,** a sports bar/rock bar; **Havana Club,** a cigar bar; and **Howl at the Moon,** a rock-'n'-roll piano bar, as well as Rams Head Live.

NEW YORK CITY

What can you say about the capital of the world that hasn't already been said? New York is just *it*: the biggest, loudest, and most historic city in the U.S., with a population that encompasses people from every country, race, religion, and social predilection on the face of the earth. From the near-perfect grid of Manhattan's streets and the vertical lines of the skyscrapers to its direct, no-nonsense natives, New York is a city of straight lines. And why not? A straight line, after all, is the fastest way to get to the point.

VISITOR INFORMATION Contact **nycgo,** New York City's official visitor information center, at **© 212/484-1222,** or visit www.nycgo.com. There are branches at several locations throughout the city, including 810 Seventh Ave. (between 52nd and 53rd sts.), at 67th Street and Central Park West, and at the southern tip of City Hall Park on the Broadway sidewalk at Park Row.

Getting to New York City & the Port

New York is served by three cruise ports: one in Manhattan, one in Brooklyn, and another in Bayonne, New Jersey, just across the Hudson.

New York City

NEW YORK
Albany ★
New York ●

UPPER WEST SIDE

West End Ave.
Amsterdam Ave.
Central Park W.

W. 65th St.
W. 64th St.
W. 63rd St.
W. 62nd Ave.
W. 61st St.
W. 60th St.
W. 59th St.
W. 58th St.
W. 57th St.
W. 56th St.
W. 55th St.
W. 54th St.
W. 53rd St.
W. 52nd St.
W. 51st St.
W. 50th St.
W. 49th St.
W. 48th St.
W. 47th St.
W. 46th St.
W. 45th St.
W. 44th St.
W. 43rd St.
W. 42nd St.
W. 41st St.
W. 40th St.
W. 39th St.
W. 38th St.
W. 37th St.
W. 36th St.
W. 35th St.
W. 34th St.
W. 33rd St.
W 32nd St.
W. 31st St.
W. 30th St.
W. 29th St.
W. 28th St.
W. 27th St.
W. 26th St.
W. 25th St.
W. 24th St.
W. 23rd St.
W. 22nd St.
W. 21st St.
W. 20th St.
W. 19th St.
W. 18th St.
W. 17th St.
W. 16th St.
W. 15th St.

65th S

CENTRA

West Drive
Central Park S.
Columbus Circle

Columbus Ave.
Ninth Ave.
Tenth Ave.
Eleventh Ave.
Twelfth Ave.
Eighth Ave.
Seventh Ave.
Broadway

DeWitt Clinton Park

THEATER DISTRICT

MIDTOWN WEST

TIMES SQUARE

Port Authority

GARMEN DISTRIC

Penn Station/ Madison Square Garden   W 32nd S

Tunnel Entrance

Chelsea Park

Intrepid Sea-Air-Space Museum

Lincoln Tunnel
← To New Jersey

Javits Convention Center

CHELSEA

Chelsea Piers Sports & Entertainment Complex

West Side Hwy.

Chelsea Piers

Hudson River

MEAT-PACKING DISTRICT

Upper Manhattan
Uptown
Midtown
Downtown

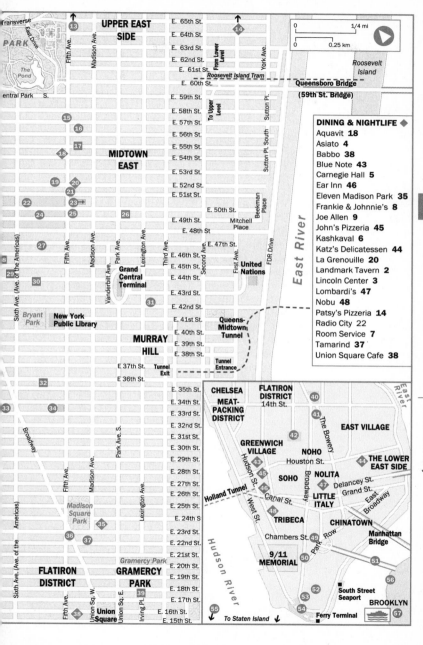

DINING & NIGHTLIFE ◆

Aquavit **18**
Asiato **4**
Babbo **38**
Blue Note **43**
Carnegie Hall **5**
Ear Inn **46**
Eleven Madison Park **35**
Frankie & Johnnie's **8**
Joe Allen **9**
John's Pizzeria **45**
Kashkaval **6**
Katz's Delicatessen **44**
La Grenouille **20**
Landmark Tavern **2**
Lincoln Center **3**
Lombardi's **47**
Nobu **48**
Patsy's Pizzeria **14**
Radio City **22**
Room Service **7**
Tamarind **37**
Union Square Cafe **38**

Manhattan's historic if utilitarian **New York Cruise Terminal** (www.nycruise. com; ☎ **212/246-5450**) is stretched out between the Hudson River and the West Side Highway, between 46th and 54th streets (enter via the vehicle ramp at 55th St.). It's frequently congested on turnaround days, though improvements in the works promise to reduce roadway congestion and improve passenger circulation. Parking is available for $35 a day, with a max fee, for any cruise from 11 to 30 nights, of $350. Two blocks away, at 11th Avenue and 46th Street, is the **Landmark Tavern** (www. thelandmarktavern.org; ☎ **212/247-2562**), one of the most beautiful and historic bars in New York. When it opened in 1868, it was on the waterfront, meaning everything between it and your ship was created out of landfill over the past century or so.

Down in the old blue-collar neighborhood of Red Hook, the **Brooklyn Cruise Terminal** (www.nycruiseterminal.com; ☎ **718/246-2794**) is located just across New York Harbor from Lower Manhattan and Governors Island, former site of the country's largest Coast Guard base. The port is easily accessible to locals driving by car, as well as to visitors flying into Kennedy, LaGuardia, and Newark airports. While Red Hook itself is industrial and gritty (if slowly gentrifying), it's just minutes from picturesque Colonial-era Brooklyn Heights and the great expanse of the **Brooklyn Bridge.** The Brooklyn terminal's most high-profile ship is the *Queen Mary 2,* which home-ports here on the western end of her transatlantic crossings. From wherever you're driving, get onto the Brooklyn-Queens Expressway and exit at Hamilton Avenue (exit 26) onto the service road. Stay to the left and make a left U-turn at the intersection of Hamilton and Clinton Street/Ninth Street, and then continue west along the westbound Hamilton Avenue service road. Take the service road to its end at Van Brunt Street. Turn left, travel 2 blocks, and then turn right onto Bowne Street to enter the terminal. Parking is $23 per day.

In Bayonne, New Jersey, the **Cape Liberty Cruise Port** (www.cruiseliberty.com; ☎ **201/823-3737**) opened in 2004 as a home port for Royal Caribbean and Celebrity vessels. I know, sailing from Bayonne doesn't sound as romantic as sailing from Manhattan, but Cape Liberty does have the advantage of being less congested. And where else can you get a view of the Statue of Liberty's butt? Located just off the New Jersey Turnpike and I-278, and approximately 15 minutes from the Newark airport, it's easily accessible to those coming from New Jersey, Long Island, and the New York boroughs of Brooklyn and Staten Island. From the New Jersey Turnpike, take exit 14A and follow signs for Route 440 S. Follow 440 to Cape Liberty Terminal Boulevard, which will be on your left. Parking is $19 per day.

If you're coming in by plane, you'll fly into one of three New York–area airports. **John F. Kennedy International Airport (JFK)** is in southern Queens, about 24km (15 miles) southeast of Midtown Manhattan. **LaGuardia Airport (LGA)** is in northern Queens, about 13km (8 miles) northeast of Midtown Manhattan. **Newark Liberty International Airport (EWR)** is in Essex and Union counties, New Jersey, about 26km (16 miles) southwest of Midtown Manhattan. For information on all three, go to the Port Authority of New York & New Jersey website at **www.panynj. gov**. Kennedy and Newark are the larger airports and accommodate both domestic and international flights. If you've arranged air transportation and/or transfers through your cruise line, a representative will direct you to shuttle buses that take you to whichever port your ship is sailing from. Yellow **taxis** are usually lined up in great numbers at the airports and can take you to any of the ports or your hotel, though the fare will be stiff. From JFK to Manhattan, yellow taxis charge a flat fee of $45 per carload, plus tolls and tip. From Newark to Manhattan, flat fees vary from $40 to $60,

THE PORTS OF EMBARKATION | New York City

depending on where you're going. There is no flat fee from LaGuardia—you pay the standard metered rate: $2.50 just to get going, then 40¢ for every fifth-mile (about 4 blocks) thereafter, with additional surcharges for peak hours (4–8pm Mon–Fri) and night fares (daily 8pm–6am). **SuperShuttle** (www.supershuttle.com; ✆ **212/258-3826**) is a cheaper shared-van alternative, costing about $21 for the first passenger and $12 for each additional to Manhattan's terminal. Twenty-four-hour advance reservations are recommended.

GETTING AROUND   The beauty of New York City is that it's so walkable and so relatively compact, with the island of Manhattan measuring only about 3km (2 miles) wide by 21km (13 miles) long—most of its streets (north of Greenwich Village, at least) follow a simple grid pattern, so it's next to impossible to lose your way. The Manhattan cruise terminal is close to the heart of Midtown, about a mile west of Times Square.

If you don't care to walk everywhere, don't hesitate to take the **subway** or **bus.** Fares for both are $2.25 a ride no matter how far you go. You can buy a **MetroCard** pass in any denomination at any subway station. Be sure to pick up a free map from a station attendant so you can be sure the subway you're on really goes where you think it does. Buses run both north-south and east-west, with routes marked (usually) at each bus stop. They're generally not fast, but they do offer something the subways don't: a view. Buses accept both MetroCards and coins, but not paper money; most have free bus maps available somewhere aboard. Route, schedule, and fare info for both subways and buses can be found at **www.mta.info**.

You can also hail one of the city's ubiquitous **yellow cabs.** The meter starts at $2.50 and increases 40¢ every fifth-mile or 90 seconds, whichever comes first.

Exploring New York City

There's much more to see and do in New York than I have space for here, so I'll concentrate on some highlights—some big touristy ones, as well as some personal favorites.

MIDTOWN   Let's triangulate from **Times Square.** Once the center of New York's entertainment industry, the whole area around 42nd Street and Broadway fell into deep, dark, sleazy blight starting in the 1960s and running right up to the early 1990s. Now, it's a corporate America theme park, overseen by the eight-story **NASDAQ** video screen (the world's largest) at 43rd Street and Broadway, nestled in among acres of other high-tech signage. Even at midnight, the whole area is bright as noon and packed with visitors, musicians, and street artists—but not very many New Yorkers. The fact is, it's a total tourist trap, but it sure is a sight.

At 44th Street, ABC's *Good Morning America* has set up a street-facing studio, while **MTV** has done the same across Broadway at 45th Street, drawing bus loads of fans. A couple of blocks away, the former porn-peddler's paradise of **42nd Street** between Seventh and Eighth avenues has been rebuilt into a family-oriented entertainment mecca. In addition to a spate of beautifully renovated theaters—including the **New Victory,** the **New Amsterdam,** and the Selwyn (aka the **American Airlines Theatre**)—the neon-bright block is chock-full with retail and amusements, including two huge movie-theater complexes and **Madame Tussaud's New York,** 234 W. 42nd St. (www.madametussauds.com; ✆ **800/246-8872**), a six-floor, new-world version of London's famous wax museum. Admission is $40 adults, and $32 kids ages 4 to 12.

Just a few blocks east, running from 48th to 50th streets between Fifth and Sixth avenues, the Art Deco buildings of **Rockefeller Center** make you feel like you're standing in a classic 1930s movie. For a dramatic approach, start at Fifth Avenue between 49th and 50th streets, where a promenade leads to the Lower Plaza, home to the famous ice-skating rink in winter and alfresco dining in summer. In December and early January, this is also the site of the city's official Christmas tree. **St. Patrick's Cathedral** (www.saintpatrickscathedral.org; ✆ 212/753-2261), one of the city's most imposing churches, is on the other side of Fifth Avenue, at 50th Street. Three blocks away, the **Museum of Modern Art,** 11 W. 53rd St., between Fifth and Sixth avenues (www.moma.org; ✆ 212/708-9400), is one of the world's great modern art museums. Admission is $25 (closed Tues).

UPTOWN To the north, starting at 59th Street, is **Central Park.** Laid out between 1859 and 1870 on a design by Frederick Law Olmsted and Calvert Vaux, the park's 340 hectares (840 acres) are, just by virtue of their continued existence amid some of the world's priciest real estate, New York's greatest marvel. Highlights include the Wollman Memorial Ice Rink, the Bethesda Fountain, Sheep Meadow (a huge sunbathing spot in summer), and the old carousel with its 58 hand-carved horses. West of the park, the **Upper West Side** is one of the city's most beautiful residential neighborhoods, its most scenic stretch running from 59th Street north to about 89th. **Lincoln Center,** located between West 62nd and 65th streets and Columbus and Amsterdam Aves., recently underwent a major renovation, and it is a beautiful, artistic sight to see. On the park's eastern edge, along Fifth Avenue between 82nd and 104th streets, is **Museum Mile,** home to the **Metropolitan Museum of Art,** at 82nd Street (www.metmuseum.org; ✆ 212/535-7710), and eight other museums. The Met is one of the country's largest and best museums, with a collection of more than two million works spanning the globe and the ages. Admission is $20 (closed Mon). Other museums in the area include the **Solomon R. Guggenheim Museum,** at Fifth Avenue and 88th Street (www.guggenheim.org; ✆ 212/423-3500), with its landmark seashell design by Frank Lloyd Wright and its collection spanning the period from the late 19th century to the present. Admission is $25 (closed Thurs).

DOWNTOWN & BROOKLYN Heading downtown from the Times Square area will take you eventually to New York's most historic districts, where the original colony of New Amsterdam got its start. From the corner of Broadway and 42nd Street, look east. That tall building with the gleaming stainless-steel spire is the **Chrysler Building**—the most beautiful skyscraper in the city. Walk toward it, stopping when you get to Fifth Avenue. Look south from here and start walking toward that other big spire ahead of you, the **Empire State Building** (www.esbnyc.com), which sits at the corner of Fifth Avenue and 34th Street and is once again the tallest building in Manhattan, since the destruction of the World Trade Center. Lines to get up to the 86th-floor observatory can be horrible at the concourse-level ticket booth, so be prepared to wait—or consider purchasing advance tickets online. Admission is $22 adults, $16 kids. You can also shell out $45 for an express ticket that lets you bypass the lines. At the observatory, you can walk out on the windy deck and look through coin-operated viewers (bring quarters) over what, on a clear day, can be as much as a 130km (80-mile) visible radius.

Back on the street, head downtown on Fifth Avenue. Where it crosses Broadway at 23rd Street, you'll see the famous **Flatiron Building** from 1902, looking like the prow of a ship. Walk south along Broadway past **Union Square,** site of protest rallies from the 1870s through today. At Broadway and 10th, **Grace Church** was designed by James Renwick, Jr., who later designed St. Patrick's. At Waverly Place, turn right and go 1 block to **Washington Square Park,** a **Greenwich Village** landmark typically full of musicians and other street performers. Meander through (and maybe take a side trip west into the warren of narrow, cozy streets that make up the Village), then walk south on La Guardia Place past Houston Street and into **SoHo.** Once the city's main arts neighborhood, it's now a center for fashion and design and a shopaholic's dream.

Après shopping, walk east to Broadway and catch the downtown R train at either Prince or Canal Street. Get off at Court Street/Borough Hall and exit at the rear of the platform. Ta-da! You're in **Brooklyn,** the Borough of Kings. Walk west on Montague Street. This is the heart of **Brooklyn Heights,** a Colonial-era village that's now a protected historic district. Wander off on some of the tree-lined side streets to see beautiful 19th-century homes. At the end of Montague, the **Brooklyn Heights Promenade** lets you onto the most spectacular Manhattan view there is, bar none. To the right, that gorgeous span between the two islands is the **Brooklyn Bridge,** completed in 1883. When built, it was the largest suspension bridge in the world, its two stone towers dwarfing every other structure in the city. To New Yorkers, it's as much a marvel now as then, because even though there are larger bridges, there are few as graceful and beautiful.

The best way to see the bridge is to walk it, and that's what you're going to do next. Walk to the end of the Promenade, up the ramp, past Cranberry Street and the playground, and go through the alley to Middagh Street. Take that to the corner of Cadman Plaza Park, where hand-lettered signs direct you to the **Brooklyn Bridge footpath.** The bridge is about 2km (1¼ miles) long, with historical plaques on its two towers and the magnificence of New York all around.

Back in Manhattan, the bridge lets you off facing **City Hall** and its surrounding park. On the far side, the 1910 **Woolworth Building** was the tallest building in the world until the Chrysler beat it out in 1929, but it remains one of New York's most beautiful. Farther down Broadway, at Fulton Street, **St. Paul's Chapel** is New York's oldest, built in 1766. George Washington prayed here on inauguration day 1789, and in 2001 it served as a refuge for 9/11 rescue workers. Thousands of small memorials left by mourners are preserved inside, along with other displays. The **9/11 Memorial** at World Trade Center, with its constant bustle of slow-motion rebuilding, is just behind the church's graveyard. You may visit the memorial but you must reserve a free visitor's pass in advance. Visit **www.911memorial.org** to use the online reservation system. Walk south to narrow little **Wall Street.** On the corner, **Trinity Church** was founded in 1697, with the present structure dating from 1846. Its small cemetery holds the graves of Alexander Hamilton and other great New Yorkers. One block down Wall is the unprepossessing entrance to the **New York Stock Exchange.** Go to the corner on Broad Street for the more ceremonial view. Next door, a statue of George Washington marks the entrance to **Federal Hall,** a reminder that the first seat of U.S. government was located here, from 1789 to 1790. In true New York fashion, it was demolished in 1812 to make room for something new.

At the very tip of Manhattan, **Battery Park** and the streets around were where the Dutch first settled "New Amsterdam" in 1625. The park's centerpiece, **Castle Clinton,** began as a fort during the War of 1812 and later served as New York's immigration facility, welcoming eight million new Americans between 1855 and 1890. You can see its more famous successor, **Ellis Island,** from the waterside, adjacent to the

Statue of Liberty. Ferries (www.statuecruises.com; ✆ **877/523-9849**) sail to both between 9am and 3pm, with tickets costing $13 for adults, $5 for kids 4 to 12, but you'll have to get there early and be prepared to wait in line. You can also buy ferry tickets in advance, online. An alternative, cheaper option is to take the **Staten Island Ferry,** which takes a 25-minute trip to Staten Island. Passengers aboard the free ferry get a beautiful view of the Statue of Liberty, Ellis Island, and the NYC skyline. They can also enjoy beers from the refreshment stand for $3 to $4 (and, rumor has it, people can BYOB).

Additionally, **NYC & Company** offers several discount passes on their website (www.nycgo.com/attraction-passes). The **New York CityPASS,** valid for 9 days, grants you access into six NYC attractions, including the Empire State Building Observatory, The Museum of Modern Art, and the American Museum of Natural History. Price: $89 for adults, $64 for children ages 6 to 17. Another great option is the **Downtown Culture Pass,** valid for 3 days. It gives you unlimited admissions to eight downtown museums, gift shop discounts, and a walking tour. Price: $25 for adults, $15 for children ages 13 to 17, and $5 for children ages 6 to 12.

Organized Tours

For an overview of town, you can join one of the red double-decker **Gray Line tour buses** (www.newyorksightseeing.com; ✆ **800/669-0051** or 212/445-0848) at the Circle Line terminal, just a few steps south of the Manhattan cruise ship piers. A 48-hour hop-on/hop-off pass is $99 for adults, $69 for kids, but there's a steep discount if you buy tickets online, in advance.

Because New York is mostly a port of embarkation, the cruise lines generally offer only a few tour choices as **shore excursions,** including several bus tours ($59–$109, 4–8 hr.). If you've got a day or two in town, though, don't bother: You can see more (and better) on your own.

Shopping

Almost every block in New York City has some interesting shop on it, from up-up-upmarket boutiques to funky little joints. Here's a quick read: The fish and herbal markets along Canal, Mott, Mulberry, and Elizabeth streets in **Chinatown** are fun for their bustle and exotica. Dispersed among them—especially along **Canal Street**—you'll find a mind-boggling collection of knockoff sunglasses and watches, cheap backpacks, discount leather goods, and exotic souvenirs. A definite highlight is the **Pearl River Chinese Emporium,** a few blocks north of Canal at 477 Broadway. Going north, **SoHo,** stretching from Broadway east to Sullivan Street, and from Houston down to Broome, is still the epicenter of cutting-edge fashion. Going up even farther, **East Ninth Street** between First and Second avenues is lined with a smart collection of boutiques that sell excellent-quality original fashions for women.

At Herald Square (where 34th St., Sixth Ave., and Broadway converge), you'll find **Macy's,** the self-proclaimed world's biggest department store. Go in if only to see the classic wooden escalators, which have been running since 1902. At **Times Square,** you can step into the giant **Toys "R" Us** flagship on Broadway and 44th Street, complete with an 18m (59-ft.) Ferris wheel. West 47th Street between Fifth and Sixth avenues is the city's famous **Diamond District,** with more than 2,600 retail and wholesale diamond and jewelry businesses. **Tiffany & Co.** reigns supreme at Fifth Avenue and 57th Street, with other big-name, big-ticket designers radiating out from the crossroads, including **Versace, Chanel, Dior,** and **Cartier.** You'll also find big-name jewelers in the area, as well as chichi department stores such as **Bergdorf Goodman, Henri Bendel,** and **Saks Fifth Avenue,** all of which help this stretch of Fifth Avenue maintain its classy cachet.

Where to Stay

There are tons of choices all over town, with rates rarely going below $200 a night, and easily running more than $400, $500, or $600—and we're not even getting into the realm of suites and penthouses. That said, there are often special promotions offered on weekends, when the business travelers have all left town.

Classic New York hotels have a tendency to charge robber-baron prices. Not so the **Waldorf-Astoria,** 301 Park Ave. (www.waldorfastoria.com; ✆ **800/WALDORF** [925-3673]), a bastion of old-school Art Deco elegance offering more than 1,000 airy rooms with high ceilings and traditional decor, all in a classy Park Avenue location. Rates: from $509. The **Algonquin,** 59 W. 44th St. (www.algonquinhotel.com; ✆ **888/304-2047** or 212/840-6800), is another legendary New York spot, its restaurant once hosting the Algonquin Round Table, a daily luncheon where Dorothy Parker, Robert Benchley, Alexander Woollcott, and other luminaries set the tone for the 1920s literary scene. The hotel makes the most of this association; its newly renovated, comfortable rooms are stocked with the latest issue of the *New Yorker,* and its publike Blue Bar is home to a rotating collection of Hirschfeld drawings. Rates: from $529.

With artistic interiors and great service, the **Muse,** 130 W. 46th St. (www.the musehotel.com; ✆ **877/692-6873** or 212/485-2400), is the hidden jewel of the Theater District, offering beautiful contemporary decor, good-size rooms with feather beds, and sumptuous bathrooms. Rates: from $469. One block south, **Grace Hotel,** 125 W. 45th St. (www.room-matehotels.com; ✆ **212/354-2323**), is another of the best moderately priced Midtown options, offering rooms designed with a modern, minimalist aesthetic, plus such niceties as a lobby swimming pool with a swim-up bar. Rates: from $278. A little farther south, the **Hotel Metro,** 45 W. 35th St. (www.hotelmetronyc.com; ✆ **800/356-3870**), is a Midtown gem that offers a surprisingly good deal. Rates: from $350.

Nestled into the residential Upper West Side, the **Lucerne,** 201 W. 79th St. (www.thelucernehotel.com; ✆ **800/492-8122** or 212/875-1000), occupies a landmark 1904 building with a magnificent terra-cotta exterior, and is only a few blocks from the Museum of Natural History. Inside, its rooms are done in a classic style, offering a real New York feel. Rates: from $290. Even more New York is the 12-room **Inn at Irving Place,** 56 Irving Place, at East 17th Street (www.innatirving.com; ✆ **800/685-1447** or 212/533-4600). An absolute jewel, it was created from two joined brownstone town houses built in 1834. Outside, only the address on the door gives away its location; inside, it's all 19th century, from the period furnishings and Persian rugs to the old-style New York grace, dignity, and charm. Rates: from $485.

Where to Eat

You can get any type of cuisine imaginable in this foodie city, from steakhouse and seafood to Chinese and Japanese to Korean, Indian, Thai, Portuguese, Argentinean, German, French, Ethiopian, Tibetan, Burmese . . . you get the picture.

In the lobby of the ornate, Art Deco MetLife building, **Eleven Madison Park,** 11 Madison Ave. (www.elevenmadisonpark.com; ✆ **212/889-0905**), serves hearty French-infused country cuisine in a magnificent, high-ceilinged setting. Four-course prix-fixe dinner: $125. To get even more French, visit **La Grenouille,** 3 E. 52nd St.

(www.la-grenouille.com; ☎ **212/752-1495**), which serves the classics with elegant perfection. Three-course prix-fixe dinner: $98. In the "best views" category, **Asiate, 80** Columbus Circle, at 60th Street (www.mandarinoriental.com/newyork; ☎ **212/ 805-8881**), in the Mandarin Oriental Hotel, might steal the show, perched 34 floors above Central Park. The Japanese/French fare is divine. Three-course prix-fixe dinner: $85. If it's Italian you're craving, go downtown to **Babbo,** 110 Waverly Place (www. babbonyc.com; ☎ **212/777-0303**), where Food Network chef Mario Batali has created the ideal setting for his exciting northern Italian cooking. Main courses: $27 to $40. For Japanese, try **Nobu,** 105 Hudson St., in TriBeCa (www.noburestaurants. com; ☎ **212/219-0500**), which also happens to have a hand in the menus on Crystal Cruise Lines' three ships. Main courses: $28 to $37.

If visiting the Lincoln Center area, walk over to 9th Avenue, and as you stroll south for 10 to 15 blocks, you will find a multitude of different restaurants, ranging from Italian to Mexican to Thai. Because one of the major ports is nearby, this area is always a great option. **Kashkaval,** 856 9th Ave. between 55th and 56th streets (www. kashkavalfoods.com; ☎ **212/581-8282**), is a gourmet-foods and cheese market in the front, and a cozy wine and cheese bar in the back. The fondue list features some unique and delicious options, and is perfect for sharing. Sharing plates: $12 to $38. **Room Service,** 690 9th Ave. between 47th and 48th streets (☎ **212/582-0999**) is a vibrant, hip Thai restaurant with a reasonable price tag. Main courses: $9 to $19.

In the Theater District, pre-theater diners can't go wrong with **Aquavit,** 65 E. 55th St. (www.aquavit.org; ☎ **212/307-7311**); be sure to mention your showtimes. The light Scandinavian cuisine won't weigh you down in your theater seat. After the show, **Joe Allen,** 326 W. 46th St. (www.joeallenrestaurant.com; ☎ **212/581-6464**), is the ultimate Broadway pub—and the meatloaf is marvelous. Main courses: $18 to $32. For a steakhouse experience in the Theater District, **Frankie & Johnnie's,** 269 W. 45th St. (www.frankieandjohnnies.com; ☎ **212/997-9494**), is a Theater District legend, in business since 1926. The steaks (especially the house sirloin) are extraordinary, and the service is old school. A second location, at 32 W. 37th St. (☎ **212/ 997-8940**), is set in a two-story former town house that was once home to legendary actor John Barrymore. Main courses: $25 to $52.

Heading downtown, the **Union Square Cafe,** 21 E. 16th St. (www.unionsquare cafe.com; ☎ **212/243-4020**), is a perennial favorite, serving new American cuisine in a cheerful setting. Main courses: $26 to $37. Holding the torch for the old Jewish Lower East Side, **Katz's Delicatessen,** 205 E. Houston St. (www.katzdeli.com; ☎ **212/254-2246**), is the choice among those who know their kreplach, knishes, and pastramis. The all-beef wieners are legendary in a town known for its dogs. For those keeping score, this is the place Meg Ryan had her fake orgasm in *When Harry Met Sally.* Main courses: $6 to $23.

For Indian food, Sixth Street between First and Second avenues is an **entire block of inexpensive Indian eats** and over-the-top decor. Just walk down the street and see which of the sidewalk touts seems most persuasive. For something fancier, head up to **Tamarind,** 41–43 E. 22nd St. (www.tamarinde22.com; ☎ **212/674- 7400**), one of the best Indian restaurants in Manhattan, offering innovative and flavorful variations on the old standards. Main courses: $18 to $34.

If you're looking for the quintessential "New York pizza," one of NYC's best-kept secrets is **John's Pizzeria.** The restaurant boasts three locations, one downtown in the West Village, one in Times Square, and one on the Upper East Side. For a more authentic, less touristy experience, venture to the downtown location, 278 Bleecker

St. between 6th and 7th avenues (☎ 212/243-1680). Be prepared to arrive early, though, as the small venue—whose walls are carved up with thousands of signatures—tends to fill up pretty quickly. It's cash only, so be prepared. An altogether different experience, the Times Square location, 260 W. 44th St. between 8th Avenue and Shubert Aly (☎ 212/391-7560), is lovely in that the building was once an old church. The Upper East Side location is at 408 E. 64th St., # 1, between 1st and York avenues (☎ 212/935-2895). A pizza pie runs from $15 to $17. Toppings are additional.

New York City After Dark

When it comes to nightlife in NYC, where to start? There's **Broadway** for world-class shows (and the **TKTS** booth in Times Square for cheapish last-minute seats: www.tdf.org/tkts); **Carnegie Hall** and **Lincoln Center** for symphonies, opera, and ballet; **Radio City** for concerts and shows; and the **Blue Note,** at 131 W. Third St., for jazz. The list goes on. Or you could just barhop. Assuming you have only a day or two to sample the Big Apple, downtown has the most interesting options, from trendoid **TriBeCa** and **SoHo** lounges, where a cosmo goes for the price of a small car, to old-time **Greenwich Village** pubs such as the **Ear Inn,** 326 Spring St. at Greenwich (☎ 212/226-9060), whose two-story brick home dates to 1817. If you want a more Woody Allen experience, Second and Third avenues between 72nd and 96th streets have no shortage of bars and restaurants where comfortably well-off uptown intellectuals might feel at home. For an Irish pub with friendly bartenders and excellent food, **Genesis,** 1708 2nd Ave. between 88th and 89th streets (☎ 212/348-5500), is an excellent choice.

For listings of current shows, plays, and live music, check out local publications such as *Time Out New York* (www.timeout.com/newyork), the *Village Voice* (www.villagevoice.com), the *New Yorker* (www.newyorker.com), and *New York* magazine (www.nymag.com).

CHARLESTON

In the closing pages of *Gone With the Wind,* Rhett tells Scarlett that he's going back home to Charleston, South Carolina, where he can find "the calm dignity life can have when it's lived by gentle folks, the genial grace of days that are gone." In spite of all the changes and upheavals over the years, Rhett's endorsement of Charleston still holds true, sans slavery and petticoats. Near-fanatical preservationists have ensured that, architecturally at least, the Old South lives on here, and they've even managed to hold on to some of that famous graciousness, too. It's one of the best-preserved cities in the South, boasting 73 pre-Revolutionary buildings and more than 600 built before the 1840s. With its cobblestone streets and horse-drawn carriages, jasmine and wisteria fragrances, and stately old homes, it's a nice little time machine of a place, totally conscious of its history but gratifyingly averse to turning itself into an Old South theme park.

Getting to Charleston & the Port

The **Port of Charleston**'s cruise ship terminal (www.port-of-charleston.com; ☎ 843/958-8298) is located at 196 Concord St., at the foot of Market Street, smack in the heart of the historic district. You can easily walk anywhere you need to go. People arrive by plane at **Charleston International Airport** (www.chs-airport.com;

© **843/767-7009**), located in North Charleston, 19km (12 miles) from the terminal. If you've made arrangements for transfers through your cruise line, a representative will meet your arriving flight and direct you to shuttle buses. **Taxis** are available to downtown for about $27.

For those arriving by car, take I-95 north or south, and then I-26 (southeast) toward Charleston. Exit at East Bay Street, and turn left onto Market Street, then right on Washington. The entrance to the terminal will be on your left. Parking lots are located near the terminal, with a shuttle service to take you to the pier. Parking is $15 per day.

GETTING AROUND   You can easily walk around the historic district right from the cruise docks.

Exploring Charleston

Charleston's streets are laid out in an easy-to-follow grid. The main north-south thoroughfares are King, Meeting, and East Bay streets. Tradd, Broad, Queen, and Calhoun streets cross the city from east to west. South of Broad Street, East Bay becomes East Battery. The cruise terminal is located in the **Downtown** neighborhood, which extends north from Broad Street to Marion Square at the intersection of Calhoun and Meeting streets. You can't miss the **Old City Market** here (see "Shopping," below), as it shoots straight at the terminal like an arrow. Meeting Street, Church Street, and all the other streets east to the waterfront are full of gorgeous homes and shady gardens, plus many of the historical attractions.

Not far from the City Market, the **Old Exchange & Provost Dungeon,** 122 E. Bay St. (www.oldexchange.com; © **843/727-2165**), served as a prison during the American Revolution, and then, in 1873, became Charleston's City Hall. Its large collection of antique chairs was donated in 1921 by the local Daughters of the American Revolution, and its dungeon (which you tour with a costumed docent) displays the only visible chunk of Charleston's original city wall, the Half-Moon Bastion. We could do without its hokey animatronic displays, though. Admission is $8 for adults and $4 for kids over 6.

One block to the north, the **Old Slave Mart Museum,** 6 Chalmers St. (www.oldslavemart.org; © **843/958-6467**), is the only surviving slave market in South Carolina, dating from 1859. Its collection of artifacts, letters, oral histories, and video documents provide visitors a sense of the real people involved in the domestic slave trade—buyers, traders, and slaves. Admission is $7 for adults and $5 for seniors and youth 5–17 (closed Sun).

The **Nathaniel Russell House,** 51 Meeting St. (www.historiccharleston.org/experience/nrh; © **843/724-8481**), is one of the finest examples of Federal architecture you'll ever see. Built in 1808, it's noted for a "free flying" staircase, spiraling unsupported for three floors. The staircase's elliptical shape is repeated throughout the house. The interiors are ornate with period furnishings, especially the elegant music room with its golden harp and neoclassical-style sofa. Admission runs $10. For a $16 combo ticket, you can also visit the **Aiken-Rhett House,** 48 Elizabeth St. (www.historiccharleston.org/experience/arh; © **843/723-1159**), built by merchant John Robinson in 1818 and then expanded by Governor and Mrs. William Aiken in the 1830s and 1850s. Like other Charlestonians of their time, the Aikens furnished their home with crystal and bronze chandeliers, classical sculpture, and paintings purchased on trips to Europe. Today, many of those objects are still in the rooms for

Charleston

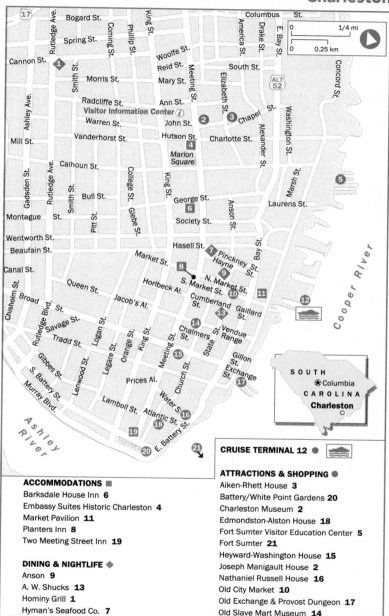

4

THE PORTS OF EMBARKATION | Charleston

CRUISE TERMINAL 12 ●

ATTRACTIONS & SHOPPING ●
Aiken-Rhett House **3**
Battery/White Point Gardens **20**
Charleston Museum **2**
Edmondston-Alston House **18**
Fort Sumter Visitor Education Center **5**
Fort Sumter **21**
Heyward-Washington House **15**
Joseph Manigault House **2**
Nathaniel Russell House **16**
Old City Market **10**
Old Exchange & Provost Dungeon **17**
Old Slave Mart Museum **14**

ACCOMMODATIONS ■
Barksdale House Inn **6**
Embassy Suites Historic Charleston **4**
Market Pavilion **11**
Planters Inn **8**
Two Meeting Street Inn **19**

DINING & NIGHTLIFE ◆
Anson **9**
A. W. Shucks **13**
Hominy Grill **1**
Hyman's Seafood Co. **7**

SOUTH
✪Columbia
CAROLINA
Charleston

which the Aikens bought them. Original outbuildings include the kitchens, slave quarters, stables, privies, and cattle sheds.

The **Charleston Museum,** 360 Meeting St. (www.charlestonmuseum.org; ℂ 843/722-2996), was founded in 1773, making it the first and oldest museum in America. The collections preserve and interpret the social and natural history of Charleston and the South Carolina coastal region, with early crafts, historic relics, and a series of hands-on exhibits for children. Admission is $10. A $16 combination ticket also gets you admission to the **Joseph Manigault House,** 350 Meeting St. (across from the museum), a three-story Federal-style town house built in 1803 for its namesake, a French Huguenot plantation owner and politician. Many rooms have been restored to their original colors, with period furniture. Outbuildings such as the kitchen, slave quarters, stable, and privy are part of the experience. A $22 combo ticket also includes the museum's **Heyward-Washington House,** 87 Church St., built in 1772 by Daniel Heyward, the "rice king" of Charleston. It was also the home of Thomas Heyward, Jr., a signer of the Declaration of Independence. President George Washington bedded down here in 1791. Many of the fine period pieces in the house are the work of Thomas Elfe, one of America's most famous cabinetmakers. Admission to either house alone is $10.

At the southernmost point of the historic area stands the **Battery** (aka the White Point Gardens), where the Cooper and Ashley rivers converge. It has a landscaped park shaded by palmettos and live oaks, with walkways lined with monuments and other war relics. Virtually every home around here is of historic or architectural interest, including the **Edmondston-Alston House,** 21 E. Battery (www.middleton place.org; ℂ 843/722-7171), an 1825 house originally built in Federal style and later modified to a Greek Revival style. Inside are heirloom furnishings, silver, and paintings. Robert E. Lee once found refuge here when his hotel uptown caught fire. Admission is $10. The house is a property of the Middleton Place Foundation, which also operates the Middleton Place estate, 23km (14 miles) northwest of town.

Head back toward the cruise terminal along the sea wall on East Battery and Murray Boulevard to absorb Charleston's riverfront ambience and catch the distant view of **Fort Sumter,** where the first shot of the Civil War was fired on April 12, 1861. Confederate forces launched a 34-hour bombardment of the fort, leading Union forces to surrender and the government in Washington to declare war. Amazingly, Confederate troops held onto Sumter for nearly 4 years, by the end of which time continual Northern bombardment had reduced it to a heap of rubble. You can visit the fort with **Fort Sumter Tours/SpiritLine Cruises** (www.spiritlinecruises.com; ℂ 800/789-3678), which runs ferries from town to the fort. You can buy tickets at Liberty Square's Fort Sumter Visitor Education Center, near the foot of Calhoun Street. The 2¼-hour tour consists of approximately 1 hour at Fort Sumter plus a 30-minute harbor cruise in each direction. Park rangers are on hand at the fort to answer questions, and you can explore gun emplacements and visit a small museum filled with artifacts related to the siege. Ferry tickets cost $17 for adults, $10 for kids; tours are offered two or three times a day, usually at 9:30am, noon, and 2:30pm, though there are seasonal variations. Call or check the website to confirm times.

Organized Tours

Narrated horse-drawn **carriage tours** are available at Market Street from several operators. **Palmetto Carriage Tours** (www.carriagetour.com; ℂ 843/723-8145) uses mule teams and takes off from the red barn behind the Rainbow Market. Tickets are available at 40 N. Market St. From there, exit out back and through the parking lot to the barn. A 1-hour tour costs $22 for adults.

In addition, the cruise lines offer the following **shore excursions:**

Historic Charleston Carriage Tour ($40, 1¼ hr.): As hokey as carriage tours may seem, this is actually a nice way to see historic Charleston. The leisurely ride just seems to match the pace of the place. You'll pass carefully restored 18th- and 19th-century homes and buildings as your guide gives some historical perspective.

Boone Hall Plantation ($79, 2½ hr.): See the historic Boone Hall Plantation, with its *Gone With the Wind* ambience. You can tour the lovely Georgian plantation house as well as the slave quarters, built from brick made on the plantation in the 1800s.

Historic Homes Walking Tour ($59, 2½ hr.): A narrated walking tour of Charleston's historic district, visiting the Nathaniel Russell House and the Edmondston-Alston House (see above) and passing the Old Exchange Building, St. Michael's Episcopal Church, Rainbow Row (the longest set of contiguous Georgian facades in the entire country), Catfish Row (a setting in *Porgy and Bess*), and the Calhoun Mansion.

Historic Charleston & Middleton Plantation ($139, 6 hr.): Middleton Plantation was established in 1741 and was once home to Arthur Middleton, a signer of the Declaration of Independence. Its formal gardens are the oldest in the United States. Tour includes a buffet lunch and a narrated drive through historic Charleston.

Shopping

Located within sight of the cruise ship docks, the **Old City Market** comprises four open-sided buildings that run from East Bay Street up to Meeting Street. The market originally sold foodstuffs, including meat, fish, and local produce, but today it's packed with vendors hawking local art, food, books, clothing, and souvenirs. One standout item here: **sea-grass baskets** woven by Gullah women, descendants of coastal slaves who maintain a distinct culture on South Carolina's islands.

King Street is known for its shopping, with antiques at the south end of the street, clothes and jewelry along the main stretch, and housewares and interior decor along North King (aka Upper King).

If you fall for the period furniture you see in the historic houses, you can buy reproductions online from the **Historic Charleston Foundation** (www.historic charleston.org), which operates the Nathaniel Russell House, the Aiken-Rhett House, and several other historic properties.

Where to Stay

There are quite a few distinctive accommodations in Charleston located within spitting distance of the cruise pier.

The **Embassy Suites Historic Charleston,** 337 Meeting St. (www.embassy suites.com; ✆ **843/723-6900**), is located close to the visitor center, on Marrion Square in the original home of the 19th-century Citadel Military College. It's listed on the National Register of Historic Places and features British West Indies Colonial plantation decor and two-room suites. Rates: from $225.

Close to the dock, the **Market Pavilion,** 225 E. Bay St. (www.marketpavilion. com; ✆ **877/440-2250**), offers opulent old-Charleston-style guest rooms with old-world decor, plaster crown moldings, mahogany touches, and four-poster beds.

There's also the wonderful rooftop Pavilion Bar and the excellent Grill 225 restaurant. Rates: from $550.

Barksdale House Inn, 27 George St. (www.barksdalehouse.com; © **888/577-4980**), is a neat, tidy, and well-proportioned Italianate building about .5km (¼ mile) north of the City Market, constructed as an inn in 1778 and later altered and enlarged. Many bedrooms have four-poster beds and working fireplaces—as if you need more heat in often-sweltering Charleston. Rates: from $159.

The **Planters Inn,** 112 N. Market St. (www.plantersinn.com; © **800/845-7082**), next to the City Market, is an opulent yet tasteful and cozy enclave of Colonial charm, and one of the finest small luxury hotels in the South. The spacious rooms have hardwood floors, marble bathrooms, and 18th-century decor. Afternoon tea is served in the lobby. The Peninsula Grill's setting has a 19th-century charm unlike any other restaurant in Charleston. The menu changes frequently, with main courses in the $26-to-$40 range. Rates: from $285.

Two Meeting Street Inn, 2 Meeting St. (www.twomeetingstreet.com; © **843/723-7322**), has the most enviable location in the city, right across from the Battery, looking over the confluence of the Charles and Ashley rivers. The house was built in 1892 as a wedding gift from a prosperous father to his daughter. Inside, the proportions are as lavish and gracious as the Gilded Age could provide. Rates: from $269.

Where to Eat

Foodies flock to Charleston for refined Low Country cookery as well as an array of French and international specialties. Among the best is **Anson,** 12 Anson St., in the City Market area (www.ansonrestaurant.com; © **843/577-0551**), which blends the grace notes of a big New York restaurant with Low Country charm and cuisine. The setting is a century-old, brick-sided ice warehouse, and the decor is full of Corinthian pilasters salvaged from demolished Colonial houses, with enough Victorian rococo for anyone's taste. Main courses: $24 to $39.

Nearby, **Hyman's Seafood Co.,** 215 Meeting St. (www.hymanseafood.com; © **843/723-6000**), occupies a location that's been in the same family since 1890, originating as a dry-goods business. Inside, multiple dining rooms and a takeout deli serve seafood platters and individual dishes, po' boy sandwiches, and more. Main courses: $18 to $43.

A. W. Shucks, 70 State St. (www.a-w-shucks.com; © **843/723-1151**), is a casual oyster bar in a restored warehouse located next to City Market, around the corner from East Bay Street. Menu highlights are oysters and clams on the half shell, tasty seafood chowders, deviled crab, and a wide beer selection. Main courses: $16 to $25.

Farther from the market area, **Hominy Grill,** 207 Rutledge Ave. (www.hominy grill.com; © **843/937-0930**), features simply and beautifully prepared dishes inspired by the kitchens of the Low Country. It has gained a devoted following among families, who come here to feast on such specialties as oven-fried chicken with spicy peach gravy. From the market, head north on Meeting Street, turn left on Calhoun, and walk 7 blocks west to Rutledge. Breakfast, lunch, and dinner are served only Monday to Friday, with brunch offered on weekends. Main courses: $12 to $17.

THE PORTS OF CALL

The Caribbean is the classic cruise destination, tailored to people who want nice white-sand beaches, tiki bars serving tropical drinks, some hot island music, and sun, sun, sun. Culture and history also have their place. In general, western Caribbean itineraries offer opportunities for visiting the ruins of Mayan cities and temple sites on the mainland, while eastern Caribbean itineraries are more likely to dock at ports that offer reminders of British, French, Spanish, and Dutch Colonial history.

5

Here's the good news: There are hardly any lousy Caribbean islands, although, depending on your likes and dislikes, you'll appreciate some more than others. Some—especially St. Thomas and Nassau—are much more touristy and commercial than others, though their large variety of bustling stores will appeal to shoppers. Others—Virgin Gorda, St. John, Jost Van Dyke, and Les Saintes, for instance—are quieter and more natural, and will appeal to those who want to walk along a calm beach or take a drive along a lonely, winding road amid lush tropical foliage. Destinations such as St. Barts and Bequia offer a low-key yachting-port atmosphere, while such ports as Key West and Cozumel are all about whooping it up.

For those who want a more European experience, the Dutch or French islands such as St. Martin or Martinique will make you feel like you are on the French Riviera. If you want to connect with friendly locals who are happy to have you as a guest in their hometown, then consider some of the destinations in the western Caribbean such as Belize, Cozumel, or Grenada; and if you want all the benefits of the Caribbean without having to leave U.S. soil, Puerto Rico or the U.S. Virgin Islands will spare you the challenges of communication and currency conversions.

PORT STRATEGIES & TIPS
Shore Excursions vs. Going It on Your Own

Participating in the shore excursions offered by the cruise lines can be a wonderful and carefree way to get to know the islands and to experience everything from island tours, snorkeling, and sailing excursions (often with a rum-punch party theme) to more physically challenging pursuits such as bicycle tours, hiking, kayaking, and horseback riding. But do you really *need* to sign up for them? The answer is: not everywhere. At some ports—Aruba, Bequia, Curaçao, and San Juan, Puerto Rico, for instance—your best bet is experiencing the island on your own. In this chapter, I'll advise you on which islands are good bets for solo exploring; tell you whether you should go it on foot or by taxi, motor scooter, ferry, or some other form of transportation; and detail the best sights to see. One downside to exploring independently is that you'll be forgoing the kind of narrative you'd get from a guide, so you may miss out on some of the historical, cultural, and other nuances of a particular island. On the other hand, you may find your own fascinating details, things that an organized tour might pass over. In some ports, touring on your own could be an inefficient use of your time, involving lots of hassles and planning, maybe costing more, and possibly incurring some risk (because of poor roads or driving conditions, for instance). In these cases, the shore excursions offered by the cruise lines are the way to go. Under each port review, I'll describe the best excursions, but these are by no means the only options available. See p. 109 for a chart rating various aspects of each island—dining, shopping, activities close to the port, and beaches and watersports. This is a good tool for deciding at a glance which ports interest you.

It's also good to keep in mind that some shore excursions have a larger impact on the environment than others. If you want to reduce your impact on the local environment, then you might want to avoid off-road dune buggy or ATV adventures, or reef SNUBA (a cross between scuba diving and snorkeling), where you get to feed the local reef fish. While the latter may be touted as eco-friendly, there is nothing friendly about disturbing the wildlife by swimming with, touching, or (gasp) eating the local animals. Luckily, the high-tech, high-impact activities are also the high-cost activities, so stick to the basics, such as snorkeling or bird-watching, and skip the Sea-Trek, SNUBA, and the like. You'll save the planet and save a bundle at the same time!

A related issue arises when perusing the lunch menu. Queen conch, all species of marine turtle, and, believe it or not, even whale or shark meat may turn up on the menu of local restaurants. These are all quite legal to consume locally, and are considered pretty darn tasty by locals and tourists alike, despite their international status as endangered or threatened species. For those with an adventurous palate or a hankering for local flavors, fear not; as long as you know they were caught in accordance with harvest laws, you can eat your fill. For those who want to tread a bit more lightly on the environment, you may prefer to stick to the grouper or mahimahi (which is still sometimes referred to as "dolphin" or "dolphin fish" but bears no relation to the marine mammal of the same name).

Keep in mind that **shore excursion prices** vary from line to line, even for the exact same tour; the prices I've listed are typical and are adult rates; children's rates for many excursions are also offered, so just ask. Keep in mind that the shore excursions are usually quite a bit more expensive than booking a similar outing with a local tour operator. The benefits are that the shore excursions are well organized, can handle large numbers of participants, and will always get you back to the ship on time.

Also note that some cruise lines may not offer all of the tours mentioned here, while others may offer even more. In some cases, the excursions fill up fast, especially on the megaships, so don't dawdle in signing up. When you receive your cruise documents, you'll probably receive a pamphlet with a listing of the excursions offered for your itinerary. Look it over, make your selections, and sign up ASAP. A few lines, such as Royal Caribbean, Celebrity, and Princess, allow you to sign up before your cruise, using your booking code on their websites. Sometimes if a tour offered by your ship is booked up, you can try to book a similar tour once you get to port. The popular

If you want to arrange a private, custom-designed excursion for your family or group of friends, or just want to save a little money on a snorkeling trip, Florida-based **Port Promotions** (www.port-promotions.com) organizes shore excursions and allows you to book them online as late as a week before your cruise. You'll get a confirmation via e-mail. Port Promotions often uses the same tour companies that the cruise lines do—though groups tend to be smaller—and rates for Caribbean tours are about 10% cheaper. If you change your mind before the excursion, you can e-mail or call Port Promotions to get a refund.

Atlantis submarine tour, for example—offered at Grand Cayman, Nassau, St. Thomas, and other islands—usually has an office or agent in the cruise terminals or nearby.

If you want to rent a car in port, make reservations in advance. **Avis** (www.avis.com; ☎ **800/331-1212**), **Budget** (www.budget.com; ☎ **800/472-3325**), and **Hertz** (www.hertz.com; ☎ **800/654-3001**) all have offices on most of the Caribbean islands in this chapter; **Dollar** (www.dollar.com; ☎ **800/800-4000**) and **National** (www.nationalcar.com; ☎ **800/227-7368**) are less represented in the region. Most rental cars in the Caribbean have manual transmissions, so if you need an automatic, be sure to specify that when renting. See "Getting Around," in the individual port listings, to see which companies have offices there. Also note that in certain ports, we advise against renting at all.

Docking, Dollars & Other Port Details

ARRIVING IN PORT Most cruise ships arrive in port sometime before 10am, though this will vary slightly from line to line and port to port. If you're a U.S. citizen, you'll rarely have to clear Customs or Immigration because your ship's purser has your passport or other ID and will have done all the paperwork for you. In most cases, you can walk down the gangway right onto the pier, but occasionally (if your ship is too big for the island's docks, for example, or if you've arrived on a busy day and all the pier space is full) your ship will have to anchor offshore and ferry passengers to land via a small boat called a tender. Once ashore, even if you've come by tender, you aren't stuck there—tenders run back and forth on a regular basis, so you can return to the ship at any time for lunch, a nap, or whatever. Tenders all look pretty much alike, so you might be confused as to which one's heading to your ship, but officers are on duty to check your ID and make sure you get to the right boat.

SCHEDULING YOUR TIME ASHORE All shore excursions are carefully organized to coincide with your time in port. If you're going it on your own, you can count on finding taxi drivers at the pier when your ship docks. In most cases, it's a good idea to arrange with the driver to pick you up at a certain time to bring you back to the port. In most ports, you can also rent a car, moped/scooter, or bicycle to get around. If you opt for the latter, be sure to get a proper safety helmet (avoid the ones with a warning label inside indicating it is a "novelty device") and be sure to wear it at all times, with the strap properly fastened. Even driving on small islands can be a hair-raising experience as locals tend to career around corners, having blown their horn to warn you. Other islands adhere to a British driving format, with drivers on the right side of the car and cars on the left side of the road.

CALLING HOME   Prices for calling home from a cruise ship are sky-high ($9–$15 per min.), so it's a better idea to call from land when you're in port. Most phones in port will take any phone card, but for some phones you'll need to purchase a local calling card from a vendor. I've included information on where to find phones in all the port reviews. Country codes are as follows: United States and Canada, 1 (from most Caribbean islands, it's just like dialing between states); Australia, 61; New Zealand, 64; the United Kingdom, 44; and the Republic of Ireland, 353. Another option is to extend your wireless coverage for international roaming at sea. Many cruise ships have cell service available. Visit **www.cellularatsea.com** for more info. Rates are determined by your carrier so be sure to check with them before boarding and calling.

SHOPPING TIPS   You'll find it all here, from jewelry (lots and lots of jewelry), perfume, and electronics to indigenous arts and handicrafts to the cheesiest tourist gimcracks. Prices vary by port. Some—such as the U.S. Virgin Islands, St. Barts, St. Martin, and Aruba—are pretty pricey, while such ports as Cozumel, Jamaica, and the Grenadines are cheaper. **Duty-free merchandise** can save you as little as 5% to as much as 50%, so if you have particular goods you're thinking of buying this way, it pays to check prices at your local discount retailer before you leave home so you'll know whether you're really getting a bargain. Many ports offer particularly good deals on **liquor,** though keep in mind that you'll pay tax when coming back into the U.S., if you buy more than your legal limit (see p. 29 for more Customs info).

It's important to understand that the clean and modern shopping malls with chain restaurants within the port complex are usually owned by the port, which is usually owned by one of the major cruise lines, meaning that a large portion of the profits from these sales go directly back to the cruise industry rather than to the local community or island residents. Although you often pay more at the port, the merchandise and food services are generally of high quality and well regulated. That said, you can get better bargains and have a more authentic experience if you venture beyond the port to do your souvenir shopping and to sample the local foods.

When shopping, be aware that some items you may see offered may not be allowed by U.S. Customs. You might be eyeing that gorgeous piece of **black-coral jewelry, carved or polished conch shell,** or **polished sea turtle bracelet,** for instance, but laws prohibiting the trade in endangered species make it illegal to bring many products made from coral and other marine animals back to the United States.

Don't Forget to Bring Some Cash When Going Ashore

After a few days of living cash free aboard ship, it doesn't even cross your mind to grab the greenbacks when you're going ashore. You get there and realize you're penniless. It's soooo frustrating, especially if you've had to take a tender in from offshore. Almost as frustrating is bringing cash and having nothing smaller than a $20 or $50 when you want to make a small purchase or leave a tip, so make sure to put some small bills in your wallet. If you happen to remember your bank card, you may be able to withdraw local currency from a local cash machine. If you do this, be sure to take out only what you think you will need on island (or on the next island on your destination if the currency will be the same).

Port	Review on Page	Overall Experience	Shore Excursions	Activities Close to Port	Beaches & Watersports	Shopping	Dining/Bars
Antigua	117	4	3	4	5	2	4
Aruba	124	5	3	4	5	4	4
Nassau, Bahamas	134	4	3	4	4	3	3
Freeport, Bahamas	141	3	2	2	3	3	3
Barbados	146	4	3	3	3	3	3
Belize	154	4	5	2	4	2	3
Bequia	161	4	2	4	4	2	4
Bonaire	167	3	4	3	5	2	3
Tortola, British Virgin Islands	177	4	3	3	3	2	3
Virgin Gorda, British Virgin Islands	185	5	3	4	4	2	3
Cozumel, Mexico	191	4	5	4	2	4	3
Costa Maya, Mexico	202	3	4	2	3	3	2
Curaçao	205	4	3	4	2	3	3
Dominica	212	3	4	3	2	3	3
Grand Cayman	221	5	5	4	5	4	3
Grand Turk	226	5	4	5	5	5	3
Grenada	232	5	3	4	3	3	3
Guadeloupe	238	4	4	5	4	4	5
Roatán, Honduras	247	4	4	3	4	4	3
Ocho Rios, Jamaica	255	4	5	4	3	2	3
Montego Bay, Jamaica	259	4	5	4	3	3	3
Key West	265	4	4	5	2	3	4
Les Saintes	278	4	2	5	3	2	3
Martinique	282	4	3	3	4	3	3
Nevis	291	4	1	4	4	2	2
Panama	295	3	4	3	2	2	2
San Juan, Puerto Rico	299	5	2	5	3	4	4
St. Barts	308	4	3	4	5	4	4
St. Kitts	314	3	3	1	3	2	3
St. Lucia	320	4	4	3	4	2	3
St. Martin	328	3	3	4	4	4	3
St. John, U.S. Virgin Islands	353	4	3	4	4	2	2
St. Thomas, U.S. Virgin Islands	346	4	4	4	4	5	3
St. Croix, U.S. Virgin Islands	359	4	4	4	4	5	3
Trinidad	337	2	2	1	2	2	3
Tobago	341	4	3	1	4	2	2

Ratings Guide: 1 = poor   2 = fair   3 = good   4 = excellent   5 = outstanding

5

THE PORTS OF CALL

Port Strategies & Tips

(Remember, corals are living animals, not rocks; a single branch of coral contains thousands of tiny coral animals, called polyps, and that beautiful conch shell was once part of a protected marine snail that takes decades to mature and reproduce.) Sea turtles, too, are highly endangered, and sea horses, while not yet protected by laws, are currently threatened with extinction. The shopkeeper selling items made from these creatures probably won't tell you they're questionable from a Customs standpoint, but the Customs agent sure will, and may fine you or at the least confiscate the item if he catches you with it. Better to just buy a cheap underwater camera and take pictures of underwater beauties on a snorkeling expedition—you get the memories, the evidence, and a little exercise to boot.

Cuban cigars are also prohibited by U.S. Customs. You'll see them all over the islands, but be aware that, *legally* speaking, you have to smoke 'em before your ship gets back to the States.

REBOARDING   Most passengers start heading back to the ship around 4pm or not much later than 5pm. By 6pm, you're often sailing off to your next destination. In some cases—for instance, in New Orleans, Nassau, St. Barts, and the British Virgin Islands—the ship may stay in port until after midnight so that passengers can stay ashore and enjoy the island's nightlife. When actually walking back aboard, you'll have to present your shipboard ID to be scanned (except aboard some small ships, which are less formal).

If a shore excursion runs late, the ship will be held until the excursion's participants are back on board. It occasionally happens, though, that a passenger goes off on his or her own, has a little too much fun, and misses the boat. If it happens to you, don't panic: The cruise line's port agent (whose offices will be at or close to the pier) will be able to get you back aboard, though it'll cost you—you'll have to either charter a boat or pay for a flight to the next port of call.

A BRIEF HISTORY OF THE CARIBBEAN

PRE-COLUMBIAN CULTURES   Every schoolchild learns that in 1492 Columbus sailed the ocean blue. He was a Johnny-come-lately, of course—people lived in the Caribbean for hundreds, even thousands, of years before Europeans arrived. Three major groups, all originally from South America, were there when Columbus arrived.

The least advanced of the native peoples, the **Ciboney,** were probably the first to arrive. Living primarily in rock shelters and caves, they formed small family groups, hunted turtles and reptiles, and collected shellfish, wild fruits, and herbs. Their rudimentary tools were made of stone.

The more advanced **Arawak** and **Carib** peoples had frequent contact with each other and shared many of the same material technologies. They farmed, hunted, and fished, and both groups used similar methods to construct canoes, build huts, weave cloth, and make pottery. Both peoples cultivated root plants—yucca, yams, arrowroot, peanuts, peppers, and gourds—and seed crops such as maize, beans, and squash. Pineapple and guava, shellfish, fish, iguanas, birds, and snakes provided additional sustenance. Men generally hunted and fished, while women farmed, cooked, wove cloth, and made household pottery and baskets.

The Arawak, by all accounts, were peaceful, gentle, and friendly. Women enjoyed considerable status, religion was based on the belief that spirits inhabited both humans and natural objects, and islands were divided into provinces ruled by chiefs.

Carib authority was less centralized. Independent villages were presided over by village chiefs, who came together to elect war chiefs for each island. Men lived together in communal houses and kept their wives, whom they treated as servants, in separate huts. Because they resisted Spain's efforts to enslave them, the Carib were vilified as bloodthirsty savages by the Spanish. In fact, the word *cannibal* comes from the Spanish name for the tribe—*caribal*. There is no evidence that the Carib practiced cannibalism—the Spanish may have made the claim to justify their assault on the tribe. The Carib were more aggressive than the Arawak, who were frequently on the receiving end of Carib raids. However, when the French and English settled the Lesser Antilles (consisting of most of the Caribbean islands except Cuba, Jamaica, and Hispaniola) in the 1630s, the Carib were friendly and provided food for the starving adventurers—they became violent only after the Europeans attacked them.

EUROPEAN "DISCOVERY" OF THE ISLANDS On October 12, 1492, Columbus became the first European to reach the New World, landing on Watling's Island in the Bahamas. This exploratory first voyage was followed in 1493 by a second and much larger expedition to establish a permanent foothold in the islands. On his second expedition, along with 1,500 men, Columbus brought horses, sheep, cattle, and hogs, as well as plants grown in Europe such as wheat, barley, grapes, and sugarcane. Landing first on Dominica, the fleet passed through and named the islands of the Lesser Antilles before arriving in Hispaniola (where Haiti and the Dominican Republic are located) in November 1494. Before returning to Spain, Columbus sighted Jamaica and explored Cuba.

ENSLAVEMENT OF THE INDIANS The Spanish crown distributed land on the islands to individual settlers, who were expected to cultivate it for 4 years. In return, they received the use of the property in perpetuity. By the time Columbus returned on his third voyage in 1498, the system had been distorted considerably, with Indian communities forced to work the land as slave laborers. Without this slave system, the Colonial economies certainly would have failed. The Spanish not only enslaved the local population, but eventually, if unintentionally, almost completely obliterated it by bringing in diseases to which the native islanders had no immunity.

DISEASE & DECIMATION Prior to the 15th century, the peoples of Europe and Africa rarely mingled, and the indigenous peoples of the Americas existed in total isolation. Consequently, a distinctive disease environment developed on each continent. Until the Europeans and Africans arrived, a host of illnesses—among them smallpox, measles, typhus, yellow fever, malaria, and tuberculosis—were unknown in the New World. The native peoples had no natural immunity to these diseases, and when exposed to them, they died in staggering numbers. In 1492, as many as six million Arawak and Carib Indians lived in the Caribbean. Within 20 years, almost all were dead. Europeans and African slaves gave each other diseases as well, and as many as a third of both groups died during their first 2 years on the islands.

GOLD FEVER The Spanish were interested in only one thing in the New World: gold. Wherever gold was found, settlers rushed in, and the meager gold sources on any given island were quickly exhausted. Undaunted, the Spanish moved on to another island, with Indian slaves in tow. Eventually, they searched farther into Mexico, Panama, and Peru, where they hit the jackpot: the unparalleled treasures of the Aztec and Inca.

Once the enormous value of the gold and silver in Mexico and Peru became clear, the Spanish ignored the Antilles except as a source of slaves. King Ferdinand authorized slaving expeditions to the Lesser Antilles and the Curaçao group in 1511. By 1520, the northern (or Leeward) islands from the Virgins to Barbuda (located next to Antigua), except for St. Kitts and Nevis, were depopulated. The inhabitants of the Curaçao group, Barbados, St. Lucia, and Tobago, were also forcibly removed, and on the remaining islands, the Carib retreated to the mountainous interiors, where they resisted would-be enslavers with considerable skill.

TREASURE SHIPS & PIRATES   The islands remained important to Spain not only as sources of slaves, but also because Spanish treasure fleets had to pass by them on their way from Mexico and Peru to Seville, the sole port in Spain authorized to receive the gold, silver, and other riches from the New World. Rulers of other European states, envious of Spain's wealth, encouraged their subjects to plunder Spanish ships. Piracy became an accepted business, and thousands of buccaneer ships, sailing from ports in France, Britain, and the Netherlands, attacked Spanish ships, as well as ports in the Caribbean and along the coast of Central America. **Sir Francis Drake** took the greatest booty, capturing an entire year's yield of Peruvian silver in 1573. To protect its treasure fleets from pirates, Spain closed its American empire to outside trade, forbidding its American colonies from trading with any other European powers. Spain also limited ocean crossings to Europe—only two heavily guarded convoys made the trip each year. While great forts were built on gold- and silver-loaded islands along the fleet route, other island settlements remained unprotected and had to fend for themselves when buccaneers came onto their shores to help themselves to food, water, and any other supplies that they needed on their long journey. Spain's focus on Peru and Mexico precluded state development of the Caribbean colonies, and for 3 centuries, most inhabitants of the forgotten islands earned modest livings as farmers and ranchers.

COLONISTS FROM NORTHERN EUROPE   The Dutch, French, and British established permanent colonies on the islands in the 1620s, initially concentrating on the smaller, still unoccupied islands of the eastern Caribbean, and moving west into the Greater Antilles (Cuba, Jamaica, and Hispaniola) after 1650. The success of these efforts often depended on events in Europe, and islands, like chips in a poker game, frequently changed hands during wars on the Continent. Governments, more interested in European affairs and with no money to spend on Colonial development, played only a limited role in the initial settlement and economic development of the islands. Individual adventurers, often acting for groups of merchants, established the first Dutch, French, and British colonies. Governments gave adventurers exclusive licenses to exploit specific areas in return for a share of the profit.

In 1618, the Dutch began to challenge Spanish control of the Caribbean by establishing its own colonies and trade in the region. During the 17th century, the Netherlands led all other European nations in manufacturing, commerce, and finance capitalism, and the nation soon dominated trade with the Far East, Africa, and the Caribbean. The **Dutch West India Company,** chartered in 1621, had a state-granted 25-year monopoly in the Americas. Between 1625 and 1635, Dutch maritime forces changed the balance of power in the Caribbean, making it possible for Dutch traders to control most of the region's commerce for decades. The Dutch established colonies on Sint Maarten (the Dutch name for St. Martin), St. Eustatius, Saba, Curaçao, Aruba, and Bonaire. Eventually, the Dutch West India Company's fortunes waned, and its monopoly expired after investors became displeased by the venture's profits. Individual traders then moved in to fill the void, and the company reorganized

A Brief History of the Caribbean THE PORTS OF CALL

to focus on the trade in West African slaves and goods to Caribbean colonies settled and controlled by other European powers.

New waves of British and French marauders followed the Dutch to the Caribbean. Tropical products such as **tobacco** and **sugar** were fetching high prices in Europe, and few investments at home promised comparable profits. The prospect of economic gain was the primary lure, but adventurers, fame seekers, and religious nationalists had their own motives for going to the Caribbean. The British and French claimed many of the same islands, but speaking in very general terms, the British settled St. Kitts, Barbados, Nevis, Antigua, Montserrat, Anguilla, the British Virgin Islands, and Jamaica, while the French established colonies on Guadeloupe, Martinique, St. Christophe (the French name for St. Kitts), and what is today Haiti. The Danish (St. Thomas, St. John, and St. Croix) and Swedish (St. Barts) came later and in much smaller numbers.

ENORMOUS SUGAR PROFITS   The Caribbean enjoyed relative peace and prosperity for much of the 1700s, and the region's economy—especially the sugar industry—grew rapidly. During the 18th century, the islands produced 80% to 90% of the sugar consumed in western Europe. Demand encouraged planters to develop large-scale plantations, which ushered in a new era of slavery. Profits and associated tax revenues convinced British and French politicians that both sugar and slavery were essential to their national economies.

SLAVERY ON AN UNPRECEDENTED SCALE   Economically, socially, and politically, slavery dominated the sugar islands to an extent never matched in human history. By the 1750s, nearly 9 out of 10 people on all the islands where sugar was grown were slaves. Conditions were brutal: Heat, disease, and backbreaking work killed slaves before they could reproduce, and sugar estates could operate only by constantly importing enormous numbers of new slaves from Africa. Except for the Spanish, all the Colonial powers supported and were directly involved in the slave trade. The genocide began even before the human cargo from Africa arrived on the islands. The trip across the Atlantic—known as the Middle Passage—claimed the lives of millions. Shackled together, subsisting on tainted water and food of minimal nutritional value, and exposed to disease, 20% of the slaves died aboard ship. As many as another third, already weakened by confinement and malnutrition, perished in their first few years on the islands. And three out of four babies born to slaves died before the age of 5.

ENGLAND & FRANCE COMPETE FOR DOMINANCE   From 1740, Great Britain and France fought throughout the world to gain commercial and Colonial supremacy. The Caribbean was a major theater of battle, but the struggle was worldwide in scope, affecting Europe, North America, Africa, and India as well. Caribbean islands, often used as bargaining chips, changed flags frequently as the balance of world power shifted between France and England. But the swing of the pendulum affected Caribbean societies and economies only superficially. Soldiers rather than civilians fought battles. Crops and plantations were largely unscathed, and planters essentially maintained power over island politics, regardless of which flag happened to be flying at any particular time. And slaves remained slaves whether an island was designated as British or French.

Islands held by both sides were vulnerable to attack, as neither the British nor the French were willing to spend the huge sums needed to protect them. The British maintained two permanent ports in the region; France had none, electing instead to send ships from Europe for specific purposes. The French fleets arrived fresh from the dockyard and in good shape, while the British ships rotted under the tropical conditions. Once they arrived in the region, however, the French fleets ran out of food, while British ships obtained provisions from their permanent naval stations. Disease also played a role: Any victory had to be won almost immediately, as a long siege would lead to staggering death rates from illnesses.

SLAVE RESISTANCE   During the height of the slave era, blacks outnumbered whites 10 to 1 on most islands. Individual slaves frequently ran away, and groups of slaves planned escapes and uprisings. In fact, slaves rebelled much more frequently in the Caribbean than in the United States, and thousands joined in widespread insurrection on dozens of occasions, destroying plantations and killing slave owners. But only the 1791 revolt on Saint-Domingue (now Haiti), led by **Toussaint L'Ouverture,** culminated in permanent liberation, with the establishment of an independent Haiti in 1804. Once liberated, some Haitians emigrated to other places, such as New Orleans, where they became known as "free people of color," and were the first black people to own property in the United States. On other islands, maroons—escaped slaves who banded together and formed their own independent communities—sought refuge in mountains and areas of dense brush and broken terrain. As planters cut down forests to create new cane estates, maroons fled to Dominica and St. Vincent, two lush, mountainous islands designated as Carib territory. Escaped slaves on the flatter, drier islands had no hiding places at all.

ABOLITION OF SLAVERY & INFLUX OF INDENTURED SERVANTS   Slavery dominated every facet of life in the Caribbean islands—it made sugar plantations possible, shaped social and familial relations, and dominated the laws and politics of the region. The abolition of slavery, therefore, represented a cataclysmic change in island life. In 1833, pressured by more frequent slave rebellions and by the large segment of the British population who increasingly found slavery morally repugnant, cruel, and economically inefficient, England permanently ended slavery in its Caribbean colonies. Inspired by the success of British abolitionists, French intellectuals pressed for emancipation, winning the fight in 1848. The Dutch abolished slavery in 1863. Many freed slaves moved off the plantations to squat on vacant land, and the loss of free labor temporarily crippled sugar production. To fill the labor void, planters recruited indentured workers (who labored under contract), primarily from India, but also from China, Indochina, and Africa's west coast.

INDEPENDENCE & ECONOMIC CHALLENGES   At the end of the 19th century, the United States succeeded the European powers as the main economic and political force in the Caribbean. After almost a century of economic decline on the islands, it was American capital that provided the means to rebuild the sugar, coffee, and banana industries. And American military power, protecting American commercial interests in the region, intervened in Cuba, Haiti, and the Dominican Republic.

In the years between the two world wars, islandwide political movements developed, paving the way for independence. Since World War II, some islands have become integral parts of larger nations, with constitutional arrangements that give their peoples management of local affairs. Puerto Rico and the U.S. Virgin Islands entered into relationships with the United States, the French Antilles were integrated into France, and the Dutch West Indies became an autonomous part of the Kingdom of the Netherlands. The major British colonies have become totally independent states, while smaller islands remaining within the British sphere enjoy home rule.

The Caribbean islands have different languages, political systems, and cultural traditions, but all face similar economic problems as they search for new sources of income to replace the declining sugar industry. Tourism is now the region's main business.

THE CRUISE LINES' PRIVATE ISLANDS

All of the major mainstream cruise lines own or lease private islands (or parts of islands) that are included as ports of call on many of their Caribbean and Bahamas itineraries. While few offer any kind of true Caribbean culture, they do offer cruisers a guaranteed beach day with all the trimmings, and a more private experience than you'd get at most ports' public beaches. Note that aside from Disney's Castaway Cay, none of the islands has a large dock, so passengers must be ferried ashore by tender boat.

CARNIVAL CRUISES & HOLLAND AMERICA LINE   Located on the Bahamian island of San Salvador, 1,000-hectare (2,500-acre) **Half Moon Cay** is a port of call on many of Carnival's eastern Caribbean and Bahamas cruises and HAL's Caribbean and Panama Canal cruises. The island also occasionally plays host to ships of sister lines Cunard and Seabourn. Passengers can take it easy on one of the many beach chairs or under a blue canvas cabana (a boon to shade worshipers), or do a little windsurfing, snorkeling, kayaking, scuba diving, deep-sea fishing, parasailing, sailboarding, aquacycling, or horseback riding. The ship's activities staff also organizes volleyball matches, tug-of-war competitions, and other games for adults, plus sandcastle building and treasure hunts for kids and teens. Facilities around the island include a food pavilion, a few bars, an ice-cream stand, a kids' play area, a post office selling exclusive Half Moon Cay stamps, a cute chapel for vow-renewal ceremonies, and several "tropical mist stations" to help keep you cool.

CELEBRITY CRUISES & ROYAL CARIBBEAN INTERNATIONAL   Many ships of sister lines Royal Caribbean and Celebrity (and, very occasionally, sister line Azamara Club Cruises) stop for a day at one of two private beach resorts, CocoCay and Labadee.

At **CocoCay** (also called Little Stirrup Cay), an otherwise uninhabited 56-hectare (138-acre) landfall in the Bahamas' Berry Islands, you'll find lots of beach, hammocks, food, drink, and watersports, plus such activities as limbo contests, waterballoon tosses, relay races, and volleyball tournaments. For snorkelers, they've even built a sunken replica of one of Bluebeard's schooners.

Labadee, an isolated, sun-flooded, 108-hectare (267-acre) peninsula along Haiti's north coast, is so completely tourist oriented that you'd never know it was attached to the rest of poverty-stricken Haiti. Labadee is, however, somewhat of a rarity among cruise lines' private islands, presenting music and dance performances to give you a small glimpse of the island's arts and culture. Five beaches are spread around the peninsula, and become progressively less crowded the farther you walk from the dock, where enormous tenders make the short trip to and from the ship. In the Columbus Cove area, a children's aquapark called Arawak Cay is full of floating trampolines, inflatable iceberg-shaped slides, and water seesaws. Kayaking and parasailing are offered from a dock nearby. At the center of the peninsula, the Haitian Market and Artisans' Market are the port's low points, full of cheesy Africanesque statues and carvings, with touts trying to lure you in. Steer clear unless you're desperate for a souvenir. When I was here last, a painter near the dock had much more interesting work for sale.

COSTA CRUISES   Passengers on Costa's eastern Caribbean itineraries spend a day at **Catalina Island,** off the coast of the Dominican Republic. This relaxing patch of paradise offers a long beach fringed by palm trees, with activities such as volleyball, beach Olympics, and snorkeling. The area adjacent to the tender dock is the busiest spot, as is to be expected, but if you walk down the beach a bit, you'll find a more private, quiet area (though the coastline gets a little rocky when you get farther out from the dock). The island has a strip of shops hawking jewelry, beachwear, and other souvenirs; a local island vendor rents jet skis and offers banana-boat rides; and the ship's spa staff sets up a cabana to do massages on the beach. Locals often offer massages as well, at rates much lower than you'll get aboard ship. Music and a barbecue round out the day.

DISNEY CRUISE LINE   A port of call on all of Disney's Caribbean and Bahamas cruises, 400-hectare (1,000-acre) **Castaway Cay** is rimmed with idyllically clear Bahamian water and fine sandy beaches.

The island's best quality is its accessibility. Unlike the other private islands, which require ships to anchor offshore and shuttle passengers back and forth on tenders, Castaway Cay's dock allows guests on Disney's large vessels to step right off the ship onto the island. Visitors can then walk or take a shuttle tram to the island's attractions. Families head to their own beach, lined with cabanas, lounge chairs, and pastel-colored umbrellas, where they can swim, explore a 5-hectare (12-acre) snorkeling course, climb around on the offshore water-play structures, or rent a kayak, paddle boat, banana boat, sailboat, or other beach equipment. Teens have a beach of their own, where they can play volleyball, soccer, or tetherball; go on a "Wild Side" bike, snorkel, and kayak adventure; or design, build, and race their own boats. Parents who want some quiet time can drop the kids at Scuttle's Cove, a supervised children's activity center for ages 3 to 12, where activities include arts and crafts, music and theater, and scavenger hunts.

Meanwhile, Mom and Dad can walk or hop the shuttle to quiet, secluded Serenity Bay, a mile-long stretch of beach in the northwest part of the island, at the end of an old airstrip decorated with vintage prop planes for a 1940s feel. Available here are 25- and 50-minute massages given in private cabanas open to a sea view on one side (sign up for your appointment at the onboard spa on the first day of your cruise to ensure that you get a spot), and the Castaway Air Bar serves up drinks.

Adult- and child-size bicycles are available for rent, and beach wheelchairs and all-terrain strollers with canopies are available free of charge. Parasailing is also available for $79 for 45 minutes (age 8 and older only, minimum weight 40kg/90 lb). A 4km (2.5-mile) round-trip biking/walking path begins at Serenity Bay, but don't go looking for scenery or wildlife—the most you'll see is the occasional bird or leaping lizard.

HOLLAND AMERICA LINE   See "Carnival Cruises & Holland America Line," above.

NORWEGIAN CRUISE LINE   NCL's private island, **Great Stirrup Cay,** is a stretch of palm-studded beachfront located about 120 miles east of Fort Lauderdale in the Bahamas' Berry Islands chain. This was the very first private resort developed by a cruise line in the Caribbean, back in 1977. Loaded with bar, lunch, and watersports facilities, the sleepy beach turns into an instant party whenever one of the NCL vessels is in port. Music is either broadcast or performed live, barbecues are fired up, hammocks are strung between palms, and rum punches are spiced and served. Passengers can ride paddle boats, sail one-person Sunfish sailboats, go snorkeling or parasailing, hop on a banana boat, play volleyball, get a massage at one of the beachside stations, lounge in a private beachfront cabana, or do nothing more than sunbathe all day long. Kids have a dedicated play area.

PRINCESS CRUISES   Most of Princess's eastern and western Caribbean itineraries offer a stop at **Princess Cays,** the line's 16-hectare (40-acre) private resort on the southwestern coast of Eleuthera in the Bahamas. A half-mile of shoreline allows passengers to swim, snorkel, and make use of Princess's fleet of Hobie Cats (catamarans), Sunfish sailboats, banana boats, kayaks, and paddle-wheelers. (If you want to rent watersports equipment, be sure to book it aboard the ship or online before your cruise to ensure that you get what you want.) There's live music, a dance area, and a beach barbecue, and anyone who wants to get away from it all (or sleep off too many rum punches) can head for the several dozen tree-shaded hammocks at the far end of the beach. Princess's local shop sells T-shirts and other clothing, plus souvenirs of the mug-and-key-chain variety, and local vendors set up stands around the island to sell conch shells, shell anklets, straw bags, and other crafts, as well as to offer hair braiding.

ROYAL CARIBBEAN & CELEBRITY CRUISES   See "Celebrity Cruises & Royal Caribbean International," above.

ANTIGUA

Though it's the largest of the British Leeward Islands, Antigua (pronounced An-*tee*-gah) is still only 23km (14 miles) long and 18km (11 miles) wide, and offers little of the glitz of some Caribbean islands. And that's its greatest asset: serenity. Antigua claims to have 365 beaches—a different one for every day of the year. Nice, relaxing beaches are close to port; **St. John's,** the island's capital and main town, is sleepy and undemanding; and the locals, usually friendly, sometimes wary, are easygoing. Sundays are especially laid-back; many shops are either closed for the day or open for business for only a few hours.

   Close to port, you can shop in historic, restored warehouses that now feature boutiques and restaurants, spend half an hour or so at a museum to get a sense of Antigua's past, or climb a gentle hill to the massive cathedral overlooking town. Not all of St. John's is charming, but the town is full of cobblestone sidewalks, weather-beaten wooden houses, and louvered verandas. The architecture is one of the town's best assets. The island's British legacy is clearly evident: Antigua has been independent since 1981, but driving is on the left, every little village has an Anglican church, and the island's greatest passion is for the sport of cricket.

   Away from St. John's, the rolling, rustic island boasts important historic sites and lots of pretty beaches. On the southern coast, **Nelson's Dockyard,** once Britain's main naval station in the Lesser Antilles, is now a well-maintained national park. Tucked away in the arid, grassy interior, **Betty's Hope,** with its picturesque windmills, conjures up Antigua's sugar-plantation past. And the **Wallings Conservation Area,** in the island's southwestern region, is the best example of the moist forests that covered Antigua before Europeans cleared the land for agriculture.

Antigua cashed in on sugar and cotton production for years. Today, tourism is the main industry. Most Antiguans are descendants of African slaves brought over centuries ago to labor in the fields. People of European, Asian, and Middle Eastern extraction are also represented in the population of 68,000.

COMING ASHORE   Most cruise ships dock at **Heritage Quay** (pronounced *Key*) in St. John's. Heritage Quay and the adjacent **Redcliffe Quay** are the main shopping areas, but duty-free stores, restaurants, taxis, and other services can be found in the surrounding blocks as well. Tourists wandering away from the duty-free shops should take care, as some of St. John's sidewalks and roads are uneven and filled with potholes. Aside from that, the town is not difficult to navigate beyond the cruise ship area. When several ships are in port, some dock at the **Deep Water Harbour Terminal,** 1.5km (1 mile) from St. John's. From there, you can either walk or take a short taxi ride into town. A handful of smaller vessels drop anchor at **English Harbour,** on the south coast.

Phone booths that take credit cards can be found on the dock, at both quays, and at Deep Water Harbour. **Cable & Wireless,** at Long and Thames streets (✆ 268/480-4237), has credit card pay phones, if you need to make a call. You'll find ATMs at both quays and at the corner of Thames and St. Mary streets.

LANGUAGE   Antigua is a former British colony, so the official language is English, often spoken with a musical West Indian lilt.

CURRENCY   Although the **East Caribbean dollar** (EC$2.70 = US$1; EC$1 = US37¢) is Antigua's official currency, the U.S. dollar is readily accepted by most shopkeepers and cab drivers, and almost all businesses post their prices in U.S. currency. Credit cards and traveler's checks are accepted by most tourist-oriented businesses as well. Prices quoted in this section are in U.S. dollars.

INFORMATION   The **Antigua and Barbuda Department of Tourism,** at the Government Complex on Queen Elizabeth Highway in St. John's (www.antiguabarbuda.org; ✆ 268/462-0480), is open Monday through Thursday from 8am to 4:30pm and Friday 8am to 3pm. If you want to get information before you leave home, the Department of Tourism also has a New York office (✆ 888/268-4227 or 212/541-4117).

CALLING FROM THE U.S.   When calling Antigua from the U.S., simply dial "1" before the numbers listed throughout this section.

Getting Around

BY TAXI   Taxis meet every cruise ship. Although meters are nonexistent, rates are fixed by the government and are posted at the taxi stand at the end of Heritage Quay's pedestrian mall. From the cruise ship dock, it's $12 to Dickenson Bay, $24 to Betty's Hope, $24 to Nelson's Dockyard, and $27 to Devil's Bridge (one way). Settle on a fare (and the currency) before hopping in. Drivers often double as tour guides; expect to pay about $30 per hour for up to four people, with a 2-hour minimum. Tip between 10% and 15% for all rides.

BY BUS   Buses are cheap (about $1.50 to almost anywhere on the island; have exact change), but service is erratic and if you have only a few hours on the island, it's definitely not a dependable form of transportation. The privately operated vehicles, mostly 12-seat vans (all have license plates beginning with "A" or "B"), run from early morning until about 6pm. If you're adventurous and want to chew the fat with Antiguan villagers, give it a whirl.

There are two bus stations in St. John's: East Bus Station, on Independence Avenue, serves the north and east; West Bus Station, near St. John's market, is the terminus for routes to the south and west (and English Harbour).

BY RENTAL CAR   Driving is on the left side. Most roads are decent, but some are narrow and full of potholes. Inadequate signage is a problem islandwide. **Avis, Budget, Hertz,** and **National** all operate on the island. Your valid driver's license and a local temporary driving permit ($20, available from all rental agencies) are required.

Best Cruise Line Shore Excursions

Nelson's Dockyard at English Harbour ($60, 3 hr.): The tour begins with a drive through the capital of St. John's and stops at Antigua's national park. A guided tour of Nelson's Dockyard includes the admiral's house, the officers' quarters, and a stop at an 18th-century inn. A short drive brings you to the Blockhouse ruins, Indian Creek, the St. James Club, and Shirley Heights, atop a rugged cliff offering spectacular views.

Helicopter to Montserrat Volcano ($285, 2 hr.): In December 1997, the Soufrière Hills Volcano on Antigua's neighboring island of Montserrat blew its top, spewing lava and ash over a huge area and burying large swaths of the island, including the former capital, Plymouth. This trip takes you over both the volcano and the char-broiled highlights of Montserrat's exclusion zone—the area declared off-limits to ground transportation.

Four-Wheel-Drive Island Tour ($102, 3 hr.): Tour the island's only remaining rainforest in a four-wheel-drive vehicle, stopping at the ruins of forts, sugar mills, and plantation houses. The excursion includes beach time.

Bird Island Catamaran Sail ($984, 5 hr.): Sail along the reef-protected north coast of Antigua into the sheltered bay of Bird Island, a designated national park, perfect for the beginning snorkeler. Venture up the trail for a fantastic view of the Atlantic Ocean from 30m (100-ft.) cliffs, and then relax on the beach.

Excursions Offered by Local Agencies

Catamaran Cruises: Every day except Sunday, **Wadadli Cats** (www.wadadlicats. com; ✆ **268/462-4792**) offers different all-day catamaran cruises. Prices, which include an open bar, buffet lunch, live music, and snorkeling equipment, start at $95. Check, though, to make sure you'll be back in time to reboard your cruise ship before it leaves. Private catamaran charters are also available.

Miscellaneous Tours: Several reputable operators offer outback eco-adventures, jeep safaris, kayak and snorkeling excursions, and bus tours of the island. Prices are reasonable, and discounts for children 11 and under are common. Inquire at **Antigua Destination Planners** (✆ **268/463-1944**) and **Wadadli Island Tours** (home page.mac.com/labarrielc/Paddles/tours.html; ✆ **268/773-0367**).

On Your Own: Within Walking Distance

St. John's has a number of attractions that are easily accessible on foot. To your right, just as you pass through immigration formalities, is **Redcliffe Quay,** Antigua's most interesting shopping complex. Most of the sugar, coffee, and tobacco produced on the island in years past were stored in the warehouses here, and before slavery was abolished on the island in 1834, the area witnessed slave auctions. The restored buildings, with their stone foundations, wooden-slat sidings, colorful shutters, and red corrugated-metal roofs, now house an array of boutiques and restaurants.

For more local color, turn right (south) once you've reached Market Street and walk 5 blocks to the **Public Market.** This is the best place to sample locally grown fruits and vegetables, and to pick up some Antiguan pottery or baskets. The market is at its most animated early in the morning, especially on Friday and Saturday. Across the street, next to the West Bus Station, fishermen hawk their catch every morning at the waterfront **Fish Market.**

Next, retrace your steps on Market Street, walking north to the intersection of Long Street, where you'll find the **Museum of Antigua and Barbuda** (www.antigua museum.org; ✆ **268/462-1469**). Although it's not the plushest exhibition space in the Caribbean, the museum traces the history of the nation from its geological birth to the present day. Housed in a former courthouse, a neoclassical structure built in 1750, it has exhibits including pre-Columbian tools and artifacts, a replica of an Arawak wattle-and-daub hut, African-Caribbean pottery, and sections dedicated to the island's naval, sugar, and slavery eras. It's open Monday through Thursday from 8:30am to 4pm, Friday from 8:30am to 3pm, and Saturday from 10am to 2pm. Admission is free, but a donation of $3 is requested.

A couple of blocks uphill from the museum, bordered by Church, Long, and New-gate streets, **St. John's Anglican Cathedral** dominates St. John's skyline with its

21m-high (69-ft.), aluminum-capped twin spires. The original St. John's, a simple wooden structure built in 1681, was replaced in 1720 by a brick building, which was destroyed during an 1843 earthquake. Upon its completion in 1847, the present baroque structure was not universally appreciated: Ecclesiastical architects criticized it as being like "a pagan temple with two dumpy pepperpot towers." The cavernous interior is entirely encased in pitch pine, a construction method intended to secure the building from hurricanes and earthquakes.

On Your Own: Beyond the Port Area

Some of Antigua's best scenery is on the opposite side of the island from St. John's, around English Harbour and its surroundings. If you want to do any sightseeing on the island, go here. One of the major historical attractions of the eastern Caribbean, **Nelson's Dockyard National Park** (www.archaeologyantigua.org/sites_seawall project.htm; ✆ **268/481-5021** or 268/481-5022) lies 18km (11 miles) southeast of St. John's, along one of the world's best-protected natural harbors. English ships used the site as a refuge from hurricanes as early as 1671, and the dockyard played a major role during the 18th century, an era of privateers, pirates, and great sea battles. Admiral Nelson's headquarters from 1784 to 1787, the restored dockyard today remains the only Georgian naval base still in use. At its heart, the **Dockyard Museum** (www. dockyardmuseum.org; ✆ **268/460-1379**), housed in a former Naval Officers' House built in 1855, traces the history of the site from its beginnings as a British Navy stronghold through its development into a national park and yachting center. Hours of operation are daily 9am to 5pm. Step into the past and walk through the lobby of the nearby **Copper and Lumber Hotel** to view its beautiful Georgian garden. Uphill and east of the Dockyard, the **Dow's Hill Interpretation Center** (✆ **268/ 481-5045**) features an entertaining 15-minute multimedia overview of Antiguan history and an observation platform that affords a 360-degree view of the park. Farther uphill, Palladian arches mark the **Blockhouse,** a military fortification built in 1787 that included officers' quarters and a powder magazine. For an eagle's-eye view of English Harbour, continue to the hill's summit, where you'll discover the **Shirley Heights Lookout,** which is arguably the most beautiful lookout point on the entire island. Fortified to defend the precious cargo in the harbor below, Fort Shirley's barracks, arched walkways, batteries, and powder magazines are scattered around the hilltop. The Lookout, with its view of the French island of Guadeloupe, was the main signal station used to warn of approaching hostile ships. The **bar** in the Guardhouse at the Lookout is *the* place to go on Sundays for live music; locals and tourists alike mingle and enjoy spirits here. The grounds of the national park, which represent 10% of Antigua's total land area, are well worth exploring. Bordered on one side by sandy beaches, the park is blanketed in cactus, tamarind, cinnamon, and turpentine trees, as well as mangroves that shelter African cattle egrets. An array of **nature trails,** which take anywhere from 30 minutes to 5 hours to walk, meander through the vegetation and offer vistas of the coast. One trail climbs to **Fort Berkeley,** built in 1704 to protect the harbor's entrance. Admission to the park is $5 for adults and free for children 11 and under. The complex, open daily from 9am to 5pm, is within walking distance of the dock at English Harbour. Free guided tours of the dockyard last 15 to 20 minutes; tipping is discretionary.

To see what's billed as the only operational 18th-century sugar mill in the Caribbean, visit **Betty's Hope** (✆ **268/462-1469**), not far from Pares village on the island's east side. On-site are twin mills, the remnants of a boiling house, and a small visitor center, which opens its doors Tuesday through Saturday from 8:30am to 4pm. Gardeners should be able to spot golden seal bushes, neem trees, and wild tamarinds on the rolling hills. Serene cows lazily saunter on the grounds.

Not far from Betty's Hope, on the extreme eastern tip of the island, **Devil's Bridge** is one of Antigua's most picturesque natural wonders. Over the centuries, powerful Atlantic breakers, gathering strength over the course of their 4,800km (3,000-mile) run from Africa, have carved out a natural arch in the limestone coastline and created blowholes through which the surf spurts skyward at high tide. In the long years before emancipation, slaves would come to Devil's Bridge and look out into the Atlantic, knowing that the next landmass was their homeland, Africa, and would commit suicide. Slaveholders would also sometimes push "disobedient" servants to their deaths in this same place. The scenery here is beautiful, and shouldn't be missed if you have time while you're on the island, but tourists must take care and should not stand anywhere near the ledge—the sea is extremely powerful here, and if a wave hits you and pushes you into the water, your chances of survival are next to none.

Another attraction for nature lovers, **Wallings Conservation Area** is Antigua's largest remaining tract of tropical rainforest. Located in the southwest, this lush wilderness area features three hiking trails and numerous opportunities to spot some of Antigua's nonhuman inhabitants: birds (purple-throated caribs, Antillean crested hummingbirds, broadwinged hawks), mammals (mongooses, bats), amphibians (tree frogs), and reptiles (lizards, snakes). Vegetation includes strangler fig, hog plum, black loblolly, mango, and silk cotton trees, as well as numerous epiphytes. If you've spent your day at Nelson's Dockyard, pass through the area on the way back to your ship via the circular **Fig Tree Drive.** Although full of potholes in places, this is the island's most scenic drive. It winds through the tropical forest, passing fishing villages, frisky goats, and old sugar mills along the way.

One of the most unique ways to take in the natural scenery of the island is to take the **Antigua Rainforest Canopy Tour** (www.antiguarainforest.com; ✆ **268/562-6363**), where you can sail above and between the trees on zip lines. A full tour lasts 2½ hours.

Shopping

Most shops of interest in St. John's are clustered in Heritage Quay and Redcliffe Quay, and on St. Mary's Street, all within easy walking distance of the cruise ship docks. Duty-free items include English woolens and linens, as well as local pottery, straw work, and rum. If you're only in the mood to shop and have lunch without wandering far from the ship, St. John's is one of the best ports of call for this. You can literally stroll down the pier from the cruise ship and have dozens of duty-free shops at your doorstep.

Redcliffe Quay, to your right as you pass through Customs, was a slave-trading and warehouse district before abolition. Tastefully renovated, it now contains interesting specialty shops, including **Jacaranda,** on Redcliffe Street (✆ **268/462-1888**), which sells spices and Caribbean art; the **Goldsmitty,** also on Redcliffe Street (www.goldsmitty.com; ✆ **268/462-4601**), which offers handmade gold jewelry; and the **Map Shop,** on St. Mary's Street (✆ **268/462-3993**), which stocks old and new map prints, sea charts, and Caribbean literature.

Located at the cruise dock, **Heritage Quay** is a run-of-the-mill shopping center with 40 duty-free shops and a vendors' hall with shops you can find in the United States, such as the Athlete's Foot and the Body Shop.

Beaches

Antiguans claim that the island is home to 365 beaches, one for each day of the year. True or not, all of them are public, and quite a few are spectacular.

Closest to St. John's, **Fort James Beach,** located 5 minutes and an $8 cab fare from the cruise ship dock, is popular with both locals and visitors. The cordoned area of the water is always safe, but farther from shore, undercurrents are occasionally strong. Volleyball and cricket are played daily. You can rent umbrellas and beach chairs, and the open-air restaurant/bar allows you to spend every minute outdoors. For a change of pace, hike up the hill to explore the authentically derelict ruins of Fort James, which once protected St. John's harbor. Another restaurant/bar at the summit offers splendid views of the area.

Farther north, a $14 cab ride from the dock, the 1km-long (½-mile) beach at **Dickenson Bay** is the island's most bustling strand, with numerous hotels, restaurants, and watersports. The water is calm, drinking and eating options abound, and chairs and umbrellas are available for rent.

Pleasant, picturesque spots on the less-developed southwest coast include unspoiled **Darkwood Beach** and nearby **Turner's Beach.** Showers, snorkeling equipment, and chairs are available. Restaurants serve fresh seafood, while bars keep you hydrated.

If you crave complete peace and quiet, head to Antigua's most beautiful beach, at **Half Moon Bay.** Isolated at the island's southeast extreme, this expanse is virtually undeveloped. Waves at the beach's center are great for bodysurfing, while the quieter eastern side is better for children and for snorkeling. A restaurant and bar are near the parking lot.

Sports

GOLF The 18-hole, par-70 **Cedar Valley Golf Club,** Friar's Hill Road (www.cedarvalleygolf.ag; *C* **268/462-0161**), is a 10-minute, $13 taxi ride from the cruise dock. The 6,142-yard golf course has panoramic views of the northern coast. Greens fees for 18 holes are $49; use of a cart is an additional $42. Club rental is $30.

SCUBA DIVING & SNORKELING Antigua's dive sites include reefs, wall drops, caves, and shipwrecks. To arrange a dive, contact **Dive Antigua,** at the north end of Dickenson Bay at the Halcyon Cove Hotel (www.diveantigua.com; *C* **268/462-3483**). Learn to scuba dive in 1 day for $100. Two-tank dives are $100 plus $28 for wet suit and other equipment. Their boat is moored at the Jolly Harbour marina along the western coast.

WATERSPORTS **Tony's Watersports** (*C* **268/462-6326**) and **SeaSports** (*C* **268/462-3355;** local calls only—no incoming international calls), both at Dickenson Bay Beach, offer a full range of watersports equipment. Prices are negotiable depending on season and demand, but sample fares are $60 per half-hour for jet skis and $45 per "figure 8" lap for water-skiing. Kayak rentals are $25 an hour.

WINDSURFING **Windsurfing Antigua Watersports** (www.windsurfantigua.net; *C* **268/461-9463**), also at Dickenson Bay Beach, specializes in 2-hour introductory lessons ($80) that are limited to four people. Experienced wind sailors can rent a full rig for $75 a day or $65 for half a day. The operation also rents Sunfish sailboats ($20 per hr.), kayaks ($20 per hr.), and snorkel gear ($10 for the day).

YACHT RACING **On Deck Ocean Racing** (www.ondeckoceanracing.com; *C* **268/562-6696**), at Catamaran Marina, Falmouth Harbour, lets you experience the thrill of yacht racing with an experienced crew. Races occur three times daily at 9am, 11am, and 1pm. Children 11 and under, and those weighing less than 80 pounds, are not permitted on board. Prices available upon request.

If you'd like to go under the water without getting wet, then try **Subcat Antigua** (www.subcatantigua.com; ☎ **268/532-7333**), where a 45-minute dive in a submarine will cost you $95 for adults and $75 for children.

Great Local Restaurants & Bars

Lunch menus on the island focus on West Indian cuisine, though you can get sandwiches, salads, and burgers as well. Antigua's local beer is **Wadadli,** the island's Carib name. The local rum is **Cavalier.**

There's no better place to watch the street life of St. John's than the second-floor wraparound veranda at **Hemingway's Veranda Bar and Restaurant,** on St. Mary's Street (www.hemingwayantigua.com; ☎ **268/462-2763**). Across from Heritage Quay, on the main road leading from the dock, it serves tasty salads, sandwiches, burgers, seafood, and refreshing tropical drinks. A definite must if you are just staying around St. John's. The restaurant is open from 8:30am Monday to Saturday, serving breakfast, lunch, and dinner.

C&C Wine Bar, Redcliffe Quay, St. John's (☎ **268/460-7025**), both a bar and a restaurant, sells South African wines, brandies, and spirits. It opens at 10:30am (closed Sun).

Commissioner Grill (☎ **268/462-1856**) is a short walk from the duty-free shops at Commissioner Alley and Redcliffe Street and specializes in West Indian Cuisine. There's plenty of seafood on the menu, but for those who don't like fish, try the chicken curry, a burger, or one of the salads. As at most restaurants on the island, the prices aren't exactly cheap—garlic shrimp will cost you $32—but you're likely to have an enjoyable meal.

If you've opted to spend all day at the beach, your best bet at Dickenson Bay is **Coconut Grove Restaurant** (www.coconutgroveantigua.net; ☎ **268/462-1538**), a quiet, open-air beachside refuge at the strand's southern extreme, complete with palm trees and superb seafood. Lunch starts at about $12.

If you're in English Harbour, stop for a lunch break at the rustic **Admiral's Inn,** in Nelson's Dockyard (☎ **268/460-1027**; admiralsantigua.com). Built in 1788, this restored brick building originally stored barrels of pitch, turpentine, and lead used to repair ships. The menu changes daily but usually features pumpkin soup and main courses such as local red snapper, grilled steak, and lobster. Lunch is around $25.

ARUBA

More of a desert island than a rainforest, Aruba has unwaveringly sunny skies, warm temperatures, and cooling breezes, along with some of the best beaches in the Caribbean—or in the world, for that matter: miles of white sugary sand; turquoise and aqua seas; warm, gentle surf; and plenty of space.

If you tire of lolling on the beach, there's scuba diving, snorkeling, windsurfing, and all the other watersports you expect from a sun-and-sea vacation. On land, you can golf, ride a horse, or drive an all-terrain vehicle over the island's outback. Away from the beach, Aruba is full of cactuses, iguanas, and strange boulder formations. Contrasting sharply with the southern shoreline's beaches, the north coast features craggy limestone cliffs, sand dunes, and crashing breakers.

Focused on shopping? The collection of stores and malls in **Oranjestad,** the island's capital, can compete with the most impressive offerings in the Caribbean. In between purchases, try your luck at one of the island's **casinos;** two are just steps away from your ship. Or grab a bite to eat: Unlike the so-so fare found in much of the Caribbean, Aruba's culinary offerings are diverse, inventive, and often outstanding.

Aruba is still part of the Netherlands, so there's a Dutch influence, which adds a nice European flavor. Though it has a few small museums and some centuries-old indigenous rock glyphs and paintings, nobody comes to Aruba for culture or history.

Only about 30km (20 miles) long and 10km (6 miles) across at its widest point, the island is slightly larger than Washington, D.C. It's the westernmost of the Dutch ABC islands—Aruba, Bonaire, and Curaçao—and lies fewer than 30km (20 miles) north of Venezuela. Aruba's largest city, Oranjestad, is on the island's southern coast, pretty far to the west. The Aruban people are as friendly as can be. With little history of racial or cultural conflicts, locals have no cause for animosity.

COMING ASHORE   Cruise ships arrive at the **Aruba Port Authority,** a modern terminal with a tourist information booth, phones, ATMs, and plenty of shops. From the pier, it's a 5-minute walk to the shopping districts of downtown Oranjestad as well as to a major bus terminal with well-run buses that will take you to beaches both near and far.

LANGUAGE   The official language is Dutch, but nearly everybody speaks English. The language of the street is often Papiamento, a local patois that combines various European, African, and indigenous American languages. Spanish is also widely spoken.

CURRENCY   The **Aruban florin (AFL)** is the official currency, but U.S. dollars are widely accepted, and most items and services are priced in both currencies. Traveler's checks and major credit cards are almost universally accepted. The exchange rate is relatively stable, at about 1.79 AFL to US$1 (1 AFL = US56¢). Prices quoted in this section are in U.S. dollars.

INFORMATION   For information, go to the **Aruba Tourism Authority,** 8 L. G. Smith Blvd., Oranjestad (www.aruba.com; ✆ **800/862-7822** or 297/582-3777). It's open Monday through Friday from 7am to 4:30pm.

CALLING FROM THE U.S.   When calling Aruba from the U.S., dial the international access code (011) before the numbers listed in this section.

Getting Around

BY TAXI   Taxis line up at the dock to take you wherever you want to go. If you need to call for a cab, the dispatch office number is ✆ **297/582-2116.** Cabs don't have meters, but fares are fixed, and every driver has a copy of the official rate table. Ask what the fare will be before getting in the car. The trip from the cruise terminal to the beach resorts will be $20 to $33. Tip between 15% and 20%. A surcharge is added on Sundays and holidays and the minimum fare is $5. Most drivers speak good English and are eager to give you a tour of the island; expect to pay $55 per hour for a maximum of five passengers.

BY BUS   Aruba has an excellent daily bus service beginning at 6am. The same-day round-trip fare between the beach hotels and Oranjestad is $2.30; a one-way ride is $1.30. Have exact change. The bus terminal is across the street from the cruise terminal on L. G. Smith Boulevard.

BY RENTAL CAR   Excellent roads connect major tourist attractions, and all the major rental companies accept valid U.S. or Canadian driver's licenses. Rent a four-wheel-drive vehicle for the rough roads in the outback. **Avis, Budget, Dollar, Hertz,** and **National** all have offices here.

BY MOTORCYCLE OR BICYCLE   Scooters and motorcycles are practical only if you plan to stick to paved roads. They're available at **Melhcor Cycle Rental,** Bubali 108B (✆ **297/587-3448**). Scooters rent for $40 per day, while ATVs go for $120 per day and Harleys are $125. At **George's Cycle Rental,** on L. G. Smith Blvd. 124 in Oranjestad (www.georgecycles.com; ✆ **297/993-2202**), you can rent scooters for $50, motorcycles for $70, and ATVs from $90 per day. Mountain bikes are available at **Eagle Beach Bike Rental,** Eagle Beach (✆ **297/587-8655**), or **Pablito's Bike**

Rental, L. G. Smith Blvd. 234 (© **297/587-8655**), where rates start at $15 per half-day and $20 for 24 hours; also at **Rancho Notorious** (© **297/586-0508**) and **Aruba Active Vacations** (© **297/586-0989**), where bike rentals are $25 per day, and **Aruba Ocean View Bikes** (© **297/587-8655**), where bikes are $15 per half-day, $20 for a full day.

Best Cruise Line Shore Excursions

In addition to the options described here, cruise lines typically offer about a dozen snorkeling, diving, sailing, and other water-oriented tours.

Off-road Adventure ($85, 4 hr.): Take off into Aruba's backcountry in a convoy of four-passenger SUVs. You'll be behind the wheel and have radio contact with your guide. A stop is made for lunch and swimming.

Island Bike Adventure ($20, half-day): Explore Aruba's undeveloped northeast coast by mountain bike. You'll pedal 15km (9 miles) and visit the Natural Bridge (cut by the sea and wind and eventually collapsed), the Bushiribana Gold Mine, the Alto Vista Chapel, and the California Lighthouse.

Aruba Beach & Snorkel Cruise ($85, 4 hr.): Travel by catamaran to snorkel at different spots, including a reef and an amazing shallow shipwreck, and then head to the beach for some swimming, sunbathing, rum punch, and a tasty lunch.

Atlantis Submarine Journey ($104, 1 hr.): Cruise 45m (150 ft.) below the sea in a submarine. During the gentle descent, you'll pass by scuba divers, coral reefs, shipwrecks, and hundreds of curious tropical fish.

Aruba Bus Tour ($20, 3 hr.): This air-conditioned bus tour rolls along part of Aruba's wild and woolly windward coastline to the (now collapsed) Natural Bridge, adjacent Baby Bridge, and the Casibari rock formations, followed by a swing through Aruba's hotel strip.

On Your Own: Within Walking Distance

Aruba's capital, Oranjestad, has a sunny Caribbean atmosphere, with Dutch Colonial buildings painted in vivid colors. The main thoroughfare, **L. G. Smith Boulevard,** runs along the waterfront and is crowded with marinas, shopping malls, restaurants, and bars. **Caya G. F. Betico Croes,** or Main Street, is another major shopping street running roughly parallel to the waterfront several blocks inland. The harbor is packed with fishing boats and schooners docked next to stalls where vendors hawk fruits, vegetables, and fish. On the other side of the Seaport Marketplace shopping mall, **Queen Wilhelmina Park** features manicured lawns, views of colorful fishing boats, and lush tropical vegetation.

If you're looking for a little culture, Oranjestad has a handful of museums that are worth a bit of your time. The recently relocated and modernized **Archaeological Museum of Aruba,** Schelpstraat 42 (www.namaruba.org; © **297/582-8979**), illustrates the island's Amerindian heritage with pottery vessels, shell and stone tools, burial urns, and skulls and bones. Admission is free; the museum is open Tuesday through Friday from 10am to 5pm and weekends 10am to 2pm.

To defend the island against pirates, the Dutch erected Fort Zoutman in 1796. In 1867, Willem III Tower, named after the then-reigning Dutch monarch, was added. Since 1992, the complex has housed the modest **Museo Historico Arubano,** Zoutmanstraat 4 (© **297/582-6099**), which displays island history from the Colonial period through the present, prehistoric Amerindian artifacts, and relics from the

Dutch Colonial period. Admission is $6; it's open Monday through Friday from 9am to noon and 1:30 to 4:30pm.

On Your Own: Touring by Rental Jeep

The best way to see Aruba's desertlike terrain is to rent a four-wheel-drive vehicle. Car-rental companies have maps highlighting the best routes to the island's attractions. A word of caution regarding the increasingly popular ATVs that zip along these same roads either alone or as part of a rental group: Their drivers are often unaccustomed to operating these, and it is best to keep an eye out and take care around corners or curves. The occasional horse caravan will also share these same roads. See "Off-Roading," below, for information on rental companies.

Following the system of roads that traces the perimeter of the island, start clockwise from Oranjestad. Drive past the hotel strip, toward the island's northwestern-most point. Here, the **California Lighthouse** affords 360-degree views of spectacular scenery—gentle sand dunes, rocky coral shorelines, and turbulent waves. The picturesque lighthouse got its name from the *California,* a passenger ship that sank off the nearby coast in 1916. Incidentally, the story that this vessel was the only ship to have heard (and ignored) the *Titanic's* distress signal is malarkey. In fact, the *Californian* (with a final *n*) of *Titanic* infamy was torpedoed by a German submarine off the coast of Greece in 1915.

From here on, your adventure will take you onto the island's moonlike terrain, past heaps of giant boulders and barren rocky coastline. The well-maintained road that links the hotel strip with Oranjestad deteriorates abruptly into a band of rubble, and the calm, turquoise sea turns rough and rowdy.

By the time you reach the **Alto Vista Chapel,** about 8km (5 miles) from the lighthouse, chances are you'll already be coated with red dust. Don't let that stop you from peeking inside the quaint pale-yellow church that was built in 1750 and renovated 200 years later. Radiating serenity from its cactus-studded perch overlooking the sea, the chapel, Aruba's first, was built by native Indians and Spanish settlers before the island had its own priest.

Farther along the northern coast, you'll approach the hulking ruins of the **Bushiribana Gold Smelter.** Built in 1872, its massive stone walls are reminders of the importance of gold mining on the island in the 19th century. Unfortunately, the walls have been marred with artless graffiti. Climb the multi-tiered interior for impressive sea views.

On the road between the Baby Bridge and the Bushiribana Gold Smelter lies a seemingly out-of-place **Ostrich Farm** (www.arubaostrichfarm.com; ℂ **297/585-9630**), where you can tour the grounds and meet the resident ostriches; the 20-minute tour is sadly lacking in any valuable information about these amazing birds, which stand nearly 2m (6½ ft.) tall and can weigh close to 135kg (300 lbs.). Visitors can, nonetheless, feed a hungry harem of females; compare and contrast the ostriches with their close kin, the emus; test the incredible strength of an egg at the hatchery; and then head back to the pavilion to browse the impressive gift shop full of carved wood and textiles shipped in from Africa. One can also sample ostrich meat at the African-themed restaurant. While the idea may be disturbing, the dark meat is surprisingly tasty and bears a striking resemblance to tender steak. The ostrich farm and restaurant are open daily from 9am to 5pm. The last tour is at 4pm.

Within sight of the smelter, **Natural Bridge** is Aruba's most photographed attraction. The former Natural Bridge collapsed in 2005, but, as luck would have it, the

Baby Bridge, right next to the former one, is almost as pretty. Rising 7.5m (25 ft.) above the sea and spanning 30m (100 ft.) of rock-strewn waters, this limestone arch has been carved out over the centuries by the relentless pounding of the surf. Because the bridge acts as a buffer between the sandy beach and the open ocean, many people come here to swim and picnic.

Next, head toward the center of the island and the bizarre **Ayó and Casibari rock formations.** Looking like something out of the Flintstones, the gargantuan Ayó rocks served Aruba's early inhabitants as a dwelling or religious site. The reddish-brown petroglyphs on the boulders suggest mystical significance. Although the Casibari boulders weigh several tons each, they look freshly scattered by some cyclopean dice roller. Look for the formations that resemble birds and dragons, and climb the trail to the top of the highest rock mound for a panorama of the area.

If you have children, or just like animals, stop by the **Donkey Sanctuary** (www. arubandonkey.org; © **297/965-6986**), half a mile from the Ayó Rock Formation, where dozens of these feral yet gentle animals are corralled, fed, and cared for. The staff will eagerly share their knowledge with you about the history and ecology of Aruba's donkeys, many of which still roam the countryside. Hours are weekdays from 9am to 4pm and weekends 10am to 3pm.

Farther east, back along the northern coast, **Arikok National Park,** Aruba's showcase ecological preserve, sprawls over roughly 20% of the island. Rock outcrops, boulders, and crevices create microclimates that support animal species found only in Aruba, including the Aruban rattlesnake, Aruban cat-eyed snake, Aruban whiptail lizard, Aruban burrowing owl, and Aruban parakeet. Iguanas and many species of migratory birds live in the park as well, and goats and donkeys graze on the hills. Examples of early Amerindian art, abandoned mines from Aruba's gold-rush past, and remains of early farms dot the park. Be sure to bring water, sunscreen, and food, and wear a hat and comfortable walking shoes. One of its premier attractions is a series of caves that punctuate the cliff sides of the area's mesas. The most popular, **Fontein Cave,** has brownish-red drawings left by Amerindians, and graffiti etched by early European settlers. Stalagmites and stalactites here look like human heads and bison; park rangers stationed at the cave will point them out. Nearby **Quadirikiri Cave** boasts two large chambers with roof openings that allow sunlight in, making flash-lights unnecessary. Hundreds of small bats use the 30m-long (100-ft.) tunnel to reach their nests deeper in the cave, as well as the 90m-long (300-ft.) passageway of **Baranca Sunu,** another cave in the area commonly known as the Tunnel of Love because of its heart-shaped entrance. Currently, the inner chambers of both caves are closed indefinitely (by the park rangers) in order to protect and replenish the bat population. In some parts of Aruba, nature takes a priority over tourists, as it should—the entire tourism industry is built on the natural beauty of the island. Despite the closures, the caves still make a worthwhile destination, if only for a glimpse inside.

Shopping

Although Aruba boasts plenty of shopping, don't expect prices to be fabulously cut-rate. Nevertheless, the island's low 3.3% duty can make prices on items such as jewelry and fragrances attractive. What's more, there's no sales tax.

Because the island is part of the Netherlands, Dutch goods, such as Delft porcelain, chocolate, and cheese, are especially good buys. Items from Indonesia, another former Dutch colony, are reasonably priced, too. If you're looking for big-ticket items, Aruba offers the usual array of watches, cameras, jewelry, Cuban cigars, premium liquor, English and German china, porcelain, French and American fragrances, and crystal. Skin and hair-care products made from locally produced aloe are also popular and practical.

Aruba's retail activity centers on Oranjestad. About 1km (½ mile) long, **Caya G. F. Betico Croes,** better known as Main Street, is the city's major shopping venue. Downtown also teems with several contiguous shopping malls that stretch for several blocks along the harbor. **Renaissance Mall** and **Renaissance Market-place** feature more than 130 stores, two casinos, 20 restaurants and cafes, and a movie theater. Just down the road, **Royal Plaza Mall** is chock-full of popular restaurants and upscale boutiques.

If your shopping appetites are still not sated, you can head over to **Paseo Herencia (Aruba's Pride),** on the high-rise district's main street. This mall contains a multiplex cinema, has a pool large enough for the Aruba synchronized swimming team (the Barracudas) to practice and perform in, and is appointed with murals and plaques to highlight the history of the island. Dozens of shops, including Nike, Lacoste, and Guess, are adjacent to restaurants such as Iguana Joe's and Moby Dick seafood restaurant, and also the new **Palm Beach Mall.**

Beaches

All of Aruba's beaches are public, but chairs and shade huts are hotel property. If you use them, expect to be charged. Shade huts located at beaches where there are no hotels, such as Baby Beach, Arashi, and Malmok, are free of charge. Visitors can rent chairs at Eagle and Bay beaches.

Palm Beach, home of Aruba's glamorous high-rise hotels, is the best spot for people-watching. This stretch of sea and white sand is also great for swimming, sunbathing, sailing, fishing, and snorkeling. It can get crowded, and with two piers and numerous watersports operators, it's also busier and noisier than Aruba's other beaches.

Separated from Palm Beach by a limestone outcrop, **Eagle Beach** stretches as far as the eye can see. The sugar-white sand and gentle surf are ideal for swimming, and although the nearby hotels offer watersports and beach activities, the atmosphere on the beach is relaxed and quiet. A couple of bars punctuate the expansive strand, and shaded picnic areas are provided for the public.

Baby Beach, at Aruba's easternmost tip, is a prime destination for families with young children. The protection of rock breakwaters makes this shallow bowl of warm turquoise water perfect for inexperienced swimmers. Giant sea-grape bushes offer shade from the sun. The beach has a refreshment stand and washrooms, but no other facilities.

Also worth seeking out is **Hadikurari (Fisherman's Huts),** where swimming conditions, in very shallow water, are excellent. The only drawback to this white-powder-sand beach is some pebbles and stones at the water's edge. This beach is known for some of the finest windsurfing on island.

Sports

CRUISES For a boat ride and a few hours of snorkeling, contact **De Palm Tours,** which has offices in eight of the island's hotels. Its main office is at L. G. Smith Blvd. 142, in Oranjestad (www.depalmtours.com; (**800/766-6016** or 297/582-4400). They offer a 4-hour cruise that visits two coral reefs and the German shipwreck

Antilla, Sunday to Friday. The cost is $77 per person (half-price for children). **Red Sail Sports** (www.redsailaruba.com; ℂ **877/733-7245** or 297/586-1603) boasts three catamarans and several sailing options. If you are looking for something fun and different from the usual catamaran sail, check out **Jolly Pirates ★** (www.jolly-pirates.com; ℂ **297/586-8107**), which features unique 4½-hour sail, snorkel, lunch, and rope-swing excursions. Friendly deckhands will astound you with their mast-climbing antics followed by an acrobatic swing into the sea—think Tarzan meets "Marine Boy." Morning cruises embark daily, and the $57 fee includes a tasty, full-service barbecue lunch. They also offer 2-hour sunset trips (Mon and Fri; $30) and 3-hour afternoon sail and snorkel tours (Tues–Thurs and Sat; $38).

HORSEBACK RIDING You can ride at **Rancho Notorious** (www.rancho notorious.com; ℂ **297/586-0508**). The price is $66 for a 1-hour tour and $70 for a 2-hour tour. The minimum age is 6 for children to ride their own horses. **The Gold Mine Ranch** (www.thegoldmineranch.com; ℂ **297/594-1317**) offers 2-hour tours starting at $65 and offers free transportation. **Rancho Ponderosa** (www.rancho laponderosaaruba.com; ℂ **297/587-1172**) has a variety of tours starting at $75 for 2 hours.

OFF-ROADING For those who want a rough-and-ready (if noisy) island adventure, several places rent all-terrain vehicles. **Melchor Cycle Rental,** Bubali 106B (ℂ **297/587-1787**), rents ATVs for $120 per day. At **George's Cycle Rental,** on L. G. Smith Blvd. 124 in Oranjestad (www.georgecycles.com; ℂ **297/993-2202**), you can rent ATVs from $100 per day. For an organized tour, check in with **DePalm Tours,** L. G. Smith Blvd. 142 (www.depalm.com; ℂ **297/582-4400**); **Rancho Daimari,** Plantage Daimari (www.visitaruba.com/ranchodaimari; ℂ **297/586-6284**); or **Rancho Notorious** (www.ranchonotorious.com; ℂ **297/586-0508**).

SCUBA DIVING & SNORKELING Aruba is no Bonaire, but it still offers enough coral reefs, marine life, and wrecks to keep scuba divers and snorkelers busy. The best snorkeling sites are around Malmok Beach and Boca Catalina, where the water is calm and shallow, and marine life is plentiful. Dive sites stretch along the entire southern coast, but most divers head for the German freighter *Antilla,* which was scuttled during World War II off the island's northwestern tip, near Palm Beach. The island's largest watersports operators, **Pelican Adventures** (www.pelican-aruba.com; ℂ **297/587-2302**) and **Red Sail Sports** (www.redsailaruba.com; ℂ **877/733-7245** or 297/586-1603) offer sailing, windsurfing, and water-skiing in addition to snorkeling and scuba diving. Two-tank dives at either outfit are around $81; one-tank dives are about $55. Two-and-a-half-hour snorkeling trips are $50; 4½-hour snorkeling excursions are $65. **JADS** (www.jadsaruba.com; ℂ **297/584-6070**) is an all-service dive club with PADI classes, a new boat, and a variety of packages. Other diving choices include **Dive Aruba** (www.divearuba.com; ℂ **297/582-7337**) and **Aruba Water Sports Center** (www.arubawatersportcenter.com; ℂ **297/586-6613**).

WINDSURFING Aruba's world-class windsurfing conditions attract wind sailors from around the world. Malmok Beach is the island's most popular windsurfing spot. Used by novices and pros alike, it has slightly gusty offshore winds, minimal current, and moderate chop. Boca Grandi, on the extreme eastern coast, is for advanced wave sailors only. **Vela Windsurf and Kiteboard Center** (www.dare2flyaruba.com; ℂ **297/586-3735**) offers beginner lessons with equipment for $150; rentals are $100 for 2½ hours.

Gambling

Aruba boasts 12 casinos, most of them casually elegant. Slot machines gear up at 10am; table games, such as baccarat, blackjack, poker, roulette, and craps, can start as early as noon; and bingo starts in the afternoon.

Two casinos are steps from the dock. At the Aruba Renaissance Beach Resort, the **Crystal Casino,** L. G. Smith Blvd. 82 (www.thecrystalcasino.com; ℂ 297/583-6000), is one of Aruba's only 24-hour casinos and probably its most elegant. The **Seaport Casino,** L. G. Smith Blvd. 9 (www.arubaseaportcasinos.com; ℂ 297/583-6000), fits in well with the surrounding shopping mall; you might think it's just another store. In addition to slots and an array of table games, it features a race- and sports-book room with a satellite linkup and wagering based on Las Vegas odds.

Great Local Restaurants & Bars

Hip and happy **Cuba's Cookin',** Renaissance Marketplace Downtown (www.cubas cookin.com; ℂ **297/588-0627**), serves flavorful Cuban dishes that are expertly prepared. Lunch is about $25.

Smokey Joe's Island Grill, J. E. Irausquin Blvd. 87, Palm Beach, across from Playa Linda (www.smokeyjoesaruba.com; ℂ **297/586-2896**), is a casual outdoor eatery featuring burgers, wings, and salads, but the ribs are its signature dish and they can be prepared several ways. Try the dry-rubbed variety, or go whole-hog and order all three types. Other options include rotisserie chicken or BBQ pulled pork. Just save room for their signature dessert: fried Oreos. Lunch is about $12.

For a Euro vibe, head over to **the Paddock,** L. G. Smith Boulevard (www. paddock-aruba.com; ℂ **297/583-2334**), which overlooks the harbor, a short walk from virtually every shop in town. You can opt for a drink, a cup of tea or coffee, a snack of sliced sausage and Gouda cheese, or a full-fledged meal. Lunch is about $15.

Salt & Pepper, J. E. Irausquin Blvd. 368A (www.saltandpepperaruba.com; ℂ **297/586-3280**), is a fresh, appealing spot that serves light meals such as salads (don't pass on the salt-and-pepper salad with salty bacon and peppery shrimp), burgers, and sandwiches, but tapas are its specialty. Most of the 30 appetizer-size dishes have a Spanish accent, but others speak Cantonese, Italian, French, or Dutch. Show up with salt-and-pepper shakers to add to their collection and you'll get a free drink on the house. Lunch is about $13.

Señor Frog's, J. E. Irausquin Blvd. 348A, The Village (ℂ **297/586-8900**), remains an overwhelmingly popular chain establishment with the die-hard party crowd for retro music, Mexican food, and—oh yeah—drinks. Twenty-somethings can be seen drinking frozen margaritas to excess just about every day of the week.

BAHAMAS: NASSAU & GRAND BAHAMA ISLAND

Technically, the 700 islands of the Bahamas aren't in the Caribbean—they're in the Atlantic Ocean, just north of the Caribbean and about 300km (185 miles) from Miami. However, because they're an important port of call on the cruise ship circuit and are part of the West Indies, they're almost always lumped together with their island neighbors to the south.

Nassau

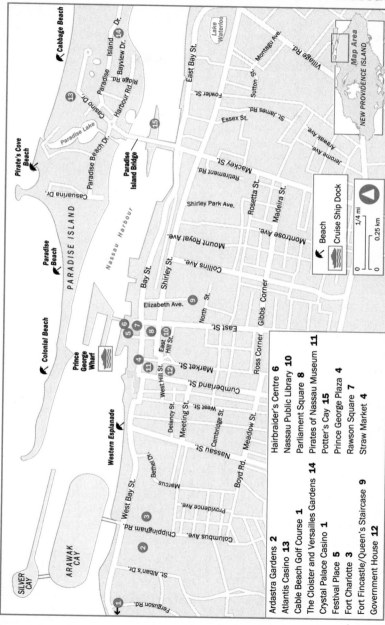

Ardastra Gardens **2**
Atlantis Casino **13**
Cable Beach Golf Course **1**
The Cloister and Versailles Gardens **14**
Crystal Palace Casino **1**
Festival Place **5**
Fort Charlotte **3**
Fort Fincastle/Queen's Staircase **9**
Government House **12**

Hairbraider's Centre **6**
Nassau Public Library **10**
Parliament Square **8**
Pirates of Nassau Museum **11**
Potter's Cay **15**
Prince George Plaza **4**
Rawson Square **7**
Straw Market **4**

If you're a seasoned cruiser, chances are you've been to the Bahamas already and might prefer an itinerary that includes more far-flung ports. If you're new to the region, the Bahamas are a great introduction, with everything you'd expect from a fun-in-the-sun vacation—postcard-perfect beaches, a full range of water activities, and warm temperatures year-round. There's a well-developed tourist infrastructure, and economic conditions are the envy of most other West Indian islands, so you won't see the kind of poverty that plagues some Caribbean islands. In many ways, the Bahamas aren't much different from, say, some parts of Florida, but you'll still be able to see and experience Colonial sights, British influences, and West Indian color—you'll know right away you're not in Kansas anymore.

The Bahamas became an independent commonwealth of Great Britain in 1973. Tourism and offshore banking account for the islands' current prosperity. About 85% of Bahamians are descended from African slaves; people of European extraction make up most of the rest of the population.

LANGUAGE   English is the official language of the Bahamas. Most people in the tourism industry speak a standard American version of the language at work. You'll also hear an island lilt and a vocabulary that reflects British, Arawak, and African influences.

CURRENCY   The legal tender is the **Bahamian dollar,** whose value is always the same as that of the U.S. dollar. Both currencies are accepted everywhere on the islands, and most stores accept traveler's checks and major credit cards.

INFORMATION   For information before you go, go to www.bahamas.com, or call the **Bahamas Tourism Board** in New York at ✆ **800/BAHAMAS** (224-2627).

CALLING FROM THE U.S.   Calling the Bahamas from the United States is as simple as phoning between states: Just dial "1" before the numbers listed throughout this section.

Nassau

The town of Nassau is the cultural, social, political, and economic center of the Bahamas. With its beaches, shopping, resorts, casinos, historic landmarks, and water and land activities, it's also the island chain's most visited destination—one million travelers a year make their way to the town, and Nassau is one of the world's busiest cruise ship ports. The Nassau/Paradise Island area comprises two separate islands. Nassau is on the northeastern shore of the 34km-long (21-mile) island of New Providence, while tiny Paradise Island, linked to New Providence by bridges, protects Nassau harbor for a 5km (3-mile) stretch. It was here that the white-sand beaches of the Atlantis Hotel and Ocean Club served as locations for James Bond in *Casino Royale.* Although the area accounts for only 2% of the nation's land area, its 175,000 residents represent 60% of the Bahamian population.

COMING ASHORE   The cruise ship docks at **Prince George Wharf** are in the center of town, near Rawson Square and adjacent to the main shopping areas. Your best bet for making long-distance phone calls is the **Bahamas Telecommunications Center (BATELCO)** phone center on East Street, about 4 blocks inland from Rawson Square.

INFORMATION   The **Bahamas Ministry of Tourism,** at Bolam House on George Street (✆ **242/302-2000**), is open Monday through Friday from 9am to 5pm. A smaller booth at Rawson Square is near the dock. You can also check out www.bahamas.com.

GETTING AROUND

Unless you hire a horse-drawn carriage, the only way to see Old Nassau is on foot. The major attractions and stores are pretty concentrated, so walking is the most convenient mode of transportation anyway. If you're really fit, you can even trek over to Cable Beach or Paradise Island.

BY TAXI   Taxis are practical for longer trips, and fares are determined by zone. From Prince George Dock (Cruise Terminal) to downtown is $6, Cable Beach is $15, South Ocean or Lyford Cay is $35, the International Airport is $22, and Paradise Island (Atlantis Hotel) is $14. A suggested tip is 15% of your fare. You can hire a five-passenger cab at $50 per hour. Taxis can be hailed on the street or taken from stands. **Meter cabs** can be ordered by calling ✆ **242/323-5111.**

BY JITNEY   Jitneys, medium-size buses that travel set routes throughout the city, are the least expensive means of transport. Fares vary depending upon the route and exact change is required. Buses operate from 6:30am to 7pm except on weekends, when service is reduced.

BY FERRY   Ferries are a common mode of transportation in the Bahamas for locals and travelers. The Fast Ferry service is designed to help you island-hop between designated main islands, while local ferries serve as water taxis that take you and locals to and from neighboring cays of a main island. Fares from the end of Casuarina Drive on Paradise Island across the harbor to Rawson Square are $5 per person. The water taxi between Paradise Island and Prince George Wharf is $6 per person.

BY HORSE-DRAWN CARRIAGE   Horse-drawn surreys are the regal (if touristy) way to see Nassau. Agree on a price before you start your ride. The average charge for a 30-minute tour is $10 per person. The maximum load is two adults plus one child 11 or under (or three small adults—if you've been spending too much time at the ship's buffet, you don't qualify). The colorfully painted surreys are available daily from 9am to 4:30pm, except when the horses rest—usually from 1 to 3pm May through October, 1 to 2pm November through April. You'll find surreys in front of the cruise port building.

BY RENTAL CAR   Most vehicles have left-hand steering, and driving is British-style. If you're used to driving on the right, it may take some time to adjust. Thankfully, traffic is seldom heavy except downtown near the port. Rental-car license plates carry the letters SD (which stands for "suicide driver," according to joking Bahamians). You must be at least 21 years of age and possess a valid driver's license. **Avis, Budget, Dollar,** and **Hertz** all have offices here.

BY MOTOR SCOOTER   Contact **Fathia Investment,** Prince George Wharf (✆ **242/356-5739**). Scooters rent for $25 an hour or $50 for a full day.

BEST CRUISE LINE SHORE EXCURSIONS

In addition to the excursions below, cruise lines typically offer a variety of snorkeling, diving, and boat tours. Avoid the terribly dull city bus tours.

Gorge on Fresh Conch at Arawak Cay

This small, man-made island across the West Bay Street shore has the freshest conch around. For a true island experience, wash it down with the local cocktail—coconut water, milk, and gin. (See "Great Local Restaurants & Bars," below.)

Harbor Cruise & Atlantis Resort ($109, 2½ hr.): A tour boat with a local guide shows you the sights (such as they are) from the water, then drops you at the fanciful Atlantis Resort for a brief tour that includes a visit to Predator Lagoon, home to sharks, barracuda, and other toothy fish. Cruise along to Fort Montague, observing the many historical points of interest and the area's local flavor.

Ardastra Gardens & City Tour ($55, 2½ hr.): Enjoy a short ride to Ardastra, home to the Bahamas' largest collection of endangered land animals. Follow limestone pathways through a tropical paradise of brilliant bougainvillea, hibiscus, and other exotic plants. Take a narrated city tour to some of the historical monuments of the Bahamas, such as Fort Fincastle. Admire the Queen's Staircase, honoring Queen Victoria's reign. Visit the Straw Market, a haven for unique island gifts and souvenirs.

Thriller Powerboat Tour ($55, 1 hr.): This is a thrill seeker's excursion, with high-speed boats roaring around the waters off Nassau, scaring the fish out of their wits. Not my personal favorite way to see . . . well, anything, but it sure is fast.

Dolphin Swim at Blue Lagoon ($179, 3½ hr.): Begin with a 30-minute scenic catamaran ride to the dolphin facility at Blue Lagoon Island. Meet the dolphins and participate in an educational lecture before the interactive program begins. Pet, kiss, hug, and feed the dolphins in small groups.

EXCURSIONS OFFERED BY LOCAL AGENCIES

You'll find guided tours on almost all of The Islands of The Bahamas. And you'll be able to select one that suits your interests exactly, ranging from shopping sprees to ecological adventures among the birds and island wildlife.

Guided Walking Tours: These 1-hour tours, arranged by the **Ministry of Tourism** (📞 242/302-2000), depart from the Welcome Center on Prince George Wharf and usually begin every hour from 10am to 2pm. Make reservations in advance. The tours include descriptions of some of the city's oldest buildings, with information on Nassau's history, customs, and traditions. The cost is $10.

Scuba Diving, Sea Scootering & Shark Dives: Try **Stuart Cove,** Southwest Bay Street, South Ocean (www.stuartcove.com; 📞 **800/879-9832** or 242/362-4171), which offers many options, including personal submarine excursions that allow non-divers to move about underwater without scuba equipment ($110). The company also offers two-tank wreck dives for certified divers ($250), all-day shark dives for $250, and snorkel excursions ($75). All dives include lunch and rental equipment. Reservations recommended.

Walking on the Ocean Floor: If you loved *20,000 Leagues Under the Sea,* you won't want to miss **Hartley's Undersea Walk,** East Bay Street (www.underseawalk. com; 📞 **242/393-8234**). For $175 per person, you'll don a breathing helmet and spend about 20 minutes walking along the ocean bottom through a "garden" of tropical fish, sponges, and other undersea life. You don't have to be able to swim, and you can wear your glasses, but some people find the high-pitched pinging noise the helmet makes underwater annoying. Ships depart from the Nassau Yacht Haven Tuesday through Saturday at 9:30am and 1:30pm. Check-in times are 9am and 1pm, respectively.

ON YOUR OWN: WITHIN WALKING DISTANCE

Walking is the best way to see the major sights of Nassau and to get a feel for the city's character and history (and to shop, shop, shop). Start at Prince George Wharf, where your ship is docked.

As you exit from the cruise ship wharf into the main port area, you'll have no choice but to pass through **Festival Place,** a barnlike hall full of little shops and stalls selling arts and crafts, T-shirts, hot sauces, and other touristy items. Outside, hawkers will encourage you to have your hair braided at the **Hairbraider's Centre.** This government-sponsored open-air pavilion attracts braiding experts from all over the island. If you want a Bo Derek look, here's your chance. If you don't, a simple "no, thanks" keeps the touts away.

Just across Bay Street from Rawson Square (inland from the wharf) are the flamingo-pink government buildings of **Parliament Square,** constructed in 1815. The House of Assembly, old Colonial Secretary's Office, and Supreme Court flank a statue of Queen Victoria, while a bust on the north side of the square honors Sir Milo B. Butler, the Bahamas' first governor general.

Built as a prison in 1798, the **Nassau Public Library,** located a block inland from Parliament Square, facing Shirley Street, is one of the city's oldest buildings, and originally served as a prison. The unpenitentiary pink paint was added after 1889, when the building reopened as a library. The books, historical prints, Colonial documents, and Arawak Indian artifacts are kept in former cells.

Slaves carved the **Queen's Staircase** out of a solid limestone cliff in 1793. Originally designed as an escape route for soldiers at Fort Fincastle, each step now represents a year in Queen Victoria's 65-year reign. Lush plants and a waterfall stand guard over the staircase, which, itself, is located a few blocks from the library on East Street. The staircase leads to **Fort Fincastle,** on Elizabeth Avenue, built in 1793 by Lord Dunmore, the royal governor. At the fort, an elevator climbs a 38m-high (125-ft.) water tower; from the top, you can look down on the entire arrowhead-shaped fort. Walk around on your own, or hire a guide (you may find some of them overeager to be hired).

Walk downhill from Fort Fincastle and back toward the waterfront, and turn left on East Hill Street past Market Street. On the left stands **Government House,** the official residence of the governor general, built in 1801. Tropical foliage lines the grounds leading to the colonial mansion, and a statue of Columbus stands over the hillside steps.

This one's for kids, but young-at-heart parents may also enjoy the **Pirates of Nassau Museum,** at King and George streets (www.pirates-of-nassau.com; ✆ **242/356-3759**), downhill from Government House. Step aboard an embattled pirate ship and come face to face with Captain Teach and his fearsome crew as they guide you through the age of piracy in the lawless Nassau of 1716. Friendly guides will entertain and engage children and adults alike. It's open daily from 9am to 6pm, except on Sunday, when it closes at noon; admission is $12 for adults, $6 for children 4 to 17. Admission includes a 45-minute self-guided tour.

On Bay Street, not far from the Pirates of Nassau, is the **Straw Market,** full of stalls selling some authentic Bahamian items and lots of objects that are actually made in Asia. There are better places to get the real thing (see "Shopping," below), but enjoy the scene anyway. Hours are roughly 7:30am to 7pm.

If you're up for more walking, **Potter's Cay,** under the Paradise Island Bridge, provides more market color. Sloops from the less populated Out Islands bring in their fresh catch. Freshly grown herbs and vegetables are also sold, along with limes, papayas, pineapples, and bananas. Stalls sell conch in several forms: raw and marinated in lime juice, as spicy deep-fried fritters, and in salad and soup.

ON YOUR OWN: BEYOND THE PORT AREA

About 1.5km (1 mile) west of downtown Nassau, just off West Bay Street, **Fort Charlotte** covers more than 40 hilltop hectares (100 acres). The largest fort in the Bahamas, it offers impressive views of Paradise Island, Nassau, and the harbor. The complex, constructed in 1788, features a moat, dungeons, underground passageways, and 42 cannons.

Parading pink flamingos are the main attraction at the lush 2-hectare (5-acre) **Ardastra Gardens, Zoo and Conservation Center,** Chippingham Road, about 1.5km (1 mile) west of downtown Nassau (www.ardastra.com; © 242/323-5806). The graceful birds obey their drillmaster's orders, and with their long-legged precision and discipline, they give the Rockettes a run for their money. The performances, accompanied by informative commentary, are presented daily at 10:30am, 2:10pm, and 4:10pm. Lory parrot feedings can be viewed at 11am, 1:30pm, and 3:30pm. The other exotic wildlife here—boa constrictors, honey bears, macaws, and capuchin monkeys—are less talented but still fascinating in their own right. Paths meander through tropical foliage that's sure to enchant gardeners. Open daily from 9am to 5pm, with gates closing at 4:30pm. Admission is $16 for adults and $8 for children 4 to 12.

The **Cloister,** on Casino Drive on Paradise Island (no phone), is part of a monastery built in the 13th century by French monks. In the 1920s, William Randolph Hearst bought it, had it disassembled, and moved it from France to his estate in San Simeon, California. The stones were stored for years because no one knew how to properly reassemble them. In 1962, Huntington Hartford, the A&P grocery-store heir and developer of Paradise Island, bought the structure from Hearst and hired a sculptor to reconstruct it on the island. It's quite an anomaly on tropical Paradise Island, but it's a serene spot. The adjacent **Versailles Gardens** feature formal vistas, tropical flowers, and classic statuary. Visitors are welcome to walk through when no wedding ceremonies are taking place. There is no admission fee.

The mythical lost city of Atlantis submerged under Bahamian waters? Sure, it sounds hokey, and all the grandiloquent hype makes you want to hate the place, but the **Dig** and **Marine Habitat** at the Atlantis Paradise Island megaresort actually end up exceeding expectations. Drawing on age-old myths of the lost city, the Dig is a fantastic world of faux ancient ruins flooded by the sea. The interconnected passageways, boulevards, and chambers, now inhabited by piranhas, hammerhead sharks, stingrays, and morays, are visible through huge glass windows. It's purported to be the largest man-made marine habitat in the world—the resort's sprawling 11-million-gallon lagoon system boasts more than 200 sea species and 50,000 individual creatures. Tickets for the guided "Discovery Tour" of the marine attractions are available at the resort's guest services desks for $39 per adult, $29 per child 11 and under. **Note:** This tour does not include use of the resort's beach or water slide, which are reserved for guests only. A day pass to the beach and aquarium costs $65, and to add the water park also will run you $135 total for adults, $85 for children ages 3 to 12. For information, check out www.atlantis.com or call © 242/363-3000.

SHOPPING

In 1992, the Bahamas abolished import duties on 11 luxury-good categories, including china, crystal, fine linens, jewelry, leather goods, photographic equipment, watches, and fragrances. Even so, true bargains are rare, as is finding much that's really worth buying. The principal shopping areas are **Bay Street** and the adjacent blocks, which are almost the first places you see when you leave your ship. Here you'll find duty-free luxury-goods stores, such as Colombian Emeralds and Solomon's

Mines, plus hundreds of other shops selling T-shirts, tourist gimcracks, duty-free booze and cigars, and recordings of Junkanoo music.

In the crowded aisles of the **Straw Market** on Bay Street, you can watch crafts-people weave and plait straw hats, handbags, dolls, place mats, and other items; be aware, though, that many of the items for sale here aren't of the best quality, nor even made locally (much of the stock is imported from Asia). If you want really beautiful handmade straw work, walk a few blocks to the **Plait Lady,** at Victoria and Bay streets, where the merchandise is vastly superior to what's peddled in the Straw Market—and it's 100% Bahamian made.

For Bahamian arts and crafts, Junkanoo masks, and jewelry, try **Island Tings,** Bay Street between East Street and Elizabeth Avenue, and **Seagrape,** West Bay Street at the Travelers' Rest restaurant (10 min. west of Cable Beach by car).

Marlborough Antiques, across the street from the Hilton British Colonial on Marlborough Street, has an eclectic and interesting collection of antiques and books.

BEACHES

On New Providence Island, sun worshipers make the pilgrimage to **Cable Beach,** which offers various watersports and easy access to shops, a casino, bars, and restaurants. The beach stretches for 6.5km (4 miles), and the waters can change quickly from rough to calm and clear. It's 8km (5 miles) from the port—you can get there by taxi for $18 or on bus no. 10 for $2.

More convenient for cruise ship passengers, but inferior to Cable Beach, the **Western Esplanade** sweeps westward from the Hilton British Colonial hotel. Facilities include restrooms, changing facilities, and a snack bar. In the months preceding the Junkanoo Carnival (celebrated Jan. 1), local bands practice their Carnival routines here.

Paradise Beach, on Paradise Island, is a ferry ride away from Prince George Wharf (see "By Ferry," under "Getting Around," above). The price of admission ($5 for adults, $1 for children) includes use of the showers and a locker. An extra $10 deposit is required for towels. Paradise Island has a number of smaller beaches as well, including **Pirate's Cove Beach** and **Cabbage Beach.** Bordered by casuarinas, palms, and sea grapes, Cabbage Beach's broad sands stretch for 3km (2 miles), but it's likely to be crowded with guests from the nearby resorts. Tranquillity seekers find something approaching solitude on Harbour Island's northwestern end, accessible by boat only. **Harbour Island's Beach** is unquestionably one of the most beautiful beaches in the world, with pure-white, powdery sand, stretching about 5km (3 miles).

Cape Santa Maria is located on Long Island, at the island's northern tip, about 15 minutes from Stella Maris, and was named by Christopher Columbus for one of his ships. The beach is in a protected bay that faces northwest. It is mostly calm and, even with strong inland winds, it is still swimmable and enjoyable. Toward its western end, there are three snorkel areas right off the beach: a mild shallow sea garden; shallow rock/low coral formations around the final western rock point; an' "Rainbow Reef," a very pretty shore rock and coral reef, ideal for snorkelers in fai'

SPORTS

GOLF The 6,453-yard, par-72 **Cable Beach Golf Course,** (© 242/677-4175), has lakes and ponds tucked picturesquely f' length encourages strong hitters to shave strokes with long Greens fees are $100 per person for 18 holes, including cart;

GAMBLING

The massive **Atlantis Casino,** in the Atlantis Paradise Island megaresort ((C) **242/363-3000**), is the largest gaming and entertainment complex in the Caribbean. Two astounding glass sculptures, the Temple of the Sun and the Temple of the Moon, anchor the vast facility and tie in with the resort's "Lost City of Atlantis" theme. Open 24 hours daily, the casino boasts nearly 1,000 slot machines and 78 gaming tables for baccarat, roulette, craps, blackjack, and Caribbean stud poker. Unlike most other casinos, the Atlantis makes no attempt at hiding what's going on outside: Huge windows provide panoramas of the adjacent marina and lagoons.

The more modest **Crystal Palace Casino,** West Bay Street, Cable Beach ((C) **242/327-6200** or 242/677-4100), part of the Wyndham Nassau Resort, is the only casino on New Providence Island. Despite tough competition from the Atlantis Casino, it stacks up well against most other casinos in the Caribbean, with 750 slot machines and more than 50 gaming tables and live poker. The oval-shaped bar extends onto the gaming floor, and the lounge offers live entertainment. It's open 3:30pm to 4:30am daily.

Taxis will take you to either casino from the cruise ship pier.

GREAT LOCAL RESTAURANTS & BARS

Conch, Bahamian "rock lobster," and boiled fish are local specialties; pigeon peas and rice are popular side dishes. The local beer is **Kalik,** and Nassau's local rum is **Bacardi.**

ON ARAWAK CAY   You'll get all the conch you can eat on Arawak Cay, a man-made island across West Bay Street from Ardastra Gardens and Fort Charlotte. Join the locals at any of the informal bars and eateries that specialize in inexpensive, local fare. Don't miss out on conch fritters or conch with hot sauce, and wash it down with a coconut-water-and-gin cocktail. Gorging on the cay is a real Bahamian experience.

IN NASSAU   If you want fancy, **Graycliff Restaurant,** West Hill Street, next to Government House (www.graycliff.com; (C) 242/322-2796), is one of the most elegant restaurants in the West Indies. It was built in the 1740s by a former privateer and became Nassau's first inn in 1844. During the American Civil War, its cellar served as a jail for war prisoners. Polly Leach, a friend of Al Capone, owned the house some time later, as did Lord and Lady Dudley, friends of the Duke and Duchess of Windsor. Royalty and celebrities have dined in the elegant surroundings for decades, enjoying the extensive wine list and hand-rolled cigars. The Continental lunches and dinners are expensive but worth it if you've squirreled away for a really special meal. Call ahead for reservations.

Much more modest, **Bahamian Kitchen,** Trinity Place, off Market Street, next to Trinity Church ((C) **242/325-0702**), is one of the best places for good, down-home Bahamian food. Specialties include lobster Bahamian-style, fried red snapper, and curried chicken. Lunch is $15.

Try the boiled-fish breakfast at the **Shoal,** Nassau Street, near Ardastra Gardens ((C) **242/323-4400**). It's a local favorite and a featured restaurant in the Ministry of Tourism's "Real Taste of the Bahamas" program, which highlights independent establishments that serve indigenous cuisine. Every cab driver knows the place, which really hops on Sunday mornings. Lunch is $20.

Café Matisse, on Bank Lane at Bay Street, behind Parliament Square ((C) **242/** 7012; cafe-matisse.com), is housed in an old colonial home and features floors, Matisse prints, and a serene outdoor courtyard. The extensive menu includes seafood, pastas, and pizzas. It's an unbeatable respite from shopping and sightseeing in downtown Nassau. Lunch is about $25.

ON PARADISE ISLAND   Among the 30-plus pricey restaurants and bars in the **Atlantis Paradise Island** resort, on Casino Drive (℃ **242/363-3000**), one merits special mention. **Mosaic** serves an affordable buffet of tropical dishes, with a special emphasis on Cuban, Caribbean, and Mediterranean cuisines. Lunch buffet is $35. For casual fare, head over to the new **Marina Village.**

Grand Bahama Island

Grand Bahama Island (often referred to as GBI), is the second-most-popular destination in the Bahamas. Freeport is the landlocked section of town, while adjacent Lucaya hugs the waterfront. Originally intended as two separate developments, the two have grown together over the years, and though they offer none of Nassau's colonial charm, they do boast plenty of sun, surf, golf, tennis, and watersports. The frenzy of the gambling and shopping scenes has been quelled in recent years by a triple punch of three hurricanes in only 2 years. While rebuilding is an ongoing process, the short-term effect is that the island's tourism sites have taken on a calmer and quieter feel.

It wasn't until the 19th century that the first permanent settlers arrived on the island. Most earned a living as fishermen or by harvesting timber. GBI remained sparsely populated until 1955, when American developer Wallace Groves joined British industrialist Sir Charles Hayward to build the tax-free city of Freeport for tourism and manufacturing. Today, tourism remains the lifeblood of the island's 50,000 residents, but with the filming of at least some of each of the *Pirates of the Caribbean* films here, the movie industry may become an even bigger source of revenue. Hollywood hounds—determined to tread in the footsteps of Johnny Depp and Orlando Bloom, meet locals hired to play extras, or ogle at the spectacular ships and props—will no doubt add to an already booming tourism industry.

COMING ASHORE   Your ship docks at a quiet port on Grand Bahama Island, where you'll find a small straw market, a cheery shopping area with phone banks, and hair-braiding stations in the middle of an industrial zone. You are best served by taking the $25 taxi ride to the **Port Lucaya Marketplace,** where you'll find most of the action. Closer to the pier, but not as bustling, is the **International Bazaar,** an $18 cab ride away.

INFORMATION   Information is available from the **Grand Bahama Tourism Board,** located in the International Bazaar in the Lucaya area (℃ **800/448-3386** or 242/352-8044). Another information booth is located at Port Lucaya (℃ **242/373-8988**).You can also check out **www.bahamas.com**.

GETTING AROUND

Once you get to Grand Bahama Island by taxi, you can explore the center of town on foot. If you want to make excursions to the west or east ends of the island, your best bet is to rent a car.

BY TAXI   Taxicabs are located at the Grand Bahama International Airport, at the Lucayan Harbour, and major hotel and tourist locations. Following are sample zoned rates for up to two passengers: from the Harbour to Royal Oasis Golf Resort & Casino, $19; to Xanadu Beach Hotel, $20; to Port Lucaya Marketplace, $27; to Taíno Beach Resort/the Ritz, $27; and to Viva Fortuna Beach, $31. You can arrange for a taxi by calling **Freeport Taxi Company** (℃ **242/352-6666**) or **Grand Bahama Taxi Union** (℃ **242/352-7101**).

BY BUS A public bus transportation system operates between both Port Lucaya Marketplace and the International Bazaar to the downtown area, and from downtown to the outlying areas of West End and East End. One-way fares are $1 within the Freeport/Lucaya area, $2 to Eight Mile Rock, $4 to West End, and $8 to McLean's Town. Exact change is required.

BY FERRY A free, government-owned ferry travels daily between Sweeting's Cay and McLean's Town. Depart Sweeting's Cay at 7:10am and 4pm, and McLean's Town at 8:30am and 5pm. Each trip takes about 20 minutes.

BY RENTAL CAR Roads are good on GBI, and traffic is light. Remember that driving is on the left side. **Avis, Dollar,** and **Hertz** all have offices here.

BY BICYCLE OR MOTOR SCOOTER In the Lucaya area, there is an official cycling path on Midshipman Road. Most hotels have bicycles for rent for about $20 per day with a $50 deposit. A two-seat scooter requires a $100 deposit and rents for about $75 a day.

BEST CRUISE LINE SHORE EXCURSIONS

Sanctuary Bay Dolphin Encounter ($129, 3¼ hr.): On this excursion you can watch, touch, and photograph Flipper, or at least one of his relatives. See the UNEXSO information below for more elaborate dolphin excursions that you can arrange on your own.

Kayaking Nature Adventure ($85, 6 hr.): Visit a protected island creek, kayak through a mangrove forest, explore the island's caves, and take a guided nature walk into Lucayan National Park. Take a dip at a beach and enjoy a picnic lunch. View several species of birds, plants, and other creatures in their natural habitats. The excursion includes lunch and beach time.

Freeport Biking Adventure ($95, 5½ hr.): This combination tour, complete with biking, sightseeing, and the beach, offers a little of everything. Take a leisurely 20km (12-mile) bike ride and explore Grand Bahama Island's sights and sounds. Ride along the shoreline through a native settlement and learn some local history. Visit the dolphins at Sanctuary Bay or just take a dip and relax on the beach.

> ### Prime People-Watching
>
> In the center of Port Lucaya's waterfront restaurant-and-shopping complex is a small square known as Count Basie Square, which looks like it came out of a little town at the turn of the century. Surrounded by balconied bars, you can sample local cocktails while watching the colorful parade of tourists and locals.

Bahamas Jeep Adventure ($100, 5½ hr.): See the best of Grand Bahama from the window of your own jeep as you drive on the left side of the road, following British tradition. See the popular Taíno Beach; Sanctuary Bay, where dolphins live; and picturesque replicas of the original New Plymouth homes. Stop on Casuarina Bridge to learn about Freeport's unique history and continue through Grand Bahama's pine forest. Take a short hike to an inland Blue Hole and then follow the Heritage Trail along the seashore walked by settlers in the 1800s. The tour concludes with a snack and time for swimming.

Alexander von Humboldt Ship ($99, 3 hr.): Named after the German naturalist and seafaring explorer, Alexander von Humboldt, the ship is more than 100 years old.

Freeport/Lucaya

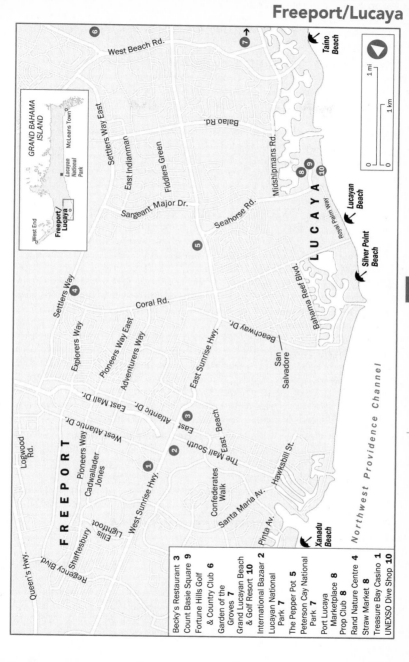

West Beach Rd.

Taino Beach

GRAND BAHAMA ISLAND

McLeans Town

Lucayan National Park

West End

Freeport/Lucaya

Settlers Way East

East Indianman

Fiddlers Green

Balao Rd.

Midshipmans Rd.

Lucayan Beach

Sargeant Major Dr.

Seahorse Rd.

Royal Palm Way

Silver Point Beach

L U C A Y A

Bahama Reef Blvd.

Settlers Way

Coral Rd.

Explorers Way

Pioneers Way East

Adventurers Way

Beachway Dr.

East Sunrise Hwy.

San Salvadore

East Mall Dr.

West Atlantic Dr.

East Atlantic Dr.

Pioneers Way

Cadwallader Jones

Logwood Rd.

Ellis Lightfoot

West Sunrise Hwy.

East Beach

The Mall South

The East Beach

Confederates Walk

Santa Maria Av.

Hawksbill St.

Pinta Av.

F R E E P O R T

Shaftesbury

Regency Blvd.

Queen's Hwy.

Xanadu Beach

Northwest Providence Channel

1 mi

1 km

Becky's Restaurant **3**
Count Basie Square **9**
Fortune Hills Golf & Country Club **6**
Garden of the Groves **7**
Grand Lucayan Beach & Golf Resort **10**
International Bazaar **2**
Lucayan National Park **7**
The Pepper Pot **5**
Peterson Cay National Park **7**
Port Lucaya Marketplace **8**
Prop Club **8**
Rand Nature Centre **4**
Straw Market **8**
Treasure Bay Casino **1**
UNEXSO Dive Shop **10**

5

THE PORTS OF CALL | Bahamas

143

Acquired by Grand Bahama Nature Tours for 3-hour daily sailing excursions, it is manned and maintained by a Bahamian crew, and powered by 25 iconic green sails. You'll be able to participate in ship activities such as assisting the captain or lifting the sails.

EXCURSIONS OFFERED BY LOCAL AGENCIES

Kayak & Bike Tours: Contact **Kayak Nature Tours** (www.grandbahamanature tours.com; ☎ **866/440-4542**) to arrange one of four excursions that fit in a cruiser's time frame. The first, to Lucayan National Park, features sea kayaking through mangroves, a nature hike, a stop at two caves, and a swim and picnic lunch at Gold Rock Beach ($89, 6 hr.). The second, to Peterson Cay National Park, includes sea kayaking to the small offshore cay, guided snorkeling, beach time, and lunch ($89, 5 hr.). The third features a leisurely bicycle ride along Taíno Beach and the settlement of Smith Point, a visit to Sanctuary Bay, a guided walk through historic settlement areas, time to shop, and lunch ($89, 6 hr.). The newest trip involves an off-road jeep convoy through the pine forests, over the canal, and down to the beach for lunch and a swim ($89, 6 hr.).

Scuba, Snorkeling, Shark Dives & Dolphin Swims: In the Bahamas, reef diving takes a back seat to theme-park-style "adventure" programs, including shark-feeding dives and swim-with-dolphins adventures. One of the premier diving and snorkeling outfitters is the **Underwater Explorers Society (UNEXSO),** at Lucaya Beach (www.unexso.com; ☎ **800/992-3483** or 242/373-1244), which offers reef and wreck dives. Two-tank reef dives are $99, shark dives are $99, and 3-hour learn-to-dive courses are $109. UNEXSO also offers several different dolphin programs. During the **Close Encounter** ($82 adults, $50 children 4–12), you will observe sea mammals from an observation deck while listening to an informative presentation; then you can wade into the waist-high water and touch the creatures. The highlight of **Swim with the Dolphins** ($169; minimum age 10; children 15 and younger must be accompanied by an adult) is swimming alongside the animals in protected waters after a briefing on dolphin behavior. The open-ocean **Ultimate Dolphins Experience** ($199; minimum age 10; children 15 and younger must be accompanied by an adult) allows you to dive with bottlenose dolphins in shallow open waters. These programs are exceedingly popular, so advance reservations are a must.

Party/Snorkel Cruises: In Freeport, **Superior Watersports** (www.superiorwater sports.com; ☎ **242/373-7863**) offers daily 5-hour party and snorkeling cruises that include equipment, lunch, and unlimited rum punch ($60 for adults, $40 for children 2–12). **Paradise Watersport,** at Club Fortuna and Island Seas Resorts (☎ **242/374-6676**), offers snorkeling cruises on a 46-foot catamaran ($40 adults, $20 children 3–12) and glass-bottom boat rides ($30 adults, $18 children 3–12).

ON YOUR OWN: BEYOND THE PORT AREA

Nothing of note is within walking distance of the port. You must take a cab over to Freeport/Lucaya for all attractions.

One of the island's top attractions, the 5-hectare (12-acre) **Garden of the Groves,** at Midshipman Road and Magellan Drive, in Freeport (www.thegarden ofthegroves.com; ☎ **242/373-5668**), was nearly destroyed due to hurricanes. It was once the private meditation garden of Freeport's founder, Wallace Groves, and features waterfalls, flowering shrubs, around 10,000 trees, tropical birds, Bahamian raccoons, Vietnamese potbellied pigs, and West African pygmy goats. The serene hilltop chapel overlooking the pond is also a popular place for exchanging vows. The garden is open daily 9am to 5pm and entry will cost you $15 for adults, $10 for kids. Admission includes a guided tour, if you so desire. Tours depart at 11am and 2pm.

A couple of miles east of downtown Freeport, the 40-hectare (100-acre) **Rand Nature Centre,** on East Settlers Way (www.geographia.com/grandbahama/rand.htm; ✆ 242/352-5438), serves as the regional headquarters of the Bahamas National Trust. Pine-land nature trails meander past native flora and wild birds, including the Bahama parrot and other animals. Other highlights include native animal displays (don't miss the boa constrictors), an education center, and a gift shop. It's open Monday through Friday from 9am to 4pm; admission is $5 for adults and $3 for kids 5 to 12.

Peterson Cay National Park, approximately 24km (15 miles) east of Freeport and less than 1km (½ mile) offshore, is accessible by boat only. Coral reefs ringing the tiny island make for great snorkeling and diving, and the serene location is perfect for a picnic. For information, contact the Rand Nature Centre, described above.

If your ship's in port late, don't miss the free nightly concert at **Count Basie Square,** in the center of Port Lucaya's waterfront restaurant-and-shopping complex. The legendary jazz bandleader who lends his name to the square had a home on Grand Bahama, and the square's vine-covered bandstand attracts steel-drum bands, limbo dancers, small Junkanoo groups, and gospel singers.

SHOPPING

The **International Bazaar,** at East Mall Drive and East Sunrise Highway, is pure 1960s kitsch, and though relentlessly cheerful, it's rather long in the tooth. Each area of the 4-hectare (10-acre), 100-shop complex once attempted to capture the ambience of a different region of the globe, but since the last few hurricanes, it's become a bit of a patchwork in terms of which country-themed shops had to close their borders and retreat. Buses marked INTERNATIONAL BAZAAR deliver passengers to the center's much-photographed Torii Gate, a Japanese symbol of welcome.

The **Port Lucaya Marketplace,** on Seahorse Road near UNEXSO, is a 2.5-hectare (6-acre) shopping-and-dining complex that, in recent years, has eclipsed the International Bazaar. This is definitely where all the action is, and because it's so close to the Lucayan Beach just across the street, it's a great way to combine dining, shopping, and beach bumming in one spot. The gingerbread trim on the pink-painted shops adds to the festive atmosphere. Many of the restaurants and shops overlook a 50-slip marina, next to the **UNEXSO Dive Shop,** where you should stop if you're in need of a wet suit, snorkel, mask, fins, underwater camera, or more prosaic items such as swimsuits, sunglasses, and hats.

The **Straw Market,** beside the Port Lucaya Marketplace, features items with a Bahamian touch—baskets, hats, handbags, and place mats. Quality varies, so look around before buying.

BEACHES

Grand Bahama Island has miles of white-sand beaches. **Xanadu Beach,** east of Freeport at the Xanadu Beach Resort, is the closest to the cruise pier, but two of the island's best are **Taíno Beach** and **Lucayan Beach,** both conveniently located on the Lucaya oceanfront. Of the two, Lucayan Beach is easiest to reach and closest to the Lucaya Marketplace. It also has plenty of beach-chair rentals, watersports, and restaurants. If total isolation is your thing, then **Gold Rock Beach,** a 20-minute ride east of Lucaya, may be the island's best. Hidden away in Lucayan National Park, it has barbecue pits, picnic tables, and a spectacular low tide. **Barbary Beach,** slightly closer to Lucaya, is great for seashell hunters, and white spider lilies in the area bloom spectacularly in May and June.

SPORTS

GOLF   **Grand Lucayan Beach & Golf Resort,** Royal Palm Way, Lucaya (www. ourlucaya.com; ✆ 866/870-7148 or 242/373-2003), offers two courses. The par-72 Lucayan course, designed by Dick Wilson, features well-protected elevated greens, fairways lined with tropical foliage, and doglegs. The par-72 links-style Reef course, designed by Robert Trent Jones, Jr., is 6,909 yards from the championship tees, with water traps on 13 of 18 holes. Greens fees are $155 for 18 holes, including cart. Club rentals are $50.

Fortune Hills Golf & Country Club, Richmond Park, Lucaya (www.geographia. com/grandbahama/golf.htm; ✆ 242/373-4500), was designed as an 18-hole course, but the back 9 holes were never completed. You can replay the front 9 for a total of 6,916 yards from the blue tees; par is 72. Greens fees are $64 per person, including cart. You can rent clubs for $20.

WATERSPORTS   **Paradise Watersport,** at Island Seas (✆ 242/374-6676), offers water-skiing ($40 for 30 min.) and parasailing ($50). Water-skiing lessons are $65 for 1 hour. **Lucaya Watersports** (www.lucayawatersports.com; ✆ 242/373-6375) offers windsurfing (rentals for $30 per hr., or 2-hr. lesson for $100) and a host of other activities, or try **Ocean Motion Watersports** (www.oceanmotionbahamas. com; ✆ 242/374-2425), at Breakers Booth on Lucayan Beach, for kayaking ($25 per hr.), banana-boat rides ($15 adults, $10 children), WaveRunners ($75 per 30 min.), water-skiing ($60 for a 2-mile run), parasailing ($75), and day passes to use the water trampoline ($10 for a half-day, $20 for a full day).

GAMBLING

The **Treasure Bay Casino,** between the Westin and Sheraton resorts at Lucaya (✆ 242/350-2001), offers gaming, dining, and live entertainment. Serious gamblers appreciate the variety of games: full-service race and sports book, craps, blackjack, minibaccarat, roulette, Caribbean stud poker, 350 slots, and 45 video poker games.

GREAT LOCAL RESTAURANTS & BARS

The most popular Bahamian beer is **Kalik.** Another brand, **Bahamian Hammerhead,** is brewed on Grand Bahama. GBI's local rums include **Don Lorenzo** and **Ricardo.**

The highest concentration of eateries can be found near Count Basie Square at the Port Lucayan Marketplace. Pubs and restaurants abound, many serving traditional Bahamian and British favorites.

On the waterfront at Lucayan Beach, the **Prop Club** (✆ 242/373-1333) has a sports-bar feel and features plenty of beach and ocean views from both indoor and outdoor tables. Pizzas and pastas dominate the menu. Lunch is $15 to $25.

The **Pepper Pot,** East Sunrise Highway, at Coral Road (✆ 242/373-7655), in a tiny shopping mall a 5-minute drive east of the International Bazaar, serves takeout portions of the best carrot cake on the island, as well as a savory conch chowder, fish, pork chops, chicken souse, sandwiches, and burgers. Lunch is $10.

BARBADOS

No port of call in the southern Caribbean can compete with Barbados when it comes to natural beauty, attractions, and fine dining. It's the perfect blend of Caribbean culture and British charm. With all it offers, you'll think the island is much bigger than it is. But what really put Barbados on world travelers' maps is its seemingly

Barbados Museum and Historical Society **12**
Barbados Wildlife Reserve **2**
Earthworks Pottery **9**
The Fish Pot **4**
Farley Hill National Park **3**
Flower Forest **5**
George Washington House and Museum **13**

Gun Hill Signal Station **10**
Harrison's Cave **8**
St. James Church **7**
St. Nicholas Abbey **1**
Sunbury Plantation House **11**
Welchman Hall Gully **6**

5

THE PORTS OF CALL | Barbados

endless stretches of pink- and white-sandy beaches, among the best in the entire Caribbean Basin. Couple that with the friendly islanders, great restaurants, and plenty of shopping, and you're nearly guaranteed a pleasurable day in this sunny country.

This Atlantic outpost was one of the most staunchly loyal members of the British Commonwealth for over 300 years, and although it gained its independence in 1966, Britishisms still remain—the accent is British, driving is on the left, cricket is a popular sport, and Queen Elizabeth II is still officially the head of state. It's also still a common vacation destination for British tourists.

Originally operated on a plantation economy that made its aristocracy rich, the island is the most easterly in the Caribbean. Topography varies from rolling hills and savage waves on the eastern (Atlantic) coast to densely populated flatlands, rows of hotels and apartments, and sheltered beaches in the southwest.

COMING ASHORE   The cruise ship pier, a short drive from **Bridgetown,** the capital, is one of the best docking facilities in the southern Caribbean. You can walk right into the modern cruise ship terminal, which has car rentals, taxi services, sightseeing tours, a tourist information office, a huge phone center (where you can make credit card calls to the U.S., send faxes, and buy phone cards and stamps), and shops and scads of vendors (see "Shopping," below).

If you want to go into Bridgetown, about 1.5km (1 mile) from the port, instead of to the beach, you can take a hot 10- to 15-minute walk or simply catch a taxi. The one-way fare ranges from $5 on up. Buses pass by the harbor frequently; the fare is $1.

LANGUAGE   English is spoken with an island lilt.

CURRENCY   The **Barbados dollar** (BD$) is the official currency. It's available in $100, $20, $10, and $5 notes; $1, 25¢, and 10¢ silver coins; and 5¢ and 1¢ copper coins. The exchange rate is BD$2 to US$1 (BD$1 = US50¢). Most stores take traveler's checks or U.S. dollars, so don't bother to convert money if you're here for only a day. Prices in this section are given in U.S. dollars.

INFORMATION   The **Barbados Tourism Authority** is on Harbour Road, Bridgetown (www.visitbarbados.org; ✆ **888/227-2236** or 246/427-2623). Its cruise terminal office, which is very well run, is always open when a cruise ship is in port.

CALLING FROM THE U.S.   When calling Barbados from the United States, you need only dial a "1" before the telephone numbers listed here.

Getting Around

BY TAXI   Taxis are not metered, but their rates are fixed by the government. Even so, drivers may try to get more money out of you, so make sure you settle on the rate before getting in. Taxis are identified by the letter z on their license plates, and you'll find them just outside of the terminal. A one-way trip from the cruise pier to Harrison's cave should be about $25 per person and a one-way trip to Paradise Beach approximately $10.

BY BUS   Blue-and-yellow public buses fan out from Bridgetown every 20 minutes or so onto the major routes; their destinations are marked on the front. Buses going south and east leave from Fairchild Street, and those going north and west depart from Lower Green and the Princess Alice Highway. Fares are about $1.

Privately owned minibuses run shorter distances and travel more frequently. These bright-yellow buses display destinations on the bottom-left corner of the windshield. In Bridgetown, board at River Road, Temple Yard, or Probyn Street. Fare is also about $1.

BY RENTAL CAR While it's a good way for those with an adventurous streak to see the island, before deciding to rent a car, Americans should keep in mind that driving is on the left side of the road and that signs are totally inadequate. Rental cars all have an H on their license plates (meaning "hired"), so everyone will know you're a visitor.

Best Cruise Line Shore Excursions

It's not easy to get around Barbados quickly and conveniently, so a shore excursion is a good idea here.

Kayak & Turtle Encounter ($75, 3½ hr.): A boat ride along the west coast brings you to the beach, where you'll clamber into your kayak for a 45-minute paddle along the shore. Once at the snorkel site, you'll be able to swim with and join your guide in feeding sea turtles.

Mount Gay Rum Distillery & Banks Beer Tour ($55, 3½ hr.): Talk about getting in the spirit. This excursion takes you for a tour and tipple at Barbados's number-one rum distillery; it then heads for the Banks Brewery for the yeasty side of things.

Horseback Riding ($115, 3½ hr.): Horse treks through the heart of the island wind past old plantation houses, sugarcane fields, old sugar factories, small villages, and, if you're lucky, green monkeys scouting for food.

Excursions Offered by Local Agencies

Island Tours: Since most cruise lines don't really offer a comprehensive island tour, many passengers rely on one of the local tour companies. **Sun Tours Barbados,** Brownes Gap, Hastings (www.suntoursbarbados.com; ✆ 246/434-8430), offers several tours that cost between $70 and $85 per person. Call ahead for reservations.

Taxi Tours: If you can afford it, touring by taxi is far more relaxing than the standardized bus tour. Nearly all Bajan taxi drivers are familiar with their island and like to show off their knowledge to visitors. The standard rate is about $35 to $45 per hour per taxi, for up to six passengers. You might want to try contacting taxi owner/driver **Aaron Francis** (✆ 246/431-9059 or 246/231-3184). He's a gem: friendly, reliable, and knowledgeable.

On Your Own: Within Walking Distance

About the only thing you can walk to is the cruise terminal. The modern, pleasant complex has an array of duty-free shops and retail stores, plus many vendors selling arts and crafts, jewelry, liquor, china, crystal, electronics, perfume, and leather goods.

On Your Own: Beyond the Port Area

Bridgetown is a friendly Caribbean city of nearly 100,000 people. If you're not up for straying far from the capital, there's plenty in town to keep you occupied for a day in Barbados. With museums, beaches, shopping, and historic sites, you'll have plenty of activities to fill your day.

Taxis from the cruise terminal into central Bridgetown will cost you about $3. Ask to be dropped off in Hero's Square near the statue of Lord Nelson. From there, it's an easy walk to the Parliament Buildings or shopping on Broad Street.

5

THE PORTS OF CALL

Barbados

But with all the natural beauty, historical monuments, and outdoor activities available on the island, no one will blame you if you skip Bridgetown's highlights and venture farther out to explore more of the island outside town.

To learn more about Barbados's rich history, visit the **Barbados Museum & Historical Society,** St. Ann's Garrison, St. Michael (www.barbmuse.org.bb; ✆ **246/427-0201**). This museum collects artifacts documenting the history of the island, its people, culture, traditions, arts, crafts, and natural beauty. Hours of operation are Monday through Saturday 9am to 5pm, and Sunday from 2 to 6pm. Admission is $7 for adults, $4 for children 17 and under.

American history buffs planning to spend time close to Bridgetown should visit the **George Washington House and Museum,** Bush Hill, the Garrison, and St. Michael (www.georgewashingtonbarbados.org; ✆ **246/228-5461**). Nineteen-year-old George Washington took his first and only international trip to Barbados in 1751 and stayed at this plantation house turned museum. The tour is rich with historical detail and includes a film viewing. Admission is $10 for adults, $2.50 for children 5 to 12.

I don't recommend wasting too much time in Bridgetown—it's hot, dry, and dusty, and the honking horns of traffic jams only add to its woes. So, unless you want to go shopping, you should spend your time exploring all the beauty the island has to offer. The tourist office in the cruise terminal is very helpful if you want to go somewhere on your own. **Welchman Hall Gully,** in St. Thomas (www.welchmanhallgully barbados.com; ✆ **246/438-6671**), is a lush tropical garden owned by the Barbados National Trust. It's 13km (8 miles) from the port (reachable by bus) and features some plants that were here when the English settlers landed in 1627. The Gully is also home to a number of green monkeys, which are originally from Africa, but arrived several hundred years ago and are now considered a distinct genetic lineage. If you're driving, take Hwy. 2 from Bridgetown. The entrance fee, which includes a self-guided tour booklet, is $10 for adults, $5 for children ages 5 to 13. Several tours are offered that range in price and activity level but all include transportation. The Gardens in the Heart tour is $55 for adults while the zip-line tour costs $125. It's open daily 9am to 4:30pm.

Many cruise ship excursions visit **Harrison's Cave,** Welchman Hall, St. Thomas (www.harrisonscave.com; ✆ **246/417-3700**). Barbados's top tourist attraction is newly renovated. Here you can see a beautiful underground world from aboard an electric tram and trailer. Admission is $30 for adults and $15 for children 16 and under. If you'd like to go on your own, a taxi ride takes about 30 minutes and costs at least $50 round-trip.

About 1.5km (1 mile) from Harrison's Cave is the **Flower Forest,** Richmond Plantation, St. Joseph (✆ **246/433-8152**). This old sugar plantation stands 255m (835 ft.) above sea level near the western edge of the "Scotland district," in one of the most scenic parts of Barbados. The entrance fee is $10.

The **Sunbury Plantation House,** 25 minutes from Bridgetown along Hwy. 5 (www.barbadosgreathouse.com; ✆ **246/423-6270**), is the only plantation great house on Barbados whose rooms are all open for viewing. The 300-year-old house is steeped in history, featuring mahogany antiques, old prints, and a collection of horse-drawn carriages. Admission is $10, half-price for children. Hours are daily 9:30am to 4:30pm. Signs along the highway will guide you in, right before Six Cross Roads.

Built in 1818, the strategically placed **Gun Hill Signal Station,** Hwy. 4, St. George (✆ **246/429-1358**), one of two such stations owned and operated by the Barbados National Trust, commands a wonderful panoramic view from east to west.

It's 19km (12 miles) from the port; the one-way taxi ride costs about $15, and the entrance fee is $5 for adults and $2.50 for kids 6 to 12. It's open Monday through Saturday from 9am to 5pm.

If it's wildlife you want, head for the **Barbados Wildlife Reserve,** in St. Peter (© 246/422-8826), on the northern end of the island. It's not exactly Animal Kingdom, but you'll see turtles, rabbits, iguanas, peacocks, green monkeys, and a caged python on this 1.5-hectare (3¾-acre) site. The entrance fee is about $12 for adults, $6 for kids 3 to 12. Hours are daily from 10am to 5pm. Just opposite is the **Farley Hill National Park,** which holds the ruins of a mansion that in the 1860s was visited by Prince Alfred, Duke of Edinburgh. Walk up the hill behind the building for breathtaking views of the island.

To see some lovely architecture, you may want to visit **St. Nicholas Abbey,** Cherry Tree Hill, St. Peter (www.stnicholasabbey.com; © 246/422-5357). Built in 1650, this classic plantation house is one of only three Jacobean mansions in the hemisphere, and believed to be the oldest house in Barbados. Hours of operation are Sunday through Friday from 10am to 3:30pm. Admission is $17 for adults, $10 for children.

Maybe it's the party life you crave. If so, don't miss the **Mount Gay Rum Tour** in Bridgetown (www.mountgay.com; © 246/425-9066). You'll get a 40-minute soup-to-nuts introduction to rum in an air-conditioned rum shop (rumor has it that of all the rum shops on the island, this is the only one with air-conditioning). Tours are offered Monday through Friday every hour from 9:30am to 3:30pm. The cost is $8 per person. There's also a "with lunch" tour option for $60.

If you're looking for some quality time in the water, but don't want to stray far from port, check out **the Boatyard,** on Bay Street in Bridgetown (www.theboatyard.com; © 246/436-2622). It's a lively nightspot that, by day, caters to cruise ship passengers. You can sign up for nearly every watersport imaginable—snorkeling, kayaking, jet-skiing—or just relax on one of their catamaran cruises. After a day on the water, hang out at Sharkey's, the Boatyard's colorful beachside bar, where you can enjoy cocktails.

Explore a shipwreck and coral reefs with **Atlantis Submarines** (www.atlantis adventures.com/barbados; © 246/436-8929) in air-conditioned comfort for $109. It's perfect for non–PADI certified people who want to see all the under-the-sea sights that are usually reserved only for scuba divers. Make reservations in advance.

Adventureland 4 X 4 Tours (www.adventurelandbarbados.com; © 246/429-3687) offers several expeditions to help you explore the natural beauty of the island. If you want to spend time in the water, sign up for the Turtle & Shipwreck Snorkel Adventure ($70), where you can swim with hawksbill and green turtles before relaxing on the beach. Or take the Congaline Adventure for some off-road fun ($88).

Shopping

The shopping mall–size cruise terminal contains duty-free shops, retail stores, a convenience store, and a plethora of vendors selling arts and crafts, jewelry, liquor, china, crystal, electronics, perfume, and leather goods. Vendors sell great local hot sauce, as well as yummy **Punch de Crème,** a creamy rum drink (you can get a free sample before buying). For rum cake, an island specialty, go to the family-owned **Calypso Island Bakery** (www.calypsorumcake.com; © 246/426-1702). The shrink-wrapped cakes last up to 6 months and make great gifts. In general, though, you'll find a wider selection of merchandise and better prices in Bridgetown.

Good duty-free buys include cameras, watches, crystal, gold jewelry, bone china, cosmetics and perfumes, and liquor (including locally produced Barbados rum and liqueurs), along with tobacco products and British-made cashmere sweaters, tweeds, and sportswear. **Cave Shepherd,** Broad Street, Bridgetown (© 246/431-2121), is the largest department store on Barbados and the best place to shop for duty-free merchandise.

Among Barbados handicrafts, you'll find lots of black-coral jewelry, but beware—because black coral is endangered, it's illegal to bring it back to the United States. Local potters turn out different products, some based on designs that are centuries old. Check out **Earthworks Pottery,** Edgehill Heights, St. Thomas (www.earthworks-pottery.com; © 246/425-0223). Crafts include wall hangings made from grasses and dried flowers, straw mats, baskets, and bags with raffia embroidery. Bajan leather work includes handbags, belts, and sandals.

In Bridgetown, **Articrafts,** on Broad Street, is a standout for Bajan arts and crafts, straw work, handbags, and bamboo items. **Pelican Craft Centre,** Harbour Road, Bridgetown, is located halfway between town and the cruise terminal. The modern center has several arts-and-crafts shops that make it an ideal location to scout around for such Barbadian souvenirs as local pottery, metal art, gift baskets, and paintings. The shops are wheelchair accessible.

Beaches

Beaches on the island's western side—the luxury resort area called the Gold Coast—are far preferable to those on the surf-pounded Atlantic side, which are dangerous for swimming. The government requires that there be access to all beaches, via roads along the property line or through the hotel entrance, so all Barbados beaches are open to the public, even those in front of the big resort hotels and private homes.

ON THE WEST COAST (GOLD COAST)   Take your pick of the beaches on the west coast, which are about a 15-minute, $8 taxi ride from the cruise terminal. A good beach for watersports, especially snorkeling, is **Payne's Bay,** with access from **Mannie's Suga Suga Restaurant** (© 246/419-4511). There's a parking area here. It can get rather crowded, but the beautiful bay makes it worth it. Directly south of Payne's Bay, at Fresh Water Bay, is a trio of fine beaches: **Brighton Beach, Brandon's Beach,** and **Paradise Beach.**

Church Point lies north of St. James Church, opening onto Heron Bay, site of the **Colony Club Hotel** (www.colonyclubhotel.com; © 246/422-2335). Although this beach can get crowded, it's one of the most scenic bays in Barbados, and the swimming is ideal. You can also order drinks at the Colony Club's beach terrace. Day passes, which allow you to use chairs, umbrellas, and towels, are $100 for the hotel area, or you can find the public beach access a bit farther down for free. Keep in mind that the public beach lacks facilities of any kind.

Snorkelers in particular seek out the glassy blue waters by **Mullins Beach.** There are some shady areas, and you can park on the main road.

ON THE SOUTH COAST   Depending on traffic, south-coast beaches are usually easy to reach from the cruise terminal. Figure on a $15-to-$20 taxi fare. **Sandy Beach,** reached from the parking lot on the Worthing main road, has tranquil waters opening onto a lagoon. This is a family favorite, with lots of screaming and yelling, especially on weekends. Food and drink are sold here.

Windsurfers are particularly fond of the trade winds that sweep across **Casuarina Beach** even on the hottest summer days. Access is from Maxwell Coast Road, across the property of the **Almond Casuarina Beach Hotel.**

Silver Sands Beach is to the east of the town of Oistins, near the very southernmost point of Barbados, directly east of South Point Lighthouse. This white-sand beach is a favorite with many Bajans, who probably want to keep it a secret from as many visitors as possible. Windsurfing is good here, but not as good as at Casuarina Beach.

ON THE SOUTHEAST COAST   The southeast coast is known for its big waves, especially at **Crane Beach,** a white-sand stretch backed by cliffs and palms that often appears in travel-magazine articles about Barbados. The **Crane Beach Resort & Residences** (℃ 246/423-6220) towers above it from the cliffs, and Prince Andrew owns a house here. The beach offers excellent bodysurfing—but this is real ocean swimming, not the calm Caribbean, so be careful. At $35 from the cruise pier, the one-way taxi fare is relatively steep, so try to share the ride with other cruise passengers.

ON THE EAST COAST   The **Soupbowl,** a beach in the village of Bathsheba, has rough waves and swimming is not encouraged, but the town is a quaint surfer's village and a good place to catch some sun.

Sports

GOLF   On the south coast of the island, the **Barbados Golf Club,** Durants, Christ Church (http://barbadosgolfclub.com; ℃ 246/428-846), is a championship public golf course that was redesigned by Ron Kirby and features two lakes on the 18-hole, par-72 course. A series of coral waste bunkers have been carved through four holes, adding to the challenge. A clubhouse, bar, and restaurant are located on the premises. Club, shoe, pull trolley, and cart rentals are available. Rates start at $105 for 18 holes. Open daily.

WINDSURFING   Experts say that Barbados windsurfing is as good as any this side of Hawaii. In fact, it's a very big business between November and April, when thousands of windsurfers from all over the world come here. **Silver Sands** is rated the best spot in the Caribbean for advanced windsurfing. **Brian Talmas deAction Beach Shop,** located right on Silver sands beach, gives lessons and rents boards. Windsurfing rentals are $68 for 3 hours, or $98 for a full day, and lessons cost $60 per hour. Take a taxi from the cruise terminal; it's about $20 for a one-way fare.

SURFING   The Soupbowl in Bathsheba, St. Joseph, on the rough Atlantic coast, is world renowned among the international surfing community. Surfboard rentals are available at a number of shops in Bathsheba. Beginners can take lessons in the calmer Caribbean water. **Zed's Surfing Adventures** (www.zedssurftravel.com) offers lessons starting at $80.

SCUBA DIVING   **The Dive Shop,** Amey's Alley, Upper Bay Street, St. Michael (www.divebds.com; ℃ 246/426-9947), offers a wide range of PADI courses, starting at $85 for the most basic class. Tank dive packages start at $70 and include equipment rental.

Great Local Restaurants & Bars

Be sure to try the tasty local delicacy, **flying fish** (you can even get it in burger form).

Right in town at the Bridgetown Marina, the **Waterfront Café** (www.waterfront cafe.com.bb; ℃ 246/427-0093) is a good place to relax after a morning of shopping. For big Caribbean spiny lobsters in Bridgetown, try **Lobster Alive,** Wesley House,

Bay Street, next to the Boathouse (www.lobsteralive.net; ☎ **246/435-0305**). Lunch daily; Sunday Jazz Brunch noon to 4pm. You can get a 1½-pound lobster for $55.

Brown Sugar, Aquatic Gap (off Bay St.), St. Michael, just below Bridgetown on Carlisle Bay (www.brownsugarbarbados.com; ☎ **246/426-7684**), is an alfresco restaurant in a turn-of-the-20th-century bungalow. The chefs prepare some of the tastiest Bajan specialties on the island. Of the main dishes, Creole-broiled pepper chicken is popular, as are the stuffed crab backs. There's a great lunch buffet Monday through Friday for $28 per person.

The Fish Pot, a restaurant in the Little Good Harbour oceanfront hotel in Shermans, St. Peter (www.littlegoodharbourbarbados.com; ☎ **246/439-3000**), is the perfect place to stop for lunch if you're spending your day north of Speightstown, Barbados's second-largest city. The menu offers Caribbean meals and seafood, and while the food is a little expensive, the views are priceless. Try the lobster with asparagus and baby corn for lunch ($45).

BELIZE

Located on the northeastern tip of Central America, bordering Mexico on the north, Guatemala to the west and south, and the Caribbean to the east, Belize combines Central American and Caribbean cultures. The area offers both ancient Mayan ruins and a 300km (185-mile) coral reef that runs the entire length of the country—it's the largest in the Western Hemisphere and the second largest in the world, supporting a tremendous number of patch reefs, shoals, and more than 1,000 islands called cays (pronounced *keys*), the largest and most populous being Ambergris Caye. The country is noted for its eco-friendly ways and, unlike many other Caribbean countries, is serious in its dedication to conservation: One-fifth of Belize's total landmass is dedicated as nature reserves, and 7,770 sq. km (3,000 sq. miles) of its waters are protected as well.

Previously known as British Honduras, Belize gained its independence from England in 1981. It has a parliamentary democracy and is a member of the British Commonwealth. Belmopan is the capital, but **Belize City** is the economic center of the country. Trying to choose which natural or man-made wonder to explore will be the most stress you'll feel in this laid-back, English-speaking nation, whose population of about 322,000 comprises Creoles, Garifuna (Black Carib Indians), mestizos (a mix of Spanish and Indian), Spanish, Mayan, English, Lebanese, Chinese, and East Indians. The country has the highest concentration of **Mayan sites** among all Central American nations; these include Altun Ha, Caracol, Cerros, Lamanai, Lubaantun, and Xunantunich (and Tikal is nearby in Guatemala). During the classic period (A.D. 250–900), there were a million Maya in Belize, and although the civilization began to decline after A.D. 900, some Mayan centers were occupied until contact with the Spanish in the 1500s. Today, Belize has joined with El Salvador, Guatemala, Honduras, and Mexico to establish **Mundo Maya (World of the Maya),** a program dedicated to the preservation of Mayan culture.

Although Belize is a year-round destination, the waters are especially clear from April to June; the dry season, lasting from February to May, coincides nicely with the cruise high season.

COMING ASHORE A multimillion-dollar, 450-sq.-m (4,840-sq.-ft.) pier called **Fort Street Tourism Village,** which caters specifically to cruise ship passengers, opened in Belize City in 2001. Although big ships still can't pull alongside because of shallow waters and must therefore tender in passengers from anchorages offshore

Belize

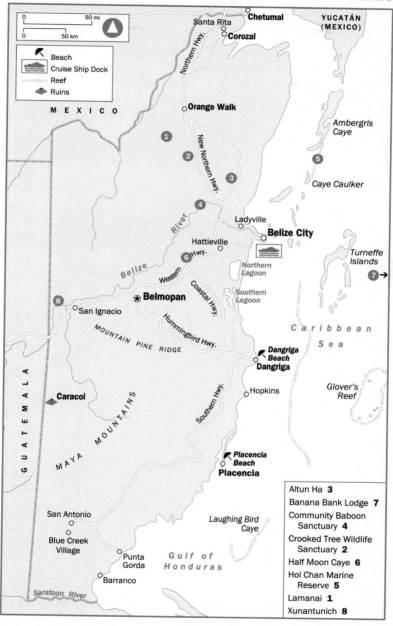

Map legend (scale): 0 — 50 mi / 0 — 50 km

Legend:
- Beach
- Cruise Ship Dock
- Reef
- Ruins

Labels on map:

YUCATÁN (MEXICO)

Chetumal
Santa Rita
Corozal

M E X I C O

Orange Walk

Ambergris Caye

Caye Caulker

New Northern Hwy.
Northern Hwy.

River

Ladyville
Belize City
Hattieville
Northern Lagoon
Turneffe Islands

Belize River
Western Hwy.
Coastal Hwy.
Belmopan
Southern Lagoon

C a r i b b e a n   S e a

G U A T E M A L A

MOUNTAIN PINE RIDGE
Hummingbird Hwy.
San Ignacio

Dangriga Beach
Dangriga

Glover's Reef

Caracol

M A Y A   M O U N T A I N S

Hopkins

Southern Hwy.

Placencia Beach
Placencia

San Antonio

Blue Creek Village

Punta Gorda

Laughing Bird Caye

Barranco

Sarstoon River

G u l f   o f   H o n d u r a s

Numbered list:

Altun Ha **3**
Banana Bank Lodge **7**
Community Baboon Sanctuary **4**
Crooked Tree Wildlife Sanctuary **2**
Half Moon Caye **6**
Hol Chan Marine Reserve **5**
Lamanai **1**
Xunantunich **8**

(a 20- to 30-min. trip each way), the spiffy pier area now offers a new shopping complex, with restaurants, tourist information, and even a tranquil Mayan-themed courtyard. Smaller ships, such as Windstar's fleet, skip Belize City completely and anchor offshore from the cays and other parts of the mainland, such as the southern Dangriga and Placencia.

LANGUAGE   English is the official language of Belize, although Spanish, Creole, Garifuna, and Mayan are spoken throughout the country as well.

CURRENCY   The **Belize dollar** (BZ$) has a fixed exchange rate of BZ$2 to US$1 (BZ$1 = US50¢), so even after a few too many rum punches, you won't have to take out your calculator here. Most establishments, as well as taxis and vendors on the street, take U.S. dollars, and most places take credit cards as well. In especially touristy areas, just be sure to ask if the price quoted is in U.S. or Belize dollars. Prices in this section are given in U.S. dollars.

INFORMATION   If you want information before you leave home, contact the **Belize Tourism Board** (www.travelbelize.org; ℂ **800/624-0686** or 501/227-2423) or the **Belize Tourism Industry Association** (ℂ **501/227-1144**). The **Belize Audubon Society** (www.belizeaudubon.org; ℂ **501/223-5004**) has a huge presence, not only for bird-watching, but also for all areas of nature conservation; the organization manages many of the country's reserves.

CALLING FROM THE U.S.   To make a call from the U.S. to Belize, dial the international access code (011), the country code (501), and then the local phone number of the establishment.

Getting Around

BY TAXI   Taxis are available at the pier, in town, and in resort areas, and are easily recognized by their green license plates. Although the taxis have no meters, the drivers do charge somewhat standard fares; ask what your fare will be prior to hiring a taxi.

BY WATER TAXI   From the **Marine Terminal,** in Belize City (ℂ **501/203-1969**), water-taxi service runs to Ambergris Caye, Caye Caulker, and various other cays. Boats leave at 9am, 10:30am, noon, 1:30pm, 3pm, and 4:30pm. The ride from Belize City to San Pedro, the main town on Ambergris Caye, is approximately 80 minutes and costs $25 round-trip. They depart eight times a day to Caye Caulker, 8am to 5:30pm, $15 round-trip.

BY PLANE   Local airlines **Tropic Air** (www.tropicair.com; ℂ **800/422-3435** or 501/226-2012) and **Maya Island Air** (www.mayaislandair.com; ℂ **800/225-6732** or 501/226-2435) offer hourly flights to Ambergris Caye, Caye Caulker, Placencia, and Dangriga. The flight to Ambergris Caye takes approximately 20 minutes, and, because you fly so low, you get a breathtaking view of the surrounding cays and atolls. Keep your eyes open for stingrays and dolphins swimming below you. Flights leave from Belize City going to San Pedro approximately every 90 minutes from 7:40am until 5:40pm; the cost is about $75 round-trip. The term "puddle jumper" really applies here: The planes can be as small as 14-seaters, and you may even get to sit next to the pilot. You can get a walk-up ticket, but it's best to reserve ahead.

BY RENTAL CAR   Not recommended. Although most of the major roads and highways are paved, lots of patches are in need of repair, which makes for a very bumpy ride.

Best Cruise Line Shore Excursions

Lamanai ($109, 7½ hr.): Lamanai is one of the largest ceremonial centers in Belize. Starting with a 45-minute drive up the Northern Highway to Tower Hill, you'll board a riverboat and head up the New River. Along the way, your guide will point out basking crocodiles, a variety of birds, delicate water lilies, and other exotic flowers. You'll pass local fishermen and, surprisingly, Mennonite farms. Upon landing, you will enjoy lunch and then tour the series of temples and the small archaeological museum.

Altun Ha ($82, 4 hr.): Meaning "water of the rock," this relatively small site was rediscovered in 1957 during expansion of the Northern Highway. This is one of the most extensively excavated sites and was an important trading post during the classical Mayan period. Many treasures were found here, and there are riveting views from the top of the temple. The tour includes lunch.

Xunantunich ($89, 7½ hr.): Also called **"Maiden of the Rock,"** Xunantunich was a major Mayan ceremonial center. After crossing the river by hand-cranked ferry, you can explore six major plazas and 25 temples and palaces, including El Castillo, the second-tallest structure in Belize. Afterward, you'll head to San Ignacio for lunch and enjoy the sounds of a marimba band.

Hol Chan Marine Reserve & Shark Ray Alley ($99, 8 hr.): You'll head north for an hour-long speedboat ride to Hol Chan (Mayan for "little channel"), 6.5km (4 miles) southeast of San Pedro on Ambergris Caye. You can snorkel the reef for about an hour, and then head off to the Shark Ray Alley, about 5 minutes away, where you'll pet southern stingrays and see nurse sharks. Visitors have also sighted eagle rays, green turtles, tarpons, barracudas, and green moray eels. Lunch is on San Pedro, where you can drink rum punch, shop, or hang out at the beach.

Cave Tubing ($119, 6½ hr.): Upon arrival at Jaguar Paw, you'll take a 45-minute hike down a jungle trail, where your guide will point out various plants and trees used by the ancient Maya for medicinal purposes. When you get to the cave, your guide will hand out flashlights and inner tubes and set you afloat, propelled by the current, through the cave system. On several occasions, you'll emerge into the sunlight before entering another cave. The float lasts about 2 hours, after which you'll have lunch. Bring a change of clothes.

Excursions Offered by Local Agencies

TAXI TOURS Generally, the excursions offered by the cruise lines are the way to go in Belize, but if you crave a more personalized experience, you can hire a taxi driver who doubles as a guide (make sure you tell the driver that you want a tour before getting into the taxi and negotiating a price). Tour guides must be licensed by the Belize Tourism Board and are recognizable with a photo ID. For a tour of Belize City, try to snag **Lasalle Tillet** of **S&L Travel & Tours** (www.sltravelbelize.com; ✆ 501/227-7593). Everyone in town seems to know him, and you'll enjoy his cheerful demeanor and insightful information.

HORSEBACK TOURS Contact **Banana Bank Lodge** (www.bananabank.com; ✆ 501/820-2020), located in Belmopan, about an hour's drive from the pier. It offers 7-hour tours through the jungle, plains, and riverbank. Larger-than-life cowboy/owner John Carr greets each of his guests personally and makes your riding experience a memorable one. The $90 cost includes a delicious traditional lunch and a tour of the lodge's grounds. A 2-hour tour costs $60. Well-trained horses are matched to each rider's ability.

FISHING EXCURSIONS Belize is a fishing mecca, with an abundance of game fish that guarantees excellent sport. The estuaries, inlets, and mouths to the many rivers are known for their tarpon, snook, and jacks; the lagoons and grass flats are known for bonefish, permit, and barracuda; the coral reefs support grouper, snapper, jacks, and barracuda; and the deeper waters offshore are home to sailfish, marlin, bonito, and pompano. One of the largest operations is the **Belize River Lodge** (www.belizeriverlodge.com; © **888/275-4843**), which offers a guided day-fishing package that includes lunch and drinks ($520 for up to two guests).

On Your Own: Within Walking Distance

Belize City is the hub of the country but is not home to its major attractions. The historic harbor district right around the pier is small and quaint. You'll find a few restaurants here, and the **Baron Bliss Park and Lighthouse** is just a short stroll away. After sailing from Portugal, Baron Bliss arrived sick with food poisoning and remained aboard his yacht for 2 months; local fisherman and administrators treated him kindly and taught him about Belize. He died soon after arriving, but not before changing his will and leaving $2 million to Belize in a trust fund. That money made possible the building of the Bliss Institute Library and Museum and a number of health clinics and markets around the country. The baron is considered Belize's greatest benefactor, and Baron Bliss Day, a national holiday, is celebrated on March 9.

Outside of the immediate port area, much of the city is run-down and poor, with narrow, crowded streets and many old colonial structures that are in need of repair. However, because tourism is an important industry in Belize, the country is making an effort to spruce up the city and reduce crime, instituting a squad of Tourism Police to patrol popular tourist areas. Officers are dressed in brown uniforms.

On Your Own: Beyond the Port Area

A 20-minute flight will get you to **Ambergris Caye,** the largest of Belize's 200 offshore islands. Everyone drives around in golf carts, and you can, too (for about $35 for an afternoon, from rental places located along the main streets and near the little airport). In San Pedro, the island's main town, the beach functions as the main street, offering plenty of shopping, restaurants, bars, and watersports. San Pedro still maintains a cozy feel, with about 4,000 year-round inhabitants, but has become a magnet due to the tourism industry. It offers some of the best fishing and diving facilities in all of Belize. The town itself is the stuff of which Caribbean postcards are born: bungalow resorts, coconut palms, and colorful houses lining streets made of sand.

Visitors typically come to Ambergris for the dizzying array of water activities offered: scuba diving, both local and chartered trips to the outer atolls, snorkeling, parasailing, and sailing, as well as snorkel tours. **Tanisha Tours** (www.tanishatours. com; © **501/226-2314**), one of the many snorkel tour outfits that line the beach, offers a wide range of daily tours ranging from $45 to $65, depending on the number of snorkel stops requested. They also offer Altun Ha Wildlife Tours ($105), a Cave Tubing and Zip Line Tour ($175), and manatee tours ($90 per person)—although your chances of spotting a bona fide manatee are about as slim as seeing a real mermaid, the allure of this mythical creature and the remote serenity of its habitat make the journey well worthwhile. Tours include lunch, beer, rum punch, and soft drinks. One favorite snorkeling destination is Shark Ray Alley, which is located at the Hol Chan Marine Preserve between Ambergris Caye and Caye Caulker. Historically, Shark Ray Alley began as a place where local fishermen cleaned their catch, thus attracting the sharks and rays that still sometimes congregate there. It can only be snorkeled, as the water is extremely shallow.

Slightly smaller **Caye Caulker** is Belize's second-most-popular cay and is even more laid-back than San Pedro, with plenty of beachfront restaurants and bars. Despite the growth of tourism, the island retains a small-village feel not found in areas with large-scale tourist development. Almost all of the businesses are locally owned, and you'll rarely see vehicles larger than golf carts on the streets. You can just hang out on the beach or plunge into one of the island's watersports, which include snorkeling, scuba, fishing, kayaking, windsurfing, sailing, and manatee-watching. Birding is also popular.

The Community Baboon Sanctuary, about 50km (30 miles) west of Belize City off the Northern Highway in the Belize District (www.howlermonkeys.org; © **501/ 220-2181**), offers a guided tour along forest trails for $7. Through a grass-roots effort, the villagers and landowners have committed to preserving the habitat necessary to ensure a healthy population of black howler monkeys (known locally as baboons). Your chance to connect with locals and see howler monkeys at close range will far offset the few mosquitoes or stray dogs you may also encounter. The sanctuary also offers river tours on the Belize Old River, where it's possible to see a myriad of tropical birds, including egrets, toucans, and parrots, as well as monkeys and iguanas idling on the riverside. The cost is $56 per couple.

Birders can also tour the **Crooked Tree Wildlife Sanctuary,** about 35 minutes from Belize City (www.belizeaudubon.org; © **501/223-5004**), which provides a habitat for more than 360 species of birds, including herons, ducks, kites, egrets, ospreys, kingfishers, and the jabiru stork—the largest flying bird in the Western Hemisphere. The sanctuary has an elevated walkway called "the Birdwalk," which is about 1km (½ mile) in length and passes through wetlands, giving visitors easy viewing access to indigenous plants and wildlife. Another worthwhile venture is a visit to the **Belize Zoo,** along the Western Highway (www.belizezoo.org; © **501/220- 8004**). First created as a haven for animals that were injured and couldn't be returned to the wild, the zoo now houses an impressive array of large cats, primates, reptiles, and birds in large, airy enclosures. Entrance fees are $15 for adults and $5 for children; the zoo offers 2-hour tours and is open from 8am to 5pm.

Shopping

In general, the best buys in Belize are wooden and slate carvings, Mayan calendars, pottery, ceramics, and Mennonite furniture. At the pier, the new **Belize Tourism Village** offers shops specializing in local souvenirs such as mahogany bowls, jewelry, clothes, assorted carvings, and artwork. A local favorite is Marie Sharp's hot sauces and jams. They're served everywhere and can be purchased to take home. On Ambergris Caye, you'll find a variety of slightly upscale gift shops, and the excursion sites all have local goods available.

Beaches

Compared to many other islands in the Caribbean, the beaches of Belize are neither the biggest nor the widest, but they are relaxing, with very clear water. Areas that offer the best sunbathing are in the cays, including **Ambergris Caye, Caye Caulker,** and **Tobacco Caye;** and on the mainland to the south, in **Dangriga** and **Placencia.** There are no beaches near Belize City.

Sports

WATERSPORTS   If you don't opt for one of your ship's dive excursions, local dive shops can customize an experience for you. Hugh Parkey's **Belize Dive Connection** (www.hpbelizeadventures.com; *C* **888/223-5403** or 501/223-4526) is conveniently located on the Radisson Pier and offers day scuba dives and snorkel trips with a yummy lunch. In San Pedro, **Aqua Dives** (www.aquascubabelize.com; *C* **800/641-2994** or 501/226-3415) is located on the beachfront and can plan your diving or snorkeling adventure. They cater to cruise passengers, offering return transportation in time for your ship's departure. A one-tank dive will run about $130; a two-tank reef dive is about $150.

In the center of Lighthouse Reef Atoll, about 80km (50 miles) due east of Belize City, the **Blue Hole** was originally a cave. The roof fell in some 10,000 years ago as the land receded into the sea, leaving an almost perfectly circular hole 300m (1,000 ft.) in diameter and about 120m (400 ft.) deep. Popularized by a Jacques Cousteau television special, it's become the most famous dive site in all of Belize.

Half Moon Caye, located at the southeast corner of Lighthouse Reef Atoll, was the first reserve to be established by the Natural Parks System Act of 1981, which specifically protected the red-footed booby bird and its rookery. Some 98 other species of birds have been recorded on the cay.

One of the newest national parks is **Laughing Bird Caye,** located 21km (13 miles) southeast of Placencia Village in the Stann Creek District. Although the cay was named for the large number of gulls that used to live here, the birds have virtually abandoned their rookery because of excessive human encroachment. Because Laughing Bird Caye is a shelf atoll with deep channels, the scuba diving and snorkeling opportunities are outstanding.

Many dive excursions include a barbecue lunch on **Goff's Caye.** Part of the Central Main Reef, it's a popular dive site itself.

Great Local Restaurants & Bars

The local beer is **Belikan,** and you can order it most anywhere. If you visit Altun Ha, you'll recognize the site as the beer's logo (or vice versa).

IN BELIZE CITY   Around the Belize Tourism Village, you'll find many pleasant restaurants within walking distance. Stroll to the Great House Hotel, 13 Cork St., to find the **Smokey Mermaid** (www.smokymermaid.com; *C* **501/223-4759**), situated in a lovely patio garden shaded by mango trees. One of its specialties is yucca-crusted snapper with a fruity salsa topping. Lobster is served year-round in such dishes as lobster Thermidor, a popular favorite. For dessert, be sure to try the coconut pie. The lunch special is $10.

At the **Stonegrill** at the **Radisson Hotel** (*C* **501/223-3333**), you can pick from several dining choices, either inside a spacious and deliciously cool dining room or out on a deck overlooking the Caribbean. A buffet lunch is about $25. A la carte meals are cooked at the table using superheated natural volcanic stones.

Dine on the water at the **Chateau Caribbean,** 6 Marine Parade (www.chateaucaribbean.com; *C* **501/223-0800**), an upscale restaurant that offers Caribbean and Asian specialties. Lunch runs approximately $26.

IN SAN PEDRO, AMBERGRIS CAYE   Most of the restaurants and bars here are on the beach, so you can just stroll along and stop at whatever place strikes your fancy.

For breakfast, seasoned travelers love **Estel's Dine by the Sea** (www.ambergris caye.com/estels; ☏ **501/226-2019**), a sandy-floored seafront restaurant with a dizzying array of breakfast options. Owners Charlie and Estella Worthington have been running this restaurant for many years, offering everything from huevos rancheros to breakfast burritos to fresh fish, tamales, *frijos,* and deliciously fresh juice. The average lunch price is $12.

Wild Mango's (☏ **501/226-2859**), on the beach, is a great option. Just north of the Sunbreeze Hotel, it is an award-winning restaurant that's considered one of the best in Belize. An entree will set you back $15 to $30. Main courses include treats such as bacon-wrapped shrimp grilled with a rum glaze and a traditional Mayan pork dish slow-cooked in banana leaves. Enjoy a beer on the outdoor covered wooden deck and drink in the ocean air. Heavenly! **Cannibal's Bar** (www.ambergriscaye.com/aiw/cannibal.html; ☏ **501/226-3706**), one of the many beach bars, boasts the motto "We'd love to have you for breakfast, lunch, or dinner!" Located on the beach just off Barrier Reef Drive and Black Coral Street, it has a great happy hour and attracts a good mix of tourists, expats, and locals.

ON CAYE CAULKER   Caye Caulker has about 25 restaurants, also mostly on the beach, offering Belizean and international cuisine, including fresh seafood. Lobster, conch, and red snapper are seasonal specialties.

Try the barracuda at **Wish Willy's** (www.wish-willy.com; ☏ **501/660-7194**), just off the main street of Caye Caulker. It's run by Maurice, from Chicago, who creates meals based on the fresh catch of the day as well as Belizean comfort food. Entrees range from about $10, and those in the know swear that it is one of the best.

Another popular restaurant is **The Sandbox,** which, true to its name, has no floor but is instead set right in the sand. Its ribs, burgers, pork chops, lobster bisque soup, and chili are all winners, and at $10 will not make much of a dent in a traveler's budget. It is highly recommended for breakfast as well. The Sandbox is on the corner of Front Street and the water taxi dock street.

FARTHER OUT   Heading west of Belize City, the very rustic **Cheers Bar & Restaurant** (www.cheersrestaurant.bz; ☏ **501/822-8014**) is kind of in the middle of nowhere, on the Western Highway at mile 31 (about 3km/2 miles from the Belize Zoo and 26km/16 miles from Banana Bank Lodge), but the food is good and it has a nice outdoor patio. Tamales, rice and beans, and daily specials are some of the offerings. Leave behind a memento T-shirt to say you were here—there are dozens of them from all over the world.

Still farther west, about 5km (3 miles) from Xunantunich, you'll find **Eva's Restaurant,** 22 Burns Ave., San Ignacio (☏ **501/804-2267**), where you can enjoy a simple but tasty lunch and check your e-mail as well. Eva's is centrally located on the main drag in San Ignacio and also offers a range of tours throughout Belize. Lunch will set you back $12.

BEQUIA

Only 18 sq. km (7 sq. miles), Bequia (meaning "Island of Clouds" in Carib, and pronounced *Beck*-way) is the largest and northernmost island in the St. Vincent and the Grenadines, only 14km (9 miles) south of St. Vincent. Sun-drenched, windswept, and peaceful, Bequia offers quiet lagoons, reefs, and long stretches of nearly deserted beaches. It's a popular stop for small-ship lines such as Clipper, ACCL, Star Clippers, and the more upscale Seabourn, SeaDream, and Windstar, which join the many yachts in Admiralty Bay throughout the yachting season. The main harbor village, **Port Elizabeth,** is known for its safe anchorage, Admiralty Bay. The bay was a haven in the 17th century for the British, French, and Spanish navies, as well as for pirates. Descendants of Captain Kydd (or Kidd) still live on the island. Today, the yachting set anchors here.

Very much a tourism-oriented island, Bequia is nevertheless anything but touristy. You'll find a few of the requisite cheesy gift shops in **Port Elizabeth,** but none of the typical cruise port giants such as Little Switzerland. Instead, the town offers one of the most attractive port settings in the Caribbean, with restaurants, cozy bars, a produce market, and crafts shops strung around the **Belmont Walkway,** a path that skirts so close to the calm bay waters that at high tide you have to skip across rocks to avoid getting your feet wet. Many ships spend the night here or make late departures, allowing passengers to take in the nightlife.

Obviously, the secluded beaches are at the top of everyone's list of Bequia's attractions. As you walk along the beaches, especially near Port Elizabeth, you'll see craftspeople building boats by hand, a method passed on by their ancestors. The friendly population of 6,000 locals is descended from seafarers and other early adventurers. The island has a rich seafaring tradition, including fishing, sailing, and boat building (though most of the handmade boats that you'll see are scale models made for the yachting set). Another tradition that remains is whaling, if only of a token, almost ritualistic sort—only about four whales are taken in any given year. Bequia was granted aboriginal rights from the International Whaling Commission to hunt a limited number of humpbacks per year. If a whale is caught, the entire island comes out to get their portion of the catch.

COMING ASHORE   Ships dock in the center of the main town, Port Elizabeth, a stone's throw from the restaurants, bars, and shops that line the waterfront.

LANGUAGE   The official and daily-use language is English.

CURRENCY   The **East Caribbean dollar** (EC$2.70 = US$1; EC$1 = US37¢) is used on Bequia; however, U.S. dollars are accepted by all businesses. It's always a good idea to ask which currency a price tag refers to. Prices quoted in this section are given in U.S. dollars.

There is a new 10% to 15% value-added tax on all restaurant, shops, and tour-operator services, so be sure to ask if the price quoted is before or after addition of the VAT.

INFORMATION   A small tourist-information booth is right on the beach by the cruise dock, but frankly, you can see almost everything there is to do from the same spot—it's a pretty small island. For information before you go, contact the **Bequia Tourist Association** (www.bequiatourism.com; ℂ 784/458-3286) or the **St. Vincent & the Grenadines Department of Tourism** (www.discoversvg.com; ℂ 800/729-1726 or 212/687-4981 in the U.S., or 784/457-1502).

CALLING FROM THE U.S.   To place a call to Bequia, you need only dial a "1" before the numbers listed in this section.

Getting Around

Ships dock in Port Elizabeth, putting you within walking distance of all the sights in town. The popular Princess Margaret Beach is within walking distance.

BY TAXI   You'll find plenty of taxis lined up right at the cruise dock to take you around the island. The fare is approximately $45 per hour, or $12 per person per hour.

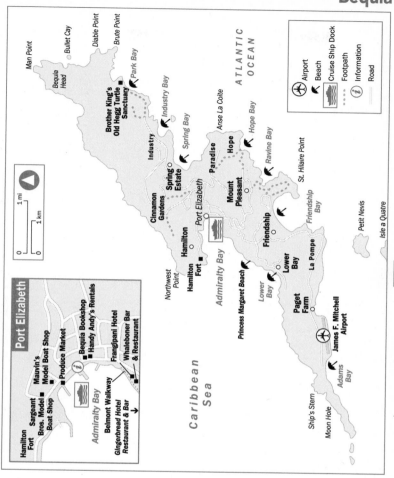

BY WATER TAXI Water taxis can be picked up at any of the jetties along the Belmont Walkway. These are perfect for destinations in Admiralty Bay (Princess Margaret or Lower Bay Beach, as well as various bars and restaurants) or for just cruising the harbor. The fixed rate for one to four persons is about $15 to any of the beaches; other rates are negotiable.

BY MINIBUS Bequia's Main Road between the wharf and the airport is served by a fleet of small, unofficial dollar-cab minibuses that cruise regular routes, picking up passengers when flagged down (some obvious bus stops are also scattered around). Tell the driver where you want to go and he'll tell you a price.

BY RENTAL CAR Rentals are available at **Handy Andy's Rentals,** on the Main Road in Port Elizabeth, to the right of the dock if you're facing inland

(© 784/458-3722). A Jeep Wrangler rents for $65 daily. **A&J Jeep Rentals** (© 784/458-3356; alvinsjeeps.bequia.net), has Suzuki Sidekicks (four doors) for approximately $60 per day.

BY BICYCLE **Handy Andy's Rentals** (see above) also rents Mongoose mountain bikes for $10.

Best Cruise Line Shore Excursions

Bequia is very much a "relax and have a drink" kind of island rather than one with a lot of definable, tourable attractions. Standard island tours ($90, 3 hr.) offer an overview and still allow you plenty of time to poke around or go to the beach. Most other excursions are sailing trips around the island and to neighboring Mustique and Tobago Cays, but I'd advise not missing Bequia—it's a lovely place.

Sailing Excursion to Mustique ($185, 7–8 hr. all-inclusive: breakfast, lunch, afternoon tea, snacks, snorkeling gear): Sail aboard a schooner to exclusive (that is, rich people own it) Mustique, just southeast of Bequia, for strolling, shopping, snorkeling, or simply lying on the beach. Complimentary drinks are included aboard ship. A shorter version of this tour travels between islands by powerboat rather than sailing ship—less romantic, but speedier ($109, 3–4 hr.).

On Your Own: Within Walking Distance

In theory, almost the entire island of Bequia is within walking distance, but only for serious walkers. I decided to test out this theory by walking from Port Elizabeth to **Hamilton Fort,** just west of town, then backtracking through the port and down to the tiny old whaling village of **Paget Farm,** near the airport on Bequia's southern tip. As the crow flies it's not much of a distance, but curving roads and hilly terrain made it a real journey that took about 4 to 5 hours round-trip, with no significant stops. If your ship is in port late and you're in good shape, it's a great way to see the island (including lovely **Friendship Bay,** on the east coast) and meet some of the local people along the way. Bring water.

For those wanting something less strenuous, strolling around Port Elizabeth itself is close to idyllic. The **Belmont Walkway** runs south from the docks right at the water's edge, fronting many restaurants, shops, and bars. This area is particularly romantic in the evenings.

Heading north from the docks along the Main Road, you'll find a homey produce market that also stocks some souvenir items. Across the street, **Mauvin's Model Boat Shop** (© 784/458-3669) is one of the visible reminders of the island's boat-building tradition, though now the money seems to lie in crafting scale models of real boats for sale to the yachting crowd. Farther along the Main Road, **Sargeant Bros. Model Boat Shop** (© 784/458-3344) is a larger shop offering the same type of merchandise. The workshop is a little more accessible here, so you can easily watch the craftsmen creating their wares (all the work is done by hand) and see models in various stages of construction. At both shops, the models are lovingly constructed and signed by the craftsman—but they're not what you'd call cheap: Prices start around $110 for a tiny model and can go up as high as $10,000 for something really fabulous. Farther along the Hamilton Main Road, in the section known as Ocar, Lawson Sargeant, descendant of one of the great schooner-building families, has opened the **Bequia Maritime Museum** (© 784/458-3896). Hours are Monday through Friday from 9:30am to 5pm, Saturday from 9:30am to 2pm, and by appointment. Admission is $5.

Use Your Ship's Facilities
Because Bequia is an extremely dry island and is very conscious of water conservation, it has no public washrooms except in restaurants. You'd be well advised to use your ship's bathroom facilities before coming ashore.

If you continue walking along the Main Road, you'll come upon a concrete walkway hanging above the water along the coast. From here, the going gets rough—many sections of the walkway have been cracked and heaved drastically off-kilter by hurricanes, and it's patched here and there with planks and other makeshift materials. At the end of the walkway, the road starts curving uphill and inland through a quiet residential area, and all the way up to **Hamilton Fort,** perched above Admiralty Bay and offering a lovely view of Port Elizabeth, though that's about all it offers—a few tiny fragments of battlements and five plugged cannons are all that remain. A taxi can take you here by another route (a good idea unless you're in decent shape and very sure-footed).

On Your Own: Beyond the Port Area

At Park Beach, on the island's northeast coast, 3km (2 miles) east of Port Elizabeth, **Brother King's Old Hegg Turtle Sanctuary** (www.turtles.bequia.net; © 784/458-3245) offers a chance to see conservation in action. Founded in 1995 by the eponymous King and dedicated to raising and releasing hawksbill turtle hatchlings, the sanctuary is a real labor of love. A main concrete swimming pool and small plastic kiddie pools allow maturing hatchlings to socialize. Orton "Brother" King and his assistants are on hand to tell you about their conservation efforts. The sanctuary is open Sunday through Friday from 10am to 5pm; it charges $5 to help keep the place going.

For touring and hiking, **Mount Pleasant** is the highest accessible point in Bequia and offers sweeping views—first over Admiralty Bay as the road winds upward, and then from the summit, down over the southern Grenadines. A reconstructed plantation house offers a glimpse into the past, with a display of petroglyph rubbings from St. Vincent that are said to be over 5,000 years old. Also, just west of Friendship Bay is a peak that locals sometimes call "the Mountain." This nearly 275m (900-ft.) hill offers an invigorating hike with a rewarding view of St. Vincent to the north, and the Grenadines to the south.

Shopping

Heading south from the pier, one of the first businesses you'll come to is the **Bequia Bookshop** (© 784/458-3905), selling books on the island's and region's culture and history, poetry, and prose by local authors, yachting guides, and a selection of other fiction and nonfiction titles, as well as truly beautiful scrimshaw pocketknives, pendants, money clips, necklaces, and pins, all made from polished domesticated camel bone rather than the traditional whalebone.

Island Things (© 784/458-3903), housed in the little gingerbread cottage next to St. Mary's church, carries a delightful selection of accessories for the home—art, woodcarvings, unusual gifts and souvenirs, and books from and about the Caribbean.

Heading in the other direction in Port Elizabeth, north from the docks, you'll find the two model-boat shops described in "On Your Own: Within Walking Distance"

5

THE PORTS OF CALL

Bequia

above, as well as a couple of open-air souvenir/crafts stalls, a produce market, and **Kennie's Music Shop** for island sounds on CD.

Not to be missed is **Spring Studios Pottery and Art Gallery** (☎ 784/457-3757), built among the ruins of the old Spring sugar estate, where it offers decorative and functional pottery items created on-site, as well as a permanent display of paintings by local and visiting artists. Spring Studios is open November through April.

Also of note is **Claude-Victorine's Atelier** (☎ 784/458-3150), located up the hill from the far end of Lower Bay Beach. It's a working studio with magnificent hand-painted silks, cushion covers, pareus, and wall hangings. **Noah's Arkade** (☎ 784/458-3424) in Belmont is a treasure-trove of locally made arts and crafts, including paintings, stained glass, hand-painted clothing, mixed media works, pottery, local spices, jams, jellies, salsas, hammocks, bags, and more. There is a weekly "meet the artist" event during certain seasons.

The **BoatHouse** is an offbeat art gallery with real island atmosphere—where Kingsley "Prop" King crafts model boats from coconut shells, and L. D. Lucy paints mystical views of island life. It is located south of Friendship, toward the airport.

Beaches

Beaches are one of the big draws on Bequia, and all are open to the public. The best on the list is **Princess Margaret Beach,** a golden-sand stretch lying just south of Port Elizabeth. To get here, take the Belmont Walkway to its end at Plantation House; from there, take the dirt path over the hill. **Lower Bay Beach** is a little farther down along the same stretch of coast.

On the northeast coast, the beach at **Industry Bay** is, despite its name, windswept and gorgeous, a scene straight out of a romance novel. Trees on the hills surrounding the bay grow up to a certain height and then level out, growing sideways due to the constant wind off the Atlantic. The seven-room **Dawn's Creole Garden Hotel** (☎ 784/458-3400) lies along this stretch. Stop in to sample Dawn's famous fish cakes and a rum punch at the **Beach Bar.**

Along the southeast coast, you might check out the uncrowded, pristine white sands at **Friendship Bay,** an area that draws many European visitors, where you can rent watersports equipment or order a drink from the bar at the hotel.

Warning: Do not under any circumstances pick or eat the small green apples you'll see growing in some spots; these are extremely poisonous.

Sports

Besides walking (see "On Your Own: Within Walking Distance," above) and biking (mountain bikes are available from Handy Andy's Rentals, right by the cruise dock), hiking the more inaccessible parts of the island can be interesting and rewarding. Some trails are marked, and special nature walks can be arranged through **Martine & Francois** (☎ 784/457-3898), specialists in dry tropical ecosystems, flora, and fauna. The company can arrange tours and hikes of all kinds, depending on tourists' specific requests, whether they be nature oriented, historical, or both.

Most of the sports here, like the rest of life on the island, center on the water. Bequia is wonderful for snorkeling and diving, as well as windsurfing, due to trade winds that provide almost year-round breezes. Kayaking is also popular in the calm beach shallows on the leeward side. Kayaks, dinghies, Hobie Cats/Lasers, and windsurfers are all available to rent along Admiralty Bay.

Dive Bequia (www.divebequia.com; ☎ 784/458-3504) and **Bequia Dive Adventures** (www.bequiadiveadventures.com; ☎ 784/458-3826), located along

Belmont Walkway right by the docks, specialize in diving and snorkeling on the lush reefs of Bequia, where you might spot manta rays. Scuba dives cost $70 for one tank, $106 for two tanks. Snorkeling trips are $20 per person, and these prices include all the necessary equipment.

Great Local Restaurants & Bars

The coastal stretch along the Belmont Walkway is chockablock with restaurants and bars. The local beer of St. Vincent and the Grenadines is **Hairoun,** which is decent but not up to the level of St. Lucia's Piton. The local rum is **Sunset.**

The **Frangipani Hotel Restaurant & Bar** (www.frangipanibequia.com; **✆ 784/458-3255**) is right on the water along the walkway. Lunch, which is served from 10am to 5pm, includes sandwiches, salads, and seafood platters. Specialties include conch chowder, baked chicken with rice-and-coconut stuffing, and an array of fresh fish. On Thursday nights, the bar hosts an excellent steel band. It's a lovely scene, with yachters, locals, cruisers from ships that have stayed late in port, and a coterie of friendly local dogs. Lunch is about $15.

Farther along the walkway, the **Whaleboner Bar & Restaurant** (**✆ 784/458-3233**) serves a nice thin-crust pizza (with toppings such as lobster, shrimp, and generic "fish"), sandwiches, fish and chips, and cold beer, either indoors or at tables in its shaded, oceanview front yard. It's a perfect casual resting-up spot after walking around the island. Lunch is about $15.

Also right along the waterfront is the **Gingerbread Hotel Restaurant & Bar** (www.gingerbreadhotel.com; **✆ 784/458-3800**), with a beautiful balcony dining room that's open throughout the day, plus a downstairs cafe that serves coffee, tea, and Italian ice cream at outdoor tables. Lunch is about $14.

Continue along the walkway for **Mac's Pizzeria** (**✆ 784/458-3474**), famous for its lobster pizzas and specialty baked goods such as breads, cakes, cookies, and the best cheesecake imaginable. Lunch is about $19.

BONAIRE

Ever wonder what's going on under all that water you've been cruising on for days? There's no better place to find out than the island of Bonaire: "Divers Paradise," as the slogan on the island's license plates says. Avid divers have flocked to this unspoiled treasure for years for its pristine waters, stunning coral reefs (which encircle the island just feet from shore), and vibrant marine life—it's simply one of the best places in the Caribbean for diving and snorkeling.

The island also offers other adventure activities such as mountain biking, kayaking, and windsurfing; if these options sound too strenuous, why not just marvel at the iguanas, fluorescent lora parrots, wild donkeys, graceful flamingos, and feral goats? As for flora, you're likely to see more cactuses in Bonaire than anywhere outside of the deserts of Mexico and the Southwest United States. Sprawling bushes of exotic succulents and permanently wind-swept divi-divi trees also abound. If you'd rather join the iguanas and just bake in the sun, Bonaire's beaches are intimate and uncrowded. In fact, the entire island is cozy and manageable. In no time at all, you'll feel it's your very own private resort.

Unspoiled Bonaire is only gently touched by development, and Bonaireans zealously protect their precious environment. Even though they eagerly seek tourism, they aren't interested in creating another Aruba, with its high-rise hotel blocks.

Spearfishing isn't allowed in its waters, nor is the taking or destruction of any coral or other living animal from the sea. Unlike some islands, Bonaire isn't just surrounded by coral reefs—it *is* the reef, sitting on the dry, sunny top of an underwater mountain.

Relying on your high-school language lessons, you might think Bonaire was colonized by the French and named for its "good air," but you'd be wrong: The name actually comes from the Caiquetio word *bonay*, which means "low country." Located 80km (50 miles) north of Venezuela and 50km (30 miles) east of Curaçao, this untrampled, boomerang-shaped refuge is one of the southernmost Caribbean islands, and forms the B in the ABC chain, along with Aruba and Curaçao. Thirty-nine kilometers (24 miles) long and 5 to 11km (3–7 miles) wide at various points, it's large enough to require a motorized vehicle if you want to explore, but small enough that you won't get lost.

The Caiquetios, members of the Arawak tribe who sailed from the coast of Venezuela a thousand years ago, were Bonaire's first inhabitants. Europeans arrived 500 years later, in 1499, when Alonso de Ojeda and Amerigo Vespucci claimed the island for Spain. The Dutch gained control in the 1630s; and, on the backs of African slave laborers, Bonaire became an important salt producer.

With the discovery of oil in Venezuela early in the 20th century, Aruba and Curaçao became refining centers, and Bonaire, too, got a piece of the pie. Tourism, the island's major industry today, developed after World War II, when Bonaire won self-rule from the Netherlands (though it remains a Dutch protectorate). The people of Bonaire are a mix of African, Dutch, and South American ancestries.

COMING ASHORE   Cruise ships dock in the port of **Kralendijk** (*Crawl*-en-dike), the island's tiny capital, commercial center, and largest town (pop. about 2,500). The dock leads to **Wilhelmina Park,** a pleasant public space named after a former Dutch queen. **Queen Beatrix Way,** the brick-paved path along the waterfront, is lined with open-air restaurants and bars. Most of the town's shopping is a block inland on **Kaya Grandi.**

Your best bet for making long-distance phone calls is **Telbo** (✆ 599/717-7000), the central phone company office, located at Kaya Libertador Simón Bolívar 8. It's open Monday through Friday until 4pm, but closed from 11:45am to 1:30pm for lunch.

LANGUAGE   Almost everyone in Bonaire speaks English, which, along with Dutch, is a required course in the local schools. The local patois and language of the street is Papiamento, a rich blend of Dutch, Spanish, Portuguese, French, English, Caribbean Indian, and several African languages. Given the island's proximity to Venezuela, you're likely to hear Spanish as well.

CURRENCY   Bonaire's official currency is the **Antillian florin,** also called the **guilder** (1.79 ANG = US$1; 1 ANG = US56¢). Don't waste your time exchanging money, though, as the U.S. dollar is as widely accepted as the local currency. Change may be a mixture of dollars and guilders. If you need cash, several ATMs are located along Kaya Grandi. Traveler's checks and credit cards are also widely accepted. Prices quoted in this section are in U.S. dollars.

INFORMATION   The **Tourism Corporation Bonaire** is located at Kaya Grandi 2, in Kralendijk (www.tourismbonaire.com; ✆ 800/266-2473 in the U.S., or 599/717-8322; fax 599/717-8408).

CALLING FROM THE U.S.   When calling Bonaire from the United States, dial the international access code (011) before the numbers listed in this section.

Map labels:

Boca Cocolishi

Mt. Brandaris

Playa Funchi

Playa Chikitu

WASHINGTON-SLAGBAAI NATIONAL PARK

Park Entrance

Boca Slagbaai

Onima

Nukove Beach

Goto Meer

Caribbean Sea

Rincón

Karpata

Santa Barbara

Spelonk

1,000 Steps Beach

Seroe Largu

Barcadera

Lagoen

No Name Beach

KLEIN BONAIRE

Kralendijk

Nikiboko

Donkey Sanctuary

Flamingo Airport

Punt Vierkant

Lac Bay

Boca Cai

Lac Bay Beach

Sorobon Beach

Salt Flats

Flamingo Sanctuary

Pekel Meer

Willemstoren Lighthouse

0   5 mi
0   5 km

Legend:
- ✈ Airport
- ⚓ Beach
- ⛵ Boating
- Lighthouse
- ▲ Mountain

Getting Around

BY TAXI Taxis greet cruise ship passengers at the pier. Although the cabs are unmetered, the government establishes rates, and drivers should produce a price list upon request. Most cabs can be hired for a tour of the island, with as many as four passengers allowed to go along for the ride. Negotiate a price before leaving, but expect to pay about $25 per person for 2 hours. You can get more information by calling the **Taxi Central Dispatch** office at ✆ **599/717-8100.**

BY RENTAL CAR Highway signs are in Dutch and sometimes English, with easy-to-understand international symbols. Driving is on the right, the same as in the States and most of Europe. A valid driver's license is acceptable for renting and driving a car.

Hop on a Mountain Bike

If you're looking for an active way to explore Bonaire, bike along the coast on a road bordered with cactus and carved-through lava and limestone. The road north from the island's capital and main town, Kralendijk, is relatively flat and passes several uncrowded beaches that are perfect for cooling off.

Avis, Budget, Hertz, and **National** all have offices here, as do a number of local companies.

BY SCOOTER, MOPED, OR MOTORCYCLE If you plan to stick close to the port area, scooters and mopeds are options. They can be rented from **Rento Fun Drive,** Kaya Grandi 4C (www.rentofun.com; ✆ **599/717-2408**), or Bonaire Motorcycle Shop, Kaya Grandi 52 (✆ **599/717-7790**). Mopeds are about $30 a day; two-seat scooters run about $32. A motorcycle (with a valid motorcycle license) will cost you about $58 per day.

BY BICYCLE For getting around town or exploring the nearby coast, try bicycling. Note that the coastal terrain is essentially flat, but the sun can be brutal even before noon. Plan your excursion as early in the day as possible. The best deals are at **Outdoor Bonaire** (www.outdoorbonaire.com; ✆ **599/791-6272** or 599/785-6272), where you can explore some of the interior on a mountain bike tour for $40 per person. **Rento Fun Drive,** Kaya Grandi 47 (✆ **599/717-2408**), rents beach cruisers and hybrids for about $15 per day.

Best Cruise Line Shore Excursions

One-Tank Scuba Excursion for Certified Divers ($129, 3½–4 hr.) or **Discover Scuba for Uncertified Divers** ($134, 3 hr.): Dive in the Bonaire National Marine Park; it's the perfect place for beginners and experts alike.

Sail & Snorkel ($65–$75, 3 hr.): The snorkeling here is some of the best you'll find in the Caribbean, and this tour takes you to the famed Bonaire National Marine Park. Ships range from catamarans to a replica junk.

North Tour & Donkey Sanctuary ($49, 3 hr.): This bus tour explores northern coastal Bonaire, visiting the flamingos at Goto Lake, the island's oldest settlement at Rincón, and the Donkey Sanctuary. If you've got a thing for donkeys, this is the tour for you.

Water Taxi to Klein Bonaire ($35, 3 hr.): Take a 30-minute boat ride to a deserted tropical island for a serene day on the beach. Pack a snack and plenty of sunscreen; there are no facilities and little shade, but beverages are provided.

On Your Own: Within Walking Distance

You can walk the length of **Kralendijk** in an hour or less. It's a sleepy town, but its residents like it that way, thank you. The **tourist office,** at Kaya Grandi 2, has walking-tour maps, but because Bonaire has always been off the beaten track, Kralendijk's highlights are modest and few. You'll probably want to stroll along the seafront with its views and restaurants, and along **Kaya Grandi,** the island's major shopping district. Just south of the town dock is **Fort Oranje,** a small fortress that has a cannon dating from the time of Napoléon, and a few artifacts excavated by local students. The town has some charming Dutch Caribbean architecture—gabled roofs you might see in Amsterdam, but painted in cheerful Caribbean colors, especially sunny ocher and terra cotta. If your ship arrives early enough, you can visit the tiny waterfront produce market.

On Your Own: Beyond the Port Area

As a day visitor, you'll probably choose to explore either the northern or southern part of the island. The coastal road north of Kralendijk is one of the most beautiful in the Antilles. Turquoise, azure, and cobalt waters stretch to the horizon on your left, while pink-coral and gray-limestone cliffs loom on your right. Towering cactuses, intimate coastal coves, strange rock formations, and panoramic vistas add to the beauty. The north also boasts Washington-Slagbaai National Park, an impressive, 5,400-hectare (13,350-acre) preserve that occupies the northwestern portion of the island, as well as Rincón, Bonaire's oldest settlement. **Bonaire Tours and Vacations** (www. bonairetours.com; © **599/717-8778**) will show you the island, both north and south, taking in the flamingos, slave huts, conch shells, Goto Lake, the Amerindian inscriptions, and other sights. You can take a half-day "Island Journey Tour," lasting 3 hours and costing from $28 per person, which allows you to see the entire northern section and the southern part as far as the slave huts.

NORTH OF KRALENDIJK   Soon after leaving Kralendijk, you'll find **Barcadera,** on the coast road across from the Bonaire Caribbean Club. This old cave was once used to trap goats. Take the stone steps down to the cave and examine the stalactites.

Just past the Radio Nederland towers, **1,000 Steps Beach** and dive site offers lovely views: picturesque coves, craggy coastline, and tropical waters of changing hues. There are actually only 67 steps; it just feels like a thousand if you're schlepping dive gear.

At the Kaya Karpata intersection, you'll see a mustard-colored building on your right. It's what's left of the aloe-processing facilities of **Landhuis Karpata,** a 100-year-old former plantation. The modest exhibits here explain the cultivation, harvesting, and processing of aloe, once a major export crop.

About 30 or 40 minutes after turning right on Kaya Karpata, you'll arrive in **Rincón,** the original Spanish settlement on the island, founded in 1527. The town eventually became the home of African slaves who worked the island's plantations. Nestled in a valley away from either coast, Rincón was hidden from marauding pirates, who plagued the Caribbean for decades. This picturesque village is home to Bonaire's oldest church, a handsome ocher-and-white structure.

The pride of Bonaire, located on the island's northern tip, **Washington-Slagbaai National Park** (www.washingtonparkbonaire.org; © **599/788-9015**) was one of the Caribbean's first national parks. Formerly two separate plantations that produced aloe and charcoal and raised goats, the park boasts more than 190 species of birds; thousands of kadushi, yatu, and prickly pear cactus; and herds of wild goats, foraging donkeys, flocks of flamingos, and what seems like billions of lizards. The scenery includes stark, desertlike hills; quiet beaches; secluded caverns; and wave-battered cliffs. You have two options: the shorter 24km (15-mile) route around the park, marked with green arrows, or the longer 35km (22-mile) track, marked with yellow arrows. You'll have plenty of opportunities to hike, swim, or snorkel either way. The unpaved roads are well marked and safe, but rugged; jeeps trump small cars. Mountain bikes are allowed in the park, but motorcycles and scooters are not, and must be left at headquarters while you hike the nearby trails. Admission is $10 for adults and

$5 for children 11 and younger; the park is open daily from 8am to 5pm except for major holidays, with the last entry at 2pm. Guide booklets and maps are available at the gate, where there's also a small museum and visitor center.

On your way back to Kralendijk, take the Kaminda Onima, which traces the island's northeastern coast to **Onima,** the site of 500-year-old Caiquetio Indian inscriptions. Some of the red-and-brown drawings depict turtles and rain; others appear to have religious significance. You'll be able to recognize snakes, human hands, and the sun among the roughly 75 inscriptions.

Before returning to Kralendijk, call on **Sherman Gibbs.** You'll find his monument to the beauty of common objects on Kaminda Tras di Montaña, the road leading back to Kralendijk. Sherman, who's as gentle as his pet iguanas, combines old detergent bottles, boat motors, buoys, car seats, and just about anything else to create a wondrously happy sanctuary. The wind and old fan blades power his TV.

SOUTH OF KRALENDIJK Just minutes south of town, dazzlingly bright salt pyramids dominate the horizon. These hills, looking more like alpine snowdrifts than sodium mounds, are created when seawater is forced into lakes by the tide and then evaporates, leaving crystallized salt behind. Farther from the road, abandoned salt-works serve as a **flamingo sanctuary.** Bonaire is one of the world's few nesting places for pink flamingos, a species that, until recently, was threatened with extinction. Thanks to the reserve, the island's flamingo population now swells to roughly 10,000 during breeding season, rivaling the island's human population of 13,000. The sanctuary is completely off limits to the public because the birds are extremely wary of humans and disturbances of any kind. But even from the road, you can spot a pink haze on the horizon, and with binoculars, you can see the graceful birds feeding in the briny pink-and-purple waters.

At the island's southern tip, restored **slave huts** stand as monuments to the inhumanity of the island's slave era. Each hut, no bigger than a large doghouse, provided crude shelter for slaves brought from Africa by the Dutch West India Company to cut dyewood, cultivate maize, and harvest salt. On Friday afternoons, the slaves trekked 7 hours in the oppressive heat to their homes and families in Rincón for the weekend, returning to the salt pans on Sunday evenings.

Located on the eastern side of the island's southern tip, the classically picturesque **Willemstoren Lighthouse,** Bonaire's first, was built in 1837. It's fully automated today and usually closed to visitors, but its magnificent setting is the real draw. Odd little bundles of driftwood, bleached coral, and rocks in the area look like something out of *The Blair Witch Project,* but they were actually constructed by fishermen to mark where boats have been left.

A few minutes up the east coast is **Lac Bay,** a lagoon that's as tranquil as the nearby windward sea is furious. The calm waters and steady breezes make the area ideal for windsurfing, and various fish come here to hatch their young. Deep inside the lagoon, mangrove trees with *Edward Scissorhands*–like roots lunge out of the water. If it weren't for the relentlessly cheerful sun, they might seem sinister. Donkeys, goats, and flamingos pepper the countryside along the way.

Just south of town, next to the airport and down a dirt road, the **Donkey Sanctuary** ★ (www.bonairenature.com/donkey; ✆ **599/9-560-7607**) provides a safe haven for many of the island's 300 to 400 wild donkeys that previously roamed the entire island and fell victim to car accidents with increasing frequency. The sanctuary is located down a bumpy dirt road just off the coastal road, south of the airport in Kralendijk. The park is open daily from 10am to 5pm. Drive-through closes at 4pm.

Entrance is $7 for adults and $3.50 for children, but additional donations are welcomed.

Shopping

You'll find most shops on **Kaya Grandi** on the adjacent streets and in small malls. But don't expect to be caught up in a duty-free frenzy in Bonaire. You'll be able to hit every store in Kralendijk before lunch, and you'll probably find greater selections and better prices at other ports. The island is a great place to buy certain items, though. Consider top-of-the-line dive watches and underwater cameras. Or how about jewelry with marine themes?

For an impressive array of unique gifts and hand-finished jewelry with a marine theme (the diamond-and-sapphire seahorse set in white gold was my favorite), check out **Jewel of Bonaire,** Kaya Grandi 38 (℗ 599/717-8890). There's also a nice selection of jewelry and hand-blown glass plates at **Atlantis** (℗ 599/717-7730).

For TAG Heuer dive watches, Cuban cigars, and Lladró porcelain, try **Littman Jewelers,** Kaya Grandi 33 (℗ 599/717-8160), which also owns the eclectic crafts shop and art gallery across the arcade called **Anything Artistique.** A third shop in the centrally located **Harborside Mall** has silk neckties, Nautica menswear, blue Delft porcelain, and an array of Cuban cigars in a climate-controlled cigar room (with the likes of Montecristos, Punch, Romeo & Julietas, and Cohibas). **Perfume Palace,** in the same mall, carries perfume and other cosmetics, including Lancôme, Estée Lauder, Chanel, Calvin Klein, and Ralph Lauren.

Benetton (℗ **599/717-5107**), Kaya Grandi 49, has smart casual wear at discounts of 20% to 30%. If batik shirts, bathing suits, or souvenir T-shirts are what you want, try **Best Buddies,** Kaya Grandi 32.

Beaches

Bonaire's beaches are narrow and full of coral, but they're clean, intimate, and uncrowded. Swimming on the tranquil, leeward coast is never a problem, but the east coast is rough and dangerous.

South of Kralendijk, **Pink Beach** was Bonaire's best strand before Hurricane Lenny washed away most of its lovely sand. The beach really is a deep pink color, from the corals that have been pulverized into sand by the waves. Bring your own cooler and towels, as there are no refreshment stands or equipment rentals to mar the panoramic setting. Enter the water at the southern end of this beach, as the northern tier has some exposed rock.

Now white-sand **Sorobon Beach,** near **Lac Bay,** is the island's best. The shallow water is especially popular with families; trees provide shade. The two windsurf concessions nearby mean that you have to contend with a bit of traffic, but they make for good entertainment, especially from a perch at one of the two beachside bars/snack shops. This is also next to the island's only nude beach, **Sorobon Beach Resort** (℗ **599/717-8080;** sorobonbeachresort.com); as a nonguest, you'll pay $15 for the privilege of disrobing, if you want to make your way past the discreet wooden fence that extends into the water and blocks the view.

North of Kralendijk, **Nukove Beach** is a small white-sand cove carved out of a limestone cliff. A narrow sand channel cuts through an otherwise impenetrable wall of elkhorn coral, giving divers and snorkelers access to the sea. Farther north is **1,000 Steps Beach,** where 67 steps (although it can feel like 1,000 on the way back up) carved out of the limestone cliff lead to the white-sand beach. This beach offers good snorkeling and diving, a unique location and view, and nearly perfect solitude.

Washington-Slagbaai National Park has a number of beaches. **Boca Slagbaai,** once a plantation harbor, draws divers, snorkelers, and picnickers. Be careful venturing into the water barefoot, though: The coral bottom can be sharp. On one side of **Playa Funchi,** flamingos nest in the lagoon; on the other, there's excellent snorkeling. The island's northernmost beach, **Boca Cocolishi,** is a perfect spot to picnic. The calm, shallow basin is good for snorkeling, but stay very close to shore. Algae make the water purplish, and the sand, formed by coral and mollusk shells, is black. At **Playa Chikitu,** the water is too treacherous for swimming, but the cove is secluded, and the sand dunes and crashing waves are beautiful.

Klein Bonaire, the small, uninhabited island about 1km (½ mile) west of Kralendijk, boasts **No Name Beach,** which features a 270m (890-ft.) white-sand strip. Parrotfish and yellowtail snappers patrol the finger, brain, and mustard hill corals, attracting snorkelers and divers. There are no facilities or shade on Klein Bonaire. A water taxi from the town pier will cost $18 round-trip.

Sports

HIKING　**Washington Slagbaai National Park** has a varied terrain; those ambitious enough to climb some of its steep hills are rewarded with panoramic views. The hiking possibilities are seemingly endless. Small hidden beaches with crashing waters by the cliffs provide ideal spots for picnics. **Outdoor Bonaire** (www.outdoorbonaire. com; ✆ 599/791-6272) can arrange hiking and climbing in the National Park.

KAYAKING　For a peaceful, relaxing time, kayak through the mangroves in Lac Bay. Proceed at your own pace in the calm waters, but take time to observe the hundreds of baby fish and the bizarre tree roots. Bring protection from the sun and the ravenous mosquitoes. Divers and snorkelers can tow a lightweight sea kayak behind them as they explore the waters of the leeward coast.

Kayak rentals and guided trips through the mangroves are available from **Bonaire Dive & Adventure,** at the southern end of Sand Dollar Condominium Resort, Kaya Gobernador N. Debrot 77A (www.bonairediveandadventure.com; ✆ 599/717-2229), and from **Jibe City,** in Sorobon (www.jibecity.com; ✆ 599/717-5233). Half-day kayak rentals cost $30 for one person and $40 for two.

The **Mangrove Info & Kayak Center,** on Kaminda Lac, the road to Lac Bay Cai (www.mangrovecenter.com; ✆ 599/790-5353), provides ecological information about the mangrove forest in addition to offering guided mangrove tours that include an option to snorkel. Prices are $27 for 1 hour and $47 for 2 hours; drinking water and snorkel gear are provided.

KITEBOARDING　This relatively extreme sport combines windsurfing with kite flying and allows boarders to sail, leap, and flip along the water's surface. On Atlantis beach, at the southern end of the island, **Kiteboarding Bonaire** (www.kiteboarding bonaire.com; ✆ 599/701-5483) helps beginners get started with 3-hour intro lessons for $225 for a private lesson, or $300 for two people. Those who've already taken an intro course and received certification are allowed to rent equipment for $100 a day and go it alone.

LANDSAILING　With less than 5 minutes of instruction and even less experience, you can be cruising at top speed around the largest landsailing track in the world. This fun sport requires little knowledge of sailing and just a rudimentary understanding of physics. Let the natural trade winds speed you along a 2,000m (6,600-ft.) figure eight. **Sun Rentals Bonaire** (www.sunrentalsbonaire.com/land-sailing-on-bonaire.html;

𝒞 866/464-1786 or 599/786-6130) offers a 1-hour rental plus a 15-minute lesson at a cost of $50, or $30 for a half-hour.

MOUNTAIN BIKING Bonaire has miles of roads, paved and unpaved, flat and hilly. The truly athletic can even follow goat paths. Take water, a map, and plenty of sunscreen. If you choose to wear a helmet (which you should), bring a baseball cap to wear underneath; it will help protect you from the sun and serve as a nice barrier between your noggin and all the noggins that wore the helmet before you. **Bonaire Dive & Adventure** (see above) conducts guided bike tours through the *kunuku* (outback) and Washington Slagbaai National Park for $65 per person.

SCUBA DIVING Much of Bonaire's allure is based on its teeming offshore reefs and dive sites. Its true beauty is under the sea, where visibility is 30m (100 ft.) and the water temperatures range from 78°F to 82°F (26°C–28°C). One of the richest reef communities in the entire West Indies, Bonaire has plunging walls that descend to a sand bottom at 40m (130 ft.) or so. Most of the diving is done on the leeward side, where the ocean is lake-flat. Bonaire has more than 80 marked dive sites and a rich marine ecosystem that includes brain, elkhorn, staghorn, mountainous star, and gorgonian coral; anemones, sea cucumbers, and sea sponges; parrotfish, surgeonfish, angelfish, grouper, blennies, frogfish, and yellowtails; and morays and sea snakes.

Bonaire Marine Park ★★ was created to protect the coral-reef ecosystem off Bonaire. The park incorporates the entire coastline of Bonaire and neighboring **Klein Bonaire.** The park is policed, and services and facilities include a visitor information center at the **Karpata Ecological Center,** lectures, slide presentations, films, and permanent dive-site moorings.

Visitors are asked to respect the marine environment and to refrain from activities that may damage it, including sitting or walking on the coral. Even a thin layer of silt can prove fatal to these delicate marine animals that make up the fragile living surface of the coral formations. Because these ecosystems are so easily destroyed, all marine life in and around Bonaire is completely protected. This means there's no fishing or collecting fish, shells, or corals—dead or alive. Spearfishing is forbidden, as is anchoring; all craft must use permanent moorings, except for emergency stops. (Boats shorter than 13 ft. may use a stone anchor.) Most recreational activity in the marine park takes place on the island's leeward side and among the reefs surrounding Klein Bonaire, a tiny island off Bonaire's coast.

Because protecting nature is taken seriously, all divers, snorkelers, windsurfers, and swimmers are required to pay a **nature fee** of $10 to $25 (this fee is included in shore-excursion rates). Tags are good for 1 calendar year and also permit admission into Washington Slagbaai National Park. A 1-day pass can also be purchased for $10 for divers and $2 for nondivers. Nondivers 11 and younger and Netherlands residents are exempt. Tags can be purchased at all dive shops as well as the tourism office at Kaya Grandi 2. An orientation dive is required for all divers. For more information, contact **STINAPA Bonaire** (www.stinapa.org; 𝒞 599/717-8444).

Dive shops are numerous, and highly professional **Bonaire East Coast Diving** (www.bonaireeastcoastdiving.com; 𝒞 599/717-5211) offers an afternoon one-tank dive for $65 where you will visit the white hole (also called the blue hole), which is one of the most popular shore-dive sites and a great place to spot tarpon among other large marine organisms.

Great Adventures Bonaire, at Harbour Village Beach Club, Kaya Gobernador N. Debrot 72 (www.harbourvillage.com; 𝒞 599/717-7500, ext. 286), is the island's poshest operation, upscale but unpretentious and friendly. It offers two of Bonaire's most beautiful boats. **Captain Don's Habitat,** Kaya Gobernador N. Debrot 103 (www.habitatbonaire.com; © **800/327-6709** or 305/438-4222 in the U.S., or 599/717-8290), attracts diving fanatics and disciples of Capt. Don Stewart, an island icon and the driving force behind the Bonaire National Marine Park. The full-service outfitter offers a photo shop and lab, plus equipment repair.

SNORKELING Thanks to shallow-water coral reefs, snorkelers can also enjoy Bonaire's awesome marine environment. The island's **Guided Snorkeling Program** includes a slide-show introduction to reef fish, corals, and sponges; an in-water demonstration of snorkeling skills; and a guided tour of one of several snorkeling sites. The cost is $25 per person. Equipment rental is about $10 more. You can arrange a tour through any of the dive shops listed above, or at **Buddy Dive Resort,** Kaya Gobernador N. Debrot 85 (© **599/717-5080**), or **Dive Inn,** Kaya C. E. B. Hellmund 27 (www.dive-friends-bonaire.com; © **599/717-8761**).

For those who want to try something different, **Outdoor Bonaire** ★ (www.outdoorbonaire.com; © **599/791-6272** or 599/785-6272) offers cave snorkeling, which combines rock climbing and exploration of small subterranean pools.

For a relaxing morning or afternoon sail and snorkel trip, board the *Woodwind* (www.woodwindbonaire.com; © **599/786-7055**). For $50 per person, the 3-hour trip includes snorkel gear and nonalcoholic beverages. Or try **Pirate Cruises** (© **599/780-9933**) with Captain Mike, aboard a 56-foot privateer ship that offers half-day sail and snorkel trips daily. If you are eager to come nose to nose with a wild turtle, he offers a turtle lover's snorkel trip aboard a 36-foot dive boat to some of the best sites for turtle encounters. All trips leave from Karel's Beach Bar Pier downtown on the waterfront and reservations can be made at ZeeZicht Restaurant across the street.

WINDSURFING Shallow waters, steady breezes, and protection from choppy waters make Lac Bay perfect for beginners and pros. Sorobon has two equipment-rental centers: **Jibe City** (www.jibecity.com; © **599/717-5233**) and **Bonaire Windsurf Place** (www.bonairewindsurfplace.com; © **599/717-2288**). Boards and sails are $70 for a full day. Two-hour beginner's lessons are $50, including equipment.

Great Local Restaurants & Bars

Kralendijk offers a variety of culinary options at generally reasonable prices. One of Bonaire's most popular restaurants, **Capriccio,** Kaya Isla Riba 1 (© **599/717-7230**), serves impeccably fresh northern Italian cuisine on the harborfront, including savory salads, homemade pastas, straight-from-the-oven focaccia, thin-crust pizzas, and more substantial fare such as mahimahi braised in onion, olives, and sun-dried tomatoes. Lunch is around $25. **La Guernica Fish and Tapas,** on Kaya Bonaire 4C (www.laguernica.com; © **599/717-5022**), specializes in tapas and has seating indoors and out as well as casual lounge seating. The hacienda decor blends well in the 150-year-old architecture. Tapas with an Italian flair and fried calamari make for a good appetizer or main course, or try the coconut shrimp with ginger sauce or the fresh tuna sashimi. Reservations are recommended. It's open daily 6 to 10pm.

Zeezicht Seaside Restaurant, Kaya Jan N. E. Craane 12 (© **599/717-8434**), is a local favorite, also on the downtown waterfront. Seviche, conch sandwiches, and a gumbo of conch, fish, shrimp, and oysters are on the menu. Mermaids, fishing nets, and paintings of pirates adorn the walls. Lunch is about $12. More popular for its waterfront location than its food, **City Café,** Caya Grandi 7 (www.citybonaire.com; © **599/717-8286**), serves burgers, pasta, sandwiches, and salads. Lunch is around $12. It's a great spot to sit at the bar and meet locals. **Karel's Beach Bar,** on the waterfront (© **599/717-8434**), is almost Tahitian in its high-ceilinged, Tiki-hut design. This popular place perches above the sea on stilts. In Bogie's Casablanca, everybody came to Rick's; in Bonaire, everybody goes to Karel's: divers, boaters, off-the-record couples—you name it.

BRITISH VIRGIN ISLANDS: TORTOLA & VIRGIN GORDA

With small bays and hidden coves that were once havens for pirates, the BVI is one of the world's loveliest cruising regions, consisting of some 60 islands and cays located in the northeastern corner of the Caribbean, about 100km (60 miles) east of Puerto Rico. Tortola, Virgin Gorda, and Jost Van Dyke (plus Anegada, 26km/16 miles to the north) are of significant size. The other islets, most of them tiny rocks and cays, have names such as Fallen Jerusalem and Ginger. Norman Island is said to have been the prototype for Robert Louis Stevenson's *Treasure Island,* and Blackbeard inspired a famous ditty by marooning 15 pirates and a bottle of rum on the rocky cay known as Deadman Bay. Yo-ho-ho!

Columbus came this way in 1493, but the British Virgins apparently made little impression on him. Although the Spanish and Dutch contested it, the English officially annexed Tortola in 1672. Today, these islands are a British Overseas territory, with their own elected government and a population of about 29,000. Despite the name, the BVI are surprisingly void of British mannerisms, accents, flags, or other reminders that this is a British territory.

The vegetation is varied and depends on the rainfall, but the lack of development has ensured that there is an abundance of greenery nearly everywhere you look. Palms and breadfruit trees grow in profusion in some parts, while other places are arid and studded with cactuses and agave.

Smaller cruise lines, such as Seabourn and Windstar, call at Tortola and the scenic Virgin Gorda and Jost Van Dyke. Unlike port calls at St. Thomas and other major ports, visits here are less bound by rigid scheduling. With the feel of a sleepy village and none of the hustle and bustle of bigger ports of call, they are also refreshingly free of megaresorts, chain restaurants, and other franchises.

LANGUAGE   English is spoken here.

CURRENCY   The **U.S. dollar** is the legal currency, much to the surprise of arriving Brits, who find no one willing to accept their pounds.

INFORMATION   For info before you go, check out www.bvitourism.com, or call the **BVI Tourist Board** in New York at © **800/835-8530** or 212/563-3117.

CALLING FROM THE U.S.   When calling the BVI from the United States, you need only dial a "1" before the numbers listed here.

Tortola

Road Town, the territory's colony's capital, sits about midway along the southern shore of 62-sq.-km (24-sq.-mile) Tortola. Once a sleepy village, it's become a bustling center since **Wickhams Cay,** a 28-hectare (69-acre) landfill development and marina, brought in a massive yacht-chartering business.

Rugged mountain peaks characterize the island's entire southern coast. On the northern coast are beautiful bays with white-sand beaches, banana trees, mangoes, and clusters of palms. An abundance of sailboats in the harbor are a testament to the popularity of sailing, which draws a large percentage of tourists and explains the lack of obvious hotels ashore, as many sailboats are rented for a week or more and serve as floating hotel rooms.

If your ship is scheduled to visit only Virgin Gorda but you want to see Tortola, you can catch a boat, ferry, or launch here and be on the island in no time, as it's only a 19km (12-mile) trip. The ferry pier is just down the road from the cruise ship pier. **Speedy's** (www.speedysbvi.com; © **284/495-5235**) seems to be the top dog, with double-decker air-conditioned ferries departing daily starting at 9am and leaving about every 1½ hours thereafter. The fee is $30 per person round-trip or $20 per person one-way, in case you wish to return via another operator. Budget plenty of time, as the ride is about 25 to 30 minutes each way.

COMING ASHORE   Visiting cruise ships dock at **Road Town Harbour,** a pleasant 5-minute walk from Main Street in Road Town. You should have no trouble finding your way around. Shopping in town is modest and pricey but well worth a relaxed stroll among the boutiques.

INFORMATION   The **BVI Tourist Board,** in the Akara Building, Wickhams Cay 1 (www.bvitourism.com; © **284/494-3134**), is open Monday through Friday from 8:30am to 4:30pm. You can pick up a copy of the *Welcome Tourist Guide* here, which prints pertinent information such as ferry schedules and special events.

GETTING AROUND

BY TAXI   Open-air and sedan-style taxis meet every arriving cruise ship. Taxis are not metered, but rates are set by the government and should be available on a printed rate sheet. To order a taxi in Road Town, call the **BVI Taxi Association** (© **284/ 494-2322** or 494/3942). Two other local taxi services, **Road Town Taxi Association** (© **284/494-8755**) and the **Waterfront Taxi Association** (© **284/494-4959** or 494-6362), are within walking distance of the cruise pier. Because all taxis are minivans that can seat up to 10 passengers, it's more economical to travel with at least three people, which can bring the per-head price to go to the beach down from $24 to $8.

BY BUS   While a government-run bus service is in the process of being implemented, local independent operators will still pick up passengers (mostly locals) who hail the passing buses and taxis. Fares for a trek across the island are about $3 to $6, but be sure to negotiate so the driver does not suddenly turn his bus into a private taxi and up the price accordingly. Island tours are also available; a 3-hour tour costs about $35 per person.

BY RENTAL CAR   I don't recommend renting a car here; roads are steep, winding, and at times downright treacherous. But if you're intent on it, **Avis, Dollar, Hertz,** and **ITGO** (the local Budget operator) all have offices here. Scooters are also available for rent, but again, due to hazardous driving conditions and a lack of road signs, it's not recommended for the faint of heart. Also keep in mind that driving here is on the left.

BEST CRUISE LINE SHORE EXCURSIONS

Town & Country Tour ($46, 3½ hr.): Tour the island in an open-air minibus, visiting the Botanical Gardens, Cane Garden Bay, Bomba's Surfside Shack at Capoons Bay, and Soper's Hole.

Norman Island Snorkeling ($64, 3 hr.): Cross the Sir Frances Drake Channel by boat to Norman Island, one of the BVI's prime snorkel sites, full of coral formations,

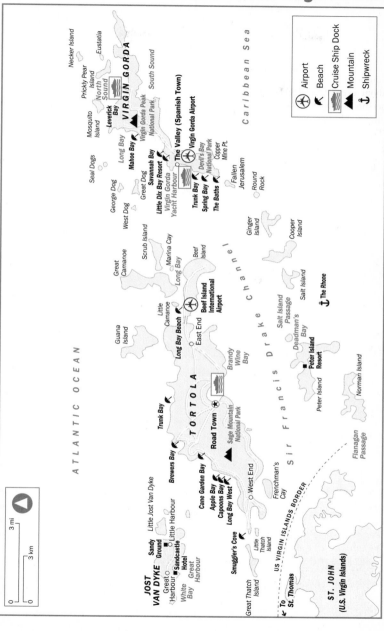

colorful fish, and a group of caves at Treasure Point, where pirate treasure is reputed to have been hidden.

Scuba Diving at the RMS *Rhone* ($149, 5½ hr.): This is a guided two-tank dive to a British ship sunk in an 1867 hurricane, her bow lying almost fully intact in 25m (80 ft.) of water and heavily encrusted/inhabited with a profusion of spectacular marine life. All divers must be certified and must have dived within the past 2 years.

EXCURSIONS OFFERED BY LOCAL AGENCIES

Bus Tours/Snorkeling Excursions/Glass-Bottom Boat Tours: Because the shore excursions here are very modest, you might consider calling **Travel Plan Tours,** Romasco Place, Wickhams Cay, Road Town (www.aroundthebvi.com; ✆ **284/494-2872**), which will take one to three people on a 3-hour guided tour of the island (about $45 a person, if there is a minimum of 2 people), a snorkeling excursion (about $75 a person, for groups of 10 or more), or an all-day catamaran sailing excursion ($125 per person, including lunch). On Virgin Gorda, **Speedy's** (www.speedysbvi.com; ✆ **284/495-5240**) offers open-air bus tours and fishing charters as well as taxis and car rentals.

Taxi Tours: You can take a 2- to 3-hour taxi tour for about $75 for up to three people. For a taxi in Road Town, call ✆ **284/494-2322.** Because all taxis are minivans that can seat up to 10 passengers, it's more economical to travel with at least three people.

ON YOUR OWN: WITHIN WALKING DISTANCE

Besides the handful of shops on Main and Upper Main streets in Road Town, there's also the J.R. O'Neal **Botanic Gardens** (✆ **284/494-4557**) right in the middle of town, across from the police station. About the size of a city block, and self-guided, with small signs identifying local and scientific names of selected plants, it's a quiet and cool oasis. It's open daily from 8:30am to 4:30pm. Entry is $3 for adults, $2 children 15 and under. Just down the street toward the town's one traffic light is the eclectic and somewhat hodgepodge **Sugar Works Museum** (no phone), a recently reopened museum which is inside a classic plantation-era building that once housed slaves working in the cotton industry. Today it contains photographs of local flora and fauna and a variety of seemingly random artifacts from distant and recent history, but the main attraction is a large hand-operated cotton press used to make bales of cotton for shipping overseas. The museum is open from 9am to 4pm daily, and admission is free.

On Main Street, near the Post Office, is the modest **Old Folk Museum,** which houses a few glass cases with artifacts and old photographs, but perhaps its most intriguing attraction is a collection of artifacts recovered from the wreck of the *Rhone,* including some well-preserved china and a porthole with glass intact. Above is a deck drawing of the sister ship to the *Rhone,* showing details such as cabin locations and the boiler room, which blew the ship into several large pieces when it went down in a storm. Way on the other side of town, but well worth the stroll along Main Street, is the recently renovated **Old Government House Museum,** in a historic building that sits on the site of an old fort replaced by a modest residence for the local governor. The original house was all but destroyed in a hurricane in 1924 but was rebuilt to a slightly less modest form which remains today a noble testament to the history of the island and truly one of the loveliest museums in the Caribbean. Opened in 2007, this historic house is furnished with eclectic period furniture and effectively evokes the modest grandeur of a governor's house from that era. In addition to restored rooms, historic accounts of the hurricane that nearly destroyed it, and records of visits from royals over the years, it houses an impressive collection of stamps in a special climate-controlled room which contains examples of every stamp issued by the BVI since the island's first post office opened. The budding or avid philatelist can head over to the **BVI Post Office** on Main Street to purchase some examples of these always-exquisite stamps. Although they bear U.S. currency, they can be used only in the British Virgin Islands, but they do make lovely souvenirs.

ON YOUR OWN: BEYOND THE PORT AREA

You mainly have nature to look at on Tortola. The big attraction is **Sage Mountain National Park** (www.bvinationalparkstrust.org; ✆ **284/494-2069**), which rises to 523m (1,716 ft.)—the highest point in the BVI and USVI—and covers 37 hectares (91 acres). The park was established in 1964 to protect those remnants of Tortola's original forests not burned or cleared during the island's plantation era. It is both the oldest national park in the British Virgin Islands and the best present-day example of the territory's native moist forests. Before you enter the park itself, you will hike through private land where you find a lush forest of mango, papaya, breadfruit, birch-berry, mountain guava, guavaberry, and fruit trees. Once inside the clearly marked gates of the park, you will find a low canopied secondary forest of native and exotic trees such as white cedar, West Indian mahogany, and fig. This is a great place to enjoy a picnic while overlooking neighboring islets and cays. Any taxi driver can take you to the mountain. Before going, stop at the tourist office (see above) and pick up a brochure with a map and an outline of the park's trails, or grab one from the tiny parks office at the entrance, which is open Monday to Friday from 9am to 5pm. The entrance fee is $3. The two main hikes are the relatively flat **Central Trail** and the more challenging **North Trail,** or the somewhat strenuous trail up to the highest point in all the Virgin Islands. Be sure to wear sturdy hiking shoes or sneakers, as the trail is quite steep and rocky. Drinking water is a must as well.

For a quiet beach day, head to **Smuggler's Cove,** a secluded spot on the West End of Tortola with white sand and calm turquoise water.

SHOPPING

Shopping on Tortola is a minor activity compared to shopping at other Caribbean ports. Only British goods are imported without duty, and they are the best buys, especially English china. You'll also find West Indian art, terra-cotta pottery, wicker and rattan home furnishings, Mexican glassware, dhurrie rugs, baskets, and ceramics. Most stores are on Main Street in Road Town.

The **Crafts Alive** village is a touristy shopping cluster a mere 5-minute walk from the pier. A variety of locally and not-so-locally made items are peddled here and at shops along Main Street. Be wary of coral figurines; black-coral, turtle-shell, or conch-shell jewelry; as well as whole or parts of conch shells and other natural trin-kets. While touted as environmentally friendly, these are often produced from pro-tected species and are technically not supposed to be traded across borders according to CITES (Convention on International Trade in Endangered Species of Flora and Fauna). While the risk of confiscation or fine is miniscule, the cumulative environ-mental impact of such commercial trade is devastating, and should be discouraged.

You can purchase and sample naturally made juices, liqueurs, and Popsicles at **Locally Yours** (✆ **284/440-2178**), all made from such locally grown fruits as guava-berry, sour sop, sea grapes, and coco plum; there's also unique Caribbean apparel.

5

THE PORTS OF CALL

British Virgin Islands

The real local treasures are the pottery, paintings, and top-rate photographs from resident artists who effectively capture the beauty of these islands and are willing to let them go for a pretty reasonable price. Check out **The Gallery,** 102 Main St. (© **284/494-2096**), for unique paper batik images of local plants and animals, or **The Allamanda Gallery** at 124 Main St. (www.virginportraits.com; © **284/494-6680**), where you can buy a $6 magnet or a $600 framed photograph featuring the natural landscape of the BVIs with an artistic and often original perspective.

A bit farther away, in Trellis Bay on Beef Island, you can find some impressive pottery and other quality handicrafts made by regional artisans at **Aragorn's Studio** (www.aragornsstudio.com; © **284/495-1849**). The **Pusser's Company Store,** Main Street, Road Town (www.pussers.com; © **284/494-2467**), offers a selection of classic travel and adventure clothing, along with unusual accessories and Pusser's famous (though not terribly good) rum, which was served aboard British Navy ships for over 300 years. A good, cheap gift item is a packet of Pusser's coasters, on which is written the recipe for that classic Caribbean rum specialty, the Painkiller.

The **Sunny Caribbee Herb and Spice Company,** Main Street, Road Town (www.sunnycaribbee.com; © **284/494-2178**), is a good spot for Caribbean spices, seasonings, teas, condiments, and handicrafts. You can buy two world-famous specialties here: West Indian Hangover Cure and Arawak Love Potion.

Soper's Hole Wharf & Marina (© **284/495-4589**), on the West End, has some shopping and restaurants. It's a 30-minute taxi ride from the cruise ship pier.

BEACHES

Most of the beaches are a 20-minute taxi ride from the cruise dock. Figure on about $20 per person one-way (some will charge less, about $6 per person if you've got a group), but discuss it with the driver before setting out. You can also ask the driver to pick you up at a designated time.

The finest beach is at **Cane Garden Bay,** which reminds me of the famous Magens Bay Beach on the north shore of St. Thomas. It's on the northwest side of the island, across the mountains from Road Town, but it's worth the effort needed to get there—you might want to take a taxi here in the morning and not head back to your cruise ship until departure time. Plan to have lunch here at any of the restaurants that overlook the beach and serve island food and fruity drinks. Try **Rhymer's** (© **284/495-4639**), where the chef will cook conch or perhaps barbecue spareribs. The beach bar and restaurant is open daily from 8am to 8pm, with main courses ranging from $15 to $25. Rhymer's rents towels.

Surfers like **Apple Bay,** also on the northwest side, but you'll have to watch out for sharks (on a recent trip, a friend saw one while surfing, and its dorsal fins were visible from the shore, though locals will testify that they are quite a way offshore and little real threat to bathers). A hotel here called **Sebastians on the Beach** (www.sebastiansbvi.com; © **284/495-4212**) caters to the surfing crowd that visits in January and February, but the beach is ideal year-round.

Brewers Bay, site of a campground, is on the northwest shore near Cane Garden Bay and is good for beach strolling and swimming. Both snorkelers and surfers come here.

The recently completed **Brandywine Bay** is man-made and lacking character, but it does have shade umbrellas and chairs along its span, restroom facilities on one end, and a beach bar/restaurant at the other.

Smuggler's Cove (sometimes known as Lower Belmont Bay) is a wide crescent of white sand wrapped around calm, sky-blue water, located on the western end of

Tortola, within walking distance of Long Bay Beach Resort. Snorkelers and surfers also like this beach.

SPORTS

SAILING   With consistent trade winds, an abundance of coves, and endless secluded beaches, the British Virgin Islands are known as one of the greatest sailing destinations in the world. If you are a seasoned sailor or a complete beginner, there are sailing charters that will fit your needs. **White Squall** (www.whitesquall2.com; ✆ **284/494-2564**) will take you and 16 of your friends (or more, but not fewer) aboard a traditional 79-foot schooner and have you back in time for your ship's departure. They also have prescheduled tours to "the Baths" (p. 186) on Monday, Wednesday, and Friday, and "the Caves" Tuesday, Thursday, and Saturday; the trips are $115 per person, including lunch, drinks, guided snorkeling, and sunbathing.

SCUBA DIVING   *Skin Diver* magazine has called the wreckage of the RMS *Rhone,* which sank in 1867 near the western point of Salt Island, the world's most fantastic shipwreck dive. It teems with marine life and coral formations, and was featured in the motion picture *The Deep.* While the vessel was trying to outrun a category 5 hurricane, its massive engine exploded and split the craft into several large sections, sending it and the 120-person crew to the sea floor below. A major portion of the hull remains sufficiently intact to be easily entered, while portions of the aft—including an intact porthole (complete with glass), a teaspoon allegedly belonging to the captain, and the massive propeller and rudder—can easily be seen on a second, shallower dive. On a recent dive, giant moray eels at least 1.5m (5 ft.) long were cruising among the scattered wreckage, giant lobsters were hiding in nearly every crevice, and a sea turtle and nurse shark were both spotted lazily gliding away from the site.

Chikuzen, an 81m (266-ft.) steel-hulled refrigerator ship that sank off the island's east end in 1981, is another intriguing dive site off Tortola, although it's no *Rhone.* The hull, still intact under about 25m (80 ft.) of water, is now home to a vast array of tropical marine life, including yellowtail, barracuda, black-tip sharks, octopus, and drum fish.

Groups of three or more can charter a private dive boat for a half or full day by contacting **UBS Dive Center** (www.scubabvi.com; ✆ **284/494-0024**). Two-tank dives for a group of three or more cost $175 per person, including instruction, equipment, snacks, and drinks. After the dive, you can choose to snorkel, island-hop, have a land tour of the island, stop for lunch at an island restaurant, or go right back to your boat. The outfitter will pick you up at Village Cay Marina; call to make arrangements beforehand. For a top-notch, full-service dive operator, call **Sail Caribbean Divers** (www.sailcaribbeandivers.com; ✆ **284/495-1675**), which operates out of Hodges Creek Marina. Its friendly staff and well-trained dive masters will cater to your needs, provide quality rental gear, and tell a colorful tale of how the wrecks came to find their final resting sites. A two-tank morning dive costs $110, while a one-tank afternoon dive is $80. They will gladly customize an excursion for both divers and snorkelers.

WINDSURFING   Gentle trade winds and clear water make windsurfing a popular sport on this laid-back island where motorized watersports are eschewed. For an introductory lesson ($100) or an hourly rental ($25), head over to **Boardsailing BVI** (www.windsurfing.vi; ✆ **800/880-SURF** [7873] or 284/495-2447) at Trellis Bay. If no one is at the stand, check next door at the cybercafe.

British Virgin Islands

GREAT LOCAL RESTAURANTS & BARS

Right on the waterfront across from the ferry dock, **Pusser's Road Town Pub** (www.pussers.com; ✆ 284/494-3897) serves Caribbean fare, English pub grub, and good pizzas. The drink to have here is the famous Pusser's rum, the same blend of five West Indian rums that the Royal Navy served to its men for more than 300 years. Honestly, it's not the world's greatest rum, but sometimes you just have to do things for the experience. Lunch is about $22.

Capriccio di Mare, Waterfront Drive, Road Town (✆ 284/494-5369), is the most authentic-looking Italian cafe in the Virgin Islands, serving a variety of coffees along with fresh pastas with succulent sauces, well-stuffed sandwiches, and great pizza. Lunch is about $15.

If you have a sweet tooth, don't miss the **Road Town Bakery,** where culinary students from the New England Culinary Institute at H. Lavity Stoutt Community College on Tortola show their skill by baking some of the planet's tastiest pastries, cookies, filled croissants, and turnovers.

For a fine *roti* (curries wrapped in flatbread) sans atmosphere—it's sparsely furnished and not too attractive—try **Roti Palace** in Road Town (✆ 284/494-4196). Lunch is about $8. For a taste of another local favorite, meat patties in a flaky crust, head over to **Crandalls** (✆ 284/494-5156) for beef, chicken, or fish patties that range in price from $2 to $5.

Over on Cappoons Bay, **Bomba's Surfside Shack** (✆ 284/495-4148) is the oldest, most memorable bar on Tortola, sitting on a strip of coastline near the West End. It's the "junk palace" of the island, covered with faded Day-Glo graffiti and laced with old license plates and rejected odds and ends of plywood, driftwood, and abandoned rubber tires. The owners must've spent their decorating budget on the sound system, which thumps mightily. It's open until midnight or later, depending on business or if it's the night of one of the island's famous full-moon parties, where the allegedly hallucinogenic mushroom tea helps visitors explore their psychedelic side. Lunch is about $15.

Wash down your conch fritters and mahimahi burger with a daiquiri at **Myett's Garden and Grille,** on Cane Garden Bay (www.myettent.com; ✆ 284/495-9649), where you can dine right on the beach among lush tropical foliage. Lunch is about $15. **Quito's Gazebo,** also on Cane Garden Bay (✆ 284/495-4837), is owned by local recording star Quito Rymer. It's a good place for West Indian fish dishes. Quito performs Tuesday and Thursday on his own and Friday and Saturday with his band. Lunch is about $15. Just down the road is the **Big Banana** (✆ 284/495-4606), serving up pizzas, burgers, and ice cream in a relaxed atmosphere where you can watch the action along the beach, including the parade of friendly dogs that seem to serve as a self-appointed beach patrol.

At **Pusser's Landing,** Soper's Hole, on the West End (✆ 284/495-4554), you can enjoy grilled fish such as mahimahi, or perhaps some West Indian roast chicken. Lunch is about $18.

Fat Hog Bob's (✆ 284/495-1010) lies in Hodge's Creek and offers a quiet getaway from town. Perched over Fat Hogs Bay, near some mangrove restoration sites, the fare ranges from salads to burgers and full entrees. The locally made salt fish cakes are recommended, as is the grilled tuna melt, smothered with cheese and served with fries and coleslaw. Lunch will set you back about $15.

Virgin Gorda

Instead of visiting Tortola, some small cruise ships put in at lovely Virgin Gorda, famous for its boulder-strewn beach known as the Baths. The third-largest island in the colony, it got its name ("Fat Virgin") from Christopher Columbus, who thought the mountain framing it looked like a protruding stomach. At approximately 15km (9 miles) long and 3km (2 miles) wide, the island is about 20km (12 miles) east of Road Town, so it's easy to take a ferry here if your ship visits only Tortola (cruise lines offer shore excursions that do this trip, too).

The island was a fairly desolate agricultural community until Little Dix Bay Hotel opened here in the early 1960s. Other major hotels followed, but privacy and solitude still reign supreme on Virgin Gorda.

COMING ASHORE Virgin Gorda doesn't have a pier or landing facilities to suit any of the large ships. Most vessels anchor offshore and tender passengers in to St. Thomas Bay, the port area and yacht harbor for Spanish Town. Ferries from Tortola also berth here.

GETTING AROUND

Taxis are available and will take visitors to the Baths and area beaches for about $6 per person each way. Entry fee to the Baths is $5 per person. For a tour of the island, contact Andy Flax of the **Virgin Gorda Tours Association,** c/o the Fischer's Cove Beach Hotel (© **284/495-5252**). It'll run you about $60 per couple; you'll get picked up at the dock if you give at least 24-hour notice. Another good option is **Speedy's,** also known as Virgin Gorda Transport (© **284/495-5240**), which usually has drivers hanging around the marina when you come ashore.

BEST CRUISE LINE SHORE EXCURSIONS

The Baths Excursion ($85, 4 hr.): All cruise lines stopping in Virgin Gorda offer a version of this trip. See "Beaches," below, for details.

Island Tour ($80, 3–4 hr.): Open-air safari buses travel around this stunning island, traveling from Leverick Bay, ascending at least partway up Gorda Peak, and stopping at the quaint capital, Spanish Town.

ON YOUR OWN: WITHIN WALKING DISTANCE

The **Virgin Gorda Yacht Harbour** at St. Thomas Bay has several restaurants and shops.

ON YOUR OWN: BEYOND THE PORT AREA

You might consider cabbing it up to glamorous **Little Dix Bay Hotel** (www.littledix bay.com; © **888-ROSEWOOD** [767-3966] or 284/495-5555), established by Laurance Rockefeller in 1965, to enjoy a lunch buffet at an outdoor pavilion that shows off Virgin Gorda's beautiful hills, bays, and sky. Aside from this, most people head for the Baths, which really is a spectacular beach (see "Beaches," below). Call the hotel for reservations.

SHOPPING

The only shopping of note here is right at the Virgin Gorda Yacht Harbor complex, with a few dive shops, boutiques, and handicraft shops. **Dive BVI** (www.divebvi. com; © **284/495-5513**) sells diving equipment and offers diving instruction for all ability levels. **Margo's Jewelry Boutique** (© **284/495-5237**) sells handcrafted gold and silver items. The **Virgin Gorda Craft Shop** (© **284/495-5137**) features

A SLICE OF paradise: JOST VAN DYKE

Covering only 10 sq. km (3¾ sq. miles), mountainous Jost Van Dyke is truly an offbeat, rarely visited retreat—unless you count the small yachts dotting Great Harbour. With no cruise pier, passengers are shuttled ashore via tender. Small-ship lines, such as Island Windjammers, will sometimes throw an afternoon party on the beach at White Bay, with the crew lugging ashore a picnic lunch for a leisurely afternoon of eating, drinking, and swimming. If your ship stays late, don't miss a trip to **Foxy's** (☎ **284/495-9258**), a well-known watering hole at the far end of Great Harbour, which is popular with the yachting set as well as locals. It's your classic island beach bar, with music pounding and drinks flowing into the wee hours.

locally made items. The **Wine Cellar** (☎ **284/495-5250**) offers oven-baked French bread and pastries, cookies, and sandwiches. **Next Wave** (☎ **284/495-5623**) sells locally handmade glassware, jewelry, handmade beach bags, and a handful of other crafts.

BEACHES

The major reason cruise ships come to Virgin Gorda is to visit **the Baths,** where geologists believe ice-age eruptions caused house-size boulders to topple onto one another to form the saltwater grottoes we see today. The pools around the Baths are excellent for swimming and snorkeling (equipment can be rented on the beach), and a crawl among the boulders, which, in places, are like caves. A cafe sits just above the beach for a quick snack or a cool drink. There is a $5 entry fee to the **Baths** if you are not visiting with a tour.

Just north of the Baths is **Spring Bay,** one of the best of the island's beaches, with white sand, clear water, and good snorkeling. Nearby is the **Crawl,** a natural pool formed by rocks that's great for novice snorkelers; a marked path leads there from Spring Bay. **Trunk Bay,** just to the north, is a wide sand beach that can be reached via a rough path from Spring Bay.

Devil's Bay National Park can be reached by a trail from the Baths. The walk to the secluded coral-sand beach takes about 15 minutes through a natural setting of boulders and dry coastal vegetation.

SPORTS

WATERSPORTS   **Kilbrides Sunchaser Scuba,** at the Bitter End Resort at North Sound (www.sunchaserscuba.com; ☎ **800/932-4286** in the U.S., or 284/495-9638), offers diving at more than 20 BVI sites, including the wreck of the RMS *Rhone.* Morning two-tank dives go for $115; afternoon one-tank dives are $80. The excursions last about 4½ hours. Wet suits rent for $10. You can also call **Dive BVI** (☎ **800/848-7078** or 284/495-5513), located at Virgin Gorda Yacht Harbour.

GREAT LOCAL RESTAURANTS & BARS

At the end of the waterfront shopping plaza in Spanish Town, **Bath and Turtle Pub,** Virgin Gorda Yacht Harbour (www.bathandturtle.com; ☎ **284/495-5239**), is the island's most popular bar and pub. You can join the regulars over a hearty breakfast of pancakes and eggs served until 10:30am. Or belly up to the bar for some midmorning guava coladas or peach daiquiris and order fried fish fingers, very spicy chili, pizzas,

Reubens or tuna melts, steak, lobster, and daily seafood specials such as conch fritters. Lunch is about $16. **Mad Dog** (www.maddogbvi.net; ✆ **284/495-5830**) is a hot-dog stop near the Baths that also serves BLTs, beer, and frozen piña coladas. Lunch is about $7. **Top of the Baths** (www.topofthebaths.com; ✆ **284/495-5497**) offers indoor and outdoor dining, lovely views, and a varied lunch menu with prices averaging about $18.

COZUMEL & THE YUCATÁN PENINSULA

On some days, up to 16 ships visit Cozumel simultaneously, making this the number-one cruise ship destination in the Caribbean. All that activity can make the port town of **San Miguel** seem more like Times Square than the sleepy, refreshingly gritty Mexican port it once was. Still, San Miguel retains its charm through its classic waterfront and unusually beautiful central square, the **Plaza Del Sol,** complete with stately trees, and surrounded by local shops and eateries. Cozumel's allure remains its friendly inhabitants, its wild beaches and manicured parks, its spectacular diving, and its proximity to the ancient Mayan ruins such as **Chichén-Itzá** and **Tulum** on the mainland of the Yucatán Peninsula. Perched on the ocean, Tulum is well known and easily accessible, but there are numerous other Mayan sites up and down the peninsula, surrounded by jungle, and impressive enough to inspire a sense of awe. You can get to know the ancient Mayans here, and don't be fooled; they did not say the world would end in 2012. Besides the ruins, you might be interested in shopping for silver jewelry and local handicrafts, and you can always sample some local tequila.

To see the ruins, you must take a rocky 45-minute ferry ride between Cozumel and **Playa del Carmen,** on the mainland. Details on Playa are included in this section. About 150km (90 miles) south of Playa del Carmen, is a relatively new port on the southern part of the peninsula; **Costa Maya,** near the sleepy fishing village of Mahajual. Costa Maya is covered in the next section. A few ships leaving from southern U.S. ports also call at **Progreso,** on the Gulf coast of the Yucatán, where the Mayan ruins and colonial architecture of nearby Mérida are the big draw.

LANGUAGE   Spanish is the tongue of the land, although English is spoken in most places that cater to tourists.

CURRENCY   The Mexican currency is the **nuevo peso (new peso).** Its symbol is the $ sign, but it's hardly the equivalent of the U.S. dollar—the exchange rate is about $12.5 pesos to US$1 ($1 peso = about US7¢). The main tourist stores gladly accept U.S. dollars and credit cards. If you want to change money, you'll find many banks within a block or so of the downtown tender and ferry pier. Prices in this section are given in U.S. dollars.

CALLING FROM THE U.S.   When calling from the U.S., you need to dial the international access code (011) and the country code for Mexico (52) before the local numbers listed here.

Mayan Ruins & Other Mainland Attractions

Because all of the sites listed here are quite far from the cruise piers, most cruise passengers visit them as part of **shore excursions.** Admission to the sites is included in the excursion prices, which typically run from $100 to $130 for Chichén-Itzá and around $75 for Tulum or Cobá. Chichén-Itzá and Cobá are all-day excursions. Visits to smaller Tulum are often paired with a visit to the Xel-Ha Eco Park, making it a full-day trek ($99). Guests are usually served free and refreshingly cold Mexican beer on the bus back after exploring the ruins.

CHICHÉN-ITZÁ   The largest and most fabled of the Yucatán ruins, Chichén-Itzá (meaning "Mouth of the Well of the Itza Family") was founded in A.D. 445 by the Mayans and later inhabited by the Toltecs of central Mexico. At its height, the city had about 50,000 residents, but it was mysteriously abandoned only 2 centuries after its founding. After lying dormant for 2 more centuries, the site was resettled and enjoyed prosperity again until the early 13th century, when it was once more relinquished to the surrounding jungle. The area covers 18 sq. km (7 sq. miles), so you can see only a fraction of it on a day trip. The following are some of the highlights:

The best known of Chichén-Itzá's ruins is the magnificent **El Castillo pyramid** (also called the Pyramid of Kukulkán), which was built with the Maya calendar in mind. The four stairways leading up to the central platform each have 91 steps, making a total of 364; when you add the top central platform, you get the 365 days of the solar year. On either side of each stairway are 9 terraces, which makes 18 on each face of the pyramid, equaling the number of months in the Maya solar calendar. On the facing of these terraces are 52 panels that represent the 52-year cycle when both the solar and religious calendars would become realigned. The pyramid's position is such that on the **spring** and **fall equinoxes,** light striking the pyramid gives the illusion of a snake slithering down the steps to join its gigantic stone head mounted at the base.

Northwest of El Castillo is Chichén's main **ball court,** the largest and best preserved such Mayan ruin anywhere. Carved on both walls of the ball court are scenes showing Mayan figures dressed as ballplayers and decked out in heavy protective padding. According to legend, the losing players paid for defeat with their lives. However, some experts say the victors were the only appropriate sacrifices for the gods. Note the lack of bleacher seating.

Temples are located at both ends of the ball court. The **North Temple** has sculptured pillars and more sculptures inside, as well as badly ruined murals. The acoustics of the ball court are so good that from the North Temple, a person speaking can be heard clearly at the opposite end, about 135m (450 ft.) away. Near the southeastern corner of the main ball court is the **Temple of the Jaguars,** a small temple with serpent columns and carved panels showing warriors and jaguars. Up the steps and inside the temple, a mural was found that chronicles a battle in a Maya village. To the right of the ball court is the **Temple of the Skulls.** Notice the rows of skulls carved into the stone platform. When a sacrificial victim's head was cut off, it was impaled on a pole and displayed in a tidy row with the others.

Follow the dirt road (actually an ancient *sacbé,* or causeway, made from a white, compacted, claylike soil that made the way visible at night) that heads north from the Platform of Venus. After about 5 minutes, you'll come to the **Sacred Cenote,** a great natural well that may have given Chichén-Itzá its name. This well was used for ceremonial purposes, not for drinking water. According to legend, sacrificial victims adorned with gold and other riches were drowned in this pool to honor the rain god Chaac. In the early 20th century, American consul and Harvard professor Edward Thompson bought the ruins of Chichén-Itzá and explored the cenote with dredges and divers, unearthing (and exporting) a fortune in gold and jade.

Due east of El Castillo is one of the most impressive structures at Chichén: the **Temple of the Warriors,** named for the carvings of warriors marching along its

The Yucatán's Upper Caribbean Coast

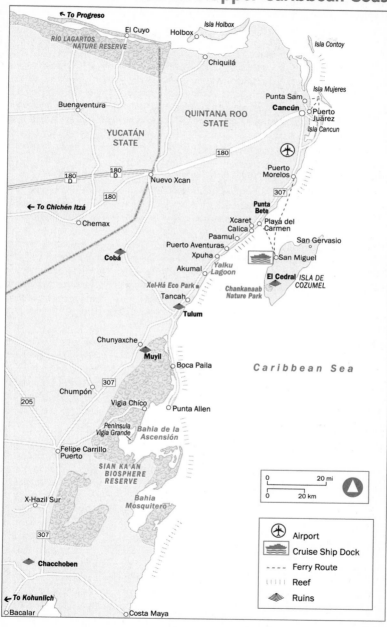

walls. It's also called the Group of the Thousand Columns for the rows of broken square pillars that flank it. A figure of high priest Chaac-Mool sits at the top of the temple, surrounded by impressive columns carved in relief to look like enormous feathered serpents. According to scholars, Chaac-Mool would tear out a sacrificial victim's heart here and then throw the body down the steps, where another priest would strip off his or her skin.

South of the temple is another group of columns (these are round) that were once an important **market,** controlling the trade in salt on the Yucatán. South of the market, a cluster of interesting ruins includes the **Observatory,** a complex building with a circular tower through whose slits astronomers could observe the cardinal directions and the approach of the all-important spring and autumn equinoxes; the **Edifice of the Nuns,** which was named for its resemblance to a European convent; and the **Church,** one of the oldest buildings at Chichén, named for its beautiful decorations. Its ceiling, with a Mayan false arch, is a stone replica of the thatched ceilings that were typical in Mayan homes of the period.

TULUM About 130km (80 miles) south of Cancún and about a 30-minute drive from Playa del Carmen, the small walled city of Tulum is the single-most-visited Mayan ruin due to its proximity to the ports. It was the only Mayan city built on the coast and the only one inhabited when the Spanish conquistadors arrived in the 1500s. From its dramatic perch atop seaside cliffs, you can see wonderful panoramic views of the Caribbean. Though nowhere near as large and impressive as Chichén-Itzá, the two cities share a similar prominent feature: a ruin topped with a temple to Kukulkán, the primary Mayan/Olmec god. Other important structures include the Temple of the Frescoes, the Temple of the Descending God, the House of Columns, and the House of the Cenote, which is a well. There's also a sliver of silky beach at the site, so bring your bathing suit for a quick refreshing dip.

COBÁ A 35-minute drive northwest of Tulum puts you at Cobá, site of one of the most important city-states in the Mayan empire. Cobá flourished from A.D. 300 to 1000, with its population numbering perhaps as many as 40,000. Excavation began in 1972, and archaeologists estimate that only 5% of this dead city has been uncovered. The site lies on four lakes. Its 32 rural hectares (79 acres) provide excellent exploration opportunities for hikers. Cobá's pyramid, Nohoch Mul, is the tallest in the Yucatán.

XCARET ECO-PARK Lying about 6.5km (4 miles) south of Playa del Carmen on the coast, Xcaret (pronounced *Ish*-car-et) is a 100-hectare (250-acre) ecological theme park with small Mayan ruins scattered about the lushly landscaped acres. Visitors can put on life jackets for a river ride, which takes them through currents running through a series of caves, or don a Sea-Trek helmet and weighted booties and walk across the ocean floor. You can also snorkel through the caves (something I highly recommend), as well as swim with dolphins, though this is the only activity not included in the cost of the excursion. The park has a botanical garden, an aquarium, a sea-turtle breeding and release facility, a dive shop, a rotating observation tower, a Mayan village, and nearly endless restaurants and shops, but the real draw is the "Xcaret Spectacular Show" that is put on every evening. You'll experience elaborate cultural shows, including a charming song-and-dance performance representing the colorful array of cultural traditions of the different regions that make up Mexico, and a reenactment of the Aztec ballgame, complete with a flaming ball that is passed between the various players. The entrance fee is $79; add a buffet lunch for $109 for adults ($48 for children under 55 in. tall). It's open daily 8:30am to 9:30pm (www. xcaret.com; © **998/881-2400**).

XEL-HA ECO-PARK South of Xcaret, Xel-Ha (pronounced *Shell*-Ha) features a sprawling natural lagoon filled with sparkling blue-green water and surrounded by lush foliage. While Xcaret attracts many Mexican visitors because of its cultural shows, the draw of Xel-Ha is its natural beauty. The use of inner tubes and life vests is included in the admission price, and you can spend a great couple of hours wending your way from one end of the snaking body of calm water to the other, accompanied by schools of tropical fish. Snorkeling gear is included with the admission fee. Xel-Ha has dolphins too. Knowledgeable, friendly, and very eco-minded guides will walk you along trails identifying local plants and take you to sacred sinkholes (called cenotes) where ancient Maya made offerings to the gods. The site is built on the natural features of the landscape, not artificially carved into the terrain the way many resorts have been. Among the natural elements you'll also find shops, restaurants, and lots of beach chairs here. Admission costs $119 for adults and about $60 for children under 55 inches (www.xelha.com; © **998/883-0470**).

Cozumel

The nearly three million cruise passengers who visit Cozumel each year have greatly changed San Miguel, which now has such trendy entertainments as Jimmy Buffet's Margaritaville and Hard Rock Cafe. However, the development is contained to the port area, about 10% of the island, which still maintains its character and natural beauty. Ashore, away from San Miguel, you'll see acres of low-lying scrub forest containing protected plants and animal species. Offshore, the government has set aside 30km (20 miles) of coral reefs as an underwater national park, including the stunning Palancar Reef, part of the Mesoamerican Barrier Reef, the world's second-largest natural coral formation.

COMING ASHORE The newest of three berths at Cozumel is **Punta Langosta,** where you'll enter a breezy, contemporary two-story mall with oodles of stores, just across from the center of town. Walk across a skyway that leaves you steps from the restaurants, shops, and cafes across the street from the port at the Plaza Del Sol. The ferries to Playa del Carmen dock about .5km (¼ mile) away. Other ships pull alongside the well-accoutered **International Pier** (3km/2 miles south of San Miguel), with its new Royal Park Mall. Another mile or so farther south is the pier at **Puerto Maya,** with shops and restaurants designed to simulate a quaint Mexican village. Both of these piers are a $10 taxi ride from town or a 30- to 45-minute walk from the heart of San Miguel. The closest beaches can be found adjacent to the International Pier.

You can make telephone calls in Cozumel from the Puerto Maya, Punta Langosta pier, and the Global Communications phone center on the International Pier, or a kiosk inside the terminal. Keep in mind that there are often lines for the phones. In town, try the **Calling Station,** Av. Rafael Melgar 27, at the corner of Calle 3 in San Miguel, 3 blocks from the ferry pier.

INFORMATION The **Department of Tourism Office,** 52 Rosados Salas between Melgar and Avenida 10, on the second floor of Plaza del Sol (© **987/869-0211**), distributes the *Vacation Guide to Cozumel* and *Cozumel Island's Restaurant Guide;* both have island maps. It's open Monday through Friday from 9am to 7:30pm, Saturday from 9am to 1pm. There are also tourist booths at the ship piers and ferry pier, open daily from 8am to 8pm. For info before you go, visit www.islacozumel.com.mx or call ✆ **800/44-MEXICO** (446-3942).

GETTING AROUND

The town of San Miguel is so small, you can walk anywhere. There is one major road in Cozumel—it starts at the northern tip of the island, hugs the western shoreline, and then loops around the southern tip and returns through the middle of the island to the capital. When leaving San Miguel, keep to the far right to find a road closer to the ocean that hugs the west coast. It's a rare experience on any island these days to be able to navigate so close to a long stretch of wild beach. Look for the openings in the vegetation on the right—they lead to the ocean. You can park and go snorkeling.

If you're driving in Cozumel, it's helpful to know that the roads parallel to the sea are called avenues, and these have the right of way. The ones running from the sea are called streets, and you have to stop at each avenue to give way.

BY TAXI   Taxi service is available 24 hours a day and taxis are easy to find at both Punta Maya and the International Pier; the trip to downtown is $10 for up to four people, and $15 for five or more, so it's good to share a ride. If you leave from San Miguel, the fare for major resorts and beaches along the west coast is $25. A good way to see the island is to hire a cab for the day; the fare starts at $40. Decide where you want to go and settle on a price before taking off—occasionally, you can bargain the price down.

BY RENTAL CAR   If you want to drive yourself, four-wheel-drive vehicles or open-air jeeps are the best rental choice. Located just 2 blocks from the ferry pier, **Blue Way Car Rental,** Avenida 5A at Calle 20A (✆ **987/872-5177**), rents cars and four-wheel-drive vehicles. A four-door economy car costs about $55 a day plus insurance and gas. The best and most convenient rentals are at **Auto Rent,** in the Hotel El Cid La Ceiba (✆ **987/872-0844**), right next to the International Pier.

BY SCOOTER   Scooters are a popular means of getting about despite heavy traffic in San Miguel, hidden stop signs, potholed roads, and a high accident rate. It's especially popular for cruise passengers to rent a scooter and drive around the entire island, which can easily be done in a half-day. **Ernestos Rental,** Carretera costera sur km. 4 Zone hotelera sur right (www.ernestosrental.com; ✆ **987/871-1223**), offers scooter rental and insurance for about $25 a day, including helmet rental (Mexican law requires that you wear one). Another friendly place is **Explore Rentadora,** at 10 Av. Norte No. 14, between Avenida Juarez and 2 Norte Col Centro (✆ **987/869-0020**).

BY FERRY   Two passenger ferries link Cozumel with Playa del Carmen, both of them with ticket booths at the main pier. The Ultramar is yellow, and larger than the Water Jet (www.mexicowaterjets.com/eng; ✆ **987/872-1588**), which is blue, white, and orange. The Ultramar has a larger, open deck and live music, while the Water Jet is a little faster with more comfortable seating. But you will most likely choose your ferry by the schedule, as they alternate times of departure. The trip takes 30 to 45 minutes and runs Monday through Saturday between 6am and 10pm. One-way fares cost $13 per person. Get a ferry schedule when you buy your ticket, but it's better to buy a one-way fare each way, to ensure the most convenient time on your way back.

BEST CRUISE LINE SHORE EXCURSIONS

See "Mayan Ruins & Other Mainland Attractions," above, for details on the big mainland excursions. In addition to those below, the cruise lines offer dozens of different snorkeling, party-boat, and underwater excursions in Cozumel.

Cozumel Island

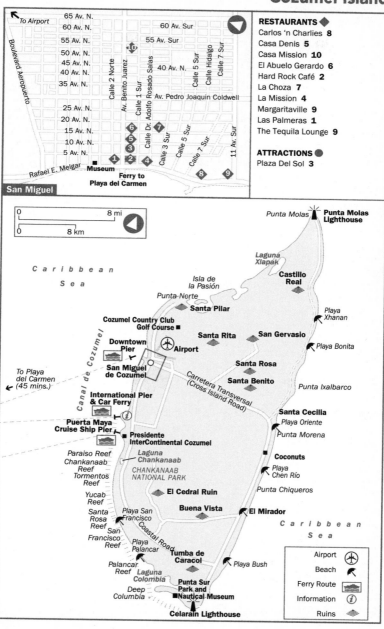

RESTAURANTS ◆
Carlos 'n Charlies **8**
Casa Denis **5**
Casa Mission **10**
El Abuelo Gerardo **6**
Hard Rock Café **2**
La Choza **7**
La Mission **4**
Margaritaville **9**
Las Palmeras **1**
The Tequila Lounge **9**

ATTRACTIONS ●
Plaza Del Sol **3**

To Airport
65 Av. N.
60 Av. N.
55 Av. N.
50 Av. N.
45 Av. N.
40 Av. N.
35 Av. N.
25 Av. N.
20 Av. N.
15 Av. N.
10 Av. N.
5 Av. N.
Boulevard Aeropuerto
60 Av. Sur
55 Av. Sur
40 Av. N.
Calle 2 Norte
Av. Benito Juarez
Calle 1 Sur
Calle Dr. Adolfo Rosado Salas
Calle 5 Sur
Calle Hidalgo
Calle 7 Sur
Av. Pedro Joaquin Coldwell
Calle 3 Sur
Calle 5 Sur
Calle 7 Sur
11 Av. Sur
Rafael E. Melgar
Museum
Ferry to
Playa del Carmen

San Miguel

0 — 8 mi
0 — 8 km

Punta Molas
Punta Molas Lighthouse

*C a r i b b e a n
S e a*

Laguna
Xlapak
**Castillo
Real**

Isla de
la Pasión
Punta Norte
Santa Pilar

Playa
Xhanan

**Cozumel Country Club
Golf Course** ■
Santa Rita
San Gervasio

**Downtown
Pier**
Airport
Playa Bonita

**San Miguel
de Cozumel**
Canal de Cozumel
Santa Rosa

To Playa
del Carmen
(45 mins.)
Santa Benito
Punta Ixalbarco

**International Pier
& Car Ferry**
Carretera Transversal
(Cross Island Road)

Santa Cecilia
Playa Oriente
Punta Morena

**Puerta Maya
Cruise Ship Pier**
**Presidente
InterContinental Cozumel**

Paraiso Reef
Chankanaab
Reef
Tormentos
Reef
Laguna
Chankanaab
CHANKANAAB
NATIONAL PARK
Coconuts
Playa
Chen Río

Yucab
Reef
El Cedral Ruin
Punta Chiqueros

Santa
Rosa
Reef
Buena Vista
El Mirador

San
Francisco
Reef
Playa San
Francisco
*C a r i b b e a n
S e a*

Playa
Palancar
Coastal Road
**Tumba de
Caracol**
Playa Bush

Palancar
Reef
Laguna
Colombia
**Punta Sur
Park and
Nautical Museum**
Airport
Beach
Ferry Route
Information
Ruins

Deep
Columbia

Celarain Lighthouse

5

THE PORTS OF CALL | Cozumel & the Yucatán Peninsula

Palancar Reef Snorkeling ($60, 4 hr.): With some of the most spectacular reefs in the world, Cozumel is a diver's paradise, but even the snorkeling is almost unmatched. In addition to colorful fish, giant sponges, and large corals, one may also see eels, rays, or even turtles.

Horseback-Riding Tours ($89, 2 hr.): Horseback-riding tours offer a chance to see Cozumel's landscape. However, although they tout visits to Mayan ruins, don't get your hopes up—there's little more than a few refrigerator-size rocks to be seen on this outing. A bus transports riders to a ranch, where the ride begins.

ATV Tours ($99, 4 hr.) For those seeking some beachside adventure, ATVs are a fun, albeit noisy, opportunity to scoot around the jungle and beach of Cozumel. Helmets and goggles are provided, and tours offer the option to travel along the beach for sweeping views of the ocean.

ON YOUR OWN: WITHIN WALKING DISTANCE

For walkers, the classic grid layout makes getting around the town of San Miguel easy, but with a twist—all odd-numbered streets are on the south side of the pier and all even-numbered streets head north. Directly across from the downtown tender docks, the main square—**Plaza del Sol** (also called *la plaza* or *el parque*)—is excellent for people-watching. The principal street along the waterfront is **Avenida Rafael Melgar,** which runs along the western shore of the island, site of the best resorts and beaches. Most of the shops and restaurants are on Rafael Melgar, although many well-stocked duty-free shops line the Malecón, the seaside promenade.

Only 3 blocks from the ferry pier, the **Museo de la Isla de Cozumel,** on Avenida Rafael Melgar between Calles 4 and 6 North (© **987/872-1434**), has two floors of exhibits displayed in what was Cozumel's first luxury hotel. Exhibits cover everything from pre-Hispanic times to the Colonial era to the present. Included are many swords and nautical artifacts; one of the displays showcases endangered species. The highlight is a reproduction of a Mayan house. A cafe on the first-floor terrace of the museum offers ocean views and traditional Mexican or American breakfasts, as well as sandwiches and salads for lunch. It's open daily from 9am to 5pm, and sometimes later; admission is $5 for adults and free for children 7 and younger.

ON YOUR OWN: BEYOND THE PORT AREA

You can rent a scooter and zip around most of the island, including its wild and natural side. Stop for a cool drink and a grilled-fish lunch at one of the beachside open-air seafood restaurants that line the coast of Cozumel. With a beer in hand and a fresh plate of ceviche, you can look out over the clear blue water with the waves gently lapping just a few feet away. Scooters can be rented from several outfits, including Auto Rent (see "Getting Around," above).

Outside of San Miguel is the **Chankanaab Nature Park** (www.cozumelparks. com), where an archaeological park, a botanical garden, and a wildlife sanctuary complement a saltwater lagoon, a beach with offshore reefs, and underwater caves. More than 10 countries have contributed seedlings and cuttings to the botanical garden here. The lagoon is occupied by some 60 species of marine life, including sea turtles, sea lions, and captive dolphins (that you can swim with for a mere $100). The shallow reefs give snorkelers and divers the opportunity to see angelfish, red grouper, and others. The lagoon, also called "little sea," became famous after Jacques Cousteau visited the island in 1958 and marveled at the lagoon's rare beauty. The quiet water offers an excellent opportunity for those who are new to snorkeling, or those with children, to explore the staggering beauty of the underwater world, with a dramatic range of coral and variety of fish. The park itself is also charming: Reproductions of Mayan dwellings are scattered throughout, and there is plenty of opportunity to wander and explore the numerous trails. There's also a wide white-sand beach with thatch umbrellas and a changing area with lockers and showers. Both scuba divers and snorkelers enjoy examining the sunken ship offshore (there are four dive shops here). The park also has a restaurant and snack stand. Admission is $21 for adults, $15 children 3 to 11, and free for children 2 and under. The 10-minute taxi ride from the downtown tender and ferry pier costs $10 for four people and $15 for five.

After driving down the dirt road to get to **Punta Sur Eco Park** at the southern tip of the island, you will feel like you've really reached land's end. On the way to the lighthouse, which still functions, you'll pass through protected environmental areas. On the right is an alligator zone. It's worth walking over the gators, on the elevated wooden walkway, to watch them wait patiently, with jaws slightly open, for a passing fish to eat. You can also climb up the observation tower for bird-watching. When you reach the Celerain Lighthouse, look around the nautical displays and pirate lore in the museum before taking the stairway to the top. There is also a well-equipped beach with palapas, hammocks, chairs, a snack bar, and snorkeling equipment. Open 9am to 4pm daily with an entrance fee of $12 for adults and $6 for children.

Because the Mayans never lived permanently on Cozumel, the ruins at **San Gervasio** (www.cozumelparks.com) are minor compared to the residential and city structures on the mainland, but the island was an important ritual site and a sanctuary for Ixchel, the goddess of the moon, water, and everything feminine in the world, including fertility. Because Mayans were required to visit the shrine at least once in their lifetime, pilgrims came across the sea from the mainland in large, wooden canoes to pay homage and make offerings of human sacrifices. There are ruins of five structures here, including the sacrificial area. Reach San Gervasio by driving east across the island to the well-marked turnoff, and then turn left and continue north 6.5km (4 miles) to San Gervasio, by either car or scooter. The ruins cost $8 to visit, which limits you to entrance to the access road. For $35, guides will show visitors what's left, including several foundations and intact columns and lintels. It's open daily from 8am to 4pm.

Cozumel's other archaeological site is **El Cedral,** situated in the center of the small rural village with the same name. Across the town square is a little church, where the first mass was held on the island. To the left, the Mayan ruins are more notable for their historical value than for their beauty—they are the island's oldest structures, and you can still see traces of original Mayan wall paintings. A small mound remains now of the original Mayan arch, together with a few ruins by the sea (the Spanish tore most of the site down, and the U.S. Army destroyed even more when they built an airfield here during World War II). El Cedral lies 3km (2 miles) inland at the turnoff at km. 17.5, east of Playa San Francisco. Guides at the site will show you around for a fee.

For those who prefer to explore the history of tequila, the **Tequila Hacienda** offers tours and samplings, where for $10 you can learn about the famous agave plant from which tequila is produced, complete with generous samples of the end result. The Tequila Hacienda is on the long road that divides Cozumel and leads to its eastern shore. They sell their own brand, called Cava Antigua, which is manufactured in Cozumel. The tequila comes in a hand-blown glass bottle, and several types can be purchased.

SHOPPING

You can walk from the ferry pier to the best shops in San Miguel. They start right across the street from the Punta Langosta pier, and are 3 to 5km (2–3 miles) from the International and Puerto Maya cruise ship piers. Because of the influx of cruise ship passengers, prices are relatively high here, but you can and should bargain. Silver jewelry is big business, and it's generally sold by weight. You can find some nice pieces, but a little comparison shopping may go a long way in sorting out the special deals from the pieces that everyone is selling. **Heritage,** Av. Rafael Melgar 341, is one of the most important jewelers in Cozumel and the exclusive distributor of Rolex watches on the Mexican Riviera. **Rachat & Romero,** Av. Rafael Melgar 101, has a wide variety of loose stones, which they can mount while you wait.

Wall-to-wall shops along the waterfront in San Miguel offer all manner of souvenirs. Hammocks, leather goods, embroidered and lace clothing, table linens, ceramics, decorative metalwork, and carved wood will intrigue and tempt you as you wander through the shops. Shops also line the perimeter of **Plaza del Sol,** adjacent to the downtown ferry pier (.5km/¼ mile or so north of the Punta Langosta pier), and several shopping arcades are accessible from the plaza, including the pleasant tree-lined **Plaza Confetti** and the **Villa Mar** complex, with several good silver-jewelry shops.

Agencia Publicaciones Gracia, Avenida 5A, a block from the ferry pier, is Cozumel's best source for English-language books, guidebooks, newspapers, and magazines. **Cinco Soleils,** at Avenida Rafael Melagar and Calle 8, is well stocked with beautiful, if pricey, handmade local goods. You'll also find **Pancho's Backyard,** a tequila bar, coffee shop, and outdoor restaurant. Sample the tequilas you're thinking about purchasing, and then take a load off your feet before heading off to your next adventure. **Bien Raices,** at Avenida 10 between Salas and Calle 1, offers an unusual range of fascinating handicrafts, including hand-carved wooden figurines and spectacular gourd lanterns. **Instrumentales Mexicanes,** at the corner of Juarez and Avenida 15, is the place to go for musical instruments from all over Mexico.

If you're docking at the **International Pier,** a bunch of nice shops in the terminal sell everything from Mexican blankets to jewelry, T-shirts, and handicrafts of all kinds. There is also a new high-end mall across the street from the port with all the shops you'd expect and prices to match. The pier at **Puerta Maya** has been newly renovated, and you might think you are in town, but it's designed to simulate a Mexican village. It boasts a wide selection of well-stocked gift shops.

BEACHES

Cozumel's best powdery white-sand beach, **Playa San Francisco,** stretches for some 5km (3 miles) along the southwestern shoreline. It was once one of the most idyllic beaches in Mexico, but resort development is threatening to destroy its old character. You can rent equipment for watersports here, as well as enjoy lunch at one of the many restaurants or bars on the shoreline. There's no admission to the beach, and it's about a $17 taxi ride south of San Miguel's downtown pier. If you land at the International Pier, you're practically at the beach already.

Playa Mia (www.playamiacozumel.com; ☎ **987/872-9030**), about 1.5km (1 mile) south of Playa del San Francisco, is a fine beach but has a big reputation as a party location, so it's likely to be wall-to-wall with your fellow cruisers. Playa Mia refers to itself as an "Adventure Beach Park" and offers several unique features, including an underwater re-creation of all of the major Mexican Mayan ruins, giving you the chance to snorkel over them. Every kind of watersport exists here, including

WaveRunners, kayaks, snorkeling, banana-boat rides, pedal boats, Sunfish sailboats, and more. It's also built up with bars, restaurants, watersports rentals, a miniature zoo, and so on, and charges a $15 entrance fee.

Several beach clubs have sprung up, one next to the other along the west coast, including **Mr. Sanchez, Carlos 'n Charlies,** and **Paradise Beach,** all with amenities, food, and good swimming. All-inclusive day rates are about $40.

You may want to consider the beach at **Chankanaab Nature Park,** and take in all the other attractions as well (see "On Your Own: Beyond the Port Area," above).

Farther south (but remember, you are still only 20 min. or 20km/12 miles from San Miguel) at the **Palancar Beach Club** (www.buceopalancar.com), you can enjoy a serene lunch under the palapas on the beach, or overlooking the sea, or at a table in the open-air dinning room and bar, and swim here for no entrance fee. (This is also the best diving site on the island—see below.) You can rent a kayak or snorkeling equipment for $10; add an hour-long boat ride to the reef for $35, or parasail for $55. Lockers, changing rooms, and outdoor showers are available. My favorite dish is deep-fried squid rings for $10.

Playa Bonita (sometimes called **Punta Chiqueros**) is one of the least-crowded beaches, despite its spectacular beauty. It is on the east side of the island, meaning that it opens out directly to the ocean, with pounding surf that has created generous amounts of fine coral sand; it lies on the east (windward) side of the island. Getting there will require renting a vehicle or throwing yourself at the mercy of a taxi driver. It sits in a moon-shaped cove sheltered from the Caribbean by an offshore reef. Waves are only moderate, the sand is powdery, and the water is clear. It has a wonderful restaurant and bar to provide succor in between rounds of snorkeling.

Farther north on the east side is **Punto Moreno Beach and Restaurant** (www.puntamorena.com.mx), where you can have lunch in a breezy, open patio by the sea. After eating, you are welcome to swim in the new saltwater pool that sparkles appealingly alongside the tables. Most of the tiny eateries that dot this side of the island can't accept credit cards because there is no electrical supply, but Punto Moreno takes cards because of a small wind generator visible on the left side of the building. Three huge fish tacos will set you back $10.

If you don't want to go far, two hotel beaches are a stone's throw north of the International Pier (facing the water, they're on the right), and they welcome day visitors to use their small beach, cabanas, pools, and changing facilities. **El Cid La Ceiba** (© 800/435-3240) charges $55 per person for the day (11am–5pm), while the **Park Royale** (© 888/774-0040) charges $70 per person for the day. Entrance fees at both include food and beverages.

SPORTS

SCUBA DIVING   Turtles and eagle rays in profusion, dozens of species of rainbow-hued tropical fish, and underwater visibility that averages 30m (100 ft.) make Cozumel one of the best diving destinations in the Caribbean. Cruisers might want to confine their adventures to the finest spot, **Palancar Reef.** Lying about 1.5km (1 mile) offshore, this fabulous water world features gigantic elephant-ear sponges and rare black coral, as well as deep caves, canyons, and tunnels. It's a favorite of divers from all over the world. At **Playa Palancar** (www.buceopalancar.com; © 987/118-5154), rent one tank for $65, or two for $90, or take a lesson for $130 with two tanks.

The best scuba outfitters are **Aqua Safari,** Avenida Rafael Melgar at Calle 5, next to the Vista del Mar Hotel (www.aquasafari.com; © 987/872-0101); **Blue Angel,** Carretera Costera Sur, km. 2.2, next to Hotel Blu (www.blueangel-scuba.com;

☎ 866/779-9986 or 987/872-1819); and **Diving Adventures,** Calle 15 Sur No. 2 (www.divingadventures.net; **☎ 987/872-3009** or 872-1631).

SNORKELING The shallow reefs at Playa San Francisco and Chankanaab Bay are among the best snorkeling spots. You'll see a world of sea creatures parading by— everything from parrotfish to sergeant majors. You can rent snorkeling equipment at Chankanaab for $10. The often photographed, shallow, white-sand sea floor full of starfish is **El Cielo,** which means "the sky." Get there by boat from Palancar Beach Club for $45—see above.

GOLF At **Cozumel Country Club** (www.cozumelcountryclub.com.mx), the 18-hole, par-72 course was designed by Jack Nicklaus, and is a Certified Audubon Cooperative Sanctuary. Book online for a special package rate of $159, which includes club rental.

GREAT LOCAL RESTAURANTS & BARS

The local beer is **Sol,** though Corona, Tecate, and Dos Equis are favored, too. On a hot day, a bottle of the stuff is manna from heaven.

The Tequila Lounge, Rafael Melgar at Calle 11 (**☎ 987/872-4421**), is an elegant bar with leather armchairs and avant-garde decor. The sea is just on the other side of the glass walls of the bar, and you can drink in the view while enjoying sushi and sophisticated cocktails. While the Tequila Lounge bears many of its namesake shot glasses on its shelves, it is also known around town as a great destination for house and lounge music.

Right across from the Punta Langosta pier is **Carlos 'n Charlies,** Av. Rafael Melgar 551 (www.carlosandcharlies.com; **☎ 987/869-1647**), Mexico's equivalent of the Hard Rock Cafe, but much wilder. Though it moved into sterile Houlihan's-style digs a few years ago, the music still blares, and dancing tourists pound back yard-long glasses of beer as if they're going out of style. Many a cruise passenger has stumbled back from this place clutching a souvenir glass as though it were the Holy Grail— dubious proof of a visit to Mexico. People come here for good times and the spicy, tasty ribs. You can dine surprisingly well on Yucatán specialties and the best chicken and beef fajitas in Cozumel.

Another party spot is the **Hard Rock Cozumel** itself, at Av. Rafael Melgar 2A (www.hardrock.com; **☎ 987/872-5271**), which serves the hard stuff as well as burgers and grilled beef or chicken fajitas. Yet another is **Fat Tuesday,** at the end of the International Pier (www.fat-tuesday.cozumel.net; **☎ 987/872-5130**), where you'll find lots of crew members on their day or night off (you can even hear their revelry from the ship). Join the fun and guzzle a 16-ounce margarita for $9 a pop or a 24-ounce version for $12. There's another Fat Tuesday near the ferry pier at the entrance to the Villa Mar complex, right next to Plaza del Sol.

For those who wish to try something a little less touristy and more authentic, we recommend **Casa Denis,** Calle 1 Sur 132, between Avenidas 5 and 10 (www.casa denis.com; **☎ 987/872-0067**). This is one of the oldest and most popular restaurants in town, located on the main plaza. Grab a seat on the open-air patio, and then take some time to admire the photos on the wall of some of the more noteworthy clientele who have dined at Casa Denis, including Jackie Kennedy Onassis and Plácido Domingo. Then select from a broad range of mouthwatering entrees such as grilled fish, fajitas, seafood tacos, or empanadas, and wash it down with the extremely generous margaritas. The restaurant has been in the family for more than 90 years; on many nights you can still find proprietor Denis Angulo overseeing what has been a lifetime passion. Cash only.

Just behind the Plaza Del Sol, **El Abuelo Gerardo,** 10th Avenida 21 Juarez and 2 Norte (℡ **987/872-1012**), is a local favorite, featuring inventive Mexican-Caribbean combinations with plenty of seafood. Open daily from 7:30am to 10:30pm, and very reasonably priced.

La Mission, Adolfo R. Salas Avenida (www.missioncoz.com; ℡ **987/872-6340**), just off the waterfront, serves the best seafood in town, with coconut shrimp and ultrafresh, grilled spiny lobster served over the shell. Live Mariachi music, big overhead fans, and a large open-air dining room surrounded by leafy plants all add to the pleasant tropical atmosphere. This local family also owns the **Casa Mission,** 55 Avenida between Juarez Avenida and 1st Street (www.missioncoz.com; ℡ **987/872-1641**), with a very different atmosphere, reminiscent of a traditional, inland hacienda (it was, and still is, the family home), with archways, large pottery vases, and folk art on the walls. The food is the same great quality and price, and there's live music here too. Coconut shrimp is $17.

Half a block from the pier, **Las Palmeras,** Avenida Rafael Melgar (www.restaurantepalmeras.com; ℡ **987/872-0532**), is ideal for casual eating. If you arrive in time, it serves one of the best breakfasts in town; at lunch, it offers tempting seafood dishes and Mexican specialties.

Two blocks from the downtown tender and ferry pier is **La Choza,** 10th Avenue #216 between Adolfo Rosado Salas and 3rd Sur (℡ **987/872-0958**), offering real local cooking that's a favorite of the town's savvy foodies.

Playa del Carmen

Playa del Carmen is an alternative to hanging around in San Miguel and is a pleasant mix of an easygoing touristy version of Mexico along the main boulevard, Avenida 5, and a more authentic version just a block or two farther west. Playa del Carmen has grown like gangbusters in the past decade, and counts among its population both international expatriates and many nationals who have moved here from other parts of Mexico. Wandering through the streets, visitors have countless opportunities to strike up conversations with those who have spent months or years relaxing and enjoying the sun, beaches, great restaurants, and laid-back ambience of Playa del Carmen. Take your snorkel, enjoy the beach, and then stroll the many shops that line Avenida 5. When the sun goes down, you can enjoy a fabulous Mexican or international meal and still make it back on the last ferry. If you can tolerate the crowds, the snorkeling is still excellent over the offshore reefs. Turtle-watching is another local pastime.

COMING ASHORE　Cruise ships calling at Cozumel offer a bundle of excursions that leave from Playa, enabling passengers to see the Mayan ruins at Tulum and Chichén-Itzá, and take all-inclusive day trips to the theme parks filled with activities on the Riviera Maya. You can take the ferry from Cozumel and hire a taxi or rent a car from Playa and see the sights on your own, or spend the day enjoying the shops and restaurants, and the attractive port area where the ferries dock.

GETTING AROUND

BY TAXI　Taxis are readily available to take you anywhere, but you can walk to the center of town, to the beach, and to most major shops.

BY RENTAL CAR　If you decide to rent a car for the day, **Budget, Hertz,** and **National** all have offices right next to the ferry pier.

BEST CRUISE LINE SHORE EXCURSIONS

Most visitors head for the Mayan ruins or one of the local eco-parks the moment they reach shore (see "Mayan Ruins & Other Mainland Attractions," on p. 187).

ON YOUR OWN: WITHIN WALKING DISTANCE

From the ferry pier, you can walk to the center of Playa del Carmen, to the beach adjacent to the pier, and to the ever-expanding shopping district, which has a seemingly endless strip of trendy boutiques and hip restaurants; this can easily fill an enjoyable afternoon. The full stroll will take you to the far side of Playa del Carmen, where the atmosphere is slightly less touristy and caters more to the local population, including a significant expat population. They know where the good restaurants are, and there is a range of appealing places just down the road. Be sure to stop off at **Ah Cacao,** Avenida 5 at Constituyentes/Calle 18, a cafe that makes to-die-for mocha, hot chocolate, and a wide range of chocolate desserts.

You can also visit one of the local beaches, **Mamitas,** on Calle 30, and then stop off at one of the many restaurants or bars on your way back.

ON YOUR OWN: ON THE YUCATÁN PENINSULA

If you take a car or taxi on your own from Playa Del Carmen, general admission for **Xcaret** (www.xcaret.net; ☏ 998/881-2400) is $79 for adults; add a buffet lunch and it's $109. See "Mayan Ruins & Other Mainland Attractions," earlier in this chapter, for a full description of the park.

Several miles farther south of Xcaret is **Xel-Ha** (www.xel-ha.com; ☏ 984/875-6000), which features a sprawling natural lagoon filled with sparkling blue-green water and surrounded by lush foliage. You can spend a great couple of hours floating your way from one end of the calm body of water to the other, stopping to see schools of tropical fish. Shops, restaurants, and lots of beach chairs pepper the area. One price covers park admission, food and drinks, snacks, snorkel equipment, life jackets, hammocks, deck chairs, and floating inner tubes. You can purchase all-inclusive tickets at $119 for adults and $60 for kids under 55 inches. (Because all meals, drinks, and equipment are included, it's a better deal if you plan to stay all day.)

Buses from Playa del Carmen come here frequently; a taxi costs about $45 one-way. See "Mayan Ruins & Other Mainland Attractions," earlier in this chapter, for a full description of the park.

No trip to the Yucatán is complete without at least one visit to a cenote—freshwater pools connecting to submerged caverns and other cenotes—which in the Mayan tradition represents the gateway to the underworld. The Yucatán offers more than 3,000 of these beautiful formations, which are the result of underground caves collapsing; they are home to a vivid variety of freshwater fish and spectacular stalactite and stalagmite formations. **Cenote Azul** is one such popular location, relatively close to Playa del Carmen at Hwy. 307, across from Xpu-Ha near Puerto Aventuras. Admission is about $7, with snorkel rental available. For those who want to try an underwater snorkeling tour of the caves, **Hidden Worlds Cenotes Park,** Hwy. 307 between Tulum and Akumal (www.hiddenworlds.com; ☏ 984/877-8535), is a great option, offering the chance to visit huge caverns. It costs $60 for 2½ hours of snorkeling, $80 for unlimited snorkeling and zip lines. Taxis run about $7 to $10 from Playa del Carmen.

For those preferring to admire the water, a horseback ride along the beach may be just the ticket. **Punta Venado** (www.puntavenado.com; ☏ 998/887-1191) offers tours through the Mayan forest and along the water, as well as ATV riding and snorkeling in a small nearby cenote.

A little farther off the beaten path but well worth the effort for foliage aficionados is a visit to the **Yaax Garden Yaax Che** (Botanical Garden), km. 320 Carr. Federal, Puerto Morelos (✆ **998/206-9233**), which is one of the most complete collections of plants of the Mayan forest. It is a lovely setting with a swinging wooden bridge and a lookout fort above the trees. There is also a display of traditional Mayan houses and lifestyle, and information on the old-fashioned methods for extracting gum from trees to make chewing gum. Many of the garden staff are former *chicleros* (gum men). Yaax Che is about 27km (17 miles) north of Playa del Carmen and is open Monday to Saturday from 9am to 4pm.

SHOPPING

The **Rincon del Sol** plaza is a tree-filled courtyard between Calle 4 and Calle 6, built in the colonial Mexican style. It has the best collection of handicrafts shops in the area, some of which offer much better quality items than the junky souvenirs peddled elsewhere, so take time to stroll. You can find the usual range of tourist fare, as well as more interesting options, such as jauntily colored tiled mirrors, hanging lamps carved out of coconuts, and Brazilian flip-flops. Several shops specialize in Mayan gear, including traditional Mayan ear candles.

Most shops are along **Avenida 5,** which runs parallel to the coast and has a pleasant pedestrian-only stretch. In between the innumerable bars and restaurants are some real gems of shops, selling must-have collectibles such as Frida Kahlo relics, cotton clothing, tiny bathing suits, candles, and jewelry for every occasion. Enjoy perusing the wares at **La Hierbabuena,** between Calle 8 and Calle 10, for Mexican mirrors and cards; **Los Milagros,** between Calle 2 and Calle 4, a gallery with work from artists from Oaxaca, Tlaquepaque, and other places around the country; and **Etenoha Ambar Gallery,** between Calle 8 and Calle 10, for jewelry with red amber and obsidian, as well as Panama hats and other treasures. **Wayan,** at Avenida 5 between Calle 2 and Calle 4, offers an all-natural clothing line and traditional crafts.

GREAT LOCAL RESTAURANTS & BARS

La Cueva Del Chango, on Calle 38, between Avenida 5 and the beach (✆ **984/147-0271**), is a gem of a restaurant that is well worth the cab fare that it costs from the pier (or the beautiful stroll down Av. 5). The crepes are divine, as is the *chile poblano* with Oaxaca cheese, which is served with both red and green sauces. Casa Del Chango also serves a wide variety of fresh juices from local ingredients, such as chaya and orange juice.

Italian expats living in Playa swear by **Romagna Mia de Davide** (✆ **984/873-2208**), Avenida Cozumel, between Calle 28 and Calle 32. With entrees such as handmade pastas and gnocchi, and savory tortes and risottos (many for little more than $10), Romagna Mia will make you cry when the ferryboat pulls out of Playa to return you to your cruise ship. Really—it's that good!

Babe's Noodles and Bar, Calle 10, between Avenidas 5 and 10 (www.babesnoodlesandbar.com; ✆ **984/803-0056**), is an excellent option for those craving international cuisine. Babe's is trendy, with small tables and low lighting, but it's popular for a reason, and that's tasty plates of Asian fusion dishes and other imaginative creations. Lunch is $8 to $14 (cash only).

There are many options for those hankering after good old-fashioned Mayan cooking: **Ajua Maya,** Calle 4, between Avenidas 5 and 10 (ajuamaya.com; ✆ **984/873-2523**), is an excellent choice for either Mayan dishes (heavy on the rice, beans, tortillas, and guacamole) or wild game, and provides an evening of entertainment to boot, with its own local band and waiters who practice the Mayan tradition of carrying precarious items such as a full table's worth of drinks on their heads. The Caesar salad is prepared tableside, with the egg yolks and anchovies mixed before your very eyes. Delicious! Lunch is about $35. **Yaxche,** Calle 8, between Avenidas 5 and 10 (www.mayacuisine.com; ℂ **984/873-2502**), is another mouthwatering option, with delicacies such as *queso relleno,* shrimp fajitas, and handmade tortillas. Lunch is about $22.

El Oasis (www.eloasismariscos.com; ℂ **984/803-2676**), Calle 12, between Avenidas 10 and 15, offers killer seviche that is large enough for a meal for about $9. They also serve a wide range of seafood options in a friendly, open restaurant and bar. Great for filling up after a day at the beach.

If you want to stay in the thick of things, there's a **Señor Frog's** (ℂ **984/873-0930**) right at the ferry pier, and a **Carlos 'n Charlies** (www.carlosandcharlies.com; ℂ **984/803-3498**) just up the street, for all the beer and shots you can stomach.

Costa Maya

While Cozumel gets the most traffic by far, another port on the Yucatán Peninsula has entered the scene: Costa Maya, near the sleepy fishing village of Mahajual (just over 150km/90 miles south of Playa del Carmen). The port has three main pavilions, which include high-end shopping areas, saltwater pools, restaurants and bars, and events and performances. There are also taxis waiting to take you to the nearby towns and beaches, and even points a little farther out.

This is a wild and beautiful place, home to Banco Chincorro, Mexico's largest coral atoll, which is part of the chain of reefs known as the Mesoamerican Barrier Reef that shadows the Costa Maya, all the way into Belize and beyond. Much of the reef along this part of the coast is protected, and populated by myriad varieties of coral, and abundant species of fish. Behind this massive natural barrier, the sea is calm, creating a shoreline with beaches perfect for swimming.

Don't confuse Costa Maya with Riviera Maya, which stretches between Puerto Morelos and Punta Allen. Costa Maya extends from Punta Allen to the border with Belize. The Mayan ruins of Kohunlich and Chacchoben are popular attractions in this area, along with the Seven Color Lagoon in Baclar; the flora and fauna of the jungle; the silky, white-sand beaches; and diving and snorkeling. Though the pavilions are attractive, fun, and comfortable, this is the least developed tourist area on the peninsula, so if you want to see a real slice of what I like to call the Mayan Caribbean, venture out and take a look.

COMING ASHORE Literally carved out of the jungle, this amenity-filled pier is the major form of development for miles around, and has pretty much everything you want: sprawling restaurants (one with a balcony, the other with outdoor seating and a stage for live music), an amphitheater for cultural dance performances, two saltwater pools, a pool bar, a trampoline, and plenty of shops. And a free tram shuttles passengers from their ships down the .5km (¼ mile) pier to the port entrance. When you leave the port, you will see a large area of bare, sun-bleached branches; these are damaged mangroves, struggling to come back after being hit hard in 2007 by Hurricane Dean.

GETTING AROUND

BY TAXI You'll find a long line of taxis just outside the pier. Because the attractions of note are fairly distant, the prices are not so cheap. Remember, if you go in a group, the cost comes down. Trips to the nearby beaches and the village of Mahajual are quite inexpensive, from $2 to $7.

BY RENTAL CAR   There are no rental-car facilities in the area yet, but the straight, flat roads are now fully paved, and rental cars will be available soon. Check agencies for availability before you leave.

BEST CRUISE LINE SHORE EXCURSIONS

The Mayan Ruins of Kohunlich ($95, 7 hr.): Located in a secluded jungle setting, this Mayan city was built between A.D. 500 and 600, during the peak of the classical period. The trail to the ruins is marked by a tree that was uprooted and replanted upside down—a means of marking sites used by the apparently brilliant, though obviously eccentric, Mexican archaeologist who first explored the site. Check out the Plaza of the Acropolis and the Temple of the Masks, where five of the eight original 2m (7-ft.) stone masks depicting the Mayan sun god Kinich Ahau are remarkably well preserved.

The Mayan Ruins of Chacchoben ($85, 4 hr.): Opened to the public in 1999, the name of this collection of temples means Red Corn, and dates back to A.D. 360, or the middle of the early classical period. This civic and religious center played an important role as a trading center for wood, jade, and colorful birds. There are more than two dozen structures; to date, less than 5% of the site has been excavated. The first temple that you'll encounter is the Temple of Venus, a tribute to fertility. The pyramids are in an excellent state of preservation, and their distinctive curved edges and soft lines are particularly beautiful.

Bike & Kayak ($69, 3 hr.): Starting off on mountain bikes, you'll pedal along a dirt road past a small mangrove lagoon with views of the coastline, then through the village of Mahajual (don't blink or you'll miss it), and finally arrive at the beach. After a short refreshment break, trade in your helmet for a paddle and pair up with a partner for a kayak trip out along the nearby reef. The small two-person kayaks are easy to handle and to launch from shore. The bike ride back includes another beach stop.

Jungle Beach Break ($45, no set time): A shuttle operates between the nearby Uvero Beach and the pier every 35 minutes, allowing you to come and go as you please. But why would you ever want to leave the snow-white beaches and crystal-blue water, not to mention the chaise longues and umbrellas, open bar, free sea kayaks, paddle boats, jet skis, and powerboats? Facilities include changing rooms with showers and an on-site snack bar (food not included in the price). Parasailing and snorkel gear rental are also available.

EXCURSIONS OFFERED BY LOCAL AGENCIES

Mayan World Adventures (www.mayanworldadventures.com.mx; ✆ **983/102-0477**) will take you on custom tours of area ruins, the Fort of the Pirates, and the Seven Colors Lagoon in Bacalar.

ON YOUR OWN: WITHIN WALKING DISTANCE

If you choose, you could stay right at the one-stop-shop pier complex and forgo a trip to the jungle, ruins, or towns. Because some ships are in port only until 1:30pm, this is an attractive option. Cultural shows daily range from a pre-Hispanic dance to a Mexican folkloric performance. There are also activities throughout the day in and around the pier, from aqua-aerobics to games and contests. Check the daily entertainment schedule posted near the restrooms for performance times and activities.

There are a number of local beach packages, some only minutes away. You can choose one at the port and a taxi will take you there for $2 to $5.

ON YOUR OWN: BEYOND THE PORT AREA

The closest town in the area is Mahajual, a fishing village and destination for a few international tourists on their way to Belize. The single main road is lined with a few small, screened-in restaurants and a miniscule grocery. On the other side of the street is a long white beach with a new walkway. The town remains rustic despite the hordes of cruise passengers who line the narrow street on port days.

The town of **Bacalar** is about 115km (70 miles) from the port and is well worth seeing. Fresh water flows underground through limestone all over the Yucatán Peninsula; at Bacalar it comes to the surface in two extraordinary formations. One is a clear, freshwater, shallow lagoon (60km/35 miles long and 2km/1¼ miles wide) with so many different shades of turquoise and blue, it is called **The Seven Colors Lagoon,** and the other is the **Cenote Azul,** a deep, circular pool surrounded by lush vegetation. (Don't confuse this one with the cenote of the same name on the Riviera Maya.) Swim in the cenote or the lagoon, or take a pontoon boat ride around the lagoon. **Club De Vela (© 983/836-0493)** will take you out on the boat. There are several nice restaurants along the waterside drive.

At Bacalar the first place you'll pass on the Coastal Road is the **Cenote Azul.** You'll park and walk down the stairs past a few vendors. You can change into swimming gear in the large (though rustic) bathrooms. Take a swim in the cenote's deep blue water. The restaurant there serves a mixed ceviche and an unusual dish of octopus in chile sauce that's worth your while. Prices start at $8.

The **Fort of the Pirates,** built in 1733, overlooks the lagoon, and once protected Bacalar from pirate attacks. The fort is well preserved and features a small museum of its history, and a large mural depicting the conquest of the Mayas by the Spanish. The entrance fee is $5; it's open from 9am to 4:30pm, closed Monday. Head south on the Hwy. 307, and make a left at the turnoff to Cenote Azul. The trip to Bacalar takes about 1¼ hours. The Caribe municipal bus goes round-trip from Mahajual to Bacalar for $8.50. A taxi will cost $106 round-trip for four people. A minivan will take 6 round-trip for $140, or rent an even bigger vehicle that will take 11 there and back for $250.

SHOPPING

Because the port at Costa Maya was constructed with the sole purpose of serving American and European cruise ship passengers, you can bet your last enchilada that shopping abounds. There are dozens of shops in a mall-like setting—some of them familiar to the seasoned cruiser, others unique. Some shops that you will likely find include **Ultra Femme,** specializing in fragrances and cosmetics cheaper than you'll find at the duty-free store; **Tanzanite International,** which sells a wide selection of gold and jewels; **Diamond International,** which usually has great bargains on jewelry and gemstones; and **Taxco Factory,** which sells "art in silver." There are also nearby *palapas* (small thatched-roof stands), where local artisans craft their wares as potential buyers look on.

BEACHES

On the way to Mahajual, along the new, wide Malecón (beach walk) that begins at the lighthouse, you'll find a beautiful stretch of white sand and clear, shallow water in front of the Quinto Sole Hotel (© **983/834-5715**). The hotel offers an all-day beach package that includes open bar ($30) or soda ($20), tables and palapas in the sand, lounge chairs, and sea kayaks. Jet skis and snorkeling equipment are available for rent. Lunch is extra; a chicken quesadilla is $10, with shrimp $12. It's a 5-minute, $2 taxi ride from the pier.

GREAT LOCAL RESTAURANTS & BARS

There are a number of eateries at the port in Costa Maya, including a **Señor Frog's** and a **Carlos 'n Charlies** (www.carlosandcharlies.com), and while both offer their standard, reliable full-service food and drinks, because of the remote location, expect a hamburger to cost a little more here (around $20).

The best restaurant in Mahajual is the **Luna De Plata,** Avenida Mahajual, km. 2 (www.lunadeplata.info; ✆ 983/125-3999), which serves gourmet Italian cuisine with homemade pasta. The lobster ravioli can't be beat. Main courses are from $8 to $30.

The Quinto Sole Restaurant, Carretera Mahahual-Xcalak, km. 0.350 (✆ **983/834-5715**), along the boardwalk before Mahajual, offers everything from whole fish to steak. Eat on the open-air deck and watch the activity along the boardwalk. Prices range from $10 to $25. The food at **Los Aluxes** along the Coastal Road in Bacalar (✆ **983/834-2817**) is Mayan Caribbean, and a fish fillet wrapped in banana leaf, seasoned with a mild, local red chile, hits the spot for flavor, texture, and presentation. You can also get a tasty steak and crème brûlée (which is more like flan here, but very good). The restaurant, decorated with wooden sculptures depicting the Maya, is steps away from a little beach with a couple swings and a slide, both over the water of the Seven Colors Lagoon. Like so many places in the Yucatán Peninsula, you can swim if you eat there. Prices are very reasonable, with main dishes costing $10 to $12. Closed Wednesday.

Toward the end of the Coastal Road, Bacalar, just below the Fort of the Pirates, is the launching area for the pontoon boats that take you out to the lagoon. The restaurant **El Muleto** is also there, and you'll find a full menu and bar, with prices starting at $8 and going to $22.

Progreso/Mérida

Visited by a fraction of the ships that call at Cozumel, Progreso has one major advantage over its rival: proximity to Chichén-Itzá, which lies only 2 hours south by motorcoach. This makes excursions to the ruins considerably cheaper than they are from Cozumel, averaging about $95 per person. Progreso itself is almost nothing but a port. Ships dock here at the end of a man-made causeway that juts out several miles into the Gulf of Mexico, and you must take a minibus up the pier. It is very difficult to visit anything on your own, and we recommend taking a tour to visit the ruins. Aside from visits to Chichén-Itzá and the smaller Mayan ruins at Uxmal and Dzibilchaltun, cruise passengers can visit Mérida, the capital of Yucatán state (about 30km/20 miles away); see pink flamingos in their natural habitat at the Celestun Estuary Nature Reserve; or take a jeep trek off-road to two local haciendas.

CURAÇAO

As you sail into the deep natural harbor of Willemstad, be sure to look for the unique "floating bridge," the Queen Emma pontoon bridge, which swings aside to open the narrow channel. Welcome to Curaçao, the largest and most populous of the Netherlands Antilles, just 56km (35 miles) north of the Venezuelan coast.

Curaçao was first discovered by the Spanish in 1499, but in 1634 the Dutch came and prospered. Because it lies outside the hurricane belt, and much of the island is an arid desert, the settlers ruled out farming and instead developed Curaçao into one of the Dutch empire's busiest trading posts. In 1915, when the Royal Dutch/Shell Company built one of the world's largest oil refineries to process crude from Venezuela, workers from 50 countries poured onto the island, and today it remains a melting pot, its population descended from a curious mixture of bloodlines, including African, Dutch, Venezuelan, and Pakistani. The oil refineries went into decline after World War II, and by the 1980s tourism had begun to develop, leading to the building of many new hotels.

Today, the island retains a Dutch flavor, especially in **Willemstad,** where the harbor is bordered by rows of pastel-colored, gabled Dutch-colonial houses. While these structures give Willemstad a storybook appearance, the rest of the island looks like the American Southwest, its desertlike landscape dotted with three-pronged cactuses, spiny-leafed aloes, and divi-divi trees bent by trade winds.

COMING ASHORE Cruise ships dock in Willemstad at a megapier just beyond the Queen Emma pontoon bridge, which leads to the duty-free shopping sector and the famous Floating Market. It's a 5- to 10-minute walk from here to the center of town, or you can take a taxi from the stand. A shopping/entertainment complex called Riffort Village recently opened in a restored fort nearby. The town itself is easy to navigate on foot. Most of it can be explored in 2 or 3 hours, leaving plenty of time for beaches or watersports. Although the ship terminal has a duty-free shop, save your serious shopping for Willemstad. There's a phone center at the cruise terminal.

LANGUAGE Dutch, Spanish, and English are spoken on Curaçao, along with Papiamento, a patois that combines the three major tongues with Amerindian and African dialects.

CURRENCY The official currency is the **Antillean florin** (1.79 ANG = US$1; 1 ANG = US56¢). Each florin (also called a **guilder**) is divisible by 100¢. Canadian and U.S. dollars, as well as euros, are accepted for purchases, so there's no need to change money. Prices in this section are given in U.S. dollars.

INFORMATION Stop by the **Curaçao Tourist Board,** Pietermaai (✆ **599/9-434-8200**), open Monday through Friday from 8am to 5pm, or at the information booth in the center of Willemstad (near the Pontoon bridge). For information before you go, visit www.curacao.com or call ✆ **800/328-7222.**

CALLING FROM THE U.S. When calling Curaçao from the United States, you need to dial the international access code (011) before the numbers listed here.

Getting Around

BY TAXI Taxis are metered, and the best place to flag one down is on the Otrobanda side of the floating bridge. Generally, there's no need to tip. Up to four passengers can share the price of an island tour by taxi, which costs about $45 per hour.

BY BUS A fleet of buses operates from Wilhelmina Plein, near the shopping center, Punda, and Otrobanda, and runs to most parts of Curaçao. You can hail a bus at any designated bus stop.

BY RENTAL CAR Driving is on the right, on paved roads. **Avis, Budget, Hertz, National,** and **Thrifty** all have offices here. The *Curaçao Traveler* magazine is free and widely distributed and has road maps and a street index Or go to www.curamap.com for a good online resource.

Curaçao

Best Cruise Line Shore Excursions

Many excursions aren't really worth the price here—you can easily see the town on your own and hop a taxi to the few attractions on the island outside of Willemstad.

Spanish Water Canoe Tour & Snorkeling ($74, 3½ hr.): At Caracas Bay Island, you'll board canoes for a 45-minute paddle alongside mangroves and rock formations. Then you'll arrive at Baya Beach, where instructors lead snorkeling sessions over a sunken tugboat.

Underwater Animal Encounter ($125, 4 hr.): Ever wanted to hand-feed a shark? Here's your chance. Suit up in scuba gear and dive into the shallow (3.5m/11-ft.) water at the Curaçao Seaquarium, where sharks and sea turtles are behind fencing,

Unlike many Caribbean islands where culture and history play a distant second to fun in the sun, Curaçao has a wealth of rich history that has been well preserved in its many museums, including Museum Kurá Hulanda, the Curaçao Museum, and the Maritime Museum. (See "On Your Own: Within Walking Distance," below.)

with holes through which you can hand them their grub, while stingrays, parrotfish, and other marine life swim around on your side. Because the water is so shallow, scuba certification isn't required.

Excursions Offered by Local Agencies

Fiesta Tours (www.fiestatourscuracao.com; © **559/9-515-9854**), a local family-run agency, will take you on a private, custom tour or a group excursion to most of the notable and scenic sites on the island; go for 2½ up to 7 hours. Their most popular excursions stop at the **Jan Kok Salt Pond** to see the flamingos and take in **Boca Tabla Caves,** or you might want to go to the **Curaçao Liqueur Factory.**

On Your Own: Within Walking Distance

The major attraction here is **Willemstad,** which you can see on foot. After years of restoration, the town's historic center full of red-roofed, pastel-colored town houses and the island's natural harbor, Schottegat, have been inscribed on UNESCO's World Heritage List. Meandering along the narrow streets and narrower alleyways is a fun way to search for bargains or get to know the locals.

The narrow channel that runs through the heart of town is **St. Anna Bay,** which is naturally deep enough to allow even large ships to berth directly in town. It divides the town into two historically separate halves. On the eastern side is Punda ("the Point" in Papiamentu), where the ornate Dutch town houses line the waterfront along Handelskade. This was the wealthy side of town and is the oldest, where Dutch merchants built homes that also served as shops and warehouses on the ground floor. The western side of town is called Otrobanda ("the Other Bank") and is marked by the historic **Fort Riffort.** Built to protect the mouth of the bay, it was run by the U.S. Army during World War II. Nazi submarines were kept out by a chain-link net that was drawn across the harbor. The fort now houses a variety of shops and restaurants as well as a brand-new megaresort and casino. While the architecture is not as lovely on this side of town, the views across the narrow channel are priceless.

By far one of the most engaging and mesmerizing sights in all of Curaçao is the **Queen Emma pontoon bridge.** A feat of engineering genius, it is motorized on one side and, about every 30 minutes, a man actually drives it to the side of the harbor so that ships and boats can pass through the channel. It's exceedingly cool to watch and adds to the already tempting appeal of finding a waterfront bistro, ordering some beers, and watching the action.

Another great way to explore is via a 75-minute **trolley tour** that takes you to the city's major highlights. The tour begins at Fort Amsterdam near the Queen Emma bridge and will set you back about $25 per adult and $15 for children 2 to 12.

A statue of **Pedro Luis Brion** dominates the square known as Brionplein, at the Otrobanda end of the Queen Emma bridge. Born in Curaçao in 1782, Brion became the island's favorite son and best-known war hero. He was an admiral of the fleet under Simón Bolívar and fought for the independence of Venezuela and Colombia.

Fort Amsterdam, site of the Governor's Palace and the 1769 Dutch Reformed church, has the task of guarding the waterfront. The church here still has a British cannonball embedded in it. The arches leading to the fort were tunneled under the official residence of the governor. A corner of the fort stands at the intersection of Breedestraat and Handelskade, the starting point for a plunge into the island's major shopping district.

A few minutes' walk from the pontoon bridge, at the north end of Handelskade, is the **Floating Market,** where scores of schooners tie up alongside the canal. Boats arrive here from Venezuela, Colombia, and various West Indian islands to sell tropical fruits and vegetables, as well as handicrafts. The modern market's vast concrete cap and rainbow-hued sunshades have not diminished the fun of watching the activity here. Either arrive early or stay late to view marine merchants setting up or storing their wares.

Between the I. H. (Sha) Capriles Kade and Fort Amsterdam, at the corner of Columbusstraat and Hanchi di Snoa, is the **Mikve Israel-Emanuel Synagogue.** Dating from 1651, the Jewish congregation here is the oldest in the New World. Next door, the **Jewish Cultural Historical Museum,** Hanchi Snoa 29 (www.snoa.com; ✆ 599/9-461-1633), is housed in two 1728 buildings that served as the rabbi's residence and the mikvah (bath), used for religious purification purposes. Entry is through the synagogue; admission is $10. Hours are Monday through Friday from 9am to 4:30pm, Sunday from 10am to 4pm.

You can walk from the Queen Emma pontoon bridge to the **Curaçao Museum,** Van Leeuwenhoekstraat (✆ 599/9-462-3873). The building, constructed in 1853 by the Royal Dutch Army as a military hospital, has been carefully restored and furnished with paintings, objets d'art, and antique furniture, and now houses a large collection from the Caiquetio tribes. On the museum grounds is a gallery for temporary exhibitions of both local and international art. Hours are Monday through Friday from 8:30am to 4:30pm, Sunday from 10am to 4pm. Admission is $5 for adults, $2.50 for children 14 and under.

A bit farther along, in Otrobanda, the **Museum Kurla Hulanda ★★**, Kipstraat 9 (✆ 599/9-434-7765), is one of the most unusual and largest museums in the Caribbean. Housed in once-dilapidated 19th-century buildings, the exhibits here display in dramatic form the dismal history of slave trading, which comprised a major component of the island's economic past. Real and re-created slave quarters and a simulated ship hull are backdrops for a vast collection of rusted shackles, chains, collars, and other torturous forms of restraint. The museum is open daily from 10am to 5pm. Admission is $10 for adults, $8 for students, and $7 for children and seniors.

If your yen for museums is still not quelled, you should visit the **Maritime Museum,** Van De Brandhof Straat 7 (www.curacaomaritime.com; ✆ 599/9-465-2327), in the historic Scharloo district, just off the harbor of St. Anna Bay. This museum boasts 40 permanent exhibits that trace the history of Curaçao, with a focus on its nautical past. Hours are Monday through Saturday from 9am to 4pm. Admission is $6 for adults, $3 for seniors and children 6 to 11, and free for children 5 and under.

On Your Own: Beyond the Port Area

Cactuses, bromeliads, rare orchids, iguanas, donkeys, wild goats, and many species of birds thrive in the 1,800-hectare (4,450-acre) **Christoffel National Park** (www. christoffelpark.org; ✆ 599/9-864-0363), located about a 30-minute taxi or car ride from the capital. Near the northwestern tip of Curaçao, the park rises from flat, arid countryside to 369m-high (1,211-ft.) St. Christoffelberg, the tallest point in the Dutch Leewards. Along the way are ancient Arawak paintings and the Piedra di Monton, a rock heap piled by African slaves who cleared this former plantation. Legend said the slaves could climb to the top of the rock pile, jump off, and fly back home across the Atlantic to Africa. The park has 30km (20 miles) of one-way trail-like roads. The shortest is about 8km (5 miles) long but takes about 40 minutes to drive because of its rough terrain. One of several hiking trails goes to the top of St. Christoffelberg; it takes about 1½ hours to walk to the summit (come early in the morning before it gets hot). There's also a museum in an old storehouse left over from plantation days. The park is open Monday through Saturday from 7:30am to 4pm, Sunday from 6am to 3pm. Admission is $12 per person. Guided tours are available.

The **Curaçao Sea Aquarium,** off Bapor Kibra (www.curacao-sea-aquarium.com; ✆ 599/9-465-6666), is the largest aquarium in the Caribbean. Created in 1984 and set in a natural lagoon, it displays more than 400 species of fish, crabs, anemones, and invertebrates such as sponges and coral, while also housing a respectable collection of flamingos, sea turtles, dolphins, sea lions, and sharks. The Shark and Animal Encounter allows divers, snorkelers, and experienced swimmers to feed, film, and photograph sharks, stingrays, lobsters, tarpons, parrotfish, and other marine life through tiny feeding holes cut into a large viewing window. You can swim with the dolphins (www.dolphin-academy.com) for $199, or dive with them in an open-water encounter for $300. Nonswimmers can get up close and personal with an assortment of invertebrates in the touch tank, watch a 3-D movie in a comfortable indoor theater, or enjoy an impressive dolphin show in the small outdoor amphitheater. The Seaquarium is adjacent to Curaçao's only full-facility, white-sand, palm-shaded beach, where you can relax or purchase lunch. Aquarium admission is $20 for adults and $10 for children 5 to 12, and includes access to the beach. Hours are daily from 8:30am to 5:30pm.

Stalagmites and stalactites are mirrored in a mystical underground lake in **Hato Caves,** F. D. Rosseveltweg (www.hatocaves.com; ✆ 599/9-868-0379). Long ago, geological forces uplifted this limestone terrace, which was originally a coral reef. The limestone formations were created over thousands of years by water seeping through the coral. After crossing the lake, you enter two caverns known as the Cathedral and La Ventana ("the Window"), where you'll see ancient Indian petroglyphs. The caves are open daily from 10am to 4pm; professional local guides take visitors through every hour. Admission is $8 for adults, $6 for children 4 to 11, and free for kids 3 and under.

Shopping

Curaçao is a shopper's paradise, with some 200 stores lining Heerenstraat, Breedestraat, and other streets in the 5-block district called the **Punda.** Many shops occupy the town's old Dutch houses.

The island is famous for its 5-pound "wheelers" of Gouda and Edam cheese. Look for good buys on wooden shoes, French perfumes, Dutch-blue Delft souvenirs, finely woven Italian silks, Japanese and German cameras, jewelry, silver, Swiss watches, linens, leather goods, liquor, and island-made rum and liqueurs, especially Curaçao liqueur, some of which has a distinctive blue color. Some stores also offer good buys on intricate lacework imported from everywhere between Portugal and China.

Suggested shops include **Bamali,** Breedestraat 2 (www.Bamali-fashion.com; ✆ 599/9-461-2258), for Indonesian-influenced clothing (mostly for women), and

Curaçao Creations, Schrijnwrekerstraat 14 (www.curacaocreations.com; ☎ **599/9-462-4516**), which sells authentic handicrafts. **Boolchands,** Breedestraat 50 (www.boolchand.com; ☎ **599/9-461-6233**), sells cameras and electronics, and **Little Holland,** Breedestraat 37 (☎ **599/9-461-1768**), has a walk-in humidor and a wide selection of cigars.

In Otrobanda, on the other side of the harbor in the old Riffort, there are a slew of high-end shops in the Renaissance Mall and **Riffort Village,** including international brands such as Brietling, Tiffany, Max Mara, Mango, and Little Switzerland. Take a shopping break at one of the many plaza cafes in the old fort complex and take a walk up on the ramparts for an expansive view of the sea.

Beaches

Curaçao has some 38 beaches, ranging from hotel sand patches to secluded coves. The seawater remains an almost-constant 76°F (24°C) year-round, with good underwater visibility, but beaches here just aren't as good as others in the region. Taxi drivers waiting at the cruise dock will take you to any of the beaches, but you'll have to negotiate a fare. To be on the safe side, arrange to have your driver pick you up at a certain time and take you back to the dock.

The **Curaçao Sea Aquarium** has the island's only full-facility, white-sand, palm-shaded beach (see "On Your Own: Beyond the Port Area," above), and aquarium admission is required. The rest of the beaches mentioned below are public.

Daaibooi is a good beach about 30 minutes from town, in the Willibrordus area on the west side of Curaçao. It's free, and popular with the locals, but there are no changing facilities.

Blauwbaai (Blue Bay) just northwest of Willemstad, is the largest and most frequented beach on Curaçao, with enough white sand for everybody. The $8 admission is well worth it. Along with showers and changing facilities, there are plenty of shady places to retreat from the noonday sun and a full-service restaurant.

This wide beach at **Playa Santa Cruz** is a multiple-use, mostly local beach dotted with palm trees, with some mangroves along one edge. The beach provides a few shade structures set back from the water, and a small bar, a restaurant, and restrooms are available at **Captain Goodlife's Beach Hut** (☎ **599/9-864-0438**). Captain Goodlife can take you in his water taxi to some secluded (private) beaches such as Love Beach, Santa Pretu, or Playa Hula—places that can be reached only by boat.

Westpunt is known for its gigantic cliffs and the divers who jump from them into the ocean below every Sunday. This public beach is on the northwestern tip of the island. Just south of Westpunt is **Knip Bay,** which has beautiful turquoise waters. On weekends, live music and dancing make the beach a lively place. Changing facilities and refreshments are available. **Playa Abao,** with crystal-turquoise water, is situated at the northern tip of the island.

Warning: Beware of stepping on the hard spines of sea urchins, which are sometimes found in these waters. While not fatal, their spines can cause several days of real discomfort. If you are unable to remove them, try the local remedies of vinegar or lime juice, which help dissolve them over the course of several days.

Great Local Restaurants & Bars

Curaçao's local beer is the very Dutch **Amstel.** The local drink is **Curaçao liqueur,** some of which has a distinctive blue color.

Gouverneur DeRouville, overlooking the waterfront, on DeRouvilleweg 9-F (www.de-gouverneur.com; ☎ **599/9-462-5999**), is a spectacular three-story structure, which was the residence of the original governor of Willemstad. Whether you sit on the balcony overlooking the water, in the courtyard, or inside the main dining room, you will appreciate the Dutch architecture almost as much as you'll enjoy the well-prepared food and professional service. The *keshi yena* (stuffed cheese) is worth the wait, and the mixed grill is cooked to perfection. Lunch is about $18.

Jaanchie's Restaurant (© **599/9-864-0126**) is a favorite among locals and visitors alike. The proprietor of this establishment is likely to greet you himself. In a rustic country-style setting with antiques and oak walls, diners are treated to savory local cuisine. The fish is among the freshest on island. My recent sampling of the grilled wahoo was perfection. You can also order delectable garlic shrimp or stewed goat. Lunch is about $14.

DOMINICA

First things first: It's pronounced "Dom-in-*eek*-a," not "Doe-*min*-i-ka." And it has nothing to do with the Dominican Republic. The Commonwealth of Dominica is an independent country, and English, not Spanish, is the official language. The only Spanish commonly understood in Dominica is *mal encaminado a Santo Domingo* ("accidentally sent to the Dominican Republic"), the phrase stamped on the many letters that make it to their proper destination only after an erroneous but common detour.

To be sure, Dominica has some rough edges. The island is poor, so don't expect luxury or up-to-the-minute technology around every corner, and not everything manmade is as beautiful as nature's handiwork. Balancing this, though, is the fact that Dominica is the lushest and most mountainous island in the eastern Caribbean. The island served as a backdrop for scenes in a couple of *Pirates of the Caribbean* movies, and many of the locations from the film can easily be recognized. The island is 47km (29 miles) long and 26km (16 miles) wide, smack-dab in the center of the arc formed by the Antilles. It's blessed with astonishing natural wonders—an abundance of clear rivers (one for every day of the year, they say), dramatic waterfalls, volcanic lakes, and foliage as gargantuan as any that H. G. Wells ever imagined on Venus. Volcanic coral reefs, every bit as biologically complex as the rainforests onshore, ring the island, and a bit farther from land, whales mate and calve.

Much of Dominica's beauty is accessible to even the most sedentary visitor. Sitting in a rowboat, you can glide up a river through swampland crowded with mangroves and exotic birds; impressive waterfalls are minutes from paved roads. You can also wend through astonishingly verdant rainforests along undemanding nature trails.

The island's people—primarily descendants of the West Africans brought over to work the plantations, plus some descendants of Europeans and Indians—are another great natural resource. Friendly and proud of their national independence, Dominica's 71,000 citizens remain, for the most part, unchanged by tourism. Don't be surprised when you're greeted with a smile and an "okay," the island's equivalent of "hi." One portion of the island's population has immeasurable ethnological significance: Concentrated in a territory in the northeast, Dominica's approximately 3,000 Carib Indians are the last remaining descendants of the people who dominated the region when Europeans arrived.

COMING ASHORE Dominica has two cruise ship ports. The most frequented is in the heart of **Roseau,** the country's capital and largest town. The other is near the northwestern town of **Portsmouth.** Banks, restaurants, a market, a tourism office, and the recommended Dominica Museum line the road opposite Roseau's berth.

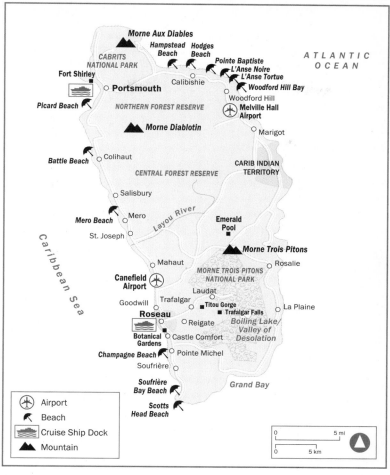

Portsmouth's port has a tourist welcome center (with an auditorium for speakers and films), shops, and instant access to Fort Shirley and Cabrits National Park.

LANGUAGE   English is Dominica's official language. Almost everyone speaks Creole as well, a patois that combines elements of French, English, and African languages. Dominica's Creole is similar to those spoken on the neighboring French islands of Guadeloupe and Martinique.

CURRENCY   The **East Caribbean dollar** (EC$2.70 = US$1; EC$1 = US37¢) is Dominica's official currency, but U.S. dollars are accepted almost everywhere. You're likely to receive change in the local currency. Most ATMs in Roseau dispense EC dollars, but a few provide an option for both currencies. Credit cards and traveler's checks are widely accepted. Prices in this section are given in U.S. dollars.

INFORMATION Dominica's **Tourism Authority** operates branches at the Roseau and Portsmouth cruise ship berths. The Roseau office is located a block from the waterfront in the downstairs of the Dominica Museum, on Dame M. E. Charles Boulevard. For information before you leave home, contact the **Dominica Tourist Office** (www.discoverdominica.com; ℂ **866/522-4057** from the U.S., or 767/448-2045). Several island businesses, including restaurants, tour operators, and other service providers, have joined forces to create another site, **www.avirtualdominica. com**, which has lots of links and some helpful information.

CALLING FROM THE U.S. When calling Dominica from the United States, simply dial "1" before the numbers listed here.

Getting Around

BY TAXI Taxis and public minivans are designated by license plates that begin with the letters H, HA, or HB. Also look for a round decal on the front of the car, which means the driver is a certified tourism operator. Fleets of both await cruise ship passengers at the Roseau and Portsmouth docks. Drivers are generally knowledgeable about sites and history. There are standard fees from the city to both airports. The fare from Melville Hall to Roseau is $50 and from Canefield to Roseau $20 per person. The vehicles are unmetered, so negotiate a price in advance and make sure everyone's talking about the same currency. You can get more information from the **Dominica Taxi Association** (ℂ **767/449-8533**). Some reputable operators are **Mally's Tour & Taxi Service** (ℂ **767/448-3114**), **Johnathan Vidal "Jon 'V'" Taxi** (ℂ **767/235-2375**), and **Ontime Taxi & Tour** (ℂ **767/449-8421**). The island served as a backdrop for the second and third installments of *Pirates of the Caribbean,* and many of these drivers were employed on set and will be happy to take you to a few of the sites where various scenes were filmed.

BY BUS Dominica has a reliable public transportation system consisting of primarily private minibus operators. Bus stops can be found at designated points throughout the city, depending on your destination. The bus fares are standardized and range from $1.50 to $11, depending on the specific route. Bus rotation is fairly frequent throughout the day.

BY RENTAL CAR Dominica's road system is extensive and relatively well maintained, considering the frequent torrential rains; but driving is on the left side, and passage through the mountains can be harrowing. You'll need a valid driver's license and a Dominican driver's permit, which costs about $12 and is usually available through rental agencies. You must be between 25 and 65 to obtain one. Don't get annoyed when other drivers sound their horns; honking usually indicates an oncoming vehicle (especially at sharp curves) or is meant as a friendly greeting. Local agencies include **Valley Rent a Car,** with offices in both Roseau and Portsmouth (www. valleyrentacar.com; ℂ **767/445-5252**), and **Garraway Rent-a-Car,** 17 Old St., in downtown Roseau (ℂ **767/448-2891**). Other options are **Best Deal Rent a Car** (ℂ **767/449-9204**), **Budget Rent-A-Car** (ℂ **767/449-2080**), and **Courtesy Car Rental** (www.dominicacarrentals.com; ℂ **767/448-7763**).

Best Cruise Line Shore Excursions

Trafalgar Falls & Sulphur Springs ($64, 5 hr.): Travel to the island interior to visit two of Dominica's most stunning wonders—beautiful Trafalgar Falls and a thermal sulfur spring so hot that your guide can actually boil an egg in its waters. You'll drive to Morne Bruce for a panoramic view of Roseau and learn about local flora and fauna at the Botanical Gardens. Next, head to the village of Trafalgar and take a 15-minute walk to view one of the Caribbean's most picturesque waterfalls. These twin falls cascade into a deep pool and are surrounded by forest, lush ferns, and tropical foliage. Finally, take another 15-minute hike to Sulfur Springs.

Carib Indian Territory ($100, 6½ hr.): Along a rugged portion of Dominica's northeastern coast, the 1,530-hectare (3,780-acre) Carib Indian Territory is home to the world's last surviving Carib Indians. Kalinago Barana Aute, the "Carib Cultural Village by the Sea," honors the diversity, history, and heritage of the Kalinago people. Visitors can enjoy the traditional crafts demonstrations and dance performances, explore an herbal medicine garden, hike the trails, and stop in the arts-and-crafts gallery. A hot meal of chicken or beef is served upon the completion of your tour and may be enjoyed at a picnic table overlooking the Caribbean.

River Tubing & Emerald Pool Adventure ($82, 3 hr.): A 40-minute drive takes you into the Layou Valley, where tubing guides will take you down the river that is lined with tall, overhanging cliffs and lush vegetation. A longer version of this tour also pays a visit to the Emerald Pool.

Dominica by 4x4 and Swimming at the Titou Gorge ($89, 3½ hr.): A jeep convoy heads up Morne Bruce for a picturesque view, stopping at the Wotten Waven Sulphur Springs before arriving at the volcanic Titou Gorge, where sheer 7m (23-ft.) black walls, rock outcrops, caves, and a thundering waterfall provide an exhilarating swimming experience. Scenes from *Pirates of the Caribbean* were filmed here.

Whale & Dolphin Safari ($72, 3½ hr.): Dominica has been hailed by some marine biologists as one of the most reliable spots for whale-watchers to see sperm whales. Board a motorized vessel and cruise to a point approximately 13km (8 miles) offshore. As you search for marine mammals, your guide provides a running commentary on the marine life found off Dominica. The deep waters surrounding Dominica are a natural breeding ground for sperm whales, and several species of dolphins are occasionally encountered.

Excursions Offered by Local Agencies

See "Sports," below, for information on scuba, snorkeling, and kayaking trips.

Canyoning: Extreme Dominica (www.extremedominica.com; ✆ 767/448-0412 or 767/276-2920) will "show you the ropes" with Dominica's newest adventure sport—canyoning. This adventure combines the get-wet fun of river tubing with the thrill of rock climbing and rappelling. Experience a hike through mesmerizing rock formations with clear pools and stunning waterfalls. The journey beneath rainforest canopy and through hidden canyons and waterfalls is truly memorable. It costs $160 for a 4- to 6-hour tour that includes round-trip transfer from the Roseau Port, equipment rental, and lunch. No previous experience is necessary. Book in advance.

Nature Tours: Dominica has several excellent tour operators who know the island's many features and intricate terrain like the backs of their hands. One truly outstanding and highly recommended operation is **Ken's Hinterland Adventure Tours,** Fort Young Hotel, Victoria Street, Roseau (www.kenshinterlandtours.com; ✆ 767/448-1660, or after hours at 448-3517), which offers tours that focus on botany, natural history, bird-watching, and whale-watching. Prices range from $60 for a half-day to $95 for a full day. Groups of four or more receive a discounted rate. Book online or walk in to the tour desk on the second-floor patio of the Fort Young Hotel.

Carib Indian Excursions: For trips through the Kalinago Barana Autê Carib Territory, you might want to make arrangements with The Carib council (www.kalinago baranaaute.com; ✆ **767/445-7979**). You can't miss with the firsthand knowledge of Carib traditions offered by the kalingo people themselves. There are local crafts available for purchase and a restaurant serving local foods. A site pass to the village plus tour costs $10. You can arrange for transport there but it will cost $175 for five people or fewer.

Caribbean Cooking: The outfitter **Jungle Trekking Adventures & Safaris** (✆ **767/440-5827**) offers several land tours with half- and full-day options, including "Cuisine a la Dominique," in which visitors are taught how to produce and present traditional Caribbean dishes by two of Dominica's hottest chefs.

Eco-Tourism Theme Park: The **Wacky Rollers Adventure Park** (www.wacky rollers.com; ✆ **767/440-4386**) is open Monday to Friday from 9am to 4pm, weekends from 12:30 to 4pm. The experiences are designed to let you interact with nature in a fun and exciting setting. There's a challenge course (with suspended platforms and bridges, zip lines, and other obstacles to conquer), as well as river-tubing safaris, river-to-ocean kayak excursions, and jeep safaris. During the week, reservations are required.

On Your Own: Within Walking Distance

IN ROSEAU   In the early 18th century, the French chose to build their largest settlement at what is now Roseau because the area had the largest expanse of flat land on the leeward coast and was well supplied with fresh water from the nearby Roseau River. The town's name comes from the river reeds (*roseaux* in French) that grow profusely around the estuary.

As you come ashore, you'll see the **Dominica Museum** (✆ **767/448-8923**), which faces the bayfront. Housed in an old market house dating from 1810, the museum's permanent exhibit provides a clear and interesting overview of the island's geology, history, archaeology, economy, and culture. The displays on pre-Columbian peoples, the slave trade, and the Fighting Maroons—slaves who resisted their white slave owners and established their own communities—are particularly informative. It's open Monday through Friday from 9am to 4pm, and Saturday from 9am to noon. Admission is $3 for adults, $1 for children ages 3 to 16.

Directly behind the museum is the **Old Market Square.** Vendors of vegetables, fruits, and other merchandise have crowded this cobbled square for centuries, and over the years the location has also witnessed slave auctions, executions, and political rallies. Today, it primarily offers handicrafts and souvenirs. The **Public Market Place,** at the mouth of the Roseau River, to your left as you leave the ship, is the Old Market Square's successor as the town's center of commercial activity. It's most colorful on Saturday mornings, when farmers and country vendors from the hills artfully display their fruits, vegetables, root crops, and flowers across the courtyards, sidewalks, and stalls of the marketplace.

It took more than 100 years to build the **Roseau Cathedral of Our Lady of Fair Heaven,** on Virgin Lane. Made of cut volcanic stone in the Gothic-Romanesque revival style, it was finally completed in 1916. The original funds to build the church were raised from levies on French planters, and Caribs erected the first wooden ceiling frame. Convicts on Devil's Island built the pulpit, and one of the stained-glass windows is dedicated to Christopher Columbus. The **Methodist Church** stands next door to the cathedral on land that once belonged to Catholics who later converted to Methodism. The Protestant church's location and the "conversion" of the land caused such discomfort in the late 1800s that a street riot ensued. Things are calmer today.

On the eastern edge of Roseau, the **Botanical Gardens** lie at the base of Morne Bruce, the mountain overlooking the town. The gardens were established at the end of the 19th century to encourage crop diversification and to provide farmers with correctly propagated seedlings. London's Kew Gardens provided exotic plants collected from every corner of the tropical world, and experiments conducted to see what would grow in Dominica revealed that *everything* does. Unfortunately, in 1979, Hurricane David destroyed many of the garden's oldest trees. One arboreal victim, an African baobab, still pins the bus it crushed, a monument to the power of the storm. At the garden's aviary, you can see sisserou and jacko parrots, part of a captive-breeding program designed to increase the ranks of these endangered species.

An explanatory booklet and pullout map titled *Self-Guided Walking Tour: Historic Roseau* is available for $5 from the **Society for Heritage Architecture Preservation and Enhancement,** or SHAPE (www.shape.dm), near the Roseau Cathedral, and from other locations.

IN PORTSMOUTH The cruise ship dock at Portsmouth leads directly to 104-hectare (257-acre) **Cabrits National Park,** which combines stunning mountain scenery, tropical deciduous forest and swampland, volcanic-sand beaches, coral reefs, and the romance of 18th-century **Fort Shirley** overlooking the town and Prince Rupert's Bay. Previous visitors to the area included Christopher Columbus, Sir Francis Drake, Admiral Horatio Nelson, and John Smith, who stopped here on his way to Virginia, where he founded Jamestown. Fort Shirley and more than 50 other major structures make up one of the West Indies' most impressive and historic military complexes. Admission is $5.

On Your Own: Beyond the Port Areas

Approximately 15 to 20 minutes by car from Roseau, **Trafalgar Falls** is actually two separate falls referred to as the mother and the father falls. The cascading white torrents dazzle in the sunlight before pummeling black-lava boulders below. The surrounding foliage grows in innumerable shades of green. To reach the brisk water of the natural pool at the base of the falls, you'll have to step gingerly along slippery rocks, so the nonballetic shouldn't attempt the climb. The constant mist that tinges the entire area beats any spa treatment. The rainbows are perpetual.

Titou Gorge, near the village of Laudat, offers an exhilarating swimming experience. Wending through the narrow volcanic gorge, you struggle against the cool current like a salmon swimming upstream to spawn. The sheer black walls enclosing the gorge loom 6m (20 ft.) above. At first, they seem sinister, but worn smooth by the water, they're ultimately womblike rather than menacing. Rock outcrops and a small cave provide interludes from the water flow, and eventually you reach the small but thundering waterfall that feeds the torrent. Scenes from *Pirates of the Caribbean* were filmed here.

Emerald Pool sits deep in the rainforest, not far from the center of the island. After walking 15 minutes along a relatively easy trail shaded by majestic trees, you reach a 15m (50-ft.) waterfall that crashes into the pool, named for the moss-covered boulders that enclose it. You can splash in the refreshing water, if you like, floating on your back to see the thick rainforest canopy and bright-blue sky arching over you.

About 6.5km (4 miles) from Portsmouth, in the midst of orange, grapefruit, and banana groves, the **Syndicate Nature Trail** provides an excellent introduction to tropical rainforests. The easy loop trail meanders through a stunningly rich ecosystem that features several species of exotic trees.

Masochists have an easy choice—the forced march through the **Valley of Desolation** to **Boiling Lake.** Experienced guides say this 6-hour hike is like spending hours on a maximum-resistance StairMaster, and an ex-Marine drill sergeant referred to it as "arduous." No joke, the trek is part of the Dominican army's basic training (of course, you won't have to carry one of your colleagues along the way). Why would any sane person endure this hell? To breathe in the harsh, sulfuric fumes that have killed all but the hardiest vegetation? Maybe to feel the thrill that comes with the risk that you might break through the thin crust that separates you from hot lava? Or could it be the final destination, the 20m-wide (65-ft.) cauldron of bubbling, slate-blue water of unknown depth? Don't even think of taking a dip in this flooded fumarole: The water temperature ranges from 180°F to 197°F (82°C–92°C). Can I sign you up? Contact **Khatts Tours** (www.khattstours.com; © **866/880-0508** or 561/210-5825). Cost is $50 per person.

When you visit **Morne Trois Pitons National Park,** you enter a primordial rainforest. Mists rise gently over lush, dark-green growth, drifting up to blue-green peaks that have earned Dominica the nickname "Switzerland of the Caribbean." Framed by banks of giant ferns, rivers rush and tumble, trees sprout orchids, green sunlight filters down through trees, and roaring waterfalls create a blue mist. One of the best starting points for a visit to the park is the village of Laudat, 11km (7 miles) from Roseau. Once here, try the **Rain Forest Aerial Tram,** at the corner of Old Street and Great George Street in Laudat (www.rainforestrams.com; © **767/448-8775**), which is open only when cruise ships are in port. For $75 per person for adults and $55 for children, you're taken on a 90-minute tour that starts at the village of Laudat, "sailing" over the rainforest through the Morne Trois Pitons National Park. Along the way, you're exposed to exotic bird life, beautiful waterfalls, and much tropical flora. They also offer a $99 combo package, **The Gorge Zip Challenge,** a zip line that lets you soar over the rainforest at high speed. It's a fun activity, but you won't be able to see much of the natural beauty of the forest. Just keep one eye on the time, as the journey back to the ship takes a while.

Shopping

In addition to the usual duty-free items—jewelry, watches, perfumes, and other luxury goods—Dominica offers handicrafts and art not obtainable anywhere else, most notably Carib Indian baskets made of dyed larouma reeds and balizier (heliconia) leaves. You can buy Carib crafts directly from the craftspeople in the Carib Indian Territory or at various outlets in Roseau. A small basket will cost about $15, and you can get a larger bell-shaped model for $43 or $48. Floor mats made from vetiver grass are another Dominican specialty.

The Art Asylum Earl Etienne's Gallery (http://avirtualdominica.com/earl etienne/mainmenu.html), at 31 Cork St., Roseau, Jimmet, is one of the island's oldest crafts shops. Etienne, one of Dominica's leading artists, also showcases his paintings here. **Frontline Cooperative,** at 78 Independence St., Roseau, specializes in books about Caribbean peoples, issues, and cooking, and also carries music CDs.

More than 100 exotic and local spices of all kinds, including pure vanilla, local honey, coffees, cocoa, various flavors of bottled rum punches, incense, and other interesting buys, are available at **Caribbean Magic Spice** in the RUINS building opposite the Old Market.

Beaches

If your sole focus is beaches, you'll likely find Dominica disappointing. The best beach on the island lies on the northwest coast. **Picard Beach** stretches for about 3km (2 miles), a strip of grayish sand with palm trees as a backdrop. It's ideal for snorkeling or windsurfing. You can drop in for food or a drink at one of the hotels along the beach.

On the northeast coast, four beaches—**Hampstead Beach, Hodges Beach, L'Anse Noire,** and **Woodford Hill Bay**—are among the island's most beautiful, although none is great for swimming. Divers and snorkelers often come here, even though the water can be rough. Watch out for the strong currents.

The southwest coast also has some beaches, but the sand here is black and rock-studded. Nonetheless, snorkelers and scuba divers flock to **Soufrière Bay Beach** and **Scotts Head Beach** for the clear waters and the stunning underwater walls.

Sports

SCUBA DIVING   Dominica's lush, beautiful scenery above water is echoed underwater in the surrounding Caribbean and Atlantic. Although the island is drained by hundreds of rivers and streams, the jagged volcanic undersea-scape prevents runoff sediment from clouding the water. Visibility ranges from 20m (65 ft.) to more than 30m (100 ft.). Visit the Dominica Watersports Association (DWA) website for the full list of dive operators: www.dominicawatersports.com/members.cfm.

Most local dive operations surpass international standards set by PADI, NAUI, and SSI, and small, uncrowded excursions are the norm. **Cabrits Dive Centre** (www. cabritsdive.com; ℂ **767/445-3010**) is Dominica's only PADI five-star dive center, and the only dive operation on the north of the island, which means yours will be the only dive group—and you'll have access to many untouched sites, pristine reefs, and an array of colorful sponges. The abundant marine life includes rare species that are at home in Dominica, such as sea horses, flying gurnards, and batfish. The dive center will provide boat or car pickup service to and from the Cabrits cruise ship dock in Portsmouth. It will also arrange transportation for passengers on ships docked in Roseau (about an hour's drive) for $120 for up to four people. Single-tank dives are $66; two-tank dives are $99. Snorkeling is also offered.

Aldive & Water Sports (www.aldive.com; ℂ **767/440-3483** or 813/254-5254) is a reputable family-owned dive operator located on the island's southern coast and a short drive from Roseau Port. Single-tank dives are $55, two-tank dives are $80, and a wreck dive is offered for $90. Guided snorkeling tours are $30 and they offer an option of getting to their site by FunCat, an electric motor–propelled aquatic lounge chair. They're a fun if utterly indulgent way to get around! If you want to redeem yourself from the image of the lazy tourist, there's also the option to kayak over to one of their snorkel sites. This dive center will provide a car pickup service from the Roseau cruise ship berth.

SNORKELING   Dominica offers nearly 30 top-notch snorkeling areas, including the popular Champagne site. Snorkelers can join a dive-boat party, participate in special snorkel excursions, or explore the coast in a sea kayak, periodically jumping overboard for a look below. The calm water on the island's leeward side is perfect for viewing the riotous colors of the sponges, corals, and 190-plus fish species native to the area. Offshore snorkeling and equipment rental can be arranged through the dive operators listed above. Prices start at approximately $45.

Great Local Restaurants & Bars

Seafood, local root vegetables referred to as "provisions," and Creole recipes are among the highlights of Dominican cuisine. *Crapaud* ("mountain chicken" in English, though it's really mountain frog) is the national delicacy. For a local beer, try **Kubuli;** for a local rum, try **Soca** or **Macoucherie.**

IN ROSEAU Try **La Robe Créole,** 3 Victoria St. (© **767/448-2896**), which gets top marks for its callaloo soup (made from the spinachlike leaves of a local vegetable called dasheen, plus coconut), lobster and conch crepes, and mango chutney. The decor features heavy stone walls, solid ladder-back chairs, and colorful madras tablecloths. Lunch is about $30.

Balisier Restaurant (www.garrawayhotel.com; © **767/449-8800**), named after a small red flower that thrives in the jungles of Dominica, was designed to maximize the views over Roseau's harbor. Lunch is $18 to $32, and might feature West Indian curries, fish Creole, or several kinds of salads.

Guiyave, 15 Cork St. (© **767/448-2930**), an airy restaurant on the second floor of a pistachio-colored, wood-frame house, features steamed fish, conch, octopus, and spareribs. Take a table on the veranda and cool off with one of the fresh-squeezed juices. How about soursop, tamarind, sorrel, cherry, or strawberry? The downstairs takeout counter offers chicken patties, spicy *rotis,* and delectable tarts and cakes. The lunch buffet is about $22.

The **Sutton Grille,** in the Sutton Place Hotel, 25 Old St. (www.suttonplacehotel dominica.com; © **767/449-8700**), boasts an airy dining area ensconced in 100-year-old stone walls. You can choose a table a few steps up from the bustle of downtown Roseau or one set back from the action. The menu, a veritable primer of Creole and other West Indian cookery, also offers a generous sprinkling of international and vegetarian dishes. Lunch is about $21.

Rainforest Restaurant, in the Papillote Wilderness Retreat (www.papillote.dm; © **767/448-2287**), is about 6km (4 miles) east of Roseau and well worth the taxi ride for lunch. Amid exotic flowers, century-old trees, and filtered sunlight, you'll dine overlooking a gorgeous vista of rivers and mountains. The array of healthful food includes flyingfish and truly delectable freshwater prawns known as *bookh.* Freshly caught kingfish is also a tasty treat. Breadfruit or dasheen puffs merit a try, if you've never had them; and we recommend the green papaya chicken salad. Lunch is about $25 and reservations are recommended.

Come to **Pearl's,** King George V Street (© **767/448-8707**), for a true taste of Dominica at a restored Creole house with a veranda. Chef Pearl's island delicacies are renowned locally. Begin with one of her tropical fruit juices, followed by freshly caught crayfish as an appetizer. Whenever lobster is available, it's served any way you want it. She also makes some mean pork chops, and her curried goat will put hair on your chest. Try the potato salad and spareribs or the codfish and plantains if you want to really go local. Lunch is around $20.

IN PORTSMOUTH If you disembark in Portsmouth, grab a table at the **Purple Turtle** (© **767/445-5296**); it's close to the dock and features lobster and crayfish, as well as lighter fare such as *rotis,* sandwiches, and salads. Lunch is about $25. If you care to stick with North American cuisine, **Tomato Fresh Food Café & Deli** (© **767/445-3334**) offers deli meats, cheeses, salads, subs, wraps, desserts, wines, and liquors to consume there or to go. **Big Papa's Restaurant (℡ 767/445-6444)** offers a relaxed seaside lunch with a variety of tasty Creole sandwiches and entrees. Lunch is about $25. **Cobra's Indian River Tours Restaurant (℡ 767/245-6332)** is located at the top of the Indian River and is a nice place to enjoy the local bird life while dining by this quiet river. Lunch is about $40. Reservations are required, as the restaurant usually caters to people on one of its hiking tours. A customized tour plus lunch starts at $90.

GRAND CAYMAN

Grand Cayman is the largest of the Cayman Islands, a British Overseas Territory 773km (480 miles) due south of Miami (Cayman Brac and Little Cayman are the others). It's the top of an underwater mountain, whose side—known as the Cayman Wall—plummets straight down for 150m (500 ft.) before becoming a steep slope that falls away for 1,800m (5,900 ft.) to the ocean floor.

Despite its "grand" name, the island is only 35km (22 miles) long and 13km (8 miles) across its widest point. Flat, relatively unattractive, and full of scrubland and swamp, Grand Cayman and its sister islands nevertheless boast more than their share of upscale, expensive private homes and condos, owned by millionaire expatriates from all over who come because of the tiny nation's lenient tax and banking laws. (Enron, the poster child of shady business dealings, reportedly had more than 690 different subsidiaries here to help it avoid paying U.S. taxes.)

Although Grand Cayman is a major tourism destination, don't expect fast-paced excitement. Island life focuses on the sea. Snorkelers will find a paradise and beach lovers will relish the powdery sands of its beaches, but party-hungry travelers in search of urban thrills might be disappointed. Come here to slow down and relax. Grand Cayman is also popular because of its laid-back civility—so civil that, until recently, ships weren't allowed to visit on Sunday.

George Town is the colony's capital and its commercial hub, and many hotels line the sands of the nation's most famous sunspot, **Seven Mile Beach.** Scuba divers and snorkelers come for the coral reefs and other formations, some of which lie within swimming distance of the shoreline.

COMING ASHORE   Cruise ships anchor off George Town and ferry their passengers to a pier on **Harbour Drive.** The short tender ride can be choppy, but the landing point couldn't be more convenient: You're let off right in the heart of the shopping district. There's a tourist information booth at the pier, and taxis line up to meet cruise ship passengers. You'll find a phone center for credit card calls and Internet access centers on Cardinal Avenue, right downtown.

LANGUAGE   English is the official language of the islands.

CURRENCY   The legal tender is the **Cayman Islands dollar** (CI 82¢ = US$1; CI$1 = US$1.21), but U.S. dollars are commonly accepted. Be sure to note which currency is referred to on price tags before making a purchase. Unless otherwise specified, prices in this section are given in U.S. dollars.

INFORMATION   The **Department of Tourism** is in Regatta Business Park, Leeward Two, Safehaven (℡ 345/949-0623). It's open Monday through Friday from 9am to 5pm. To get info before you go, contact the New York office of the **Cayman Islands Department of Tourism** (www.caymanislands.ky; ℡ 877/422-9626 or 212/889-9009).

CALLING FROM THE U.S. When calling Grand Cayman from the U.S., you need only dial a "1" before the numbers listed here.

Getting Around

BY TAXI Taxi fares are fixed; typical one-way fares to the nearest beach will be about $7 per person. **Holiday Taxi** (✆ **345/947-1066**) offers 24-hour service.

BY RENTAL CAR The roads are good by Caribbean standards, so driving around is relatively easy, as long as you remember to drive on the left side of the road. **Avis, Budget, Dollar,** and **Hertz** all have offices here.

BY MOTOR SCOOTER OR BICYCLE The terrain is relatively flat, so motor scooters and bicycles are another way to get around. **Island Scooter Rental,** at Bernard Drive in Industrial Park (✆ **345/949-2046**), offers shuttle service to and from George Town and rents scooters for $56 per day.

Best Cruise Line Shore Excursions

Cruise lines typically offer about 30 shore excursions here, most of them of the swimming, snorkeling, sailing, submarine, and glass-bottom boat variety.

Stingray City ($71, 2–3 hr.): The waters off Grand Cayman are home to Stingray City, one of the world's most unusual underwater attractions. Set in the very shallow waters of North Sound, about 3km (2 miles) east of the island's northwestern tip, the site was discovered in the 1980s when fishermen noticed scores of stingrays showing up to feed on offal they dumped overboard. Today, anywhere from 30 to 100 relatively tame stingrays swarm around visiting snorkelers like aquatic basset hounds, eager for handouts. Stingrays are very gentle creatures, but never try to grab one by the tail—their barbed stingers are indeed poisonous, and although they are very rarely a genuine threat to one's life, they can inflict a lot of pain.

Atlantis Submarine Excursion ($99, 1½ hr.): Those looking for some underwater adventure can sign up for a deep-sea dive on a 48-passenger sub, which takes you down to 30m (100 ft.) through coral canyons, with an automatic fish feeder drawing swarms of colorful marine creatures.

Island Bicycle Tour ($74, 3 hr.): A great way to really get a feel for an island—and get some exercise—is via bicycle. You'll pick up your touring mountain bike at the Beach Club Colony Hotel, ride along the coastline for views of Seven Mile Beach, and then journey inland en route to the north side of the island to ride along the coast again.

Excursions Offered by Local Agencies

Stingray City: If the tours on your ship get booked, about half a dozen entrepreneurs lead expeditions to Stingray City, and usually a few tour agents wait around the terminal in George Town to snare cruise passengers as they debark. **Moby Dick Tours** (www.mobydicktours.com; ✆ **480/626-5429**) will pick you up from the terminal and take you to the Stingray City sandbar for a morning of snorkeling. The price is $45 for adults and $40 for children 11 and under.

Taxi Tours: If you want to see the island, you can grab a taxi in port and take a tour. Taxis should cost about $50 per hour and can hold up to five people. A 3-hour tour covers all the sights in a leisurely fashion. Make sure to stop in the town called Hell and send a postcard home.

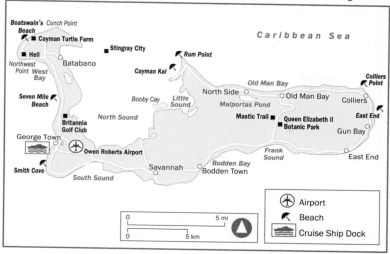

On Your Own: Within Walking Distance

The capital, **George Town,** can easily be explored in an afternoon; stop by for its restaurants and shops (and those famous offshore banks)—not sights. The town does have a clock monument to King George V, and the post office on Edward Street is the oldest government building in use in the Caymans. Stamps sold here are collected avidly.

The **Cayman Islands National Museum,** Harbour Drive (www.museum.ky; ✆ 345/949-8368), is housed in a veranda-fronted building that once served as the island's courthouse. Today the formal exhibits include a collection of Caymanian artifacts collected by Ira Thompson beginning in the 1930s, and the museum incorporates a gift shop, theater, cafe, and more than 2,000 items portraying the natural, social, and cultural history of the Caymans. Hours are Monday through Friday from 9am to 5pm, and Saturday from 9am to 1pm. Admission is $5 for adults and $3 for children.

You might also go to **Hell,** a town at the north end of West Bay Beach named for a jagged piece of rock. You can guess what the postmistress will stamp your postcard to send back to the U.S., but you probably don't want to mail one to Grandma.

The **National Gallery of the Cayman Islands,** Esterley Tibbetts Highway (www.nationalgallery.org.ky; ✆ 345/945-8111), is a nonprofit educational organization that supports the growth of the Cayman Islands art scene. It offers an average of eight exhibitions per year of both local and international art. The gallery is open Monday through Friday from 9am to 5pm, Saturday from 11am to 4pm. Admission is free but donations are accepted.

On Your Own: Beyond the Port Area

North of George Town, at Northwest Point, **Boatswain's Beach** (www.boatswains beach.ky; ✆ 345/949-3894), pronounced "*Boe*-suns," is a newly renovated 9-hectare (22-acre) marine park that includes a snorkeling lagoon, a predator tank full of sharks and green moray eels, a separate tank for dolphin swims, an aviary, a nature trail, three restaurants, and other mostly marine-oriented displays. The facility also includes the **Cayman Turtle Farm ★**; the only green-sea-turtle farm of its kind in the world. Once the islands had a multitude of turtles in the surrounding waters (which is why Columbus called the islands "Las Tortugas"), but today these creatures are sadly few in number, and the green sea turtle has been designated an endangered species protected by an international trade agreement. (Thus, while it is legal to eat farmed turtle meat, it is illegal to bring turtle parts or products into the United States.) The turtle farm was radically upgraded and enlarged in the wake of hurricane damage in 2004, and reopened in September 2006 in new premises across the road from its previous location. Its main function involves providing the local market with edible turtle meat (preventing the need to hunt turtles in the wild) and replenishing the waters with hatchling and yearling turtles. The graceful turtles here range in size from 170g to 270kg (6 oz.–600 lb.). At a snack bar and restaurant, you can sample turtle dishes if you so desire. The turtle farm is open daily from 8am to 5:30pm (last admission is at 4:30pm). Admission, which includes full access to the entire facility as well as the tour, costs $45 for adults and $25 for children ages 2 to 12, and is free for children younger than 2. You can also tour just the turtle farm for $30 for adults and $20 for children 2 to 12.

Those searching for the quieter side of Grand Cayman should check out the eastern part of the island, where you're more likely to find empty beaches than brand-name resorts. On the way to **East End,** just before Old Isaac Village, you'll see the onshore sprays of water shooting up like geysers. These are called blowholes, and they sound like the roar of a lion. **Pedro St. James National Historic Site,** Savannah (www.pedrostjames.ky; ✆ **345-947-3329**), is a restored great house dating from 1780, when only 400 people lived on the island. It lasted until 1970, when it was destroyed by fire. Now rebuilt, it is the centerpiece of a new heritage park with a visitor center and an audiovisual theater with a laser light show. Because of its size, the great house was called "the Castle" by generations of Caymanians. Its primary historic importance dates from December 5, 1831, when residents met here to elect Cayman's first legislative assembly. You can explore the house's wide verandas, rough-hewn timber beams, gabled framework, mahogany floors and staircases, and wide-beam wooden ceilings. Admission is $10 for adults, and free for those 12 and under. Hours are daily from 9am to 5pm.

On 26 hectares (64 acres) of rugged wooded land, **Queen Elizabeth II Botanic Park,** off Frank Sound Road, North Side (www.botanic-park.ky; ✆ **345-947-3558**), offers visitors a 1-hour walk along a short (1km/.5-mile) trail through wetlands, swamps, dry thicket, and mahogany trees. If you're lucky, you may spot a blue iguana, a species endemic to Grand Cayman, which once had fewer than 15 left in the wild. Thanks to the Blue Iguana Recovery Programme, the population has been boosted to 650 individuals. You may also see hickatees (the freshwater turtles found only on the Cayman Islands and in Cuba), the rare Grand Cayman parrot, or the anole lizard, with its cobalt-blue throat pouch. There are six rest stations along the trail, plus a visitor center and a canteen, a heritage garden, a floral garden, and a lake. Admission is $10 for adults, free for children 12 and under. Hours are daily from 9am to 5:30pm (6:30pm in summer).

Nearby, the **Mastic Trail,** west of Frank Sound Road, is a restored 200-year-old footpath through a 2-million-year-old woodland area in the heart of the island. Named for the majestic mastic tree, the trail showcases the reserve's natural attractions, including a native mangrove swamp, traditional agriculture, and an ancient woodland area. You can follow the 3km (1.75-mile) trail on your own, but we recommend taking a 3-hour guided tour for $15 per person. Call ✆ **345/945-6588** to make a reservation. The trail, adjacent to the Botanic Park, is about a 45-minute drive from George Town.

Shopping

There's duty-free shopping here for silver, china, crystal, Irish linen, and British woolen goods, but we've found most prices to be similar to those in the U.S. You'll also find rum and cigar shops. There are some lovely art galleries that sell local art. Please don't succumb and purchase turtle or black-coral products, both of which are highly endangered species and protected. You'll see them everywhere, but it's illegal to bring them back into the United States and most other Western nations.

Some standout shops include **Artifacts Ltd.,** Harbour Drive, on the harborfront across from the landing dock (www.artifacts.com.ky; ✆ **345/949-2442**), for antique coins, silver, china, and back issues of many highly prized Cayman stamps; the **Jewelry Centre,** Cardinal Avenue (✆ **345/949-0070**), one of the largest jewelry stores in the Caymans; and the **Kennedy Gallery West Shore Centre** (www.kennedy gallerycayman.com; ✆ **345/949-8077**), specializing in paintings by local artists. **Pure Art** (www.pureart.ky; ✆ **345/949-9133**) sells works from local artists.

Beaches

Grand Cayman's **Seven Mile Beach,** which begins north of George Town, is an easy taxi ride from the cruise dock and has sparkling white sands with a backdrop of casuarina trees. The beach is really about 9km (5½ miles) long, but who are we to quibble with tradition? It's lined with condominiums and plush resorts, and is known for its array of watersports and its translucent aquamarine waters. Because the beach is on a relatively tranquil side of Grand Cayman, there is no great tide and the water is generally placid and inviting, ideal for families, even those with small children. The average water temperature is a balmy 80°F (27°C). It tends to be crowded near the big resorts, but the beach is so big you can always find some room to spread out your towel. There are no peddlers to hassle you, and the beach is for the most part kelp free and beautifully maintained.

Many beaches on the east and north coasts of Grand Cayman are relatively desirable, layered in many cases with pale sand and protected in some cases by offshore barrier reefs, so waters are generally tranquil. The best windsurfing on Grand Cayman is off the eastern shore, with particularly good conditions on the beaches adjacent to the Morritt's resorts. One of our favorites is on the north coast, bordering **Cayman Kai.** This beach is a Caribbean cliché of charm, with palm trees and beautiful sands, along with changing facilities. You can snorkel along the reef to Rum Point.

Sports

GOLF   Plentiful sunshine and light breezes make conditions perfect for golf year-round. Grand Cayman boasts the Caribbean's only Jack Nicklaus–designed course, **the Britannia Club** (www.britanniavillas.net/golf.aspx; ✆ **345/949-8020**), which features a 9-hole championship layout that doubles as an 18-hole executive course. Located on the North Sound, this links-style course features rolling hills and long carries over water.

SCUBA DIVING & SNORKELING   Coral reefs and other formations encircle the island and are filled with marine life, which are protected by local law from any form of disruption. It's easy to dive close to shore, so boats aren't necessary, but plenty of boats and scuba facilities are available, as well as many dive shops renting scuba gear to certified divers. An easily accessible dive operator and leader in the Caribbean is **Red Sail Sports** (www.redsailcayman.com; ✆ **877/733-7245** or 345/945-5965), which offers full-day resort courses (1-day trial courses to practice breathing underwater) as well as excursions for experienced divers. The staff is helpful and highly professional. **Ocean Frontiers** (www.oceanfrontiers.com; ✆ **800/348-6096** or 345/947-0000) is another good choice.

SKATEBOARDING   In the Caribbean? Apparently so. The **Black Pearl Skate and Surf Park** (www.blackpearl.ky; ✆ **345/947-0755**) is not to be missed for the adventurous family with teens or tweens who are bored or antsy from too many days at sea. Boasting the world's largest outdoor concrete skate park and highest surf machine, Black Pearl is the perfect attraction for those looking to let the kids burn off some unspent energy! You and the kids can skate the day away for $28 (including equipment and pads) or hang ten at the wave pool for $75 an hour. Rentals and lessons are available.

WINDSURFING   The best place for windsurfing on the island is the beachfront resort of **Morritt's Tortuga Club & Resort** at the East End (✆ **345/947-7449**). There, Tortuga Divers, an outfit that's associated with Red Sail Sports, charges $60 for 1 hour, $125 for 3 hours. A 1-hour lesson can be arranged for $80, which is followed by a 1-hour practice session that's included in the price. The favorable windsurfing conditions here result from nearly constant winds blowing in from offshore, and an offshore reef that protects the waters of the lagoon in most cases from unpredictable waves.

Great Local Restaurants & Bars

A favorite local beer is **Stingray,** and popular local rums are **Tortuga and Seven Fathoms.**

A short walk (less than 1km/½ mile) south of the pier is **Paradise Bar & Grill,** on Harbour Drive (✆ **345/945-1444**). It's a great open-air seaside cafe for a sandwich, chicken fingers, and a couple of cool Stingray beers or a frozen drink. Lunch will cost you about $14.

Near Boatswain's Beach, **Cracked Conch by the Sea,** West Bay Road (www.crackedconch.com.ky; ✆ **345/945-5217**), serves some of the island's freshest seafood, including the inevitable conch, plus meat dishes such as beef, jerk pork, and spicy combinations of chicken. Lunch is about $25.

Rackham's Pub & Restaurant, at 93 N. Church St. (✆ **345/945-3860**), offers open-air dining with a beautiful view of boats sailing into port. The extensive menu has plenty of fresh seafood. Lunch is about $16.

Befitting its name, the **Lighthouse Restaurant** (www.lighthouse.ky; ✆ **345/947-2047**) is located right on the sea and features a great patio for oceanside dining; it is about a 30-minute taxi ride away. Try the cracked conch fritters with jerk mayonnaise, lobster gnocchi, or grilled yellowfin tuna steak with mixed peppercorn sauce. Lunch is about $25.

GRAND TURK

Welcome to the Caribbean's newest cruise port. Just about 11km (7 miles) long and 2km (1¼ miles) wide, with 3,700 residents, Grand Turk has long been known as one of the top five diving destinations in the world, owing to the fact that, just a few hundred meters from shore, the shallow continental shelf suddenly plunges 2,130m (7,000 ft.) straight down, with healthy coral reefs and great visibility. The whole western shore of the island is a protected underwater park. Above water, things are practically perfect as well, with an average temperature of 83°F (28°C) and an amazing 320 days of sunshine a year. The temperature can climb pretty high in the summer, but the surprisingly strong trade winds keep things comfy.

Grand Turk

While ships have visited Grand Turk in the past, the island really wasn't equipped to handle a massive influx of passengers until the **Grand Turk Cruise Center** opened in February 2006, its deepwater pier able to accommodate even the largest megaships. Carnival was the prime mover behind the pier, leasing 15 hectares (37 acres) from the government, and the duty-free building. The cruise center will welcome all ships, not just Carnival lines.

About 5km (3 miles) from the pier is charming **Cockburn Town,** a sleepy half-mile stretch that also happens to be the administrative capital of the Turks and Caicos Islands. Along its streets, Bermudan-influenced colonial buildings mix with simple gift shops, guesthouses, and a couple of laid-back bars, plus miles of public powder-white beaches. Islanders describe the ambience here as the way the rest of the Caribbean was 25 years ago. A bit neglected over the years, Grand Turk received a $7-million boost from Carnival for infrastructure improvements, ranging from pedestrian crossings to the creation of ready-made tourist attractions based on the island's substantive history.

COMING ASHORE Located on the south side of Grand Turk, the **Grand Turk Cruise Center** may seem to arriving passengers like one of the cruise lines' private islands, with its carefully placed landscaping between the dock and the beach. Its advantages, of course, are that it's part of a real country, and passengers don't have to tender ashore, as the cruise pier can accommodate the largest ships. At the cruise center beyond, you can get visitor info, rent a car, make phone calls, shop duty-free, or catch a taxi or water taxi into Cockburn Town, 5km (3 miles) away.

LANGUAGE English is spoken everywhere.

CURRENCY The official currency is the **U.S. dollar,** but there's a local currency called the TCI crown (of equal value with the dollar) and a quarter, both of which make nice souvenirs.

INFORMATION Visitor centers can be found right in the cruise center and on Front Street in Cockburn Town. For info before you go, go to **www.turksandcaicostourism.com** or call ⓒ **800/241-0824** in the U.S.

CALLING FROM THE U.S. No country calling code is required—just dial as you do from home, with a "1" and the area code.

Getting Around

BY TAXI Taxi fares from the port to Cockburn Town run about $15, but get a quote from the driver before you commit.

STANDING ON top OF THE WORLD

Walking out on the eastern trail leading from the lighthouse at the northern end of the island, you can brace yourself against the strong trade winds, marvel at the beautifully eroded cliff faces below, perhaps spot giant manta rays or humpback whales in the turquoise waters, and let your mind drift back to a time when the islanders stood near where you're perched, waving lanterns and guiding ships to their doom on the rocks below so they could plunder their treasures. (See "On Your Own: Within Walking Distance," below.)

Looking for the Green Flash

After your day in Grand Turk, once you're back aboard ship, keep your eyes peeled for the Green Flash, a solar phenomenon in which the sky flashes green for about 10 to 20 seconds after the sun goes down. Because green light rays bend more drastically than their red and orange counterparts, they remain visible for just a tad longer. There are not many places in the world where you can see the flash, but Grand Turk is one of them—at least on days when the sky conditions are very calm.

BY BUS   There's no public transportation on the island, but one shore excursion offered by the cruise lines is a bus loop, which allows you to hop off and on at will (see below).

BY RENTAL CAR   The island is small enough to explore on foot or by a few short rides in a taxi—but if you want one, car-rental desks are located at the cruise terminal. Be sure to book ahead, as supplies are limited. Also be prepared to drive on the left side of the road.

Best Cruise Line Shore Excursions

In addition to the excursions listed here, **whale-watching** will be added to ships' offerings on an ad hoc basis. It has to be the right season and the right weather, but the Atlantic humpback whales travel down Turk's Passage and trench on the western side of the island every year, heading for their breeding grounds south of Grand Turk, where they take care of their calves from January to April. Aside from looking for whales, the main thing to do in Grand Turk is get underwater.

Scuba Diving ($119–$135, 2¾ hr.): Many consider Grand Turk the best diving in the Caribbean, and it's on many lists of the top-five diving destinations in the world. With the continental shelf plunging just 275m (900 ft.) offshore, you can scuba right from the beach. You won't get better conditions anywhere in the Caribbean than Grand Turk, with its tranquil, clear waters and protected reef. Experienced divers will be wowed by the manta rays, whale sharks, sea turtles, and beautiful colors of the third-largest coral reef in the world. Even a first-timer can get to the reefs via a resort course, with intensive one-on-one instruction followed by a half-hour of diving.

Catamaran Sailaway to Cotton Cay Beach & Snorkeling: ($89, 3 hr.): If you're not up for scuba, you can at least go snorkeling to experience the beauty of Grand Turk's undersea world. Snorkeling trips departing from the cruise terminal typically visit Horseshoe Reef (with depths averaging 2–4m/6½–13 ft.) and a reef off of Round Cay, one of Grand Turk's best dive locations.

Hop-On, Hop-Off Island Tour ($45, 2–3 hr.): Air-conditioned buses loop around the island whenever there's a ship in port, letting booked excursionists see things at their leisure. A wristband allows entry to various tourist venues along the route, including Cockburn Town's Millennium Clock Tower and restored 1800s prison; Lighthouse Park, with its namesake 1852 light and two nature trails; the Turks and Caicos National Museum, which has some information on John Glenn's splashdown off Grand Turk in 1962; and the Philatelic Bureau. Anyone who's ever collected stamps will know that Turks and Caicos are well known for their beautiful stamps, created almost solely for collectors. Stops are located approximately every half-mile along the route, with many sited close to island attractions. Buses arrive at each stop approximately every 15 minutes.

Bike & Hike ($75, 3 hr.): Get a great look at Grand Turk from the seat of a bicycle and on foot. Departing from the cruise terminal, pedal toward town, making your way to the Salt Pans, where you can learn about Grand Turk's salt-raking past. Then make your way to the northwest end of the island for fantastic east- and west-coast views. En route, you will stop for an easy hike and your guide will point out the various flora and fauna you will see along the way.

Excursions Offered by Local Agencies

The only local tour operators are the dive shops. For instance, walk a couple minutes north of the cruise center along the beach and you'll find **Oasis Divers** (© 800/892-3995). On Duke Street is **Grand Turk Diving** (www.gtdiving.com; © 649/946-1559), which offers two-tank morning dives at $95. An afternoon single-tank dive costs $80. Rental equipment is also available. NAUI courses at all levels are offered. Snorkeling and cay trips are available for nondivers. The owners and operators are among the more experienced divers on the island, and they know where to find marine life in a kaleidoscope of colors. **Blue Water Diver,** on Front Street (www.grandturkscuba.com; ©/fax **649/946-2432**), offers single dives, PADI registration, and dive packages, and even runs trips to Salt Cay. These people are first-rate and will tell you many facts and legends about diving in their country (like the fact that the highest mountain in the Turks and Caicos is 2,400m/7,900 ft. tall, but only the top 42m/140 ft. are above sea level). Scuba divers flock here to enjoy panoramic "wall dives" on the vertical sides of the reefs. A single-tank dive costs $80, with a two-tank dive going for $115. A PADI-instruction resort course is priced at $160. Full PADI certification is $450. Advance reservations are strongly recommended.

On Your Own: Within Walking Distance

People go to Grand Turk mainly to swim, snorkel, dive, or do nothing but soak up the sun. Other activities include bird-watching, horseback riding, heritage walks, and golf. You might also want to stroll over to the lighthouse that was brought in pieces from the United Kingdom, where you can brace yourself against strong trade winds and marvel at the eroded cliffs below. Built in 1852, the lighthouse has been restored and still works, guarding the northern tip of the island.

Passengers could easily spend their whole day just hanging out at the cruise center, whose biggest structure by far is the two-story, 1,580-sq.-m (17,000-sq.-ft.) **Margaritaville Cafe** (www.margaritavillecaribbean.com), the largest stand-alone Jimmy Buffett franchise in the Caribbean. Wastin' away again? Behind the restaurant is a giant amoeba-shaped swimming pool with swim-up bar, slide, cabanas, and infinity-edge view. It's open to the public and, because it's only 1m deep, makes a great place to hang out with the younger kids. If you're up for a walk along the beach, the powder-white sound stretches for about a mile north of the cruise center, though just past Oasis Divers, you'll need to take to the nearby road to make your way around a fenced-in Customs pier. Just north of this pier lies **Governor's Beach** (see "Beaches," below) and another 180m (590 ft.) of pristine beach before you reach a rocky shoreline. If you're looking for a quiet place to lounge away from your fellow passengers, then this area of beach is worth the 20-minute walk.

On Your Own: Beyond the Port Area

Cockburn Town's historic district is centered on Duke and Front streets, where some houses built of wood and limestone stand along the waterfront. Historic government buildings surround a small plaza where cannons and a bronze plaque mark the spot where Christopher Columbus allegedly first set foot in the New World, on October 14, 1492. Columbus's logbook notes landfall at a bean-shaped island, but there's no absolute proof that said bean was Grand Turk.

Also on Front Street is the **Turks and Caicos National Museum** (www.tc museum.org; ℂ **649/946-2160**), a 180-year-old house originally constructed from timbers salvaged from shipwrecks. Half the museum exhibits artifacts from the West Indies' most complete archaeological excavation of a Spanish sailing ship that sank sometime before 1513. Most of the exhibits consist of everyday objects used by the crews and officers. The remainder of the museum is devoted to the island's natural history, salt industries, plantation economy, and the pre-Columbian inhabitants. The website provides information about ongoing explorations for other sunken ships. The museum offers a private tour for $25, where guests will learn details about the oldest shipwreck in the Caribbean and early island life. Reserve in advance. It's open Monday to Saturday 9am to 1pm. Admission is $5.

Shopping

Grand Turk isn't particularly known for its arts and crafts, though you will find shops at the cruise center and at the island's various attractions and museums, plus a couple along Duke Street, which borders the western beach in the downtown area.

Beaches

The cruise terminal's powder-white sandy beach is just steps from the pier, and you'll find lounge chairs and hammocks; bartending staff come by to take your drink order. For $20 a day, you can rent a clamshell that provides shade for two lounge chairs. You can also get a taste of the underwater view that makes Grand Turk famous by snorkeling, with equipment available for rent or purchase.

On the island's southwest coast, below Cockburn Town, **Governor's Beach** is one of the few Blue Flagged beaches in the Caribbean, which means it's passed stringent tests for water quality, cleanliness, and lifeguard availability. It's also reputed to have the best snorkeling on the island. Right next door is **Waterloo,** the governor's mansion, a pretty structure with the curved stucco architecture characteristic of Bermudan buildings.

Sports

BIKING Bikes are available for rent at the cruise center and in town. Apart from the Ridge (which is where all the fancy accommodations are springing up), the roads are quite flat, and most of the attractions and sights are an easy bike ride away. Call **Tony's Rentals** (www.tonyscarrental.com; ℂ **649/946-1879**), where bicycles cost $20 for the day and the friendly advice is free.

BIRD-WATCHING Grand Turk plays host to more than 190 species of birds, but the most impressive sight has to be the greater flamingos fishing in the salt ponds of the island in spring and summer.

In Cockburn Town, just behind the historic waterfront, the island in the town's saltwater pond was once used to quarantine sick sailors. Today it's a favorite of birders, who come to see flamingos, pelicans, and herons feeding in the shallow waters.

WATERSPORTS   Because of the delicate reef system, such watersports as jet-skiing and banana-boating are not allowed. Snorkeling and scuba diving, which can be done right from shore, are the water activities not to be missed (see "Best Cruise Line Shore Excursions" and "Excursions Offered by Local Agencies," above). Deep-sea and flats fishing are also fabulous in these waters.

Great Local Restaurants & Bars

For something with a slightly more upscale feel, head toward the other end of Duke Street to the **Guanahani Restaurant,** in Bohio Dive Resort (© **649/946-2135**). You'll find an eclectic menu featuring fish (of course), juicy jerk chicken, and some delicious desserts. Lunch runs $25 to $35.

Secret Garden, located in the Salt Raker Inn on Duke Street (© **649/946-2260**), is a casual eatery and an island favorite. Try for a lunchtime seat in the garden of the covered patio. Lunch specials are tasty and include a different curry every day or homemade fish cakes. Sandwiches are always available, including one made with grouper. Top off your meal with Key lime pie or a slice of rum cake. It's open Thursday to Tuesday 7:30am to 2:30pm. Lunch specials are $14 to $22.

GRENADA

The southernmost nation of the Windwards, Grenada (Gre-*nay*-dah) is one of the lushest places in the Caribbean. Called the "Spice Island," it has extravagant fertility—a result of the gentle climate and volcanic soil—which produces more spices than anywhere else in the world: clove, cinnamon, mace, cocoa, tonka beans, ginger, and a fifth of the world's supply of nutmeg. The beaches are white and sandy, and the populace (a mixture of English expatriates and islanders of African descent) is friendly. Once a British crown colony but now independent, the island nation also incorporates two smaller islands: Petite Martinique and Carriacou, neither of which has many tourist facilities.

Crisscrossed by nature trails, Grenada's interior is a jungle—in 1904 the government protected 1,200 hectare (3,000 acres)—with oleander, bougainvillea, purple and red hibiscus, crimson anthurium, bananas, breadfruit, bird-song, ferns, and palms. There are 37 species of bamboo alone. The island's tropical scenery and natural bounty attract visitors who want to snorkel, sail, fish, hike on jungle paths, or loll the day away on the 3km (2-mile) white-sand Grand Anse Beach, one of the best in the Caribbean.

St. George's, the country's capital and major port, rises on three sides around a protected bay formed by the deep crater of a long-dead volcano. With its charming Georgian colonial buildings, pastel walls, and red-tile roofs—the tiles were brought by European trade ships as ballast—the view has been compared to Portofino, Italy. The damage to buildings and roofs wrought by Hurricane Ivan in 2004 has since been repaired; though not all roofs were retiled, red remains a prominent feature of the landscape. In addition to the lovely frangipani and flamboyant trees, the city is flanked by old forts that offer spectacular views for those who venture up the steep city streets.

COMING ASHORE   Passengers disembarking at the Melville Street Cruise Terminal (which can accommodate two ships) exit directly through the modern Esplanade Shopping Mall. Out of the Esplanade, you pass though the Sendall Tunnel—a major feat of engineering when it was built in 1894—and onto the picturesque Carenage

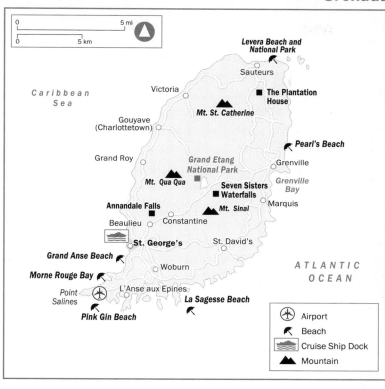

waterfront of St. George's. Passengers on the few smaller ships that now anchor in the old harbor are tendered ashore and disembark at the Inner Harbour and exit directly onto the Carenage waterfront. Unlike some ports of call designed primarily as tourist destinations, the old harbour of St. George's remains a working commercial port, with the occasional rusty barge, and has the look and feel of an old-world waterfront. Many visitors say it's part of the charm. The city of St. George's, with its traditional architecture, shops, and restaurant, is only a short (but steep) walk away from the pier; a taxi into the center of town costs about $6. To get to Grand Anse, you can take a regular taxi or a water taxi (see "Getting Around," below).

There are several pay phones inside the Melville Street Cruise Terminal and a local phone center nearby, where you will find both LIME and Digicel telephone providers. Though there are about six highly visible yet ancient London-style red phone booths midway around the Carenage, less than a half-mile from the terminal, most don't contain working phones.

LANGUAGE   English is the official language spoken on this island.

CURRENCY   The official currency is the **East Caribbean dollar** (EC$2.70 = US$1; EC$1 = US37¢). Always determine which dollars—EC or U.S.—you're talking about when discussing a price. Credit cards and traveler's checks are commonly accepted in tourist areas. Prices in this section are given in U.S. dollars.

INFORMATION ·Go to the **Grenada Board of Tourism,** on the Carenage in St. George's (© **800/927-9554** or 473/440-2279), for maps and information; it's open Monday through Friday from 9am to 5pm. To get information before you go, check out www.grenadagrenadines.com or call the Florida office at © **561/588-8176.**

CALLING FROM THE U.S. When calling Grenada from the United States, you need only dial a "1" before the numbers listed here.

Getting Around

St. George's can easily be explored on foot, although parts of the town are steep as the streets rise up from the harbor.

BY TAXI Taxi fares are set by the government. Most cruisers take a cab from the pier to somewhere near St. George's. You can also tap most taxi drivers as a guide for a day's sightseeing. The charge is about $50 per hour for a group of one to four persons; be sure to negotiate a price before setting out, and make sure you're both talking about the same currency. The ride from the pier to Grand Anse Beach is about $15 per carload.

BY TROLLEY The trolley, called the **Grenada Discovery Train** (www.grenada discoverytrain.com; © **473/405-6698**), is patterned after a 1900s steam locomotive, though it's painted the unlikely color of bright yellow. Sightseeing tours leave every 45 minutes from the **Cruise Ship Terminal** just outside the Esplanade Mall. The "train" takes you on a narrated scenic tour and makes a number of stops at places like **Fort George** and the **National Museum.** The hop-off/hop-on concept allows you to stay and look around for 45 minutes until the next one comes by. You won't miss it—it rings its bell frequently. Purchase tickets at the Cruise Terminal kiosk. Tour times start at 2 hours for $19 adults, $15 children.

BY MINIVAN Minivans, used mostly by locals, charge 75¢ to $4.40. All minivans depart from the new terminal on Melville Street in St. George's. The most popular run is between St. George's and Grand Anse Beach.

BY WATER TAXI Water taxis are an ideal way to get around the harbor and to Grand Anse Beach (the round-trip fare is about $8). All water taxis depart from the Esplanade area of St George's.

BY RENTAL CAR I don't recommend driving here, as the roads are very narrow and winding, and the local drivers are bold and macho behind the wheel; even a taxi ride can be an exercise in panic control.

Best Cruise Line Shore Excursions

Because of Grenada's lush landscape, we recommend spending at least a few hours touring its interior, one of the most scenic in the West Indies.

Hike to Seven Sisters Waterfalls ($79, 3½ hr.): This is a hearty walk along a muddy path that winds through the thick, pristine Grand Etang rainforest. At the end of the approximately 1.5km (1-mile) trail, a 40-minute hike, there's a set of beautiful waterfalls. Passengers are free to take a swim in the natural pools created by the force of the falls. It's gorgeous and lots of fun. Don't forget to wear your bathing suit and maybe a pair of waterproof sandals or shoes.

Rainforest/Grand Etang Lake Tour ($54, 4 hr.): This is a great way to experience Grenada's lush, cool, dripping-wet tropical interior. Via bus, you travel past the red-tiled roofs of St. George's en route to the Grand Etang Lake, set within an extinct volcanic crater some 530m (1,740 ft.) above sea level. A profusion of floating plants encroaching upon its edges gives it the appearance of an emerald wetland more so than a crystal blue lake. On the way, you drive through rainforests and stop at a spice estate. Some tours include a visit to Annandale Falls and Fort Frederick.

Excursions Offered by Local Agencies

Island Tours: Contact **Sunsation Tours** (www.grenadasunsation.com; *C* 473/444-1594), which offers full-day, half-day, and private tours to the island's homes and gardens, markets, and more. Guided hikes and tours are also available from **Grenada Tours** (www.grenadatours.com; *C* 473/440-1428), where they are passionate that no visit to Grenada is complete without exploring the rainforest preserve and historical sites.

On Your Own: Within Walking Distance

In St. George's, you can visit the **Grenada National Museum,** at Young and Monckton streets (*C* 473/440-3725), set on the foundations of an old French army barracks and prison built in 1704. Small and eclectic, it houses ancient petroglyphs and other archaeological finds, a rum still, and various Grenada memorabilia, including the island's first telegraph and two notable bathtubs: the wooden barrel used by the fort's prisoners and the carved marble tub used by Joséphine Bonaparte during her adolescence on Martinique. The most comprehensive exhibit illuminates the native culture of Grenada. The museum is open Monday through Friday from 9am to 4pm, Saturday from 10am to 1pm. Admission is $2.50 for adults and $1 for children.

If you're up for a good hike, walk around the historic Carenage from the cruise terminal, and then head up to **Fort George,** built in 1705 by the French and originally called Fort Royal. You can pick up a rudimentary walking-tour map from the cruise terminal to help you find interesting sites along the way. The fort ruins and the 200- to 300-year-old cannons are worth a peek, and the 360-degree panoramic views of the entire harbor area are spectacular. This is also the site of the assassination of the prime minister and death of several citizens during the political upheaval in 1983 that resulted in U.S. intervention. Despite that unsettling event, the island is quite peaceful and politically stable.

On Your Own: Beyond the Port Area

You can take a taxi up Richmond Hill to **Fort Frederick,** which the French began building in 1779. The British retook the island in 1783 and completed the fort in 1791. From its battlements, you'll have a panoramic view of the harbor and the yacht marina.

Grenada's cultural center, **The Spice Basket,** Beaulieu (www.spicebasket grenada.com; *C* 473/437-9000), sits above St. George's. This is a lush locale brimming with theater, music, a restaurant, folk arts and a gift shop, and two museums. There is even a **Cricket Heritage Center** (the only one of its kind in the Caribbean) called the **High Five** that illustrates the importance of the sport to island culture. Open Tuesday to Sunday from 9am to 5pm; restaurant and bar open 11am to 10pm.

Don't miss the mountains northeast of St. George's. If you don't have much time, **Annandale Falls,** a tropical wonderland where a 15m-high (50-ft.) cascade drops into a basin, is just a 15-minute drive away, on the outskirts of the **Grand Etang Forest Reserve.** The overall effect is almost Tahitian. You can have a picnic surrounded by liana vines, elephant ears, and other tropical flora and spices. Annandale Falls Centre offers gift items, handicrafts, and samples of the island's indigenous spices. Nearby, a trail leads to the falls, where you can enjoy a refreshing swim.

If you've got more time and want a less crowded spot, the even better **Seven Sisters Waterfalls** are farther into Grand Etang, an approximately 30-minute drive and then a 1.5km (1-mile) or so hike along a muddy and sometimes steep trail. It's well worth the trip, and you'll really get a feel for the power and beauty of the tropical forest here. The falls themselves are lovely—be careful, though, as it's awfully slippery on those rocks. Enjoy a relaxing swim in the cool water after your sweaty hike.

Opened in 1994, 180-hectare (445-acre) **Levera National Park** has several white-sand beaches for swimming and snorkeling, although the surf is rough. Offshore are coral reefs and sea-grass beds. Inland, the park contains a mangrove swamp, a lake, and a bird sanctuary. It's a hiker's paradise. About 24km (15 miles) from the harbor, the park can be reached by taxi, bus, or water taxi.

Shopping

The local stores sell luxury imports, mainly from England, at prices that are not quite at the duty-free level, and you can find some fine local handicrafts, gifts, and art here. There are now better shopping opportunities at the new Cruise Ship Mall on the Esplanade than there once were.

Spice vendors besiege you wherever you go, including just outside of the cruise terminal. If you're not interested, a polite "I just bought some from another vendor" usually works. But you really should take at least a few samples home with you. The spices here are fresher and better than any you're likely to find in your local supermarket, so nearly everybody comes home with a hand-woven basket full of them. Nutmeg products are especially popular. The Grenadians use every part of the nutmeg: They make the outer fruit into a tasty liqueur and a rich jam, and ground the orange membrane around the nut into a different spice called mace. You'll see the outer shells used as gravel to cover trails and parking lots. **Arawak Islands,** Building No. 15 in Frequente Industrial Park, St. George's (www.arawak-islands.com; © 473/444-3577), is the factory and outlet for these locally made products. Some other worthwhile shops include **Art Fabrik,** Young Street (www.artfabrikgrenada.com; © 473/440-0568), for batik shirts, shifts, shorts, skirts, T-shirts, and the like; **Sea Change Bookstore,** the Carenage (© 473/440-3402), for recent British and American newspapers; and **Tikal,** Young Street (© 473/440-2310), for handicrafts from Grenada and around the world. Some local artists make lovely and affordable glass jewelry and other small trinkets.

If you chance upon a local selling a sea turtle or queen conch shell or coral chunks, don't dial the conservation authorities yet. Harvesting marine turtles is still practiced in Grenada during regulated seasons, although from a sustainability perspective it should be frowned upon. If someone tries to sell you one such souvenir, you may want to explain that due to their international protected status, it could be confiscated upon entry to your home country.

Beaches

Grenada's **Grand Anse Beach,** with its 3km (2 miles) of wide sugar-white sands, is one of the best beaches in the Caribbean. The calm waters and a great view of St.

George's make the scene complete. There are several restaurants beachside, and you can join a banana-boat ride or rent a Sunfish sailboat or just loll in the gentle surf skipping stones. From the port, it's about a 10-minute, $10 taxi ride, although you can also take a water taxi from the pier for only $6 round-trip. Take heed of the signs warning beachgoers to steer clear of the toxic fruit and bark of the local manchineel trees.

If you like your waters more turbulent, visit the dramatic **Pearl's Beach,** north of Grenville on the Atlantic coast. The light-gray sand stretches for miles and is lined with palm trees. You'll practically have the beach to yourself.

Sports

SCUBA DIVING & SNORKELING   While Grenada once offered an underwater world rich in fish and coral, extensive damage from Hurricane Ivan will take years to undo. In an effort to enhance the underwater sites, and at the same time provide infrastructure for new reef growth, a local artist sank numerous life-size concrete sculptures, including people holding hands in a circle, a man seated at his desk toiling at a typewriter, and an eerie bridelike figure holding flowers and wearing a bonnet. Visibility is often up to 35m (115 ft.). Off the coast is the wreck of the nearly 590-foot ocean liner *Bianca C.* Novice divers should stick to the west coast; the more experienced might search out the sites along the rougher Atlantic side. *Note:* Grenada doesn't have a decompression chamber. In the event of an emergency, divers must be taken to the facilities on Barbados or Trinidad.

Aquanuts (www.aquanautsgrenada.com; ☏ 473/444-1126), the premier diving outfit on Grenada, has three locations on the island and also offers snorkeling trips. American-run **Eco-Dive,** at Coyaba Beach Resort and the Grenada Grand Beach Resort, both on Grand Anse Beach (www.ecodiveandtrek.com; ☏ **473/444-7777**), offers diving and snorkeling jaunts to reefs and shipwrecks teeming with marine life. Diving instruction is available.

Great Local Restaurants & Bars

A favorite local beer is **Carib;** a favorite local rum is **Clarkescourt,** which comes in a variety of flavors, including coconut, spice, and lime.

Local food and traditional cooking are making a huge comeback in Grenada, with festivals and certifications for local cooks. For an excellent chance to enjoy food from old-time island recipes in a classic setting, try the **Plantation House** (aka the Betty Mascoll Morne Fendue Plantation House), at St. Patrick's (www.mornefendue plantation.com; ☏ **473/442-9330**), 40km (25 miles) north of St. George's. The house was built in 1912 of chiseled river rocks held together by a mixture of lime and molasses. Betty Mascoll was born that same year and lived here right up until her death in 1998. Guests dine as an upper-class family did in the 1920s. Lunch is likely to include a yam-and-sweet-potato casserole or curried chicken with lots of island-grown spices. The most famous dish is the legendary pepper-pot stew, which includes pork and oxtail, tenderized by the juice of grated cassava. The proprietor, Dr. Jean Thompson, and the veteran staff need time to prepare, so it's imperative to call ahead. They serve a three-course, fixed-price ($20) lunch Monday through Saturday from 12:30 to 3pm.

The New Nutmeg (☏ **473/435-9525**), overlooking the Carenage with a view of the waterfront from its second-floor location, is newly renovated with an inventive menu that mixes local food with international fare. Try the Calaloo lasagna or a burger of Grenadian beef infused with local spices. On Wednesdays and Fridays the lunch buffet features BBQ pork and Creole chicken and fish stew, among others dishes (including local vegetables), all for $10. Originally from Nevis, chef Keithly Liburd opened here after Windjammer Cruises went out of business, closing his kitchen on the Yankee Clipper. His special "seasoning pepper" is not hot but uniquely flavorful. **Ocean Grill,** at the end of the Carenage (*C* **473/440-9747**), offers fresh fish prepared with West Indian flair, accompanied by a gorgeous view of the harbor. Lunch is about $25.

If you're an adventurous eater, take the steep hike up to **Deyna's Tasty Food,** on Melville Street (*C* **473/440-6795**), where you can order "Deyna's Fix Up," a small sampling of everything on the menu. While the downstairs venue is informal and usually filled with locals, the upstairs venue is more formal and less crowded. Wash everything down with bush tea, made from black sage leaves, or Lime Squash, a local drink. Lunch will cost you about $12.

You can also try **Creole Shack** (*C* **473/435-7422**), located upstairs at Andall's Supermarket on Melville Street. This cafeteria-style eatery opens daily at 11am for lunch and, judging from the waiting crowd, is popular among the locals. Queue up and slide your tray down the line, where you can get a dollop of everything from pepper-pot stew to locally cooked swordfish. Vegetarians will delight in the abundance of well-prepared options, including vegetable casserole, fresh okra, and callaloo (a local vegetable that cooks up and tastes like creamed spinach), all for about $12, including a glass of freshly squeezed juice.

For an elegant dining experience in a serene beachside enclave, take a taxi to **Aquarium Restaurant** at Maca Bana Villas Point Salines (www.aquarium-grenada. com; *C* **473/444-1410** or 473/439-5355), where you can gorge on lobster or just enjoy a burger in a rustic seaside restaurant at the bottom of a cliff tucked under some rocks. It's enchanting, despite the steep hike from the parking lot down the steps to the water and restaurant. Bring your swimsuit if you want to take a dip, or just stroll on the beach and watch the pelicans dive or the locals fish. Lunch is about $20.

Don't be confused by the popular dish called **lambie,** which is not lamb, but is the local name for conch. Another favorite local taste is the sweet and refreshing drink called a **bently,** made from lime juice, sugar, and club soda with a splash of angostura bitters. Or try the bright red **sorrel,** made from flowers boiled in local spices and served over ice. Be wary, however, of a medicinal and very bitter-tasting concoction made from boiled bark called a **mauby,** which is often taken to help cleanse your intestines and is reputed to be so effective at lowering blood pressure that one local claimed that a single sip could put her in the hospital.

GUADELOUPE

Take the things you love about France: sophistication, great food, and an appreciation of the good things in life. Add the best of the Caribbean: nice beaches, a relaxed pace, and warm, friendly people. Finally, combine with efficiency and modern convenience. *Voilà!* Guadeloupe. And once you leave the crowded, narrow streets of Pointe-à-Pitre, the commercial center and main port, you'll see that the island is more developed and modern than many others in the region.

Guadeloupe's Creole cuisine, a mélange of French culinary expertise, African cooking, and Caribbean ingredients, is reason enough to get off the ship, regardless of how much you're enjoying the food on board. And if shopping is your favorite sport, you'll have ample opportunity to stock up on French perfumes, clothes, and other luxury products. For the more adventurous, there's a volcano, scuba diving, surfing,

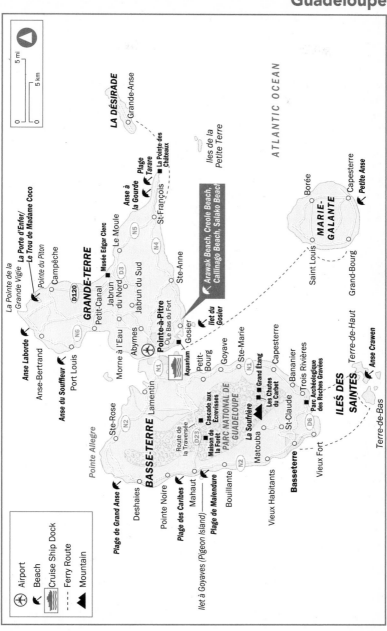

and hiking to spectacular mountain waterfalls. Of course, you can always work on your tan at one of the island's many beaches. Or maybe you'll just want to sit at a sidewalk cafe, sip your espresso while glancing through a copy of *Le Monde,* and watch the world go by.

Guadeloupe, the political entity, is an overseas region of France that includes the islands of Les Saintes, La Désirade, Marie-Galante, and Guadeloupe itself. The name *Guadeloupe,* however, usually refers to two contiguous islands—Basse-Terre and Grande-Terre—separated by a narrow seawater channel, the Rivière Salée. Nestled between Antigua and Dominica, these two islands are shaped like a 1,373-sq.-km (530-sq.-mile) butterfly. The eastern wing, the limestone island of **Grande-Terre,** is known for its white-sand beaches, rolling hills, sugarcane fields, and resort areas. Pointe-à-Pitre, your port of debarkation, is here. The butterfly's larger, volcanic western wing, **Basse-Terre,** is dominated by the national park of Guadeloupe, a mountainous rainforest replete with waterfalls and La Soufrière, a brooding, still occasionally troublesome volcano. The capital of Guadeloupe, also called Basse-Terre, is at the southern tip of this western wing.

Of Guadeloupe's population of 400,000, about 80% are descended from African slaves, with those of European and East Indian ancestry making up most of the remaining 20%. Sugar, rum, bananas, and melons are the island's main exports today.

COMING ASHORE   Cruise ships dock at the modern **Centre Saint-John Perse,** adjacent to downtown Pointe-à-Pitre, Grande-Terre's main city. The terminal has shops, restaurants, cafes, a small tourist office, and phones.

LANGUAGE   French is the official language, but you'll often hear islanders speaking a local Creole among themselves. Don't expect to get too far with only English unless you're at one of the busier tourist areas. Bring a phrase book. Guadeloupeans are nice people; meet them halfway.

CURRENCY   Guadeloupe is an overseas region of France, so the **euro** (€) is now the official currency (.75€ = US$1; 1€ = US$1.32). Each euro is divisible by 100¢. You'll have no trouble using your credit cards here. There are also numerous *distributeur de billets* (ATMs) in downtown Pointe-à-Pitre. While most vendors do not accept them, prices in this section are given in U.S. dollars.

INFORMATION   In Pointe-à-Pitre, the main **tourist office** *(Comité du Tourisme des Iles de Guadeloupe)* is at 5 Square de la Banque (© **590/82-09-30**), a 5-minute walk from the port. It's open Monday through Friday from 8am to 5pm, Saturday from 8am to noon. For advance information, visit **www.lesilesdeguadeloupe.com**.

CALLING FROM THE U.S.   When calling Guadeloupe from the United States, dial the international access code (011) and 590 before the numbers listed in this section. The numbers listed already have a 590 prefix, but that's not the same 590: You need to dial 590 twice (bureaucracy in France is just as inscrutable as anywhere). **Telecartes** phone cards make local and international calls easier and less expensive. They're sold at post offices and other outlets marked TELECARTE EN VENTE ICI, and are used in phone booths (marked TELECOM) found all over. Many phones also accept credit cards for long-distance calls.

Getting Around

BY TAXI   Metered taxis await cruise passengers at the Pointe-à-Pitre pier. Rates are regulated, but they can be expensive. Taxis can be hired for private tours, but you'll have a hard time finding a driver who speaks English. Negotiate a price before setting out, and make sure all terms are clear, to avoid an unpleasant scene later. General radio cab dispatch numbers include ℂ **590/20-74-74,** 590/21-12-21, and 690/35-18-02.

BY BUS Buses are inexpensive, comfortable, and efficient. Almost all play zouk, an upbeat local music (at reasonable decibel levels), and some have videos. Signs (ARRET-BUS) indicate bus stops, but you can wave down a driver anywhere along the road. Pay the driver or the conductor as you get off. The fare from Pointe-à-Pitre to Gosier is about $2.

BY RENTAL CAR Guadeloupe's road system is one of the best in the Caribbean, and traffic regulations and road signs are the same as elsewhere in France. Driving is on the right. Reserve a car before leaving home, especially during high season. **Avis, Budget, Hertz,** and **Thrifty** all have offices on the island. Your valid driver's license from home will be honored. Almost all rentals have standard transmissions. Be forewarned that Guadeloupeans are skillful but aggressive drivers; don't tarry in the passing lane.

Best Cruise Line Shore Excursions

La Soufrière Volcano Trek ($78, 5½ hr.): Located in the Parc National de Guadeloupe, the still-simmering La Soufrière volcano rises to 1,440m (4,720 ft.), flanked by banana plantations and lush vegetation. In 1975, ashes, mud, billowing smoke, and tremors proved that the volcano is still active, and today, you can smell sulfurous fumes and feel the heat through the soil as steam spews from the fumaroles. An hour-long uphill hike takes you to the summit, which looks like another planet.

Carbet Falls ($67, 4 hr.): After driving through the banana plantations and rainforests of Basse-Terre's south side, hike 30 minutes to picturesque Carbet Falls, where you're free to swim in the refreshing water. Wear sturdy walking shoes.

Pigeon Island ($58, 4½ hr.): First pass through Guadeloupe's national park, a lush and mountainous tropical rainforest, on the Route de la Traversée. At Pigeon Island, board a glass-bottom boat for a 90-minute ride around a beautiful coral reef now designated the Cousteau Underwater Reserve. Marvel at the numerous fish, corals, and other marine life.

Excursions Offered by Local Agencies

Hiking Tours: Basse-Terre's **Parc National** (national park) has about 300km (185 miles) of well-marked trails. Some meander through tropical rainforests to waterfalls and mountain pools; others focus on the La Soufrière volcano, geology, animals, and vegetation. Free maps and brochures in English can be obtained from the **National Park Office,** Habitation Beausoleil, Montéran, Boite Postal 13, St-Claude 97120 (ℂ **590/80-86-00**). The park office will also provide visitors with a list of local agencies offering excursions.

Snorkeling Tours: To snorkel in the Cousteau Underwater Reserve, contact **Nautilus** (www.lesnautilus.com; ℂ **590/98-89-08**), located at the Bouillante town dock, south of Malendure. It offers 90-minute guided tours in glass-bottom boats several times daily; at least 15 minutes are reserved for snorkeling and refreshments. The cost is $35 to $40.

On Your Own: Within Walking Distance

Walking is the best way to browse, shop, and visit the museums. Pointe-à-Pitre's narrow streets and congested sidewalks are bustling with activity, and its markets are among the Caribbean's most colorful. The largest, **Marché St. Antoine,** at the corner of rues Frébault and Peynier, is well known for its playful, sassy vendors, who sell tropical produce and spices in madras bags. **Marché de la Darse,** on the waterfront at the foot of place de la Banque, offers exotic fruits, vegetables, and souvenirs. The **place Gourbeyre flower market,** next to the cathedral, is ablaze with tropical blooms, including roses de porcelaine and alpinias.

Lined with royal palms, scarlet flamboyants, and traveler's palms, the renovated **place de la Victoire** commemorates Victor Hugues's defeat of the English in 1794. It's the largest public space in town and is bordered with restaurants and cafes. The nearby **Cathedral of St-Pierre and St-Paul,** built in 1871, has an iron framework designed to withstand earthquakes and hurricanes. Three churches destroyed by successive earthquakes form its foundation.

The **Musée Municipal Saint-John Perse,** 9 rue de Nozières, near rue Achille-René Boisneuf (② **590/90-01-92**), chronicles the life of native son Alexis Léger, who won the Nobel Prize for literature in 1960 under the nom de plume Saint-John Perse. The museum is housed in one of the city's most beautifully restored colonial mansions, an urban chalet with ornate friezes, voluted consoles, and wrought-iron galleries. Open windows allow breezes into the main parlor, which is furnished with bourgeois furniture. In addition to many of the poet's personal effects, the museum displays photographs documenting Guadeloupean life from the turn of the 20th century to the 1930s; you can buy postcards of some of them in the gift shop. The museum is open Monday through Friday from 9am to 5pm, Saturday from 8:30am to noon. Admission is $4 for adults, $2 for students.

The **Musée Schoelcher,** 24 rue Peynier (② **590/82-08-04**), tells the story of Victor Schoelcher, the key figure in the move to abolish slavery in Guadeloupe. The powerful exhibits, housed in a renovated mansion, include a slave-ship model, a miniature guillotine, china from Bordeaux with scenes from *Uncle Tom's Cabin,* and racist caricatures published in Parisian journals. Particularly moving is an 1845 census document that lists slaves as nothing more than plantation animals. The museum is open Monday through Friday from 9am to 5pm; admission is $2 for adults, $1 for students and children.

On Your Own: Beyond the Port Area

Guadeloupe is too large to tour in a single day. You'll have to choose among Grande-Terre, northern Basse-Terre, and southern Basse-Terre.

ON GRANDE-TERRE   The **Aquarium de la Guadeloupe,** near the Bas du Fort Marina just east of Pointe-à-Pitre (www.guadeloupeaquarium.com; ② **590/90-92-38**), is compact but has an impressive collection of exotic fish, corals, and sponges from the Caribbean and the Pacific. Come face to face with hugging sea horses, sleeping nurse sharks, and graceful sea turtles. Don't miss the polka-dot grouper known as *mérou de Grace Kelly.* Explanatory markers are in both French and English. The souvenir shop sells hand-painted folk art, jewelry, and fish- and sea-themed trinkets and T-shirts. It is open daily from 9am to 7pm; admission is $15 for adults, $10 for children 5 to 12, and free for those 4 and under.

La Pointe des Châteaux (Castle Point), at Grande-Terre's easternmost point, is an impressive seascape spectacle. Angry Atlantic waves bash black-limestone rocks and jagged cliffs with a roughness reminiscent of Brittany's Finistère coast or England's Land's End. For the best views of the island of La Désirade, follow the path leading to the point where the land falls off abruptly to the ocean.

Farther north, **La Porte d'Enfer** is a quaint little cove and beach protected from the furious Atlantic by an outcrop of limestone cliffs. The name means "Hell's Gate," but swimming close to shore in the turquoise water is usually safe. Don't venture out too far, though; the next cove, **Le Trou de Madame Coco (Madame Coco's Hole),** is where (according to legend) the sea stole Madame Coco and her parasol as she promenaded along the edge. **La Pointe de la Grande Vigie,** at the northernmost tip of the island, has paths that lead to the edge of spectacular cliffs with dramatic views of Porte de l'Enfer and, on a clear day, the island of Antigua. Cactuses and other succulents grow everywhere.

Along the northern coasts of Grande-Terre and Basse-Terre, **La Réserve Naturelle du Grand Cul-de-Sac Marin** is one of the Caribbean's largest marine reserves.

ON BASSE-TERRE Basse-Terre's greatest attraction is the **Parc National de la Guadeloupe** (www.guadeloupe-parcnational.com; ℭ **590/80-86-00**), 30,000 hectares (74,000 acres) of tropical rainforests, mountains, waterfalls, and ponds. UNESCO designated the park a World Biosphere Reserve in 1992. Its approximately 300km (185 miles) of well-marked trails make it one of the best places for hiking in the entire Caribbean. Pick up information and maps at park entrances. **La Maison de la Forêt (Forest House)** is 30 minutes from Pointe-à-Pitre on the Route de la Traversée, which bisects the park; it's the starting point for easy walking tours of the surrounding mountainous rainforest. English-language trail-guide booklets describe the plant and animal life. It's closed on Monday. Nearby, the **Cascade aux Ecrevisses (Crayfish Falls),** a slippery 10-minute walk from the roadside, is nice for a cooling dip. To the south, the steep hike to the three falls of **Les Chutes du Carbet (Carbet Falls)** is among Guadeloupe's most beautiful excursions (one of the falls drops 20m/66 ft., the second 108m/354 ft., the third 123m/404 ft.). The middle fall, the most dramatic, is the easiest to reach. On the way up, you'll pass **Le Grand Etang (Great Pond),** a volcanic lake surrounded by tree-size ferns, giant vining philodendrons, wild bananas, orchids, anthuriums, and pineapples.

The park's single greatest feature is the still-simmering volcano **La Soufrière,** rising to 1,440m (4,720 ft.) and flanked by banana plantations and lush vegetation. In 1975, ashes, mud, billowing smoke, and tremors proved that the volcano is still active, and today you can still smell sulfurous fumes and feel the heat through the soil as steam spews from the fumaroles. The summit is like another planet: Steam rises from two active craters, large rocks form improbable shapes, and roars from the earth make it difficult to hear your companions. Go with an experienced guide (see "Hiking Tours" under "Excursions Offered by Local Agencies," above). On your way down, don't miss **La Maison du Volcan** (www.maisonduvolcan.fr), the volcanology museum in St-Claude.

Gardeners should save a couple hours to visit the **Domaine de Valombreuse** (www.valombreuse.com; ℭ **590/95-50-50**), a 2.4-hectare (6-acre) floral park with exotic birds, spice gardens, and 300 species of tropical flowers. Created in 1990, and close to the town of Petit Bourg, the park has a riverside restaurant and a superior gift shop. It's open daily from 9am to 6pm; admission is about $15 for adults and $8 for children 6 to 12.

Parc Archéologique des Roches Gravées, on Basse-Terre's southern coast in the town of Trois-Rivières (ℭ **590/92-91-88**), has the West Indies' largest collection of Arawak Indian petroglyphs. The animal and human images etched on boulders date from between A.D. 300 and A.D. 400. Paths and stone stairways meander through the tranquil grounds. The park is currently undergoing a renovation, but tour guides will escort you through the grounds every hour on the hour starting at 9am (except noon). It's open daily from 8:30am to 4:30pm; admission is waived during renovations.

Parc National de la Guadeloupe is located about 6km (4 miles) from Pointe Noire. When you reach Mahault, you'll see Route de la Traversée, the Transcoastal Highway, on your left. This is the best route to explore the scenic wonders of Parc National de Guadeloupe, passing through a tropical forest as you travel between the capital, Basse-Terre, and Pointe-à-Pitre.

To preserve Parc National, Guadeloupe has set aside about one-fifth of its entire terrain. Easily accessible via modern roads, this is a huge tract of mountains, tropical forests, and gorgeous scenery, and one of the largest and most spectacular parks in the Caribbean.

The park is home to a variety of tame animals, including titi (a raccoon, adopted as the park's official mascot) and such birds as the wood pigeon, turtledove, and thrush. Small exhibition huts devoted to the volcano and forest, or to coffee, sugarcane, and rum, are scattered throughout the park. Parc National has no gates, no opening or closing hours, and no admission fee.

You can hike for a mere 15 minutes or stretch out your adventure for an entire day. The 300km (185 miles) of trails here take in rainforests and the wooded slopes of the Soufrière volcano, and pass by hot springs, rugged gorges, and rushing streams. (See also "Hiking," under "Sports," below.)

From Mahault, you drive slowly in a setting of giant ferns and luxuriant vegetation. Six kilometers (4 miles) after the fork, you reach **Les Deux Mamelles (The Two Breasts),** where you can park your car and go for a hike. Some of the trails are for experts only; others, such as the **Pigeon Trail,** will bring you to a summit of about 780m (2,560 ft.), where the view is impressive. Expect to spend at least 3 hours going each way. Halfway along the trail, you can stop at **Forest House;** from that point, many lanes, all signposted, branch off on trails that will take anywhere from 20 minutes to 2 hours.

The most enthralling walk in the park is to the **Chute de l'Ecrevisse ★**, the "Crayfish Waterfall," a little pond of very cold water at the end of a .5km (.3-mile) path. This spot in the tropical forest is one of the most beautiful spots on the island. The pool found at the base of the falls is an ideal place for a cooling swim. In just 10 minutes, you can reach this signposted attraction from the Corossol River Picnic Area. To the left of the Route de la Traversée, a short trail parallels the Corossol River, ending at the crayfish falls.

After the hike, the main road descends toward **Versailles,** a village about 8km (5 miles) from Pointe-à-Pitre. If you don't take the Route de la Traversée at this time but want to continue exploring the west coast, you can head south from Mahault until you reach the village of Bouillante, which is exciting for only one reason: You might encounter the former French film star and part-time resident, Brigitte Bardot.

Shopping

Parlez-vous Chanel? Hermès? Saint Laurent? Baccarat? If you do, you'll find that Guadeloupe has good buys on almost anything French—scarves, perfumes, cosmetics, crystal, and other luxury goods—and many stores offer a 20% discount on items purchased with foreign currency, traveler's checks, or credit cards. You can also find local handcrafted items, madras cloth, spices, and rum at any of the local markets.

Right at Pointe-à-Pitre's port, the **Centre Saint-John Perse** has about 20 shops that frequently offer lower prices than can be found elsewhere in town. **L'Artisan Parfumeur** sells French and American perfumes, as well as tropical scents.

Rue Frébault, directly in front of the port, is one of the best shopping streets for duty-free items. **Rosébleu,** 5 rue Frébault, offers china, crystal, and silver from Christofle, Kosta Boda, and other high-end manufacturers. **Phoenicia,** 8 rue Frébault and 121 bis rue Frébault, has large selections of French perfumes and cosmetics. For men's and women's fashions, as well as for cosmetics and perfumes, browse through **Vendôme,** 8–10 rue Frébault. If you find yourself overdosing on froufrou, duck into **Tati,** at rues Frébault and Abbé Grégoire; this venerable old department-store chain is France's answer to Kmart. It's famous for its antifashion pink-plaid shopping bags and makes a great stop for inexpensive basics.

The French Antilles are where the beguine began, so if you're in the market for French Antillean music or French-language books, visit **Librairie Général,** 46 rue Schoelcher. It has a small selection of English-language books as well.

If you really want to see all the best shops, like in Paris, just take a taxi to the **Commercial Center Destrelland** in Baie Mahault; you'll have a great choice of shops and markets.

Beaches

Beaches on Grande-Terre's southern coast have soft, white sand. Those on the Atlantic coast have wilder water and are less crowded. The convenient **Bas du Fort/Gosier hotel area** has mostly man-made strips of sand with rows of beach chairs, watersports shops, and beach bars. Changing facilities and chairs are available for a nominal fee. The tiny, uninhabited **Ilet Gosier,** across Gosier Bay, is a quieter option, popular with those who want to bare it all. You can take a fishing boat to the island from Gosier's waterfront. The wide strip of white sand at **Ste-Anne,** about 30 minutes from Pointe-à-Pitre, is lined with shops and food stands. **Plage Tarare,** just before the tip of Pointe des Châteaux, is the most popular nude beach.

On Basse-Terre, the **Plage de Grande Anse** is a long expanse of ocher sand. A pleasant walk north from Deshaies, it offers changing facilities, watersports, boutiques, and outdoor snack bars. Farther south, the gray expanse of **Plage de Malendure** is alive with restaurants, bars, and open-air boutiques. It's the departure point for snorkeling and scuba trips to the **Cousteau Underwater Reserve,** off Pigeon Island.

French visitors here often like to go nude, and topless sunbathing is common at hotels (less so on village beaches). There is no finer nude beach than **Pointe Tarare,** a 45-minute drive from Gosier. This beach lies east of St-François at Pointe des Chateaux. It's one of the island's most pristine, tranquil beaches, but there's no shade to protect you from the fierce noonday sun. You can snorkel here, if the water's not kicking up. There's a good restaurant by the car park. Sunday is family day at the beach. *Warning:* The tourist office recommends that women who come here be accompanied.

If you're not a nudist, you can enjoy the lovely strip of white sand at **Anse de la Gourde,** lying between St-François and Pointe des Chateaux. It has good sand, but it tends to become crowded on weekends. There's no shade at the **Creole Beach** fronting Creole Beach Hotel, although you can retreat to the bar there for a drink. A stone retaining wall blocks access to the water. Nearby, the **Salako Beach** has more sand and is set against a backdrop of palms that provide some shade. Part of this beach also leads up to a jetty. This is a fine sandy beach (although a little too crowded at times) and it also contains a snack bar. Also nearby, **Arawak Beach** is a gorgeous spot, with plenty of swaying palm trees providing a bit of shade on the beige sands. It is protected by jetties. Close at hand, **Callinago Beach** is smaller than Arawak, but still has a pleasant crescent of beige sand and palms.

South of Pointe Noire, also on the west coast, is **Plage des Caraïbes,** with its calm waters and sandy strip. This beach has picnic facilities, a shower, and toilets.

Other good beaches are found on the offshore islands, **Iles des Saintes** (see below) and **Marie-Galante.**

Sports

HIKING   The **Parc National de la Guadeloupe** (www.guadeloupe-parcnational. com; ✆ **590/80-86-00**) contains some of the best hiking trails in the Caribbean. Hikers cut through the deep foliage of rainforest, passing waterfalls and cool mountain pools, hot springs, and rugged gorges along the way. The big excursion country, of course, is around the volcano, La Soufrière.

SCUBA DIVING   Guadeloupe is more popular for scuba diving than any of the other French-speaking islands. The allure is the relatively calm seas and **La Réserve Cousteau,** a kind of French national park with many intriguing dive sites, where the underwater environment is rigidly protected. Jacques Cousteau once described the waters off Guadeloupe's Pigeon Island as "one of the world's 10 best diving spots." Sergeant majors become visible at a depth of 9m (30 ft.), spiny sea urchins and green parrotfish at 20m (65 ft.), and magnificent stands of finger, black, brain, and star coral at 25m (80 ft.). Reacting to the rich diversity of underwater flora and fauna, which thrive at relatively shallow—and relatively safe—depths, several entrepreneurs have set up shop. One of these is **Les Heures Saines,** Rocher de Malendure, Bouillante (www.heures-saines.gp; ✆ **590/98-86-63**), whose trio of dive boats departs three times a day, at 8am, 10am, and 2:30pm, for explorations of the waters within the reserve. With all equipment included, dives—depending on the level of expertise of the participants, and the intended destination—cost from $74 each. Novices, at least for the very first time they engage in the sport, pay $86 for what is referred to as a *baptême* (baptism).

SNORKELING   Beachside stands at virtually all the resorts on Grande-Terre's southern coast rent snorkeling equipment for about $15 a day. The St-François reef and the Ilet de Gosier are especially recommended.

Great Local Restaurants & Bars

Many restaurants change their hours from time to time and from season to season, so call in advance for reservations and exact hours. Most, but not all, restaurants accept major credit cards.

The local beer is **Corsaire,** while the local coffee is **Bonka.** Local rums come in a variety of flavors—such as *bois bandé* (made with the bark of the bois bandé tree), shrubb (orange and vanilla), and lemon—and are painstakingly nurtured at small rum estates such as **Séverin, Longueteau, Damoiseau, Bologne,** and **Montebello.** Local producers compare their slow, time-honored process to that used to make cognac.

AT POINTE-À-PITRE   Located in the Marina, **Côté Jardin** (✆ **590/90-91-28**) is one of the finest, most upscale independent restaurants in Guadeloupe, with an allegiance to the tenets of French cooking that you might expect in France itself. Because of its fine food and its sense of Gallic style, no one really cares that there isn't a water view. Surrounded by potted flowers and shrubs, with a view over palm trees and reproductions of paintings by Miró and Matisse, you'll dine in a white-and-green room with a hint of Provence. Menu items focus on fresh shellfish, much of which comes from fish tanks near the restaurant's entrance. Lunch will run about $65. It is open Monday through Friday for lunch and dinner, as well as for lunch on Saturday.

In the heart of Pointe-à-Pitre, **El Bistrot Sucré-Salé** (© **590/21-22-55**) is always filled at lunchtime with deal makers and office workers. The decorative theme revolves around jazz, with portraits of Louis Armstrong, Billie Holiday, and Miles Davis. The charming Marius Pheron, the Guadeloupe-born owner who did an 18-year stint in Paris, offers filets of snapper served with pommes soufflés and black pepper or marmalade of onions, meal-size salads, entrecôte steaks, and an impressive medley of grilled fish. Lunch is around $45.

ON GRANDE-TERRE   Cafes and bistros line the marina in St-François, and you can't go wrong at any of the lunch spots. On the waterfront, try the rustic and charming **Les Pieds dans l'Eau,** on rue de la République (© **590/88-60-02**), where you can get a grilled lobster for under $30. Another option is **Man Michel** (© **590/88-72-79**), where lunch will cost about $45.

The marina area of Bas du Fort in Gosier is also lined with restaurants. If you enjoy people-watching, park yourself at any French cafe and feast your eyes on the beautiful people—French tourists and yachties—mingling with one another.

ON BASSE-TERRE   In Deshaies, Lucienne Salcède's family has run **Le Karacoli** (© **590/28-41-17**), one of Guadeloupe's best seaside restaurants, for almost 30 years. Sit on the beachfront terrace in the shadow of almond and palm trees, and let the waves hypnotize you. The island of Montserrat is visible in the distance. Try a rum aperitif or two, then bliss out on cod fritters, stuffed christophine, and avocado *féroce* (a peppery purée) before moving on to Creole lobster or conch. It's open daily from noon to 2pm (closed the entire month of Sept). Reservations are imperative on weekends. Lunch is about $45.

ROATÁN, HONDURAS

Roatán, the largest of Honduras's Bay Islands, is also the most visited destination in the country. It has been on the cruise map for a number of years, but only recently has graduated to the major leagues, with such lines as Carnival, Princess, HAL, Norwegian, Costa, and Royal Caribbean scheduling calls at its port. Be warned, however, that the destabilizing coup in Honduras in 2009 weakened the country's institutions and has resulted in Honduras's having the highest per capita murder rate on the globe, including the killing of 18 opposition journalists. As a result, all 158 U.S. Peace Corps volunteers were ordered out of the country in January 2012, and the situation has severely affected the tourism industry.

Measuring almost 64km (40 miles) in length, Roatán has a total landmass of 127 sq. km (49 sq. miles). The island has a mountainous backbone and is surrounded by the world's second-largest barrier reef, which allows for superb diving as well as excellent fishing. An added bonus is that the beaches and towns are much less crowded than in such places as Cozumel, and the place is still charmingly rough around the edges, though English seems as widely spoken as Spanish.

Roatán is a prime eco-tourism destination, with wildlife reserves, marine mammal encounters, reef diving, and other watersports. At the western tip of the island, **West Bay** has Roatán's best beach, while the community of **West End** (just 5 min. away) is full of bars, souvenir shops, and restaurants—from Thai and Italian spots to countless Honduran restaurants serving traditional local foods such as *sopa de gallina* (chicken broth seasoned with basil and spearmint) and *platos tipico* (tortillas with beef and rice and beans). Most cruise passengers head here or take a shore excursion.

COMING ASHORE   Ships dock either in Port of Roatán, located in Coxen Hole, or the new Mahogany Bay Cruise Center, in Dixon Cove, the latter of which offers a welcome center along with a variety of retail outlets, including two themed bars, a restaurant, and several shops.

LANGUAGE   **Spanish** is the main language in Honduras, but most people on the Bay Islands speak English as well. The native languages of Lenca, Miskitu, and Garifuna are also spoken in some regions.

CURRENCY   Honduras's currency is the **Honduran lempira** (19 HNL = US$1; 1 HNL = US5¢), but U.S. dollars are widely accepted as well throughout the Bay Islands. Some establishments may charge an additional fee for processing credit cards. All prices in this section are in U.S. dollars.

CALLING FROM THE U.S.   To place a call to Honduras, you need only dial **011** before the numbers listed in this section.

Getting Around

You'll find plenty of **taxis** lined up right at the cruise dock to take you around the island. Unfortunately, some taxis try to rip off customers with outlandish fares on days when ships are in port, so be sure to settle on a price before getting in. A daily rate for an island tour should cost about $100 (for the whole taxi, not per person), while the average trip between the pier and West End or West Bay should cost between $8 and $11 per person. **Water taxis** are a good option to get between West End and West Bay. It's about a 10-minute ride and costs $3. Look for the dock near Foster's Bar in West End. The return trip from West Bay has two easily identifiable pickup spots. **Bicycle rentals** are available at **Captain Van's** (www.captainvans.com; ✆ **504/403-8751**) in West End for $10 per day. They also offer full- and half-day excursions tailored to the cruise ship passenger.

Best Cruise Line Shore Excursions

Coral Cay Snorkel Adventure ($69, 5½ hr.): Take a 15-minute bus ride to the Coral Cay Marine & Nature Park, where certified snorkel guides will lead you through the marine park's labyrinthine coral reefs, home to tropical fish, brain coral, sea fans, and other marine life—maybe even sea turtles and nurse sharks.

Certified Dolphin Dive ($169, 2 hr.): Take a short ride to Anthony's Key Resort and the Roatán Institute for Marine Sciences, where you'll head out by boat with a dive guide, dolphin behaviorist, and videographer. You'll spend 45 minutes observing, photographing, and playing with the dolphins in the open ocean, in a one-tank dive at depths of up to 18m (60 ft.). Divers need a certification card to participate. Nondivers can take part in a dolphin swim also offered on the property ($75, 2½ hr.).

Garifuna Experience & Mangrove Tunnel ($75, 4 hr.): A 30-minute bus ride takes you to Roatán's northeast shore to experience the culture of the Garifuna

Roatán

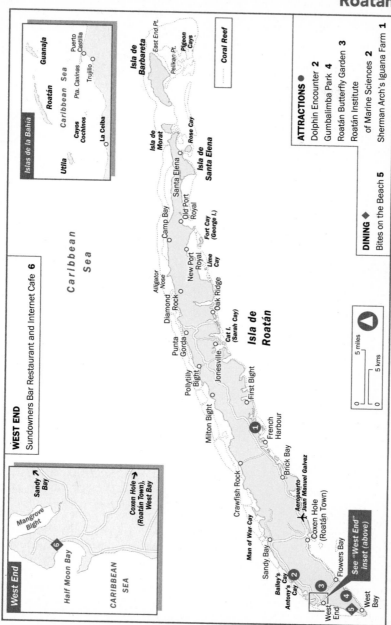

Islas de la Bahía

Utila

Guanaja

Cayos
Cochinos

Roatán

Puerto
Castilla

Pta. Caxinas
Trujillo

La Ceiba

Caribbean
Sea

Caribbean
Sea

West End

Sandy
Bay

Mangrove
Bight

Coxen Hole
(Roatán Town),
West Bay

Half Moon Bay

CARIBBEAN
SEA

WEST END

Sundowners Bar Restaurant and Internet Cafe **6**

Isla de
Barbareta

East End Pt.

Pelikan Pt.

Pigeon
Cays

Coral Reef

Isla de
Morat

Rose Cay

Santa Elena

Isla de
Santa Elena

Camp Bay

Old Port
Royal

Port Cay
(George I.)

Alligator
Nose

Diamond
Rock

New Port
Royal

Lime
Cay

Punta
Gorda

Oak Ridge

Cat I.
(Sarah Cay)

Isla de
Roatán

Pollytilly
Bight

Jonesville

First Bight

Milton Bight

French
Harbour

Brick Bay

Crawfish Rock

Man of War Cay

Aeropuerto
Juan Manuel Galvez

Coxen Hole
(Roatán Town)

Sandy Bay

Bailey's
Antony's Cay
Cay

Flowers Bay

See "West End"
inset (above)

West
End

West
Bay

0   5 miles

0   5 kms

ATTRACTIONS ●

Dolphin Encounter **2**
Gumbalimba Park **4**
Roatán Butterfly Garden **3**
Roatán Institute
of Marine Sciences **2**
Sherman Arch's Iguana Farm **1**

DINING ◆

Bites on the Beach **5**

people, descendants of slaves who settled here in 1797. The tour includes a dance performance, crafts and cooking demonstrations, and a little dose of history; it also includes a visit to a stilt village and a 30-minute boat ride through canals with the intertwined boughs of mangrove trees as roofing overhead.

Pirates, Birds & Monkeys at Gumbalimba Park ($54, 3 hr.): Gumbalimba Park is a one-stop shop for all things Roatán: a tropical bird and animal sanctuary with resident macaws and capuchin monkeys; hiking trails through a botanical garden full of orchids and heliconia; a beach destination and watersports center—with a restaurant and "pirates' cave" thrown in for good measure. This tour basically gives you access to all of that, to explore at your leisure. They also offer canopy zip-line tours using a three-cable safety system.

Excursions Offered by Local Agencies

Roatán Tourist Info Centers (www.roatantouristinfo.com; ✆ **504/3336-5597**), in the West Bay and West End, offers activity tickets, glass-bottom boat rides, sailing, canopy tours, jet-skiing, kayak rentals, and more.

On Your Own: Within Walking Distance

Just steps from the pier is **Mohagany Beach,** complete with white sand, a beach volleyball court, and various watersports vendors. If you prefer not to walk, you can always ride the "magical flying beach chair," a ski-lift-type device that sails you over the walkway and deposits you directly on the beach. An all-day pass is $12.

The area around the Coxen Hole piers holds few attractions, just lots of tourist shops. Mahogany Bay has a welcome center, shops, restaurants, and bars just off the docks.

On Your Own: Beyond the Port Area

West End is the most popular village on the island, with restaurants, bars, shopping, and proximity to West Bay.

If you want something a little different, head to the village of French Harbour, about 25 minutes from Coxen Hole on the south side of the island. On the outskirts, in French Key, **Sherman Arch's Iguana Farm** is home to 2,700 iguanas of four different species. Getting there is easy: Take a taxi along the road leading east from French Harbour toward the Fantasy Island Hotel. You can take a tour, feed and pet the lizards, and greet the resident yellow-necked parrots and macaws that live on the property. The iguana is heavily hunted, and as a protected creature, it should not be molested or harassed! The best time to see these critters is before noon, as early afternoon is feeding time and the iguanas know it. Admission is $8 per person and the farm is open daily from 8am to 4pm. You'll see a clearly marked sign showing the detour toward the farm.

Roatán Butterfly Garden (www.roatanbutterfly.com; ✆ **504/445-4481**) in the West End offers the usual assortment of native and exotic butterflies in a safe and picturesque setting. It's open Sunday through Friday 9am to 5pm. Admission is $7 for adults and $5 for children 9 and under.

In Sandy Bay, **Carambola Botanical Gardens** (www.carambolagardens.com; ✆ **504/9961-5760**) is located across the road from Anthony's Key Resort. This 16-hectare (40-acre) site includes trails that wend through lush jungle vegetation, up to picturesque cliffs with magnificent views. The admission is $10 for adults and $15 if you want a guided tour. Children 7 and under are free.

Barrio Dorcas Ranch (www.barriodorcasranch.com; © **504/9555-4880**), between Sandy Bay and West End, offers horseback rides for around $60, including transportation to and from the pier. They also offer "Saddle and Swim" or "Saddle and Sail" packages that include either a boat ride or a swim in the ocean as part of the experience. Sail options require a minimum of four passengers, and reservations must be made in advance.

Spa Baan Suerte (www.spabaansuerte.com; © **504/445-3059**) in Sandy Bay is a boutique day spa that caters to both male and female cruise ship passengers. Nestled into one of Roatán's most beautiful gardens, this peaceful sanctuary offers treatments that run the gamut from $100 milk-and-honey baths to a ginger scrub costing $140 to a $150 Mayan mud wrap.

Shopping

The best place to find souvenirs on the island is in West Bay, with a single-lane dirt road that has a variety of shops selling Honduran-made goods, including Lenca pottery that is unique to the country. Of course, there is plenty of shopping to be done at the **Mahogany Bay Cruise Center** terminal (www.mahoganybaycc.com; © **504/445-2221**). Another cluster of shops can be found at the **Town Center at Port of Roatán at Coxen Hole** (to see a current listing of shops, go to www.portofroatan.com).

Yaba Ding Ding Roatán Gallery of Local Arts & Crafts (www.yabadingding.com) is a gift shop and art gallery selling local batik, tie-dye, paintings, woodcarvings, candles, and more. It is located in the Bonilla Building, on the waterfront in central Coxen Hole. Another worthwhile shop is **Waves of Art** (www.waves-of-art.com), which boasts fair-trade products and works by local artists. **Evelyn Gift Shop** and **Pink Shack** both carry handmade crafts and locally designed wearables.

Beaches

The best beaches on the island are **Half Moon Bay** and **West Bay.** Half Moon Bay is a small beach right at the entrance to West End, and is bordered by a fossilized, raised coral. The reef passes right along the mouth of Half Moon Bay, an easy swim from shore. West Bay is about 5 minutes from West End. Scattered with resorts, this beach is blessed with powdery white sands and the reef is an easy swim from the shore. Boat transfers are available from West End, and you can rent kayaks along the beach.

Sports

WINDSURFING & KITESURFING **Wind & Fun Windsurfing School** (www.windsurfhonduras.com; © **504/445-3292**), at Sandy Bay, or **Kite Honduras** (© **504/3312-8439**), at the Marble Hill Farms in Punta Blanca, will outfit you with windsurfing and kitesurfing gear and offers lessons.

SAILING & KAYAKING **Roatán Tourist Info Center** (www.roatantouristinfo.com; © **504/3336-5597**) will meet you at spots around the island (including at the cruise ship pier) to charter a small or medium-size vessel for the afternoon. **Sea Breeze Inn** (www.seabreezeroatan.com; © **504/445-4026**) on the West End has sea-kayak rentals in West End. **Roatán Marine Park Office** (www.roatanmarinepark.com; © **504/445-4206**) on the West End offers snorkel-gear rentals and some info on responsible eco-tourism. **Subway Watersports** at Palmetto Bay Plantation (www.subwaywatersports.com; © **504/445-5707**) also has a location at

Turquoise Bay Resort (📞 **504/413-2229**). The office offers watersports including scuba, snorkeling, fishing, sailing, kayaking, and water-skiing.

SCUBA DIVING & SNORKELING Dolphin encounters, snorkeling, and dives can all be arranged at the Roatán Institute for Marine Sciences (www.anthonyskey. com; 📞 **800/227-3483** or 504/445-3026) at Anthony's Key Resort. Along the West End there are plenty of dive shops to choose from, including **Coconut Tree Divers** (www.coconuttreedivers.com; 📞 **504/445-7214**), **Native Sons Divers** (www. nativesonsroatan.com; 📞 **504/445-4003**), **Reef Gliders** (www.reefgliders.com; 📞 **504/8913-5099**), **Sueño del Mar Dive Center** (www.suenodelmar.com; 📞 **504/445-4343**), **Tyll's Dive** (www.tyllsdive.com; 📞 **504/9698-0416**), and **West End Divers** (www.westenddivers.com; 📞 **504/445-4289**). The average cost of a one-tank dive is $45 and a two-tank dive will set you back about $90. Most diving here includes relatively undisturbed reefs, flats, and wall dives. The discover-scuba course is $100 and includes all equipment. For the advanced diver, there is a wreck (a 90m/300-ft.-long vessel called *Odyssey*, sunk in 2002), but the shark diving is supposed to be some of the best in the Caribbean.

ZIP-LINE & CANOPY TOURS So many zip-line tours, so little time. Maybe it's the call of the jungle, or perhaps the sudden popularity of this new adrenaline rush, but whatever the cause, there are plenty of ways to answer the call. **Monkey Trail Canopy** (📞 **504/9914-9196**) and **South Shore Canopy Tour** (www.southshore canopy.com; 📞 **504/904-7855**) are both near West Bay. **Pirates of the Caribbean Canopy** (www.roatanpiratescanopy.com; 📞 **504/455-7576**) is east of French Harbour, and **Mayan Jungle Canopy Tour** (www.tropicalrez.com; 📞 **877/540-9692** or 504/408-5108) is at Sandy Bay. All offer similar adventures that include a heart-stopping ride above the jungle canopy while strapped into a harness.

Great Local Restaurants & Bars

Restaurants in Roatán seem to come and go with the monthly high tide. While you won't find a Starbucks or McDonald's, you will find many charming family-owned eateries, many of which serve fresh seafood and home-baked goods, and cater to the cruise ship passenger. For a charming waterfront setting, try **Bite on the Beach** (www.biteonthebeach.net; 📞 **504/403-8064**). Located on West Bay Beach, it's open from noon to 8pm, serves a full lunch menu, and has a full bar. **Sundowner Bar, Restaurant and Internet Cafe** (www.roatanonline.com/sundowner; 📞 **504/445-457**), in Half Moon Bay at West End Village, will go so far as to pick up and drop off cruise ship passengers, and offers free drinks to any visitor who can show they just arrived on the island. If you are more inclined to work than drink or snorkel, bring your laptop and check your e-mail while enjoying lunch and the beachfront views. Lunch costs about $10.

JAMAICA

A favorite of North American honeymooners, Jamaica is a mountainous island 160km (100 miles) south of Cuba and about 150km (90 miles) west of Haiti. It's the third largest of the Caribbean islands, with some 10,990 sq. km (4,240 sq. miles) of predominantly green terrain, a mountain ridge peaking at 2,256m (7,400 ft.) above sea level, and, on the north coast, many beautiful white-sand beaches rimming the clear blue sea.

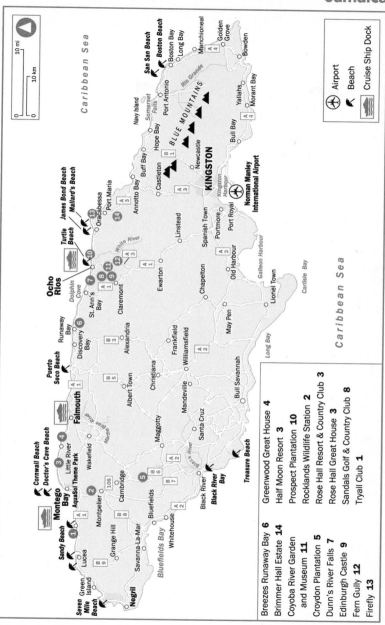

Jamaica

Caribbean Sea

Montego Bay
Falmouth
Ocho Rios
Negril
KINGSTON

BLUE MOUNTAINS

Caribbean Sea

Legend:
- ✈ Airport
- ✓ Beach
- 🛳 Cruise Ship Dock

Breezes Runaway Bay **6**
Brimmer Hall Estate **14**
Coyoba River Garden and Museum **11**
Croydon Plantation **5**
Dunn's River Falls **7**
Edinburgh Castle **9**
Fern Gully **12**
Firefly **13**

Greenwood Great House **4**
Half Moon Resort **3**
Prospect Plantation **10**
Rocklands Wildlife Station **2**
Rose Hall Resort & Country Club **3**
Rose Hall Great House **3**
Sandals Golf & Country Club **8**
Tryall Club **1**

One of the most densely populated nations in the Caribbean, with a vivid sense of its own identity, Jamaica has a history rooted in the plantation economy and some of the most impassioned politics in the Western Hemisphere, all of which leads to a sometimes turbulent day-to-day reality. You've probably heard, for instance, that the island's vendors and hawkers can be pushy and the locals not always the most welcoming to tourists; while there's some truth to this, I've had nothing but positive experiences on many visits to Jamaica.

Since its opening in 2011, the port in Falmouth has become the favored port of call for cruise ships. For more information about the ports, see www.cruisejamaica.com. Ships also dock at either Ocho Rios, on the lush northern coast, or at the city of Montego Bay ("Mo Bay"), 108km (67 miles) to the west. These ports offer comparable attractions and some of the same shopping possibilities. Port Antonio, 106km (66 miles) to the east of Ocho Rios, is an option for smaller ships.

LANGUAGE   The official language is English, but most Jamaicans speak a richly nuanced Creole English (locally called patois) that primarily evolved from English and has African grammatical features. It also includes some elements of the Spanish, Taíno, French, Chinese, Portuguese, and East Indian languages.

CURRENCY   The unit of currency is the **Jamaican dollar,** designated by the same symbol as the U.S. dollar ($). The exchange rate is around J$84 = US$1 (J$1 = US1¢). Visitors can pay in U.S. dollars, but should always find out if a price is being quoted in Jamaican or U.S. dollars—there's a big difference! Prices in this section are given in U.S. dollars.

INFORMATION   For info before you go, contact the **Jamaica Tourist Board (JTB)** (www.visitjamaica.com; ✆ **800/233-4582** or 305/665-0557). The information booths in the ports are discussed below. The JTB will assist you with booking tours and hiring taxis in all ports.

CALLING FROM THE U.S.   When calling Jamaica from the United States, you need only dial a "1" before the numbers listed here.

Shore Excursions Offered in All Ports

Because there's little to see or do besides shopping near the docks at either Ocho Rios or Montego Bay, most passengers sign up for shore excursions. The following are usually offered from all of Jamaica's ports.

Dunn's River Falls Tour ($102, 4 hr.): These falls cascade 180m (590 ft.) to the beach and are the most visited attraction in Jamaica, which means they're hopelessly overcrowded when a lot of cruise ships are in port. Visitors are allowed to climb, slip, and slide their way up the falls, so wear a bathing suit, and bring aqua-socks (or rent them on-site for $5). This tour usually visits other local attractions as well, with time allocated for shopping. *Note:* The falls are much closer to Ocho Rios than to Mo Bay, so tours from the latter typically cost around $110 and require a 2¼-hour drive each way, for a total of 7½ hours.

Chukka River Tubing Safari ★★ ($85, 3½ hr.): After a scenic van ride deep into the jungles, small groups of passengers and guides sit back in colorful river tubes and glide downriver, passing by towering bamboo and other lush foliage. It alternates between peaceful and exhilarating—especially when you hit the rapids. If you're docking in Ocho Rios, this tour is usually on the White River. If in Montego Bay, it's on the Great River. This trip is much more interesting than the popular **Martha**

Brae River Rafting, which takes you down the river on two-seat bamboo rafts. The cost is a little more, but worth it.

Horseback-Riding Excursion ($92, 3 hr.): Riders will love this trip. After a 45-minute ride from the stables through fields, you'll gallop along the beach and take your horse bareback into the surf for a thrilling ride while the horse paddles in slow motion through the cool water. Bring your swimsuit and wear closed-toe shoes.

Appleton Estate Rum Tour ($90, 4 hr.): This popular shore excursion gives you an inside look at the rum-making process. From the 18th-century-style extraction from sugarcane to the modern-day distillation, the tour gives you an overview of the history of rum in Jamaica. You also have the opportunity to juice your own cane and sample the many varieties of rum that Appleton produces.

Excursions Offered by Local Agencies

CCS Tours (www.ccstoursjamaica.com; ☎ **876/952-2007**) specializes in tours for cruise ship passengers and schedules tours to match the time constraints of the cruise ship schedule. It is actually cheaper to book the tours directly with them or the other tour operators featured at the JTB booth. All excursions are licensed and insured.

Chukka Caribbean Adventures (www.chukkacaribbean.com/jamaica.php; ☎ **877/424-8552**), named after a unique form of polo started in Jamaica, offers a variety of exciting "soft-adventure" tours from all ports. ATV safaris, river tubing, horseback riding in the surf, canopy tours, and dog sledding (many of the dogs were rescued by the Jamaica Society for the Prevention of Cruelty to Animals, or JSPCA, and a percentage of this tour goes to that organization) are just a few of the active tours offered that explore the natural and cultural highlights of the island. We suggest that you check out their website for options. They have a Green Globe (www.greenglobe.org) certification for sustainable tourism. My favorite tour is the **"Zion Bus Tour"** ($84) from Ocho Rios, traveling through the beautiful mountains of St. Ann to the village of Nine Mile, the birthplace and final resting place of reggae legend and global icon Bob Marley.

Ocho Rios

Once a small fishing port, Ocho Rios welcomes a couple of ships every day during high season. Though the area has some of the Caribbean's most fabled resorts, and Dunn's River is just a 5-minute taxi ride away, the town itself is not much to see, despite there being a few outdoor local markets within walking distance. Don't expect to shop in the markets without a lot of hassle and a lot of very pushy hawking of merchandise—some of which is likely to be ganja, the locally grown marijuana. (Remember, it may be readily available, but it's still illegal.) In recent years, the government has been making an effort to keep things saner around the markets, employing a veritable army of blue-uniformed "resort patrol" officers on bikes to help keep order.

COMING ASHORE Most cruise ships dock at the **Port of Ocho Rios,** near Dunn's River Falls and adjacent to Island Village and several shopping options. The terminal has bathrooms and a phone center.

INFORMATION You'll find the Ocho Rios office of the **Jamaica Tourist Board** at the Ocean Village Shopping Centre (www.visitjamaica.com; ☎ **876/974-2582**), open Monday through Friday from 8:30am to 4:30pm, Saturday from 9am to 1pm. There's also a small information stand right at the dock.

GETTING AROUND

BY TAXI Taxis are your best means of transport. Your safest bet is to get a taxi from the pier; there will be lots of them waiting, and fixed rates are posted. The official Jamaica Tourist Board taxis, which are licensed by the government, display JTB decals. All others are gypsy cabs, which you should avoid. If you're getting into a taxi from somewhere else on the island, always agree on a fare before you get in.

BEST CRUISE LINE SHORE EXCURSIONS

In addition to the excursions offered from all Jamaican ports (see "Shore Excursions Offered in All Ports," above), tours to the following nearby attractions are also offered from Ocho Rios.

Prospect Plantation & Dunn's River Falls ($118, 4½ hr.): About 5km (3 miles) east of town, Prospect Plantation offers a taste of Jamaica's Colonial days (sans slavery), with a tractor-drawn jitney taking you among seasonal crops that include bananas, sugarcane, coffee, pineapple, and papaya. The trip includes a stop at Dunn's River Falls (see "Shore Excursions Offered in All Ports," above).

Coyaba River Garden & Dunn's River Falls ($59, 3 hr.): About a mile from town, Coyaba River Garden and Museum was built on the grounds of the former Shaw Park plantation; it displays artifacts from the Arawak, Spanish, and English settlements in the area. The gardens are filled with native flora, a cut-stone courtyard, and fountains. Like many of the other tours in Ocho Rios, it hits Dunn's River Falls on the way back.

Dolphin Cove ($115, 2 hr.): Various excursions to this beachfront site allow you to gander at, touch, or swim with the resident dolphins. For about $10 more, you can add 1½ hours at Dunn's River Falls.

ON YOUR OWN: WITHIN WALKING DISTANCE

Adjacent to the cruise pier, **Island Village** is a 1.5-hectare (3¾-acre) entertainment-and-shopping complex developed by Island Records' Chris Blackwell. Attractions include a museum of Jamaican art, a casino, an outdoor concert venue, an indoor theater, a beach with watersports, shopping (lots of it), and a branch of **Jimmy Buffett's Margaritaville** (www.margaritavillecaribbean.com; © **876/675-8976**).

ON YOUR OWN: BEYOND THE PORT AREA

South of Ocho Rios, **Fern Gully** was originally a riverbed. Today, the main A3 road winds some 200m (650 ft.) through a rainforest filled with wild ferns, hardwood trees, and lianas. For the botanist, there are hundreds of varieties of ferns; for the less plant minded, roadside stands sell fruits and vegetables, carved-wood souvenirs, and basketwork. The road runs for about 6.5km (4 miles).

Near Lydford, southwest of Ocho Rios, are the remains of **Edinburgh Castle.** This was the lair of one of Jamaica's most infamous murderers, a Scot named Lewis Hutchinson, who used to shoot passersby and toss their bodies into a deep pit. The authorities got wind of his activities, and although he tried to escape by canoe, he was captured by the navy and hanged in 1773. Rather proud of his achievements (evidence of at least 43 murders was found), he left £100 and instructions for a memorial to be built. It never was, but the 1763 castle ruins remain. To get to Lydford, take

---

Cruise Booze

If you step inside the small cruise "terminal" in Ocho Rios, you'll find a shop called Cruise Booze, with a tasting station where you can sample a ton of different rums, including a 150-proof white rum.

the A3 south until you reach a small intersection directly north of Walkerswood, and then follow the signposts west.

The 1817 **Brimmer Hall Estate,** Port Maria, St. Mary's (© **876/994-2309**), 34km (21 miles) east of Ocho Rios, is a working plantation where you're driven around in a tractor-drawn jitney to see the tropical fruit trees and coffee plants. Knowledgeable guides tell you about the processes necessary to produce the fine fruits of the island. Afterward, you can relax beside the pool and sample a wide variety of drinks, including one called "Wow!" The **Plantation Tour Eating House** offers typical Jamaican dishes for lunch. There's also a souvenir shop with a good selection of ceramics, art, straw goods, woodcarvings, rums, liqueurs, and cigars. Tours run daily, if there are enough people. Hours are Monday through Friday from 9am to 3pm. Admission is $18 for adults, $7.50 for children, and free for kids 4 and under.

About 1.5km (1 mile) from the center of Ocho Rios, at an elevation of 126m (413 ft.), **Coyaba River Garden and Museum,** Shaw Park Road (www.coyabagardens. com; © **876/974-6235**), was built on the grounds of the former Shaw Park plantation. The Spanish-style museum displays artifacts from the Taíno, Spanish, and English settlements in the area. The gardens are filled with native flora, Spanish architecture, fountains, and the spectacular Mahoe waterfalls. It's open daily from 8am to 5pm. Admission is $10 for adults, $5 for children.

At the 180m (590-ft.) **Dunn's River Falls,** on the A3 (www.dunnsriverfallsja.com; © **876/974-2857**), you can relax on the beach, splash in the waters at the bottom of the falls, or climb with a guide to the top and drop into the cool pools higher up between the cascades of water. The beach restaurant provides snacks and drinks; dressing rooms are also available. If you're planning to climb the falls, wear aquasocks or sneakers to protect your feet from the sharp rocks and to prevent slipping.

About 5km (3 miles) east of Ocho Rios along the A3, the working **Prospect Plantation** (www.prospectplantationtours.com; © **876/974-5335**) is often a shore-excursion stop. On your leisurely ride by covered jitney, you'll see why this section of Jamaica is called the "garden parish of the island." You'll see pimiento (allspice), banana, cassava, sugarcane, coffee, cocoa, coconut, pineapple, and the famous leucaena "Tree of Life"—plus, for what it's worth, Jamaica's first hydroelectric plant. Horseback riding is available on three scenic trails. The rides vary from 1 to 2¼ hours; you'll need to book a horse at least an hour in advance. Visit the website for several touring options; reservations are required.

Firefly, Grants Pen (www.firefly-jamaica.com; © **876/725-0920**), 30km (20 miles) east of Ocho Rios above Oracabessa, was the home of Sir Noël Coward and his longtime companion, Graham Payn, who, as executor of Coward's estate, donated it to the Jamaica National Heritage Trust. The recently restored house is as it was on the day Sir Noël died in 1973. It is open Monday through Thursday and Saturday from 9am to 5pm. Admission is $10 for adults, $5 for children 11 and under.

SHOPPING

Shopping in Ocho Rios is not as good as in Montego Bay and other ports, but if your money's burning a hole in your pocket, you can wander around the Ocho Rios Craft Park, opposite the **Ocean Village Shopping Centre,** off Main Street. Some 150 stalls stock hats, handbags, place mats, woodcarvings, and paintings, plus the usual T-shirts and jewelry. More luxurious items can be found at **Island Village** near the pier and **Soni's Plaza,** on Main Street. For more local craft items, try **Coconut Grove Shopping Plaza,** a collection of low-slung shops linked by walkways and shrubs. Right in the heart of Ocho Rios, the **Island Plaza** shopping complex has paintings by local artists, local handmade crafts (be prepared to do some haggling), carvings, ceramics, and even kitchenware—plus T-shirts, of course. At all of these places, prepare yourself for aggressive selling and fierce haggling. Every vendor asks too much for an item at first, which gives him or her the leeway to negotiate the real price.

Wassi Art, on Bougainvillea Drive, Great Pond (www.wassiart.com; ✆ **876/974-5044**), offers unique, Jamaica-themed pottery done by local artists. It is about 4km (2½ miles) from the center of Ocho Rios. The clay used is hand-dug from the Blue Mountains and carefully crafted into vessels representing the colors of nature found on the island. They also offer free tours of the studio, which allows you to meet some of the artists.

If you'd like to flee the hustle and bustle of the Ocho Rios bazaars completely, take a taxi to **Harmony Hall,** Tower Isle, on the A3 (www.harmonyhall.com; ✆ **876/975-4222**), about 6.5km (4 miles) east of Ocho Rios. One of Jamaica's great houses, the restored house is now a gallery selling paintings and other works by Jamaican artists. The arts and crafts here are of high quality—not the usual mass-produced assortment you might find at the beach. While there, you can enjoy lunch at **Toscanini's** (✆ **876/975-4785**) Italian Restaurant. Italian chef Ricci features a changing menu based on the freshest ingredients available. Lunch is around $30.

BEACHES

Island Village, adjacent to the port, has a beach with watersports. The **Sunset Jamaica Grande Resort,** on Main Street (www.sunsetjamaicagrande.com; ✆ **876/974-2201**), has two beaches, shared by hotel guests and cruise ship passengers. The beaches, located at the North and South Towers, can sometimes be overcrowded. You might also want to check out the **James Bond Beach** in Oracabessa, at the east end of Ocho Rios. It has a spacious facility.

SPORTS

GOLF SuperClubs' 18-hole, par-72 **Breezes Runaway Bay,** at Runaway Beach near Ocho Rios (✆ **876/973-7319**), is one of the better courses in the area, although it's nowhere near the courses at Montego Bay. Greens fees are $80 for 18 holes, $35 for carts, and $30 for clubs (caddies are mandatory, so add $30 to these rates).

The 18-hole, par-71 **Sandals Golf & Country Club,** at Ocho Rios (✆ **876/975-0119**), is also open to the public, charging a special cruise rate of $75 for 18 holes. Clubs are an additional $60, while carts are an extra $40. Caddies, which are required, are $12 for 9 holes and $25 for 18 holes. The course lies about 200m (660 ft.) above sea level. To get here from the center of Ocho Rios, travel along the main bypass for 3km (2 miles) until Mile End Road; turn right at the Texaco station and drive for 8km (5 miles).

GREAT LOCAL RESTAURANTS & BARS

The favorite local beer is **Red Stripe,** the local dark rum is **Appleton,** and few Jamaican homes are without **Wray & Nephew Overproof** white rum. There are a number of restaurants and bars in Ocho Rios; among the best is **Bibi Bips,** 93 Main St. (✆ **876/974-7438** or 974-8759).

Ocho Rios Jerk Centre, on Da Costa Drive (✆ **876/974-2549**), serves up lip-smacking jerk pork and chicken. Don't expect anything fancy; just come for platters of meat. Lunch is about $20.

For a special lunch, **Almond Tree Restaurant,** in the Hibiscus Lodge Hotel, 83 Main St., 3 blocks from the Ocho Rios Mall (© **876/974-2813**), is a two-tiered patio restaurant overlooking the Caribbean, with a tree growing through its roof. Lobster Thermidor is the most delectable item on the menu. Lunch is about $35.

Evita's Italian Restaurant, Eden Bower Road, 5 minutes south of Ocho Rios (www.evitasjamaica.com; © **876/974-2333**), is run by a flamboyant Italian and is the premier Italian restaurant in Ocho Rios. It serves pastas and excellent fish dishes, as well as unique choices such as jerk spaghetti and pasta Viagra (don't ask). Lunch is around $20.

The Ruins at the Falls, 17 Da Costa Dr. (www.ruinsjamaica.com; © **876/974-8888**), centers on a 12m (40-ft.) cascading waterfall framed by orchids, ferns, and other water-loving plants. Almost any seat in the restaurant offers a nice view of the falls. The menu is a mixture of Jamaican, Chinese, and other international cuisine. Lunch is around $25.

For authentic Jamaican seafood, visit **Fisherman's Beach** restaurant along the shore between Island Village and Reynolds Pier. A longtime favorite of locals, Fisherman's Beach serves fish caught fresh by local fishermen and prepared in front of you. It is not fancy, but the food is reasonably priced and flavorful. Lunch is about $12.

If you're looking for a bar, check out **Ocean's 11 Watering Hole,** Lot no. 6, Fisherman's Point Row (© **876/974-6896**). It overlooks a boardwalk-style waterfront pier and is open daily from 8am to midnight. **John Crow's Tavern,** Main Street (© **876/874-5895**), has more of a sports bar feel than a vacation spot, but it is quickly becoming a favorite with locals and cruise ship passengers alike. Lunch is around $15.

Montego Bay

Montego Bay (also referred to as "Mo Bay") is sometimes less of a hassle to explore than the port at Ocho Rios, plus it has better beaches, shopping, and restaurants, as well as some of the best golf courses in the Caribbean (superior even to those in Puerto Rico and the Bahamas). Like Ocho Rios, Montego Bay has its share of traffic and urban annoyances, but there's much more to see and do here.

There's little of interest in the town itself except shopping, although the good stuff in the environs is easily reached by taxi or shore excursion.

COMING ASHORE   Montego Bay has a modern cruise dock with lots of conveniences, including duty-free stores, phones, tourist information, and plenty of taxis to meet all ships.

INFORMATION   You'll find the **Jamaica Tourist Board** office at Praise Concourse Plaza, 18 Queens Dr. (© **876/952-4425**). It's open Monday through Friday from 9am to 5pm.

GETTING AROUND

BY TAXI   If you don't book a shore excursion, a taxi is the way to get around. See "Getting Around," under "Ocho Rios," earlier in this chapter, for taxi information, as the same conditions apply to Mo Bay.

BEST CRUISE LINE SHORE EXCURSIONS

Mo Bay is the starting point for excursions to several interesting plantations and great houses, in addition to the excursions described under "Shore Excursions Offered in All Ports," earlier in this chapter.

The **Montego Bay Marine Park** (www.mbmp.org; ✆ **876/940-4465**), a marine preserve in the heart of Montego Bay, hosts an interesting assortment of marine life. You can snorkel, or take a tour with **Calico Sailing & Undersea Tours** (www.calicojamaica.net; ✆ **876/952-5860**) for a fish's-eye view of a marine area in various stages of renewal and preservation. Admission is $50; reservations are required.

Rose Hall Great House ($50, 3½ hr.): This is the most famous plantation home in Jamaica. Built about 2 centuries ago by John Palmer, it gained notoriety from the doings of "Infamous Annie" Palmer, wife of the builder's grandnephew, who supposedly dabbled in witchcraft and took slaves as lovers, killing them when they bored her. Annie was also said to have murdered several of her husbands while they slept, and eventually suffered the same fate herself. Many Jamaicans insist the house is haunted. Take a picture of her mirror and see if her ghost appears in the photo.

Greenwood Great House ($49, 3½ hr.): More interesting to some than Rose Hall, the Georgian-style building was the residence of Richard Barrett, a first cousin of Elizabeth Barrett Browning. On display are the family's library, portraits, antiques, and period musical instruments.

Croydon Plantation Tour ($65, 6 hr.): A guided tour of this mountain estate includes a short walk over gently sloping terrain, with a lot of great views. Stops are made for refreshments and seasonal fresh fruits, and, at the end, you get a traditional Jamaican-style lunch.

ON YOUR OWN: WITHIN WALKING DISTANCE

There's nothing really. You'll have to take a taxi to the town for shopping, or else sign up for an excursion.

ON YOUR OWN: BEYOND THE PORT AREA

It's a unique experience to have a Jamaican doctor bird perch on your finger to drink syrup, or to feed small doves and finches from your hand, or simply to watch dozens of birds flying in for the evening at **Rocklands Wildlife Station,** Anchovy, St. James (✆ **876/952-2009**). Lisa Salmon, known as the "Bird Lady of Anchovy," established this sanctuary. It's perfect for nature lovers and bird-watchers alike. Rocklands is less than a mile outside Anchovy on the road from Montego Bay. It is open daily from 9am to 5:30pm; admission is $20 for adults and $10 for children 5 to 12.

SHOPPING

The main shopping areas are at **Montego Freeport,** within easy walking distance of the pier; **City Centre,** where most of the duty-free shops are, aside from those at the large hotels; and **Holiday Village Shopping Centre.**

Old Fort Craft Market, a shopping complex with nearly 200 vendors licensed by the Jamaica Tourist Board, fronts Howard Cooke Boulevard up from Gloucester Avenue in the heart of Montego Bay, on the site of Fort Montego. With a varied assortment of handicrafts, this is browsing country. You'll see a selection of wall hangings, hand-woven straw items, and hand-carved wood sculptures; you can also get your hair braided. Vendors can be aggressive, so be prepared to either negotiate or walk away should you choose not to buy. A simple "no, thank you, I am just looking" should suffice. However, persistent bargaining on your part could lead to substantial discounts. Be sure to visit **Sam Sharpe Square,** off St. James Street, in honor of one of Jamaica's nine National Heroes. Sam Sharpe was captured and hung there for spurring the slave rebellion of 1831.

You can find the best selection of handmade souvenirs at the **Crafts Market,** near Harbour Street in downtown Montego Bay. Straw hats and bags, wooden platters, baskets, musical instruments, beads, carved objects, and toys are all available here. That "jippijappa" hat will come in handy, if you're going to be out in the island sun.

Try the **Gallery of West Indian Art,** 11 Fairfield Rd. (www.galleryofwestindian art.com; ✆ 876/952-4547), for the best selection of local folk art—as well as an absolutely fantastic, and reasonably priced, collection of Cuban, Jamaican, and Haitian fine art. And the nearby **Klass Kraft Leather Sandals,** 44 Fort St. (✆ 876/ 952-5782), offers sandals and leather accessories made on location.

The Shoppes at Rose Hall (✆ 876/953-3245), along the North Coast Highway and across from Rose Hall, offers an array of upscale stores with jewelry, watches, clothing, and other unique luxury gift items.

BEACHES

Doctor's Cave Beach (✆ 876/952-2566), on Gloucester Avenue across from the **Doctor's Cave Beach Hotel** (www.doctorscave.com; ✆ 876/952-4355), helped launch Mo Bay as a resort in the 1940s. Admission to the beach is about $6 for adults, half-price for children up to 12. Dressing rooms, chairs, umbrellas, and rafts are available for a $6 rental fee per item.

One of the premier beaches of Jamaica, **AquaSol Theme Park** (✆ 876/979-9447) is at Walter Fletcher Beach in the heart of Mo Bay. It's noted for tranquil waters, which makes it a particular favorite for families with children. Changing rooms are available, and lifeguards are on duty. There's also a restaurant for lunch. The beach is open daily, with an admission of $8 for adults and $5 for children ages 3 to 11.

If you want to skip the public beaches, you could head for **Sunset Beach Resort and Spa** (www.sunsetbeachresort.com; ✆ 876/979-8800). It stands on its own peninsula 5km (3 miles) from the port. It offers cruise ship passengers a day pass for $80 for adults and $40 for children 3 to 15, which allows you access to a white-sand beach, swimming pools (one with a swim-up bar), watersports, and the Pirate's Paradise water park with tubes and slides. The pass also includes food and beverages. This is a great option for families with young children.

SPORTS

GOLF **Cinnamon Hill Golf Course** (✆ 876/953-2984), at **Rose Hall Resort & Country Club** (www.rosehallresort.com; ✆ 876/953-2650), has a noted 18-hole, par-71 course with an unusual and challenging seaside and mountain layout, designed by Robert Von Hagge. The 90m-high (300-ft.) 13th tee offers a rare panoramic view of the sea, and the 15th green is next to a 12m (40-ft.) waterfall, once featured in a James Bond movie. A fully stocked pro shop, a clubhouse, and a professional staff are among the amenities. Greens fees are $169, all inclusive.

The regal 18-hole, par-72 course at the **Tryall Club,** 19km (12 miles) from Montego Bay (www.tryallclub.com; ✆ 876/956-5660), has often been the site of major golf tournaments, including the Jamaica Classic Annual and the Johnnie Walker Tournament. The 18-hole, par-72 course, designed by Ralph Plummer, has been called "among the most beautiful golf courses in the world." This tricky, wind-swept course offers stunning views and unique natural hazards. Greens fees are about $150, plus $30 for a cart.

The **Half Moon Rock Resort,** at Rose Hall (www.halfmoongolf.com; ☎ **876/ 953-2560**), features an 18-hole, par-72 championship course designed by Robert Trent Jones, Sr. Greens fees are about $150, plus $30 for a mandatory caddy.

HORSEBACK RIDING The best horseback riding is offered by the helpful staff at the **Rocky Point Riding Stables,** at the Half Moon Club, Rose Hall (www. horsebackridingjamaica.com; ☎ **876/953-2286**). The stables, built in the colonial Caribbean style in 1992, are the most beautiful in Jamaica. A 90-minute beach ride is $80 per person.

RAFTING **Mountain Valley Rafting,** 31 Gloucester Ave. (☎ **876/956-4920**), offers excursions on the Great River, departing from the Lethe Plantation, about 15km (9 miles) south of Montego Bay. Bamboo rafts are designed for two, with a raised dais to sit on. In some cases, a small child can accompany two adults on the same raft, although you should exercise caution when doing so. For $55, a half-day experience includes transportation to and from the pier, an hour's rafting, a garden tour of the Lethe property, and a taste of Jamaican liqueur.

GREAT LOCAL RESTAURANTS & BARS

Gloucester Avenue, also known as the "Hip Strip," is Montego Bay's entertainment center. Lined with restaurants, bars, and souvenir shops, it is especially happening in the afternoon and after dark.

The open-air **Pork Pit,** 27 Gloucester Ave., near AquaSol Theme Park (☎ **876/ 952-1046**), is the best place for the famous Jamaican jerk pork and jerk chicken. Many beachgoers come here for a big, informal lunch at picnic tables encircling the building. Order half a pound of jerk meat with a baked yam or baked potato and a bottle of Red Stripe beer. Prices are very reasonable; lunch is about $12.

The **Native Restaurant,** Gloucester Avenue (☎ **876/979-2769**), continues to win converts with such appetizers as jerk reggae chicken, ackee and saltfish (an acquired taste), smoked marlin, and steamed fish. The boonoonoonoos, billed as "A Taste of Jamaica," is a big platter with a little bit of everything, including meats and several kinds of fish and vegetables. Lunch is about $20.

Stop by **Jerky's Bar & Grill,** 29 Alice Eldmire Dr. (☎ **876/684-9101**), for authentic jerk chicken or pork done in the style of Boston Bay, Port Antonio, the origin of jerk cooking. Along with your jerk meat, enjoy roasted breadfruit or yams and a cold Red Stripe at the bar. It's open from 11am until the last person finishes his or her beer and jerk pork. It is on the same road that takes you to Rose Hall. Lunch is about $12.

Coral Cliffs Entertainment Resort, Gloucester Avenue (www.coralcliff jamaica.com; ☎ **876/952-4130**), is a gaming and entertainment center open 24/7. Tons of arcade games and more than 120 slot machines with blinking lights tempt you to win back your vacation expenditures. In between slots, you can replenish at the **Rum Jungle Café & Bar,** with a choice of more than 100 rums and a list of specialty drinks.

Falmouth

The capital of the parish of Trelawny, Falmouth has the largest collection of intact colonial Georgian architecture in the Caribbean. At one time, it was one of the busiest ports in Jamaica, hosting as many as 30 tall ships in any given day exchanging

European goods for rum and sugar. The popularity of the new port of call for Royal Caribbean's Oasis-class ships has once again put Falmouth on the map. The terminal and shops have been well designed to complement the local Georgian architecture.

EXCURSIONS OFFERED BY LOCAL AGENCIES

Chukka Tours offers a number of tours from Falmouth, including one with historical highlights and a beach break. See the Good Hope Estate House in a horse-drawn carriage, or choose the High Tea experience on the estate. Adventurous types can choose from river tubing, kayaking, zip-line plunges, horseback riding, and ATV trails (www.chukkacaribbean.com; ✆ 877/424-8552).

If river rafting is your thing, the long wooden poles stitched together will take you down 3 miles of the Martha Brea River with **Martha Brea River Rafting** (www.jamaicarafting.com; ✆ 876/940-6398).

ON YOUR OWN: BEYOND THE PORT AREA

Visit the **Outameni Experience,** Coopers Pen, Trelawny (www.outameni.com; ✆ 876/954-4035), for a 90-minute trip through Jamaican history and culture. In this interactive encounter, a time traveler will take you on a journey from the first inhabitants of Jamaica, the Taíno, through slavery, Colonialism, and to modern times. You will test your maypole dance skills, sample a variety of Jamaican snacks, and try out dance-hall moves—all while learning about the rich cultural history that influences Jamaican culture today. It is less than 1 hour from Ocho Rios or Montego Bay.

Green Grotto Caves, Runaway Bay (www.greengrottocavesja.com; ✆ 876/973-2841), is a natural limestone labyrinth that is about 1,500m (5,000 ft.) long and 12m (40 ft.) deep. It has numerous chambers, light holes, interesting formations, and a subterranean lake. The occasional unearthed pottery provides evidence of Taíno occupancy, and the caves have also sheltered runaway slaves, Spanish fleeing from the British, and smugglers running arms to Cuba. Admission is $20 adults and $10 children 4 to 12.

Cranbrook Flower Forest (✆ 876/878-4287), 29km (18 miles) west of Ocho Rios, describes itself as a "unique experience of peace and natural beauty." Starting from the unusual turquoise orchids at the entrance, each step through the gardens brings you to another sighting of the flora, both endemic and introduced, of the island. There are nature trails that lead to the head of the river and several wading streams, sure to be a delight for bird-watchers, garden enthusiasts, and nature lovers. Chukka's canopy tours include a visit to the gardens, but you can go on your own via taxi. Admission is $10 for adults and $5 for children 11 and under, or book an on-site tour for $40.

On the road between Falmouth and Ocho Rios, you will pass the town of Duncans. Ask the driver to point out the **Sober Robin Inn,** which was the house where famed Jamaican calypso and folk singer Harry Belafonte spent his childhood with his grandparents.

Columbus Park, on the Queen's Highway/A1, is almost equidistant between Falmouth and Ocho Rios, and is a free open-air museum in Discovery Bay. It is alleged that this is where Columbus first set foot in Jamaica. The park has historical relics of Jamaica's past and offers a breathtaking view of **Discovery Bay.**

Port Antonio

"Day-O," the folk song popularized by Harry Belafonte, was sung by men bringing bananas down the rivers to the town of Port Antonio for export. Jamaican tourism started here when empty banana boats returning from the States brought well-heeled tourists to Jamaica. If you are lucky enough to be on one of the ships that dock here, you are in for a treat. If not, you could hire a taxi or take one of the tours from Ocho Rios. The new road allows you to take the trip from Ocho Rios in less than 2 hours. Ships dock at the **Errol Flynn Marina** (www.errolflynnmarina.com; © 876/715-6044). With white-sand beaches and active coral reefs, it is currently the only Blue Flag–certified (www.blueflag.org) port in Jamaica.

EXCURSIONS OFFERED BY LOCAL AGENCIES

CCS tours (www.ccstoursjamaica.com; © 876/952-2007) offers several options to Port Antonio, or you could hire a taxi and go on your own.

Rio Grande Rafting (5 hr.), first popularized by Errol Flynn, is a 2½-hour trip along the Rio Grande through the tropical and subtropical forests of the North Coast. You might even meet a farmer bringing his goods to market on your way to the sea. With lush greenery, sounds of birds, and smells of flora, it is one of the best rafting experiences in Jamaica. At the end of your trip, refresh with a drink and snack at the **Rafters Rest,** St. Margaret's Bay (© 876/993-5778).

Somerset Falls (4 hr.), along the A4 just past Hope Bay, is one of the many spectacular waterfalls found in Jamaica. The Daniels River plunges through a gorge into a shallow cave where a guide will row you for a closer look. It is a less crowded option than Dunn's River, and you can stay and swim in the cool aquamarine-colored waters and have a snack and drink at the bar/restaurant.

ON YOUR OWN: BEYOND THE PORT AREA

Visit the **Maroon Cultural Center** in Charlestown, Buff Bay, to view cultural artifacts and learn about Queen Nanny, the only female of Jamaica's National Heroes and the Windward Maroons of Jamaica, slaves who escaped from the British and formed their own sovereign communities in the Blue Mountains. You may have the opportunity to experience the drumming that characterizes the spiritual vibrancy of the community and their connection to the ancestors.

Jamaican jerk originated in **Boston Beach** and began with the Taíno tradition of using pimento to season and smoke wild pigs. It was later perfected by the Maroons, who used additional spices from Africa and Spain to preserve meats. You can smell the sweet smoke as you approach the Boston beach, which is the jerk center of Jamaica . . . and the world, for that matter. I recommend having lunch at Boston Beach and then heading for either **Frenchman's Cove** or **San San Beach** for a rest, swimming, and/or snorkeling before you head back to Port Antonio or Ocho Rios.

BEACHES

The beaches of Port Antonio are less crowded than those of Montego Bay and Ocho Rios. At **Frenchman's Cove Resort** (www.frenchmans-cove-resort.com; © 876/993-7270), a small river winds its way through the grounds to the sea, where you will find a small but serene white-sand beach. The recent hurricanes pushed the white sand up the river, rendering the water a clear aquamarine blue that is flanked by lush tropical greenery. The entrance fee is $6. **San San Beach** is a long but narrow strip of white sand. The water is calm, and you can snorkel near Pellew Island, described as a pristine piece of Jamaican rock and jungle, in an almost unspoiled marine ecosystem.

GREAT LOCAL BARS & RESTAURANTS

If you want to travel from Ocho Rios to Port Antonio, the A3/A4 is the main highway that connects the major port cities on the North Coast. Allow for at least 2½ hours each way. If you are in Port Antonio, you could ask for assistance from the Jamaica Tourism Board desk in the marina.

Mockingbird Hill (www.hotelmockingbirdhill.com; ✆ **876/993-7267**) is an award-winning, environmentally friendly inn tucked away in the foothills of the Blue Mountains. The restaurant, **Mille Fleurs,** serves up "creative Caribbean" cuisine with views of the Blue Mountains and Port Antonio. The menu changes daily, but with such dishes as coriander-and-coconut mahimahi and ackee quiche, it is a fusion of global Caribbean flavors. It is open for lunch from noon to 2:30pm. Meals are about $35. Owners Barbara and Shireen strive to protect the local environment with carbon-offsetting programs and local environmental initiatives. Visit the website to learn how you can engage in sustainable tourism on your holiday.

KEY WEST

No other port of call offers such a sweeping choice of fine dining, easy-to-reach attractions, street entertainment, and roguish bars as does this heavy-drinking, fun-loving town at the very end of the fabled Florida Keys. It's America's southernmost city, located at Mile Marker 0, where U.S. Route 1 begins, but it feels more like a colorful Caribbean outpost mixed with a dash of New Orleans. It is also the largest predominantly wooden historic district in the U.S.; as you wander, keep your eyes peeled for bronze markers denoting historic houses and other historic landmarks.

You only have a day here, so flee the busy cruise docks and touristy Duval Street for a walk through hidden and more secluded byways, such as Simonton, Caroline, or William streets. Or you might want to spend your day sunbathing, diving, or snorkeling.

COMING ASHORE   Ships dock at **Mallory Square** (Old Town's tourist central), at the nearby Westin Resort's **Pier B,** and at the U.S. Navy base's **"Outer Mole" pier.** All are on the Gulf side of the island. Passengers arriving at the navy pier must take an official shuttle bus the short distance to and from Mallory Square, as individuals are not permitted to transit the base on their own.

LANGUAGE   You can speak English here. Remember, you're in the U.S. of A.!

CURRENCY   **U.S. dollars** are used here.

INFORMATION   Right near the cruise docks, the **Greater Key West Chamber of Commerce,** 510 Greene St. (www.keywestchamber.org; ✆ **305/294-2587**), provides information on tours and fishing trips. *Pelican Path* is a free walking guide that documents the history and architecture of Old Town, while *Sharon Well's Walking and Biking Guide to Old Key West* contains a bunch of walking tours. For advance info, contact the **Florida Keys & Key West Tourism Council** (www.fla-keys.com; ✆ **800/352-5397**).

Getting Around

The island is only 6.5km (4 miles) long and 3km (2 miles) wide, and getting around is so easy that many locals do without cars, using "conch cruisers" (in other words, bicycles) instead. The most popular attractions, including the Harry S Truman Little White House and the Key West Museum of Art and History, are all within walking distance of Mallory Square—even the farthest attraction (Key West Butterfly and Nature Conservancy) is only about a mile down Duval.

BY TAXI Island taxis operate around the clock, but are small and not suited for sightseeing tours. They will, however, take you to the beach and arrange to pick you up at a certain time. Services include **Maxi-Taxi Sun Cab System** (© 305/294-2222), **Pink Cabs** (© 305/296-1800), and **Five Sixes Taxi** (© 305/296-6666). Prices are uniform; the meter starts at $2.75 and adds 60¢ per ⅕ mile.

BY TRAM The **Conch Tour Train** (www.conchtourtrain.com; © 305/294-5161) is a narrated 90-minute tour that takes you up and down all the most interesting streets and offers commentary on 100 local sites, giving you lots of lore about the town. It's the best way to see Key West in a short time. The depot is located at Mallory Square, near the cruise ship docks. Trains depart every 30 minutes. Most ships sell this as an excursion, but you can also do it on your own; departures are daily from 9am to 4:30pm and cost $29 per person; children 12 and under are free. The trip has only one stop where passengers can get on and off (the Historic Seaport and the station depot at the corner of Front and Duval). Tickets can be purchased online, for a discount.

If you want more flexibility and are booking on your own, try the **Old Town Trolley** (www.trolleytours.com; © 305/296-6688). It's less popular than the Conch Tour Train, but it lets you get off to explore a particular attraction, and then reboard another of its trolleys later. Professional guides recount relevant history about Key West throughout the 90-minute route. The trolleys operate daily from 9am to 4:30pm, with departures every 30 minutes from convenient spots throughout town. You can board the trolley near the cruise docks (look for signposts). Tours cost about $29 per person; children 12 and under are free. Tickets can also be purchased online for a small discount.

BY BUS The cheapest way to see the island is by bus, which costs only $2 for adults, 50¢ for seniors and children 6 and older.

BY MOTOR SCOOTER OR BICYCLE One of the largest and best places to rent a bicycle or motorbike is **Keys Moped and Scooter Rental,** with three locations: 500 Truman Ave.; 523 Truman Ave., about a block off Duval Street; and 513 South St. (© 305/294-0399). Cruise ship passengers might opt for a 4-hour motor-scooter rental for about $30, the 9am-to-5pm rental for $45, or the all-day (24-hr.) rental for $60. One-speed, big-wheeled "beach-cruiser" bicycles, with soft seats and big baskets for toting beachwear, rent for about $15 for 8 hours.

BY RENTAL CAR Walking or cycling is better than driving in Key West, but if you do want to rent, **Avis, Budget, Dollar, Thrifty,** and **Hertz** all have offices here, as do **Tropical Rent-a-Car,** 1300 Duval St. (© 305/294-8136), which rents electric cars only, and **Enterprise Rent-a-Car,** 2834 N. Roosevelt Blvd. (www.enterprise.com; © 800/325-8007 or 305/292-0220). If you're visiting in winter, make reservations at least a week in advance.

Best Cruise Line Shore Excursions

In addition to the Conch Tour Train described above, most lines offer walking tours and sometimes bike tours for those who like the services of a guide. But this is really a port to explore on your own.

Catamaran Party Cruises ($60, 3 hr.): The popular Fury catamarans take passengers to a reef for some snorkeling. This excursion finishes the trip back to shore with lots of music and booze.

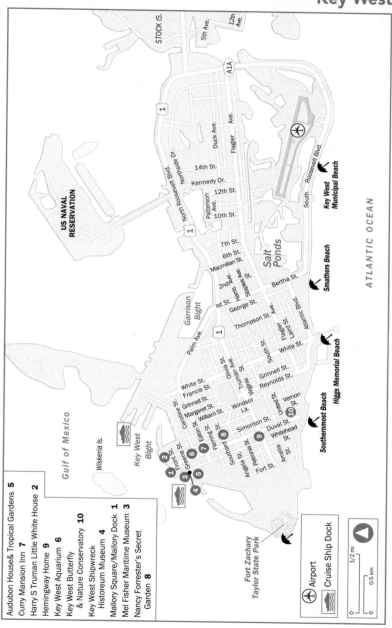

Audubon House& Tropical Gardens **5**
Curry Mansion Inn **7**
Harry S Truman Little White House **2**
Hemingway Home **9**
Key West Aquarium **6**
Key West Butterfly
& Nature Conservatory **10**
Key West Shipwreck
Historeum Museum **4**
Mallory Square/Mallory Dock **1**
Mel Fisher Maritime Museum **3**
Nancy Forrester's Secret
Garden **8**

✈ Airport
🚢 Cruise Ship Dock

0 ___ 1/2 mi
0 ___ 0.5 km

5

THE PORTS OF CALL | Key West

Excursions Offered by Local Agencies

Glass Bottom Boat Tours' *The Pride of Key West* (www.furykeywest.com; ✆ **305/296-6293**) departs at noon for a 2-hour excursion to the only living barrier reef in the continental U.S., which is also the third-largest barrier reef in the world. The ship departs from the Westin Marina at Front and Greene streets. The cost is $45 for adults, $23 for children ages 6 to 12. Discounts are available if you book online.

Dolphin Safari Charters (www.safaricharters.com; ✆ **305/747-0453**), 2319 Roosevelt Blvd., offers small-scale excursions with a maximum of six people. This family-run business will take your group out to see bottlenose dolphins in the wild. The 3½-hour trips depart at 8:30am and noon and include snorkel gear, beverages, and snacks. The cost is $89 per person or $69 for children 10 and under.

On Your Own: Within Walking Distance

The **Harry S Truman Little White House,** 111 Front St. (www.trumanlittlewhite house.com; ✆ **305/294-9911**), is part of the 42-hectare (104-acre) Truman Annex, near the cruise ship docks. Originally the home of the navy base commander, Truman commandeered it for use as a vacation home during his presidency. Today it remains just as he left it, decorated in perfect late-1940s style. By the time the guides get through their well-organized hour-long tour, you'll feel as if you've gone back in time. Admission is $17 for adults, $5 for children ages 5 through 12.

The **Hemingway Home,** 907 Whitehead St. (www.hemingwayhome.com; ✆ **305/294-1136**), provides a similar if less formal look back at the island's old days. "Papa" lived here with his second wife, Pauline, completing *For Whom the Bell Tolls* and *To Have and Have Not* in the studio annex out back. Hemingway had a gaggle of polydactyl (many-toed) cats, whose descendants still live on the grounds. While not exactly feral, some of these feline residents prefer their privacy while others are happy to be petted. A good rule of thumb is to avoid the ones that act coy and aloof, but if they come up to you, feel free to indulge in an endless buffet of petting and belly scratches, with unlimited purrs at no extra cost. Because the cats reside both within the house and on the grounds, be sure to bring allergy medicine if you are inclined to sneeze at the sight of cat hair. The home is open daily from 9am to 5pm; admission is $13 for adults and $6 for children.

Audubon House & Tropical Gardens, 205 Whitehead St., at Greene Street (www.audubonhouse.com; ✆ **877/294-2470** or 305/294-2116), is dedicated to the 1832 Key West sojourn of the famous naturalist John James Audubon. The ornithologist didn't live in this three-story building, but it's filled with his engravings. The main reason to visit is to see how wealthy sailors lived in Key West in the 19th century. And the lush tropical gardens alone are worth the admission, which is $10 for adults, $6.50 for students, and $5 for children 6 to 12. Hours are from 9:30am to 5pm daily.

On the waterfront at Mallory Square, the **Key West Aquarium,** 1 Whitehead St. (www.keywestaquarium.com; ✆ **305/296-2051**), in operation since 1932, was the first tourist attraction built in the Florida Keys. The aquarium's special feature is a touch tank, where you can feel a horseshoe crab, sea squirt, sea urchin, starfish, and, of course, conch, the town's mascot and symbol. It's worth taking a tour, as the guides are knowledgeable and entertaining—and you'll get to pet a shark, if that's your idea of a good time. The aquarium is open daily from 10am to 6pm; admission is $15 for adults and $7 for children 4 to 12.

The Key West Shipwreck Historeum Museum, 1 Whitehead St. (www.ship wreckhistoreum.com; ✆ **305/292-8990**), is another combination of entertainment and education. Actors portraying 19th-century master wrecker (an expert in ship-wreck recovery) Asa Tift and his crew draw visitors into their warehouse, filled with recovered objects from a real wreck and videos explaining the history, techniques, and even modern-day practitioners of shipwrecking. The museum also includes one of the best aerial views of the city at the top of its 20m (65-ft.) wreck-spotting tower. Hours are 9:40am to 5pm daily. The cost is $15 for adults and $7 for children 4 to 12.

Another great bird's-eye view of Old Key West awaits at the top of the **Curry Mansion,** 511 Caroline St. (www.currymansion.com; $\textcircled{C}$ **800/253-3466** or 305/294-5349), home of Key West's first millionaires. Although the mansion operates as a bed-and-breakfast, tourists can explore many of its 22 rooms, filled with memorabilia dating to the 1800s. Everything is hands-on, which means that you can play the antique piano or make a move on the chess board in the parlor. But the best part about the mansion is the widow's watch, a small perch at the very top of the house that gives 360-degree views of the town, the cruise ships, and the sea. Admission for nonguests is $5 for adults, $1 for children ages 3 to 12.

The late treasure hunter Mel Fisher used to wear heavy gold necklaces, which he boasted were worth a king's ransom. He wasn't exaggerating. After long and risky dives, Fisher and his associates plucked more than $400 million in gold and silver from the shipwrecked Spanish galleons *Santa Margarita* and *Nuestra Señora de Ato-cha,* which were lost on hurricane-tossed seas some 385 years ago. Now this extraor-dinary Spanish treasure—jewelry, doubloons, and silver and gold bullion—is displayed at the **Mel Fisher Maritime Museum,** 200 Greene St. (www.melfisher.org; $\textcircled{C}$ **305/294-2633**), near the docks. It's open daily from 9:30am to 5pm. Admis-sion is $13 for adults, $11 for students, and $6 for children 6 to 12.

Nancy Forrester's Secret Garden, 1 Free School Lane, off Simonton between Southard and Fleming streets (www.nfsgarden.com; $\textcircled{C}$ **305/294-0015**), is the most lavish and verdant garden in town. Some 150 species of palms and thousands of other plants, including orchids, climbing vines, and ground covers, are planted here, creat-ing a blanket of lush, tropical magic. It's a 20-minute walk from the docks, near Key West's highest point, Solares Hill. Pick up a sandwich at a deli and then picnic at the tables in the garden. It's open daily from 10am to 5pm; admission is $10.

At the **Key West Butterfly & Nature Conservatory,** 1316 Duval St. (www.keywestbutterfly.com; $\textcircled{C}$ **800/839-4647** or 305/296-2988), a different kind of natu-ral adventure awaits. The center is home to thousands of butterflies, from 50 to 60 different species, all of which have free rein over a large greenhouse with walking paths for visitors. No need to chase the insects to get good photos, either; they fill the space, often landing on nearby plants or even on the shoulders and heads of specta-tors (a sign of good luck, according to conservatory staff). The flurry of butterflies, decorated in a full spectrum of colors, can be both awe-inspiring and overwhelming, especially if you visit during peak hours of activity, when the sun is at its highest point. Hours of operation are daily 9am to 5pm. The cost is $12 for adults, $8.50 for children 4 to 12 years old, $9 for seniors and military personnel, and free for children 3 and under.

If your ship leaves late enough, you can take in a unique local celebration: viewing the sunset from **Mallory Dock.** Sunset-watching is good fun all over the world, but in Key West it's been turned into a carnival-like, almost pagan celebration. People from all over begin to crowd Mallory Square even before the sun starts to fall, bring-ing the place alive with entertainment—everything from string bands to a unicyclist wriggling free of a straitjacket to a juggler tossing around machetes and flaming sticks.

The main entertainment, however, is that massive fireball falling out of view, a sight that's always greeted with hysterical applause.

On Your Own: Beyond the Port Area

Nothin'. That's the beauty of Key West: Everything worthwhile is accessible on foot.

Shopping

Within a 12-block radius of Old Town, you'll find a mix of tawdry and outrageously overpriced merchandise, as well as tasteful boutiques and exquisite art galleries. If you're in the market for some Key West kitsch, this is the neighborhood for you. Shopping by cruise ship passengers has become a joke among Key West locals, but that's their problem. I say be proud of your flamingo snow globe and floppy straw hat. What else says "vacation" better?

Among the less kitschy alternatives, a few standouts are located much farther along **Duval Street,** the main drag leading to the Atlantic, and on hidden back streets. Among them are **Archeo,** 1208 Duval St. (www.archeogallery.com; © 305/294-3771), selling works of art by tribes from the Middle East and northern Africa, including stunning rugs hand-woven by tribeswomen in Iran; and the **Lucky Street Gallery,** 1130 Duval St. (www.luckystreetgallery.com; © 305/294-3973), boasting an eclectic selection of paintings, photos, and sculpture, all without a fluorescent-colored beach scene in sight. This end of Duval is also home to boutiques offering clothing and accessories that are unique but far more, shall we say, toned down than their counterparts closer to port. You can reach all of these stores from the cruise ship docks via a 15- to 20-minute stroll.

Even if you don't find anything you'd like to bring home, it's worth a quick stroll through **Fast Buck Freddie's,** 500 Duval St. (www.fastbuckfreddies.com; © 305/294-2007), for sheer size alone. The closest thing you'll find to a department store in Old Town, Freddie's carries everything from souvenir hot sauce and hokey palm-tree wall hangings to designer clothing from the likes of Kenneth Cole and Lacoste.

Key West Aloe, Inc., 410 Duval St. (www.keywestaloe.com; © 800/445-2563), is aloe, aloe, and more aloe; the shop's stock includes shaving cream, after-shave lotion, sunburn ointments, and fragrances for men and women based on tropical essences such as hibiscus, frangipani, and white ginger. **Key West Hand Print Fashions and Fabrics,** 201 Simonton St. (www.keywestfashions.com; © 800/866-0333 or 305/292-8951), sells bold, tropical prints—hand-printed scarves with coordinated handbags and rack after rack of busily patterned sundresses that will make you look jaunty on deck.

Haitian Art Company, 1100 Truman Ave. (www.haitian-art-co.com; © 305/296-8932), claims to inventory the largest collection of Haitian paintings in the U.S. Prices range from $15 to $5,000. **Key West Island Bookstore,** 513 Fleming St. (© 305/294-2904), is well stocked with books on Key West and has Florida's largest collection of works by and about Hemingway. In the rear is a rare-book section where you may want to browse, if not buy.

Beaches

Beaches are not too compelling here. Most are man-made, often with sand imported from the Bahamas or mainland Florida. Those mentioned below are free and open to the public daily from 8am to sunset. There are watersports rentals and a few facilities, mostly locals hawking beach umbrellas, food, and drinks.

The beach at **Fort Zachary Taylor State Park** (www.fortzacharytaylor.com; ℂ 305/292-6713) is the best and the closest to the cruise ship docks, a 20-minute walk away. This 20-hectare (50-acre) man-made beach is adjacent to historic Fort Taylor, once known as Fort Forgotten because it was buried under tons of sand. To get here, go through the gates leading into Truman Annex. One watering hole near the end of the beach is the raffish **Green Parrot Bar** (www.greenparrot.com; ℂ 305/294-6133).

A 25-minute walk from the harbor near the end of White Street, one of the main east-west arteries, leads to **Higgs Memorial Beach,** where you'll find lots of sand, picnic tables sheltered from the sun, and fewer of your fellow cruise ship passengers.

In the 1950s, **Southernmost Beach** drew Tennessee Williams, but today it's more likely to fill up with visitors from the area motels. Facilities include watersports rentals and a nearby restaurant. The beach lies at the foot of Duval Street on the Atlantic side, across the island from the cruise ship docks.

Smathers Beach, named in honor of one of Florida's most colorful former senators, is the longest (about 2.5km/1½ miles) in town. Unfortunately, it's about a $12 one-way taxi ride from the cruise docks. The beach borders South Roosevelt Boulevard. *Note:* There's no shade here.

Sports

FISHING As Hemingway, an avid fisherman, would attest, the waters off the Florida Keys are some of the world's finest fishing grounds. You can follow in his wake aboard the 39-foot *Linda D IV* and *Linda D V* (www.charterboatlindad.com; ℂ 800/299-9798 or 305/296-9798), which offer the best deep-sea fishing here. Full-day charters for up to six people are $995; half-day charters are $675. Full-day shared charters go for $250 per person. Make arrangements as far in advance as possible.

GOLF Redesigned in 1982 by architect Rees Jones, the 18-hole, par-70 **Key West Resort Golf Club,** 6450 E. Junior College Rd. (www.keywestgolf.com; ℂ 305/294-5232), lies 4km (2½ miles) from the cruise docks, near the southern tip of neighboring Stock Island. It features a challenging terrain of coral rock, sand traps, mangrove swamp, and pines. Greens fees are $95, including cart. The course is a 10- to 15-minute, $20 taxi ride from the dock one-way.

SCUBA DIVING The largest dive outfitter is **Captain's Corner,** 125 Ann St. (www.captainscorner.com; ℂ 305/296-8865 or 305/304-0437), located just a few blocks from the cruise docks. The five-star PADI operation has five instructors, a well-trained staff, and a 59-foot dive boat that was used by Timothy "James Bond" Dalton during the filming of *License to Kill.* To reach the departure point, walk to the end of Greene Street. Wreck dives are $95 per person including all equipment. Be warned, however, that the waters off Key West are not the same as tranquil warm Caribbean waters, and can instead have strong currents, murky visibility, and dangerous consequences. On a recent wreck dive by a contributing author, several divers lost gear to the strong current, one depleted his air struggling against the tide, and none was able to complete the dive.

Great Local Restaurants & Bars

RESTAURANTS All of the restaurants listed below are within an easy 5- to 15-minute walk from the docks, except for Camille's and El Siboney, which are more than a mile away. Several raw bars near the dock area offer seafood, including oysters and clams, although the king here is conch—served grilled, ground into burgers, made into chowder, fried in batter as fritters, or simply raw in a conch salad. Even if you don't have lunch, at least sample the local favorites: a slice of Key lime pie with a Cuban coffee. The pie's unique flavor comes from the juice and minced rind of the piquant Key lime. I suggest you go straight for the best: the **Blond Giraffe Key Lime Pie Factory** (www.blondgiraffe.com; ☎ **305/295-6776**). In addition to slices, entire pies, and just about every Key lime–flavored thing you could dream up, the factory also offers a treat that, to our knowledge, is entirely unique to Key West: whole slices of key lime pie that are frozen, dipped in chocolate, and served on a stick like a Popsicle. Do not, I repeat, do not pass this up. There are five Blond Giraffe stores in Key West.

Cruise ship passengers on a return visit to Key West often ask for the Rose Tattoo, a historic old restaurant named for the Tennessee Williams film partially shot on the island. The restaurant, one of Key West's finest, is now the **Bagatelle,** 115 Duval St., at Front Street (www.bagatellekeywest.com; ☎ **305/296-6609**). Look for daily specials or stick to the chef's better dishes, such as conch seviche (thinly sliced raw conch marinated in lime juice and herbs). Lunch is about $24.

Blue Heaven, 729 Thomas St. (www.blueheavenkw.com; ☎ **305/296-8666**), is an outdoor oasis dive that serves some of the best food in town, including fresh local fish, most often grouper or red snapper. Its hot and spicy jerk chicken is as fine as that served in Jamaica. Lunch is about $18. Breakfast is served until noon daily and is reported by some to be the best in the U.S.

For quick and easy diner food with a side of local flavor, don't miss **Harpoon Harry's,** 832 Caroline St. (www.harpoonharryskeywest.com; ☎ **305/294-8744**), offering your typical short stacks and omelets alongside Cuban staples such as grilled toast and strong Cuban coffee. The front of the diner looks out to the water, making it a convenient stop for a late breakfast off the boat. Meals range from $8 to $20.

If you're looking for a more civilized start to your day, head to **Banana Café,** 1211 Duval St. (www.banana-cafe-key-west.com; ☎ **305/294-7227**), a French creperie with spectacular daily specials and outdoor seating that's removed from the hustle and bustle of the port. Breakfast is served until 3pm, and breakfast and lunch are both $7 to $18.

Key West's original raw bar is the **Half Shell Raw Bar,** Land's End Marina, at the foot of Margaret Street (www.halfshellrawbar.com; ☎ **305/294-4902**), offering fresh fish, oysters, and shrimp direct from its own fish market. Lunch is about $18. To be honest, though, I prefer **Turtle Kraals Wildlife Bar & Grill,** Land's End Village, at the foot of Margaret Street (www.turtlekraals.com; ☎ **305/294-2640**). Try the tender Florida lobster, spicy conch chowder, or perfectly cooked fresh fish (often dolphin fish with pineapple salsa, or baked stuffed grouper with mango-crab-meat stuffing). Lunch is around $20.

Pepe's Cafe, 806 Caroline St., between William and Margaret streets (www.pepescafe.net; ☎ **305/294-7192**), is the oldest eating house in the Florida Keys, established in 1909. Diners sit under slow-moving paddle fans at tables or dark-pine booths with high backs. Choose from zesty homemade chili, perfectly baked oysters, fish sandwiches, and Pepe's deservedly famous steak sandwiches. Lunch is about $15.

Camille's, 1202 Simonton St., at Catherine Street (www.camilleskeywest.com; ☎ **305/296-4811**), is a hip, unpretentious cafe that serves the best breakfast in town and offers the best lunch value. Try a sandwich made from the catch of the day and served on fresh bread, then finish off with some of the great Key lime pie. Breakfast is about $8, and lunch is about $12.

El Siboney, 900 Catherine St. (www.elsiboneyrestaurant.com; © **305/296-4184**), though off the beaten path (ask a local for directions), is the place for time-tested Cuban favorites such as *ropa vieja* (shredded meat stew), roast pork with garlic and tart sour oranges, and paella Valenciana. Lunch is around $14.

For a sweet treat, stop for ice cream at **Flamingo Crossing,** 1105 Duval St., at Virginia Street (© **305/296-6124**).

BARS   Key West is a bar town, and because many ships stay in town late, you'll likely have an opportunity to do some carousing. Most places recommended below offer fast food to go with their drinks. The food isn't the best on the island, but it usually arrives shortly after you order it, which suits most rushed cruise ship passengers just fine. Try some of the favorite local beer, **Key West Ale.**

Heavily patronized by cruise ship passengers, **Captain Tony's Saloon,** 428 Greene St. (www.capttonyssaloon.com; © **305/294-1838**), is the oldest active bar in Florida and is tacky as can be. The 1851 building was the original Sloppy Joe's, a rough-and-tumble fisherman's saloon. Hemingway drank here from 1933 to 1937, and Jimmy Buffett got his start here before opening his own bar and going on to musical glory. The name refers to Capt. Tony Tarracino, a former Key West mayor and rugged man of the sea who owned the place until 1988.

The current **Sloppy Joe's,** 201 Duval St. (www.sloppyjoes.com; © **305/294-5717**), is the most touristy bar in Key West, visited by almost all cruise ship passengers, even those who don't normally go to bars. It aggressively plays up its association with Hemingway, although the bar stood on Greene Street back then (see above). Marine flags decorate the ceiling, and the ambience and decor evoke a Havana bar from the 1930s.

Jimmy Buffett's Margaritaville, 500 Duval St. (www.margaritaville.com; © **305/292-1435**), is the third-most-popular Key West bar with cruise ship passengers. Although Buffett is not actually from Key West, his cafe is decorated with pictures of him. And, yes, it sells T-shirts and Margaritaville memorabilia in a shop off the dining room. His margaritas are without competition, but then they'd have to be, wouldn't they?

One of the strangest phenomena you'll experience in Key West is the tourists' apparent desire to be insulted while drinking. You'll find singing comedians in any of a handful of bars on Duval Street, but the most popular is **Irish Kevin's,** 211 Duval St. (www.irishkevins.com; © **305/292-1262**). The dive is open all day and long into the night, with constant live entertainment by guys with guitars who will definitely have something to say about your Hawaiian shirt, the city you came from, and the woman you came in with.

Open-air, very laid-back, and sometimes very loud, the **Hog's Breath Saloon,** 400 Front St. (www.hogsbreath.com; © **305/296-4222**), near the cruise docks, has been a Key West tradition since 1976. Drinking is a sport here, especially among the fishermen who come in after a day chasing the big one, as well as the biker types who show up anytime. Live entertainment is offered from 1pm to 2am.

For a real local hangout within an easy walk of the cruise docks, head to **Schooner Wharf,** 202 William St., Key West Bight (www.schoonerwharf.com; © **305/292-3302**), the most robust and hardest-drinking bar in Key West. It draws a primarily young crowd, many of whom work in the tourist industry or on the local fishing boats.

You'll also find locals in more laid-back locales such as **the Green Parrot Bar,** 601 Whitehead St. (www.greenparrot.com; © **305/294-6133**). This is the site of a thriving live, local music scene—jazz, blues, swing, and country, mostly—but the bar also hosts a laid-back happy hour daily from 4 to 7pm, where you'll find employees from some of the more touristy bars hanging out before starting their shifts.

Meanwhile, the local sailors and fishermen head over to **Finnegan's Wake,** 320 Grinnell St. (www.keywestirish.com; ✆ **305/293-0222**), a truly authentic Irish pub with an extensive and creative food menu.

LA ROMANA, DOMINICAN REPUBLIC

Along Dominican Republic's Southeastern Coast lie vast sugarcane fields surrounding some of the Caribbean's most beautiful resorts and beaches of La Romana and Bayahibe. Founded in the early 19th century, La Romana was originally a sugar-producing region that was also developed as a commercial port for the transport of sugarcane and wood. Today, La Romana is an emerging destination hungry for tourists and eager to please. Its greatest attraction is to avid golfers, who can choose from world-class courses with such colorful names as Teeth of the Dog, and Dye Fore.

COMING ASHORE   Still in its cruise-terminal infancy, La Romana has two terminals where cruise ship passengers come ashore. One dock is on the **La Romana** side of the harbor; the other is at **Casa de Campo,** the resort side of the harbor. If you dock at La Romana, it's a 15-minute walk to the downtown area, or a pricey cab ride if you're lucky enough to snag a taxi. There is little to do in town so your best bet may be either to head over to the resort **Casa de Campo** or to find a taxi and head out to see some of the island's attractions.

LANGUAGE   Spanish is the official language; however, many employees in hotel and tourist destinations speak relatively good English, as well as French, German, and Italian.

CURRENCY   The Dominican peso (RD$) is the official currency. Visitors can pay in U.S. dollars most places, but should always find out if a price is being quoted in Dominican pesos or U.S. dollars. Prices in this section are given in U.S. dollars.

INFORMATION   For additional information on transportation, where to go, attractions, brochures, images, and more, visit www.GoDominicanRepublic.com.

CALLING FROM THE U.S.   When calling Dominican Republic from the United States, you need only dial a "1" before the numbers listed. To call Europe and South America from Dominican Republic, visitors need to dial "011" along with the area code and phone number.

Getting Around

There is little to see at the cruise pier. The closest amenity is the über-upscale **Casa de Campo** resort, where you can spend the day watching polo or indulging in spa treatments. The cruise lines usually offer a free shuttle to and from the resort if you dock at the more distant cruise terminal. If you miss the shuttle, you can take a taxi the 6km (4 miles) to the resort for about $15 to $20.

The Dominican Republic is the second-largest country in the Caribbean, and attractions can be a long distance away from one another, so be sure to budget time carefully for more distantly located excursions. If you venture off on your own, be sure to negotiate price, distance, and travel time before you agree on any terms, and make sure you have effectively communicated when you need to be back at the cruise terminal.

La Romana, Bayahibe & Altos de Chavón

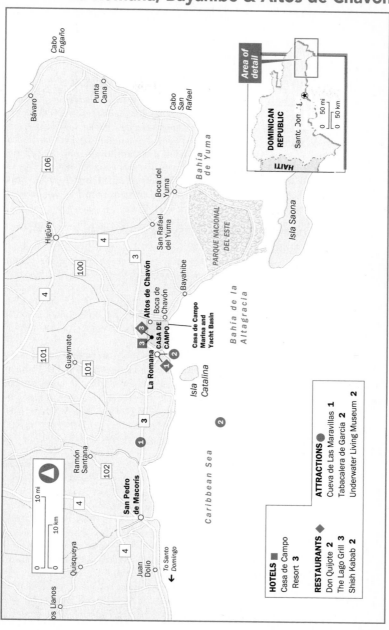

Area of detail

HAITI

DOMINICAN REPUBLIC

Santo Domingo

0   50 mi
0   50 km

Cabo Engaño

Bávaro

Punta Cana

Cabo San Rafael

Bahía de Yuma

106

Boca del Yuma

Higüey

4

San Rafael del Yuma

Isla Saona

3

100

Altos de Chavón

4

Boca de Chavón

Bayahibe

PARQUE NACIONAL DEL ESTE

101

Guaymate

CASA DE CAMPO

Casa de Campo Marina and Yacht Basin

101

La Romana

Bahía de la Altagracia

101

3

3

3

1

2

Isla Catalina

Isla

2

Ramón Santana

102

San Pedro de Macorís

1

Caribbean Sea

4

Quisqueya

Juan Dolio

4

To Santo Domingo

Los Llanos

0   10 mi
0   10 km

HOTELS ■
Casa de Campo
Resort **3**

RESTAURANTS ◆
Don Quijote **2**
The Lago Grill **3**
Shish Kabab **2**

ATTRACTIONS ●
Cueva de Las Maravillas **1**
Tabacalera de Garcia **2**
Underwater Living Museum **2**

Best Cruise Line Shore Excursions

Taino Indian Cave and La Romana–Cueva de Las Maravillas ($80, 3 hr.): The "Cave of Wonders" is located between San Pedro de Macoris and La Romana. The cave system is easily accessible and has a variety of interesting rock formations in addition to hundreds of pictographs, petroglyphs, and other rock art left here by the Taino Indians, who once inhabited this area.

On Your Own: Within Walking Distance

The two nearby towns are **Marina** and **Altos de Chavón.** Both are new but were designed to look like old Mediterranean or Spanish villas complete with bumpy cobblestones and breathtaking views of the water. Altos de Chavón was actually conceived in part by Roberto Copa, a former Paramount Studios set designer. Today, Altos de Chavón is an artists' hub, with studios, craft workshops, and art galleries. The Center's School of Design is associated with Parsons in New York City. In the center of the village are a **Greek-style amphitheater** and the **Church of St. Stanislaus.** The surrounding shops and restaurants are similarly contrived and upscale, both charming and charmless in a very Disney sort of way.

On Your Own: Beyond the Port Area

Cueva de Las Maravillas, the "Cave of Wonders," is located between San Pedro de Macoris and La Romana. The fascinating cave system contains hundreds of well-preserved pictographs, petroglyphs, and engravings from the Taino Indians who once inhabited it thousands of years before. The dwelling is easily accessible, with an excellent lighting system, ramps, a footpath, and an elevator. It is home to some archaeologically important rock art as well as natural rock formations such as stalactites, stalagmites, and columns. The Cave of Wonders is open Tuesday through Sunday from 10am to 5pm.

Cigar aficionados can take the opportunity to visit **Tabacalera de Garcia** (www. TabacaleradeGarcia.com), the largest handmade cigar factory in the world, and makers of such fine Dominican cigars as Montecristo, Romeo & Juliet, U. Upmann, Don Diego, Santa Damiana, VegaFina, and Onyx, among others. Here you will see the handwork of the cigar industry's most experienced craftsmen (and -women). Their Cigar Shop carries the best selection and prices of premium Dominican cigars. Tours are offered by appointment Monday through Friday from 8am to 5pm, and Saturday from 8am to noon.

Fascinating underwater archaeological exhibits are located at the **Underwater Living Museum,** off the coast of the Bayahibe hotel zone. Shipwrecked galleons dating back to the early 18th century have been re-created here to portray how they looked when originally discovered by marine biologists. Both snorkelers and scuba divers frequent the museums. Among its many offerings is the **Cara Merchant Pirate Ship,** the ship Captain William Kidd commandeered and then abandoned in 1699 as he raced to New York in an attempt to clear his name of piracy charges. Discovered off Catalina Island in 2008, this bona fide sunken ship has been turned into a "living museum" as well as a research site.

Parque Nacional del Este (National Park of the East) is home to more than 500 flora species, 300 types of birds, and long stretches of beaches and underwater wonders. It's one of the most visited and protected areas in the country. While here, visitors can hike, discover ancient Taino ruins, or do a little bird-watching.

Shopping

Cruise passengers will most likely stop at **Casa de Campo/Altos de Chavón,** which houses more than 45 retail stores with resort apparel, native jewelry, original art and ceramics, and of course plenty of fine cigars.

El Artístico, approximately 3km (2 miles) west of La Romana, is known for selling Dominican art, jewelry, and Dominican icons made from pounded metal and bright colors. The nearby resort **Casa de Campo** also houses more than 45 retail stores with resort apparel, native jewelry, original art and ceramics, fine cigars, and more. Guests can visit shops throughout Marina and Altos de Chavón, and throughout the towns of La Romana and Bayahibe.

Beaches

Recognized for their exceptionally fine sand and pristine waters, La Romana and Bayahibe comprise some of the most beautiful beaches in the Caribbean. The beaches within the Bayahibe hotel zone are internationally recognized as certified Blue Flag beaches, which guarantee high-quality clean coastal waters and beaches along with proper environmental management and safety measures. These beaches include **Isla Saona, Playa Minitas, Playa Dominicus, Bayahibe, Palmilla, Catalinita,** and **Isla Catalina.**

Sports

GOLF Casa de Campo Resort (www.casadecampo.com.do) seems to have the corner on the market for golf enthusiasts. Among their world-class offerings are **Dye Fore, Teeth of the Dog,** and **The Links.**

Another worthwhile option is **La Estancia Golf Course** at La Estancia Golf Resort (www.laestancia.do).

Great Local Restaurants & Bars

In the center of the town, directly in front of the Parque Principale, you will find **Don Quijote,** Diego Avila Street No. 42 (② **809/556-2827**). The fare is international seafood, familiar and reliable. You can't beat the seafood paella, and the lobster Creole-style is inventive. Finish with a strong Dominican coffee. Daily 11am to 11pm. Lunch is about $22.

The **Lago Grill,** at the Casa de Campo Resort, Dolores Tajeda, Minitas Beach (www.casadecampo.com.do/restaurant-lagogrill; ② **809/523-3333**), serves Caribbean American with a twist of lemon, lime, coconut, or nearly any other fruit you can name. At the fresh-juice bar, choose from 25 tropical varieties. Dine in a replica of a palm-frond-covered Taíno hut that catches the breezes from the nearby golf course. The lunch buffet includes sandwiches, burgers, and *sancocho,* the famous Dominican stew. Buffet price is $28. Daily 7 to 11am and noon to 3pm.

For a change of pace from Dominican in an informal setting, try **Shish Kabab,** Calle Francisco del Castillo Marquez 32 (② **809/556-2737**). While this Middle Eastern eatery specializes in (what else?) kabobs, there are other Middle Eastern specialties such as baba ghanouj, as well as not–so–Middle Eastern options such as shish kebab pizza and skewered grouper. The cost of lunch is about $15. Open 10am to midnight, closed Mondays.

LES SAINTES

You want charming? The islets of Les Saintes (pronounced "Lay *Sant*") are irresistibly so: pastel-colored gingerbread houses with tropical gardens, hills that slope down to miniature beaches, and picturesque bays with pelicans, sailboats, and turquoise water. Only two of the islands in this French archipelago off the southern coast of Guadeloupe are inhabited: **Terre-de-Bas** and its more populous neighbor, **Terre-de-Haut** (more populous, in this case, meaning it has about 1,700 inhabitants). Terre-de-Haut (pronounced "T'air *d'Oh*"), with only one village—the straightforwardly named Le Bourg ("The Town")—is the destination of most visitors. Some say it's what Saint-Tropez was like before Brigitte Bardot. For a U.S. point of reference, think Fire Island, Provincetown, Martha's Vineyard, or Sausalito with a French-Caribbean twist. "Nautical" and "quaint" are the watchwords.

But Les Saintes, also known as Iles des Saintes, isn't a fantasy park built to look enchanting. Although tourism is important to the island's economy, most people here still make their living from the sea. The population of Terre-de-Haut is mainly Caucasian, all fisher folk or sailors and their families who are descended from Breton corsairs (pirates). Just don't mention that to the locals, lest they become insulted at such an accusation! Les Saintois, as the locals are called, are widely regarded as the best fishermen in the Antilles. These very skilled sailors maneuver large boats called *saintoies*. Despite their charming appearance, they are a serious lot, and it's this underlying saltiness that keeps the place from being cloyingly sweet.

COMING ASHORE   Cruise ships dock at **Le Bourg,** in Terre-de-Haut. The village has two main streets, both parallel to the bay and lined with cafes, restaurants, and souvenir shops. Telephones at the dock require a *telecarte,* a prepaid phone card sold at the post office (a 10-min. walk from the dock; take a right) and other outlets marked TELECARTE EN VENTE ICI. Some phones now accept U.S. calling cards or major credit cards for long-distance calls.

LANGUAGE   The official language is French, but many islanders speak Creole with one another. Few locals feel comfortable with English, though, so take the opportunity to practice your high-school French. Most everyone is helpful and friendly, especially if you smile and make an effort. That said, the reserved and formal mannerisms of this French island's residents can come off as detached or impersonal.

CURRENCY   Les Saintes is part of the larger archipelago of Guadeloupe, an overseas region of France, so the **euro** (€) is now the official currency (.75€ = US$1; 1€ = US$1.32). Each euro is divisible by 100¢. You can withdraw euros from the ATM next to the tourism office (see "Information," below). Prices in this section are given in U.S. dollars.

INFORMATION   If you take a right on the main road after you leave the ship, you'll see signs for the **tourism office** (OFFICE DU TOURISME) at rue Jean Calot just to the left of the port (© **590/99-58-60**). The office is manned Monday through Friday from 8am to 1pm, then 2 to 5pm. Be aware that you may be placed on hold for quite a while with no apology, as the staff is small. While their English is good, the accent over the phone can lead to some confusion when asking questions. If you can, it's better to head down for a face-to-face meeting. It's less than a 5-minute walk. Most printed information available here is in French, but the maps are helpful even if you don't understand the lingo. For info before you go, call the **French Government**

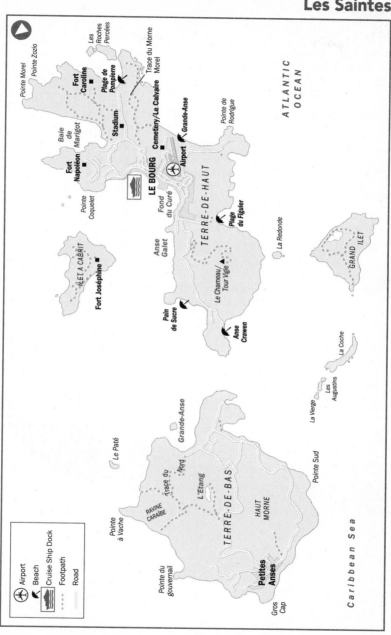

Les Saintes

Tourist Office in Canada (℡ **514/288-6989**), which is manned by a friendly but not very informative operator. Your best bet is to log on to either **www.lesilesde guadeloupe.com** or **www.omtlessaintes.fr**.

CALLING FROM THE U.S. When calling Les Saintes from the U.S., dial the international access code (011) and 590 before the numbers listed here. Yes, the numbers listed here already begin with 590, but an effort by the French telephone authorities to standardize procedures requires that you dial those three digits twice. Really.

Getting Around

If you're reasonably fit, there's no reason you can't walk wherever you want to go. If you're the type who runs 8km (5 miles) a day, you can hike up Le Chameau, traipse around Fort Napoléon, head over to Plage de Pompierre, and complete the Trace des Crêtes, with time for a meal or swim before returning to the ship.

BY TAXI The island has a handful of minivans that serve as taxis. Each seats six to eight passengers, and most drivers offer 3-hour tours of the island for about $15 per person (be aware, though, that English is not widely spoken). You'll find the cabs parked directly in front of the cruise ship dock. There is also a local bus station behind the church.

BY SCOOTER Terre-de-Haut is less than 6.5km (4 miles long) and 3km (2 miles) wide. Aside from tourist vans and the occasional private car, four-wheeled vehicles are rare (at last count, there were fewer than three dozen). Scooters rule the roads. Scores of them await you just off the dock along Le Bourg's main road. Expect to pay about $40 for a two-seater for the day. A $400 deposit (credit cards accepted) is required.

BY BICYCLE You can rent bicycles for between $15 and $20 along Le Bourg's main road. The island is hilly, though. You'd do better to rent a scooter or walk.

Best Cruise Line Shore Excursions

Don't expect any. This is a wander-around-at-your-own-pace kind of place. See "Sports," below, for scuba, snorkeling, and fishing excursions you can arrange through local agencies.

On Your Own: Within Walking Distance

Everything is within walking distance of the dock. On the way to the tourism office and the ATM, you'll pass Le Bourg's **stone church.** It's humble, but worth the couple of minutes it takes to peek inside.

Fort Napoléon looms over Le Bourg's picturesque bay. The French started building this stone bastion after they regained Les Saintes from the British in 1815, but didn't complete it until 1867. Today, it houses engaging, detailed exhibits that cover the entire history of the islands, including life before Columbus, European expansion into the New World, early French settlements, the Battle of Les Saintes, and the development of the fishing industry. You can wander through barracks, dungeons, and the grounds, which feature an impressive array of cactuses and succulents. Pick up the English-language brochure that describes the vegetation when you purchase your ticket; admission is about $5 for adults and $2 for children 11 and under. You can also rent a cassette that provides excellent English commentary as you walk through the museum. The fort is open a brief 3½ hours a day, daily from 9am to 12:30pm, so make it your first destination.

If you're up for some hiking, the **Trace du Morne Morel trail** traces the spine of one of Terre-de-Haut's hills just north of the airport and offers remarkable views of beaches, cliffs, and neighboring islands. Although clearly marked, the path is rocky and challenging—you have an advantage if you're part goat. Wear sunscreen and bring water.

Be sure to stop for a few minutes at the **cemetery** next to the airport. You'll notice several graves adorned with conch shells, which signify a sea-related death. On Saturday nights, refrigerator-size speakers are brought in, makeshift food stands are set up, and the cemetery becomes a huge open-air disco. In the same vicinity is **Le Calvaire,** a giant Christ statue at the summit of a hill; numerous steps ascend to great panoramas.

Chameau means "camel" in French, and with a bit of imagination, you can see that **Le Chameau,** the highest point on Terre-de-Haut, looks sort of like the hump of a dromedary. The concrete road to the 300m (1,000-ft.) summit is off-limits to all motorized vehicles; mercifully, it's shaded much of the way. After 30 to 60 minutes of arduous climbing, you're rewarded with spectacular views of the entire archipelago, Guadeloupe, and Dominica. **Tour Vigie,** a military lookout dating from the time of Napoléon, crowns the mountain; unfortunately, it's usually locked.

Shopping

Little boutiques that sell beachwear, T-shirts, jewelry, and knickknacks line the streets. Be sure to stop by Pascal Foy's **Kaz an Nou Gallery,** behind the church. You can watch him make *Cases Creoles,* miniature carved wooden Creole houses in candy colors. They're becoming collectors' items. **Galerie Martine Cotten,** at the foot of the dock, features the work of an artist originally from Brittany who celebrates the natural beauty and fishing traditions of Les Saintes. Beyond the town hall, **Ultramarine** is a tiny cottage where you can buy unusual dolls, clothes, T-shirts, and handcrafted items from France, Haiti, and Africa. **Galerie Marchande Seaside,** a group of shops situated around a patio, is just up the street after you turn right from the pier. Art, gifts, antiques, jewelry, lace, beachwear, and ice cream are all available.

Beaches

Beaches with golden sand are tucked away in almost all of the island's coves. Calm, crescent-shaped **Plage de Pompierre** (sometimes spelled Pont Pierre) is shaded by sea-grape bushes, as well as almond and palm trees. A 15-minute walk from the dock, it boasts soft white sand, shade from coconut palms, and quiet seclusion. The gentle water in the cliff-encircled cove is a stunning aquamarine. Because the bay is a nature preserve, fishing and anchoring are prohibited. It's the island's most popular sunbathing spot, so your best bet is to go early or late.

Grande Anse, near the airfield, is large, but there's no shade, and the rough surf has a strong undertow. Although swimming is prohibited, the cliffs at either end of the beach and the powerful breakers make for a dramatic seascape. The usually deserted **Figuier,** on the southern coast, has excellent snorkeling. **Pain du Sucre Bay** is undoubtedly the most beautiful beach on the island.

Sports

FISHING   Going out to sea with a local fisherman is one way to experience the nautical heritage of Les Saintes. Most of the local sailors will be delighted to take you out, if you can communicate well enough to negotiate a price. Most fishermen are stationed next to the cruise ship dock; just follow the waterfront to the fishing boats.

Don't leave anything unattended while swimming at Plage de Pompierre. Savvy goats hide out in the scrub behind the beach, patiently scoping out the action. Once you go into the water, they'll make a beeline for your unattended picnic basket and treat themselves to anything edible.

SCUBA, SNORKELING & OTHER WATERSPORTS Some visitors travel to the Iles des Saintes for the day just to go scuba diving; the underwater world has attracted deep-sea divers as renowned as Jacques Cousteau. For scuba diving and snorkeling, go to **La Dive Bouteille Centre Nautique des Saintes** (www.divebouteille.com; ✆ **590/99-54-25**), at the Plage de la Colline, west of town past the market. One-tank dives run about $68. You can also rent sea kayaks and windsurfing equipment here. Another option is **Pisquettes** (www.pisquettes.com; ✆ **590/99-88-80**). Both charge competitive rates and have staffs well versed in the esoterica of the region's many dive sites.

Great Local Restaurants & Bars

Virtually every restaurant in Terre-de-Haut offers seafood that couldn't be fresher, and many feature Creole dishes. A local favorite is *thazard fumé* (smoked kingfish).

Many restaurants are closed for lunch. **Le Triangle** (✆ **590/99-50-50**), on Rue de Noit, has outdoor and indoor seating with views of the sea. Lunch is about $26. **Le Fringale** (✆ **590/98-14-65**), on Jean Calot, the pedestrian street overlooking the water, serves French and Creole dishes as well as pasta and fresh seafood. Lunch is about $29. For pasta, pizza, or salad, try the seaside terrace at **La Saladerie** (✆ **590/99-53-43**), on the way to Fort Napoléon. Lunch is about $30. Another option is **Café de la Marine,** on the bay and main street (✆ **590/99-53-78**), which serves thin-crust pizzas and seafood. Lunch here is $26.

The island's oldest *boulangerie* (bakery) is **Le Petit Saintois,** on the beachfront. If you stop in at the right time, you can get a crusty baguette hot from the oven. Or if you'd rather have something cold, try one of the Italian gelati at **Tropico Gelato** (✆ **590/99-88-12**). Turn right off the dock; it's a couple of storefronts down on your right.

MARTINIQUE

Fairy-tale romance and horrific disaster: Who could resist such an enticing combination? As if being the birthplace and childhood home of Empress Joséphine, sweetheart and wife of Napoléon, weren't enough, Martinique mesmerizes with the epic tragedy that befell St-Pierre one fair day in 1902: bustling cosmopolitan capital one minute, devastated volcanic graveyard of 30,000 souls the next. Love and death make quite a one-two punch, but they're just the hook. Look a bit deeper to appreciate Martinique's subtler attractions—quaint seaside villages, colonial ruins, and captivatingly beautiful rainforests and beaches.

Madiana, or "Island of Flowers," was the Carib name for the island, and hibiscus, bougainvillea, and bird of paradise grow in lush profusion alongside mango, pineapple, banana, and papaya. Like Guadeloupe and St. Barts, Martinique is as French as Bordeaux, and you'll find everything from baguettes to Balenciaga here. But with African and New World roots forever entwined, Creole cuisine and traditions continue to flourish. About 80km (50 miles) long and 35km (22 miles) wide, the island features a diverse topography. Rainforests drape the volcanic mountains of the north;

Martinique map

Martinique Passage

Macouba
Basse-Pointe
Grand Rivière

Leyritz — N1 — Le Lorrain

ATLANTIC OCEAN

Ajoupa-Bouillon
Le Marigot
Mt. Pelée
Le Prêcheur
N1
Morne Rouge
Ste-Marie
Tartane
St-Pierre
Caravelle Peninsula
Morne des Esses
Anse Turin ■ **Musée Paul Gauguin**
Trinité
Le Carbet
Jardin de Balata ■ N3
Gros-Morne
N2
Balata
N4
Bellefontaine
Carbet Peak St-Joseph
Robert
Case-Pilote
N1
Schoelcher
Le François
Fort-de-France
N1 Lamentin
Lamentin International Airport
Pointe du Bout
Mt. Vauclin N6
Anse Mitan
N5
Vauclin
Anse-à-l'Ane
Trois Ilets
Caribbean Sea
D7
Grande Anse
Musée de La Pagerie
Anses-d'Arlets
Le Diamant D7
Rivière-Pilote
D37
Ste-Luce
Le Marin
Diamant Beach
D18A
Cap Chevalier
Le Rocher du Diamant
Ste-Anne
Grand Anse des Salines
Pointe des Salines
St. Lucia Channel

Legend:
- Airport
- Beach
- Cruise Ship Dock
- Mountain

5

THE PORTS OF CALL | Martinique

small, rounded hills and enclosed valleys mark the central plain; and white-sand beaches ring the arid, flat south.

During the 18th and 19th centuries, France and England vied for the island. In 1946, Martinique became an overseas department of France, and, in 1974, it achieved regional status—the French minister of the interior appoints a prefect, but the island's citizens elect representatives to the national legislature in Paris and the regional legislature in Fort-de-France.

Most of Martinique's 380,000 residents are descendants of African slaves, but others of European, Asian, and Middle Eastern ancestry add to the melting pot. Attesting to the generally amicable relations among the various peoples, every shade of skin color is represented.

COMING ASHORE   Most cruise ships dock in the heart of Fort-de-France, at the **Pointe Simon Cruise Dock,** which has quays for two large vessels. Because Martinique is a popular port of call, ships also dock at the **Passenger Terminal** at the main harbor, a cargo port on the north side of the bay, a $12 cab ride from the center of town.

LANGUAGE   French is Martinique's official language, but you can get by with English at most restaurants and tourist attractions. You'll also hear Creole on the street. Because many of the island's service employees work hard to improve their English, cruisers who speak no French find Martinique easier to navigate than Guadeloupe, the other big French Caribbean island. Ask for English-language brochures and commentaries when sightseeing; most sites have them.

CURRENCY   Martinique is an overseas region of France, so the **euro** (€) is now the official currency (.75€ = US$1; 1€ = US$1.32). Each euro is divisible by 100¢. Prices in this section are given in U.S. dollars.

There are numerous *distributeur de billets* (ATMs) in downtown Fort-de-France, and you'll have no trouble using your credit cards and traveler's checks as well. You can change money on the waterfront at **Change Caraïbe,** 4 rue Ernest Deproge (© **596/60-28-40**), or a block inland at **Change Point Change,** 14 rue Victor Hugo (© **596/63-80-33**).

INFORMATION   The **tourism office** (© **596/60-27-73**) opens its doors at the pier in Fort-de-France when ships come in. For info before you go, visit www.martinique.org.

CALLING FROM THE U.S.   When calling Martinique from the U.S., dial the international access code (011) and 596 before the numbers listed here. The numbers listed here already begin with 596, but an effort by the French telephone authorities to standardize procedures requires that you dial those three digits twice.

Getting Around

BY TAXI   Travel by taxi is convenient but expensive. Most cabs are metered, but they do offer flat rates for touring the island. Taxis wait for ships at the cruise pier, and several English-speaking drivers give tours of the island for roughly $65 an hour for up to four passengers. Local laws demand that any bona fide Martiniquais cab must contain a working meter. For specific itineraries—wherein a passenger tells the driver where he or she wants to go—the meter must be on and functioning. **Radio Taxi** (© **596/63-63-62**), the island's largest dispatcher, advises us that if a taxi driver quotes a flat rate to a passenger instead of turning on the meter, you're being robbed, and you should immediately get out and find another cab. For an idea of prices, approximate rates between Fort-de-France and any hotel of La Pointe du Bout are $85, but only $65 from Lamentin Airport to any hotel of La Pointe du Bout. Between 7pm and 6am, a 40% surcharge is assessed. The rule about using a taxi's meter does not apply to passengers who want to hire a taxi for a general tour of the island. Touring the island by taxi can be so expensive, and so easily corrupted by the whims of the individual driver, that it is often a better deal to rent your own car for the day, despite the island's many rutted (but often panoramic) roads.

BY BUS   For trips beyond Fort-de-France, collective taxi-minibuses are a cheap but iffy alternative. These privately owned minivans (look for the TC sign) generally seat eight and have flexible routes and unpredictable schedules. Often crowded and sometimes less than comfortable, they're widely used by adventurous tourists nonetheless, particularly those who speak some French. A one-way ride to Grande Anse des Salines beach is about $65. Vans leave from a parking lot at Pointe Simon, in the heart of Fort-de-France.

BY FERRY To reach La Pagerie (Empress Joséphine's birthplace), the island's golf course, horseback-riding stables, and the resort area of Pointe du Bout, take one of the orange ferries operated by **Pyétrolettes du Soleil** or the white or blue ferries run by **Madinina Vedettes** from Quai d'Esnambuc, east of the cruise dock, in Fort-de-France. The ferry trip takes 15 minutes. Once you reach the other side of the bay, you will need to take a 3km (2-mile) taxi ride to Pointe du Bout. Round-trip ferry tickets are about $8 per person; boats leave at least once an hour.

BY RENTAL CAR Martinique's size and myriad attractions make renting a car especially worthwhile. You'll drive on the right on roads that are often steep and bumpy, but almost always scenic. Renters need a valid driver's license and must be at least 21. **Budget** has an office at 30 rue Ernest-Desproges, La Baie, Cruise Terminal, Fort-de-France, in addition to one at Lamentinthe airport (www.budget.com; ✆ 800/472-3325 in the U.S. and Canada, or 596/42-16-79). **Avis** is located at Lamentin Airport (www.avis.com; ✆ 800/331-1084 in the U.S. and Canada), as is **Hertz** (www.hertz.com; ✆ 800/654-3001 in the U.S. and Canada, or 596/51-01-01).

Regardless of which company you choose, you'll be hit with a value-added tax (VAT) of 8.5% on top of the final bill, plus either a charge of around $40 if you ask the car to be delivered to you, or an airport pickup charge of about $30 if you retrieve your car at the airport. Collision damage waivers (CDWs), which eliminate some or all of your financial responsibility in the event of an accident, cost between $18 and $37 per day at Budget and Hertz, and usually a bit more at Avis. Of these three car-rental companies, the rates at Budget tend to be the least expensive, although that depends on a wide array of seasonal variations.

Best Cruise Line Shore Excursions

Rainforest & Plantations 4WD Safari ($99, 4½ hr.): Take your off-road vehicle through tropical forests and sugarcane plantations (stopping to sample the crop) to a banana plantation and a distillery, where you'll do short tours.

Martinique Snorkeling ($69, 3 hr.): Across the bay from Fort-de-France, the reef at Anse Dufour offers excellent snorkeling for experts and novices. It's filled with marine animals, including French grunts, blackbar soldierfish, and silversides. Snorkeling equipment is provided, as are professional instruction, supervision, and transportation.

Excursions Offered by Local Agencies

See "Sports," later in this section, for more options.

Adventure Excursions & Hiking: Martinique's lush, mountainous northern half provides myriad adventure opportunities. **Cama Shipping** (✆ 596/71-31-00), based in Fort-de-France, offers many tours, including a 4-hour jeep adventure that takes you through the heart of Martinique, into the green forest, around the volcano Mt. Pelée, through banana plantations, and to a rum distillery. It costs around $85 per person.

Horseback Treks: Pros and novices are both accommodated on morning horseback rides offered by **Ranch Jack,** in Morne Habitué (www.ranchjack.com; ✆ 596/68-37-69). The daily promenades pass over hills, through fields, and onto beaches, and guides provide a running commentary on the history and botany of the island. Transportation to and from the cruise dock can be arranged. The price of a half-day excursion with refreshments is about $80.

On Your Own: Within Walking Distance

Fort-de-France is a bustling, cosmopolitan town with 100,000 residents and an unmistakable French air. Part New Orleans, part French Riviera, it's full of ocher buildings, ornate wrought-iron balconies, cascading flowers, and tall palm trees. The town's narrow streets, cluttered with boutiques and cafes, climb from the bowl of the sea to the surrounding hills, forming a great urban amphitheater. There's plenty here to keep you busy.

At the eastern end of downtown, **La Savane** is a broad formal park with palms, mangoes, and manicured lawns, perfect for a promenade or a rest in the shade. Its most famous feature is the **Statue of Empress Joséphine,** carved in 1858 by Vital Dubray. Like a variation on the Venus de Milo, this white-marble empress is headless: Napoléon's Little Creole was unceremoniously decapitated and doused with red paint in 1995 by locals who remembered her role in reinstating slavery on the island in the early 1800s. Near the harbor, at the edge of the park, you'll find vendors' stalls with handmade crafts, including baskets, beads, bangles, woodcarvings, and straw hats.

Across the street, the **Bibliothèque Schoelcher (Schoelcher Library),** 21 rue de la Liberté (no phone), is one of Fort-de-France's great Belle Epoque buildings. Named in honor of Victor Schoelcher, one of France's most influential abolitionists, this elaborate structure, designed by French architect Henri Pick, was first displayed at the 1889 Paris Exposition. Four years later, the red-and-blue Romanesque portal, Egyptian lotus-petal columns, iron-and-glass cupola, and multicolored tiles were dismantled and then reassembled piece by piece at the present site. The interior light, mosaics, and tile floor are glorious. The proud repository of Schoelcher's 10,000-volume book collection, as well as an impressive archive of colonization, slavery, and emancipation documents, is open Monday 1 to 5:30pm, Tuesday through Friday 8:30am to 5:30pm, and Saturday 8:30am to noon. It charges no admission.

Another Henri Pick masterpiece, **Cathédrale St-Louis,** on rue Victor Schoelcher at rue Blénac, was built in 1895. The religious centerpiece of the island, it's an extraordinary iron building where a number of the island's former governors are buried beneath the choir loft. A contemporary of Gustave Eiffel (of Eiffel Tower fame), Pick used massive iron beams to support the walls, ceiling, and spire. A grand example of Industrial Revolution architecture, it's been likened to a Catholic railway station. The organ, stained-glass windows, and ornamented interior walls are well worth a look and can be viewed every morning except Saturday.

Built in 1640, **Fort St-Louis,** Boulevard Alfassa, dominates the rocky promontory east of La Savane. A noteworthy example of 17th- and 18th-century military architecture, it first defended Fort-de-France in 1674 against Dutch invaders; beginning in 1762, it was the site of numerous battles between French and English forces. Today, the bastion remains the French navy's headquarters in the Caribbean. It isn't open to the public for tours but does have an area with beautiful views of the ocean.

Fort St-Louis, built in the Vauban style on a rocky promontory, guards the port. **Fort Tartenson** and **Fort Desaix** also stand on hills overlooking the port.

The best of Fort-de-France's many museums, the **Musée Départemental Archéologie Precolombienne Préhistoire,** 9 rue de la Liberté (© **596/71-57-05**), traces 2,000 years of Martinique's pre-Columbian past with more than a thousand relics from the Arawak and Carib cultures. Spread over three floors, the detailed exhibits document various pottery and tool styles, burial practices, agricultural methods, social and religious customs, and changes that occurred after the arrival of Europeans. The museum has exhibits from the years from 3000 B.C. to A.D. 1635, but stops shortly after the arrival of the first French colonials on Martinique in the early 1600s. In other words, it's mostly an ethnological museum. Across the street from La Savane, it's open Monday from 1 to 5pm, Tuesday through Friday from 8am to 5pm, and Saturday from 9am to noon. Admission is about $5 for adults, $4 for students, and $2 for children 11 and under. The tiny gift stand sells pottery reproductions.

The **Musée Régional d'Histoire et d'Ethnographie,** 10 bd. du Général de Gaulle (© **596/72-81-87**), is housed in one of Fort-de-France's best-preserved examples of colonial architecture and is devoted to an illumination of the island's agrarian past (and the slave culture that made it possible). Expositions showcase the late-19th-century volcanic eruption that leveled St-Pierre, slavery and its effects on the island's society, and explorations of the sugarcane industry. The museum's permanent exhibition re-creates the interior of a bourgeois villa at the turn of the 20th century; various temporary photography exhibits depict life in Martinique over the past 150 years. Admission is $5.

On Your Own: Beyond the Port Area

Martinique is much too large to tackle in a single day. You'll have to make some tough choices about which of its many museums, plantations, floral parks, and natural wonders to visit. Below are two suggested itineraries for the day.

NORTH OF FORT-DE-FRANCE   Less than 8km (5 miles) north of Fort-de-France, on the scenic Route de la Trace (N3), **L'Eglise Sacré Coeur de Balata** overlooks the capital and its bay. This quiet village church is anything but typical: Built in 1924, it's a one-fifth-scale replica of the wedding-cake-pretty Sacré Coeur Basilica that crowns Montmartre in Paris. Rather than the white stone of the Paris original, this unintentionally whimsical copy uses gray freestone.

Martinique's Carib name, Madiana, means "island of flowers." To see what the Caribs were talking about, stroll through the **Jardin de Balata** (www.jardindebalata. fr; © **596/64-48-73**). Just minutes north of the Sacré Coeur church, this lush, Edenic garden showcases 200 species of plants, trees, and tropical flowers, including towering ferns, lotuses, alpinias, porcelain roses, anthuriums, and heliconias. This tropical botanical park was created by Jean-Philippe Thoze on land around a Creole house that belonged to his grandmother. He has also restored the house, furnishing it with antiques and historic engravings. The garden is open daily from 9am to 5pm. Admission is about $11 for adults, $5.50 for kids 11 and under.

Yes, it's hot outside, but things could be worse. One of Martinique's must-see attractions, the village of **St-Pierre,** on the northwest coast, was the cultural and economic capital of Martinique until 8am on May 8, 1902, when Mt. Pelée, the hulking volcano that dominates the northern tip of the island, exploded in fire and lava. All but 1 of St-Pierre's 30,000 inhabitants was incinerated, buried in ash and lava, or asphyxiated by poisonous gas. The town once hailed as the "Paris of the Antilles" suddenly became the "Pompeii of the Caribbean." It never regained its splendor, and today, it's no more than a sleepy fishing village, home to fewer than 5,000 souls. In lieu of walking from one ruin to another, you can hop on the rubber-wheeled trolley known as the Cyparis Express, which departs from the Musée Volcanologique (see below). The 1-hour tours operate Monday through Friday; half-hour tours run on the weekends. The fee is about $10 for adults and $5 for kids.

The town's touristic potential hasn't been grotesquely exploited: Aside from the ruins, the only other point of interest is the **Musée Volcanologique,** rue Victor Hugo (© **596/78-15-16**). Founded by American volcanologist Franck A. Perret, this one-room exhibit traces the story of the cataclysm through pictures and relics excavated from the debris, including petrified spaghetti, lava-encrusted teapots, twisted musical instruments, a human skull, and distorted clocks that stopped at the hour of destruction. The museum is open daily from 9am to 5pm; admission is $4 for adults and free for children 7 and under.

A few miles south of St-Pierre, **Le Carbet** is where Columbus landed in 1502. The first French settlers arrived in 1635, and the French painter Paul Gauguin lived here for 5 months in 1887. Too ill to return to France after a failed quest for "noble savages" in Panama, the artist wrote that "only in Martinique was I able to feel truly myself." An unassuming museum devoted to Gauguin and his Martinican works, the **Musée Paul Gauguin,** Anse Turin (© **596/78-22-66**), sits relatively close to the hut the painter once occupied. It boasts no original paintings, but it does have reproductions of the dozen pictures he composed on the island—precursors of his later, more famous Tahitian works. Also on display are biographical texts and self-pitying letters he wrote to his wife back in France. Other exhibits include Creole costumes and contemporary island art. The museum has extensive English commentary and is open daily from 9am to 5pm. Admission is about $8 for adults, $2 for children ages 8 to 17, and free for kids 7 and under.

SOUTH OF FORT-DE-FRANCE Marie Josèphe Rose Tascher de la Pagerie was born in 1763 in the quaint little village of Trois Ilets, across the bay from Fort-de-France. As Joséphine, she became the wife of Napoléon Bonaparte in 1796 and empress of France in 1804. Although reviled by some historians as ruthless and selfish, she's revered by some on Martinique as having been uncommonly gracious. A small museum, the **Musée de la Pagerie** (© **596/68-34-55**), sits in the former estate kitchen building where Joséphine once gossiped with her slaves. Displays include the bed that she slept in until she departed for France at age 16, portraits of her and of Napoléon, invitations to Parisian balls, bills attesting to her extravagance as the empress, and letters, the most notable being a passionate missive from lovelorn Napoléon. The plantation house itself was destroyed in a hurricane, but the kitchen and partially restored ruins of the sugar mill and church remain (the latter is in the village itself). The museum is open Tuesday through Sunday from 9am to 3pm; an English-speaking guide is usually on hand. Admission is $8 for adults, $4 for children 15 and under.

One of Martinique's best-known geological oddities is **Le Rocher du Diamant (Diamond Rock),** a craggy, multifaceted protrusion of an island that juts upward from the sea to a height of 172m (564 ft.) in the bay south of Trois Ilets. This Gibraltar of the Caribbean, as it is sometimes called, figured prominently in a daring British invasion in 1804, when the British proclaimed Diamond Rock a man-of-war (actual ships were in short supply) and proceeded to equip the islet with guns. The garrison held out for 18 months, completely dominating the passageway between the rock and the coast of Martinique. On a misty day, the rock looks more like the Loch Ness Monster emerging from the depths than a diamond. Intrepid foreigners sometimes visit Diamond Rock, but the access across the strong currents of the channel is risky.

You'll have passed through a number of quaint coastal villages by this time, but none sweeter than **Sainte-Luce.** Absurdly picturesque with its blindingly white stucco walls, red-tile roofs, turquoise sea, and multicolored fishing boats, this town is pure sun-drenched maritime serenity. Swim or snorkel off the small but pleasant beach, meditate on horizon-dominating Diamond Rock, or check out the village boutiques and cafes. For an unhurried taste of French island life, this is as good a place as any to spend the day.

Shopping

The main shopping district in Fort-de-France is bound by rue Ernest Deproge (on the waterfront), La Savane, rue Lamartine, and rue de la République, with **rue Victor Hugo** being the single-most-important stretch. Stores generally open during the week at 9am and close at 5pm; most close for lunch, usually between 1 and 3pm. On Saturday, shops are open in the morning only; on Sunday, virtually all are closed.

Martinique offers a good selection of French luxury items—perfumes, fashionable clothing, luggage, crystal, and dinnerware—at prices that can be as much as 30% to 40% lower than those in the States. Unfortunately, because some luxury goods, including jewelry, are subject to a hefty value-added tax, the savings are ultimately less compelling. Duty-free divas invariably make **Nocibe/Roger Albert,** 7 rue Victor Hugo, their first stop. This well-known outlet frequently has the best buys on French perfume, china, and crystal. **Cadet-Daniel,** 72 rue Antoine Siger, is its chief competitor. Compare and save.

Martinican goods, such as rum, Creole jewelry, madras fabric, folk paintings, and hand-woven baskets, are good buys and more representative of the island. The **open-air market** in La Savane, at rue de la Liberté and rue Ernest Deproge, has the best selection of these items. For sheer Caribbean color, stroll through the enclosed **produce market** on rue Isambert near rue Blénac; built in 1901, it's another work of architect Henri Pick.

Centre des Métieres d'Art, rue Ernest Deproge, near the tourism office, is one of the best arts-and-crafts stores in Martinique. Pass over the junk and focus on the more accomplished handmade items, including ceramics, painted fabrics, and patchwork quilts.

The French consider libations an art, and aficionados consider Martinican rum among the world's finest. **La Case à Rhum,** in the Galerie Marchande, 5 rue de la Liberté, stocks all the local brands and allows sample nips to help you decide which bottle to buy.

If you find yourself across the bay in Pointe du Bout, stop by **La Belle Matadore,** Immeuble Vermeil Marina (midway between the La Pagerie Hôtel and the Méridien Hôtel). This boutique takes the history and tradition of Creole jewelry seriously, and virtually every piece for sale replicates designs developed during slave days by *matadores* (prostitutes), midwives, and slaves.

Beaches

Serious beach bunnies hop south of Fort-de-France to **Grand Anse des Salines,** widely regarded as Martinique's nicest strand. At the island's extreme southern tip, about an hour from the capital by car, it features coconut palms, views of Diamond Rock, and white sand that seems to go on for miles. During summer holidays and weekends, it's busy with families and children, but during the week, it's often quiet and uncrowded. Beachside stands offer refreshment.

Conveniently located across the bay from Fort-de-France, **Pointe du Bout** is Martinique's most lavish resort area. Aside from a marina and a variety of watersports, the area has some modest man-made white-sand beaches. The sandy, natural beaches at nearby **Anse Mitan** and **Anses d'Arlets** are popular with both swimmers and snorkelers. However, the steepness of Martinique's shoreline leaves something to be desired; the water declines steeply into depths, and no reefs ring the shores. The neighboring beach is **Anse-à-l'Ane,** an ideal place for a picnic. Set on the island's southwestern coast, about 40 minutes by taxi from the airport, this village offers a good beach, open to the prevailing southern winds. **Le Diamant (Diamond Beach),** on the Martinique mainland, offers a sandy bottom, verdant groves of swaying palms, and many different surf and sunbathing possibilities. The entire district has developed in recent years into a resort, scattered with generally small hotels.

Beaches north of Fort-de-France have mostly gray (they like to call it silver) volcanic sand. The best of the bunch is **Anse Turin,** just to the side of the main Caribbean coastal road, between St-Pierre and Le Carbet. Extremely popular with locals and shaded by palms, it's where Gauguin swam when he called the island home.

Martinique has no legal nudist beaches, but toplessness is as common here as anywhere in France. As a rule, public beaches lack changing cabins or showers, but hotel lockers and changing cabanas can be used by nonguests for a charge.

Sports

GOLF   When Robert Trent Jones, Sr., designed **De L'as Golf Martinique** (© 596/52-04-13) in 1976, he chose a picturesque, historic site: the seaside hills neighboring La Pagerie, the birthplace of Empress Joséphine. About 30km (20 miles) from Fort-de-France, this good, tough, 18-hole, 6,640-yard, par-71 course features emerald hills, swaying palms, constant vistas of the turquoise sea, and, thankfully, year-round trade winds that help keep things cool. Facilities include a pro shop, golf academy, bar, restaurant, and tennis courts. English-speaking pros are at your service. Greens fees and cart rental run about $65 for 18 holes, $32 for 9 holes. A set of clubs is another $25.

HIKING   Inexpensive guided hikes, sometimes within the boundaries of the **Parc National Régional de la Martinique,** are organized year-round by the **CRRPM** (Centre Régional des Randonnés Pedestres de la Martinique). This organization also gives out maps of recommended hikes within Martinique, and offers advice about routings and access to departure points for walks and hill treks. You can call the park's administrative headquarters at © **596/64-42-59** for more information.

HORSEBACK RIDING   The premier riding facility on Martinique is **Ranch Jack,** Esperanze, Trois-Ilets (© **596/68-37-69**). It offers morning horseback rides for both experienced and novice riders, at a cost of about $70 to $80 for a 4-hour ride (at 8:30am or 2:30pm). Jacques and Marlene Guinchard make daily treks across the beaches and fields of Martinique, with a running explanation in English of the history and botany of the island. Cold drinks are included in the price, and transportation is usually free to and from the hotels of nearby Pointe du Bout. Four to 15 participants are needed to book a tour. This is an ideal way to discover both the botany and the geography of Martinique.

JET-SKIING   Also on the grounds of the Carayou Hotel is an outfit specializing in jet-skiing, **Jet Caraibes** (www.jetcaraibes.com; © **696/44-67-24**). A 30-minute rental of a jet ski costs about $80.

SCUBA DIVING & SNORKELING   Favorite dives in the coastal waters off Martinique include the caves and walls of Diamond Rock and the dozen ships sunk by the 1902 volcanic eruption at St-Pierre. (The most popular wreck, the metal-hulled *Roraima,* was made famous by Jacques Cousteau and rests on a slant in 45m/150 ft. of water.)

For cruisers, the most convenient dive operators are across the bay from Fort-de-France in Pointe du Bout. **Espace Plongée,** at the **Kalenda Resort** (formerly the

Hôtel Méridien; http://planetebleue-plongee.com; ☏ **800/442-5917** or 596/66-01-79), and **Planète Bleue,** at the Pointe du Bout marina (☏ **596/66-08-79**), are among the island's best operators. If you want to dive around St-Pierre, try **UCPA** (☏ **596/78-21-03**). Single-tank dives with all equipment run about $65.

The waters of Pointe du Bout and nearby Anse Mitan and Anse Dufour are popular with snorkelers, as are the small bays of Ste-Anne and Anses d'Arlets on the southwest coast. Snorkeling equipment from on-site vendors runs about $12.

WINDSURFING An enduringly popular sport in the French West Indies, *la planche à voile* (windsurfing) is available at most of the large-scale hotels. One of the best-equipped (and longest-lived) of Martinique's windsurfing centers is **Windsurf Club Martinique,** which occupies a site directly on the beachfront of the Hotel Carayou (www.windsurf-kite-martinique.com; ☏ **596/66-19-06**). Lessons cost about $135 per hour, and boards, depending on their make and model, rent for about $50 per hour. A half-day rental costs about $100.

Great Local Restaurants & Bars

Hey, it's France: Expect great food. More than any other island in the French West Indies, Martinique gives French and Creole cuisine equal billing. If you're on a mission to sample the booze of every port of call, Martinique's local beer is **Lorraine;** among the island's best rums are **Clement, Depaz,** and **Saint James.** Too early in the day for demon rum? Slake your thirst with **Didier,** the Caribbean's only naturally carbonated spring water.

AT POINTE DU BOUT Just minutes by ferry car from the resorts of Pointe du Bout, **La Villa Créole,** Anse Mitan (www.la-villa-creole.fr; ☏ **596/66-05-53**), serves down-home Creole staples such as *accras de morue* (codfish beignets), *boudin Créole* (Creole blood sausage), and *féroces* (avocado, codfish, and manioc hush puppies). Don't leave your garden table without indulging in the chocolate fondant with bittersweet chocolate–and–pear sauce. Lunch is about $35. The nearby **Au Poisson d'Or,** Anse Mitan (☏ **596/66-01-80**), a rustic roadside eatery, offers more Creole choices such as grilled conch in coconut milk and stewed shrimp, as well as lobster soup and shark in hot sauce. Lunch is about $30.

Le Dôme (☏ **596/75-75-77**) is set on the uppermost (eighth) floor of a hotel in the Valmenière district, midway between Fort-de-France's commercial center and the airport—far from the neighborhoods and haunts visited by the leisure-industry crowd. This establishment caters almost exclusively to a clientele of business travelers, many of whom come from the French mainland. Outfitted with a contemporary decor, it boasts large bay windows through which diners enjoy a view that sweeps along the island's coastline. Menu items blend traditional French cuisine with Antillean ingredients, sometimes in very creative ways. The best examples include a cream of christophine (Caribbean squash) soup with crayfish; ground rack of lamb served with a sauce made from cocoa powder and red wine; and filet of John Dory with yellow bananas and anise. Lunch is about $50.

NEVIS

Off the beaten tourist track, south of St. Martin and north of Guadeloupe, Nevis is the junior partner in the combined Federation of St. Kitts and Nevis, which gained self-government from Britain in 1967 and became a totally independent nation in 1983. Nevis's 1998 referendum for separation from its larger partner failed by the slimmest of margins, and while there is still a movement toward independence—which would make Nevis the smallest country in the world (and probably won't be happening anytime soon)—the dual-island nation, for the most part, lives in peaceful coexistence.

Though smaller than St. Kitts and lacking a major historic site, such as Brimstone Hill Fortress, Nevis is nevertheless the more appealing and upbeat of the two islands. When viewed from its sister island, about 3km (2 miles) away, Nevis appears to be a perfect cone, rising gradually to a height of 970m (3,180 ft.). Columbus first sighted the island in 1493, naming it Nuestra Señora de las Nieves, Spanish for "our lady of the snows," because its peak reminded him of the Pyrenees. Settled by the British in 1628, Nevis became a prosperous sugar-growing island as well as the most popular spa island of the 18th century, when people flocked in from other West Indian islands to visit its hot mineral springs.

Nevis's two most famous residents were **Admiral Horatio Nelson,** who married a local woman here in 1787, and **Alexander Hamilton,** who was born here and went on to find fame as a drafter of the American Federalist Papers, as George Washington's treasury secretary, and as Aaron Burr's unfortunate dueling partner. Today, the island's capital city, Charlestown, has a lovely mixture of port-town exuberance and small-town charm, and the popular Pinney's Beach is just a knockout.

COMING ASHORE   Only small ships call on Nevis, docking right in the center of **Charlestown** and/or dropping anchor off the coast of **Pinney's Beach.**

LANGUAGE   English is the language of both Nevis and St. Kitts.

CURRENCY   The local currency is the **East Caribbean dollar** (EC$2.70 = US$1; EC$1 = US37¢). Many shops and restaurants quote prices in U.S. dollars. Always determine which currency the locals are talking about. We've used U.S.-dollar prices in this section.

INFORMATION   The **Nevis Tourism Authority** is in the historic Treasury Building, on Main Street near the docks (www.nevisisland.com; ✆ **869/469-7550**). Hours are Monday through Friday from 8am to 4pm, Saturday from 8am to noon. For information before you go, call ✆ **866/556-3847.**

CALLING FROM THE U.S.   When calling St. Kitts or Nevis from the United States, you need dial only a "1" before the numbers listed here.

Getting Around

BY TAXI   The entirety of Charlestown is accessible on foot, but if you want to visit Pinney's Beach or elsewhere on the island, you can hop a taxi in Charlestown. The cost to Pinney's is about $8. Taxi drivers double as guides on Nevis, so if you want to take a general tour of the island, negotiate a price with your driver.

BY RENTAL CAR   Because driving is on the left side in Nevis and most of the worthwhile sites are within walking distance or easily reached by taxi, I don't recommend renting a car here.

Best Cruise Line Shore Excursions

Few organized excursions are offered on Nevis. Some of the small ship lines offer a day at **Pinney's Beach** as part of their regular visit, and might also offer hiking and snorkeling options, but the island is so small and easy to negotiate on your own that organized excursions aren't really necessary. If you want some local commentary, you can hire a taxi driver to give you an island tour. (See "Getting Around," above.)

To St. Kitts · The Narrows · Newcastle · Newcastle Beach · Mosquito Bay · Vance W. Amory International Airport · Oualie Beach · Under the Sea Sealife Education Centre · Fort Ashby · Long Haul Bay · Pinney's Beach · Cotton Ground · Huggins Bay · ATLANTIC OCEAN · Nevis Peak · Charlestown · Bocane Ceramics · New River · Caribbean Cove · Fig Tree · Hermitage Plantation · Peak Haven Villiage Experience · White Bay · Bath · Montpelier · Gingerland · Botanical Garden · White Bay Beach · Saddle Hill · Caribbean Sea · Indian Castle Beach

Charlestown · Government Rd. · Grove Park Cricket Ground · Governor's House · Jews' Burial Ground · Police · Nelson Museum · Cradock Rd. · Chapel St. · Happy Hill Alley · Main St. · Prince William St. · Court House & Library · Island Rd. · Island Hopper · Prince Charles St. · Cotton Ginnery · Alexander Hamilton Birthplace/Museum of Nevis History · Market · Gallows Bay

Airport
Beach
Cruise Ship Dock
Mountain

On Your Own: Within Walking Distance

If your ship docks in Charlestown, you're dead center in a perfect walking-tour opportunity. Charlestown is a lovely little place, laid-back in somewhat the same manner as St. John, but with some of the really rural character of sister island St. Kitts.

If you head left from the docks and walk a little ways (maybe .5km/¼ mile) along Main Street, you'll come to the **Museum of Nevis History at the Birthplace of Alexander Hamilton** (www.nevis-nhcs.org/nevishistory.html; © 869/469-5786), where the road curves just before the turnoff to Island Road. It's a rustic little two-level house set right on the coastline. On the first floor is the Museum of Nevis History and gift shop (admission is $5 for adults, $2 for children 11 and under), but in all honesty, you'll do just as well to skip it and just appreciate the outside, taking a moment to read the historic plaque. Hours are Monday to Friday 9am to 4pm, Saturday 9am to noon.

Backtracking along Main Street, you'll pass several serviceable, if unremarkable, shops (see "Shopping," below). Keep walking through the center of town, saying hello to the occasional mama goat and kids you'll pass, and then turn left onto Government Road. One block up on the left, you'll find the **Jews' Burial Ground,** with graves from 1684 to 1768. Stones left atop the graves attest to the visitors who have been there before you to pay their respects. When I was there, the dead were being enter-tained with reggae music coming from the doorway of a shop across the street, while a breeze stirred the few trees on the property. All in all, not a bad resting spot.

Backtrack to Main Street, turn left, and continue on past the Grove Park Cricket Ground, bearing left when the road forks. Head up the hill and then turn at the first right, which will bring you to the **Nelson Museum** (www.nevis-nhcs.org/nelson museum.html; © **869/469-5786**). A very small, very homemade kind of place, it's nonetheless an interesting spot, and well worth the $5 admission ($2 for children 12 and under). The museum traces the history of Admiral Horatio Nelson's career enforcing England's Navigation Acts in the Caribbean. It also houses artifacts from Nevis's Carib, Arawak, and Aceramic peoples; a small display on Nevis today; and a number of wonderful clay artworks, including a replica of the old "Coolie Man's Store," by local artist Gustage "Bush Tea" Williams. The museum is open Monday through Friday from 8am to 4pm, Saturday from 9am to noon.

On Your Own: Beyond the Port Area

The 3-hectare (7½-acre) **Botanical Garden of Nevis** (www.botanicalgardennevis. com; © **869/469-3509**) is located 5km (3 miles) south of Charlestown on the Montpelier Estate. Fountains, ponds, and re-creations of Mayan sculptures dot the grounds, which are open Monday through Saturday from 9am to 4pm. Admission is $16 for adults, $10 for children. Also on-site are a restaurant and a gift shop.

The island of Nevis is essentially one big cone, sloping upward on all sides to Nevis Peak in the center. Hiking even halfway up the mountain is a strenuous climb, but pays off with spectacular views and sightings of monkeys, birds, and rare plants. Under no circumstances should you hike this mountain alone; not only is it unsafe, but you'll miss out on your guide's explanations of your surroundings. **The Peak Heaven Village Experience,** Zetland Village, Gingerland (www.peakheavennevis. com; © **869/665-6926**) offers various tours and guided walks, including an old sugar mill and village huts. Admission is $12 per person; guided tours are extra. Stay and have lunch atop Nevis Peak on an outdoor dining deck at the **Coal Pot Restau-rant.** Lunch is about $20.

Shopping

Nevis is not a shopping hub on the order of St. Thomas, or even the much more laid-back St. John. In fact, it's no kind of shopping hub at all. Still, there are a few shops worth poking your head into, most of them along Main Street, right in the port area.

Island Hopper, on Main Street, a block north of Prince Charles Street (© **869/469-0893**), is the best shop in town for visitors, stocking a huge selection of batik clothing. Across from Island Hopper is **Pemberton Gift Shop,** Main Street (© **869/469-5668**), which is sparse but does carry a selection of T-shirts, gift items, and a shelf of CSR (Cane Spirit Rothschild), the local cane-sugar liquor. **Jerveren's Fash-ions,** in the Cotton Ginnery complex right at the pier (© **869/469-0062**), has a decent selection of T-shirts and gifts.

Collectors can browse the range of Nevis stamps at the **Nevis Philatelic Bureau at the Head Post Office,** on Market Street (www.nevisisland.com/Philatelic.htm; © **869/469-5535**). It's next to the public market, 1 block south and 1 block east of the docks.

Outside of Charlestown awaits a more down-to-earth shopping scene. For hand-made goods, check out the **Nevis Crafthouse** on the main road north of the city

(℃ **869/469-5505**). This is the home base of a cooperative of weavers who make rugs, baskets, and plenty of other goodies out of the grass growing right outside their window—meaning that these are some truly native goods.

It's a bit off the beaten path, but if you're in the market for uniquely Nevisian ceramics, **Bocane Ceramics and Gift Studio** in Stoney Grove (www.bocane ceramics.com; ℃ **869/469-5437**) is your place. Local artist Cheryl "Cherrianne" Liburd has filled the shop with platters, vases, bowls, plates, and more, all decorated brightly in a Caribbean palette with such images as small cottages, lizards, and monkeys that are clearly inspired by the local surroundings. Some of my favorites are vases shaped like sliced-open coconuts, as well as the entire line of dishes painted to resemble palm fronds. Bocane also sells homegrown honey and locally produced hot sauce—a real killer blend of peppers, so consume at your own risk.

Beaches

The name to know on Nevis is **Pinney's Beach,** located north of Charlestown. A lovely spot for swimming, snorkeling, beachcombing, or just sitting back and watching the pelicans divebomb into the surf, it's home to the Four Seasons Resort, reopened in late 2000 after being obliterated by 1999's Hurricane Lenny. As a counterpoint to conspicuous luxury, the rickety **Sunshine's Bar and Grill** sits right on the beach, offering beer and other refreshments.

Oualie Beach, just north of Pinney's Beach, isn't as popular as its sister to the south, but is no less pristine. Visitors here are protected from rough waves by reefs far out into the bay, so the water is usually safe for small children. Behind the beach sits **Oualie Beach Resort** (www.oualiebeach.com; ℃ **869/469-9735**), with a restaurant, bar, and live open-air music available to all beachgoers.

Great Local Restaurants & Bars

Pinney's Beach isn't just a spectacular stretch of shoreline—it's also home to some of the best dining experiences in Nevis. **Sunshine's Bar and Grill** (℃ **869/469-5817**) serves up grilled seafood and barbecued meats alongside its signature "Killer Bee" rum punch. By night, this is a crowded locals' hangout, but cruisers stopping by for lunch should have no problem claiming one of Sunshine's flag-decorated beachfront cabanas for an afternoon of dining, drinking, and dipping into the sea. Lunch will set you back about $18. **Oualie Beach Resort** (www.oualiebeach.com; ℃ **869/469-9735**) is just up the beach, with an open-air restaurant and bar hangout, as well as free beach lounges. **Double Deuce Restaurant** (www.doubledeucenevis.com; ℃ **869/469-2222**), also on Pinney's Beach, is another ultracasual lunch spot serving fresh fish from the grill on a patio just steps from the sea. Lunch will cost you about $45. If you're so inclined, you can spend an entire day on the beach at any of these beachside eateries; locals often hang out on Pinney's Beach from the afternoon well into the evening, and we encourage you to do the same.

PANAMA

The Panama Canal is an awesome feat of engineering and human effort that rivals the pyramids of Egypt and the Great Wall of China. Construction began in 1880 and wasn't completed until 1914, at the expense of thousands of lives. The vast majority of the original structure and equipment is still in use.

Passing through the canal takes about 8 hours from start to finish and is a fascinating procedure—the route is about 80km (50 miles) long and includes passage through three main locks, which, through gravity alone, raise ships over Central America and down again on the other side. Between the locks, ships pass through artificially created lakes such as the massive **Gatun Lake,** 26m (85 ft.) above sea level. It often costs ships about $100,000 to pass through, with fees based on each ship's weight. Your ship will line up in the morning, mostly with cargo ships, to await its turn through the canal. While it's transiting, there will be a running narration of history and facts about the canal by an expert who's brought on board for the day.

Forget about all the images of Panama that you saw on the news in the 1980s. Panama is now one of Latin America's success stories, with a thriving economy, a growing tourist infrastructure, an expanding expatriate community, and a real-estate boom that makes it an ideal investment spot for people looking to buy vacation homes. In addition to being home to one of the greatest engineering feats of all time, it also has a national park within city limits and lush rainforests just a 20-minute drive out of the capital.

COMING ASHORE   The Cristobal Pier is located in Colón, Panama, on the eastern side of the Panama Canal. Cruise ships docking here generally enter the locks and are then raised up to Gatun Lake, where they tender passengers ashore for their shore excursions. The Colón 2000 terminal is generally for cruise ships that are docking in Colón for the entire day and not entering the Panama Canal. The terminal building features lounge areas, an Internet cafe, a duty-free mall, restaurants, and native-crafts boutiques.

LANGUAGE   Spanish is the language of choice, but many Panamanians speak English.

CURRENCY   The local currency, the Panamanian balboa (B), is equivalent to the U.S. dollar.

INFORMATION   You can find visitor information at the **Tourist Bureau (℃ 507/ 526-7000)** or in Colón (℃ **507/475-2301**). If you prefer the computer, you can visit www.visitpanama.com.

CALLING FROM THE U.S.   When calling Panama from the United States, you need to dial "011" before the numbers listed here.

Colón

In compliance with a treaty signed between the United States and Panama in 1977, canal operations passed from American to Panamanian hands at the stroke of midnight on December 31, 1999. Not only did the transition go smoothly, but the canal changeover spurred government agencies and private developers in Panama to expand the canal zone's tourism infrastructure—not simply trying to attract as many ships as possible, but developing new attractions at the canal's Atlantic entrance to lure cruise passengers off their ships and into Panama's interior on shore excursions and for pre- and postcruise stays. Even ships not transiting the canal are being wooed, with a long-term goal of making the city of Colón a home port for cruise ships sailing to the southern Caribbean.

The linchpin project in the new canal-area developments is **Colón 2000,** a $45-million private port development that opened in October 2000 near the canal's Caribbean entrance, and that is capable of handling any size cruise vessel—even the 100,000-ton-plus ships that are too large to pass through the canal. Colón 2000's developer, Corporación de Costas Tropicales, has created a tour company, **Adventuras 2000** (www.colon2000.com), that offers a series of shore excursions highlighting

Panama

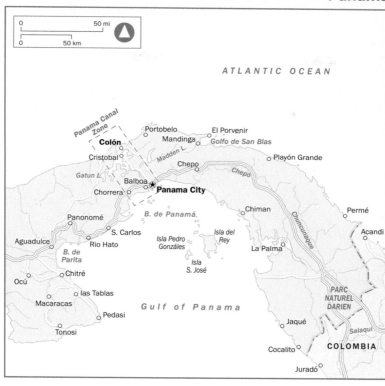

Panama's history, culture, and diverse natural attractions (see "Best Cruise Line Shore Excursions," below). The project has opened many new jobs to locals, who are being trained as bilingual tour guides, drivers, and so on.

Colón 2000's glass-and-marble terminal building has a large lounge, an Internet cafe, a huge duty-free shopping mall (part of the Colón Free Zone, the second-largest tax-free zone in the world), restaurants, and crafts shops. Unfortunately, the town surrounding the splashy new development remains depressed, so there's no question that passengers calling here should book an organized tour; the city of Colón is known for being poverty-stricken and extremely unsafe, so tourists absolutely should not wander around town.

Another new development in Colón, the **Cristobal Cruise Terminal** (Pier 6), offers piers for two ships of any size and has a duty-free shopping area, restaurants, and phones. A rail line here, connecting Colón and the capital of Panama City, is in the planning stages.

BEST CRUISE LINE SHORE EXCURSIONS

The excursions listed below represent a sampling of those offered from Colón.

Emberá Indian Village Tour ($119, 3½ hr.): Today, Panama's Emberá indigenous people live much as they did in the early 16th century, when their first tourist—Vasco

Nunez de Balboa, who "discovered" the Pacific Ocean—came through. You'll travel by dugout canoe up the Chagres River, visit the Emberá village, witness a performance of traditional dance, and (surprise, surprise) have an opportunity to purchase handicrafts.

Kayaking the Canal ($132, 9 hr.): You'll travel to Sol Meliá Resort, where you'll spend about an hour kayaking amid the plant life, mammals, and birds. Then you'll head by bus to the Gatun Locks for a look at the canal's workings. A buffet lunch is served.

Panama City Tour ($99, 5½–6 hr.): Visit the ruins of Old Panama, founded in 1519 by Pedro Arias Davila and destroyed in 1671 by the pirate Sir Henry Morgan; head to colonial Panama, built to replace the original capital; and then visit the Miraflores Locks for a look at the canal.

Monkey Watch ($84, 5½ hr.): After a 30-minute ride at high speed through the heart of the Panama Canal, the boat will slow down and enter the labyrinth of jungle-covered islands of Lake Gatun. Wildlife is plentiful in this protected area; you are likely to encounter capuchin monkeys, three-toed sloths, howler monkeys, toucans, turtles, butterflies, crocodiles, and more.

Panama City & the Surrounding Environs

If you're not in the mood to shop in the Colón Free Zone, take a tour of Panama City. It's sophisticated, with a modern downtown area, but still has Spanish colonial remnants in Casco Antiguo. If you want to discover Panamanian city life, this is the place to go, not Colón.

Visit the Calzada de Amador (Amador Causeway), where you can take in views of the city skyline and the Bridge of the Americas. When you want to stop for food, go to **Café Barko** on the Flamingo Island section of the causeway, which specializes in Panamanian cuisine and seafood. You won't be disappointed.

Picturesque Casco Antiguo is wonderful to stroll around during the day if you stay near the area surrounding **Plaza de la Indepencia.** Walk around the Plaza during the day to enjoy the magnificent details of the colonial architecture, but don't wander too far from the plaza after sundown. The area becomes unsafe at night.

Metropolitan Nature Park is the only rainforest within a capital city in the Americas. Observe toucans, woodpeckers, and parrots within their natural habitat. **Soberania Rainforest** is just 25km (16 miles) out of Panama City. Abundant with wildlife—including 500 different bird species—you'll see monkeys, sloths, crocodiles, and other animals that you'll never find in your own backyard.

Exploring the rainforest is a must if you're in Central America, but do it with a guide, as you don't want to risk getting lost in unfamiliar terrain.

Ports Along the Canal Route

The **San Blas Islands** are a beautiful archipelago and home to the Kuna indigenous people, whose craftswomen are well known for their colorful, hand-embroidered stitching. If you get a chance to go ashore, the tiny women, dressed in their traditional molas (bright, intricately appliquéd blouses), sell all manner of this textile art in square blocks and strips, which make great pillow covers or wall hangings. They cost about $10 each, but don't try to bargain too much—the women will go only so low before standing firm.

In Costa Rica, many ships call at **Puerto Caldera** on the Pacific side or **Puerto Limón** on the Atlantic side. There's nothing to see at either cargo port, but both are great jumping-off points for tours (offered by all visiting ships) of the country's lush, beautiful rainforests, which are alive with some 850 species of birds, 200 species of mammals, 9,000 species of flowering plants, and about 35,000 species of insects. After a scenic bus ride, the tour will take you on a nature walk through the jungle or a mild whitewater-rafting trip.

In Guatemala, most Panama Canal–bound ships call at **Puerto Quetzal,** on the Pacific coast; a few may call at **Santo Tomas** on the Caribbean side. Both are used as gateways to Guatemala's spectacular Mayan ruins at **Tikal.** They're the country's most famous attractions and are also considered the most spectacular, with more than 3,000 temples, pyramids, and other buildings of the ancient civilization—some of them dating as far back as A.D. 300—nestled in a thick, surreal jungle setting. Excursions here are neither cheap nor easy—a 10-hour tour involves buses, walking, and a 1-hour flight, and costs about $650—but the journey is well worth the effort. Tours to the less spectacular Mayan sites in Honduras are also offered from Puerto Quetzal, as are several overland tours of Guatemala's interior.

PUERTO RICO

San Juan, the capital of Puerto Rico, has the busiest ocean terminal in the West Indies and is one of the cruise trade's most important ports. Cruise groups overwhelm many ports of call by their sheer size, but San Juan absorbs cruise passengers with ease. The San Juan metropolitan area, home to about a third of Puerto Rico's four million people, is one of the largest and most sophisticated urban centers in the Caribbean, offering all the amenities of a modern major city: great shopping, interesting neighborhoods, beautiful people, excellent restaurants, glamorous bars and nightclubs, and fine museums. It also offers some of the drawbacks: traffic, crowded sidewalks, and, in some areas, crime (avoid the La Perla neighborhood, along the north-central edge of Old San Juan).

Founded in 1521 by Spanish conquistador **Juan Ponce de León,** the city is one of the oldest in the New World. The cobblestone streets of the hilly old section of the city—**Old San Juan,** the ancient walled city on San Juan Island—are lined with brightly painted colonial town houses, ancient churches, intimate parks, and sun-drenched plazas. Like the pyramids of Egypt and the Great Wall of China, Old San Juan's Spanish colonial forts and city walls are United Nations World Heritage Sites. Another attraction is the people: Puerto Ricans are warm, quick to laugh, and proud of their multicultural heritage, a distinct blend of Amerindian, Spanish, African, and North American influences that is present in the culture of the island, from salsa music to Puerto Rican cuisine.

San Juan's shopping ranks among the Caribbean's best, and the city's historic sights, beaches, gambling, and other diversions make it, overall, the number-one port of call in the region. You'll find some of the Caribbean's best restaurants here, as well as sprawling beaches with high-rise luxury hotels reminiscent of those in Miami.

Old San Juan is the prime tourist haunt, but there's much more to the metropolitan area. Other interesting neighborhoods include **Santurce,** linked with San Juan Island by a causeway; **Condado,** a strip of beachfront hotels, restaurants, casinos, and nightclubs on a peninsula stretching from San Juan Island to Santurce; **Hato Rey,** the business center; **Río Piedras,** site of the University of Puerto Rico; and **Bayamón,** an industrial and residential quarter. **Isla Verde,** another resort zone, is connected to the rest of San Juan by an isthmus. Rumor has it that a second cruise ship pier will be greatly expanded on the other side of the island, near the quaint city of **Ponce.** In addition to art, history, museums, and beaches, many of the interior-based natural attractions are equally accessible from San Juan and Ponce.

COMING ASHORE Cruise ships dock in historic **Old San Juan,** a short walk from the Plaza de la Darsena, Old San Juan's main bus station, and most of its historic treasures. During periods of heavy volume—such as Saturday and Sunday in midwinter, when as many as eight cruise ships dock on the same day—additional, less convenient piers are used. Many of Old San Juan's shops and attractions are within walking distance of these docks. Over the next few years, this area will be expanded with more docks and attractions to the east of the current piers. For information about the port, contact the **Port of San Juan** (✆ 787/723-2260).

LANGUAGE Spanish is the native tongue, but most people on the island also speak English (both are the official languages here). The farther you venture from San Juan, the more likely it is you'll have to practice your Spanish.

CURRENCY Puerto Rico is part of the United States (as an unincorporated territory), so the **U.S. dollar** is the coin of the realm. Canadian currency is accepted, albeit reluctantly, by some of San Juan's bigger hotels. Credit cards and traveler's checks are widely accepted.

INFORMATION For advice and maps, drop by the **Tourist Information Center** at La Casita, near Pier 1 (✆ 787/722-1709). For info before you go, contact the **Puerto Rico Tourism Company** (www.prtourism.com; ✆ 800/223-6530).

CALLING FROM THE U.S. Calling Puerto Rico from the continental United States is as simple as dialing between U.S. states: Just dial "1" before the numbers listed here.

Getting Around

Driving in congested San Juan is frustrating, and parking in some areas is impossible. You're better off walking around Old San Juan. Take buses or taxis to Condado, Ocean Park, and Isla Verde.

BY TAXI Taxis operated by the Tourist Transportation Division are metered in San Juan, but the fare structure between major tourism zones is standardized. The set rates from the cruise ship piers are $10 to Old San Juan, $15 to Condado, and $20 to Isla Verde. You can also hire a taxi for $35 per hour. If the meter's used, the initial charge is $3, plus 10¢ for each additional ⅟₁₃th of a mile and $1 for each suitcase ($2 for each suitcase after the third). The minimum fare is $3. After 10pm, there's a night surcharge of $1 to the meter reading. To order a cab, call **Metro Taxi** (✆ 787/725-2870) or **Borican Taxi** (✆ 787/843-6000).

BY TROLLEY When you tire of walking around Old San Juan, board one of the free trolleys. They depart from Plaza de la Marina and piers 2 and 4, but you can hop on anywhere along the route.

BY BUS The **Metropolitan Bus Authority** operates extensive bus service in the greater San Juan area. Bus stops are marked by signs that read PARADA, and terminals are in front of Pier 4. For route and schedule information, call ✆ 787/250-6064.

BY RENTAL CAR Puerto Rico has expressways as well as thousands of miles of other paved roads, so travel by car is pretty effortless, except in metropolitan San Juan, where traffic can be heavy and nightmarish—the 500-year-old streets in Old San Juan just weren't built with cars in mind. Driving is on the right side of the road,

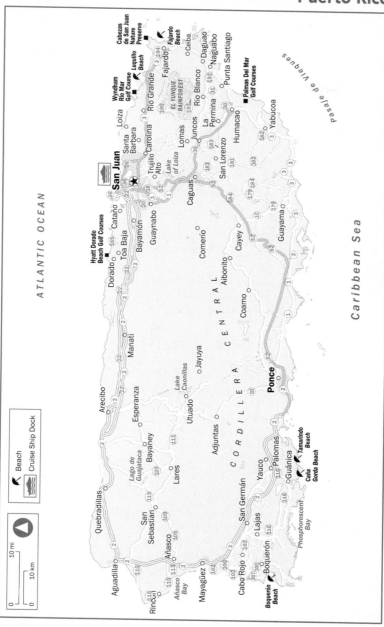

Puerto Rico

ATLANTIC OCEAN

Caribbean Sea

pasaje de Vieques

Beach
Cruise Ship Dock

10 mi
10 km

San Juan

Ponce

Cabezas de San Juan Nature Preserve
Fajardo Beach
Ceiba
Daguao
Naguabo
Punta Santiago
Fajardo
Luquillo Beach
Wyndham Rio Mar Golf Course
Río Grande
Río Blanco
Palmas Del Mar Golf Courses
EL YUNQUE RAINFOREST
La Pernina
Humacao
Yabucoa
Loíza
Santa Barbara
Carolina
Trujillo Alto
Lomas
Juncos
Lake of Loíza
San Lorenzo
Caguas
Guaynabo
Cataño
Bayamón
Hyatt Dorado Beach Golf Courses
Toa Baja
Dorado
Comerio
Cayey
Guayama
Manatí
Aibonito
Coamo
Arecibo
Jayuya
Lake Caonillas
Utuado
Ponce
Esperanza
Bayaney
Lago de Guajataca
Adjuntas
Lares
CORDILLERA CENTRAL
Palomas
Tamarindo Beach
Caña Gorda Beach
Guánica
Quebradillas
San Sebastián
Yauco
San Germán
Lajas
Phosphorescent Bay
Aguadilla
Rincón
Añasco Bay
Añasco
Mayagüez
Cabo Rojo
Boquerón
Boquerón Beach

5

THE PORTS OF CALL | Puerto Rico

301

and all other U.S. rules apply. Signs are in Spanish, though; the metric system is used for distance markers (kilometers rather than miles) and at gas stations (liters instead of gallons); but, confusingly enough, speed limits are posted in miles per hour. **Avis, Budget, Dollar,** and **Hertz** all have offices here.

Best Cruise Line Shore Excursions

Unless you want a guide to offer historic perspective ($45, 2½ hr.), don't bother with organized tours of Old San Juan—it's easy enough to get around on your own. On the other hand, if you explore somewhere farther afield, an organized tour is a good idea.

El Yunque Rainforest Drive ($55, 4–5 hr.): One of Puerto Rico's most popular attractions, El Yunque covers more than 11,000 hectares (27,000 acres) and receives up to 500cm (200 in.) of rain per year. There are 240 different tropical trees, more than 50 orchid species, 150 varieties of ferns, 68 types of birds, and millions of tiny coquí tree frogs. After arriving at Baño Grande, a natural swimming hole, hike half an hour along the Camimitillo trail and see parrot nests, giant ferns, orchids, and palms. Listen for the song of Puerto Rico's national symbol, the tiny coquí tree frog. After a short stop at an interpretive station, proceed to the Yokahu observation tower and Coca waterfall.

Tropical Horseback Riding ($100, 3½ hr.): Once you reach the ranch, you'll meet your horse, briefly learn the ropes, and then ride down a beautiful beach. Take a quick swim during the refreshment stop.

City Tour & Bacardi Rum Distillery ($49, 4 hr.): After a tour of the old city, with a stop at the San Cristóbal fort, you'll travel to the Bacardi distillery to learn about the Puerto Rican sugar and rum industries, watch giant fermenting tanks transform sugarcane into rum, and get a taste for yourself.

Excursions Offered by Local Agencies

If you're staying in a hotel before or after your cruise, book excursions at your hotel's tour desk. Otherwise, try **Rico Suntours,** 176 Calle San Jorge, San Juan (www.ricosuntours.com; ℂ 787/722-2080), or **Castillo Tours & Travel Services,** 2413 Calle Laurel, Punta La Marias, Santurce (www.castillotours.com; ℂ 787/791-6195). For serious adventure, rock climbing, rappelling, cave exploring, or canyoneering, your best bets are **Aventuras Tierra Adentro,** 268-A Av. Piñero, Río Piedras (www.aventuraspr.com; ℂ 787/766-0470), or **Acampa,** 1211 Av. Piñero, San Juan (www.acampapr.com; ℂ 787/706-0695). You can also check *Que Pasa* magazine for more detailed information.

Shopping

San Juan has some great bargains—prices are often even lower than those in St. Thomas—and U.S. citizens pay no duty on items bought in Puerto Rico. Every tourist zone offers ample shopping opportunities, but the streets of the **Old Town,** especially **Calle San Francisco** and **Calle del Cristo,** are the major venues. Local handicrafts can be good buys, including *santos* (hand-carved wooden religious figures), needlework, straw work, hammocks, guayaberas (lightweight shirts worn untucked), papiermâché masks, and paintings and sculptures by local artists. **El Alcazar,** 103 Calle San José, has the largest collection of antique furniture, silver, and art objects in the Caribbean. You'll need help to wade through the massive inventory, though—it fills several buildings. Smaller but still impressive, **Olé,** 105 Calle Fortaleza, has antique *santos,* coins, and silver. It's also the place to get a custom-fitted Panama hat.

San Juan at a Glance

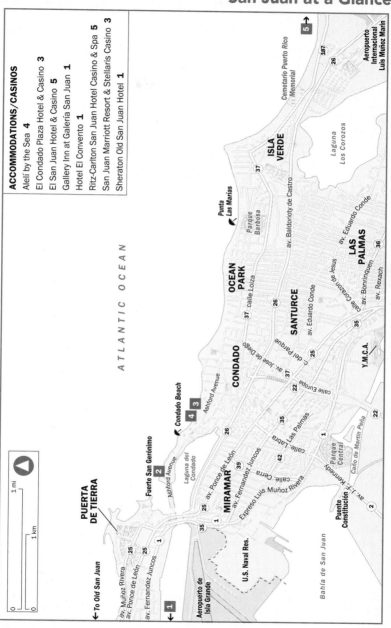

ACCOMMODATIONS/CASINOS

Alelí by the Sea **4**
El Condado Plaza Hotel & Casino **3**
El San Juan Hotel & Casino **5**
Gallery Inn at Galería San Juan **1**
Hotel El Convento **1**
Ritz-Carlton San Juan Hotel Casino & Spa **5**
San Juan Marriott Resort & Stellaris Casino **3**
Sheraton Old San Juan Hotel **1**

SAN JUAN AS A PORT OF embarkation

Puerto Rico is the number-one port of embarkation in the Caribbean, with more than 1.2 million visitors embarking on 700 cruises every year from here. Most cruise lines have packages that include hotel rooms on the island.

Getting to San Juan & the Port   Luis Muñoz Marín International Airport (📞 **787/791-1014**) is on the city's east side, about 12km (7½ miles) from the port. Taxi fares from the airport are fixed at $12 to Isla Verde, $18 to Condado and Ocean Park, and $22 to Old San Juan and the cruise ships. The ride to the port takes at least 30 minutes—longer if traffic is heavy, which it often is.

WHERE TO STAY

In Old San Juan   The quietly elegant **Hotel El Convento,** 100 Calle del Cristo (www.elconvento.com; 📞 **800/468-2779** or 787/723-9020), is Puerto Rico's most famous lodging. A former Carmelite convent, it offers large rooms, many with views of the Old Town. Rates: $345–$705 winter, $180–$555 summer. The **Sheraton Old San Juan Hotel,** 100 Brumbaugh St. (www.sheratonoldsanjuan.com; 📞 **800/325-3535** or 787/721-5100), is

on the waterfront across the street from the cruise ship docks. Rooms are comfortable, and Old San Juan is a step away. Rates: $275–$885. Set on Old San Juan's highest hill, with a sweeping view of the sea, **Gallery Inn at Galería San Juan,** 204 Calle Norzagaray (www.the galleryinn.com; 📞 **866/572-2783** or 787/722-1808), was the home of a Spanish aristocrat in the 1700s. Many of the rooms open onto patios, fountains, and gardens. Art is everywhere, contributing to the hotel's cultured, contemplative, bohemian ambience. Rates: $275–$380.

In Condado   The original high-rise, high-glamour section of modern San Juan, Condado boasts numerous hotels, restaurants, and clubs. Among its best hotels are the **El Condado Plaza Hotel & Casino,** 999 Ashford Ave. (www. condadoplaza.com; 📞 **866/317-8934** or 787/721-1000; rates: $339–$1,249), and the **San Juan Marriott Resort & Stellaris Casino,** 1309 Ashford Ave. (www. marriott.com; 📞 **800/464-5005** or 787/722-7000; rates: $275–$545). **Alelí by the Sea,** 1125 Sea View St., a block off Ashford Avenue (📞 **787/725-5313**), is a small, charming option on the beach.

Eclectika, 205 Cruz, has exactly what you would think—an eclectic mix of art representing the diverse background of peoples on Puerto Rico. Although much of the art is not of the island, the variety is fun eye candy that is bound to catch your attention.

Natural, Inc., 257 Calle San Francisco, offers a variety of unique jewelry, inexpensive T-shirts, and many items made from eco-friendly materials.

La Casa de Las Casitas & Handcraft, 208 Calle Fortaleza, has authentic handicrafts, including wonderful locally made paintings starting at $30. **Galería Botello,** 208 Calle del Cristo, once the home of late Puerto Rican artist Angel Botello, sells his paintings and sculptures, as well as antique *santos.*

Old San Juan's best book and music store, **Cronopios,** is at 255 Calle San José. Most titles are in Spanish, but there are plenty in English too. Looking for Puerto Rican novels? Try *The House on the Lagoon,* by Rosario Ferré, or *The Renunciation,* by Edgardo Rodríguez Julia. And pick up some salsa CDs while you're browsing. On the same block is **Arte & Mascaras,** 250 Calle San Jose, with authentic Puerto Rican masks. Ena sells masks from families who have been practicing the tradition for more than 100 years.

Rooms are basic but clean; the big draws are the sound of the surf just outside your window and the low rates. Rates: $80–$120.

Motels in Condado include the **Holiday Inn Express,** 1 Mariano Ramirez Bages, off Ashford Avenue at Joffre Street (www.hiexpress.com; ✆ **800/315-2621** or 787/724-4160; rates: $144–$207), and **San Juan Comfort Inn–Condado Lagoon Hotel,** 6 Clemenceau St. (www.comfortinn.com; ✆ **787/721-0170;** rates: $110–$240).

In Isla Verde   Similar to Condado in atmosphere and abundance of hotels, but more recently developed, Isla Verde has a number of dazzlingly deluxe resort complexes, including the **El San Juan Hotel & Casino,** 6063 Isla Verde Ave. (www.elsanjuanhotel.com; ✆ **866/317-8935** or 787/791-1000; rates: $229–$2,300), and the **Ritz-Carlton San Juan Hotel Casino & Spa,** 6961 Ave. of the Governors (www.ritzcarlton.com; ✆ **800/241-3333** or 787/253-1700; rates: $345–$972). At the other end of the spectrum, motels include the **Howard Johnson Carolina,** 4820 Isla Verde Ave. (www.hojo.com; ✆ **787/728-1300**). Rates: from $115.

SAN JUAN AFTER DARK

The San Juan club scene is hot. In general, people get pretty dressed up, so forget about T-shirts or shorts. The newly renovated **Brava,** in the Wyndham El San Juan Hotel & Casino, 6063 Isla Verde Ave. (www.bravapr.com; ✆ **787/791-2781**), attracts a rich and beautiful crowd, as well as hundreds of wannabes. On weekends, you may have to wait a couple hours to get in. In the Old Town, head for **Club Lazer,** 251 Calle del Cruz (✆ **787/725-7581**), where you can dance the night away to the sounds of salsa and merengue. San Juan's exuberant gay scene is easily the Caribbean's best, and no club in town surpasses the energy of **Krash,** 1257 Av. Ponce de León, Santurce (✆ **787/722-1131**).

For a mellow and sophisticated atmosphere in Old San Juan, try **Carli Café Concierto,** on Plazoleta Rafael Carríon (www.carlisworld.com; ✆ **787/725-4927**), a bistro offering live piano and jazz music.

Designer outlet shops include **Polo Ralph Lauren,** 201 Calle del Cristo; **Coach,** 158 Calle del Cristo; **Dooney & Bourke,** 200 Calle del Cristo; and **Tommy Hilfiger,** 206 Calle del Cristo.

Beaches

Puerto Rico is ringed by hundreds of miles of sandy beaches, and you won't have to leave San Juan to play in the surf. Perhaps the most famous beach in the Caribbean, **Condado Beach,** at the western end of Ashford Avenue, is the backyard playground of Condado's resort hotels. A favorite of families, it can get pretty crowded in winter. The beaches of **Isla Verde,** behind the hotels and condominiums along Isla Verde Avenue, are less rocky and are excellent for people-watching. If you're looking for a more picturesque, sedate scene, head to **Ocean Park,** north of McLeary Street. The waters here are sometimes choppy, but they're still swimmable. If you walk past the swimmable areas, you can sometimes catch surfers braving the waves. Popular with college students on weekends, the beach is also very gay-friendly. Condado Beach, Isla Verde, and Ocean Park all have white sand, palm trees, ocean breezes, beautiful bodies, and ample eating and drinking options. Snorkeling gear and other watersports equipment are available to rent.

If you're anxious to get out of the city, **Luquillo Beach,** about 50km (30 miles) east of San Juan, near the town of Luquillo, stretches along a vast coconut grove. Coral reefs protect the clear lagoon from the fierce Atlantic, and a "Sea Without Barriers" facility caters to people with physical disabilities. Be aware, however, that some sections of the beach aren't as well maintained as they once were.

All *balnearios*—government-run beaches with dressing rooms, showers, lifeguards, snack bars, and parking—are open to the public. They're closed on Monday; however, if Monday is a holiday, the beaches will be open that day but closed the next. Be aware that if it is raining, the facilities will also be closed. Hours are 9am to 5pm in winter, 9am to 6pm during the off season. If you find a secluded spot, be vigilant about your surroundings: Solitude is nice, but there's safety in numbers.

Sports

DEEP-SEA FISHING Many say that **Mike Benitez Marine Services** (www. mikebenitezsportfishing.com; (¢ 787/723-2292), which has chartered boats out of San Juan for more than 40 years, sets the standard by which the others are judged. **Capt. Bill Burleson** (www.puertoricodeepseafishing.com; (¢ 787/850-7442) operates charters off the southeast coast. For both companies, expect to pay $700 for a half-day excursion and $990 for an extended half-day, for up to six anglers.

GOLF Puerto Rico is a golfer's dream, but you'll need to sign up for a ship excursion or rent a car to reach the major courses from San Juan. Situated on about 400 hectares (1,000 acres) and with 72 holes, **Dorado Beach Resort** ((¢ 787/626-1001), about 50km (30 miles) west of San Juan, offers the greatest concentration of golf in the Caribbean. Greens fees, including cart, at the Dorado Beach East Course are $250 for play before 1pm and $185 after 1:30pm. Greens fees, including cart, at the Plantation Sugarcane and The Pineapple courses are $137 for 18 holes before 1pm and $89 after 1:30pm. Club rentals are $55. The West Course is currently being renovated.

All four 18-hole courses here were designed by Robert Trent Jones, Sr. Jack Nicklaus ranks the 4th hole at the Dorado Beach East course as 1 of the 10 best-designed holes in the world.

The **Palmas del Mar** (www.palmasdelmar.com; (¢ 787/285-2700), 72km (45 miles) east of San Juan, has two courses: the par-71 Palm course designed by Gary Player, and the newer 18-hole Flamboyan course designed by Rees Jones. Greens fees for 18 holes are $150 at the Palm and $180 at the Flamboyan, including cart. Reservations can be made by calling the Palmas Athletic Club (www.palmaspac.com; (¢ 787/656-3020).

The **Wyndham Rio Mar Beach Resort and Spa** (www.wyndhamriomar.com; (¢ 800/474-6627 or 787/888-6000), 30km (20 miles) from San Juan in Rio Grande, also has two 18-hole courses, one designed by Tom and George Fazio, the other by Greg Norman. Greens fees, including cart, are $190 (or $130 for play after 2pm).

SCUBA DIVING & SNORKELING Puerto Rico offers excellent diving and snorkeling, but the best sites aren't within easy reach of San Juan. **Caribe Aquatic Adventures** (www.caribeaquaticadventure.com; (¢ 787/281-8858) will take you to sites around the capital or near Fajardo on the northeast coast. Caribe operates out of the Normandie (Av. Muñoz-Rivera, at the corner of Calle Los Rasales in Puerta de Tierra). A local reef dive is $65 and a local snorkel tour is $55. Much more interesting trips to Fajardo, which include a picnic, require a minimum of four passengers; cost is $145 per person for two dives for a maximum of six people. Those who wish to snorkel may join the Fajardo excursion and pay only $95. The Fajardo excursion must be booked a week in advance; the local reef dive or snorkel trip, a day in advance.

PADDLEBOARDING, KITEBOARDING & KAYAKING **Velauno Paddle-boarding,** 2430 Calle Loiza (www.velaunopaddlboarding.com; ℂ **787/728-8716**), rents paddleboards (also called SUPs, or stand-up paddleboards) for $40 an hour or $80 for the day and offers 1-hour beginner lessons for $100. Velauno also offers SUP eco-tours, where you will gently paddle through Condado Lagoon, for $200 for four people. **Kiteboarding Puerto Rico,** 2434 Loiza St. (www.kiteboardingpr.com; ℂ **787/374-5329**), offers Get Wet beginner lessons starting at $175. **Goodwind Puerto Rico,** in the Hosteria del Mar Hotel (www.kitegoodwinds.com; ℂ **787/605-5235**), offers an introductory lesson for $60 per hour for groups of three.

If you're spending an extra night on the island, be sure not to miss the luminescent bay off of Fajardo. There are single-celled bio-flagellates that glow when they are disturbed, but you can see them only at night. Plan to stay overnight in the town and reserve a kayaking trip ahead through **Kayaking of Puerto Rico** (www.kayaking puertorico.com; ℂ **787/435-1665;** from $45 with snacks). If you would rather see the bay by catamaran, try **East Island Excursions** (www.eastislandpr.com; ℂ **877/937-4386** or 787/860-3434).

Gambling

Casinos are one of San Juan's biggest draws, and most large hotels have one. They're generally open daily from noon (slots from 10am) to 4am, and many never close. Dress, usually informal during the day (though no bathing suits, flip-flops, or tank tops), becomes impressive in the evenings. The **Casino at the Ritz-Carlton,** Avenue of the Governors, Isla Verde (www.ritzcarlton.com/en/properties/sanjuan/casino; ℂ **787/253-1700**), is the largest in Puerto Rico. Combining elegant 1940s decor with tropical fabrics and patterns, it's one of the plushest entertainment complexes in the Caribbean. The **InterContinental San Juan,** 5961 Isla Verde Ave. (ℂ **800/496-7621** or 787/791-6100), is another elegant place to rendezvous. One of its Murano glass chandeliers is "longer than a bowling alley." Most convenient for cruise ship passengers is the bustling **Sheraton Old San Juan Hotel & Casino,** 100 Brumbaugh St. (www.sheratonoldsanjuan.com; ℂ **787/721-5100**), directly across from Pier 3.

Great Local Restaurants & Bars

San Juan has some of the best restaurants in the Caribbean and a variety of cuisines that only a major city can offer. A favorite local beer is **Medalla.** The most famous local rum is **Bacardi,** in all of its varieties; **Don Q** is also popular.

In Old San Juan, **Amadeus,** 106 Calle San Sebastián (www.amadeuspr.com; ℂ **787/722-8635**), offers nouvelle Caribbean dishes and features an intimate courtyard in back. Lunch is about $25. **El Patio de Sam,** practically next door at 102 Calle San Sebastián (ℂ **787/723-1149**), is a popular gathering spot for expatriates, journalists, and shopkeepers. The hearts of palm salad is crisp and fresh, and the olive bites are a must-have snack. Lunch is around $15.

A wonderful vegetarian option is **Café Berlin,** 407 Calle San Francisco (ℂ **787/722-5205**). Located north of Plaza Colón and perfect for people-watching, the cafe boasts sidewalk seating and a comfortable dining area with the large windows.

Offering free wireless Internet and their signature "manjito" frozen mango mojitos ($8), this is the perfect setting to rest your weary feet after shopping. Try the delicious Tofu Griega, a large entree with ginger, peppers, walnuts, goat cheese, and cubes of tofu ($14). Lighter fare includes soups, salads, and sandwiches.

The unpretentious **La Bombonera,** 259 Calle San Francisco (✆ **787/722-0658**), famous for its homemade Puerto Rican meals and 1940s diner atmosphere, has attracted the island's literati and Old San Juan families for decades. Lunch is about $12. A kitschy experience not to be missed (especially for brunch) is San Juan's trailblazing *nuevo Latino* bistro, **Parrot Club,** 363 Calle Fortaleza (www.oofrestaurants.com; ✆ **787/725-7370**), which blends Spanish, Taíno, and African cuisines. It's decorated with a variety of wooden parrots, local art, and a great attitude. Stop by for brunch or lunch (each about $35).

If you crave fresh seviche, you can enjoy the raw bar delights at **Aguaviva,** 364 Calle Fortaleza (www.oofrestaurants.com; ✆ **787/722-0665**), home to a wonderful selection of fresh oysters and a large variety of fish. For the adventurous, try the seviche sampler ($49 for all six, $25 for three, $18 for two); the Blue Marlin and Red Snapper are favorites.

In Condado, **Miró Marisquería Catalana,** 76 Condado Ave. (✆ **787/723-9593**), serves seafood and traditional Catalonian dishes. Lunch is around $22. For stylish but relaxed beachfront dining and sublime Caribbean delicacies, no place beats **Pamela's,** 1 Calle Santa Ana, in Ocean Park (www.numero1guesthouse.com; ✆ **787/726-5010**). You'll savor every bite. Lunch is about $32.

An exquisite and expensive culinary adventure is to be had at **Pikayo** (✆ **787/721-6194**), located in the Museo de Arte de Puerto Rico. Hop in a cab and enjoy this modern restaurant, filled with fantastic art. Not to be missed is the octopus seviche and the juiciest swordfish you have ever tasted. Once you're there, walk around the museum and enjoy a wide spectrum of art. It's open for dinner only.

ST. BARTHÉLEMY (ST. BARTS)

Chic, sophisticated St. Barts (or, technically, St. Barthélemy, a name nobody ever uses) is internationally renowned as one of the ritziest refuges in the Caribbean, rivaled only by Mustique as the preferred island retreat of the rich and famous. Forget historic sites or ambitious watersports programs. You go to St. Barts for the relaxation, the French cuisine, the white-sand beaches, and the ultimate in comfort.

From early fans Nureyev, Baryshnikov, and Buffett to later enthusiasts Mick Jagger, Princess Di, Calvin Klein, Madonna, and Naomi Campbell, the glitterati who have played here form a veritable who's who of fabulousness. Despite its transformation over the past couple of decades into a celebrity hot spot, St. Barts retains its charm, serenity, natural beauty, and Gallic flavor. Just 24km (15 miles) from St. Martin, the island's 21 sq. km (8 sq. miles) of dramatic hills and pristine white-sand beaches are decidedly French, like a peaceful slice of the Côte d'Azur transplanted in the Caribbean. Since 2007, St. Barts has been part of a Territorial Collectivity, no longer directly ruled by Guadeloupe as a municipality. A combination of things—including the roller-coaster terrain, strict zoning and construction laws, and a local consensus that stratospheric pricing is the surest way to maintain exclusivity—protects the island from massive development that would certainly change its character.

First inhabited about 3,000 years ago by Ciboney Indians, then later by Arawaks (A.D. 200) and Caribs (A.D. 1000), St. Barts was first spotted by Europeans in 1496, when Christopher Columbus named the island after his baby brother, Bartolemeo.

St. Barthélemy (St. Barts)

THE PORTS OF CALL

5

In sharp contrast to most Caribbean islands, where descendants of African slaves form the majority, the 7,000 year-round residents of St. Barts are primarily of French ancestry, mostly from Brittany and Normandy. Many affluent Americans and Europeans have villas on the island—some living in the Caribbean year-round, others making seasonal visits.

Occasionally you'll see St. Bartians dressed in the provincial costumes of Normandy and speaking Norman French. In little **Corossol,** more than anywhere else, people sometimes follow customs brought from 17th-century France.

COMING ASHORE Cruise ships anchor off **Gustavia,** the main town, and ferry passengers via tenders to the dollhouse-size harbor and dock General de Gaulle. Phones and ATMs are in the immediate vicinity of the harbor. The post office (or PTT), which also serves as a telecommunications center, is located at the back corner of the harbor opposite the dock.

You can check your e-mail at the first-floor offices of **Centre @lizes,** on rue de la République (© **590/29-89-89**), a few blocks to the right of the dock. Internet access is about $8 per 30 minutes. Be sure to ask for an American keyboard: The position of letters on French keyboards is not significantly different, but it's just enough to cause frustration. It's open Monday through Saturday from 8:30am to 7:30pm, Sunday from 3 to 7pm (May–Nov, it's closed for lunch).

LANGUAGE   French is the official language, but virtually everyone speaks English as well.

CURRENCY   St. Barts is part of the French overseas region of Guadeloupe, so the **euro** (€) is the official currency (.75€ = US$1; 1€ = US$1.32). You'll have no trouble using Visa, MasterCard, and traveler's checks. Prices mentioned in this section are in U.S. dollars.

INFORMATION   The **Comite Territorial du Tourisme,** adjacent to the dock on quai Général de Gaulle (✆ **590/27-87-27;** us.franceguide.com), is open Monday through Friday from 8:30am to 6pm and from 8:30am to 12:30pm on Saturday.

CALLING FROM THE U.S.   When calling St. Barts from the United States, dial the international access code (011) and 590 before the numbers listed here, which also begin with 590. That's right: If you want to make a connection, you have to dial 590 twice. It's just one of those oddities that makes the world go round.

Getting Around

BY TAXI   Taxis meet cruise ships at Gustavia's harbor. Because the island is so small, no destination is too distant. Dial ✆ **590/27-66-31** for service if you don't spot a cab. The fare ranges from approximately $10 to $22, depending on your destination.

BY RENTAL CAR   If you love adventure, rent a Suzuki Samurai: Zipping up and down the island's jagged, picturesque hills is more thrilling than riding most amusement-park rides. Local drivers are alert and competent, but they tend to drive aggressively and the roads aren't exactly in top condition. Automatic transmissions are in short supply, so reserve in advance: If you're not already adept at using a stick shift, St. Barts is not the place to learn. All valid foreign driver's licenses are honored. *Warning:* Honk your horn furiously while going around the island's blind corners to avoid having your fenders sideswiped. **Avis, Budget, Hertz,** and **National** have offices here, as do local firms **Turbé Car Rental** (✆ **590/27-71-42**); **Tropic'all Rent,** rue du Roi Oscar II, Gustavia (✆ **590/27-64-76**); and **Europcar** (✆ **590/ 27-74-34**). Driving is on the right. Never drive with less than half a tank of gas on St. Barts. The island has only two gas stations: one near the airport, the other in Lorient. Both are closed on Sunday, but the airport station has a pump that accepts credit cards any time of day, any day of the week.

Best Cruise Line Shore Excursions

Jet-Set Boat & Beach Excursion ($225, 4 hr.): Circumnavigate St. Barts in a 39-foot cruiser, then tender ashore at St. Jean Beach for a swim, a snorkel, or drinks from the open bar.

St. Barts on Horseback ($75, 1½ hr.): Travel to northern St. Barts for a relaxed guided ride through the island's outback.

Excursions Offered by Local Agencies

Easy Time offers a variety of tours all around the island, including hiking on fairly rugged terrain to some of the island's natural sites. A guided historical walk around Fort Gustavia and other monuments and museums takes 2½ hours and costs about $33. A 3-hour scenic tour of the island will take you to beaches and villages and provide some refreshments for about $78. There are full-day tours of different parts of the island with a gourmet meal and some shopping. The price varies depending on your preferences, but start at about $185. You need to book at least 24 hours in advance (www.stbartheasytime.com; ℭ **690/63-46-09**).

On Your Own: Within Walking Distance

Aside from shopping, eating, and hanging out in sidewalk cafes, cruisers sticking close to port can visit Gustavia's modest points of interest. **St. Bartholomew's Church,** rue Samuel Fahlberg, dates from the 1850s and features limestone and volcanic-stone walls, as well as imported pitch-pine pews. Its tiny Anglican, English-speaking congregation is an anomaly on this overwhelmingly French Catholic island.

Evidence of St. Barts's faint but lingering Swedish presence, the **Wall House,** rue Duquesne, is a staid stone building near the harbor's mouth, across from the dock. Once a Swedish home, the structure was rebuilt after fire devastated it (and much of Gustavia) in 1852. Since 1989, it has housed the **Territoril Museum** (ℭ **590/29-71-55**), an unfocused but respectable introduction to the history, sociology, ethnology, economy, and ecology of the island. The most interesting items include Amerindian artifacts, rustic farm furnishings, clothing used by early French settlers, and photos documenting hurricane devastation. The exhibits are open Monday to Friday from 8:30am to 1pm and 2:30 to 5pm, and Saturday from 9am to 1pm. Admission is about $3 for those older than 12.

On Your Own: Beyond the Port Area

Visiting the tiny fishing village of **Corossol** is a vibrant way to experience the St. Barts of the past. About 10 minutes by taxi from the dock, this quaint, totally unchic hamlet is home to traditional folk who still live off the sea. It's your best bet for spotting women in traditional 17th-century bonnets and for watching roadside vendors weave items from palm fronds. On the town's waterfront, stop by **Le Regal** (ℭ **590/27-85-26**) and have a beer or a bite with the locals.

Shopping

A duty-free port, St. Barts is a good place to buy liquor, perfume, and other French luxury items. Good deals on apparel, crystal, porcelain, and watches can also be found, especially during May, the biggest sale month. Moisturizer mavens can stock up on the island's own cosmetic line, **Ligne St. Barth.** Shops are concentrated in Gustavia and St. Jean, where the quality-to-schlock ratio is as high as anywhere in the Caribbean. Most shops and offices close for a long lunch, usually from noon to 2pm.

If you're looking for big-name brands, you'll find them all in Gustavia, from **Burberry** and **Cartier** to **Hermès** and **Roberto Cavalli.** But there are also plenty of sophisticated local boutiques worth exploring.

In Gustavia, **Carat,** rue de la République; **Fabienne Miot,** rue de la République; and **Diamond Genesis,** rue du Général de Gaulle, offer an array of fine jewelry, some handcrafted on the premises. **St. Barth Style,** rue Lafayette, near rue du Port, stocks fashionable beachwear, while **Sabina Zest,** cours Vendôme, carries cotton voile, silk, linen, and lace clothes and accessories, all made in St. Barts. High-style women's fashion is also available at **Stéphane & Bernard,** rue de la République, behind Carat.

Both men's and women's shoes can be found at **Human Steps,** rue de la France. And **Privilège,** rue du Roi Oscar II, is your best bet for perfumes and cosmetics.

Le Comptoir du Cigare, rue du Général de Gaulle, sells cigars from Cuba and the Dominican Republic along with connoisseur-quality rums, while **Pipiri Art Gallery,** rue du Général de Gaulle, features the work of local artists—and is also a boutique and restaurant with a delightful garden.

In St. Jean, **Kiwi Saint Tropez** and **Pain de Sucre** stock chic beachwear; **Bleu Marine** has French and Italian women's fashions; **Elysees Caraïbes** sells high-style handbags and luggage; and **Boutique Iléna** offers gorgeous lingerie.

Beaches

The 16 beaches of St. Barts are first-rate. Few are ever crowded, even during the peak season, and all are public and free. There is no such thing as a private beach on St. Barts (even if some beachfront hotels claim so). Beaches are easily accessible by taxi from the cruise pier, and you can make arrangements with your driver to be picked up later at a specific time and place. As St. Barts is a French island, toplessness is common at all beaches. Full nudism is officially prohibited, but bathers at several sites—Saline and Gouverneur, to name a couple (see below)—flout the rules. Defying a common stereotype, most nude bathers on the island actually have attractive bodies.

Shell Beach, just a short walk from the harbor in Gustavia, is the most convenient place to soak up the sun if your time is limited. The water is calm, and **Do Brazil** (www.dobrazil.com; ✆ 590/29-06-66), a lively fusion restaurant right on the beach, is an ideal spot for lunch or for watching the sunset. You can also grab a sandwich to go at **Zen Beach Bar** (✆ 590/27-19-39), a snack bar below.

St. Jean, the busiest and most social beach on the island, is protected by a coral reef; its calm waters attract families and watersports enthusiasts, including windsurfers and the occasional surfer. Near the end of the airport's incredibly short runway, St. Jean also provides numerous eating, drinking, shopping, and people-watching opportunities.

Gouverneur, on the south-central coast, is quiet and relatively remote. Its idyllic setting and unspoiled beauty make it number one with locals and discerning visitors who want privacy and serenity. (The steep and winding drive to the beach is an experience in itself.)

Farther east, in a wild and rustic area that was once the site of salt ponds, **Saline** is reached by a 3-minute walk over a sand dune. It's most famous for its adult environment and nude bathers. Plan on eating lunch at one of the many nearby dining spots (see "Great Local Restaurants & Bars," below).

For a more serious hike, start at the end of the beach at Flamands and trek about 20 minutes to **Colombier.** This beach is magnificent—and you'll enjoy the views of the rugged coast along the way. Shade and snorkeling are found here, and you can pack a lunch and spend the day. Locals call it Rockefeller's Beach because for many years David Rockefeller owned the property surrounding it.

If you'd rather skip the trek, just stay at **Flamands,** which boasts great bodysurfing waves. If you long to feel a part of the St. Barts scene, park yourself on a lounge chair on the sand in front of the **Isle de France** hotel and splurge on a salad or sandwich at the restaurant, **La Case de L'Ile** (www.isle-de-france.com; ✆ **590/27-61-81**). A light lunch will cost you about $42. (Don't say I didn't warn you.)

Sports

HIKING   **Easy Time** tours has a number of different hikes of varying difficulty (rated from 1 to 6) to beautiful sites, some in the rocky interior of the island. Hiking

St. Barthélemy (St. Barts)

THE PORTS OF CALL

the summit at Grand Fond is a 3-hour climb at difficulty level 5 and costs about $65. But it's easier—level 2—to go to the natural pools from Grand Fond and it costs about $42. It's been said that guide Helen Bernier knows every rock, flower, and critter on the island. You'll be hiking with a maximum of seven people, and meals are not included. Wear walking shoes, and bring a hat, water, and swimwear. You need to book at least 24 hours in advance (www.stbartheasytime.com; ☏ **690/63-46-09**).

SAILING, SCUBA DIVING & SNORKELING   **Jicky Marine Service,** quai du Yacht Club (www.jickymarine.com; ☏ **590/27-70-34**), operates from the marina across the harbor from the busier side of Gustavia. Most dive sites served by this five-star PADI operator are a 10- to 20-minute boat ride from the harbor; depths vary from 3 to 30m (10–100 ft.). Reef dives are the rule, although one wreck dive for more experienced divers is a possibility. One-tank dives are about $98; two-tank dives are about $170, including beverages and all equipment. The operation also offers half-day snorkeling cruises (about $95, including snorkeling gear, a French snack buffet, and an open bar) and catamaran or sloop charters (starting at $875 for half a day, including cheese, fruit, beverages, and music). The price pays for a maximum of eight people and includes a crew. Call for Christmas and New Year's rates.

Vendors at both St. Jean and Grand Cul de Sac rent snorkel gear and other watersports equipment—jet skis, Sunfish sailboats, and so on.

WINDSURFING   Try **CARIB Waterplay,** near the Tom Beach Hotel at St. Jean (☏ **690/61- 8081**), or **Windwave Power,** at Grand Cul de Sac (☏ **590/27-82-57**). Expect to pay about $50 an hour for a full rig.

Great Local Restaurants & Bars

Mix lots of rich, discerning diners with the French tradition of culinary expertise, and it's no wonder that so many of the island's restaurants consistently receive high accolades. It's a pity that some of the best open only for dinner, well after your ship has gone out to sea. As luck would have it, enough serve lunch to assure you one of the best meals of your cruise.

IN GUSTAVIA   If you're interested in seeing and being seen, make a beeline for **Le Select,** rue de la France at rue du Général de Gaulle (☏ **590/27-86-87**), the epicenter of Gustavia's social life for more than 50 years. This cafe's tables rest in a tree-shaded garden a block from the harbor. A full bar is available to complement the burgers, salads, and other simple fare. Salty locals, celebrities, and chic tourists are among the clientele. The classic, funky ambience supposedly inspired Jimmy Buffet's "Cheeseburger in Paradise." Lunch costs around $20.

AT ST. JEAN   **Eden Rock** (www.edenrockhotel.com; ☏ **590/29-79-99**) has three restaurants at St. Jean beach: one on the rock promontory that bisects the strand, one next to the ocean, and one in the sand, aptly dubbed the Sand Bar, which serves lunch for about $45. Traditional French cuisine, seafood, and tropical drinks are the trio's strong suits. For great pizza and friendly ambience, try the **Hideaway** (☏ **590/27-63-62**), where lunch will be around $25. You can relax on the open-air terrace or get your order to go. If you're more in the mood for a sandwich and want to get back to the sun, head to **KiKi-e Mo** (☏ **590/27-90-65**), an Italian gourmet shop that whips up tasty, relatively inexpensive light fare to go. Lunch is about $15.

Grilled fish and seafood are the highlights at **La Plage,** in the chic Le Tom Beach Hotel (www.st-barths.com/tom-beach-hotel; ☏ **590/27-53-13**). This beachfront restaurant has made waves in St. Barts—in fact, it's the hottest dining address in town. Lunch costs around $35.

St. Barts is so expensive that many visitors opt to buy at least one of their meals (perhaps a "gourmet lunch to go" package) from a takeout deli. The most centrally located of the island's epicurean delis is **La Rôtisserie,** St. Jean Centre Commercial Vaval (© **590/29-75-69**), which is proud of its endorsement by Fauchon, the world-famous food store in Paris. On display are bottles of wine, crocks of mustard, pâté, herbs, caviar, chocolate, and exotic oils and vinegars, as well as takeout and (very French) platters sold by the gram. *Plats du jour,* with portions suitable for one, cost from $7.50 to $23.

IN LORIENT For a *très* French experience, have a café au lait and a pain au chocolat at the sunny **La Petite Colombe** (© **590/29-74-30**), which will cost you about $8.

AT SALINE A handful of restaurants are within walking distance of the Saline beach. Upscale but still relaxing, **Le Tamarin** (© **590/27-72-12**) specializes in inventive Creole dishes. The menu focuses on light, summery meals that go well with the streaming sunlight and tropical heat. Service can be erratic, but if you're in a rush, you shouldn't be here. If you have to wait, you can order an aperitif in one of the hammocks stretched under a tamarind tree. Lunch is around $55.

AT PUBLIC If you're lucky enough to be on a ship that stays in port past sunset, get yourself to **Maya's** (© **590/27-75-73**) for sunset cocktails or dinner. Feast your eyes on an unbeatable view of the sea and the glamorous clientele while enjoying flavorfully prepared fresh seafood. Dinner is about $65. If, alas, your ship leaves port earlier, you can at least enjoy the food at **Maya's to Go** (© **590/29-83-70**), located across from the airport in St. Jean. It offers pastries, sandwiches, quiche, and salads.

ST. KITTS

Somewhat off the beaten tourist track, south of St. Martin and north of Guadeloupe, St. Kitts forms the larger half of the combined Federation of St. Kitts and Nevis, which gained self-government from Britain in 1967 and became a totally independent nation in 1983. The two islands are separated by only about 3km (2 miles) of ocean, and although the citizens of Nevis, in the past, have expressed a strong urge for independence from St. Kitts, in recent years this movement has died down and the dual-island nation, for the most part, lives in peaceful coexistence.

St. Kitts—or St. Christopher, a name hardly anyone uses—is by far the more populous of the two islands, with some 36,000 people. It was the first English settlement in the Western Hemisphere, and during the plantation age, its 176 sq. km (68 sq. miles) enjoyed one of the richest sugarcane economies in the Caribbean—until 2005, when it ceased the production of sugarcane for export. Cane fields still climb the slopes of a volcanic mountain range, and you'll see ruins of old mills and plantation houses as you drive around the island.

St. Kitts is lush and fertile, dotted with rainforests and waterfalls, and boasting some lovely beaches along its southeast coastline. After being hit by several successive hurricanes in the late 1990s, a push to improve the amenities and infrastructure of the country, among other efforts at wooing tourists to bring in badly needed cash,

has proved fruitful. The bulk of the island's revenue now comes from tourism, followed by agriculture.

The island is crowned by the 1,156m (3,793-ft.) **Mt. Liamuiga,** a crater that, thankfully, remains dormant. The island's most impressive landmark is the **Brimstone Hill Fortress,** one of the Caribbean's most impressive forts. The capital, **Basseterre,** is rife with old-time Caribbean architecture and has a few worthwhile landmarks, but overall the city offers little to hold the interest of visitors.

COMING ASHORE **Port Zante** has undergone rebuilding and expansion, and can now accommodate up to four ships. The port, which stretches from the center of town into the deep offshore waters, offers duty-free shopping, restaurants, a hotel/casino, and a welcome center.

LANGUAGE English is the language of both St. Kitts and Nevis.

CURRENCY The local currency is the **East Caribbean dollar** (EC$2.70 = US$1; EC$1 = US37¢). Many shops and restaurants quote prices in U.S. dollars. Always determine which currency locals are talking about. We've used U.S.-dollar prices in this section.

INFORMATION You can get local information at the **St. Kitts Tourism Authority,** Pelican Mall, Bay Road, in Basseterre (✆ **869/465-4040**), open Monday through Friday from 8:30am to 5pm. For info before you go, go to www.stkittstourism. com or call ✆ **800/582-6208.**

CALLING FROM THE U.S. When calling St. Kitts or Nevis from the United States, you just need to dial a "1" before the numbers listed here.

Getting Around

BY TAXI Taxis wait at the docks in Basseterre and in the Circus, a public square near the docks at the intersection of Bank and Fort streets. Since most drivers are also guides, this is the best means of getting around the island. Taxis aren't metered, so you must agree on the price before heading out. Always ask if the rates quoted are in U.S. dollars or East Caribbean dollars.

BY RENTAL CAR **Avis** and **Thrifty** have offices on the island, as do local rental agencies **Cool Profile** (✆ **869/465-4448**) and **Williams Car Rental** (✆ **869/663-6119**). Road conditions are good, but keep in mind that driving is on the left side.

Best Cruise Line Shore Excursions

Brimstone Hill Fortress ($60, 3 hr.): Among the largest and best preserved of all the forts in the Caribbean, Brimstone Hill (www.brimstonehillfortress.org) dates from 1690, when the British fortified the hill to help recapture Fort Charles, located below, from the French. Tours typically include a visit to the beautiful **Romney Gardens** (featuring giant ferns, orchids, poinsettias, and "the Tree," a 350-year-old Saman tree). You can also shop at **Caribelle Batik,** one of the island's most popular boutiques, where you'll find rack after rack of Indonesian-style, hand-printed clothes.

Mt. Liamuiga Volcano Hike ($109, 6 hr.): The name of this dormant volcano, in the northwest area of the island, means "fertile land" in the Carib Indian language. It has been dormant since 1692, and today its summit is a major goal for hikers. On this excursion, you'll hike about 1,156m (3,793 ft.) to the summit, traveling along narrow trails and through the island's rainforest. It takes about 3 hours to reach the top. Refreshments are offered before the hike back down. This is a great trip if you're in shape.

Mountain Biking & Beach Tour ($78, 4 hr., minimum height 1.5m/60 in.): From the pier, you'll ride through Basseterre and then out through sugarcane fields and up 450m (1,475-ft.) Olivees Mountain, where you'll enjoy the views and the refreshments. After the ride down, you'll stop at Friar's Bay for a swim and snack. It's a nice way to see this lush island.

St. Kitts Scenic Railway ($99, 3½ hr.): Take a scenic ride on the "Sugar Train," a deluxe, double-decker train that follows the same tracks built in 1912 to haul cane from the fields to the sugar mills. Learn about the island's culture, people, and history while you view abandoned windmills and chimneys from old sugar estates, along with a canopy of rainforest vegetation along the slopes of Mt. Liamuiga.

Excursions Offered by Local Agencies

Rainforest Tours: For a great rainforest walk in the thickets around Romney Gardens, contact Addy of **Addy's Nature Tours** (www.addysnaturetours.com; ✆ **869/465-8069**). He knows the flora and fauna of St. Kitts like the back of his hand and delivers a satisfying, personal rainforest experience, ending his tour by sharing a plate of his wife's tasty homemade banana bread and some fresh guava and passion fruit juices.

Hikes: Call **Greg's Safaris** (www.gregsafaris.com; ✆ **869/465-4121**) to arrange full-day hikes to Mt. Liamuiga ($105 per person) or assorted half-day hikes around the island ($65). The owner, Greg Pereira, is a local folklore and botanical expert.

Taxi Tours: You'll find a fleet of taxis waiting at the dock as you disembark from your ship. Taxi drivers will take you on a 3-hour tour of the island for about $70. Lunch can be arranged at one of the local inns. Try the lunch buffet at **Rawlins Plantation,** in Mount Pleasant (www.rawlinsplantation.com; ✆ **869/465-6221**).

On Your Own: Within Walking Distance

The capital city of **Basseterre,** where the docks are located, has typical British colonial architecture and a few shops. Drop by the **marketplace,** where country people bring baskets brimming with mangoes, guavas, soursop, mammee apples, and wild strawberries and cherries just picked in the fields. Tropical flowers abound.

The town is built around a so-called **Circus,** the town's round square. A tall green Victorian clock stands in the center of the Circus. After Brimstone Hill Fortress, **Berkeley Memorial Clock** is the most photographed landmark of St. Kitts. In the old days, wealthy plantation owners and their families used to promenade here.

St. George's Anglican Church, on Canyon Street (walk straight up Church St. or Fort St. from the dock), is the oldest church in town and is worth a look. **Independence Square,** a stone's throw from the docks along Bank Street, is pretty, with its central fountain and old church, but there's no good reason to linger unless it's to sit in the shade and toss back a bottle of Ting, the local grapefruit-based soda. Once an active slave market, it's surrounded by private homes of Georgian architecture.

On Your Own: Beyond the Port Area

Brimstone Hill Fortress ★ (www.brimstonehillfortress.org; ✆ **869/465-6211**), 14km (9 miles) west of Basseterre, is a major stop. This historic monument, among the largest and best preserved in the Caribbean, is a complex of bastions, barracks, and other structures ingeniously adapted to the top and upper slopes of a steep-sided 240m (790-ft.) hill. The fortress dates from 1690, when the British attempted to recapture Fort Charles from the French. In 1782, an invading force of 8,000 French troops bombarded the fortress for a month before its small British garrison, supplemented by local militia, surrendered. When the British took the island back the next year, they proceeded to enlarge the fort into the "Gibraltar of the West Indies." In all, the structure took 104 years to complete.

Today, the fortress is the centerpiece of a national park with nature trails and a diverse range of plant and animal life, including the green vervet monkey. Perched on the upper slopes of a steep hill, it's a UNESCO World Heritage Site. It's also a photographer's paradise, with views of mountains, fields, and the Caribbean Sea. On a clear day, you can see six neighboring islands. From below, the fort presents a dramatic picture, poised among diabolical-looking spires and outcroppings of lava rock. Its name comes from the odor of sulfur released by nearby undersea vents.

Visitors can enjoy self-guided tours among many ruins and restored structures, including the barrack rooms at Fort George, which contain an interesting museum. The gift shop stocks prints of rare maps and paintings of the Caribbean. Admission is $8 for adults, $4 for children. The Brimstone Hill Fortress National Park is open daily from 9:30am to 5:30pm.

You can visit the site where a large tamarind tree in the hamlet of **Half-Way Tree** once marked the boundary between the British- and French-held sectors.

It was near the hamlet of **Old Road Town** that Sir Thomas Warner landed with the first band of settlers and established the first permanent colony to the northwest at Sandy Point. Sir Thomas's grave is in the cemetery of St. Thomas Church.

A sign in the middle of Old Road Town points the way to **Carib Rock Drawings,** all the evidence that remains of the former inhabitants. The markings are on black boulders, and the pictographs date from prehistoric days.

Into the Volcano

Mount Liamuiga was dubbed "Mount Misery" long ago, but it sputtered its last gasp around 1692. This dormant volcano on the northeast coast is today one of the major highlights for hikers on St. Kitts. The peak of the mountain often lies under cloud cover.

The ascent to the volcano is usually made from the north end of St. Kitts at Belmont Estate. The trail winds through a rainforest and travels along deep ravines up to the rim of the crater at 788m (2,585 ft.). The actual peak is at 1,156m (3,793 ft.). Figure on 5 hours of rigorous hiking to complete the round-trip walk.

The caldera itself is some 120m (390 ft.) from its rim to the crater floor. Many hikers climb or crawl down into the dormant volcano. However, the trail is steep and slippery, so be careful. At the crater floor is a tiny lake along with volcanic rocks and various vegetation.

Shopping

Basseterre is not a shopping town, but it does offer a growing list of retail stores and dining establishments, including gift shops and duty-free outlets. Items such as paintings, pottery, jewelry, jams, teas, and handmade batik fabrics are local specialties. Visitors browsing the art galleries, antiques dealers, and shops will find locally made items as well as familiar brand names. Many shops are located in one of five malls (Pelican Mall, Shoreline Plaza, TDC Mall, Port Zante, and Palms Arcade); others are scattered across the island and within Basseterre.

Artist **Kate Spencer's Gallery** (www.katedesign.com; ✆ 869/465-7740), out in the country in Mount Pleasant, about 23km (14 miles) away, is worth a visit, as is **Brown Sugar,** on Bay Road in Basseterre (www.mybrownsugar.com; ✆ 869/499-4664), owned and operated by local clothing designer Judith Gumbs. For brand names, head over to the **Polo Company** (✆ 869/466-5282) located on Fort Street in Basseterre; it carries Timberland, Tommy Hilfiger, and Gap for men and women.

At Romney Manor, you'll find **Caribelle Batik** (www.caribellebatikstkitts.com; ✆ 869/465-6253), one of the island's most popular boutiques for Indonesian-style, hand-printed, brightly colored clothes. The Brimstone Hill excursion and the rainforest hike typically include a stop here. If you're coming on your own, look for signs indicating a turnoff along the coast road, about 8km (5 miles) north of Basseterre in the town of Old Road.

Beaches

Most visitors to St. Kitts are primarily concerned with its beaches. The narrow peninsula in the southeast contains the island's salt ponds and also boasts the best white-sand beaches (approach via the winding, hilly road for a dramatic and gorgeous view). All beaches, even those that border hotels, are free and open to the public. However, you must usually pay a fee to use a hotel's beach facilities.

Until the Dr. Kennedy Simmonds Highway (named for the nation's first prime minister) opened in 1989, it was necessary to take a boat to enjoy the beautiful, unspoiled beaches of the southeast peninsula. To travel this road is one of the pleasures of a visit to St. Kitts. Not only will you see some of the island's most beautiful scenery, but you'll also pass lagoonlike coves and fields of tall guinea grass. If the day is clear (and it usually is), you'll have a panoramic vista of Nevis.

You'll find the best swimming at **Conaree Beach,** 5km (3 miles) from Basseterre; **Frigate Bay,** with its talcum-powder-fine sand; and the twin beaches of **Banana Bay** and **Cockleshell Bay,** at the southeast corner of the island. If you're lucky, the green vervet monkeys may come down from the hillside behind the beach to say hello as well. Food and drink are available. (**Beware:** The monkeys have been known to steal drinks from unsuspecting tourists.)

The beaches in the north of St. Kitts are numerous but are of gray volcanic sand and much less frequented than those of the southeast peninsula. Beachcombers like to visit them, and they can be ideal for sunbathing, but swimming is much better in the southeast, as waters in the north are often turbulent. Bodysurfing is popular here. **Dieppe Bay,** another black-sand beach on the north coast, is good for snorkeling and windsurfing but not for swimming. **Warning:** If you should be on this beach during a tropical shower, do not seek shelter under the dreaded manchineel trees, which have rounded leaves and small green fruit. They are poisonous—rain falling off the leaves will feel like acid on your skin.

Sports

GOLF The **Royal St. Kitts Golf Club** (www.royalstkittsgolfclub.com; © 869/466-2700) is less than a 10-minute drive from the cruise port. Greens fees at the recently remodeled championship golf course are $180 for 18 holes and $130 for 9 holes during high season (cart rental included); rates are cheaper May through October. A cab from the cruise terminal will cost you about $20 for up to four people.

HORSEBACK RIDING **Trinity Stables** (www.trinityinnapartments.com; © 869/465-3226) charges $60 for a half-day tour through a rainforest. Or you may get to see the wild lushness of the North Frigate Bay area and the rather desolate Conaree Beach on the beach ride for $50. You must call for a reservation; you'll then be told where to meet and offered advice, including what to wear.

SCUBA DIVING & SNORKELING Practically unknown as a dive destination, the waters surrounding St. Kitts boast plentiful and virtually untouched coral reefs, shoals, hot water vents, shallows, sloping canyons, walls, and swim-through caverns that are all home to colorful marine life at depths of 12 to 60m (40–200 ft.). One recently discovered and excavated dive site is located at **White House Bay,** where the wreck of a 1740s English troopship rests.

One of the best diving spots is **Nag's Head,** at the southern tip of St. Kitts. This is an excellent shallow-water dive for certified divers, starting at 3m (10 ft.) and extending to 20m (70 ft.). You'll see a variety of tropical fish, eagle rays, and lobster here. Another good site is **Booby Shoals,** between Cow 'n' Calf Rocks and Booby Island. Booby Shoals has abundant sea life, including nurse sharks, lobster, and stingrays. Dives here are up to 9m (30 ft.) in depth and are good for both certified and beginning divers.

Local dive operators include **Dive St. Kitts,** at Bird Rock Beach Hotel (www.divestkitts.com; © 869/465-1189), **Pro Divers,** at Fisherman's Wharf (www.prodiversstkitts.com; © 869/466-3483), and **Kenneth's Dive Center** in Basseterre (www.kennethsdivecenter.com; © 869/465-2670). Single- or two-tank dives depart from the Port Zante dock at 9am and return by 1pm. Two-tank dives with equipment run about $105; snorkeling excursions, $45.

Great Local Restaurants & Bars

The favorite local beer is **Carib,** brewed right on the northern edge of Basseterre. There's a local sugarcane drink called **CSR (Cane Spirit Rothschild)** that tastes a bit like Brazilian *cachaça,* but with a slight licorice flavor, and is usually mixed with the Jamaican grapefruit soda **Ting** or with the locally produced **Brinley Gold Vanilla Rum** (also available in coffee, lime, coconut, and mango flavors; look for the Brinley Rum shop at the port, or visit **www.brinleygoldrum.com**). Sometimes the local rum is too strong to bring on a plane, so be prepared to drink it before you go home if that is the case!

For kicking back on the beach, **Island Oasis** sports bar at the start of Frigate Bay Strip is a big draw for those who want to catch a cricket match or other sporting event on a big-screen TV. The Kittitians are passionate about their national pastime and eager to introduce the sport to newcomers.

For some of the best baby back ribs in town, head to **Ballahoo Restaurant** (www.ballahoo.com; © 869/465-4197), located at Basseterre's most picturesque intersection (the Circus, right by the cruise dock). Seafood platters, such as garlic shrimp, curried conch, or fresh lobster, are served with salad and rice. The conch chowder goes fast so arrive early to get your fill! Lunch ranges from $10 up to $35.

There are also a number of pastry shops nearby, or you can try the *roti* and other local favorites at **Excelsior Restaurant** on New Street (© 869/465-6693). Lunch will cost about $15. In Fortlands, on Wigley Avenue, **Serendipity** (www.serendipitystkitts.com; © 869/465-9999) has a patio overlooking Basseterre, the Caribbean Sea, and Nevis beyond. Lunch will cost about $20.

ST. LUCIA

With a turbulent history shared by many of its Caribbean neighbors, St. Lucia (pronounced *Loo*-sha), second largest of the Windward Islands at about 622 sq. km (240 sq. miles), changed hands often during the Colonial period—it was British seven times and French seven times. Today, though, it's an independent state that's become one of the most popular destinations in the Caribbean, with some of the finest resorts. The heaviest development is concentrated in the northwest, between the capital of Castries and the northern end of the island, where there's a string of white-sand beaches. The interior boasts relatively unspoiled green-mantled mountains and gentle valleys, as well as the volcanic **Soufrière.** Two dramatic peaks, the **Pitons,** rise along the southwest coast.

Castries, the capital, is a large harbor surrounded by hills. Because of fires that devastated many of its older structures, the town today has touches of modernity, with glass-and-concrete buildings, although there's still an old-fashioned Saturday-morning market on Jeremie Street. The country women dress in traditional cotton headdress to sell their luscious fruits and vegetables, while weather-beaten men sit close by playing warrie (a fast game played with pebbles on a carved board) or dominoes using tiles the color of cherries.

COMING ASHORE   Most cruise ships arrive at a fairly new pier at **Pointe Seraphine,** within walking distance of the center of Castries. Unlike piers on other

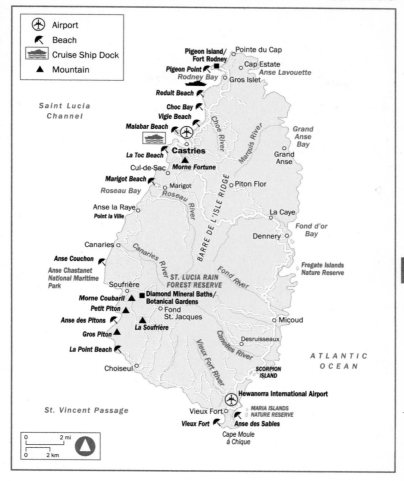

Legend:
- ✈ Airport
- 🏖 Beach
- 🚢 Cruise Ship Dock
- ▲ Mountain

Saint Lucia Channel

Pigeon Island/ Fort Rodney
Pointe du Cap
Pigeon Point
Cap Estate
Anse Lavouette
Rodney Bay
Gros Islet
Reduit Beach
Choc Bay
Vigie Beach
Choc River
Marquis River
Grand Anse Bay
Malabar Beach
Castries
La Toc Beach
Grand Anse
Cul-de-Sac
Morne Fortune
Marigot Beach
Marigot
Piton Flor
Roseau Bay
Roseau River
BARRE DE L'ISLE RIDGE
Anse la Raye
Point la Ville
La Caye
Canaries
Canaries River
Fond d'or Bay
Dennery
Anse Couchon
Fond River
Anse Chastanet National Maritime Park
ST. LUCIA RAIN FOREST RESERVE
Fregate Islands Nature Reserve
Soufrière
Morne Coubaril ▲
Diamond Mineral Baths/ Botanical Gardens
Petit Piton ▲
Fond St. Jacques
Anse des Pitons
Micoud
Gros Piton ▲
La Soufrière
Desruisseaux
La Point Beach
Vieux Fort River
Canelles River
ATLANTIC OCEAN
Choiseul
SCORPION ISLAND
St. Vincent Passage
Hewanorra International Airport
Vieux Fort
MARIA ISLANDS NATURE RESERVE
Vieux Fort
Anse des Sables
Cape Moule á Chique

0   2 mi
0   2 km

islands, this one boasts St. Lucia's best shopping. You'll also find a visitor information bureau. Phone cards are sold for use at specially labeled phones.

If Pointe Seraphine is too crowded (not too likely, as two megaships can pull alongside at once), your ship might dock at **Port Castries,** on the other side of the colorful harbor. There's a shopping terminal here called La Place Carenage, with duty-free stores and telephones.

Some smaller vessels, such as Star Clippers', Seabourn's, and Clipper's, anchor off **Rodney Bay** to the north or **Soufrière** to the south and carry you ashore by tender.

LANGUAGE   English is the official language, but most locals also speak Creole.

CURRENCY   The official monetary unit is the **East Caribbean dollar** (EC$2.70 = US$1; EC$1 = US37¢). Prices quoted in this section are in U.S. dollars, which are accepted by nearly all hotels, restaurants, and shops.

INFORMATION   The **St. Lucia Tourist Board** is at Vide Bouteille, outside Castries (✆ 758/452-4094). The board runs a visitor information bureau at Pointe Seraphine, which is open Monday through Friday from 9am to 5pm. For info before you go, check out **www.stlucianow.com** or call the U.S. office at ✆ **800/456-3984** or 212/867-2950.

CALLING FROM THE U.S.   When calling St. Lucia from the United States, you need only dial a "1" before the numbers listed here. It is not necessary to dial "1" when calling from a cellular telephone.

Getting Around

BY TAXI   Most taxi drivers have been trained to serve as guides. Their cars are unmetered, but the government fixes tariffs for all standard trips. Be sure to determine whether the driver is quoting a rate in U.S. or Eastern Caribbean dollars. There is an official taxi association servicing both Pointe Seraphine and La Place Carenage; this association will have standard fares posted. You can also hire a taxi to go to Soufrière on your own: A 3- to 4-hour tour for four passengers will cost about $150, including a beach stop, photo ops, shopping, and sightseeing. From Castries, the fare to Marigot Bay should be $35 to $40. To Rodney Bay, the fare is $25 to $32 one-way. For more information, call **Holiday Taxi** (✆ **758/452-6067**) or the **Taxi Association** (✆ **758/454-6136**).

BY RENTAL CAR   Driving is on the left, and roads are decent (but not great). The roads are narrow and not always clearly marked. I wouldn't recommend renting a car, but if you're set on it, **Avis** (www.avis.com; ✆ **800/332-1818**), **Budget** (www.budget.com; ✆ **758/452-9887**), and **Hertz** (www.hertz.com; ✆ **800/654-3001**) all have offices here, as does **Courtesy Rent-A-Car** (✆ **758/452-8140**). Avis's rates begin at $83 per day, and Hertz's begin at $78 per day. You can sometimes save money by booking through one of the local car-rental agencies, where rates begin at $68 per day, depending on size. **Cool Breeze Car Rental,** New Development, Soufrière (✆ **758/459-7729**), is a good bet if you're docked in the south. Prices are $70 and up. Expect to pay more if you want A/C and an automatic transmission.

Drive carefully and honk your horn while going around the blind hairpin turns. You'll need a St. Lucia driver's license ($15), which you can purchase at the office when you pick up your rental car.

BY BUS   **Minibuses** (with such names as "Lucian Love") and **jitneys** connect Castries with main towns such as Soufrière. They're cheap (about $2–$3), but they're generally overcrowded and often filled with produce on its way to market. Buses for Cap Estate, in the northern part of the island, leave from Jeremy Street in Castries, near the market. Buses going to Vieux Fort and Soufrière depart from Bridge Street in front of the department store.

BY HELICOPTER   In addition to providing the fastest mode of transport on this island (preferred by such visitors as Harrison Ford), **St. Lucia Helicopters** (www.stluciahelicopters.com; ✆ **758/453-6950**) offers the island's most dramatic sightseeing. The 10-minute "North Trip," costing $85 per person, flies you over Castries, the major resort hotels, the elegant Cap Estate homes, Pigeon Point, Rodney Bay, Rat Island, and the more turbulent Atlantic coast. The longer 20-minute "South Tour," costing $140 per passenger, flies over Castries, the banana plantations, beautiful Marigot Bay, fishing villages, the lush rainforest, the Pitons, the Soufrière volcano, and even remote waterfalls, rivers, and lush valleys. A tour combining both the north and the south costs $175 per person.

Best Cruise Line Shore Excursions

Because of the difficult terrain, shore excursions are the best way to see this beautiful island in a day or less. In addition to the sampling below, most ships typically offer bus tours (many visiting the island's banana plantations) and snorkeling cruises.

Pigeon Island Sea Kayaking ($69, 3 hr.): After transferring to Rodney Bay, you'll make the approximately 30-minute paddle out to the island, where you'll have time to swim, kayak some more, or make the steep climb up to Fort Rodney. From the summit of the fort, you'll have great views of the Pitons, and if you're lucky you'll even be able to see Martinique. (See below for more info.)

Rainforest Bicycle Adventure ($60, 4½ hr.): After being dropped off by bus in the middle of the forest, you'll ride past banana plantations and the Errard Falls waterfall, stopping to sample various fruits that grow along the roadside. Some time for swimming is usually included at the falls.

Jungle Biking ($104, 4½ hr.): This tour takes you by boat to the Jungle Biking facility, located on an 18th-century sugar plantation within the Anse Chastenet Resort. Here you can explore 19km (12 miles) of trails at your own pace. Beach time is included at the end.

Soody Nature Hike & Mineral Waterfall ($49, 4 hr.): Drive along the west coast through fishing villages, banana plantations, and the edge of the rainforest before arriving at Soufrière, location of the Pitons and the Diamond Botanical Gardens. A guided hour-long hike through the volcanic forest introduces you to the island's flora and fauna; it ends up at a therapeutic sulfuric waterfall where you can take a dip to cure what ails you.

Beach Snorkel ($70, 3½ hr.): Snorkeling is spectacular around St. Lucia. This trip departs the Castries harbor by boat, traveling an hour en route to the island's marine reserve, which has an area set aside especially for snorkeling. There's also a supersize 7-hour ($119) version of this trip that includes a buffet lunch.

Excursions Offered by Local Agencies

Horseback Treks: North of Castries, **Trim's National Riding Stables** (©758/450-8273) offers picnic trips to the Atlantic side of the island, with a barbecue lunch and drinks included. Departure is at 10am. The fee is $85 for a 2-hour ride.

On Your Own: Within Walking Distance

Castries has a very colorful **Central Market,** right near the dock, which is worth a visit. The airplane hangar–size emporium sells local food, trinkets, and produce. Buy some banana ketchup or local cinnamon sticks to take home.

The principal streets of Castries are William Peter Boulevard and Bridge Street. Don't miss a walk through town: People are very friendly, and **Jeremie Street** is chockablock with variety stores of the most authentic local kind, selling everything from spices to housewares.

A Roman Catholic cathedral stands on **Columbus Square,** which has a few restored buildings. Take a gander at the enormous 400-year-old "rain" tree, also called a "no-name" tree, which grows in the Derek Walcott Square, named after the St. Lucian Nobel Prize winner for literature. The nearby Government House is a late Victorian structure.

Beyond Government House lies **Morne Fortune,** which means "Hill of Good Luck." Actually, no one's had much luck here, certainly not the French and British soldiers who battled for Fort Charlotte. The fort switched nationalities (from French to English, and vice versa) many times. You can visit the 18th-century barracks, complete with a military cemetery, a small museum, the Old Powder Magazine, and the Four Apostles Battery—four grim, muzzle-loading cannons. The view of the harbor of Castries is panoramic from this point. You can also see north to Pigeon Island or south to the Pitons. To reach Morne Fortune, head east on Bridge Street.

On Your Own: Beyond the Port Area

Bananas are St. Lucia's leading export, so if you're being taken around the island by a taxi driver, ask him to stop at one of the huge plantations. Most island tours include a drive through one of the plantations as a matter of course. We suggest a look at one of the three biggest: the **Cul-de-Sac,** just north of Marigot Bay; **La Caye,** on the east coast in Dennery; or the **Roseau Estate,** south of Marigot Bay.

An ideal spot for picnics and nature walks is St. Lucia's first national park, **Pigeon Island National Landmark** (www.slunatrust.org; ✆ **758/452-5005**). It was originally an island but is now joined to the northwest shore of the mainland by a very environmentally unfriendly causeway that has disrupted offshore currents, thereby upsetting the local fishing industry. The 18-hectare (45-acre) island got its name from the red-neck pigeon, or ramier, which once made this island home. The best way to get to Pigeon Island National Landmark is to take a taxi and arrange to be picked up in time to return to your ship (the trip is 30 min., at most, back to the docks). Some small ships anchor here and bring passengers ashore by tender. Hours are daily from 8:30am to 5pm; admission is $7.50 for adults, $2 for children 6 to 12.

The island's **Interpretation Centre** contains artifacts and a multimedia display of local history, covering everything from the Amerindian settlers of A.D. 1000 to 1782's Battle of Saints, when Admiral Rodney's fleet set out from Pigeon Island and defeated the French admiral De Grasse. Right below the interpretation center is a cozy pub called the **Captain's Cellar** (www.captainscellarpub.com; ✆ **758/450-0253**), located in what was formerly a soldier's mess. From the tables outside, you get views of the crashing surf on the Atlantic coast, just a few steps away. From the center, you can walk up the winding and moderately steep path to a lookout from which you can see Martinique.

Pigeon Island's west coast has two white-sand beaches. There's also a restaurant, **Jambe de Bois** (Leg of Wood; ✆ **758/452-0321**), named after a peg-legged pirate who once used the island as a hideout.

Soufrière, a fishing port and St. Lucia's second-largest settlement, is dominated by the dramatic Pitons, Petit Piton and Gros Piton. These two pointed peaks rise right from the sea to 740m and 785m (2,420 ft. and 2,580 ft.), respectively. Formed by lava and once actively volcanic, these mountains are now cloaked in green vegetation, with waves crashing around their bases. Their sheer rise from the water makes them such visible landmarks that they've become the very symbol of St. Lucia.

Near the town of Soufrière lies the famous "drive-in" volcano, **La Soufrière,** a rocky lunar landscape of bubbling mud and craters seething with fuming sulfur. You can literally drive into an old crater and walk between the sulfur springs and pools of hissing steam. The fumes are said to have medicinal properties. A local guide is usually waiting nearby; if you do hire a guide, agree—then doubly agree—on what the fee will be.

Nearby are the **Diamond Mineral Baths** (www.diamondstlucia.com; © 758/459-7155), surrounded by a tropical arboretum. They were constructed in 1784 by order of Louis XVI, whose doctors told him that these waters were similar in mineral content to the waters at Aix-les-Bains. The baths were built to help French soldiers who had been fighting in the West Indies recuperate from wounds and disease. Later destroyed, they were rebuilt after World War II. The water's average temperature is 106°F (41°C). You'll also find another fine attraction here: a waterfall that changes colors (from yellow to black to green to gray) several times a day. Regular admission is $5, but for an extra $6 you can bathe and benefit from the recuperative effects of the baths yourself. It's open daily from 10am to 5pm (Sun until 3pm).

Shopping

Many stores sell duty-free goods and will deliver tobacco products and liquor to the cruise dock. Keep in mind that you are allowed to purchase only one bottle of liquor here (in St. Thomas, you can buy five). You'll find some good, but not remarkable, buys in bone china, jewelry, perfume, watches, liquor, and crystal. Souvenir items include designer bags and mats, local pottery, and straw hats—again, nothing remarkable. *Tip:* If your cruise is also calling in St. Thomas, let the local vendors know; it may make them more amenable to bargaining.

Built for cruise ship passengers, **Pointe Seraphine** has the best collection of shops on the island. You must present your cruise pass when making purchases here. Liquor and tobacco will be delivered to the ship.

Gablewoods Mall, on Gros Islet Highway, 3km (2 miles) north of Castries, has one of the densest concentrations of stores on St. Lucia, along with three restaurants. Because this mall is near some lovely beaches (and near the Sandals St. Lucia Resort), it's possible to plan a day that combines shopping and sunbathing. Another shopping venue is **Rodney Bay Mall,** which is both larger and newer.

At **Caribelle Batik,** Howelton House, Old Victoria Road, the Morne (© 758/452-3785), just a 5-minute taxi ride from Castries, you can watch St. Lucian artists creating intricate patterns and colors through the ancient art of batik, which involves application of removable wax before dyes are applied; the waxed area repels the dye. They also own a sister store, **Sea Island Cotton,** in Rodney Bay Mall.

Eudovic Art Studio, Goodlands, Morne Fortune (© 758/452-2747; eudovicart. com), sells woodcarvings by St. Lucia native Vincent Joseph Eudovic and some of his pupils. Take a taxi from the cruise pier.

Southwest of Soufrière, just past the small village of Choiseul, **Choiseul Craft Centre,** La Fargue (www.choiseulstlucia.com; © 758/454-3226), is a government-funded retail outlet and training school that perpetuates the tradition of handmade Amerindian pottery and basket ware. Some of the best basket weaving on the island is done here, using techniques practiced only in St. Lucia, St. Vincent, and Dominica. Look for place mats, handbags, woodcarvings (including bas-reliefs crafted from screw pine), and pottery. The center is open Monday through Friday from 8:30am to 4:30pm.

Beaches

If you don't take a shore excursion, you might want to spend your time on one of St. Lucia's famous beaches, all of which are open to the public, even those at hotel properties (but you must pay to use a hotel's beach equipment). Taxis can take you to any of the island's beaches, but I recommend that you stick to the calmer shores along the western coast, as the rough surf on the windward Atlantic side makes swimming potentially dangerous.

Leading beaches include **Pigeon Island,** off the northern shore, with white sand and picnic facilities; **Vigie Beach,** north of Castries, with fine sand; **Marigot Beach,** south of Castries, framed on three sides by steep emerald hills and skirted by palm trees; and **Reduit Beach,** between Choc Bay and Pigeon Point, with fine brown sand. Just north of Soufrière is a beach connoisseur's delight, **Anse Chastanet** (www.ansechastanet.com; ✆ **758/459-7000**), boasting an expanse of white sand at the foothills of lush green mountains. This is a fantastic spot for snorkeling. **Choc Bay** is a long stretch of sand and palm trees on the northwestern coast, convenient to Castries and the big resorts. Its tranquil waters lure swimmers and especially families (including locals) with small children. The 3km (2-mile) white-sand **Malabar Beach** runs parallel to the George F. L. Charles Airport runway, in Castries, to the Rendezvous resort. The dramatic crescent-shaped bay of **Anse des Pitons** is at the foot of and between the twin peaks of the Pitons, south of Soufrière. The Jalousie Plantation transformed the natural black-sand beach by covering it with white sand; you walk through the resort to get to it. It's popular with divers and snorkelers. While here, you can ask about a very special beach reached only by boat: the black volcanic sands and tranquil waters of **Anse Couchon.** With its shallow reefs, excellent snorkeling, and picture-postcard charm, this beach has become a hideaway for lovers. It's south of Anse-le-Raye.

You'll find miles of white sand at the beach at **Vieux Fort,** at the southern end of the island. Reefs protect the aqua blue waters here, rendering them tranquil and ideal for swimming. At the southern end of the windward side of the island is **Anse des Sables,** which opens onto a shallow bay swept by trade winds that are great for windsurfing.

Sports

BOATING   The most dramatic trip offered is aboard the 138-foot brig *Unicorn* (www.seaspraycruises.com; ✆ **758/452-8644**), used in the filming of the three *Pirates of the Caribbean* films and the TV miniseries *Roots*. Passengers sail from Rodney Bay in Castries to Soufrière and the twin peaks of the Pitons. A full-day sail costs $110 for adults, $50 for children ages 2 to 12.

DEEP-SEA FISHING   The waters around St. Lucia are known for their game fish, including blue marlin, sailfish, mako sharks, and barracuda, with tuna and kingfish among the edible catches. Most hotels can arrange fishing expeditions. Call **Mako Watersports** (✆ **758/452-0412**), which offers half-day fishing trips from $600 or full-day trips from $1,100. Excursions start at $100 per person. **Captain Mike's** (www.captmikes.com; ✆ **758/452-7044**) also conducts fishing trips, renting boats by the half-day for $550 or a whole day in the $800-to-$1,000 price range. Scheduled fishing tours will run you only $85 per day, or for the nonfisherman there is a $45 whale-watch tour.

GOLF   St. Lucia has an 18-hole golf course (6,815 yards, par 71) at the **St. Lucia's Golf and Country Club,** Cap Estate, at the northern end of the island (www.stluciagolf.com; ✆ **758/450-9905**). Greens fees are $145 for 18 holes, $105 for 9 holes. There are no caddies, but carts are included, and Callaway clubs can be rented for $50. Hours are daily from 7am to 6pm. Reservations are needed.

HIKING   A tropical rainforest covers a large area in the southern half of St. Lucia, and the St. Lucia Forest and Lands Department manages it wisely. This forest reserve divides the western and eastern halves of the island. There are several trails, the most popular of which is the **Barre de l'Isle Trail,** located almost in the center of St. Lucia, southeast of Marigot Bay; it's a fairly easy trail that even children can handle. There are four panoramic lookout points with dramatic views of the sea where the Atlantic and the Caribbean meet. It takes about an hour to walk this 2km-long (1.25-mile) trail, which lies about a 30-minute ride from Castries. Guided hikes can usually be arranged through the major hotels or through the **Forestry Department Tour Guide Office** (⌀ 758/468-5645 or 758/468-5648). Tours cost $10 per person or $5 for children ages 2 through 12, and range in length.

SCUBA DIVING   In Soufrière, **Scuba St. Lucia** (www.scubastlucia.com; ⌀ 758/459-7755), located in the **Anse Chastanet Resort** (⌀ 758/459-7000), is a five-star PADI dive center offering great diving and comprehensive facilities. The resort is at the southern end of Anse Chastanet's .4km (¼-mile) secluded beach. Some of St. Lucia's most spectacular coral reefs—many only 3 to 6m (10–20 ft.) below the surface—provide shelter for sea creatures just a short distance offshore. Many PADI instructors offer five dive programs a day. Experienced divers can rent any equipment they need. A 2- to 3-hour introductory lesson costs $115 and includes a short theory session, equipment familiarization, development of skills in shallow water, a tour of the reef, and all equipment. Single dives cost $45 with equipment, and for the photographer in you, Reefmaster digital cameras rent for $35. Hours are from 8am to 6pm daily.

Another full-service scuba center is available on St. Lucia's southwest coast at the **Jalousie Plantation,** at Soufrière (www.jalousieplantation.com; ⌀ 758/456-8000). The PADI center offers dives in St. Lucia's National Marine Park; there are numerous shallow reefs near the shore. The diver certification program is available to hotel guests and other day visitors ages 12 and up. Prices for a single dive start at $85. There's a daily resort course for noncertified divers, which includes a supervised dive from the beach and costs $90. All prices include equipment, tax, and service charges.

WATERSPORTS   The best all-around watersports center is **St. Lucian Watersports,** at the Rex St. Lucian Hotel (⌀ 758/452-8351). For those with fantasies of retro-1950s beach fun, try water-skiing. A lesson starts at $45, or a 10- to 15-minute ride runs $20 for those more experienced (about three rounds, depending on how good you are). Snorkeling is free for guests of the hotel; nonguests pay $10 per hour for equipment.

Great Local Restaurants & Bars

A really, really great local beer is **Piton**—very refreshing on a hot day, like Corona but better. A favorite local rum is **Bounty.**

IN RODNEY BAY   Chef Jacky Rioux, of **Jacques Waterfront Dining** (www.jacquesrestaurant.com; ⌀ 758/458-1900), has traveled the world, picking up ideas for a fusion cuisine that combines market-fresh ingredients with French cooking methods. Lunch is about $60.

AT MARIGOT BAY   **Doolittle's,** at the Marigot Beach Club (www.marigotbeachclub.com; ⌀ 758/451-4974), showcases Caribbean and international dishes. To reach the place, you'll have to take a ferryboat across Marigot Bay. The ferry runs to and from the Moorings Marigot Bay Resort about every 10 minutes throughout the day and evening. Lunch is about $40.

Just down the road is **J.J.'s Paradise** (www.jj-paradise.com; © 758/451-4076). Chef/owner Gerard (J.J.) Felix is one of the island's best cooks and most welcoming hosts. In lush foliage, the restaurant frames the edge of Marigot Bay. The fish and seafood are freshly caught and seasoned with locally grown herbs and fruits from island gardens.

IN THE SOUFRIÈRE AREA   **Dasheene Restaurant & Bar,** in the Ladera Resort (www.ladera.com; © 758/459-7323), serves the most creative cuisine in St. Lucia. Your best bet is the catch of the day, likely to be kingfish or red snapper, grilled to perfection. The menu changes often but some winners are the dumpling-and-callaloo soup, the fresh pumpkin risotto with red-pepper coulis, and the banana-stuffed pork with ginger-and-coconut sauce. The restaurant is perched atop a 300m (1,000-ft.) ridge and is framed by the rising twin peaks of the Pitons. Everything is locally produced, including the furniture. Lunch is about $25.

Lifeline Restaurant (© 758/459-7232) is the best part of the Hummingbird Beach Resort complex. Tables are set on a stylish veranda adjacent to the sands of Hummingbird Beach. The cuisine focuses on such West Indian dishes as Creole-style conch, lobster, burgers, steaks, and filets of both snapper and grouper, punctuated with such American staples as burgers and BLTs. A tiny gift shop on the premises sells batik items crafted by staff members. Lunch is about $24.

The **Edge Restaurant,** in the Harmony Marina Suites, Rodney Bay Lagoon (www.edge-restaurant.com; © 758/450-3343), is a new sushi bar and restaurant owned and operated by celebrated chef Bobo Bergstrom. In addition to an intriguing fusion of European and Caribbean cuisine, with a touch of Asian flavor, the Edge offers indoor/outdoor dining with a view of the boats moored at the nearby marina. Lunch will cost about $50.

ST. MARTIN/SINT MAARTEN

Who can resist a two-for-one sale? On the island of St. Martin/Sint Maarten, you get two cultures, two nationalities, and two different experiences for the price of one. Occupying the bend where the Lesser and Greater Antilles meet, about 240km (150 miles) southeast of Puerto Rico, this is the smallest territory in the world that is shared by two sovereign states: France, with 52 sq. km (20 sq. miles), and the Netherlands, with 44 sq. km (17 sq. miles). On February 22, 2007, the French side was officially detached from Guadeloupe and became a separate French overseas collectivity with its own local administration. The two nations have shared the island in a spirit of neighborly cooperation and mutual friendship for more than 350 years. Although the border between the two sides is virtually imperceptible—a monument along the road marks the change in administration—each side retains elements of its own heritage. The French side, with some of the best beaches and restaurants in the Caribbean, emphasizes quiet elegance. French fashions and luxury items fill the shops, and the fragrance of croissants mixes with the spicy aromas of West Indian cooking. The Dutch side, officially known as Sint Maarten, reflects Holland's anything-goes philosophy: Development is much more widespread, flashy casinos pepper the landscape, and strip malls make the larger towns look as much like Anaheim as Amsterdam. The 100% duty-free shopping has turned both sides of the island into a bargain-hunter's paradise.

St. Martin's first inhabitants, the Stone Age hunter-gatherer Ciboneys, arrived as early as 1800 B.C. The first Dutch and French colonists arrived in the early 17th

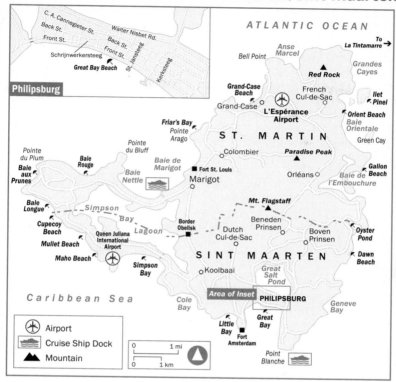

century, and exchanged some martial rumblings before deciding, in 1648, to just get along, splitting the island roughly in two. Coffee, sugar, rum, and salt brought relative prosperity to the island, but not to the slaves brought over from Africa. Tourism supplanted agriculture as the major industry in the last half of the 20th century.

Today, the Dutch side holds a slight population edge: 37,850 people to the French side's 37,000. Most locals are descendants of African slaves, but residents born in France, Holland, and the U.S. occupy many of the villas and condominiums around the island.

COMING ASHORE   Most cruise ships dock on the Dutch side, at **A. C. Wathey Pier,** about 1.5km (1 mile) southeast of Philipsburg. Many passengers take water taxis (which cost about $10 round-trip) to the smaller **Captain Hodge Pier,** at the center of town, but others choose to take regular taxis or walk the distance on a newly renovated boardwalk. The Wathey Pier has credit card phones, cafes and bars, and a shopping area. For its part, Hodge Pier offers access to phones, tourist information, and taxis.

Smaller vessels sometimes dock on the French side of the island, at **Marina Port la Royale,** adjacent to the heart of Marigot. The waterfront here features restaurants, shopping arcades, and a tourist office. The pier accommodates only one ship at a time, so passengers on subsequently arriving vessels are tendered ashore.

LANGUAGE   Surprise, surprise: The official language on the Dutch side is Dutch, and the official language on the French side is French. Most people on both sides also speak English. Among locals on the street, a patois is often spoken: Papiamento on the Dutch side, Creole on the French.

CURRENCY   The legal tender in Dutch St. Martin is the **Netherlands Antilles florin,** also called the **guilder** (1.79 ANG = US$1; 1 ANG = US56¢), while the official currency on the French side is the **euro** (.75€ = US$1; 1€ = US$1.32). U.S. dollars are widely accepted on both sides, though, so there's no need to change money. Most prices are quoted in U.S. dollars too, so you're spared the work of calculating exchange rates. Credit cards and traveler's checks are also readily accepted. ATMs abound in both Philipsburg and Marigot. Prices in this chapter are given in U.S. dollars.

INFORMATION   On the Dutch side, the **St. Maarten Tourist Bureau,** Vineyard Office Park, W. G. Buncamper Road 33, Philipsburg (http://en.vacationstmaarten.com; ℭ 721/549-02300), is open Monday through Friday from 8am to 5pm. There's a smaller but more conveniently located satellite office at the town pier. For information before you go, go to www.st-maarten.com or call ℭ **800/786-2278.**

On the French side, the **St. Martin Tourist Office,** adjacent to the pier at Marina Royale in Marigot (ℭ 590/87-57-21), is open Monday through Friday from 9am to 5pm. For advance info, go to www.iledesaintmartin.org or call ℭ **212/745-0945.**

CALLING FROM THE U.S.   When calling Dutch St. Maarten from the United States, simply dial the international access number (121) before the numbers listed here. Calling French St. Martin requires more of an effort: Dial 011, then 590 before the numbers listed. Yes, 590 appears in our listed numbers, but those three digits must be dialed twice to make a connection.

Getting Around

BY TAXI   Taxis on both sides of the island are unmetered. Agree on a rate and currency before getting in. Dutch law requires that drivers list government-regulated fares, which assume two passengers (each additional passenger is another $8). Shorter rides, including the route between Marigot and Philipsburg, average around $18; longer trips can climb to $25-plus. Drivers, who greet cruisers in both Philipsburg and Marigot, expect at least a $1 tip for short runs, more for extended 2-hour sightseeing trips around the island. To call a taxi on the Dutch side, dial ℭ **721/545-4317.** On the French side, dial ℭ **590/87-56-54.**

BY MINIVAN   Privately owned and operated minivans are a reasonable way to get around, if you don't mind frequent stops, potential overcrowding, and the local zouk and soca music that's usually playing (a plus or a minus, depending on your tastes). These jitneys run daily from 7am to midnight and serve much of the island. The most popular run, between Philipsburg and Marigot, has almost constant service. Fares range from about $2 to $5. The vans, which have signs to indicate their destination, can be hailed anywhere on the street.

BY RENTAL CAR   Rental cars are a great way to make the most of your day and see both sides of the island. Driving is on the right side, roads are generally in decent shape, and signage is in either international symbols or English. Parking can be a headache in both Philipsburg and Marigot, and road construction and drawbridges sometimes exacerbate congestion. Away from the two main towns, however, zipping along is a breeze. **Avis, Budget,** and **Hertz** all have offices here.

Best Cruise Line Shore Excursions

America's Cup Sailing Regatta ($109, 3 hr.): Get a taste of nautical exhilaration by competing in a race aboard an America's Cup–winning sailboat. This hands-on, extremely popular excursion lets you grind winches, trim sails, and duck under booms—after professionals have trained you, of course. Alternatively, sit back and watch others do all the work.

Ilet Pinel Snorkeling Tour ($45, 3½ hr.): After a scenic bus ride to the French town of Cul-de-Sac, along the northeast coast, hop on a tender to the small offshore island of Ilet Pinel for some of St. Martin's best snorkeling.

Hidden Forest Hike ($85, 4 hr.): You'll take a 45-minute drive to Loterie Farm, where you'll do a 2-hour hike through the tropical forest, eventually emerging at Pic Paradise, the island's highest point. Along the way, your guide will point out a secret freshwater spring and the island's famous guavaberry trees. Return to Loterie for a complimentary rum or fruit punch and a typical Caribbean farmhouse lunch.

Butterfly Farm & Marigot ($49, 3½ hr.): After a scenic drive through both the French and the Dutch sides of the island, walk through a surrealistic enclosed garden that features hundreds of exquisitely beautiful and exotic butterflies from around the world. Amusing guides identify species, describe courtship and mating rituals, and give tips on attracting butterflies to your garden at home. Afterward, absorb the Creole charm and French atmosphere of Marigot.

Excursions Offered by Local Agencies

Horseback Treks: The **Bayside Riding Club,** Coconut Grove, next to the Butterfly Farm (© **590/87-36-64**), offers 1½-hour riding expeditions through the Nature Marine Reserve that conclude on an isolated beach, where horses and riders enjoy a cool postride romp in the water. The price of $95 per person includes a complimentary drink at a bar on the beach. Half-hour pony rides with a handler, for the little ones, are $35. Riders of all experience levels are welcome.

Mountain-Biking Tours: On the Dutch side, **TriSport,** in Simpson Bay (www.trisportsxm.com; © **721/545-4384**), offers 2½- to 3-hour tours of varying difficulty for $49 per person. It also arranges kayaking, hiking, and snorkeling trips.

Scuba Diving: Of the island's 40 dive sites, the 1801 British man-of-war HMS *Proselyte,* which sank to a watery grave on a reef 1.5km (1 mile) off the coast, is the most popular. Other favorites include Ilet Pinel, for shallow diving; the Green Key barrier reef; and Flat Island, for its sheltered coves and geologic faults. On the Dutch side, Aqua Mania Adventures, Simpson Bay (www.stmaarten-activities.com; © **721/544-2640**), employs some of the most knowledgeable guides on the island. Dives range from $55 to $100. Snorkel tours range from $45 to $85 per person.

On Your Own: Within Walking Distance

Shopping, sunbathing, and gambling are the pastimes that interest most cruisers who hit this island, but folks with a taste for culture and history can make a day of it here as well.

ON THE DUTCH SIDE Directly in front of the Philipsburg town pier, on Wathey Square, the **Courthouse** combines northern European sobriety with Caribbean

One of the best things about St. Martin is that once you're here, it's easy to visit the more serene and unspoiled neighboring islands of Anguilla or St. Barts. To get to **Anguilla,** simply take the *Voyager* ferry, which leaves every 30 minutes from Marigot Bay and arrives on Anguilla just 10 minutes later. You do not need a reservation, but one is recommended. The cost is about $50 round-trip.

Intrepid travelers in search of natural beauty, quiet, and understated glitz may find a trip to **St. Barts** worth the time, money, and potentially queasy stomach.

The *Voyager* to St. Barts (www.voy12. com; *C* **590/87-10-68**) departs from one of two locations on the French side of St. Martin; it takes between 40 minutes and 1½ hours, depending on your departure point, and can be extremely choppy. The round-trip fare is about $90 for adults, $45 for children ages 2 to12. Reservations are recommended. *Note:* The only trip back to St. Martin leaves St. Barts at 4:30pm Monday through Saturday (5:30pm on Sun), so be sure you have ample time to make it back to your ship before it leaves port!

brightness. Originally built in 1793 of freestone and wood, this venerable old building has suffered numerous hurricanes but has been restored after each tempest and continues to house government offices. East of the Courthouse, down a little shopping alley, the tiny **Sint Maarten Museum,** 7 Front St. (www.speetjens.com/museum; *C* **721/542-4917**), features modest, cluttered exhibits that focus on the island's history and geology. Admission is $1, and it is open Monday through Friday from 10am to 4pm, Saturday from 10am to 2pm. The street-level gift shop stocks handicrafts, postcards, and books.

Fort Amsterdam is the Dutch side's most important colonial site. Since 1631, the fort has looked out over Great Bay from the hill west of Philipsburg. The fort was the Netherlands' first military outpost in the Caribbean. The Spanish captured it 2 years later, making it their most significant bastion east of Puerto Rico. Peter Stuyvesant, who later became governor of New Amsterdam (now New York), lost his leg to a cannonball while trying to reclaim the fort for Holland. The site provides grand views of the bay, but ruins of the walls and a couple of rusty cannons are all that remain of the original fort.

ON THE FRENCH SIDE   **Fort St. Louis** is Marigot's answer to Fort Amsterdam. Built in 1767 to protect the waterfront warehouses that stored the French colony's agricultural riches, this bastion frequently fired its cannons on hostile British raiders from Anguilla. After restorations and modification in the 19th century, the fort was eventually abandoned. You'll find cannons, crumbling walls, and a French flag flapping in the breeze. The short climb up the hill flanking Marigot Bay's north end affords splendid vistas. As a respite from the sun, duck into **Marigot's Museum of Saint Martin** (*C* **590/29-22-84**), next to the St. Martin Tourist Office and adjacent to the marina. Much more thorough and scholarly than its Philipsburg counterpart, this institution boasts a first-rate collection of Ciboney, Arawak, and Carib artifacts excavated from the island's Amerindian sites, plus a reproduction of a 1,500-year-old burial mound. Another display details the history of the plantation and slavery era, and early-20th-century photographs trace the island's modern development. The museum is open Monday through Friday from 9am to 4pm, Saturday from 9am to 1pm. Admission is $8 for adults, $3 for children ages 2 to 12.

Shopping

This island is a true free port—no duties are paid on any item coming in or going out—and neither side has a sales tax.

ON THE DUTCH SIDE Shops in the much busier Dutch side are concentrated in **Philipsburg,** along Front Street and, to a lesser extent, Back Street and the numerous alleys radiating from them. The district is largely nondescript, but you'll find all the usual suspects—the omnipresent jewelry and luxury-item shop **Little Switzerland** and a host of other gift shops—as well as some quirky local boutiques. In general, prices in the major stores are nonnegotiable, but at small, family-run shops, you can try your luck with a little polite bargaining. The T-shirt and souvenir epicenter is in the open-air market behind the Courthouse, in front of the town pier.

Guavaberry Emporium, 8–10 Front St., sells Guavaberry "island folk liqueur," an aged rum with a distinctive fruity, woody, almost bittersweet flavor; it's available only on St. Martin. Stop by for a variety of drinks made at their bar and make sure to buy a custom painted bottle to bring home as a souvenir. Try a free sample of the Guavaberry Colada. Parrotheads in search of all things Jimmy Buffett should cross the street to **Last Mango in Paradise,** 17 Front St., for CDs, T-shirts, and more—you name it, they got it. Be sure to bring your camera and take a picture with Shark-man in front of the store.

Walking west, Old Street, off Front Street, features a couple dozen boutiques, including **Colombian Emeralds** and the **Belgian Chocolate Shop.** For cigars, **La Casa del Habano,** 24 Front St., has Cohibas, Montecristos, and the like; **Lipstick,** 31 Front St., is your best bet for perfumes and cosmetics. Next door, **Dutch Delft Blue,** 29 Front St., stocks the distinctive blue-and-white porcelain. Don't miss the adorable clothing shop **C'Est La Vie,** 40 bd. de Grand Case, filled with T-shirts and shorts adorned with their slogan.

ON THE FRENCH SIDE Marigot features a much calmer, more charming and sophisticated ambience, with waterfront cafes where you can rest your weary feet. Many shops here close their doors for a 2-hour lunch break starting at 1pm.

The wide selection of European merchandise is skewed toward an upscale audience, but French crystal, perfume, liqueur, jewelry, and fashion can be up to 50% less expensive than in the States. Be sure to stop by the **West Indies Mall** (www.sxm-shopping.com/westindiesmall) on the Marigot waterfront. Many luxurious boutiques fill the three-story building overlooking the water, including **Lancel, L'Occitane,** and **Diamond Creations,** which sells fine jewelry.

At Marina Port la Royale, **Havane Boutique** offers casual and high-fashion French clothing for women, while **L'Epicerie** stocks caviar, foie gras, and a host of French wines. For chic women's clothing, especially Italian styles, start your search at **Cocolito,** rue de la République. **Goldfinger,** rue de la République, is one of many purveyors of bracelets, necklaces, and watches, while **Beauty & Scents,** rue du Général de Gaulle, has your favorite perfumes and cosmetics.

An inviting open-air crafts market sprawls along the waterfront next to boulevard de France every day, while on Wednesday and Saturday, another open-air market stretches from the base of Fort St. Louis to the wharves below, offering a colorful array of homegrown produce, tropical fruits and spices, and fresh fish. On market days, look for **Fifi's Rum Store,** which offers 20 flavors of rum (and lets you sample them).

Beaches

Beach lovers, rejoice: The island has more than 30 beautiful white-sand beaches, some social, some serene. The busier ones boast bars, restaurants, watersports, and hotels, where changing facilities are usually available for a small fee. Toplessness is ubiquitous; nudism is common on the French side, and increasingly found on the Dutch side as well.

ON THE DUTCH SIDE   **Great Bay Beach** is your best bet if you want to stay in Philipsburg. This 1.5km-long (1-mile) stretch is convenient, but because it borders the busy capital, it lacks the tranquillity and cleanliness of the more remote beaches. The water is calm, though, and all the amenities of Philipsburg are a step away.

Just west of the airport, on the west side of the island, **Maho Beach** boasts a casino, shade palms, and a popular beachside bar and grill. Its biggest attraction, however, seems to be its views of takeoffs and landings (keep your belongings outside the flight path; jumbo jets sometimes blow items into the surf).

Farther west, **Mullet Beach** borders the island's golf course. Shaded by palm trees and crowded on weekends, it's popular with swimmers and snorkelers. On-site vendors rent an array of watersports equipment.

Just around the corner to the west, but miles away mentally, lies perfectly serene **Cupecoy Beach.** Set against a stunningly beautiful backdrop of mysterious caves and sandstone cliffs that provide morning shade, this beach has no facilities, but a vendor at the parking lot rents beach chairs and umbrellas. The clientele is adult: primarily in the buff, quiet, and, not infrequently, gay. The surf can be strong, and aficionados claim that the sun here is more intense than anywhere else on the island.

ON THE FRENCH SIDE   Far and away the island's most visited strand, **Orient Bay,** on the northeast coast, fancies itself the "Saint Tropez of the Caribbean." Hedonism is the name of the game here: plenty of food, drink, music, and flesh (a naturist resort occupies the beach's southern tip, but nudism isn't confined to any one area). Watersports abound.

South of Orient Beach, the waveless waters of **Coconut Grove** or **Galion Beach** are shallow 30m (100 ft.) out. Protected by a coral reef, this area is number one with kids and popular with windsurfers.

On the island's west coast, just north of the Dutch border, **Baie Longue (Long Bay)** is one of the island's longest beaches and another refuge for adults seeking peace and quiet. There are no facilities, but this wild beach bordering some of the island's grandest mansions is popular with the rich and (sometimes) famous. The water and sand here are silky.

Friar's Bay Beach, outside of Marigot, is a quiet sheltered cove at the end of a bumpy road, offering gorgeous views of the neighboring island Anguilla on clear days. This spot is ideal for children as the water is calm. Beach chairs, umbrellas, and food are available on the beach.

Sports

SNORKELING   Tiny coves and calm offshore waters make St. Martin a snorkeler's paradise. **Dawn Beach,** on the Dutch east coast, is one of the best snorkeling sites on the island; rent equipment from vendors near **Mr. Busby's Beach Bar** (© 721/543-6828), which is right on the beach. Also worthy are the Dutch side's **Maho Beach** and the French side's **Baie Rouge** and **Ilet Pinel,** the latter of which can be reached by ferry from Cul-de-Sac (about $5 per person, round-trip). Most hotels and restaurants at these sites rent equipment for about $15.

WATERSPORTS Most of the large hotels on Orient Beach offer an array of watersports adventures, often from makeshift kiosks on the beach. Two independent operators function from side-by-side positions near the Esmeralda Hotel: **Kon Tiki Watersports** (✆ 590/87-46-89) and **Bikini Watersports** (✆ 690/33-33-14 or 590/87-43-25). Jet skis and WaveRunners go for about $60 for 30 minutes, $100 for an hour; parasailing is $50 for a single rider and $90 for a double.

Gambling

Slot machines and game tables can be found in the Dutch side's dozen casinos. Most of the heavy betting takes place after dark, but a handful of casinos open before noon. In the heart of Philipsburg on Front Street, **Coliseum Casino** (✆ 721/543-2101), **Diamond Casino** (www.diamondcasinosxm.com; ✆ 721/543-2565), and **Rouge et Noir** (www.casinorougeetnoir.com; ✆ 721/542-2952) all open at 11am, early enough to snag cruisers.

West of Philipsburg, **Hollywood Casino,** at the Pelican Resort, Simpson Bay (www.casinosxm.com; ✆ 721/544-2503), features a panoramic view of the water and offers craps, roulette, blackjack, stud poker, and slots after 1pm. Farther west, **Casino Royale,** Maho Bay (www.playmaho.com; ✆ 721/545-2590), has roulette, Caribbean stud poker, craps, blackjack, baccarat, minibaccarat, and slots, also after 1pm; and **Atlantis World Casino,** Cupecoy Bay (www.atlantisworld.com; ✆ 721/545-4601), has baccarat, blackjack, craps, poker, roulette, and Texas hold 'em.

Great Local Restaurants & Bars

The indigenous rum liqueur is the fruity and slightly bitter **Guavaberry.** If you are skeptical, be sure to stop by the Guavaberry Emporium (see above) and have the friendly bartenders make you a Guavaberry drink.

ON THE DUTCH SIDE As might be expected, food is usually better on the French side, but Dutch St. Maarten has a number of appealing restaurants, too. You can even enjoy a *très* French dining experience right in Philipsburg at **L'Escargot,** 96 Front St. (www.lescargotrestaurant.com; ✆ 721/542-2483), a bright-yellow house with snails painted all over it, in case you don't know French. Try the crispy duck in a pineapple and banana sauce, the Dover sole, or rack of lamb. Lunch is about $35.

On the pier, **Taloula Mango's Carib Café** (www.taloulamango.com) offers tapas, burgers, pizza, pasta, salad, and island favorites such as blackened mahimahi and chicken curry. Lunch is about $22.

Over in Simpson Bay, feast on crispy coconut shrimp on the water at **Turtle Pier** (✆ 721/545-2562). Lunch is about $18.

ON THE FRENCH SIDE On the Marigot waterfront, **Mini Club,** rue des Pêcheurs (✆ 590/87-50-69), is one of the oldest restaurants in town. Savor the rich flavors of spicy conch stew, Creole-style fresh fish, or other West Indian and French dishes on the bright-yellow upstairs terrace. Lunch is about $35.

For light salads, sandwiches, and ice-cream concoctions, claim a harborside table at **La Vie en Rose,** at rue de la République and boulevard de France (✆ 590/87-54-42). Open for more than 20 years, this restaurant offers an extensive menu, ranging from red snapper filet in champagne sauce to sautéed foie gras with gingerbread toast. The restaurant is open for lunch.

In Grande-Case, a stroll down "restaurant row" (boulevard de Grand-Case) will lead you to seemingly endless dining options. Unfortunately, many of the finest are open only for dinner, after your ship has left the port. However, more and more are

5

open all day and offer fun options for breakfast and lunch as well. **Le Petite Auberge des Iles** (© 590/87-56-31), in Marigot at the Marina Port la Royale, is a charming and cozy destination that's open for lunch and dinner. There are many other nice restaurants in Grand Case that you can explore, such as **Le Pressoir** and **Le Tastevin,** which both have a terrace on the ocean, and **Le Cottage,** which has an excellent soufflé for dessert.

TRINIDAD & TOBAGO

The southernmost islands in the Caribbean chain, Trinidad and tiny Tobago (which together form a single nation), manage to encompass nearly every facet of Caribbean life. Located less than 15km (9 miles) east of Venezuela's coast, Trinidad is large (the biggest and most heavily populated Caribbean island) and diverse, with an industrial, cosmopolitan capital city, Port of Spain, and an outgoing, vibrant culture that combines African, East Indian, European, Chinese, and Syrian influences. Little sister Tobago is the more natural of the two, with rainforested mountains and spectacular secluded beaches.

Trinidad and Tobago won independence from Britain in 1962 and became a republic in 1976, but some British influences, including the residents' love of cricket, remain. Trinidad profited from oil, and the islands are still the Western Hemisphere's largest oil exporters. This is not to say that Trinidad is rich, and in fact there are few big hotel or resort chains and most establishments have a mom-and-pop feel.

The music of Trinidad is another treasure. The calypso, steel-pan, and soca styles that originated here have influenced musical trends worldwide. These rhythmic, soulful sounds are a main feature of Carnaval, the Caribbean-wide bacchanalian celebration held each year on the Monday and Tuesday before Lent. Among all the Carnaval celebrations in the Caribbean, Trinidad's is king.

The local people are charming and friendly, and love to talk. With a literacy rate of 97%, the populace is full of well-informed conversationalists. You'll find Trinis (as residents call themselves) happy to socialize with visitors and discuss just about anything.

To say Trinidad is a laid-back island is an understatement, so when you arrive, don't expect everything to be running on schedule and as posted. In fact, don't be surprised if you arrive for lunch to find the proprietor absent and the restaurant locked up tight. While business is important, the locals value fun, friends, and family more, and if the mood strikes or the sunshine is calling, it's business as usual to close shop for the day and follow the sunshine to the beach or the party. Luckily, the locals are so friendly, they just may invite you to join them, or at least give you the scoop on whatever it is you need or desire.

LANGUAGE   The official language is English, but like many of their Caribbean neighbors, Trinis speak it with a distinct patois. Hindi, Creole, and Spanish are also spoken among various ethnic groups.

CURRENCY   The unit of currency is the **Trinidad and Tobago dollar,** sometimes designated by the same symbol as the U.S. dollar ($) and sometimes just by "TT" (TT$6 = US$1; TT$1 = US16¢). Vacationers can pay in U.S. dollars, but be sure you know what currency prices are being quoted in, and try to get change in U.S. dollars. Local ATMs mainly dispense TT notes. Prices in this section are given in U.S. dollars.

CALLING FROM THE U.S.   When calling Trinidad and Tobago from the United States, you need only dial "1" before the numbers listed here.

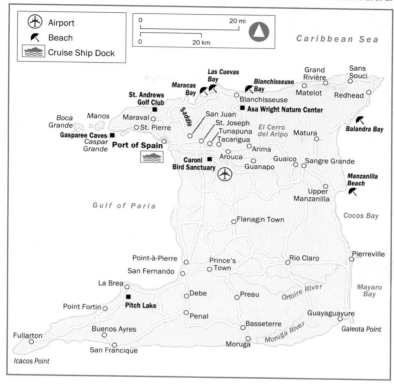

Airport
Beach
Cruise Ship Dock

Caribbean Sea

Las Cuevas Bay
Maracas Bay
St. Andrews Golf Club
Boca Grande
Manos
Maraval
Gasparee Caves
Caspar Grande
Port of Spain
Saddle
San Juan
St. Joseph
Tunapuna
Tacarigua
Blanchisseuse Bay
Blanchisseuse
Asa Wright Nature Center
Grand Rivière
Matelot
Sans Souci
Redhead
El Cerro del Aripo
Matura
Balandra Bay
Arima
St. Pierre
Caroni Bird Sanctuary
Arouca
Guanapo
Guaico
Sangre Grande
Manzanilla Beach
Upper Manzanilla
Cocos Bay
Gulf of Paria
Flanagin Town
Point-à-Pierre
San Fernando
Prince's Town
Rio Claro
Pierreville
La Brea
Debe
Preau
Ortoire River
Mayaro Bay
Point Fortin
Pitch Lake
Penal
Basseterre
Guayaguayure
Galeota Point
Fullarton
Buenos Ayres
San Francique
Moruga
Moruga River
Icacos Point

Trinidad

Trinidad is one of the most industrialized countries in the Caribbean, and it shows—if you're looking for a sleepy, quiet Caribbean retreat, go to Tobago instead. Trinidad's capital and commercial center, **Port of Spain,** is an energetic, bustling metropolis of 300,000. There are few distinct attractions—Port of Spain isn't necessarily a tourist city—but the central shopping area at the south end of Frederick Street is a colorfully crowded mix of outdoor arcades and air-conditioned minimalls. **Independence Square,** in the heart of Port of Spain, is the place to get a taxi, find a bank, and get good, cheap food. There are mosques, shrines, and temples here, and locals gather at **Woodford Square** to hear public speakers or attend outdoor meetings.

Note: While Port of Spain is interesting and not threatening by day, it's unsafe at night, and strolling around is not recommended if your ship happens to be in port late.

COMING ASHORE Cruise ships visiting Trinidad dock at Port of Spain's 1.5-hectare (3¾-acre) cruise terminal, built in the early 1990s to accommodate the island's growing cruise traffic. The complex, which includes a shopping mall and car-rental agencies, is within easy walking distance of the center of town. Steel-pan musicians and colorfully dressed dancers usually greet arriving passengers. Outside the terminal, there's a crafts market with T-shirts, straw items, and other souvenirs.

INFORMATION The **Tourism Development Corporation of Trinidad and Tobago (TDC),** Level I Maritime Centre, 29 Tenth Ave., Barataria (www.gotrinidad andtobago.com; ☎ **800/816-7541** or 868/675-7034), is open Monday through Friday from 8am to 4:30pm.

GETTING AROUND

BY TAXI Taxis are available at the cruise terminal. The registered taxi association here is the **Trinidad and Tobago Tourist Transport Association.** These drivers are trained tour guides, identifiable by their dark pants and shirts with printed taxi association monograms. Their car license plates begin with the letter H (for "hiring car"). The taxis are unmetered, but the Port Authority posts fares on a board by the main entrance. Always establish a fare before loading into the taxi and shoving off. Private cabs can be relatively expensive.

BY VAN Maxitaxis (minivans operating regular routes within specific zones) have a yellow stripe and are lower priced than taxis. There are also route taxis, which are shared cabs that travel along a prescribed route and charge about $2 to $4 to drop you at any spot along the way.

BY RENTAL CAR Driving is on the left. Trinidad has a fairly wide network of roads, and streets in town are generally well marked, but traffic is frequently heavy. Few of the major U.S.-based car-rental firms have franchises on the island, so you'll likely have to make arrangements with a local firm (go over the terms and insurance agreements carefully). Count on spending about $75 to $125 per day or more, with unlimited mileage included. Your best bet is one of the firms maintaining offices at Piarco Airport. These include **Econo-Car Rentals** (☎ **868/669-2342**), **Thrifty** (☎ **800/847-4389** or 868/669-0602), and the simply named **Auto Rentals** (☎ **868/669-2277**). *Warning:* Although these local car-rental firms technically accept reservations, a car may not be waiting for you, even if you reserve ahead of time.

> ### Bitters Sweet
>
> Try a drink made with Angostura Bitters: This local specialty contains citrus-tree bark and is made from a secret recipe. Just a few drops are enough to add zing to any drink.

BEST CRUISE LINE SHORE EXCURSIONS

Caroni Bird Sanctuary ($64, 3 hr.): One of Trinidad's ecological wonders, the Caroni Bird Sanctuary is a pristine network of dense mangroves, remote canals, and shallow lagoons, and is the breeding grounds of the famed scarlet ibis. Embark on a motorized flat-bottom boat to ply the calm waters of the canal and lagoons. Keep a watchful eye out for heron, osprey, and the scarlet ibis, just a few of the 130 bird species typically found in this unique wetland ecosystem. This is a world-class destination for bird-watchers and outdoor enthusiasts.

Asa Wright Nature Center ($89, 6 hr.): Set within 80 hectares (200 acres), about 360m (1,180 ft.) up into Trinidad's rainforested mountains, the center is known to bird-watchers throughout the world. You can see hummingbirds, toucans, bellbirds, manakins, several varieties of tanagers, and the rare oilbird. Hiking trails line the grounds. A Creole-style buffet lunch is served at the center's Old Plantation House.

Maracas Beach Getaway ($59, 4 hr.): Enjoy a scenic ride up island, through windy mountain roads and breathtaking scenic vistas, to Maracas Beach, Trinidad's most beautiful and popular beach. When the sun, surf, and sand get you hungry, head across the street for a "shark and bake" sandwich (a local favorite made with fresh slabs of shark and fried bread).

Maracas Waterfall Hike ($64, 3½ hr.): Hike to the magnificent Maracas Waterfall, hidden in the Maracas Valley, and then cool off in one of the pools at the base of the falls. The 90m (300-ft.) falls are situated in the upper part of the valley and are a 45-minute hike from the starting point. Along the way, guides make stops to point out interesting flora and fauna.

Port of Spain Highlights & Cultural Show ($59, 3½ hr.): Begin an informative scenic tour of Port of Spain that passes by the seven colonial houses at the Queen's Park, the Royal Botanical Gardens, and the President's House, a gracious 19th-century mansion set on the garden grounds. Then relax and enjoy the spirited cultural show, featuring calypso singers, the vibrant music of steel drums, colorful folkloric costumes, and the ever-popular fire limbo.

ON YOUR OWN: WITHIN WALKING DISTANCE

Among Port of Spain's chief centers of activity, **Independence Square,** a stone's throw from the cruise complex, isn't really a square at all, but parallel streets running east and west and connected at one end by a pedestrian mall. The scene here resembles a Middle Eastern bazaar, with a dense thicket of pushcarts, honking cabs, produce hawkers, and inquisitive shoppers moving to the irresistible beat of soca, reggae, and calypso music blaring from nearby stores and sidewalk stands. Some parts of the square have become run-down, and some locals consider the area less than safe. Visitors should keep an eye out for pickpockets and petty thieves.

Woodford Square, laid out by Ralph Woodford, Trinidad's early-19th-century British governor, is among the most attractive areas in town, full of large, leafy trees surrounding a rich lawn with landscaped walkways. This area has traditionally served as a center for political debates, discussions, and rallies. The **Cathedral of the Holy Trinity,** built in 1818 by Woodford, lies on the square's south side. The church's carved roof was designed as a replica of Westminster Hall in London. Inside the church is a memorial statue of Woodford himself. To reach the square, take Independence Square North and then go left on Abercromby Street, or take Wrightson Road to Sackville Street.

On the square's western border is **Red House,** an imposing (and, yes, red) Renaissance-style edifice built in 1906. Today, it houses Trinidad's parliament. The building was badly damaged in 1990, when militants took the prime minister and parliament members hostage.

A little farther north of the city center is **Queen's Park Savannah,** originally part of a large sugar plantation, and now a public park with 32 hectares (80 acres) of open land and walkways, with great shade trees. A depression at the park's northwest section, known as the Hollows, features flower beds, rock gardens, and small ponds and has become a popular picnic spot. Most streets heading north from the cruise complex end at the park.

There are a number of notable sights along the park's outer, western edge, including the **Magnificent Seven,** a row of seven colonial buildings constructed in the late 19th and early 20th centuries. The buildings include Queen's Royal College, White Hall (the prime minister's office), and Stollmeyer's Castle, which was designed to resemble a Scottish castle—complete with turrets.

Beyond the northern edge of Queen's Park Savannah lies the **Emperor Valley Zoo** (www.zstt.org; © **868/622-3530**), featuring local animals such as tropical toucans and macaws, porcupines, monkeys, and various snakes. The zoo emphasizes colorful tropical plants, which are in evidence all over the grounds. It's open daily from 9am to 6pm; admission is $4 adults, $2 for children.

The 28-hectare (70-acre) **Royal Botanical Gardens** are east of the zoo. Laid out in 1820, the gardens are landscaped with attractive walkways and great flowering trees, among them the wild poinsettia, whose bright red blossom is the national flower. The **President's House,** built in 1875 as the governor's residence, is adjacent to the gardens and is open daily from 6am to 6pm.

ON YOUR OWN: BEYOND THE PORT AREA

All out-of-town attractions are covered in "Best Cruise Line Shore Excursions," above.

SHOPPING

Shopping in the Port of Spain area means crafts, fabrics, and fashions made by local artists, a range of spices, and colorful artwork. Most of the shopping opportunities lie in the area around Independence Square, particularly near Frederick and Queen streets.

Art lovers will find a handful of galleries and studios featuring the work of local and regional artists. **Art Creators,** at Seventh Street and St. Ann's Road, in the Aldegonda Park section, is a serious gallery offering year-round exhibits of both emerging and established artists. **Aquarela Galleries,** 1A Dere St., exhibits the work of recognized and up-and-coming Trini artists, and also publishes high-end art books.

Art Potters Ltd., at the cruise terminal, is a pottery specialist. For crafts outside of the terminal area, try the **Trinidad and Tobago Blind Welfare Association,** 118 Duke St. (© 868/624-4675), with accessories and gifts of rattan and other natural materials, all made by blind craftsmen.

For distinctive gifts and apparel, hire a cab to take you to the **Hotel Normandie,** 10 Nook Ave., in the St. Ann's section (www.normandiett.com; © 868/624-1181), where the **Signature Collection** (© 868/624-2958) shops feature clothing and jewelry by some of the country's top designers.

Music is one of Trinidad's signature products, and the latest soca and reggae can be purchased at **Crosby Music Center,** 54 Western Main Rd., in the St. James area (© 868/622-7622).

BEACHES

Unlike its tiny sister Tobago, Trinidad does not have many beautiful beaches. The beaches that do exist lack that manicured polish of more upscale islands. The most popular of the beaches is **Maracas Bay,** a scenic but steep and winding 40-minute journey from Port of Spain. The drive takes you over mountains and through a lush rainforest. As you near the beach, the coastal road descends from a cliffside. The beach itself is wide and sandy, with a small fishing village on one side and the richly dense mountains in the background. There are lifeguards, changing rooms and showers, and areas for picnics. You'll also see a stand selling "shark and bake" sandwiches.

SPORTS

GOLF   The oldest and best-known golf course on the island is the 18-hole, par-72 **St. Andrews Golf Club,** in the suburb of Maraval (www.golftrinidad.com; © 868/629-0066). Also known as Moka Golf Course, it was established in the late 19th century. Greens fees are $85 for 18 holes and $45 for 9. There are no carts, and caddies, mandatory for nonmembers, cost $25; club rentals are $25.

GREAT LOCAL RESTAURANTS & BARS

Trinidad is home to some of the most diverse culinary styles in the Caribbean, a result of its African, Chinese, English, French, Indian, Portuguese, Spanish, and Syrian influences. A favorite local beer is **Stag,** and a favorite local rum is **Vat 19 Old Oak.**

Battimamzelle, at the Coblentz Inn (www.coblentzinn.com/restaurant.html; ℂ 868/621-0541), is one of the best restaurants in the Port of Spain. Its decor—red-and-yellow walls adorned with flower paintings and red lampshades with imprints of *battimamzelles* (dragonflies) on them—is often called "Mexicanish." Grilled chicken, coconut shrimp, and the Chancelor's Steak are just a few of the regular menu items. The barbecued kingfish, when available, is brushed with fresh guava and served with pumpkin. A children's menu is offered upon request. Lunch is about $35.

Angelo's, 38 Ariapita Ave. (ℂ 868/628-5551), is a quality Italian restaurant located in a charming colonial house. Lunch is around $35.

Tobago

Tobago is the antithesis of its larger cousin, as peaceful, calm, and easygoing as Trinidad is loud, crowded, and frenetic. Tobago's idyllic natural beauty makes it one of the greatest escapes in the Caribbean. The island is filled with magical white-sand beaches, languid palm trees, and clear blue water, and you'll find lots of spots for diving and snorkeling. There are also magnificent rainforests and hundreds of tiny streams and waterways carved into a steep crest of mountains that rise about 600m (2,000 ft.) and snake down the island's center. The bird life and nature trails here are impressive.

Unlike bustling Trinidad, Tobago is sleepy, and Trinidadians come here, especially on weekends, to enjoy the wide, sandy beaches. The legendary home of Daniel Defoe's Robinson Crusoe, Tobago is only 43km (27 miles) long and 12km (7½ miles) wide. The people are hospitable and their tiny villages seem to blend in with the landscape. The island's villagelike capital and main port, **Scarborough,** lies on the southern coast. Surrounded by mountains, its bay provides a scenic setting, but the town itself is rather plain. Most of the shops are clustered in streets around the local market.

COMING ASHORE   Most cruise passengers arrive at a small but orderly cruise terminal in central **Scarborough.** There's usually a fleet of taxis ready to go just outside the terminal, and detailed cab rates are posted inside the terminal at the main entrance. Larger ships must anchor offshore and transfer passengers to the terminal via tenders. There are a number of phones inside the terminal.

INFORMATION   The small information booth at the terminal in Scarborough is open Monday through Friday from 9am to 3pm. For info before you go, go to www. gotrinidadandtobago.com or call ℂ **212/682-7272.**

GETTING AROUND

BY TAXI   Taxi is the preferred mode of transportation for visitors here; the island is small enough that any location worth visiting can be reached this way. Distances can be deceptive, though, because some of the roads are in very bad shape and others wind along the coast and twist through the mountains. There is no road that completely circles the island. As in Trinidad, visitors should use registered drivers who are part of the **Trinidad and Tobago Tourist Transport Association;** see the Trinidad taxi section for more information.

BY RENTAL CAR   There's really no need for a cruise passenger to rent a car on Tobago.

BEST CRUISE LINE SHORE EXCURSIONS

Pigeon Point Beach Trip ($63, 5½ hr., including lunch): By taxi, you'll head toward Tobago's most popular beach, where you'll find a restaurant, a bar, restrooms, and small cabanas lining the beach. You have your pick of watersports, including snorkeling and banana-boat rides (for a fee, of course).

Argyle Falls ($64, 4 hr.): A taxi takes you from the quaint fishing village of Charlotte and along the picturesque windward road to the town of Roxborough. Here you will disembark for a short hike through the verdant Main Ridge Forest Reserve, the oldest rain forest in the Western Hemisphere and home to many exotic birds. Continue to Argyle Falls, a scenic three-tiered waterfall, where you can relax or swim in the refreshing cascading water.

Buccoo Reef Snorkeling ($55, 3 hr.): From Pigeon Point, board a glass-bottom boat for the ride out to Buccoo Reef for your snorkeling dip. From there, you'll head off to the Nylon Pool, a sand bank named for its stunningly clear water.

Glass-Bottom Boat & Snorkel ($65, 3 hr.): It's about a 10-minute drive from Charlotte to Speyside. Across the bay from Speyside is Goat Island and Bird of Paradise Island, both surrounded by some of the most spectacular reefs in Tobago—ideal sites for glass-bottom boat viewing and snorkeling. Pass over the Japanese and Coral Gardens, dive sites where various species of fish, coral, and sponges are visible through the crystal-clear water. When the boat drops anchor, snorkel and swim, or just relax on board the boat.

ON YOUR OWN: WITHIN WALKING DISTANCE

The well-restored, British-built **Fort King George,** dating from 1777, overlooks Scarborough's east side. There's no charge to enter the grounds. The fort offers a great view of Tobago's Atlantic coast. Other historic buildings here include **St. Andrew's Church,** built in 1819, and the **Courthouse,** built in 1825. The small **Tobago Museum** (© 868/639-3970) is located in the fort's old barracks guardhouse; it charges $2 admission and is open Monday through Friday from 9am to 4:30pm.

Scarborough's **Botanical Gardens** are situated between the main highway and the town center, less than .5km (¼ mile) from the cruise dock, but they are not much more than a glorified public park with a few marked trees.

Other than this, there aren't many attractions within walking distance of the cruise terminal, and even the terminal shops are small and limited.

SHOPPING

There simply isn't much here beyond the shops inside the cruise terminal and the sporadic crafts merchants at the popular beaches at Fort King George. It's best to put aside the shopping excursions for another port and simply enjoy Tobago's relaxed atmosphere and fine beaches.

BEACHES

On Tobago, you can still feel like Robinson Crusoe in a solitary sandy cove—at least until Saturday, when the Trinidadians fly over for a weekend on the beach. **Pigeon Point,** near the southern tip of Tobago on the Caribbean side, is the best beach on an island filled with great beaches. Set against a backdrop of royal palms, this beach is becoming increasingly commercial. Facilities include food kiosks, crafts shops, a diving concession, paddle-boat rentals, changing rooms in thatched shelters, and picnic tables. Pigeon Point is also the jumping-off point for snorkeling cruises to **Buccoo Reef.**

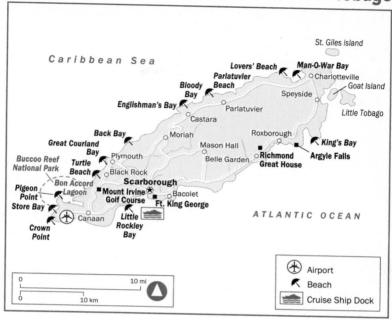

Store Bay, south of Pigeon Point, has white sands and good year-round swimming (there's a lifeguard too). Vendors hawk local wares here, and glass-bottom-boat tours depart for Buccoo Reef. **Parlatuvier Beach** and **Bloody Bay,** on Tobago's Caribbean coast, are tranquil, secluded, and beautiful. Another good beach, **Back Bay,** is an 8-minute walk from the Mount Irvine Bay Hotel. Along the way, you'll pass a coconut plantation and an old cannon emplacement. Snorkeling is generally excellent, even in winter. Near Fort Bennett and south of Plymouth, **Great Courland Bay,** known for its calm, gin-clear waters, is one of the longest sandy beaches on the island and the site of several hotels and a marina. It's flanked by **Turtle Beach,** named for the turtles that nest here.

Near the little fishing village of Charlotteville, **Man-O-War Bay** is one of the finest natural harbors in the West Indies. It has a long, sandy beach and a government-run rest house. Sometimes local fishermen will hawk the day's catch (and clean it for you as well).

The true beach buff will head for **King's Bay** in the northeast, south of the town of Speyside near Delaford. Against a backdrop of towering green hills, the crescent-shaped, gray-sand beach is one of the best places for swimming.

SPORTS

GOLF About 8km (5 miles) from Pigeon Point, the championship 18-hole, par-72 course at the **Mount Irvine Bay Hotel & Golf Club (© 868/639-8871)** is among the most scenic in the Caribbean. The clubhouse sits on a promontory and offers great views of the sea. This 6-hectare (15-acre) resort, established in 1972, stands on the site of an 18th-century sugar plantation. The grounds slope down to a good sandy beach. Greens fees for 9 holes are $30; 18 holes are $48. Club rentals cost $25.

SCUBA DIVING   Tobago is virtually surrounded by shallow-water reefs filled with colorful marine life, easily visible through the clear water. All kinds of diving experiences, from beginner-level dives to drift diving for experienced divers at Grouper Ground, are available. **Tobago Frontier Dive,** at Pigeon Point (www.frontierdiverstt. com; ⓒ **868/683-7210**), offers rentals and resort courses, catering to both beginners and experienced divers.

GREAT LOCAL RESTAURANTS & BARS

There are several moderately priced restaurants in Tobago, including the **Café Havana,** at the Half Moon Blue Hotel on Bacolet Street, Scarborough (www.half moonblue.com; ⓒ **868/639-3551**), which occupies a restored colonial home that once served as Tobago's first guesthouse. Today, it's a bistro serving French wines, light snacks, salads, and soups. Lunch is about $18.

The beach at Store Bay is lined with a row of cheap food stands offering *rotis* (chicken or beef wrapped in Indian turnovers and flavored with curry), "shark and bake" sandwiches, crab with dumplings, and fish lunches.

Even cruise passengers visiting for the day should consider **Kariwak Village Restaurant** (ⓒ **868/639-8442**) in the Kariwak Village hotel, Local Road, Store Bay. The owner grows herbs and vegetables in an on-site organic garden, and the chefs prepare one of the choicest menus on the island. Lunch is about $17.

One of the very few restaurants in the Caribbean designed as a treehouse, **Jemma's Seaview Kitchen** (ⓒ **868/660-4066**) is a short walk north of the hamlet of Speyside, on Tobago's northeastern coast. Although the simple kitchen is firmly anchored to the shoreline, the dining area is set on a platform nailed to the massive branches of a 200-year-old almond tree that leans out over the water. Lunch platters include shrimp, fish, and chicken. No liquor is served, but you can BYOB. Lunch costs around $25.

La Tartaruga (www.latartarugatobago.com; ⓒ **868/639-0940**) is casual yet elegant, with lots of color and local artwork. The island's most gracious host, Gaetano, "table hops," always concerned about your welfare; diners almost invariably tell him how tasty his Italian-inspired cuisine is. Many of the dishes will appeal to the vegetarian. The luscious desserts are homemade daily, and everything is backed up by the best wine cart on the island. Lunch will cost between $12 and $25.

U.S. VIRGIN ISLANDS: ST. THOMAS, ST. JOHN & ST. CROIX

Ever since Columbus discovered the Virgin Islands during his second voyage to the New World in 1493, they have proven irresistible to foreign powers seeking territory, at one time or another being governed by Denmark, Spain, France, England, Holland, and, since 1917, the United States.

Vacationers discovered **St. Thomas,** the largest of the islands, right after World War II and have been flocking here in increasing numbers ever since to enjoy its fine dining, elegant resorts, and, in recent years, shopping. Tourism and U.S. government programs have raised the standard of living to one of the highest in the Caribbean, and today, the island is one of the busiest and most developed cruise ports in the West Indies, often hosting more than six ships a day during the peak winter season.

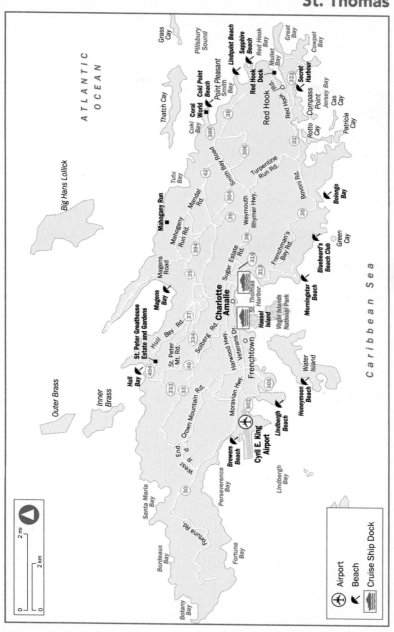

Charlotte Amalie (pronounced Ah-*mahl*-yah), named in 1691 in honor of the wife of Denmark's King Christian V, is the island's capital and has become the Caribbean's major shopping center. With its white houses and bright red roofs glistening in the sun, the island's capital is one of the most beautiful towns in the Caribbean. In addition to its shopping, the town is also filled with historic sites, such as Fort Christian, an intriguing 17th-century building constructed by the Danes. The town's architecture reflects the island's culturally diverse past. You'll pass Dutch doors, Danish red-tile roofs, French iron grillwork, and Spanish-style patios.

By far the most tranquil and unspoiled of the islands is **St. John,** the smallest of the lot, more than half of which is preserved as the gorgeous Virgin Islands National Park. A rocky coastline, forming crescent-shaped bays and white-sand beaches, rings the whole island, with miles of serpentine hiking trails that lead past the ruins of 18th-century Danish plantations and let onto panoramic ocean views.

St. Croix, the largest of the USVIs, gets nowhere near as many visitors as St. Thomas, making for a more tranquil port experience. The island's major attraction is Buck Island Reef National Monument, an offshore park full of gorgeous coral reefs.

The largest number of cruise ships dock in St. Thomas's Charlotte Amalie, but a few anchor directly off St. John or tie up at the Anne Abramson Pier in Fredericksburg, St. Croix. Those that dock in St. Thomas usually offer excursions to St. John, but if yours doesn't, it's quite easy to get there on your own via water taxi or ferry.

LANGUAGE   English is spoken on all three islands.

CURRENCY   The **U.S. dollar** is the local currency.

INFORMATION   For information before you go, contact the **U.S. Virgin Islands Department of Tourism** (www.visitusvi.com; © **800/372-8784**). Another useful resource is their interactive online phone book (www.viphonebook.com), which you can use to look up phone numbers and addresses of local businesses and residents.

CALLING FROM THE U.S.   When calling the Virgin Islands from the States, you just need to dial a "1" before the numbers listed in this section. Please note that while most cellphone carriers consider the islands part of their national plan, you may pick up a signal from neighboring British Virgin Islands, which is considered international roaming and can be very expensive. This is more common on St. John, which is only a stone's throw away. In the event this occurs, most carriers will credit your account when you call them upon your return.

St. Thomas

With a population of about 50,000 and a large number of American expatriates and temporary sun-seekers in residence, tiny St. Thomas isn't exactly a tranquil tropical retreat. You won't have any beaches to yourself. Shops, bars, and restaurants (including a lot of fast-food joints) abound here, and most of the locals make their living off the tourist trade. Most native Virgin Islanders are the descendants of slaves brought from Africa. In fact, Charlotte Amalie was one of the major slave-trading centers in the Caribbean.

COMING ASHORE   Most cruise ships anchor at **Havensight Mall,** at the southern end of Charlotte Amalie Harbor, 2.5km (1½ miles) from the town center. The mall has a tourist information office, restaurants, a bookstore, a bank, a U.S. post office, phones that accept long-distance credit cards, and a generous number of duty-free shops. Many people make the long, hot walk to the center of Charlotte Amalie,

Carnival

The annual **Carnival** celebration, held after Easter, is a spectacular event, with echoes of the islanders' African heritage. "Mocko Jumbies," people dressed as spirits, parade through the streets on stilts nearly 6m (20 ft.) high. Steel and *parang* (a type of folk music) bands, "jump-ups" (Caribbean hoedowns), and parades bring the event to life. Events take place islandwide, but most of the action is on the streets of Charlotte Amalie. Contact the visitor center in St. Thomas for a schedule of events.

but it's not a scenic route in any way—you may want to opt for one of the open-air taxis for about $5 per person.

If Havensight Mall is clogged with cruise ships, your ship will dock at the **Crown Bay Marina,** to the west of Charlotte Amalie. A taxi is your best bet—the 30-minute walk into Charlotte Amalie feels longer on a hot day and isn't terribly picturesque. A taxi ride into town from here costs about $7 per person.

INFORMATION The **U.S. Virgin Islands Department of Tourism** has offices at the pier in Charlotte Amalie (✆ 340/774-8784), open Monday through Friday from 8am to 5pm, Saturday from 9am to 3pm, and Sunday from 9am to 1pm. Stop by and pick up *St. Thomas This Week,* which includes maps of St. Thomas and St. John. There's also an office at the Havensight Mall.

GETTING AROUND

BY TAXI Taxis are the chief means of transport here. They're unmetered, but a guide of point-to-point fares around the island is included in most of the tourist magazines. A typical fare from Havensight Mall to Magens Bay, for a day at the beach, runs from $10 per person or $7 per person in a shared cab. Surcharges, one-third of the price of the excursion, are added after midnight. You'll pay $2 to $4 per bag for luggage. For 24-hour radio-dispatch taxi service, call ✆ 340/774-7457. If you want to hire a taxi and a driver (who just may be a great tour guide) for a day, expect to pay about $40 per person for 2 hours of sightseeing in a shared car, or $55 per hour for two to four people.

BY BUS Comfortable and often air-conditioned, the government-run **Vitran** buses serve Charlotte Amalie and the countryside as far away as Red Hook, a jumping-off point for St. John. You rarely have to wait more than 30 minutes during the day. A one-way ride costs $1. For routes, stops, and schedules, call ✆ 340/774-5678.

BY TAXI VAN Less structured and more erratic are "taxi vans," privately owned vans, minibuses, and open-sided trucks operated by local entrepreneurs that transport 8 to 12 passengers to multiple destinations on the island. They make unscheduled stops along major traffic arteries and charge varied fares—for example, it may cost $5 to $8 for a trip out to Red Hook. If you look like you want to go somewhere, one will likely stop for you. They may or may not have their final destinations written on a cardboard sign displayed on the windshield.

BY FERRY Ferries run every 2 hours from Charlotte Amalie to St. John until 5:30pm and all day hourly from Red Hook to St. John. The ride from Charlotte Amalie takes about 45 minutes and costs $12 one-way. The ferry from Red Hook departs every hour on the hour, takes 20 minutes, and costs $6. For information, call ✆ 340/776-6282.

BY SEAPLANE Daily seaplane shuttles between St. Thomas and St. Croix are available for $228 round-trip. Booking in advance is strongly recommended. Flights depart every 15 to 45 minutes in both directions; flight time is a mere 18 minutes, but figure 30 minutes from dock to dock. For more information, contact **Seaborne Airlines,** 34 Strand St., Christiansted (www.seaborneairlines.com; C **340/773-6442**).

BY RENTAL CAR No need to rent a car here.

BEST CRUISE LINE SHORE EXCURSIONS

In addition to the excursions below, a bajillion booze cruises, island tours, and beach/snorkeling tours are offered here. The waters off these islands are rated among the most beautiful in the world.

Coral World & Island Tour ($65, 3 hr.): Coral World Ocean Park and Undersea Observatory is St. Thomas's number-one attraction. The 1.5-hectare (3¾-acre) complex features a three-story underwater observation tower 30m (100 ft.) offshore, plunging into the depths to provide views of tropical fish, coral, sharks, and other sea beasts. In the Marine Gardens Aquarium, saltwater tanks display everything from sea horses to sea urchins, and a touch pool lets you fondle some. Another tank is devoted to sea predators, including circling sharks. From here, you zip around the island for a brief tour, visiting Cassie Hill for great views of St. John and the British Virgin Islands.

Kayaking Tour of the Marine Sanctuary ($90, 3½ hr.): Kayak from the mouth of the marine sanctuary at Holmberg's Marina and spend nearly an hour paddling among the mangroves while a naturalist explains the mangrove and lagoon ecosystem. This trip includes 30 minutes to snorkel or walk along the coral beach at Bovoni Point.

St. John Eco-Hike ($74, ½ hr.): Take the ferry to St. John for a walkabout through the Virgin Islands National Park. The Lind Point Trail ascends about 75m (250 ft.) to the Lind Point Overlook for views of St. John, St. Thomas, and the surrounding islands. An expert guide discusses the park's ecosystem and St. John's cultural history while you walk to Honeymoon Beach for a little swimming.

Water Island Bike Trip ($76, 3½ hr.): After a ferry ride to Water Island, a 5-minute bus ride brings you to the island's highest point, from which you get a nice downhill ride. Your guide will point out various historic sights and wildlife en route to Honeymoon Beach, where you can swim and enjoy a drink.

EXCURSIONS OFFERED BY LOCAL AGENCIES

St. John Yachting/Snorkeling Excursion: Many yachts and catamarans are available for snorkel and scuba excursions and champagne sails.

For a more personal experience, the six-passenger *Fantasy* (www.daysailfantasy.com; C **340/775-5652**) departs from the American Yacht Harbor at Red Hook (on the east coast of St. Thomas) daily at 9:30am, sailing to St. John and nearby islands for swimming, snorkeling, beachcombing, or trolling. The normal full-day trip departs at 9:30am and returns at 3:30pm. Depending on availability, shorter sailings can be arranged. The cost is $140 per person, including an open bar, a hot lunch served on board, a guided tour, and snorkel and fishing gear. Call to book in advance.

ON YOUR OWN: WITHIN WALKING DISTANCE

Depending on your level of energy, you can either walk from the port into **Charlotte Amalie** (about 2.5km/1½ miles) or take a taxi. In days of yore, seafarers from all over the globe flocked to this old-world Danish town, including pirates and, during the Civil War, Confederate sailors. The old warehouses that once held pirates' loot still stand and, for the most part, house shops. The main streets (called Gades here, in honor of their Danish heritage) are a veritable shopping mall, usually packed with

Charlotte Amalie

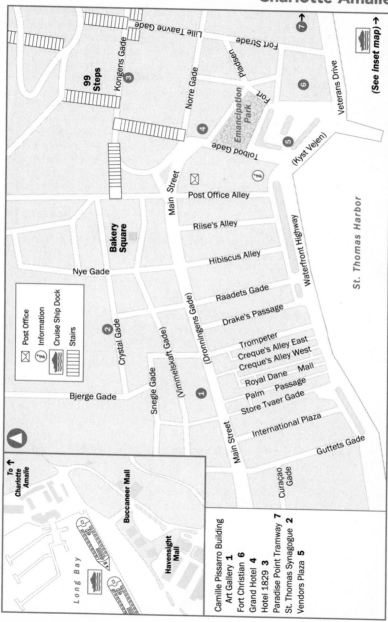

Legend:
- ⊠ Post Office
- ⓘ Information
- 🚢 Cruise Ship Dock
- ▥ Stairs

Map labels:

99 Steps

Lille Taavne Gade
Kongens Gade
Norre Gade
Fort Strade
Pladsen
Fort
Emancipation Park
Tolbod Gade
(Kyst Vejen)
Veterans Drive

Main Street
Post Office Alley
Riise's Alley
Hibiscus Alley
Nye Gade
Bakery Square
Raadets Gade
Drake's Passage
Trompeter
Creque's Alley East
Creque's Alley West
Royal Dane Mall
Palm Passage
Store Tvaer Gade
International Plaza
Guttets Gade
Curacao Gade

Crystal Gade
Snegle Gade
(Vimmelskaft Gade)
(Dronningens Gade)
Bjerge Gade
Main Street

Waterfront Highway
St. Thomas Harbor

To ↑
Charlotte
Amalie

Buccaneer Mall
Havensight Mall
Long Bay

Key:

Camille Pissarro Building
Art Gallery **1**
Fort Christian **6**
Grand Hotel **4**
Hotel 1829 **3**
Paradise Point Tramway **7**
St. Thomas Synagogue **2**
Vendors Plaza **5**

(See inset map) →

visitors. Sandwiched among the shops are a few historic buildings, most of which can be covered on foot in a couple hours.

Before starting your tour, stop off at the so-called **Grand Hotel,** near Emancipation Park. No longer a hotel, it contains a restaurant, a bar, shops, and a visitor center. There are views of the harbor below from the wood-paneled pub/restaurant at **Hotel 1829** (www.hotel1829.com; ✆ **340/776-1234**), one street farther up Government Hill. Here you can go on a self-guided tour of the hotel and **Blackbeard's Castle** (www.blackbeardscastle.com; ✆ **800/524-2002** or 340/776-1234), where you can go up in the pirate's tower, see life-sized bronze pirate statues, shop at the **Treasure company,** or stroll through the botanical gardens. Hours are Monday to Saturday 9am to 2pm and cost $14 for adults, $5 for children. Stray behind the seafront shopping strip (Main St.), and you'll find pockets of 19th-century houses and the truly charming, cozy, brick-and-stone **St. Thomas Synagogue** (✆ **340/774-4312**), built in 1833 by Sephardic Jews. There's a great view from here as well. It's located high on the steep-sloping Crystal Gade.

Dating from 1672, **Fort Christian,** 32 Raadets Gade, rises from the harbor to dominate the center of town. Named after the Danish king Christian V, the structure has been everything from a governor's residence to a jail. Many pirates were hanged in its courtyard.

The **Paradise Point Tramway** (✆ **340/774-9809**) affords visitors a dramatic view of Charlotte Amalie's harbor at a peak height of 210m (700 ft.). The tram travels from the Havensight area to Paradise Point in just 15 minutes, where riders disembark to visit shops and a popular restaurant and bar. A day pass is $21 for adults, $11 for children 11 and under.

ON YOUR OWN: BEYOND THE PORT AREA

Twenty minutes from downtown Charlotte Amalie is **Coral World Ocean Park** ★★, 6450 Coki Point, off Route 38 (www.coralworldvi.com; ✆ **340/775-1555**), the number-one attraction in St. Thomas. The 1.5-hectare (3¾-acre) complex features a three-story underwater observation tower 30m (100 ft.) offshore—you'll see sponges, fish, coral, and other underwater life in their natural state through the windows. In the Marine Gardens Aquarium, saltwater tanks display everything from sea horses to sea urchins. An 80,000-gallon reef tank features exotic Caribbean marine life. Another tank is devoted to sea predators, including circling sharks. By far, the most exciting of interactions is a guided swim with a friendly sea lion followed by a photo op with one before you dry off. It's well worth the additional $74 price tag. Other a la carte add-ons include Sea-Trek, shark or turtle encounters, and a ride in a semisubmersible craft. Coral World is open daily from 9am to 5pm. Admission is $19 for adults and $10 for children 3 to 12. Call to confirm the summer schedule, which may vary.

West of Charlotte Amalie, **Frenchtown** was settled by French-speaking citizenry who were uprooted when the Swedes invaded their home of St. Barts. These settlers were known for wearing cha-chas, or straw hats. Many of the people who live here today are the direct descendants of those long-ago residents. The colorful fishing village contains several interesting restaurants and taverns. To get here, take a taxi down Veterans Drive (Rte. 30) west and turn left at the sign to the Admirals Inn.

The lush **St. Peter Greathouse Estate and Gardens,** at St. Peter Mountain Road (Rte. 40) and Barrett Hill Road (www.greathousevi.com; ✆ **340/774-4999**), ornaments 4.5 hectares (11 acres) on the volcanic peaks of the island's northern rim. It's the creation of Howard Lawson DeWolfe, a Mayflower descendant who, with his wife, Sylvie, bought the estate in 1987 and set about transforming it into a tropical paradise. It's filled with some 200 varieties of plants and trees, including an umbrella plant from Madagascar. There's also a rainforest, an orchid jungle, waterfalls, and reflecting ponds. From a panoramic deck, you can see some 20 of the Virgin Islands. The house itself is worth a visit; its interior is filled with local art. The estate and gardens are open daily from 9am to 4pm. Admission is $8 for adults, $5 for children ages 3 to 12.

SHOPPING

St. Thomas is famous for its shopping opportunities. As in St. Croix and St. John, American shoppers can bring home $1,600 worth of merchandise without paying duty—twice the amount of other Caribbean islands. You'll sometimes find well-known brand names at savings of up to 40% off stateside prices, but you'll often have to plow through a lot of junk to find the bargains. The main goodies are jewelry, watches, cameras, china, and leather.

Many cruise ship passengers shop at the **Havensight Mall,** where the ships dock, but the major shopping goes on along the harbor of **Charlotte Amalie. Main Street** (or Dronningens Gade, its old Danish name) is the main shopping area. Just north of Main Street is merchandise-loaded **Back Street,** or Vimmelskaft. Many shops are also spread along the Waterfront Highway (also called Kyst Vejen). Running between these major streets is a series of side streets, walkways, and alleys, all filled with shops. All the usual Caribbean megatourist shops sell all the usual jewelry, watches, perfume, gift items, and so on; but there are a number of other interesting, more unique shops. Just do a little comparison shopping from place to place and be a little cautious of people trying to lure you into their shop and offering you a special rate if you bring in others from your group.

The **Camille Pissarro Building Art Gallery,** upstairs at 14 Dronningens Gade, is in the house where the impressionist painter Pissarro was born on July 10, 1830. In three high-ceilinged and airy rooms, you'll see all the available Pissarro paintings (both originals and reproductions) relating to the islands. Many prints and cards by local artists are available, too, as well as original batiks.

Huddled under oversize parasols, hundreds of street vendors ply their trades in a designated area called **Vendors Plaza,** at Veterans Drive and Tolbod Gade. It's open Monday through Saturday from 7:30am to 5:30pm, plus Sunday if a cruise ship is expected. Food vendors set up on sidewalks outside.

BEACHES

St. Thomas has some good beaches, all of which are easily reached by taxi. Arrange for your driver to return and pick you up at a designated time. All the beaches in the U.S. Virgin Islands are public, but some still charge a fee. If you're going to St. John, you may want to do your beaching there, as they are somewhat nicer.

ON THE NORTH SIDE Located across the mountains, 5km (3 miles) north of the capital, **Magens Bay** was once hailed as one of the world's 10 most beautiful beaches, but its reputation has faded. Though still beautiful, it isn't as well maintained as it should be and is often overcrowded, especially when many cruise ships are in port. It's less than a mile long and lies between two mountains. Admission is $5 for adults and 50¢ for children 11 and under. Changing facilities, bathrooms, a snack bar, picnic tables, snorkel gear, and float rentals are available. There's no public transportation here, so take a taxi. The gates are open daily from 6am to 6pm (you'll need insect repellent after 4pm).

Located in the northeast near Coral World, **Coki Point Beach** is good, but it, too, becomes overcrowded when cruise ships are in port. Snorkelers come here often, as do pickpockets—protect your valuables. Lockers can be rented at Coral World, next door. An East End bus runs to Smith Bay and lets you off at the gate to Coral World and Coki.

ON THE SOUTH SIDE   On the south side, **Morningstar Beach** lies about 3km (2 miles) east of Charlotte Amalie at the Marriott Frenchman's Reef and Morningstar Beach Resort. You can wear your most daring swimwear here, and you can also rent sailboats, snorkeling equipment, and lounge chairs. The beach can be easily reached via a cliff-front elevator at the Marriott.

Also on the south coast, **Bluebeard's Beach Club** (formerly known as Limetree Beach) offers a secluded setting and is a quick ride from the cruise ship pier.

Bolongo Bay lures those who love a serene spread of sand. You can feed hibiscus blossoms to iguanas, rent snorkeling gear and lounge chairs, or try a variety of watersports, including parasailing. There's no public transportation, but it's about a $15 taxi ride from Charlotte Amalie. Unlike Magens Bay (see above), where there's only a snack bar, Iggy's Restaurant is right on Bolongo's beach.

Brewers Beach, one of the island's most popular, lies in the southwest near the University of the Virgin Islands, also along the Fortuna bus route.

ON THE EAST END   Small and special, **Secret Harbour** sits near a collection of condos. With its white sand and coconut palms, it's a veritable cliché of Caribbean charm. No public transportation stops here, but it's an easy taxi ride east of Charlotte Amalie heading toward Red Hook.

Sapphire Beach is one of the finest on St. Thomas, set against the backdrop of the Doubletree Sapphire Beach Resort and Marina, where you can lunch or order drinks. Windsurfers like this beach a lot. You can rent snorkeling gear and lounge chairs here. A large reef lies close to the shore, and there are great views of offshore cays and St. John. To get here, take the East End bus from Charlotte Amalie, going via Red Hook. Ask to be let off at the entrance to Sapphire Bay; it's a short walk to the water.

SPORTS

GOLF   Designed by Tom and George Fazio, **Mahogany Run,** Mahogany Run Road, on the north shore (www.mahoganyrungolf.com; ✆ **800/253-7103** or 340/777-6250), is one of the most beautiful courses in the West Indies. This 18-hole, par-70 course rises and drops like a roller coaster on its journey to the sea. Cliffs and crashing sea waves are the ultimate hazards at the 13th and 14th holes. The golf course is a $10 to $20 taxi ride from the cruise dock. Greens fees are $165 ($115 after 1:30pm) during high season, and include cart. Tee times may be booked online.

SCUBA DIVING & SNORKELING   The waters off the U.S. Virgin Islands are rated one of the "most beautiful areas in the world" by *Skin Diver* magazine. Thirty spectacular reefs lie just off St. Thomas alone. **Dive In!** at the Doubletree Sapphire Beach Resort and Marina, Smith Bay Road, Route 36 (www.diveinusvi.com; ✆ **866/434-8346** or 340/777-5255), offers a two-tank morning dive for $110 and a one-tank afternoon dive at $80. PADI certification courses are offered, and snorkeling trips are available.

GREAT LOCAL RESTAURANTS & BARS

IN CHARLOTTE AMALIE   In downtown Charlotte Amalie, **Beni Iguana's Sushi Bar,** in Havansite Mall (www.beniiguanassushibar.com; ✆ **340/777-8744**), was the first sushi bar on St. Thomas. Lunch is around $30.

Greenhouse, Veterans Drive (www.thegreenhouserestaurant.com; ✆ 340/774-7998), attracts cruise ship passengers with daily specials, including American fare and some Jamaican-inspired dishes. Lunch is about $22. **Virgilio's,** 18 Dronningens Gade (✆ 340/776-4920), is a good northern Italian restaurant that serves excellent lobster ravioli. Lunch is about $25. The entrance is on a narrow alleyway running between Main and Back streets.

In the Secret Harbour Beach Resort, **Cruzan Beach Club,** 6280 Estate Nazareth Bay (www.sunsetgrillevi.com; ✆ 340/714-7874), offers tiki-bar dining in an open-air setting. Lunch is about $20.

IN & AROUND RED HOOK   You can mingle with locals at the fun, happening **Duffy's Love Shack** (www.duffysloveshack.com; ✆ 340/779-2080). Duffy's serves standard American dishes with Caribbean flavors. The open-air restaurant has lots of bamboo and a thatched roof over the bar. Even the menu appears on a bamboo stick, like an old-fashioned fan. The lunch selection is loaded with familiar favorites (burgers and salads) with a retro Polynesian flair (such as the flaming pu-pu platter). Lunch is about $20.

At Bolongo Bay Beach Resort, **Iggy's Beach Bar & Grill** (www.iggiesbeachbar.com; ✆ 800/524-4746) offers one of the most laid-back and tasty seaside dining experiences on the island. The restaurant is billed as "where locals and visitors meet." Once finished with lunch (about $19), prepare to be lured into a game of beach volleyball.

IN FRENCHTOWN   West of town, **Bella Blue,** 24-A Honduras Rd. (www.bella bludining.com; ✆ 340/774-4349), puts a heavy emphasis on seafood—sometimes prepared in unusual ways. Other dishes include a mouthwatering Wiener schnitzel. Lunch is about $25. **Craig & Sally's,** 22 Honduras Rd. (www.craigandsallys.com; ✆ 340/777-9949), serves dishes that, according to the owner, are not "for the faint of heart, but for the adventurous soul"—roast pork with clams, filet mignon with macadamia-nut sauce, and grilled swordfish with a sauce of fresh herbs and tomatoes. Lunch is about $20. Lunch is served Wednesday through Friday only.

St. John

A tiny gem of an island, lush St. John lies about 5km (3 miles) east of St. Thomas across Pillsbury Sound. It's the smallest and least populated of the U.S. Virgins, only about 11km (7 miles) long and 5km (3 miles) wide, with a total land area of some 49 sq. km (19 sq. miles). The island was slated for big development under Danish control, but a slave rebellion and the decline of the sugarcane plantations ended that idea.

Since 1956, more than half of St. John's landmass, as well as its shoreline waters, have been set aside as the **Virgin Islands National Park** (www.virgin.islands.national-park.com; ✆ 340/776-6201), and today the island leads the Caribbean in eco-tourism. Miles of winding hiking trails lead to panoramic views and the ruins of 18th-century Danish plantations. Mysterious geometric petroglyphs incised into boulders and cliffs can be seen all over the island (ask a guide to point them out if you can't find them). These figures, of unknown age and origin, have never been deciphered. Because St. John is easy to reach from St. Thomas and the beaches are spectacular, many cruise ship passengers spend their entire day here.

COMING ASHORE   Cruise ships cannot dock at either of the piers in St. John. Instead, they moor off the coast at **Cruz Bay,** sending in tenders to the National Park Service Dock, the larger of the two piers. Most cruise ships docking at St. Thomas offer shore excursions to St. John's pristine interior and beaches.

If your ship docks on St. Thomas and you don't take an organized shore excursion to St. John, you can get here from Charlotte Amalie by ferry. Ferries leave the Charlotte Amalie waterfront for Cruz Bay at 1- to 2-hour intervals, from 9am until around 5:30pm. The last boat leaves Cruz Bay for Charlotte Amalie at 3:45pm. The ride takes about 45 minutes and costs $12 each way, $5 for children 2 to 11. Another ferry leaves from the Red Hook pier on St. Thomas's eastern tip more or less every hour, on the hour, starting at 6am and ending at midnight. It's a 30-minute drive from Charlotte Amalie's port to the pier at Red Hook; the ferry trip takes another 20 minutes each way. The one-way fare is $6 for adults, $3 for children 11 and under. Schedules can change without notice, so call ✆ 340/776-6282 for more information on either ferry. You can take a Vitran bus from a point near Market Square (located near the west end of Main St. in Charlotte Amalie) directly to Red Hook for $1 per person, or negotiate a price with a taxi driver.

GETTING AROUND

BY TAXI The most popular way to get around is by surrey-style taxi. Typical fares from Cruz Bay are $8 to Trunk Bay, $9 to Cinnamon Bay, and $13 to Maho Bay. Taxis wait at the pier. In the very unlikely event you don't see one, you can call **St. John Taxi Service** (✆ **340/693-7530**). Almost any taxi at Cruz Bay can take you on a 2-hour tour of the island; it will cost around $45 per person for three or more riders, but fares are negotiable.

BY RENTAL CAR The extensive Virgin Islands National Park has kept the island's roads undeveloped and uncluttered, opening onto some of the most panoramic vistas anywhere. Renting a vehicle is the best way to see these views, especially if you like to linger at particularly beautiful spots. Open-sided jeeplike vehicles are the most fun of the limited rentals here. There's sometimes a shortage of cars during the busy midwinter season, so try to reserve early. **Avis** and **Hertz** both have offices here. Remember to drive on the left (even though steering wheels are on the left, too—go figure). Your car is likely to come with just enough fuel to get you to one of the island's two gas stations, so fill 'er up. Due to the distance between stations, it's never a good idea to drive around St. John with less than half a tank of gas.

BEST CRUISE LINE SHORE EXCURSIONS

Island Tour ($65, 4–5 hr.): Because most ships tie up in St. Thomas, tours of St. John first require a ferry or tender ride to Cruz Bay in St. John. Then you board open-air safari buses for a tour that includes a stop at the ruins of a working plantation (the Annaberg Ruins), as well as a pause at Trunk Bay or one of the other beaches. The island and sea views from the coastal road are spectacular.

ON YOUR OWN: WITHIN WALKING DISTANCE

Most cruise ship passengers dart through **Cruz Bay,** a cute little West Indian village with interesting bars, restaurants, boutiques, and pastel-painted houses. **Wharfside**

Spend a Day at Salt Pond

Take a drive, or a dollar-bus, east past Coral Bay and get out at Salt Pond. Bring food and plenty of water and enjoy the beautiful panoramic views of the Atlantic and Caribbean from the **Ram's Head Trail.** When you return to the beach, have lunch under a shady tree and snorkel out to the point for a different view of this island park. (See "Beaches," below.)

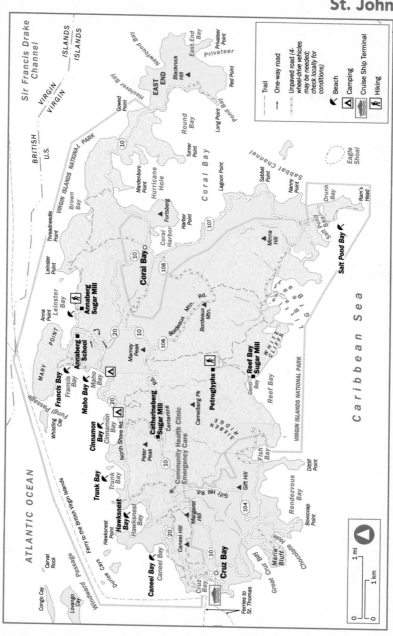

⚠ Drivers Beware

Remember: Drive on the left. This comes as a surprise to many U.S. visitors, who expect that U.S. driving practices will hold here. Speed limits are 20 mph in towns, 35 mph outside towns. St. Thomas has a high accident rate, as tourists are not used to driving on the left, the hilly terrain hides blind curves and entrance ramps, roads are narrow and poorly lit, and drivers often get behind the wheel after too many drinks. Double-check whether your own car insurance will cover you on the island, or whether your credit card will provide coverage. If not, to be on the safe side, consider getting **collision-damage insurance,** which usually costs an extra $20 to $35 per day. Be aware that even with this insurance, you could still get hit with a whopping deductible: The Hertz deductible is the full value of the car; at Avis and Budget, it's $500.

Village, near the dock, is a complex of courtyards, alleys, and shady patios with a mishmash of boutiques, restaurants, fast-food joints, and bars. Down the road from the dock is **Mongoose Junction** (see "Shopping," below).

ON YOUR OWN: BEYOND THE PORT AREA

In November 1954, the wealthy Rockefeller family began acquiring large tracts of land on St. John. They then donated more than 2,000 hectares (4,940 acres) to the Department of the Interior for the creation of the **Virgin Islands National Park,** which Congress voted into existence on August 2, 1956. Over the years, the size of the park has grown steadily; it now totals 5,109 hectares (12,625 acres), including more than two-thirds of St. John's landmass, plus submerged land and water adjacent to the island. Stop off first at the **visitor center,** right on the dock at St. Cruz (✆ 340/776-6201), where you'll find some exhibits and learn more about what you can see and do here. You can explore the park on the more than 30km (20 miles) of biking trails; rent your own car, jeep, or mini-moke; or hike. If you decide to hike, stop at the visitor center first to pick up maps and instructions. The starting points of some trails are within walking distance, while others can be reached by taxi for about $5 to $20. Trails can also be reached by Vitran bus service for $1. All trails are well marked and entrance is free.

Within the park, try to see the **Annaberg Ruins,** Leinster Bay Road, where the Danes founded thriving plantations and a sugar mill in 1718. You'll find tidal pools, forests, hilltops, wild scenery, and the ruins of several Danish plantations. It's located off North Shore Road, east of Trunk Bay on the north shore. On certain days of the week (dates vary), guided walks of the area are given by park rangers. Check at the visitor center.

SHOPPING

Compared to St. Thomas, St. John is a minor shopping destination, but the boutiques and shops at **Cruz Bay** are generally more interesting than those on St. Thomas. Most of them are clustered at **Mongoose Junction** (www.usvi.net/shopping/mongoose), in a woodsy area beside the roadway, about a 5-minute walk from the ferry dock. **Bamboula** (www.bamboulastjohn.com; ✆ 340/693-8699) has an unusual and appealing collection of gifts from the Caribbean, Haiti, India, Indonesia, and Central Africa. **Donald Schnell Studio** (www.donaldschnell.com; ✆ 800/253-7107 or 340/776-6420) deals in handmade pottery, sculpture, and blown glass.

The Fabric Mill (© 340/776-6194) features silk-screened and batik fabrics and clothing. Upstairs, **Portico** (© 340/776-9600) sells home furnishings, rugs, and housewares from around the world. **R and I Patton Goldsmithing** (www.patton gold.com; © 800/626-3445 or 340/776-6548) has a large selection of locally designed jewelry, made with sterling silver, gold, and precious stones. In case you forgot your Tevas or need a new bathing suit, check out **Big Planet Adventure Outfitters** (www.big-planet.com; © 340/776-6638), which stocks lots of outdoor-gear brands.

BEACHES

For a true beach lover, missing the great white sweep of **Trunk Bay** would be like touring Europe and skipping Paris. Trouble is, the word is a little more than out. This gorgeous beach is usually overcrowded, and there are sometimes pickpockets lurking about. The beach has lifeguards and rents snorkeling gear to those wanting to explore the underwater trail near the shore. Both taxis and "safari buses" to Trunk Bay meet the ferry as it docks at Cruz Bay.

Caneel Bay, the stomping ground of the rich and famous, has seven perfect beaches on its 69 hectares (170 acres), but only one—**Honeymoon Beach**—that's open to the public. Because it's the closest beach to Cruz Bay (and is very beautiful, if a bit narrow and windy), it's often overcrowded. Safari buses and taxis from Cruz Bay will take you along North Shore Road.

The campgrounds of **Cinnamon Bay** and **Maho Bay** have their own beaches. Snorkelers find good reefs here, and it's a great place to spot turtles and schools of parrotfish. Changing rooms and showers are available. There's also **Hawksnest Bay,** on the island's north shore. It's known as the beach locals frequent during peak tourist season.

Francis Bay Beach and **Watermelon Cay Beach** are just a couple more of the beaches you'll encounter traveling eastward along St. John's gently curving coastline. Watermelon is actually an island in Sir Francis Drake Channel, and it's far from a melon, with a reef of rainbow-hued fish surrounding it. It lies right offshore, and you can easily swim across to it along with the starfish gliding through turtle-grass beds. To reach Watermelon, follow the Leinster Bay Trail for just over 1km (.75 mile) along the Sir Francis Drake Channel, which is studded with islands. Francis Bay Beach lies near the Annaberg Plantation. Locals come here for Sunday barbecues, and snorkelers explore its shallow reef washing up on the bay's rock-strewn northern shore. Swimming among the algae-covered rocks are the territorial damselfish, French grunts, and even "Christmas tree worms" with their feathery tentacles. The beach at **Leinster Bay** is another haven for those seeking the solace of a private sunny retreat. You can swim in the bay's shallow water or snorkel over the spectacular and colorful coral reef, perhaps in the company of an occasional turtle or stingray.

The remote **Salt Pond Bay** is known to locals but often missed by visitors. It's on the beautiful coast in the southeast, adjacent to **Coral Bay.** The bay is tranquil, but the beach is somewhat rocky. It's a short walk down the hill from a parking lot. The snorkeling is good, and the bay has some fascinating tidal pools. The Ram Head Trail begins here and, winding for about 1.5km (1 mile), leads to a belvedere overlooking the bay. Facilities are meager but include an outhouse and a few tattered picnic tables.

If you want to escape the crowds, head for **Lameshur Bay Beach,** along the rugged south coast, west of Salt Pond Bay and accessible only via a bumpy dirt road. The sands are beautiful and the snorkeling is excellent. You can also take a 5-minute stroll down the road past the beach to explore the nearby ruins of an old plantation estate that was destroyed in a slave revolt.

Does St. John have a nude beach? Not officially, but lovely **Solomon Bay Beach** is a contender, although park rangers sometimes ask people to put their swimwear back on. Leave Cruz Bay on Route 20 and turn left at the park service sign, about .5km (¼ mile) past the visitor center. Park at the end of a cul-de-sac, and then walk along the trail for about 15 minutes. Go early, and you'll practically have the beach to yourself. The beach interests snorkelers of all levels of experience. Also on the north shore and to the immediate south of Salomon is the aptly named **Honeymoon Beach,** where couples often openly display their affection.

SPORTS

HIKING　The network of trails in Virgin Islands National Park is the big thing here. The visitor center at Cruz Bay hands out free trail maps of the park. Because you don't have time to get lost—you don't want the ship to leave without you—it's best to bring a map or set out with someone who knows his or her way around. Both **Maho Bay Camps** (✆ 800/392-9004 or 340/715-0501) and **Cinnamon Bay Camp-ground** (www.cinnamonbay.com; ✆ 340/776-6330) conduct nature walks. St. John has the most rewarding hiking in the Virgin Islands. The terrain ranges from arid and dry (in the east) to moist and semitropical (in the northwest). The island has more than 800 species of plants, 160 species of birds, and more than 20 trails maintained beautifully by the island's crew of park rangers. Much of the land on the island is designated as **Virgin Islands National Park.** Visitors must stop by the **Cruz Bay Visitor Center,** where you can pick up the park brochure, which includes a map of the park, and the *Virgin Islands National Park News,* which has the latest information on park activities. It's important to carry a lot of water and wear sunscreen and insect repellent when you hike.

St. John is laced with a wide network of clearly marked walking paths. At least 20 of these originate from Northshore Road (Rte. 20) or from the island's main east-west artery, Centerline Road (Rte. 10). Each is marked at its starting point with a pre-planned itinerary; the walks can last anywhere from 10 minutes to 2 hours. Maps are available from the national park headquarters at Cruz Bay.

One of my favorite hikes, the **Annaberg Historic Trail** (identified by the U.S. National Park Service as trail no. 10), requires only about a 1km (.5-mile) stroll. It departs from a clearly marked point along the island's north coast, near the junction of Routes 10 and 20. This self-guided tour passes the partially restored ruins of a manor house built during the 1700s. Signs along the way give historical and botanical data. Visiting the ruins is free. If you want to prolong your hiking experience, take the **Leinster Bay Trail,** which begins near the point where trail no. 10 ends. It leads past mangrove swamps and coral inlets rich with plant and marine life; markers iden-tify some of the plants and animals. A memorable hike that includes a stop for snor-keling is **Ram's Head and Salt Pond,** which is located east of Coral Bay. The dollar bus runs every hour, in each direction, and there are local stop schedules posted along its route. Take the bus to the last stop, Salt Pond, and walk the 5-minute trail to the beach. From there you can continue on this scenic 45-minute hike that takes you to the top of Ram's Head, where you can enjoy views of the Caribbean and Atlantic. When you get off the bus, ask the driver when it will depart back toward the docks.

KAYAKING & WINDSURFING　The **Cinnamon Bay Watersports Center,** on Cinnamon Bay Beach (✆ 340/776-6330), rents kayaks and Hobie monohull sailboats. The windsurfing here is some of the best anywhere, for both beginners and experts.

SCUBA DIVING & SNORKELING Low Key Watersports, Cruz Bay (www. divelowkey.com; ℂ 800/835-7718 or 340/693-8999), offers two-tank, two-location wreck dives on its own custom-built dive boats for $175. It also arranges day-sailing charters, kayaking tours, deep-sea sport fishing, and snorkel tours, and rents water-sports gear, including masks, fins, snorkels, and dive skins. **Cruz Bay Watersports,** at the Westin and in Cruz Bay (www.divestjohn.com; ℂ 340/776-6234), is a PADI and NAUI five-star diving center. Two-tank dives are $100, one-tank dives are $80, and "Wreck of the *Rhone*" Dives are $185. Snorkel tours are available daily.

GREAT LOCAL RESTAURANTS & BARS

St. John has some posh dining, particularly at such luxury resorts as Caneel Bay, but it also has West Indian establishments with plenty of local color and flavor. Many of the restaurants here command high prices, but you can lunch almost anywhere more reasonably. If your ship happens to be staying late, you are in luck; dinner is often an event on St. John, as it's about the only form of nightlife on the island.

IN CORAL BAY Skinny Legs (www.skinnylegs.com; ℂ 340/779-4982) offers a nice selection of Caribbean pub fare, including hamburgers, hot dogs, and mahimahi sandwiches. Lunch is about $12. In **Wharfside Village** (www.wharfsidevillage.com) at Cruz Bay, the upscale **Waterfront Bistro** (www.thewaterfrontbistro.com; ℂ 340/777-7755) offers a lovely view of the harbor. Lunch is about $22. For a more casual meal and drinks, try the **Beach Bar,** downstairs (ℂ 340/777-4220), with the same view to go with your burgers and bar food. Lunch is about $17.

St. Croix

More tranquil and less congested than St. Thomas, St. Croix is rocky and arid on its eastern end (which, incidentally, is the easternmost possession of the U.S.) but more lush in the west, with a rainforest of mango and mahogany, tree ferns, and dangling lianas. Rolling hills and upland pastures make up much of the area between the two extremes, and the vivid African tulips are just one of the many tropical flowers that add a splash of color to the landscape, which is dotted with the ruins of sugarcane plantations. The major St. Croix attractions are the coral reefs of **Buck Island Reef National Monument,** located offshore. There are some fine beaches here as well, including Sandy Point, Sprat Hall, and Rainbow Beach.

Although large cruise ships moor at Frederiksted, most of the action is really in **Christiansted,** located on a coral-bound bay about midway along the north shore and featuring more sights and better restaurants and shopping. Showing 2½ centuries of Danish influence in its architecture, the town is being handsomely restored, and the entire harborfront area is a National Historic Site. St. Croix's population is descended from both Africa and Europe, and some families have been here for 10 generations, with roots dating back to Colonial times.

COMING ASHORE Only cruise ships no longer than 107m (350 ft.) can land directly at the dock at **Christiansted.** Others moor at newly renovated **Ann Abramson Pier** at **Frederiksted,** a sleepy town that springs to life only when the ships arrive. There's space for two megaships, and both piers have information centers and phones. A representative from the **St. Croix Tourism Office** can be reached at ℂ 340/772-0357, Monday to Friday from 8am to 5pm.

I suggest you spend as little time as possible in Frederiksted and head immediately for Christiansted, some 27km (17 miles) away. It's easy to explore either town on foot

5

THE PORTS OF CALL

U.S. Virgin Islands

Because of its well-preserved 18th- and 19th-century Danish architecture (particularly evident at Fort Christiansvaern), Christiansted has been designated a National Historic Site. In the late 1700s, it was a crown colony of Denmark and one of the Caribbean's major ports. Today many street signs are still in Danish. (See "On Your Own: Within Walking Distance," below.)

(it's the only way, really). You might want to consider one of the shore excursions outlined below to see more of the island, especially its underwater treasures.

Although St. Croix is relatively safe, it's wise to stay on the beaten path and watch your belongings on the beaches (as you should on any island).

GETTING AROUND

BY TAXI   The **St. Croix Taxicab Federation** (✆ **340/778-1088**) offers door-to-door service. Taxis are unmetered, and rates are set from point to point. It costs $25 to $30 to go from Christiansted to Frederiksted. On cruise ship days the Taxi Federation has agreed to reduce that fare by half, but be sure to agree on a fare before you get in. Taxi tours are a great way to explore the island; the cost is $100 for one to four people for 4 hours.

BY BUS   Air-conditioned buses run between Christiansted and Frederiksted about every half-hour weekdays between 5:30am and 9pm, weekends till 7:30pm. The main stop in Christiansted is on Hospital Street, near the National Park office; the main stop in Frederiksted is on Budhoe Park, near Fort Frederik and King Street. The fare is $1 for adults, 75¢ for children ages 3 to 12, and 75¢ for seniors. For more information, call ✆ **340/778-0898.**

BY SEAPLANE   Daily seaplane shuttles between St. Croix and St. Thomas are available for $228 round-trip. Booking in advance is strongly recommended. Flights depart every 15 to 45 minutes in both directions; flight time is a mere 18 minutes, but figure 30 minutes from dock to dock. For more information, contact **Seaborne Airlines,** 34 Strand St., Christiansted (www.seaborneairlines.com; ✆ **340/773-6442**).

BY RENTAL CAR   I don't recommend renting a car here.

BEST CRUISE LINE SHORE EXCURSIONS

Buck Island Tour/Snorkeling ($87; 6½ hr.): The most popular tour in St. Croix takes you to a tropical underwater wonderland of blue water, a dazzling rainbow of sea life and colorful coral reefs, sailing aboard either a glass-bottom catamaran or a speedboat. An experienced guide provides snorkel lessons. A shorter, 4½-hour version of this tour is available for $60.

Salt River Kayak Tour ($89, 4 hr.): The Salt River Bay National Historic Park and Ecological Preserve, on the island's northern shore, is the only site that Columbus is known to have landed on in what is now U.S. territory. The park today is in a natural state, with the largest mangrove forest in the Virgin Islands, sheltering many endangered animals and plants. You'll kayak for about 2 hours through secluded estuaries, birding areas, and mangroves, including a visit to the site of the original Carib village explored by Columbus and his men.

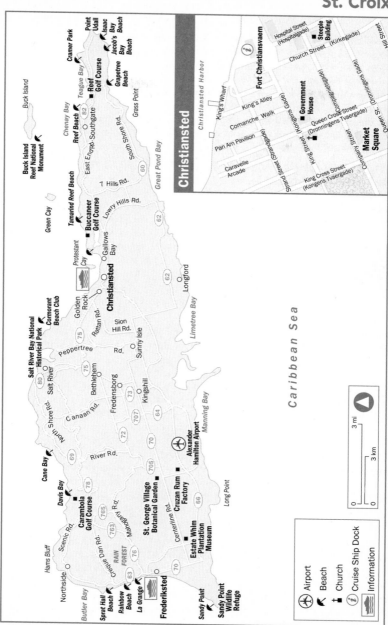

St. Croix

Christiansted

Hospital Street (Hospitalgade)
Steeple Building
Church Street (Kirkegade)
Fort Christiansvaern
King's Wharf
Christiansted Harbor
King's Alley
Government House
Comanche Walk
Pan Am Pavilion
Queen Cross Street (Dronningens Tvaergade)
Caravelle Arcade
King Street (Kongens Gade)
Strand Street (Strandgade)
Company Street (Kompagniegade)
Queen Cross Street (Dronningens Gade)
Queen St. (Dronningens Gade)
King Cross Street (Kongens Tvaergade)
Hill Street
Market Square

Point Udall
Isaac Bay Beach
Cramer Park
Jacob's Bay Beach
Teague Bay
Reef Golf Course
Grapetree Beach
Grass Point
Chenay Bay
Reef Beach
East End Rd.—Southgate
82
South Shore Rd.
Great Pond Bay
60
Buck Island
Buck Island Reef National Monument
7 Hills Rd.
Tamarind Reef Beach
Buccaneer Golf Course
Green Cay
Lowry Hills Rd.
62
Protestant Cay
Gallows Bay
Golden Rock
Christiansted
Longford
62
Rattan Rd.
Sion Hill Rd.
Limetree Bay
Salt River Bay National Historical Park
Cormorant Beach Club
Peppertree Rd.
Sunny Isle
75
Salt River
80
Bethlehem
Fredensborg
Kingshill
73
Manning Bay
Canaan Rd.
72
707
64
Cane Bay
69
North Shore Rd.
River Rd.
70
Alexander Hamilton Airport
705
Davis Bay
78
Caribbean Sea
Carambola Golf Course
765
Maroon Rd.
St. George Village Botanical Garden
Cruzan Rum Factory
Centerline Rd.
66
Long Point
763
Creque Dam Rd.
RAIN FOREST
76
Estate Whim Plantation Museum
Hams Bluff
Scenic Rd.
Sprat Hall Beach
Rainbow Beach
63
La Grange
70
Frederiksted
Northside
Butler Bay
Sandy Point
Sandy Point Wildlife Refuge

0   3 mi
0   3 km

Airport
Beach
Church
Information
Cruise Ship Dock

St. Croix Heritage Tour ($61, 6 hr.): Visit St. George Village Botanical Garden, the Cruzan Rum Factory, the Estate Whim Plantation Museum, and a patch of rainforest in the company of a local guide, stopping for lunch along the way.

EXCURSIONS OFFERED BY LOCAL AGENCIES

Horseback Tour: On this 1½-hour tour, run by **Paul and Jill's Equestrian Stables,** Sprat Hall Plantation, Route 58 (www.paulandjills.com; ✆ **340/772-2880**), for $90 you'll climb the hills of St. Croix's western end and pass ruins of abandoned 18th-century plantations and sugar mills. The stables are set on the sprawling grounds of the island's oldest plantation, and are known throughout the Caribbean for the quality of the horses and the exceptionally scenic forest trails. The grounds also boast an exquisite tropical fruit orchard. Both beginner and experienced riders are welcome. Make reservations in advance.

ON YOUR OWN: WITHIN WALKING DISTANCE

IN FREDERIKSTED   Frederiksted is a throwback to a sleepier, bygone era, when the Caribbean was less commercialized. If you decide to hang around and enjoy the atmosphere and historical buildings, relax with a cup of coffee and freshly made muffin, or a cocktail, from Polly's cafe near the pier. It's also worth checking out russet-colored **Fort Frederik** (✆ **340/772-2021**), next to the cruise ship pier. Some historians claim it was the first fort to sound a foreign salute to the U.S. flag, in 1776. The structure, at the northern end of Frederiksted, has been restored to its 1840 look. You can explore the courtyard and stables, visit the police museum, peruse exhibits of antique cannons and clothing, and see photographs of life on St. Croix in the days of yore. Admission is $3 for adults, free for children 15 and under. The fort is open Monday through Friday from 8am to 5pm.

IN CHRISTIANSTED   Start off at the **visitor bureau** (www.usvitourism.vi; ✆ **340/773-0495**), a yellow building with a cedar roof near the harbor. It was built as the Old Scalehouse in 1856 to replace a similar older structure that burned down. In its heyday, all taxable goods leaving and entering the harbor were weighed here. The scales could once accurately weigh barrels of sugar and molasses of nearly a ton.

Follow Hospital Street to the **Steeple Building,** or Church of Lord God of Sabaoth (✆ **340/773-1320**), which was completed in 1753 as St. Croix's first Lutheran church. It contains an exhibit on island heritage in general and the church in particular, with photos and artifacts. The building was deconsecrated in 1831 and has served at various times as a bakery, a hospital, and a school. Admission is $3 for adults, free for children 15 and under, and also includes entry to **Fort Christiansvaern** (✆ **340/773-1460**), the best-preserved colonial fortification in the Virgin Islands. The National Park Service maintains the fort as a historic monument, overlooking the harbor. Its original star-shaped design was at the vanguard of the most advanced military planning of its era. Hours are Monday through Friday from 8am to 5pm, Saturday and Sunday from 9am to 4:45pm. Admission is $3.

ON YOUR OWN: BEYOND THE PORT AREA

Salt River, on the island's northern shore, is the only site that Columbus is known to have landed on in what is now U.S. territory. To mark the 500th anniversary of the arrival of Columbus, former President George H. W. Bush signed a bill creating the 410-hectare (1,015-acre) **Salt River Bay National Historic Park and Ecological Preserve.** The landmass includes the site of the original Carib village explored by Columbus and his men, along with the only Taíno ball court (used for ceremonial sporting events) ever discovered in the Lesser Antilles.

The park today is in a natural state. It has the largest mangrove forest in the Virgin Islands, sheltering many endangered animals and plants, plus an underwater canyon attracting scuba divers from around the world. The **St. Croix Environmental Association,** 5032 Anchor Way, Gallows Bay (www.stxenvironmental.org; ✆ 340/773-1989), conducts tours of the area. Hours are Monday through Friday from 9am to 5pm.

The **Cruzan Rum Factory,** West Airport Road, Route 64 (www.cruzanrum.com; ✆ 340/692-2280), distills the famous Virgin Islands rum. Guided tours depart from the visitor pavilion Monday through Friday from 9am to 4pm; the cost is $5 for adults, $1 for children 17 and under.

Restored by the St. Croix Landmarks Society, the **Estate Whim Plantation Museum,** Centerline Road, about 3km (2 miles) east of Frederiksted (www.stcroix landmarks.org; ✆ 340/772-0598), is composed of only three rooms and is unique among the many old sugar plantations dotting the island, with 1m-thick (3¼-ft.) walls made of stone, coral, and molasses. Also on the grounds are the estate's original kitchen, a museum store, servants' quarters, and tools from the 18th century. The ruins include remains of the plantation's sugar-processing plant, complete with a restored windmill. It's open Monday through Saturday, 10am to 4pm. Admission is $10 for adults, $5 for children ages 3 to 12.

The **St. George Village Botanical Garden of St. Croix** (www.sgvbg.org; ✆ 340/692-2874) is a much-loved Eden of tropical trees, shrubs, vines, and flowers, located 6.5km (4 miles) east of Frederiksted off Queen Mary Highway. Hours are daily from 9am to 5pm. Admission is $8 for adults, $6 for seniors, and $1 for children 12 and under.

SHOPPING

Americans get a break here, as they can bring home $1,600 worth of merchandise from the U.S. Virgin Islands without paying duty—double the amount allowed from most other Caribbean ports. Liquor here is duty-free, too.

The **King's Alley Complex,** a pink-sided compound created right on the Christiansted waterfront following the hurricanes of 1995, is filled with the densest concentration of shopping options on St. Croix. There are a number of worthwhile specialty shops in Christiansted as well.

Coconut Vine (✆ 340/773-1991), in the Pan Am Pavilion, Strand Street, is one of the most colorful and popular boutiques on the island, specializing in hand-painted batik for both men and women. **Many Hands** (✆ 340/773-1990), also in the Pan Am Pavilion, sells Virgin Islands handicrafts, spices and teas, handmade pottery, local art, and more. **Nelthropp and Low** (www.nelthropp-low.com; ✆ 340/773-0365) sells and repairs fine gold jewelry. **Sonya Ltd.** (www.sonyaltd.com; ✆ 340/778-8605), 1 Company St., focuses on traditional Caribbean hook bracelets.

BEACHES

Beaches are the biggest attraction on St. Croix. The drawback is that getting to them from Christiansted or Frederiksted isn't always easy. Taxis will take you, but they can be expensive. From Christiansted, you can also take a ferry to the **Hotel on the Cay,** a palm-shaded island in the harbor.

NEAR FREDERIKSTED   Most convenient for passengers arriving at Frederiksted is **Sandy Point,** the largest beach in all of the U.S. Virgin Islands. Its waters are shallow and calm, perfect for swimming. You may remember this beach from the last scene of the movie *The Shawshank Redemption.* Sandy Point is also the nesting ground for endangered leatherback, hawksbill, and green sea turtles, which lay their eggs every year between early April and early June. Parts of the beach are roped off during this time, but you can watch these fascinating creatures from outside of the protected areas.

On Route 63, a short ride north of Frederiksted, is the inviting **Rainbow Beach,** with white sand and ideal snorkeling conditions. **Sprat Hall Beach** is another good beach in the vicinity, also on Route 63, about 5 minutes north of Frederiksted. You can rent lounge chairs here, and there's a bar nearby.

I highly recommend **Cane Bay** and **Davis Bay.** They're both the type of beaches you'd expect to find on a Caribbean island—palms, white sand, and good swimming and snorkeling. Cane Bay attracts snorkelers and divers with its rolling waves, coral gardens, and drop-off wall. It's near Route 80 on the north shore. Bodysurfers are drawn to nearby **Davis Beach,** also off Route 80, in the vicinity of the Carambola Beach Resort. There are no changing facilities here.

NEAR CHRISTIANSTED   At **The Palms at Pelilcan Cove** (www.palmspelican cove.com/beach.php), about 8km (5 miles) west of Christiansted, palm trees shade some 370m (1,200 ft.) of white sand. A living reef lies just offshore, making snorkeling ideal.

SPORTS

GOLF   St. Croix has the best golfing in the U.S. Virgin Islands, hands down. In fact, guests staying on St. John and St. Thomas often fly over to St. Croix for a day, just to play. On the northeast side of the island is the 18-hole, par-72 **Carambola Golf Course** (www.golfcarambola.com; ✆ **340/778-5638**), designed by Robert Trent Jones, Sr., who called it "the loveliest course I ever designed." Golfing authorities consider its collection of par-3 holes to be the best in the Tropics. Greens fees are $95 to $130, including cart.

The 18-hole, par-70 **Buccaneer,** 3km (2 miles) east of Christiansted (www.the buccaneer.com; ✆ **800/255-3881** or 340/773-2100, ext. 738), is a challenging 5,685-yard course with panoramic vistas. Players can knock the ball over rolling hills right to the edge of the ocean. Greens fees are $100 including cart.

The 3,100-yard, 9-hole, par-35 **Reef Golf Course,** at Teague Bay (✆ **340/773-8844**), is over on the east end of the island. Greens fees are $20 (yes, that's correct), plus $15 per person for those wishing to rent a cart, and $8 for clubs.

SCUBA DIVING   Divers love St. Croix's sponge life, beautiful black-coral trees, and steep drop-offs near the shoreline. This island is home to the largest living reef in the Caribbean. Its fabled north-shore wall begins in 7.5 to 9m (25–30 ft.) of water and drops—sometimes almost straight down—to 4,023m (13,200 ft.). There are 22 moored diving sites. Favorites include **Salt River Canyon,** the coral gardens of **Scotch Banks,** and **Eagle Ray,** filled with cruising eagle rays. **Pavilions** is another good dive site, boasting a pristine coral reef. The best site of all, however, is **Buck Island,** an underwater wonderland with a visibility of more than 30m (100 ft.) and an underwater nature trail. All minor and major agencies offer scuba and snorkeling tours to Buck Island.

Divers who really care about the reef should head to **Dive Experience** (www.divexp.com; ✆ **800/235-9047** or 340/773-3307), an outfitter with a friendly style that welcomes both beginner and experienced divers. Owner Michelle Pugh, who is in the Women's Diver Hall of Fame, opened this dive shop 25 years ago on the premise that the reef deserves protection. She founded a program called Anchors Away, which sets up moorings so boats won't damage the reef with anchors, and she continues to raise funds to maintain these moorings, now used by all dive boats on the island. Two-tank dives are $100 and one-tank dives are $85.

GAMBLING

St. Croix's first casino opened in 2000 on the east side of the island, at the **Divi Carina All-Inclusive Resort,** 25 Estate Turner Hole (www.divicarina.com; **℃ 340/ 773-9700**). It takes approximately 45 minutes by taxi and costs about $30 per person to get here from Frederiksted. The casino opens at noon.

GREAT LOCAL RESTAURANTS & BARS

Favorite local beers include **Carib** and **Blackbeard's** (made on St. Thomas); the preferred local rum is **Cruzan.**

IN FREDERIKSTED Blue Moon, 7 Strand St. (**℃ 340/772-2222**), is a popular bistro in Frederiksted, offering upscale burgers and salads. Lunch is about $18. It is closed for lunch on Monday and Saturday, but offers an award-winning brunch on Sundays.

IN CHRISTIANSTED Harvey's, 11B Company St. (**℃ 340/773-3433**), features the thoroughly zesty cooking of island matriarch Sarah Harvey. The main dishes are the type of food Sarah was raised on: barbecue chicken, barbecue spareribs (barbecue is big here), broiled snapper, and lobster when she can get it. Lunch is about $15.

Across from Government House, **Tommy T's Paradise Cafe,** 53B Company St., at Queen Cross Street (**℃ 340/773-2985**), serves burgers and New York deli–style sandwiches throughout the day—everything from a Reuben to a tuna melt. Lunch is about $12 (cash only).

Fort Christian Brew Pub, King's Alley Walk (**℃ 340/713-9820**), has one of the best harbor views in Christiansted. As the only restaurant/microbrewery in the Virgin Islands, it serves beer, plus burgers, sandwiches, and Cajun cuisine. Lunch is around $14.

Index